International Comparisons of Real Product and Purchasing Power

UNITED NATIONS
INTERNATIONAL
COMPARISON PROJECT:
PHASE II

International Comparisons of Real Product and Purchasing Power

Produced by
The Statistical Office of
The United Nations and
The World Bank

Irving B. Kravis • Alan Heston • Robert Summers

in collaboration with Alicia Civitello, Samvit P. Dhar,
Meera Mehta, Carl Otto, and Alfonso Uong

Published for the World Bank
The Johns Hopkins University Press • Baltimore and London

The views and interpretations in this book are those of the
authors and should not be attributed to the World Bank or its
affiliated organizations, to the United Nations, or to any
individual acting in their behalf. The designations employed
and the presentation of material in this publication do not
imply the expression of any opinion whatsoever on the part of
the Secretariat of the United Nations concerning the legal status
of any country, territory, city, or area, or of its authorities,
or concerning the delimitations of its frontiers or boundaries.

LIBRARY OF CONGRESS CATALOG CARD NUMBER 77-17251
ISBN 0-8018-2019-7 (CLOTH)
ISBN 0-8018-2020-0 (PAPER)

Contents

v

Preface

THIS VOLUME REPRESENTS A FURTHER STEP in the work of the United Nations Statistical Office toward the development of a comprehensive and reliable system of estimates of real gross domestic product (GDP) and purchasing power of currencies based on detailed price comparisons among countries. A description of the earlier aspects of this work was set out in the introduction to the first report on the United Nations International Comparison Project (ICP): *A System of International Comparisons of Gross Product and Purchasing Power* (Johns Hopkins University Press, Baltimore and London, 1975).

Phase I of the ICP as described in that publication was devoted to a large degree to the development of a methodology for a system of international comparisons. The methodology was applied to ten countries: Colombia, France, Federal Republic of Germany, Hungary, India, Italy, Japan, Kenya, the United Kingdom, and the United States. Product and purchasing-power comparisons for the reference year 1970 were presented for these countries.

In the present report the methodology has been extended to cover six other countries—Belgium, Iran, Republic of Korea, Malaysia, Netherlands, and Philippines—for 1970, and the opportunity has been taken to revise the Phase I comparisons for the original ten countries. Data are also presented to show how the sixteen countries compared during the year 1973. The results of the comparison have been presented in terms of per capita quantities and purchasing-power parities for real GDP as a whole, its three main components (consumption, investment, and government), and for thirty-four summary subaggregates. Besides the presentation of the 1970 and 1973 intercountry comparisons, the comparisons have further been extended to a longer, eleven-year period, 1965–75, though for GDP per capita only.

As in the Phase I report, the international comparisons reported upon here are both multilateral and binary comparisons. The more traditional binary presentations compare each country in succession with the United States. The multilateral comparisons treat all the countries simultaneously, so that the base country is used simply as a numéraire. The quantity comparisons for GDP and its components are thus independent of the country chosen as the numéraire. From an international point of view, where the interest is in many different countries taken together rather than in particular pairs, multilateral comparisons are the more relevant ones.

During Phase II, the ICP continued as a wide international cooperative effort involving many institutions and persons in many countries. In organization the ICP was a joint responsibility of the United Nations Statistical Office, the World Bank, and the International Comparison Unit of the University of Pennsylvania. The major operational responsibility rested with the United Nations Statistical Office, and the director of that office exercised the general supervision over the development of the project. The immediate responsibility for technical guidance and supervision rested with the project director, who divided his efforts between the work at the University of Pennsylvania and at the United Nations.

The World Bank provided essential financial support from its own resources and organized a consortium of contributors that included the bilateral aid agencies of Denmark, the Federal Republic of Germany, Norway, the Netherlands, and the United States. Hungary and the United Kingdom made technical experts available to assist certain developing countries participating in ICP work.

As in Phase I, the responsibility for coordinating collection, collation, and transmission of the required data for each of the participating countries rested mainly with the national statistical authorities. In particular, mention may be made of the following institutions:

> COLOMBIA: mainly the Departamento Administrativo Nacional de Estadística (DANE) and also the Centro de Estudios Desarrollo Económico (CEDE) at the Los Andes University and the Banco de la República.
>
> HUNGARY: Central Statistical Office.
>
> INDIA: Central Statistical Organisation of the Department of Statistics.
>
> IRAN: Economic Statistics Affairs Directorate of the Bank Markazi.
>
> JAPAN: Bureau of Statistics of the Office of the Prime Minister, and the Economic Research Institute of the Economic Planning Agency.
>
> KENYA: Central Bureau of Statistics, Ministry of Finance and Planning.
>
> REPUBLIC OF KOREA: Statistics Department of the Bank of Korea and the Bureau of Statistics of the Economic Planning Board.
>
> MALAYSIA: Jabatan Peangkaan Malaysia, Wisma Statistik.
>
> PHILIPPINES: National Census and Statistics Office of the National Economic and Development Authority and other related government agencies.
>
> UNITED KINGDOM: Central Statistical Office in the Cabinet Office, Economic and Statistics Division of the Departments of Industry, Trade, and Prices and Consumer Protection, Statistics Divisions of the Department of Employment, and the Department of Environment.
>
> UNITED STATES: Office of Federal Statistical Policy and Standards, Bureau of Labor Statistics, and National Income and Wealth Division of the Bureau of Economic Analysis, Department of Commerce.

All information about five of its member countries—Belgium, France, Federal Republic of Germany, Italy, and Netherlands—was supplied in the desired form by the Statistical Office of the European Communities in Luxembourg.

A large number of persons in these and other agencies made important contributions in providing the data and as critics and advisers. At the risk of slighting some whose contribution has not come to the attention of the central staff, mention may be made of Jorge A. Celis, Alvaro Velásquez-Cock, and Roberto Pinilla Peña of Colombia; Hughes Picard and Jean-Michel Rempp of France; Mária K. Köszegi, Ádám Marton, Albert Rácz, Szabolcs Ráth, György Szilágyi, László Vuics, and Mihály Zafir of Hungary; Uma Roy Choudhury, Girdhar Gopal, Ram Murti, C. S. Pillai, Ved Prakash, and Paramjit Singh of India; F. W. Daftari, G. H. Shahkarami, M. Tajdar, Said Ziyai, and Hassan Zoghi of Iran; Michio Matsuda, Sadanori Nagayama, and Tsutomu Noda of Japan; Parmeet Singh of Kenya; Woong Soo Rhee and Hong-Bae Kim of the Republic of Korea; R. Chander and Kwok Kwan Kit of Malaysia; Lilia H. Constantino, Tito Mijares, and Pablo Samson of the Philippines; Ross Arnett, William Berry, Ken Dalton, and Allan H. Young of the United States; and

Hugo Krijnse-Locker and Vittorio Paretti of the EEC. The insight that the ratio of expenditure shares at national prices to expenditure shares at international prices could be regarded as measuring each country's relative price structure was offered by Benjamin B. King of the World Bank.

Statistical assistance in the work of the central staff was provided by Sharon Bond, Daniel Gottlieb, Helen Hirschfeld, K. C. Lee, and Chad Leechor, and secretarial services by Myrtle Campbell and Susan Long. Mrs. Long typed the successive versions of the text and many of the tables with remarkable patience, speed, and accuracy; the remainder of the tables were efficiently typed by Mrs. Campbell.

Elinor Yudin Sachse provided professional support and effective liaison with the World Bank. The text was edited by Robert Faherty; the index was prepared by Rachel C. Anderson; and book design and production was supervised by Brian J. Svikhart.

International
Comparisons of
Real Product and
Purchasing Power

Chapter 1

The Nature of the Report and the Main Results

THE PURPOSE OF THE UNITED NATIONS International Comparison Project (ICP) is to compare the purchasing power of currencies and the real gross domestic product (GDP) per capita of different countries.

It is well known that the usual method of converting the GDPs of different countries to a common currency, usually U.S. dollars, at existing exchange rates is misleading because exchange rates do not necessarily reflect the purchasing power of currencies. The ICP, as will be seen in a later section of this chapter, has found that the purchasing power of a country's currency over GDP can be as much as three times its dollar exchange rate, and thus the real GDP per capita is three times the value shown in an exchange-rate conversion. The unsatisfactory nature of exchange-rate conversions has become even clearer in the past few years under the new regime of managed floating rates. Changes in exchange rates of as much as 20 percent within the space of a year have not been unusual even among major currencies. Exchange-rate conversions thus sometimes show substantial changes in relative gross domestic products between pairs of countries when no such real change has actually occurred.

The first phase of the ICP was reported on in an earlier volume—*A System of International Comparisons of Gross Product and Purchasing Power.*[1] That phase had two objectives. The first was to develop methods for a system of comparisons that could be applied to a large number of countries. The second, partly as an end in itself and partly as an aid in the methodological work, was to make a start at actual comparisons. To meet these objectives, arrangements were made for the participation of ten countries, including a number of industrial countries, and, at the same time, some representatives of countries with different social systems, in different geographical regions, and at different income levels. The Phase I countries were Colombia, France, the Federal Republic of Germany, Hungary, India, Italy, Japan, Kenya, the United Kingdom, and the United States.

For all ten of these countries, *A System* contained comparisons of real gross domestic product per capita and of the purchasing powers of currencies

The Three Phases of the ICP

---

1. Irving B. Kravis, Zoltan Kenessey, Alan Heston, and Robert Summers, *A System of International Comparisons of Gross Product and Purchasing Power* (Baltimore: Johns Hopkins University Press, 1975). Hereafter referred to as *A System*. At certain points, this source is borrowed from freely without further citation.

with a 1970 reference date. For six of the countries, there were also comparisons with a 1967 reference date. Comparisons of both per capita quantities and purchasing-power parities (or price levels) were presented not only for GDP as a whole, but also for the three main components of GDP—consumption, investment, and government—and for 34 subaggregates. As will be explained more fully in the next section, these comparisons were based on data supplied by the countries on prices, expenditures, and sometimes quantities for 153 detailed final expenditure categories.[2] These 153 detailed categories, which exhaust GDP, represent the most disaggregated classifications used by the ICP.

Both binary and multilateral comparisons were presented. In the former each country was compared individually with the United States; in the latter all the countries were compared simultaneously. These two types of comparisons, and reasons for preferring the multilateral ones, are explained later in this chapter.

What is new in this report?

The present volume is a report on Phase II of the ICP. Comparisons of real gross domestic product per capita and of purchasing powers of currencies for sixteen countries and two reference dates are presented. The comparisons include revised 1970 and new 1973 estimates for the ten Phase I countries, and both 1970 and 1973 estimates for six new countries—Belgium, Iran, the Republic of Korea, Malaysia, the Netherlands, and the Philippines. For all sixteen countries and the two reference years, comparisons are provided for GDP as a whole, the three main components of GDP (consumption, investment, and government), and the thirty-four subaggregates. As in *A System*, both multilateral and binary comparisons are presented. (See Chapters 4 and 5, respectively.) In this introductory chapter, however, only the preferred multilateral results are given.

In addition, indexes of real GDP per capita for the sixteen countries (but not for any breakdowns) are estimated for each of the other years in the period 1965–75. These are obtained by extrapolating the 1970 and 1973 (and 1967) results to other years on the basis of each country's own price and quantity changes. (See Table 1.4 for extrapolations to 1974 and 1975 and Chapter 4 for the full set of extrapolations.)

Although the methodology of the present report follows closely that of its predecessor, the opportunity is taken here to clarify certain matters, particularly some issues relating to the concept of international prices. Also, the effects of expanding the system from ten to sixteen countries and related matters dealing with the precision of the estimates are treated.

What is still to be done?

Work has already been started on Phase III of the ICP, which includes more than thirty countries with a 1975 reference date. Phase III, targeted for completion in 1979, will expand significantly the proportion of the world for which comparisons of real income are made.

Plans for the maintenance and expansion of the system of international

---

2. The 34 subaggregates are listed in Summary Multilateral Tables 4.1–4.10 and in Summary Binary Tables 5.1–5.30. (The count of 34 is obtained by excluding any entry in these tables that represents an aggregation of other entries.) These subaggregates are also referred to as "summary categories" since they represent more aggregated categories than the 153 "detailed categories." The latter may be found listed in Appendix Tables 4.1–4.5 and in Appendix Table 5.1. Subsequent references to 36 summary categories include two categories—increase in stocks (ICP 18.000) and exports less imports (ICP 19.000)—that are excluded from most tabulations because their sometimes negative signs make the meaning of quantity comparisons problematic. They are, however, included at the aggregative levels (in capital formation and GDP).

comparisons after Phase III have not been fully formulated. If reasonably current comparisons are to be provided on a continuous basis, however, the broad outlines of what will be required are clear:

- Keeping the estimates up to date will require the selection of future benchmark years for which a full set of comparisons would be made—that is, comparisons like those carried out for the sixteen Phase II countries with 1970 and 1973 reference dates. These benchmark years might initially be at five-year intervals.
- Abbreviated methods must be developed to extrapolate the benchmark comparisons to years falling between the benchmarks. This may be done for only GDP as a whole or for GDP and its three main components and perhaps also for the thirty-four subaggregates.
- A way must be found to make comparisons for the countries that cannot be accorded the full ICP treatment. It is unrealistic to believe that it will be possible in the near future to carry out benchmark estimates for all 188 countries and areas for which GNP is reported in the 1975 edition of the *World Bank Atlas* or even for all 155 entities for which tables are included in the 1975 U.N. *Yearbook of National Accounts Statistics*.
- It would be desirable to develop a method that would make it possible to express the real GDPs per capita—and the components of the GDPs—for the different countries in the different years in constant prices.

Exploratory work along all these lines is under way, but only an effort to extrapolate benchmark results to other years is reported upon in the present volume.

ICP Methods in Brief

Because of the emphasis on the methodological purposes in the Phase I report, special care was taken in *A System* to set out fully the methods and procedures that were followed. Particularly in connection with the multilateral methods, for which new ground had to be broken, *A System* described in detail the various alternative aggregation procedures that might have been followed at each stage in producing price and quantity indexes. The advantages and disadvantages of each of the alternatives were indicated; the reasons were given for each choice that was made; and, for the major aggregates, the results produced by the alternative methods were displayed.

The same degree of detail about the methods is not included in the present report, nor is as much attention given to alternative methods, because such efforts would needlessly duplicate *A System*. The reader who wishes a full account of ICP methodology is referred to the earlier book.

In this volume, a brief sketch of the basic methodology is offered in this chapter, and a somewhat longer summary is given in Chapter 3. In addition, Chapter 3 treats certain methodological problems that rose afresh or required reexamination in the course of preparing the new estimates in this report.

By way of introduction, it may be explained that the basic methodological thrust was to obtain quantity comparisons by means of price and expenditure comparisons. Expenditures (E), prices (P), and quantities (Q) are linked together in the familiar identity $E = P \cdot Q$. It follows that for any pair of countries, j and k, with respect to commodity i,

$$\frac{E_{ij}}{E_{ik}} = \frac{P_{ij}}{P_{ik}} \cdot \frac{Q_{ij}}{Q_{ik}}.$$

Thus, the availability of any two of the three ratios makes it possible to derive the third. Expenditures for detailed categories were or could be made available from each country's national accounts. Direct quantity comparisons—that is, direct estimates of Q_{ij}/Q_{ik}—are difficult to make for many detailed categories. The ICP category women's clothing, for example, is so heterogeneous that quantity data for each type and quality are difficult to obtain. Also, the quantity ratios (Q_{ij}/Q_{ik}) for individual types and qualities may be expected to exhibit wide dispersion relative to the corresponding price ratios. Hence, primary reliance has been placed on direct price comparisons because they are easier to obtain and because the sampling variance of the quantity ratios derived from them will be smaller than that of the direct quantity ratios.

Organizing the data

The final expenditures on GDP used in the ICP comparisons correspond in the main to the concepts and definitions of the U.N. System of National Accounts (SNA).[3] It was, however, necessary to flesh out and make more specific the commodity classifications suggested in the SNA. A standard classification of the final expenditures on GDP, consisting of 153 detailed categories, was established. Of these categories, 110 were in ICP "consumption" (for example, beef); 38 were in ICP "capital formation" or "investment" (for example, trucks); and 5 were in ICP "government" (for example, expenditure on skilled blue-collar employees). All expenditures on health care, education, and recreation—other than those of a purely governmental nature (for example, licensing, or setting drug standards)—were classified in ICP consumption. This was done to ensure that the international comparisons for those sectors were independent of the manner in which the financing of these services was divided between the public purse and householders. Each participating country was asked to allocate its expenditures on GDP to the detailed categories provided by the ICP classification system.

Prices for each of the fifteen "partner" countries were compared with the prices for the United States for most of the 153 detailed categories. In each case the comparisons were made for from one to a dozen representative items in common use. The identification of equivalent representative items was a focal point for much of the work. It involved the exchange of expert members of the staffs of the national statistical offices and the ICP, consultations with industry experts and government experts outside of the statistical offices, and the use of samples, catalogs, and price sheets. The price comparison for each item yields a price ratio indicating the number of units of a country's currency that are required to buy what can be bought in the United States with one U.S. dollar.

Binary comparisons

For a binary comparison between a partner country and the United States, the purchasing-power parity (PPP) for each detailed category was calculated as the geometric mean (usually unweighted)[4] of the price ratios for the item. (The PPP gives the number of units of a country's currency that have the same purchasing power for the category as a U.S. dollar.) The quantity comparison for most detailed categories was then derived by dividing the PPP for the category into the ratio of the partner country expenditure to the U.S. expenditure. For a few categories, such as education and health care, in which price comparisons were difficult to make, the quantity comparisons were estimated directly on the basis of quantity data, and the PPPs were derived indirectly by division of the quantity ratio into the expenditure ratio.

The PPPs and quantity comparisons for the 153 detailed categories of final expenditure were then aggregated into 36 summary categories (such as

---

3. U.N. Statistical Office, *A System of National Accounts,* Studies in Method, Series F, No. 2, Rev. 3 (New York: United Nations, 1968).
4. Unweighted because, in the absence of expenditure data at the item level, no estimate of the relative importance of different items was available.

meat, transport equipment), the three main components (consumption, capital formation, and government), and GDP itself.[5]

The aggregation method was relatively straightforward in the case of the binary comparisons. Each of the fifteen partner countries was paired in turn with the United States. The usual practice was followed by presenting, for each pair of countries, two quantity indexes, one in which the quantity indexes for various categories were aggregated with the given country's ("own") weights and the other in which they were aggregated with U.S. weights. A similar process was then followed for the price indexes. For both the quantity and the price indexes, the geometric mean of the own-weighted and U.S.-weighted indexes—the so-called Fisher "ideal" index—is also given.[6]

These traditional binary comparisons have the advantages of familiarity and easy interpretation. They possess to the utmost degree what has come to be called "characteristicity"—that is, the results are influenced only by the commodities, prices, and weights of the countries being compared because the data associated with all other countries are ignored.[7] When the purpose is solely to compare a particular pair of countries, a binary comparison is normally the best possible answer.

Multilateral comparisons

International comparisons, however, involve more than two countries for many, if not most, purposes. For example, sharing the burden of the financial support of international organizations requires simultaneous comparisons of all countries rather than comparisons of particular pairs. Simultaneous comparisons are also required by aid donors, whether national or international entities, that want to use relative incomes of potential recipients in order to determine the allocation of grants or soft loans. Analytical studies, particularly those seeking insights into economic development, are often based on cross-section data and require comparative real product figures for a large number of countries.[8] For these and other situations in which many countries must be considered in relation to each other, binary comparisons have serious disadvantages. The number of possible binary comparisons quickly becomes astronomical; even for the sixteen Phase II countries, there are 120 possible pairs. What is more important, however, binary comparisons will not, if carried out in the traditional way, define a cardinal scaling of countries with respect to real GDP per capita that does not depend upon the choice of the base country.

For these reasons, much of the effort in Phase I was devoted to developing methods to produce simultaneous comparisons with certain desired statistical properties. For example, the methods yield comparisons that possess the aforementioned property of "base-country invariance"; that is, the country selected as the base serves simply as a numéraire without affecting the unique cardinal scaling.

The methods cover both of the stages distinguished above in the discussion of binary comparisons: first, combining item data to obtain price or quantity

---

5. Each country's PPP can be converted into a price level comparison (with the United States equal to 100) by dividing it by the exchange rate (currency units per U.S. dollar) and multiplying by 100.

6. The name is derived from Irving Fisher, *The Making of Index Numbers* (Boston: Houghton Mifflin, 1922).

7. The term "characteristicity" was suggested in Laszlo Drechsler, "Weighting of Index Numbers in Multilateral International Comparisons," *Review of Income and Wealth*, March 1973, pp. 17–34.

8. A real product is a final product (that is, something that is bought for its own use and not for resale) that is valued at common prices in two or more countries and, therefore, is valued in comparable terms internationally.

indexes for each country at the detailed category level; and, second, averaging the price or quantity indexes for the different categories to obtain the price or quantity indexes at various levels of aggregation.

The need for special multilateral methods at the first of these levels arises from the fact that the items priced for a given category vary somewhat from one country to another. The method developed, the "country-product-dummy" method (CPD),[9] uses all the prices available, even though there are some holes in the typical tableau of item prices (items on the row stubs and countries in the column headings), to produce transitive price comparisons that do not vary with the base country.[10]

The PPPs directly obtained from the CPD method are used to derive (indirect) quantity ratios from expenditure ratios as in the binary comparisons—that is, by division of the PPPs into the expenditure ratios. In the multilateral comparisons, as in the binary comparisons, direct quantity comparisons and indirect price comparisons were made for some categories.

The method of aggregating the quantities of the detailed categories in the multilateral comparisons turned on the use of a set of "international prices" for the various categories. These international prices were then employed to value the category quantities of each of the countries in "international dollars" so that the category quantities could be added together to get total GDP. The international price for a category is defined as the quantity-weighted average of the category prices observed in each country after they have all been made commensurate by being divided by their respective country PPPs. The international prices have been estimated using a procedure devised by R. C. Geary and amplified by S. H. Khamis. The ICP inputs for the Geary-Khamis formulas are (1) the category PPPs for the various countries, obtained mainly by the CPD method, and (2) all the category quantities of the countries obtained by dividing these PPPs into the appropriate category expenditures of each country.

Without any adjustment of the quantity weights, the international prices and therefore the estimates of per capita GDPs would depend fortuitously on which countries fell within the ICP set. If the ICP countries were unrepresentative of all the countries in the world, this would affect the ICP results. Therefore, weights were used that in effect allowed each ICP country to affect the calculation of international prices in a way that reflected the prevalence of countries worldwide with its economic structure.[11]

It should be added that an international dollar has the same purchasing power over the U.S. GDP as a whole as a U.S. dollar, but its purchasing power over individual categories is different, because it is determined by the structure of international prices. The price and quantity relationships among the countries would be the same if some other country was taken as the numéraire country, even though the results would be described in terms of "international pounds," "international marks," or the like.[12]

9. See Chapter 3.

10. Transitivity is achieved if the indexes expressing the price or quantity relationships between any two among three or more countries are the same whether derived from an original-country comparison between them or from the comparison of each country with any third country. In the case of three countries, where I is a price index and j, k, and l are countries, there is transitivity when $I_{j/k} = I_{j/l} \div I_{k/l}$, where $I_{j/k}$ is the PPP for the jth country relative to the kth country.

11. See the discussion of "supercountries" in Chapter 3.

12. See Chapter 3 for a discussion of the dependence of the international prices on the choice of a numéraire country. It remains true, however, that the resulting quantity relationships do not depend upon the numéraire country.

The Main Results

*GDP in national currencies,
U.S. dollars, and inter-
national dollars*

In this section the main results of Phase II are summarized, first, regarding GDP; second, regarding the three principal components of GDP (consumption, capital formation, and government); and, third, regarding the commodity and service components of GDP.

Table 1.1 shows the GDPs of the sixteen Phase II countries in 1970 and 1973, first in national currencies, then in U.S. dollars after conversion by means of exchange rates, and finally in international dollars (I$).[13] Only the last set of figures applies a common measuring rod—a set of international prices—to the quantities constituting the GDPs of the various countries.

Attention is directed first to the GDP figures that are converted to U.S. dollars by means of exchange rates (columns 3 and 4), since this is the type of comparison most usually cited. According to this measure the GDP of most of the countries was less than 10 percent of that of the United States, and for five of the countries it was less than 1 percent in each year. Japan had the highest GDP, about 20 percent of the United States in 1970 and 31 percent in 1973.

The exchange-rate–converted figures imply that between 1970 and 1973 the United States lost substantial ground relative to the other countries. Indeed, the sum of the dollar GDPs of the fifteen countries in 1973 amounted to 121 percent of the U.S. total as against only 92 percent of the U.S. total in 1970.

These increases cannot, however, be taken at face value. They are the result of changes in exchange rates and domestic inflation as well as of changes in real income. The depreciation of the U.S. dollar between the two years relative to the currency of most countries, measured by the decline in the number of foreign currency units required to buy one U.S. dollar (compare the column 2 figures in 1970 and 1973), accounted for some of the largest individual country changes (for example, those of Germany and Japan).

Of course, the whole point of the ICP is to go behind these exchange-rate–converted dollar comparisons. The comparisons relying on exchange rates do not explicitly reflect the differing relative purchasing powers of currencies; they apply quite variable measures of value to the quantities in each country's GDP. The ICP results, on the other hand, are obtained by applying a common set of prices, expressed in international dollars, to the quantities of the commodities and services entering into each country's final expenditures on GDP. Within a particular year—1970 or 1973—the quantities valued in international dollars are comparable from country to country for GDP as a whole or for any given subaggregate thereof. As explained earlier, a 1970 international dollar has the same purchasing power over U.S. GDP as a whole as a 1970 U.S. dollar, but its purchasing power over individual categories (for example, bread, tractors) is different because it is determined by the structure of world prices. The same is true for a 1973 international dollar.

The comparisons in international dollars tell a very different story from the exchange-rate–converted GDPs. In 1970 the international dollar figures are consistently higher than the exchange-rate–converted figures (except, of course, for the United States, which is standardized to be the same); exchange-rate conversions understated the real GDP of all the other countries relative to that of the United States.

Between 1970 and 1973, the depreciation of the U.S. dollar relative to the

13. The basis for ordering the countries in Table 1.1 will be made clear when Table 1.2 is discussed below.

Table 1.1. Gross Domestic Product in National Currencies, in U.S. Dollars at Official Exchange Rates, and in International Dollars, 1970 and 1973

Country	Currency unit	GDP in national currency (millions) [a] (1)	Official exchange rate per U.S. dollar (2)	GDP in U.S. dollars converted at official exchange rate		GDP in international dollars (I$)	
				Millions of U.S. dollars (3)	U.S.=100 (4)	Millions of international dollars [b] (5)	U.S.=100 (6)
			1970				
Kenya	shilling	11,499 (P)	7.1429	1,610	0.16	3,406	0.35
India [c]	rupee	403,749 (P)	7.499	53,840	5.49	179,233	18.27
Philippines	peso	41,363 (F)	6.0652	6,820	0.70	21,222	2.16
Korea, Republic of	won	2,577,402 (F)	310.42	8,303	0.85	18,677	1.90
Colombia	peso	130,872 (F)	18.352	7,131	0.73	17,888	1.82
Malaysia	M. dollar	12,404 (F)	3.0797	4,028	0.41	9,511	0.97
Iran [d]	rial	884,100 (F)	76.38	11,575	1.18	28,055	2.86
Hungary	forint	321,458 (P)	30.0	10,715	1.09	21,127	2.15
Italy	lira	57,937 [e](P)	627.16	92,380	9.41	126,428	12.88
Japan	yen	70,894 [e](F)	358.15	197,945	20.17	294,036	29.96
United Kingdom	pound	50,772 (P)	0.4174	121,639	12.40	168,731	17.19
Netherlands	guilder	114,573 (P)	3.6166	31,680	3.23	42,857	4.37
Belgium	B. franc	1,263,310 (P)	49.656	25,441	2.59	33,250	3.39
France	franc	783,248 (P)	5.5289	141,664	14.44	177,908	18.13
Germany, F.R.	DM	679,407 (P)	3.6465	186,318	18.99	227,249	23.16
United States	dollar	981,290 (P)	1.0	981,290	100.00	981,290	100.00
			1973				
Kenya	shilling	16,114 (P)	7.0012	2,302	0.18	4,731	0.36
India [c]	rupee	576,785 (P)	7.742	74,501	5.72	227,626	17.47
Philippines	peso	70,237 (F)	6.7629	10,386	0.80	30,283	2.32
Korea, Republic of	won	4,965,700 (F)	398.54	12,460	0.96	30,782	2.36
Colombia	peso	235,968 (F)	23.813	9,909	0.76	24,892	1.91
Malaysia	M. dollar	17,488 (F)	2.4426	7,160	0.55	13,351	1.02
Iran [d]	rial	1,971,800 (F)	68.72	28,693	2.20	56,833	4.36
Hungary	forint	415,103 (P)	24.59	16,881	1.30	29,128	2.24
Italy	lira	80,818 [e](P)	583.0	138,624	10.64	159,953	12.28
Japan	yen	111,004 [e](F)	272.19	407,818	31.30	432,232	33.17
United Kingdom	pound	71,629 (P)	0.4078	175,647	13.48	210,103	16.13
Netherlands	guilder	165,379 (P)	2.7956	59,157	4.54	56,905	4.37
Belgium	B. franc	1,753,041 (P)	38.977	44,976	3.45	45,416	3.49
France	franc	1,109,047 (P)	4.454	249,000	19.11	245,491	18.84
Germany, F.R.	DM	916,716 (P)	2.6725	343,018	26.33	296,940	22.79
United States	dollar	1,302,920 (P)	1.0	1,302,920	100.00	1,302,920	100.00

Sources: GDP in national currency: The GDP figures are those reported for ICP purposes by participating countries or, in the case of the member countries of the European Common Market, by the Statistical Office of the European Communities. Adjustments to the 1973 figures for rent subsidies have been made in a number of cases on the basis of the estimates available for 1970. Exchange rates: Annual average market rates as reported in International Monetary Fund, *International Financial Statistics*, February 1977, except for Colombia, for which average implicit rates are used; Kenya and Philippines, for which average par rates are used; and Hungary, for which exchange rates for 1970 are from United Nations, *Statistical Yearbook*, 1971, p. 605, and for 1973 from the Hungarian Central Statistical Office. GDP in international dollars: Per capita figures from Summary Multilateral Tables 4.5 and 4.10 multiplied by population figures in Table 1.2.

a. (F) refers to estimates based on the 1952 version of the U.N. System of National Accounts (SNA); (P) refers to estimates based on the current (1968) version. See U.N. Statistical Office, *A System of National Accounts*, Studies in Methods, Series F, No. 2, Rev. 3 (New York: United Nations, 1968). For the few cases among the countries in which estimates have been available on both the former and the current bases, the GDP aggregates have differed by amounts ranging up to 4.6 percent, with neither version consistently yielding a higher aggregate than the other.

b. The 1970 international dollar has the same *overall* purchasing power as a 1970 U.S. dollar, and the 1973 international dollar the same as a 1973 U.S. dollar. The 1970 and 1973 figures in column (5) thus differ because of both price and quantity changes between the two years.

c. Reference year beginning 1 April of year indicated.

d. Reference year beginning 21 March of year indicated.

e. Billions.

Japanese yen and the currencies of some of the European countries sharply reduced the differences between comparisons with the United States based on U.S. dollars and comparisons based on international dollars. In fact, in the case of three of the countries, the former figures actually exceeded the latter.

Some overall indication of the difference between the two sets of estimates is given by the fact that in 1970 the GDP of the United States measured in international dollars was 28.3 percent lower than the aggregate GDP of the fifteen other countries, whereas measured in exchange-rate–converted figures it was 8.9 percent higher; in 1973 it was 30.1 percent lower measured in international dollars and 17.6 percent lower measured by the exchange-rate figures. In both years the GDP of the United States in international dollars was higher than that of the six current members of the Common Market that are included in the Phase II countries (Belgium, France, the Federal Republic of Germany, Italy, the Netherlands, and the United Kingdom); their aggregate was 79 percent of the U.S. aggregate in 1970 and 78 percent in 1973. By contrast, the figures were 61 percent for 1970 and 77.5 percent for 1973 using exchange-rate–converted comparisons.

For many purposes it is more useful to consider international comparisons of GDP per capita rather than aggregate GDP. It is the per capita figures that will be used in the balance of this book, beginning with those set out in Table 1.2. In this table the countries are arrayed in order of increasing real GDP per capita (that is, in international dollars) for 1970. The exchange-rate–converted figures are also shown. Of course, for any country the ratio between its real GDP and its exchange-rate–converted GDP is the same whether expressed in terms of the aggregate figures of Table 1.1 or in terms of the per capita figures of Table 1.2.

With the countries arrayed in order of increasing real GDP per capita, the systematic relationship between the ICP estimates and the exchange-rate–derived figures may be clearly seen: the ratio of real GDP per capita to exchange-rate–converted GDP per capita—referred to as the "exchange-rate–deviation index" (column 7)—falls as per capita real GDP rises. This phenomenon can be explained in terms of what may be referred to as a "productivity differential" model, which has been offered at various times by Ricardo, Viner, Harrod, and Balassa.[14] The model turns on the impact of differences in the productivity gap between high- and low-income countries for traded and nontraded goods. International trade tends to drive the prices of traded goods, mainly commodities, towards equality in different countries. With equal or nearly equal prices, wages in the traded goods industries in each country will depend upon productivity. Wages established in the traded goods industries within each country will prevail in the country's nontraded goods industries. In nontraded goods industries, however, international productivity differentials tend to be smaller. Consequently, in a high-productivity country high wages lead to high prices of services and other nontraded goods, whereas in a low-productivity country low wages produce low prices. The lower a country's income, the lower will be the prices of its home goods and the greater will be the tendency for exchange-rate conversions to underestimate its real income relative to that of richer countries.

As the exchange-rate–deviation index indicates, the 1970 real GDP per

14. D. Ricardo, *The Principles of Political Economy and Taxation* (London: J. M. Dent and Sons, 1911), p. 87; J. Viner, *Studies in the Theory of International Trade* (New York: Harper and Brothers, 1937), p. 315; R. F. Harrod, *International Economics* (New York and London: Pitman Publishing Co., 1947), Chapter 4; and Bela Balassa, "The Purchasing Power Parity Doctrine: A Reappraisal," *Journal of Political Economy*, December 1964, pp. 584–96.

capita of the fifteen partner countries relative to that of the United States ranged from more than 20 percent higher than indicated by the exchange-rate–converted figures in the cases of France and the Federal Republic of Germany to more than three times as great in the cases of India and the Philippines.

The depreciation of the U.S. dollar relative to European currencies between 1970 and 1973 brought European/U.S. exchange rates into closer alignment with purchasing-power parities; the exchange-rate–deviation index for all the

Table 1.2. Population and per Capita Gross Domestic Product in National Currencies, in U.S. Dollars at Official Exchange Rates, and in International Dollars, 1970 and 1973

Country	Currency unit	Population (thousands) (1)	Per Capita GDP In national currency (2)	In U.S. dollars converted at official exchange rates U.S. dollars (3)	U.S.=100 (4)	In international dollars [a] International dollars (5)	U.S.=100 (6)	Exchange-rate–deviation index (7)=(5)÷(3) (7)
1970								
Kenya	shilling	11,230	1,024	143	2.99	303	6.33	2.12
India	rupee	541,000	746	99	2.07	331	6.92	3.35
Philippines	peso	36,850	1,122	185	3.86	576	12.0	3.11
Korea, Republic of	won	32,190	80,068	258	5.39	580	12.1	2.25
Colombia	peso	20,580	6,359	347	7.24	869	18.1	2.50
Malaysia	M. dollar	10,390	1,194	388	8.10	915	19.1	2.36
Iran	rial	28,860	30,633	401	8.37	972	20.3	2.42
Hungary	forint	10,340	31,089	1,036	21.6	2,043	42.7	1.97
Italy	lira	53,660	1,079,706	1,722	36.0	2,356	49.2	1.37
Japan	yen	103,720	683,513	1,908	39.8	2,835	59.2	1.49
United Kingdom	pound	55,520	914	2,190	45.7	3,039	63.5	1.39
Netherlands	guilder	13,030	8,793	2,431	50.8	3,289	68.7	1.35
Belgium	B. franc	9,640	131,050	2,639	55.1	3,449	72.0	1.31
France	franc	50,770	15,427	2,790	58.2	3,504	73.2	1.26
Germany, F.R.	DM	60,650	11,202	3,072	64.1	3,747	78.2	1.22
United States	dollar	204,880	4,790	4,790	100.0	4,790	100.0	1.00
1973								
Kenya	shilling	12,480	1,291	184	2.97	379	6.12	2.06
India	rupee	577,000	1,000	129	2.08	394	6.37	3.06
Philippines	peso	40,120	1,751	259	4.18	755	12.2	2.91
Korea, Republic of	won	34,070	145,750	366	5.91	904	14.6	2.47
Colombia	peso	22,500	10,487	440	7.11	1,106	17.9	2.51
Malaysia	M. dollar	11,310	1,546	633	10.2	1,180	19.1	1.86
Iran	rial	31,410	62,776	914	14.8	1,809	29.2	1.98
Hungary	forint	10,430	39,799	1,619	26.2	2,793	45.1	1.72
Italy	lira	54,910	1,471,828	2,525	40.8	2,913	47.0	1.15
Japan	yen	109,100	1,017,451	3,738	60.4	3,962	64.0	1.06
United Kingdom	pound	56,020	1,279	3,136	50.6	3,750	60.6	1.20
Netherlands	guilder	13,440	12,305	4,402	71.1	4,234	68.4	0.96
Belgium	B. franc	9,740	179,984	4,618	74.6	4,663	75.3	1.01
France	franc	52,130	21,275	4,777	77.2	4,709	76.1	0.99
Germany, F.R.	DM	61,980	14,791	5,535	89.4	4,791	77.4	0.87
United States	dollar	210,410	6,192	6,192	100.0	6,192	100.0	1.00

Sources: Column 1 contains mid-year population estimates: Kenya, Hungary, Italy, Malaysia, the Netherlands, the Philippines, and the United States from United Nations, *Monthly Bulletin of Statistics,* May 1977; Belgium, France, and the Federal Republic of Germany from Statistical Office of the European Communities, 1976, *National Accounts Aggregates 1960–75, Yearbook 1976;* Colombia, India, Iran, Japan, the Republic of Korea, and the United Kingdom provided by the countries for the ICP. Columns 2 and 3 are calculated from data in column (1) and Table 1.1. Column 5 is taken from Summary Multilateral Tables 4.5 and 4.10.

a. The 1970 international dollar has the same *overall* purchasing power as a 1970 U.S. dollar, and the 1973 international dollar the same as a 1973 U.S. dollar. The 1970 and 1973 figures in column 5 thus differ because of both price and quantity changes between the two years.

European countries is closer to 1 in 1973 than in 1970. The same is less uniformly true for the five lowest-income countries in Table 1.2; for the Republic of Korea and Colombia, two of the four countries with currencies that depreciated against the dollar,[15] the exchange-rate–deviation index is higher in 1973 than in 1970, although only marginally so in the second case.

The large changes in exchange rates between the two years underline the unreliability of comparisons based on exchange-rate conversions. The exchange-rate–converted figures in the case of the Federal Republic of Germany, for example, suggest that its per capita GDP relative to that of the United States rose from 64.1 percent in 1970 to 89.4 percent in 1973. In fact, Germany's per capita real GDP (that is, measured in international dollars) declined slightly relative to that of the United States, from 78.2 percent to 77.4 percent. Because of the ICP methods, the latter result is much more closely in accord with the relative growth of the real per capita GDP (that is, as measured in constant internal prices) between the two years in the two countries; real GDP per capita increased by 9.5 percent in Germany and by 11.6 percent in the United States.[16] (The decline in the German index—from 78.2 percent to 77.4 percent—does not precisely match the implied 2.1 percent decrease because international prices, rather than the prices of Germany and the United States, are used to derive the Table 1.2 figures for each year.)

The variation in the exchange-rate–deviation index from country to country means that the relative per capita income levels of the countries cannot be inferred from exchange-rate–converted GDP per capita. For only one pair of countries, however, does the ordinal ranking based upon international prices differ from that based upon exchange-rate conversions. In both years, the use of international prices produces a slightly higher per capita GDP for India than for Kenya, which is the opposite of the result obtained when exchange rates are used to convert the countries' GDPs to U.S. dollars.

The discussion so far has focused on indexes based on the United States, and this indeed will remain the standard method of summarizing the results of the ICP. As explained above, however, the choice of the United States as the numéraire country and the expression of values in terms of international dollars do not determine the per capita quantity relationships either at the detailed category level, at summary category levels, or at higher levels of aggregation. Any other country could have been selected as the numéraire without affecting the quantity relationships such as those in column 6 of Tables 1.1 and 1.2. Of course, all the value figures such as those in column 5 of the two tables would be altered by a common factor when expressed in terms of a different currency, and all of the index comparisons (column 6) would be altered by a common factor to make the value figure for the new numéraire country equal to 100. Any one of the sixteen countries can legitimately be selected as the base country and the real per capita GDPs of the other countries can be expressed as a ratio to the real per capita GDP of that country. The full matrix of the relationships is presented in a convenient

15. Compare the 1970 and 1973 figures in Table 1.1, column 2.

16. The figures on GDP in constant prices and the population figures for the two countries are taken from United Nations, *Monthly Bulletin of Statistics,* July 1976. The same issue of the *Bulletin* contains per capita GDP figures converted to U.S. dollars by means of exchange rates (in Special Table C) that are very similar to the exchange-rate–converted figures reported in Table 1.2. The footnote in the *Bulletin* warning against intertemporal comparisons of real per capita product based on such exchange-rate–converted GDPs should be taken seriously. Since the intertemporal relations are untrustworthy, it is also difficult to know the year for which the comparisons are closest to the true relationship.

Table 1.3. Relative Gross Domestic Product per Capita. All Pairs of Countries, 1970 and 1973

(Percent)

Base country	Kenya	India	Philip-pines	Korea, Republic of	Co-lombia	Malaysia	Iran	Hungary
1970								
Kenya	100.0	109.2	189.9	191.3	286.6	301.8	320.5	673.7
India	91.5	100.0	173.8	175.1	262.4	276.3	293.4	616.7
Philippines	52.7	57.5	100.0	100.7	150.9	159.0	168.8	354.8
Korea, Republic of	52.3	57.1	99.3	100.0	149.8	157.8	167.5	352.2
Colombia	34.9	38.1	66.3	66.8	100.0	105.3	111.8	235.1
Malaysia	33.1	36.2	62.9	63.4	95.0	100.0	106.2	223.2
Iran	31.2	34.1	59.2	59.7	89.4	94.2	100.0	210.2
Hungary	14.8	16.2	28.2	28.4	42.5	44.8	47.6	100.0
Italy	12.9	14.1	24.4	24.6	36.9	38.9	41.3	86.7
Japan	10.7	11.7	20.3	20.5	30.7	32.3	34.3	72.1
United Kingdom	10.0	10.9	18.9	19.1	28.6	30.1	32.0	67.2
Netherlands	9.2	10.1	17.5	17.6	26.4	27.8	29.6	62.1
Belgium	8.8	9.6	16.7	16.8	25.2	26.5	28.2	59.2
France	8.7	9.5	16.4	16.6	24.8	26.1	27.7	58.3
Germany, F.R.	8.1	8.8	15.4	15.5	23.2	24.4	25.9	54.5
United States	6.3	6.9	12.0	12.1	18.1	19.1	20.3	42.7
1973								
Kenya	100.0	104.1	199.1	238.3	291.8	311.4	477.3	736.7
India	96.1	100.0	191.3	229.0	280.4	299.2	458.7	707.9
Philippines	50.2	52.3	100.0	119.7	146.6	156.4	239.7	370.0
Korea, Republic of	42.0	43.7	83.5	100.0	122.4	130.7	200.3	309.1
Colombia	34.3	35.7	68.2	81.7	100.0	106.7	163.6	252.4
Malaysia	32.1	33.4	63.9	76.5	93.7	100.0	153.3	236.6
Iran	21.0	21.8	41.7	49.9	61.1	65.2	100.0	154.3
Hungary	13.6	14.1	27.0	32.4	39.6	42.3	64.8	100.0
Italy	13.0	13.5	25.9	31.0	38.0	40.5	62.1	95.9
Japan	9.6	10.0	19.1	22.8	27.9	29.8	45.7	70.5
United Kingdom	10.1	10.5	20.1	24.1	29.5	31.5	48.2	74.5
Netherlands	9.0	9.3	17.8	21.3	26.1	27.9	42.7	66.0
Belgium	8.1	8.5	16.2	19.4	23.7	25.3	38.8	59.9
France	8.1	8.4	16.0	19.2	23.5	25.1	38.4	59.3
Germany, F.R.	7.9	8.2	15.8	18.9	23.1	24.6	37.8	58.3
United States	6.1	6.4	12.2	14.6	17.9	19.1	29.2	45.1

way in Table 1.3, which takes each country in turn as the base country. For example, the table shows that the 1973 real per capita GDP of India was 43.7 percent of that of the Republic of Korea, whereas the relationship of Korea to Malaysia was 76.5 percent. (The corresponding exchange-rate–converted figures calculated from column 3 of Table 1.2 are 35.2 percent and 57.8 percent, respectively.)

Table 1.4 reverts to comparisons on a U.S. base and offers estimates of real GDP per capita in international dollars for some additional years— 1967, 1974, and 1975. The 1970 and 1973 figures are repeated from Table 1.2 as a matter of convenience.[17] The 1967 figures are based on those pub-

17. As noted in the tables, direct comparisons of the value aggregates (in international dollars) should not be made between the two years. It would be wrong, for example, to think that the real per capita GDP of the Philippines went up by a factor of 754.8/575.9 between 1970 and 1973. The reason is that the purchasing powers of the 1973 and 1970 international dollars are not the same.

Italy	Japan	United Kingdom	Nether-lands	Belgium	France	Germany, F.R.	United States	Base country
				1970				
776.8	934.7	1,002.0	1,084.4	1,137.2	1,155.4	1,235.4	1,579.1	Kenya
711.2	855.7	917.3	992.8	1,041.1	1,057.7	1,131.0	1,445.7	India
409.1	492.3	527.7	571.1	598.9	608.5	650.6	831.7	Philippines
406.1	488.6	523.8	566.9	594.5	605.0	645.8	825.5	Korea, Republic of
271.1	326.2	349.6	378.4	396.8	403.2	431.1	551.0	Colombia
257.4	309.7	332.0	359.3	376.8	382.8	409.3	523.2	Malaysia
242.4	291.6	312.6	338.3	354.8	360.5	385.4	492.7	Iran
115.3	138.7	148.7	161.0	168.8	171.5	183.4	234.4	Hungary
100.0	120.3	129.0	139.6	146.4	148.7	159.0	203.3	Italy
83.1	100.0	107.2	116.0	121.7	123.6	132.2	168.9	Japan
77.5	93.3	100.0	108.2	113.5	115.3	123.3	157.6	United Kingdom
71.6	86.2	92.4	100.0	104.9	106.5	113.9	145.6	Netherlands
68.3	82.2	88.1	95.4	100.0	101.6	108.6	138.9	Belgium
67.2	80.9	86.7	93.9	98.4	100.0	106.9	136.7	France
62.9	75.7	81.1	87.8	92.1	93.5	100.0	127.8	Germany, F.R.
49.2	59.2	63.5	68.7	72.0	73.2	78.2	100.0	United States
				1973				
768.4	1,045.1	989.3	1,116.9	1,230.0	1,242.2	1,263.8	1,633.4	Kenya
738.4	1,004.3	950.7	1,073.3	1,182.0	1,193.7	1,214.4	1,569.6	India
385.9	524.9	496.9	560.9	617.8	623.9	634.7	820.4	Philippines
322.4	438.5	415.1	468.6	516.1	521.2	530.3	685.4	Korea, Republic of
263.3	358.1	339.0	382.7	421.5	425.7	433.1	559.7	Colombia
246.8	335.6	317.7	358.7	395.0	398.9	405.8	524.5	Malaysia
161.0	219.0	207.3	234.0	257.7	260.3	264.8	342.2	Iran
104.3	141.9	134.3	151.6	167.0	168.6	171.6	221.7	Hungary
100.0	136.0	128.8	145.3	160.1	161.7	164.5	212.6	Italy
73.5	100.0	94.7	106.9	117.7	118.9	120.9	156.3	Japan
77.7	105.6	100.0	112.9	124.3	125.6	127.7	165.1	United Kingdom
68.8	93.6	88.6	100.0	110.1	111.2	113.2	146.2	Netherlands
62.5	85.0	80.4	90.8	100.0	101.0	102.7	132.8	Belgium
61.9	84.1	79.6	89.9	99.0	100.0	101.7	131.5	France
60.8	82.7	78.3	88.4	97.3	98.3	100.0	129.2	Germany, F.R.
47.0	64.0	60.6	68.4	75.3	76.1	77.4	100.0	United States

Note: Each table entry gives the GDP per capita of the country named at the top of the column relative to that of the country named at the beginning of the row.

lished in *A System,* adjusted only to take account of revisions in expenditures on GDP for that date that have become available to the ICP since the publication of the Phase I report.[18] The 1974 and 1975 figures are extrapolations of the 1973 comparisons derived by the "international price" method described later in Chapter 4. The method is designed to ensure that changes in the terms of trade since the benchmark year are incorporated in the year for which the extrapolations are performed. For this purpose, the net foreign balance (exports minus imports) is treated differently from the rest of GDP, which is referred to as "domestic absorption." The real per capita quantity change in domestic absorption for each country is calculated in a straightforward manner using the expenditure data from national accounts in current

18. The most notable revision was for the United Kingdom, for which the index rose from 61.0 in the Phase I report to 61.9.

**Table 1.4. Indexes of Real Gross Domestic Product per Capita in
International Dollars, 1967, 1970, 1973, 1974, and 1975**

(United States =100)

Country	1967	1970	1973	1974	1975
Kenya	5.64	6.33	6.12	6.23	6.09
India	6.93	6.92	6.37	n.a.	n.a.
Philippines	n.a.	12.0	12.2	13.1	13.9
Korea, Republic of	n.a.	12.1	14.6	15.9	16.9
Colombia	n.a.	18.1	17.9	19.4	19.8
Malaysia	n.a.	19.1	19.1	21.8	19.9
Iran	n.a.	20.3	29.2	36.7	40.8
Hungary	37.6	42.7	45.1	49.6	n.a.
Italy	n.a.	49.2	47.0	47.7	47.1
Japan	48.3	59.2	64.0	63.2	65.1
United Kingdom	61.9	63.5	60.6	60.5	62.0
Netherlands	n.a.	68.7	68.4	70.3	70.5
Belgium	n.a.	72.0	75.3	79.2	78.3
France	n.a.	73.2	76.1	78.6	79.5
Germany, F.R.	n.a.	78.2	77.4	78.9	79.2
United States	100.0	100.0	100.0	100.0	100.0

n.a. Not available.
Sources: For 1967, benchmark ICP estimates from Summary Multilateral Table 14.9 in Irving B. Kravis, Zoltan Kenessey, Alan Heston, and Robert Summers, *A System of International Comparisons of Gross Product and Purchasing Power* (Baltimore: Johns Hopkins University Press, 1975), adjusted for subsequent revisions in GDP figures; for 1970 and 1973, benchmark ICP estimates from Table 1.2; for 1974 and 1975, extrapolated from 1973 by the international price method described in Chapter 4.

prices and the implicit deflators for consumption, capital formation, and government. The quantity change is applied to domestic absorption for the benchmark year (1973) valued in international dollars to derive domestic absorption for the extrapolation year (1974 or 1975), also valued in benchmark-year international dollars. The per capita net foreign balance is also valued in benchmark-year international dollars and the two components of per capita GDP are then added to obtain a total that is expressed as an index number relative to the corresponding U.S. total.

Most of the countries in Table 1.4 have rising indexes relative to the United States, reflecting the relatively slow rate of real per capita GDP growth in the United States. The main exceptions are Malaysia, Italy, the United Kingdom, and the Federal Republic of Germany, which maintained nearly constant indexes relative to the United States, and India, which experienced some decline between the two earlier years and 1973. Not surprisingly, the most spectacular increase among the ICP countries was that of Iran: relative to the United States, Iran's per capita real GDP doubled between 1970 and 1975. The Republic of Korea's index also rose substantially relative to the United States and to the other countries; Hungary, Belgium, Japan, and France were other relative gainers. The combination of rapid growth in Japan and slow growth in the United Kingdom brought about a reversal between 1970 and 1973 in their rank order position with respect to real per capita GDP. Similar extrapolations of the benchmark data are made for other years in the 1965–75 period in Chapter 4.

Consumption, capital formation, and government

The three main components of GDP—consumption, capital formation, and government—for the benchmark years (1970 and 1973) are presented in Tables 1.5 and 1.6. Table 1.5 shows the breakdown of the components in national currencies and by percentage share of GDP. Table 1.6 presents the same breakdown in international dollars, the corresponding percentage shares, and, for each of the three components, per capita quantity indexes with the United States equal to 100.

These figures may be analyzed in a number of ways and, for the most part, the reader is left to follow his own interests. An illuminating way of thinking through the implications of the two tables, however, is presented in Table 1.7.

Table 1.7 shows the relation of the price structure of each country to the structure of international prices. Specifically, the figures in the table represent for each country the ratio of the share of a given component in expenditure on GDP in national (own) prices (from Table 1.5) to the share of the component in expenditure on GDP in international prices (from Table 1.6). This ratio may be written as:

$$R_{ij} = \frac{P_{ij}Q_{ij} / \sum_{i=1}^{3} P_{ij}Q_{ij}}{\Pi_i Q_{ij} / \sum_{i=1}^{3} \Pi_i Q_{ij}},$$

where P_{ij} and Q_{ij} are the domestic price and quantity of the ith component in the jth country, and Π is the international price. The value of R_{ij} for GDP as a whole is 1 (both the numerator and the denominator would be 1 for all of GDP). Consequently, a value of more than 1.00 for a given country in a given component indicates that, relative to the relationship of the country's prices to international prices for its GDP as a whole, the country's prices for that particular component are high. A figure below 1.00, on the other hand, indicates that a component is cheap in the country's structure of relative prices compared to the world structure of relative prices.

Table 1.7 indicates that for these broad aggregative categories the general features of the relative price structures of the countries remained the same in the two years despite the fact that the period 1970–73 was marked by unusual changes in rates of inflation and in exchange rates. Where a particular component differs substantially from 1.00 in one year, it almost invariably differs substantially in the same direction in the other year. That is not to say the differences between the two years are always trivial: for nine of the sixteen countries, the figure for at least one of the three components changed by more than 5 percentage points.

In both years, the deviations of consumption from the overall price relationship for GDP as a whole tend to be smaller than the deviations of either of the other major components. This is to be expected because consumption is such a large proportion of GDP (generally 55 to 75 percent in own prices). As the 1970 data for Japan indicate, however, it is not a necessary occurrence.

Larger deviations are found in the capital formation component. The pattern of these deviations is particularly interesting because investment is so strategic for economic development. The figures indicate that capital goods are relatively expensive (figures above 1.00) in the four lowest-income countries and relatively inexpensive (figures below 1.00) in the six highest-income countries. The picture presented by the six middle-income countries is mixed with no clear pattern.

These results can, of course, be seen directly in Tables 1.5 and 1.6. A comparison of Tables 1.5 and 1.6 shows that the share of capital formation of the four lowest-income countries is reduced, sometimes quite sharply, when the valuation basis is shifted from national to international prices. For example, the share of capital formation in the Philippines in 1970 is reduced from 21 percent in national prices (line 6 of Table 1.5) to 13 percent in international prices (line 6 of Table 1.6). For the six highest-income countries, the opposite is true; the share of capital formation rises when international prices replace national prices.

Table 1.5. Gross Domestic Product and Its Main Components in National Currencies and by Percentage Distribution, 1970 and 1973

(National currencies in millions, except lira and yen in billions)

Category	Kenya (shillings)	India (rupees)	Philip-pines (pesos)	Korea, Republic of (won)	Colombia (pesos)	Malaysia (M. dollars)	Iran (rials)	Hungary (forints)
1970								
In national currencies								
1. Consumption	8,028	304,716	30,498	1,924,330	95,854	8,171	545,400	194,226
2. Capital formation	2,322	67,362	8,571	434,707	26,466	2,891	221,700	102,290
3. Government	1,149	31,671	2,294	218,365	8,552	1,342	117,000	24,942
4. GDP	11,499	403,749	41,363	2,577,402	130,872	12,404	884,100	321,458
Percentage distribution								
5. Consumption	70	75	74	75	73	66	62	60
6. Capital formation	20	17	21	17	20	23	25	32
7. Government	10	8	6	8	7	11	13	8
8. GDP [a]	100	100	100	100	100	100	100	100
1973								
In national currencies								
1. Consumption	10,658	437,698	50,366	3,460,572	168,176	10,763	907,000	239,085
2. Capital formation	3,892	96,639	16,044	1,129,393	52,304	4,642	797,100	147,257
3. Government	1,565	42,448	3,828	375,735	15,488	2,083	267,700	28,761
4. GDP	16,114	576,785	70,237	4,965,700	235,968	17,488	1,971,800	415,103
Percentage distribution								
5. Consumption	66	76	72	70	71	62	46	58
6. Capital formation	24	17	23	23	22	27	40	35
7. Government	10	7	5	8	7	12	14	7
8. GDP [a]	100	100	100	100	100	100	100	100

The entries in Table 1.7 indicate that government is relatively inexpensive (figures below 1.00) in the low-income countries and relatively expensive (figures above 1.00) in the high-income countries. Once again, these findings have their reflection in the shares of expenditure shown in Tables 1.5 and 1.6. When international prices rather than local prices are used for evaluation, expenditure shares are 4 to 10 percentage points higher in the four low-income countries and 1 to 3 percentage points lower in the six high-income countries. Of course, if international prices shrink the share of capital formation in the four lowest-income countries and expand the share in the six highest-income countries, they must in each case have offsetting effects on the share of one or both of the other components. Most of the compensation is found in government.

The standard of comparison most commonly used is the U.S. structure of prices, not the international price structure. Thus, in Table 1.8 purchasing-power parities relative to the United States and price level indexes with the United States as the base country are presented.

Much the same story emerges from this table as the one that came out of Tables 1.5, 1.6, and 1.7. Capital formation in the four lowest-income countries is characterized by PPPs that are high (line 2) relative to the PPPs for GDP as a whole (line 4) and, correspondingly, by price indexes that are high (line 7) relative to the price level index for GDP as a whole (line 9). Because the countries are arrayed in order of increasing per capita incomes, one must go well to the right in the table before finding cases in which capital goods are cheap relative to GDP as a whole (Italy, the United Kingdom, the Netherlands, France, and the Federal Republic of Germany, in one or both years). The paucity of these cases indicates that the prices of capital goods

Italy (lire)	Japan (yen)	United Kingdom (pounds)	Netherlands (guilders)	Belgium (B. francs)	France (francs)	Germany, F.R. (DM)	United States (dollars)	Category
				1970				
								In national currencies
39,106	38,678	35,128	72,185	823,040	498,029	410,434	670,090	1. Consumption
13,727	28,775	10,301	30,278	337,510	212,678	209,174	174,720	2. Capital formation
5,104	3,441	5,343	12,110	102,760	72,541	59,799	136,480	3. Government
57,937	70,894	50,772	114,573	1,263,310	783,248	679,407	981,290	4. GDP
								Percentage distribution
67	55	69	63	65	64	60	68	5. Consumption
24	41	20	26	27	27	31	18	6. Capital formation
9	5	11	11	8	9	9	14	7. Government
100	100	100	100	100	100	100	100	8. GDP [a]
				1973				
								In national currencies
55,629	60,694	50,729	101,927	1,158,533	709,119	564,085	885,960	1. Consumption
16,959	44,367	13,144	45,733	441,360	301,354	264,450	255,731	2. Capital formation
8,230	5,943	7,756	17,719	153,148	98,574	88,181	161,229	3. Government
80,818	111,004	71,629	165,379	1,753,041	1,109,047	916,716	1,302,920	4. GDP
								Percentage distribution
69	55	71	62	66	64	62	68	5. Consumption
21	40	18	28	25	27	29	20	6. Capital formation
10	5	11	11	9	9	10	12	7. Government
100	100	100	100	100	100	100	100	8. GDP [a]

Sources: As in Table 1.1.
a. Percentages may not add to 100 because of rounding.

are relatively cheap in the United States compared with the prices in the consumption and government sectors. Of course, the internal price structures of different countries (each relative to the price structure of the United States) are being compared, so it does not contradict the point made earlier to observe that, in terms of a common currency (for example, U.S. dollars), capital goods in very poor countries tend to be low in price relative to the same goods in rich countries. The reason is that the (U.S. dollar) prices of commodities and services in the consumption and government sectors in poor countries are even further below the corresponding prices in rich countries than are the prices of capital goods. In India, for example, capital goods were priced at 37 percent of the U.S. price level in 1970, whereas the prices of consumption and government were 32 percent and 14 percent, respectively.

The inferences drawn from the earlier tables about prices for government services are also reflected in Table 1.8. Government, with its large component of employee compensation, tends to be low in the relative price structure of low-income countries and high in the upper-income countries.

For the most part, an examination of more detailed subaggregations is left to Chapter 4, but the dichotomy between the commodity and service components of GDP is explored briefly here. Table 1.9 shows per capita quantity indexes for these two components, first, based on the conversion of each country's expenditures by means of exchange rates and, second, in real terms by valuing all the quantities at average international prices. "Services" are defined to include categories in which expenditures are entirely on per-

Comparisons for the commodity and service components of GDP

Table 1.6. Per Capita Gross Domestic Product and Its Main Components in International Dollars, by Percentage Distribution, and in Indexes of Quantity per Capita, 1970 and 1973

Category	Kenya	India	Philip-pines	Korea, Republic of	Colombia	Malaysia	Iran	Hungary
1970								
Valuation at international prices (international dollars)								
1. Consumption	209	234	444	416	617	602	647	1,347
2. Capital formation	45	50	73	87	175	217	224	520
3. Government	50	47	58	77	77	96	102	176
4. GDP	303	331	576	580	869	915	972	2,043
Percentage distribution of GDP valued at international dollars								
5. Consumption	69	71	77	72	71	66	67	66
6. Capital formation	15	15	13	15	20	24	23	25
7. Government	16	14	10	13	9	10	10	9
8. GDP	100	100	100	100	100	100	100	100
Per capita quantity indexes based on international prices (United States=100)								
9. Consumption	6.4	7.2	13.6	12.7	18.9	18.5	19.8	41.3
10. Capital formation	4.7	5.3	7.7	9.1	18.3	22.8	23.5	54.6
11. Government	8.6	8.2	10.1	13.4	13.4	16.8	17.6	30.5
12. GDP	6.3	6.9	12.0	12.1	18.1	19.1	20.3	42.7
1973								
Valuation at international prices (international dollars)								
1. Consumption	258	270	569	618	780	736	972	1,767
2. Capital formation	58	58	110	184	235	313	628	792
3. Government	62	66	75	101	92	131	209	234
4. GDP	379	394	755	904	1,106	1,180	1,809	2,793
Percentage distribution of GDP valued at international dollars								
5. Consumption	68	68	75	68	70	62	54	63
6. Capital formation	15	15	15	20	21	26	35	28
7. Government	16	17	10	11	8	11	12	8
8. GDP	100	100	100	100	100	100	100	100
Per capita quantity indexes based on international prices (United States=100)								
9. Consumption	6.1	6.4	13.5	14.7	18.5	17.5	23.1	42.0
10. Capital formation	4.4	4.3	8.2	13.7	17.5	23.3	46.7	59.0
11. Government	9.8	10.3	11.7	15.8	14.3	20.5	32.7	36.6
12. GDP	6.1	6.4	12.2	14.6	17.9	19.1	29.2	45.1

sonnel (for example, domestic services, teachers, and government employees), repairs of various kinds, rents, public transport and communication, public entertainment, and household services. All of the other categories of GDP in this rough classification are regarded as "commodities."

When indexes with the United States equal to 100 are based on the use of exchange rates to convert all figures to U.S. dollars, it appears that other countries consume relatively larger quantities of commodities than of services (compare columns 1 and 2). Further, the ratio of the commodity index to the service index (with the United States equal to 100 in both cases) tends to be highest in the lowest-income countries and shows a tendency to diminish as real GDP per capita rises, though not without interruptions. For example, in 1970 the average ratio for the four lowest-income countries was 2.2, whereas

Italy	Japan	United Kingdom	Nether- lands	Belgium	France	Germany, F.R.	United States	Category
				1970				
								Valuation at international prices (international dollars)
1,560	1,609	2,038	2,051	2,276	2,149	2,111	3,261	1. Consumption
631	1,084	696	964	941	1,065	1,376	953	2. Capital formation
165	142	305	274	232	291	259	576	3. Government
2,356	2,835	3,039	3,289	3,449	3,504	3,747	4,790	4. GDP
								Percentage distribution of GDP valued at international dollars
66	57	67	62	66	61	56	68	5. Consumption
27	38	23	29	27	30	37	20	6. Capital formation
7	5	10	8	7	8	7	12	7. Government
100	100	100	100	100	100	100	100	8. GDP
								Per capita quantity indexes based on international prices (United States=100)
47.9	49.3	62.5	62.9	69.8	65.9	64.7	100.0	9. Consumption
66.2	113.7	73.0	101.2	98.8	111.8	144.5	100.0	10. Capital formation
28.6	24.8	52.9	47.6	40.3	50.5	45.1	100.0	11. Government
49.2	59.2	63.5	68.7	72.0	73.2	78.2	100.0	12. GDP
				1973				
								Valuation at international prices (international dollars)
1,994	2,252	2,618	2,540	3,149	2,857	2,692	4,209	1. Consumption
692	1,514	756	1,360	1,211	1,477	1,747	1,343	2. Capital formation
227	196	377	334	302	375	352	640	3. Government
2,913	3,962	3,750	4,234	4,663	4,709	4,791	6,192	4. GDP
								Percentage distribution of GDP valued at international dollars
68	57	70	60	68	61	56	68	5. Consumption
24	38	20	32	26	31	36	22	6. Capital formation
8	5	10	8	6	8	7	10	7. Government
100	100	100	100	100	100	100	100	8. GDP
								Per capita quantity indexes based on international prices (United States=100)
47.4	53.5	62.2	60.3	74.8	67.9	63.9	100.0	9. Consumption
51.5	112.7	56.3	101.2	90.2	110.0	130.0	100.0	10. Capital formation
35.4	30.7	59.0	52.2	47.2	58.6	55.1	100.0	11. Government
47.0	64.0	60.6	68.4	75.3	76.1	77.4	100.0	12. GDP

Note: Figures for components may not add to GDP totals because of rounding.
Sources: Summary Multilateral Tables 4.5 and 4.10.

that for the four highest-income countries (excluding the United States) was 1.6. On this basis, one would be led to believe that low-income countries are even poorer in their flows of services than in their flows of commodities.

These results, however, depend upon the valuation of the goods in each country at its own prices. When all goods, including both commodities and services, in each country are valued at a common set of prices—average international prices—a different picture emerges (columns 4 and 5). The indexes reflecting the relative flow of services are larger, especially for the low-income countries. Further, the sharp difference between the per capita absorption of services and commodities virtually disappears; the quantity indexes for services are much closer to those for commodities. Indeed, there

Table 1.7. Relation of National Price Structures to the International Price Structure,[a] 1970 and 1973

Category	Kenya	India	Philip-pines	Korea, Republic of	Colombia	Malaysia	Iran	Hungary
			1970					
Consumption	1.01	1.07	0.96	1.04	1.03	1.00	0.93	0.92
Capital formation	1.36	1.10	1.63	1.13	1.01	0.98	1.09	1.25
Government	0.61	0.55	0.55	0.63	0.73	1.03	1.27	0.90
GDP	1.00	1.00	1.00	1.00	1.00	1.00	1.00	1.00
			1973					
Consumption	0.97	1.11	0.95	1.02	1.01	0.99	0.86	0.91
Capital formation	1.57	1.13	1.56	1.12	1.05	1.00	1.17	1.25
Government	0.59	0.44	0.55	0.68	0.79	1.07	1.17	0.83
GDP	1.00	1.00	1.00	1.00	1.00	1.00	1.00	1.00

Table 1.8. Purchasing-Power Parities and Price Indexes for Gross Domestic Product, Consumption, Capital Formation, and Government, 1970 and 1973

Category	Kenya (shillings)	India (rupees)	Philip-pines (pesos)	Korea, Republic of (won)	Colombia (pesos)	Malaysia (M. dollars)	Iran (rials)	Hungary (forints)
			1970					
Purchasing-power parities (currency units per U.S. dollar)								
1. Consumption	3.42	2.40	1.86	143.0	7.53	1.30	29.1	13.9
2. Capital formation	5.13	2.77	3.55	173.0	8.22	1.43	38.4	21.2
3. Government	1.79	1.07	0.92	76.0	4.64	1.16	34.5	11.9
4. GDP	3.38	2.25	1.95	138.0	7.32	1.30	31.5	15.2
5. Exchange rate	7.1429	7.499	6.0652	310.42	18.352	3.0797	76.38	30.00
Price index (U.S.=100)								
6. Consumption (1÷5)	48	32	31	46	41	42	38	46
7. Capital formation (2÷5)	72	37	59	56	45	46	50	71
8. Government (3÷5)	25	14	15	24	25	38	45	40
9. GDP (4÷5)	47	30	32	44	40	42	41	51
			1973					
Purchasing-power parities (currency units per U.S. dollar)								
1. Consumption	3.31	2.81	2.20	164.0	9.58	1.29	29.7	13.0
2. Capital formation	5.90	3.18	4.01	199.0	10.95	1.45	44.7	19.7
3. Government	1.68	0.93	1.06	91.0	6.27	1.17	34.0	9.8
4. GDP	3.41	2.53	2.32	161.0	9.48	1.31	34.7	14.3
5. Exchange rate	7.0012	7.742	6.7629	398.54	23.813	2.4426	68.72	24.59
Price index (U.S.=100)								
6. Consumption (1÷5)	47	36	33	41	40	53	43	53
7. Capital formation (2÷5)	84	41	59	50	46	59	65	80
8. Government (3÷5)	24	12	16	23	26	48	49	40
9. GDP (4÷5)	49	33	34	40	40	5÷	50	58

Italy	Japan	United Kingdom	Nether-lands	Belgium	France	Germany, F.R.	United States	Category
				1970				
1.02	0.96	1.03	1.01	0.99	1.04	1.07	1.00	Consumption
0.88	1.06	0.89	0.90	0.98	0.89	0.84	0.90	Capital formation
1.26	0.96	1.05	1.27	1.21	1.12	1.27	1.16	Government
1.00	1.00	1.00	1.00	1.00	1.00	1.00	1.00	GDP
				1973				
1.01	0.96	1.01	1.03	0.98	1.05	1.10	1.00	Consumption
0.88	1.05	0.91	0.86	0.97	0.87	0.79	0.90	Capital formation
1.31	1.08	1.08	1.36	1.35	1.12	1.31	1.20	Government
1.00	1.00	1.00	1.00	1.00	1.00	1.00	1.00	GDP

Source: Appendix Table 4.6.
a. Ratio of share of each component in GDP in national prices to the share of that component in GDP in international prices.

Italy (lire)	Japan (yen)	United Kingdom (pounds)	Netherlands (guilders)	Belgium (B. francs)	France (francs)	Germany, F.R. (DM)	United States (dollars)	Category
				1970				
								Purchasing-power parities (currency units per U.S. dollar)
466.0	231.0	0.309	2.69	37.4	4.55	3.20	1.00	1. Consumption
453.0	286.0	0.298	2.69	41.6	4.40	2.80	1.00	2. Capital formation
498.0	201.0	0.273	2.93	39.7	4.25	3.29	1.00	3. Government
458.0	241.0	0.301	2.67	38.0	4.40	2.99	1.00	4. GDP
627.16	358.15	0.4174	3.6166	49.656	5.5289	3.6465	1.00	5. Exchange rate
								Price index (U.S.=100)
74	64	74	74	75	82	88	100	6. Consumption (1÷5)
								7. Capital formation
72	80	71	74	84	80	77	100	(2÷5)
79	56	65	81	80	77	90	100	8. Government (3÷5)
73	67	72	74	77	80	82	100	9. GDP (4÷5)
				1973				
								Purchasing-power parities (currency units per U.S. dollar)
508.0	247.0	0.346	2.98	37.8	4.76	3.38	1.00	1. Consumption
493.0	297.0	0.343	2.77	41.3	4.32	2.70	1.00	2. Capital formation
552.0	232.0	0.306	3.29	43.4	4.21	3.37	1.00	3. Government
505.0	257.0	0.341	2.91	38.6	4.52	3.09	1.00	4. GDP
583.00	272.19	0.4078	2.7956	38.977	4.454	2.6725	1.00	5. Exchange rate
								Price index (U.S.=100)
87	91	85	107	97	107	126	100	6. Consumption (1÷5)
								7. Capital formation
85	109	84	99	106	97	101	100	(2÷5)
95	85	75	118	111	95	126	100	8. Government (3÷5)
87	94	84	104	99	101	116	100	9. GDP (4÷5)

Sources: Summary Multilateral Tables 4.3 and 4.8.

Table 1.9. Comparison of Per Capita Quantity Indexes for Commodity and Service Components of Gross Domestic Product Based on Exchange-Rate Conversions with Real Indexes Based on International Dollars, 1970 and 1973

(United States=100)

Country	Indexes based on exchange-rate conversion			Real indexes based on international dollars			Exchange-rate–deviation indexes		
	Com-modities (1)	Ser-vices (2)	GDP (3)	Com-modities (4)	Ser-vices (5)	GDP (6)	(4)/(1) (7)	(5)/(2) (8)	(6)/(3) (9)
				1970					
Kenya	3.5	2.3	3.0	5.6	8.3	6.3	1.62	3.62	2.10
India	2.9	0.9	2.1	6.5	8.1	6.9	2.28	9.00	3.32
Philippines	5.1	2.1	3.9	10.8	15.1	12.0	2.14	7.36	3.11
Korea, Republic of	7.0	2.9	5.4	11.8	13.0	12.1	1.69	4.45	2.25
Colombia	8.1	5.9	7.2	15.8	24.1	18.1	1.95	4.08	2.50
Malaysia	9.7	5.7	8.1	18.8	20.0	19.1	1.94	3.53	2.36
Iran	10.2	5.6	8.4	19.1	23.4	20.3	1.87	4.18	2.42
Hungary	28.4	11.3	21.6	40.7	47.6	42.7	1.43	4.21	1.97
Italy	42.7	25.6	35.9	49.2	49.1	49.2	1.15	1.92	1.37
Japan	50.7	23.3	39.8	61.3	53.9	59.2	1.21	2.31	1.49
United Kingdom	50.8	38.1	45.7	62.7	65.5	63.5	1.24	1.72	1.39
Netherlands	59.9	36.9	50.8	72.0	60.1	68.7	1.20	1.63	1.35
Belgium	62.4	44.0	55.1	68.5	81.1	72.0	1.10	1.84	1.31
France	67.2	44.6	58.3	75.4	67.6	73.2	1.12	1.52	1.26
Germany, F.R.	76.7	45.0	64.1	83.0	66.0	78.2	1.08	1.47	1.22
United States	100.0	100.0	100.0	100.0	100.0	100.0	1.00	1.00	1.00
				1973					
Kenya	3.4	2.2	3.0	5.4	8.0	6.1	1.57	3.57	2.05
India	2.8	0.9	2.1	5.8	7.9	6.4	2.04	8.87	3.07
Philippines	5.6	1.9	4.2	11.2	14.7	12.2	1.98	7.76	2.92
Korea, Republic of	7.9	2.8	5.9	15.2	13.1	14.6	1.92	4.72	2.47
Colombia	8.1	5.6	7.1	15.3	24.5	17.9	1.89	4.40	2.52
Malaysia	12.2	7.1	10.2	18.7	19.9	19.1	1.53	2.80	1.87
Iran	19.2	7.8	14.8	29.1	29.5	29.2	1.52	3.77	1.98
Hungary	34.4	13.3	26.1	43.4	49.5	45.1	1.26	3.73	1.73
Italy	46.4	32.0	40.8	45.9	49.9	47.0	0.99	1.56	1.15
Japan	75.4	36.9	60.4	65.8	59.3	64.0	0.87	1.61	1.06
United Kingdom	54.0	45.4	50.6	58.5	65.8	60.6	1.08	1.45	1.20
Netherlands	81.6	54.6	71.1	72.0	59.0	68.4	0.88	1.08	0.96
Belgium	82.4	62.4	74.6	69.8	89.4	75.3	0.85	1.43	1.01
France	86.9	61.8	77.1	77.3	72.7	76.1	0.89	1.18	0.99
Germany, F.R.	102.5	68.8	89.4	80.7	68.7	77.4	0.79	1.00	0.87
United States	100.0	100.0	100.0	100.0	100.0	100.0	1.00	1.00	1.00

Sources: Summary Multilateral Tables 4.1 and 4.5; Tables 4.15 and 4.17.

is actually a tendency for the relationship to twist around. The low-income countries usually have higher quantity indexes for services than for commodities, whereas the opposite is often true of the higher-income countries. Thus, the actual relative composition of GDP quantities between poor and rich countries is different from what would be inferred from exchange-rate conversions.

One notable difference that will be set out more fully in Chapter 4 is with respect to the relation between expenditures on services and per capita GDP. The general view of this relationship is that the share of income spent on services tends to rise as per capita incomes increase. This is indeed found to be the case for the sixteen ICP countries when the share of service expenditures is calculated in each country's own prices. When international prices are used to value each country's quantities, however, the proportion spent on services declines as per capita GDP rises.[19] As this implies, it is the rise in prices of services and not the rise in quantities that plays the main role in pushing up service expenditures as incomes increase.[20]

The underlying factors at work can be explained in terms of the productivity differential model referred to earlier. Services, which are nontraded goods, are very cheap in low-income countries; hence exchange-rate conversions greatly understate the true quantities of services in low-income countries relative to those in high-income countries. Indeed, the low prices of services in the price structure of the low-income countries encourage their use and lead to quantities that are high relative to the quantities of the relatively more expensive commodities. In the case of commodities, therefore, although the understatement of real quantities by exchange-rate conversions is substantial, it is much less than in the case of services. In 1970 for the four lowest-income countries, for example, the average exchange-rate–deviation index for commodities is 1.87, whereas that for services is 5.43. Both indexes tend to decline with rising income so that for the four highest-income countries (excluding the United States) the figures are 1.12 for commodities and 1.61 for services.

A fuller examination of these matters, particularly of the price relationships, as well as an explicit treatment of traded and nontraded goods will await Chapter 4.

19. See Table 4.15.
20. See Table 4.17.

Chapter 2

Data and Procedures

THE DATA AND PROCEDURES USED IN PHASE II of the International Comparison Project (ICP) are set out in this chapter. Enough will be said here to enable the reader to understand the sources of data and the methods of handling data that were common to Phase I and Phase II, but all the details given in the Phase I report are not repeated.[1] More information is provided, of course, for the six new countries included in Phase II.[2] Explanations are also given for the revisions in the product and price comparisons that have been made in the 1970 estimates for the ten original countries.[3] The changes are attributable to: revisions in estimates of expenditures; additional price and quantity data received after the Phase I report was completed; corrections of errors; minor refinements of methods; and, in the case of multilateral comparisons, the addition of new countries to the process of estimating the purchasing-power parities and the average international prices of categories of gross domestic product.

The General Approach to Phase II Data Requirements

Because our two reference years, 1970 and 1973, were so close together, it was not considered imperative that a full set of benchmark data be gathered from each country for both years. Most of the countries provided detailed expenditure and price data for only one of the reference years. For example, for Hungary the 1970 data are official, whereas the 1973 data are not. The data for the other year have in most cases been estimated by the ICP staff largely by extrapolation. The extrapolation was carried out with data for both years for summary categories that were supplied by each country on an "updating worksheet," a copy of which appears in Appendix 1 to this chapter. Specifically, the updating worksheet calls for 1970 and 1973 expenditures on GDP, its three major components, and thirty-six subaggregates (or summary categories) in both current and constant prices.[4] An implicit deflator for each summary category was obtained simply by dividing the 1973 expenditure in current prices by the 1973 expenditure in 1970 prices.[5] In some cases the constant price series was based on a year other than 1970 and the series had first to be shifted to a 1970 base for this purpose. Of course, there would have been better comparability in the extrapolators if the constant price series

---

1. See Irving B. Kravis, Zoltan Kenessey, Alan Heston, and Robert Summers, *A System of International Comparisons of Gross Product and Purchasing Power* (Baltimore: Johns Hopkins University Press, 1975); referred to as *A System*.

2. Belgium, Iran, the Republic of Korea, Malaysia, the Netherlands, and the Philippines.

3. Colombia, France, the Federal Republic of Germany, Hungary, India, Italy, Japan, Kenya, the United Kingdom, and the United States.

4. Two of the summary categories, "increase in stocks" and "net exports of goods and services," are often omitted in the tables that give comparative data. This explains some subsequent references to thirty-four summary categories.

5. For the "net foreign balance" summary category, the use of the current average exchange rate as the PPP for each year achieves the same purpose.

of the countries had all been prepared on the basis of relative prices in a common year.

For the countries that supplied detailed data for 1970, each *detailed* category expenditure in 1973 was estimated as the product of the corresponding 1970 expenditure and the factor of change between 1973 and 1970 exhibited in the *summary* category that embraced the *detailed* category. For example, in the United Kingdom the expenditures in current prices of the "milk, cheese, and eggs" summary category went up by 35.1 percent between 1970 and 1973; thus, the United Kingdom's 1970 expenditures for the three detailed categories—fresh milk, milk products, and eggs and egg products—were also increased by 35.1 percent to get the corresponding 1973 expenditures.

Similarly, on the price side, each 1973 item price in a detailed category was extrapolated from its 1970 counterpart by multiplying the 1970 item price by the price change between 1973 and 1970 as indicated by the implicit deflator in the appropriate summary category. To illustrate, for the United Kingdom the 1973 prices of all of the items in the fresh milk, milk products, and eggs and egg products detailed categories were made 30 percent greater than their counterparts in 1970 because the ratio of the 1973 expenditure in current prices for the milk, cheese, and eggs summary category to the 1973 expenditure in 1970 prices was 1.30.

Where detailed data were provided for 1973 rather than 1970, the 1970 figures were estimated from those of 1973 in an equivalent way. The original ten Phase I countries and Belgium and the Netherlands provided detailed data only for 1970, except that many U.S. item prices were available for both years. Most of the data provided by Iran, the Republic of Korea, Malaysia, and the Philippines refer to 1973 but, as described below, some data refer to 1970 instead of or in addition to 1973.

These rather cumbersome extrapolation methods of deriving a full set of detailed price and expenditure data for each of the two reference years were employed to ensure that full use was made of all the primary price data available in each year—exclusively or primarily 1970 for twelve countries, and mainly but not exclusively 1973 for the other four countries—and still include all sixteen countries in each year. Because all of the countries were to be asked to provide a full set of detailed estimates for 1975, the Phase III reference year, full sets of data were not requested for both 1970 and 1973.

The classification of final expenditure on GDP adopted by the ICP is set out in Appendix 2 to this chapter. The ICP classification follows closely the classifications of the U.N. System of National Accounts (SNA).[6]

Two of the three major SNA components of GDP are modified for ICP purposes: first, SNA's private final consumption expenditure (PFCE) is replaced by the ICP's final consumption expenditure of the population (CEP); and, second, SNA's government final consumption expenditure (GFCE) is replaced by the ICP's public final consumption expenditure (PFC). SNA's gross fixed capital formation is unchanged except that in ICP aggregations the term gross capital formation (GCF) is used to include net change in stocks and net exports as well as gross fixed capital formation. (To facilitate exposition, the term "consumption" is used for CEP, "government" for PFC, and "capital formation," or sometimes "investment," for GCF.)

The main modifications affecting CEP and PFC relate to rents and to govern-

The Expenditure Data

The expenditure framework

6. U.N. Statistical Office, *A System of National Accounts,* Studies in Method, Series F, No.2, Rev. 3 (New York: United Nations, 1968).

ment expenditures for health care, education, and recreation. The modifications were made to ensure that comparisons for these groupings were independent of the degree to which a country's expenditures for them are made collectively by the society on the one hand and out of household budgets on the other. Therefore, all public expenditures in health care, education, and recreation other than those of a clearly governmental character (for example, the licensing of physicians) were transferred to ICP consumption. Although this may change the relative sizes of consumption and government, it leaves total SNA gross domestic product unaltered. The detailed categories involved in these transfers of expenditures are listed in Table 2.1.

The other major ICP modification of the SNA does change total GDP. All rent subsidies extended by government to households have been added to gross rents and to the SNA concept of GDP. The importance of these subsidies in many countries relative to the value of gross rents paid by tenants

Table 2.1. Government per Capita Expenditures Transferred to Final Consumption Expenditure of Population, 1970 and 1973

Category	Kenya (shillings)	India (rupees)	Philippines (pesos)	Korea, Republic of (won)	Colombia (pesos)	Malaysia (M. dollars)	Iran (rials)	Hungary (forints)
1970								
Rents	0.00	0.00	0.00	0.00	0.00	0.00	0.00	342.36
Drugs and medical preparations	0.37	0.23	0.26	21.31	0.00	1.39	74.64	260.83
Medical supplies	0.12	0.10	0.40	4.04	0.00	0.21	0.87	80.56
Therapeutic equipment	0.00	0.13	0.32	0.84	0.00	0.29	2.88	0.00
Physicians' services	2.23	0.42	0.43	15.78	29.45	5.92	29.97	101.35
Dentists' services	0.00	0.00	0.08	1.80	5.83	1.27	5.02	7.93
Other medical services, nurses, and the like	3.02	0.62	1.78	8.57	0.73	3.13	7.66	106.67
Hospitals	8.53	1.06	1.27	18.45	10.74	3.42	36.94	413.15
Public entertainment	0.13	0.09	0.00	0.22	0.87	0.49	0.00	126.21
Other recreational and cultural activities	0.00	0.11	0.00	13.76	0.24	0.21	0.00	46.91
First- and second-level teachers	27.96	7.82	25.83	1,333.36	86.64	40.70	454.92	453.38
College teachers	1.39	1.02	0.65	194.75	24.88	1.42	63.44	46.52
Physical facilities for education	3.87	0.40	0.48	115.22	13.95	1.68	11.61	237.62
Educational books and supplies	1.59	0.24	0.60	90.56	2.58	0.81	7.38	24.66
Other educational expenditures	1.85	0.46	0.85	154.27	5.39	0.95	14.41	103.00
Other services	0.00	0.00	0.36	72.69	0.00	0.00	147.41	105.22
1973								
Rents	0.00	0.00	0.00	0.00	0.00	0.00	0.00	405.27
Drugs and medical preparations	0.39	0.32	0.39	34.78	0.00	1.68	162.21	324.45
Medical supplies	0.13	0.14	0.61	6.63	0.00	0.26	1.62	100.19
Therapeutic equipment	0.00	0.18	0.49	1.38	0.00	0.35	5.95	0.00
Physicians' services	2.35	0.59	0.65	24.54	38.18	7.16	73.64	126.08
Dentists' services	0.00	0.00	0.12	3.67	7.56	1.54	34.10	9.88
Other medical services, nurses, and the like	3.19	0.88	2.72	14.47	0.93	3.78	14.55	132.69
Hospitals	9.01	1.50	1.94	30.03	13.96	4.13	105.89	514.00
Public entertainment	0.17	0.11	0.00	0.03	1.56	0.59	57.31	155.42
Other recreational and cultural activities	0.00	0.14	0.00	5.25	0.44	0.26	35.02	57.72
First- and second-level teachers	29.35	9.57	39.59	1,573.26	169.11	49.26	729.07	606.52
College teachers	1.46	1.28	0.99	965.42	48.58	1.72	276.98	62.22
Physical facilities for education	4.06	0.49	0.73	169.97	27.20	2.04	6.37	317.93
Educational books and supplies	1.67	0.29	0.91	108.75	5.02	0.98	136.90	32.98
Other educational expenditures	1.95	0.56	1.30	185.38	10.53	1.15	120.98	137.78
Other services	0.00	0.00	0.55	72.79	0.00	0.00	184.65	126.46

(or imputed to householders) would lead to a distortion in the pattern of final expenditure if they were excluded. A corresponding adjustment to rents paid—that is, in the price of housing space—is made in developing the purchasing-power parities for the countries affected.

The full adjustments relating to rents and to transfers from government to consumption were made for Phase II by some countries on a more approximate basis than the Phase I adjustments; for a few countries, the adjustments were made by the ICP staff on the basis of the Phase I proportions with the approval of the countries.

The three major components of GDP—consumption, capital formation, and government—were divided, as already indicated, into 36 summary and 153 detailed categories. The 153-category breakdown required a substantial expansion of the detail provided in the SNA. The way in which the detailed categories—110 in consumption, 38 in capital formation, and 5 in govern-

Italy (lire)	Japan (yen)	United Kingdom (pounds)	Netherlands (guilders)	Belgium (B. francs)	France (francs)	Germany, F.R. (DM)	United States (dollars)	Category
				1970				
0.00	1,108.75	5.48	0.00	129.67	4.51	8.34	2.45	Rents
85.72	888.93	4.21	0.77	124.27	0.06	11.76	29.26	Drugs and medical preparations
16.77	900.50	0.43	0.00	1.76	0.00	4.45	3.87	Medical supplies
68.95	180.29	1.19	0.31	60.48	0.79	4.98	5.87	Therapeutic equipment
1,802.09	1,071.15	4.88	2.99	649.69	34.57	27.98	11.88	Physicians' services
0.00	230.43	1.40	0.00	0.00	0.00	0.00	4.29	Dentists' services
1,615.73	946.78	8.92	7.37	762.66	33.13	42.03	1.75	Other medical services, nurses, and the like
3,570.63	767.45	11.67	3.22	581.95	6.15	29.38	16.56	Hospitals
0.00	0.00	2.83	0.00	0.00	0.00	0.00	10.51	Public entertainment
0.00	0.00	0.00	0.00	0.00	0.00	0.00	0.00	Other recreational and cultural activities
33,734.63	12,547.24	19.25	355.26	5,114.42	450.52	216.08	165.63	First- and second-level teachers
4,001.12	1,015.23	3.03	46.20	747.93	66.73	43.26	23.66	College teachers
2,230.71	2,473.97	5.08	76.36	721.68	26.02	40.69	19.15	Physical facilities for education
380.17	907.25	1.86	14.20	137.45	4.00	1.91	1.72	Educational books and supplies
1,192.69	1,075.01	3.46	14.20	192.01	4.23	14.62	4.56	Other educational expenditures
0.00	0.00	3.96	0.00	0.00	0.00	0.00	14.31	Other services
				1973				
0.00	1,710.36	8.19	0.00	162.11	6.39	10.92	3.16	Rents
134.77	1,337.31	6.05	1.26	183.06	0.10	18.17	45.55	Drugs and medical preparations
25.50	1,354.72	0.62	0.00	2.57	0.00	6.87	6.02	Medical supplies
107.45	271.31	1.71	0.52	89.12	1.17	7.70	9.09	Therapeutic equipment
2,819.16	1,611.37	7.02	4.99	956.98	51.51	43.24	16.04	Physicians' services
0.00	346.47	2.02	0.00	0.00	0.00	0.00	5.93	Dentists' services
2,527.77	1,424.38	12.80	12.28	1,123.31	49.38	64.94	2.36	Other medical services, nurses, and the like
5,587.32	1,154.90	16.76	5.36	857.19	9.15	45.40	23.88	Hospitals
0.00	0.00	4.21	0.00	0.00	0.00	0.00	12.64	Public entertainment
0.00	0.00	0.00	0.00	0.00	0.00	0.00	0.00	Other recreational and cultural activities
48,328.17	19,679.19	29.78	508.41	7,595.17	643.30	321.49	220.77	First- and second-level teachers
5,731.20	1,592.12	4.68	66.15	1,110.68	95.28	64.38	30.42	College teachers
3,196.14	3,879.93	7.85	109.30	1,071.77	37.16	60.55	28.13	Physical facilities for education
544.53	1,422.55	2.87	20.31	204.11	5.72	2.84	2.02	Educational books and supplies
1,708.25	1,686.53	5.36	20.31	285.11	6.04	21.77	9.06	Other educational expenditures
0.00	0.00	5.80	0.00	0.00	0.00	0.00	23.89	Other services

ment—are combined to constitute summary categories and the content of the detailed categories may be seen by examining the ICP classification in Appendix 2 to this chapter. With only minor changes, this classification conforms to the corresponding classification presented as an appendix to Chapter 3 of the Phase I report.

Accounting problems

Before the details of the Phase II expenditure data are considered, some conceptual and accounting problems and difficulties that may diminish the international comparability of the data should be noted.

TREATMENT OF NET PURCHASES OF RESIDENTS ABROAD. In principle, the CEP total, like the SNA total or private consumption expenditure, should include the consumption expenditure of residents both within the domestic territory and abroad and should exclude the consumption expenditure of nonresidents within the domestic territory. In the SNA it is recommended that the breakdown of consumption expenditure refer to purchases within the domestic territory only and that an overall adjustment be made for net purchases of residents abroad.

The data on the CEP supplied by the Statistical Office of the European Communities for most of its member countries are based on the "domestic" concept of expenditure rather than the "national" concept recommended in the SNA. An adjustment has been made in these cases to the CEP total for net purchases of residents abroad as required for ICP purposes and as recommended by the SNA. A corresponding adjustment has also been made in net exports of goods and services where, according to ICP requirements and SNA recommendation, a counterentry should be made. In principle, the GDP total should in all cases be unaffected by these adjustments.

TREATMENT OF FINAL CONSUMPTION EXPENDITURE OF PRIVATE NONPROFIT INSTITUTIONS. A similar problem arises in the treatment of final consumption expenditure of private nonprofit institutions serving households. In the SNA there is no provision for an independent breakdown by object of such expenditure or for the distribution of the total to the appropriate categories of private final consumption expenditure. Instead, this expenditure is recorded in the form of an overall addition to the final consumption expenditure of households that for ICP purposes is assigned to "other services, n.e.s." (ICP 08.400). In future ICP work these expenditures will be distributed to other categories by prorating, if a better method is not available. In the present report, quantity comparisons for the other services category are not reliable: other categories of consumption are probably slightly underestimated in countries with relatively large reported expenditures on the other services category, and they are probably slightly overestimated in countries with relatively small reported miscellaneous expenditures. Of course, aggregate consumption and GDP are not affected.

TREATMENT OF PURCHASES IN HOTELS, RESTAURANTS, AND THE LIKE. According to the SNA, all expenditures of households in hotels, restaurants, and similar establishments should be recorded together as part of the major expenditure category "other goods and services, n.e.s." A footnote in the SNA indicates that it is desirable to have outlays on food, beverages, and tobacco also recorded separately. This is again a change from the former SNA, in which the individual elements of such expenditure were to be allocated to the appropriate individual categories. This creates problems for those countries following the commodity flow method in estimating the breakdown of private final consumption expenditure. In accordance with the present SNA, the ICP classification provides separate categories for all final (nonbusiness) expenditures in restaurants and cafes (ICP 08.310) and in hotels and similar lodging places (ICP 08.320).

STATISTICAL DISCREPANCY. In a number of countries, the independent estimate of GDP obtained from the expenditure approach differs from the one obtained from the income side (or "cost structure" as it is referred to in the U.N. *Yearbook of National Accounts Statistics*). This difference is usually entered as a separate item, either in the expenditure or in the income breakdown, in order to make the two breakdowns add to the same GDP total. When a country places the discrepancy in its income breakdown, the implication is that the expenditure approach provides a better measure of its GDP. No problem is created for the ICP in this instance. When the discrepancy is entered in the expenditure breakdown, however, the implication is that the income total is the more reliable measure of its GDP and that the total of expenditures either overstates or understates GDP by the amount of the statistical discrepancy. In these cases, therefore, the preferred GDP figure for international comparison would include not only consumption, capital formation, and government but also a statistical discrepancy.

The statistical discrepancy could have been treated as a separate category in the comparisons, but then it would have been necessary, either implicitly or explicitly, to factor it into price and quantity components in order to obtain the correct price and quantity comparisons for GDP as a whole. The ICP adopted the alternative of allocating the statistical discrepancy to the various expenditure categories. Such allocations were carried out for the four countries that reported the statistical discrepancy on the expenditure side: India, Iran, the Republic of Korea, and the Philippines. Advantage was taken of whatever information was available for the inclusion or exclusion of ICP categories in the prorating. For example, the relatively firm estimates of public final consumption expenditure and net exports of goods and services were maintained at their original values; that is, they were excluded from the prorating.

The same practice was followed in the occasional instances in which other unallocated expenditures were reported. In the case of India, for example, the category of "errors and omissions," reported as part of gross capital formation, was prorated exclusively among the reported components of private capital formation. The Indian statistical discrepancy was prorated among the original components of CEP—that is, among the components of private consumption expenditure before adjustment for public sector transfers. (The government expenditures on both capital and CEP categories were not included in the prorating because public expenditure figures were regarded as complete, being based on an actual analysis of budget documents.)

Allocating the statistical discrepancies and "errors and omissions" in this way will introduce error in the expenditures of categories that were correctly reported. But the benefits of allocation are convenience of computation, presentation, and analysis. Computationally, the fact that the statistical discrepancy can be negative presents difficulties in using the Geary-Khamis aggregation technique noted in Chapter 1. Even if the statistical discrepancy were positive, however, an appropriate PPP would have to be assigned to the statistical discrepancy category, which in turn would require an assumption about its distribution. In terms of presentation and analysis, the quantity ratios are probably more comparable between countries when the discrepancy is allocated. If left unallocated, the effect is to understate (or overstate) expenditures and quantities for some categories, and thus to lead to an underestimate (or overestimate) of the country's relative quantities in ICP comparisons. Allocating the discrepancy may cause errors in some particular categories, but on average the expenditure in each category will be closer to being correct. On balance, then, it appears better to allocate.

*Treatment of the
expenditure data*

As already noted, revisions in estimates of national accounts supplied the ICP by the countries since the Phase I report have been incorporated in the present work, making possible more accurate comparisons than were previously published. These new numbers have improved the consistency of each country's 1970 GDP estimates with its 1973 GDP estimates. In a few cases the revisions have made a notable difference (as much as 4 or 5 percent) in total GDP, but in more instances it is the allocation of nearly the same total to the different expenditure categories that is altered. In part, these changes arise from the normal process of statistical revision. Some changes, however, are the result of improved methods of national accounting adopted by the reporting country. The latter type of change has been particularly important in the case of India. The Phase II estimates for Indian consumer expenditures have been independently obtained through the commodity flow approach, whereas the previous estimates for 1970–71 had been obtained by updating 1967–68 figures through the use of the trends in prices and production of commodities between 1967–68 and 1970–71.[7] Some revisions, both in the overall aggregates and in the individual components, are attributable to a changeover from the old version of the SNA (1953) to the present one (1968). In a few instances, the ICP's source of expenditure data within the country changed after Phase I, and this change led to substantial changes in the expenditure figures.

Both 1970 and 1973 expenditures in current prices for the thirty-six summary categories were provided on a consistent basis on the updating worksheet for the ten Phase I countries.

As indicated above, the detailed 153-line breakdown of GDP for 1973 was obtained in most cases by prorating the estimates of 1973 expenditures for the summary categories to their component detailed categories according to the 1970 distribution. Where additional information was available on the more detailed distribution, the prorating procedure was modified appropriately. For example, independent estimates of the transfers of government expenditure to the private sector sometimes made possible independent prorating of the public and private components within the summary category.

The expenditure estimates reported in summary form for 1973 are generally comparable with those the countries submit for publication to the international statistical agencies or publish themselves. In a number of cases, however, the more detailed estimates probably do not meet the same standards. The basic information for national accounting purposes is sometimes not adequate to provide reliable estimates of the detailed breakdown of private consumption expenditure. The reported distributions may be derived from partial data, or from more firmly based estimates for adjoining years. Thus, in some cases, the breakdown of expenditures to the detailed categories as given in Appendix Tables 4.1–4.5 and Appendix Table 5.1 represents extremely crude estimates, some by the ICP staff, that are not of sufficient quality to be published. These materials are offered so that re-

---

7. The 1967–68 details, in turn, had been developed by distributing the residually obtained aggregate figure of private consumption expenditure primarily on the basis of consumer expenditure patterns revealed by India's National Sample Survey for that year. The CEP estimate was obtained by subtracting gross capital formation, government final consumption expenditure, and net exports from total gross domestic product, itself obtained through the value-added approach.

search workers may aggregate the data in ways different from those followed here, if they wish. These worksheet data should not be regarded as independently reliable estimates of expenditures in the detailed categories that can stand on their own. This caveat is equally applicable to corresponding quantity comparisons.

The Phase II estimates of per capita GDP in national currencies for the original ten Phase I countries differ from the previously published estimates as follows:

Comparisons of Phase II and Phase I 1970 expenditure data

Country	Percent difference of current estimates from Phase I estimates
Colombia	+4.0
France	−4.3
Germany, F.R.	−0.6
Hungary	−0.1
India	+1.4
Italy	+1.7
Japan	−5.1
Kenya	−0.3
United Kingdom	+2.4
United States	−0.2

The large difference in the case of Japan results in part from the change in the ICP's source of expenditure data. The new figures are provided by the source for the official national accounts statistics. A major cause of the difference, however, appears to have been a failure in Phase I to deduct some expenditures from government after they were properly transferred to consumption. Another large change, that for France, is attributable mainly to a changeover to the 1968 SNA: the French 1970 GDP is 4.3 percent lower on the new SNA basis than on the old.[8] The change for Colombia results not so much from a revision of the GDP as from a downward revision in the population estimate. A lower population estimate is also the main source of the small increase in the Italian GDP per capita.

Although the total GDP estimates are changed very slightly except for Colombia, France, and Japan, there are sometimes quite substantial revisions in the allocation of GDP to the various ICP categories. An illustration of an unusually large change is the increase in the United Kingdom's per capita expenditure for the miscellaneous category of producers' durable goods (ICP 17) from £2.3 to £9.4. The most radical general revision in the distribution of expenditures is that for Colombia for which a completely new set of estimates was provided to the ICP. Fortunately, for most countries, the revisions represent much smaller changes in expenditures.

Since the purchasing-power parities (PPPs) for aggregates such as producers' durables can be considered expenditure-weighted averages of the PPPs of their underlying detailed categories, changes in the allocation of expenditures to different categories can make a significant difference in the PPPs for the aggregates. This shows up particularly for producers' durable goods and construction, because in some countries the PPPs differ substantially from one underlying category to another.

These remarks should underline the statement made earlier and emphasized in the Phase I report that the reliability of the estimates diminishes as one moves from total GDP to successively more disaggregated categories.

8. The 1970 GDP for France is reported on both bases in U.N. Statistical Office, *Yearbook of National Accounts Statistics, 1974* (New York: United Nations, 1974).

Consumption

As in Phase I, the price comparisons for most categories of consumers' goods followed well-established procedures for identifying matching qualities of goods in each country and the United States. First, a list of specifications was used to make a tentative selection of items for price comparison and, then, verification procedures were applied to ensure that the qualities of the items matched.

Price collection in individual countries

The list of consumers' goods specifications, consisting of nearly 1,000 items, represented a substantial evolution from the Phase I list that was initially drawn from specifications of the U.S. Bureau of Labor Statistics. The list used in Phase II incorporated many suggestions of both the ten original and the six new countries. Thus, by the end of Phase II, less than half of the specifications were based on descriptions of the Bureau of Labor Statistics.[9] In particular, new specifications for restaurant food and furniture were required to represent patterns of consumption found in the Republic of Korea, the Philippines, and Malaysia. These specifications are proving useful in Phase III for the new Asian countries that are being drawn into the ICP comparisons.

The verification procedures included exchanges of descriptive materials and samples, solicitation of expert advice from relevant industries, and visits by ICP pricing experts to various countries. The visits enabled the ICP and the country experts to visit shops jointly to examine goods about which quality questions could not be resolved at a distance.

Revisions of 1970 prices for the original ten countries

In the course of preparing this Phase II report, a thorough review of the 1970 price comparisons made for the original ten countries was undertaken. In a few instances, particularly for India and the United States, it was possible to incorporate a few new prices unavailable at the time the work on the Phase I report went to press.[10] In other instances, errors in prices were found and corrected. A few misclassifications were caught (for example, vermouth had been erroneously classified as spirits instead of wine); mistakes in the conversion of local quantity units to the standard ICP unit (for example, kilograms) were corrected; and still other clerical errors were put right.

The gratifyingly few errors that have been detected by and large have had negligible impacts on the overall results. Two of the errors, however, warrant comment: First, a clerical error resulted in the overestimation of each U.S. rent by approximately 7.5 percent.[11] The result was to understate the PPPs of the other countries and to overstate to a corresponding degree their housing quantities relative to that of the United States. Since the proportion of expenditure on rent in the countries varied between 2 percent and 9 percent

9. The total number of specifications was reduced from 991 in Phase I to 979 by the end of Phase II. This was a net reduction resulting from the addition of new specifications or variants and the exclusion of specifications that no country priced.

10. In addition, the Indian prices, originally reported on a calendar year basis, were adjusted to the fiscal year beginning 1 April. The adjustment factor was based on the implicit price deflators underlying the CEP component of GDP estimates at current and at 1960–61 prices. The data used for this purpose were taken from Government of India, Central Statistical Organisation, Department of Statistics, Ministry of Planning, *National Accounts Statistics 1960–61—1974–75* (New Delhi, October 1976). The adjustment factor was, however, worked out for an overall basis purely for reasons of operational convenience.

11. See *A System,* p. 123. The entry of the standard factor for city size is in error. The figure under the heading "log rent" at the bottom of the left column on the page should be 0.0404 instead of 0.1130. The correct rent in the illustration is $56.00 rather than $60.21 as reported.

of total GDP, the correction of this error produced downward adjustments of real GDPS per capita relative to the United States of less than two-thirds of a percentage point. Second, Japanese prices for local transport were entered per kilometer rather than per ride of approximately 3 kilometers. The correction had the result of cutting the Japan/United States quantity comparison for local transport substantially, and the Japanese comparison of total GDP per capita was reduced by nearly one-half of a percentage point.

In a few cases, the Phase II comparisons were improved by the addition of specifications or by the better matching of items. In the refrigerator category (ICP 04.31), for example, an intermediate-size class of 6 to 13 cubic feet was added to the small-size class of 2 to 5 cubic feet and the large-size class of 14 cubic feet. Although the prices of refrigerators in each size class were expressed on a per cubic foot basis, the new item improved the representativeness of the sample in some countries.

The PPPs derived from quantity comparisons, particularly in the health and education areas, were revised because additional 1970 quantity data previously unavailable were obtained for almost all of the countries.

There were also some minor refinements of methods that affected the results. These affected mainly "other services, n.e.s." (ICP 08.4) for which the PPP was inferred from the PPPs of other categories.

The impact of the expenditure revision for 1970 for the Phase I countries has been shown above. The following figures show the percentage change in the overall PPPs for 1970 between the Phase I and the Phase II estimates. (The PPPs upon which these figures are based were estimated using the Fisher formula in the binary comparisons.) They indicate that the effects of revisions in prices on the overall PPPs (that is, for GDP) range from −1.8 to +4.7 percent. The figures do not, however, provide a pure measure of the effect of the price revisions, because the changes also include the effects of the minor changes in methods and of changes in expenditure weights.

Country	Percentage difference of Phase II PPP from Phase I
Colombia	−1.2
France	−0.4
Germany, F.R.	−0.9
Hungary	−1.8
India	+4.7
Italy	−1.7
Japan	+3.3
Kenya	+2.5
United Kingdom	+2.0

BELGIUM AND THE NETHERLANDS. Prices for Belgium and the Netherlands, provided by the Statistical Office of the European Communities, were gathered during a November 1970 survey. In addition to the common list of specifications developed for its member countries, the EC Statistical Office priced a number of ICP specifications in its survey. Both in Belgium and in the Netherlands prices were collected in ten different towns, five large and five small, with six outlets (namely, two department stores, two supermarkets, and two specialized shops) covered in each town.

IRAN. In Iran more than half of the prices were among those collected for the regular national consumer price index (CPI), which is based on pricing in thirty-five cities. These prices referred to 1970. The balance were collected in Teheran during two months of 1973; these were converted to a

Price collection in the new countries

national average through the use of place-to-place price relationships for related CPI items. Special adjustments were made to the prices of a few items:

- Bread. The price for white bread was obtained as a weighted average of the prices of four local varieties of flat bread and machine-made loaves.
- Stainless steel flatware. Since ordinary table knives are not usually a part of the standard place setting, the Iranian price for the smaller setting was adjusted upward to account for the weight difference between the Western place setting and that of Iran.
- Brooms. Since the normal variety is without a handle—though some brooms with handles are available—the average retail price of a handle was added to the CPI price in order to synthesize a broom price that conforms to the ICP specifications.

MALAYSIA. Eighty percent of the Malaysian prices—also for 1973—came from the regular CPI collection covering 3,400 outlets in ninety urban and rural towns in West Malaysia (on the Malay Peninsula). The remaining prices were specially collected in 1973–75 in the larger cities of West Malaysia. The 1970 prices were extrapolated from those of 1973 by the use of the regularly compiled indexes.

Relatively few adjustments were necessary outside of the clothing and furniture categories. Other than having to adjust poultry prices from live-weight to deadweight, no difficulties were encountered with food purchased for home consumption. Restaurant pricing was more difficult because of the nature of the typical meal. The regular CPI price set included family-style meals, such as a whole roasted chicken and other dishes meant to be combined according to individual preference. For example, a diner might choose a combination of soup, noodles, and meat or a combination of rice, meat, and vegetable. Many meals are taken in open stalls where it is difficult to judge relative qualities or portion sizes. For Phase II, only a fish platter was compared; for 1975, however, several Asian specifications will be added that will more adequately cover this type of dining.

Clothing prices were secured mostly by pricing material and adding a tailoring charge, although some items, particularly men's clothing and underclothing, were widely available ready-made.

Furniture presented the greatest problems. Upholstered furniture is not in common use because of climate, and it is found only in the homes of higher-income families or foreigners. Kitchen furniture is commonly a collapsible, formica-topped, composition-board table accompanied by any number of molded plywood or plastic chairs. The common table size is much larger than that used in other countries, but this was offset by the use of less expensive materials. Bedrooms are usually furnished with only a bed, a chest, and a wardrobe; Western-style suites are not common. In Phase III more matches will be available because of newly added specifications for furniture more common to the Asian countries.

REPUBLIC OF KOREA. Consumer prices for 239 specifications for the years 1970 and 1973 were provided for the Republic of Korea by the country's Bureau of Statistics. Special ICP pricing was carried out in nine cities in 1975 and these prices were then deflated to refer to 1970 and 1973. More than 60 percent of the specifications were adapted from the regular CPI collection.

Here too furniture was a problem area because the average Korean home contains little Western-style furniture. People dine sitting on floor cushions around a table about one-foot high. They sleep directly on the floor, using straw mats and heavy quilts, rather than on bedsteads. Closer coordination with Japan has produced more matches for Phase III.

Food away from home again presented difficulties. Most Korean meals are one dish, consisting of a base of either rice and barley or noodles topped with a combination of vegetables, egg, meat, and fish. The meal is accompanied by several varieties of kimchi (a fermented cabbage) and tea. Bread and separate vegetable dishes are usually not served. A few of these dishes were compared, taking into account quality and quantity of contents. One Western dish was also compared—a hamburger, which is now a popular snack among the young.

PHILIPPINES. ICP prices were collected in 1973 by the Philippine Bureau of Census and Statistics in Manila and nineteen trading centers in nine regions. The coverage of prices—more than 350 specifications in all—was the widest of any of the Asian countries. About half of the prices came from regular pricing; the other half were specially collected. There were no major problems with these data. Some of the same kinds of special adjustments were necessary as for the countries just discussed: broom prices had to be adjusted to include a handle, and restaurant meals had to be composed of selected separate dishes to form a meal matching a specification. The customary manner of furnishing homes caused the greatest difficulties, for the same reasons as in the case of Malaysia.

The number of items actually priced in each new Phase II country is set out in Table 2.2.[12]

Categories requiring special treatment

Automobiles (ICP 6.11) and rents (ICP 3.11) require a special treatment not needed by other detailed categories. In the usual case, a set of reasonably homogeneous items can be defined such that a subset of items can be priced in each country. The use of the "country-product–dummy" method (CPD), which is explained in Chapter 3, makes it possible to estimate category PPPs even though each item has not been priced in each country. The heterogeneous character, however, of the individual automobiles and dwelling units found in the ICP countries makes impossible direct pricing everywhere or

Table 2.2. Number of Consumer Goods Priced by Six Phase II Countries

Group	Target [a]	Belgium	Nether-lands	Iran	Malaysia	Korea, Republic of	Philip-pines
Food, beverages, and tobacco	67	113	114	74	73	78	107
Clothing and footwear	50	40 [b]	39 [b]	47 [b]	42 [b]	38 [b]	46 [b]
Gross rents	7	18	18	10	8	8	15
House furnishings and operations	37	47	47	33 [b]	35 [b]	33 [b]	45
Medical care	23	17 [b]	17 [b]	18 [b]	15 [b]	19 [b]	36
Transport and communications	21	21	21	24	22	19 [b]	21
Recreation and education	22	46	46	22	22	22	39
Other goods and services	16	26	27	19	18	22	44
Total	243	328	329	247	235 [b]	239 [b]	353

a. The minimum number of specifications countries were asked to price. Where prices for additional specifications were available or easily obtained, countries were encouraged to provide them.

b. Less than the target number.

12. For the number of items priced by the Phase I countries, see Table 6.1 in *A System*, p. 81.

even nearly everywhere of a standard set of automobiles and a standard set of dwelling units. Few particular kinds of automobiles or dwelling units are typical in more than a few countries. In these cases, it is easier to gather, for an adequate sample of units, information about prices and key price-determining characteristics. Quality matching can be based upon the so-called hedonic regression technique which is described at length in *A System*.[13] The price of a car or dwelling unit is conceived to be related to its various physical characteristics. Experience has shown that it is quite possible to find for each country an empirical formula through multiple regression analysis that enables one to estimate what the price would be for any closely specified kind of car or dwelling unit. By selecting a series of "standard" cars or dwelling units, the price of which can be estimated from the equation for each country, the matching of quality is achieved.

Some details of the selection and pricing of standard cars and dwelling units appear in the following sections. Readers wishing additional information should consult *A System*.

Automobiles

In eleven of the sixteen countries, all automobile models with a significant volume of sales were selected for the regressions. Five countries—Colombia, India, Iran, Kenya, and the Republic of Korea—had too few automobile models to make regressions possible. The number of automobile models used in estimating the regression equations varied from eleven for Hungary to eighty for the United States. The number of standard cars for which prices were estimated and then used in the subsequent averaging process to get individual country PPPs ranged from four to nine. (The last two lines of Table 2.3 display the detailed information for all sixteen countries.)

PRICE ESTIMATES. Hedonic regression equations were computed for each of the eleven countries where data permitted. These regressions relate the natural logarithm of an automobile's price, stated in U.S. dollars (the domestic price converted at the exchange rate), to some subset of the automobile's characteristics, listed in the stubs of Table 2.3. Because the regressions were computed for the purpose of estimating prices of standard cars rather than for structural analysis of automobile pricing, the criterion for deciding which characteristics to use as independent variables was intentionally loose. A *sensible* quest for high coefficients of determination ($\bar{R}^2$) was a guiding principle. If the coefficient of a characteristic was of the expected sign and had an associated *t*-value at least equal to unity in absolute value, the characteristic was included as an independent variable.[14] High multicollinearity between values of characteristics precluded the possibility of a more restrictive criterion.[15] Although the multicollinearity makes structural analysis difficult, in the present case price estimates for most of the standard cars turn out not to vary much across alternative formulations of the estimating equation.

The quantity of sales plays two roles in the estimation process. One role that sales fills in all the equations is to serve as weights reflecting the relative

13. See *A System*, Chapters 8 and 9.
14. The negative coefficient of "number of cylinders" in the Malaysian regression seems to violate the "expected sign" rule. Extra cylinders, however, increase an automobile's weight. The negative sign indicates that extra cylinders in the Philippine case adds less to an automobile's cost than the extra weight of the cylinders would suggest.
15. Multicollinearity refers to the correlation among the explanatory variables. High multicollinearity means that the variables are highly correlated and, as a result, the estimates of the regression coefficients are highly imprecise.

importance of different models. This was done to place in perspective the influence of autos with special, unusual price characteristics. In addition, the possible distorting effects on price comparisons arising from economies of scale (in production) makes necessary the use of sales as an independent variable.[16]

The parameter estimates of the eleven regressions appear in Table 2.3. The scattering of blank entries throughout the table indicates that the critical characteristics determining automobile prices varied from country to country. In some cases, however, the selection of characteristics depended upon data availability. Certainly, one should not infer that the differences arose entirely out of differences in conditions of production. In many countries, particularly the less affluent ones, there is no domestic production of cars so the hedonic regression quite possibly reflects a number of technologies associated with different exporting countries.

Table 2.4 gives the weight and horsepower distribution of the automobiles sold in each country. Ten cells in the table are heavily outlined. These cells were chosen as the basis for selecting the standard cars to be priced and compared in the eleven countries for which the hedonic regression technique was used. The specific cars chosen for pricing, one per box, are listed in Table 2.5. The selections were made to give representation to a variety of cars, ranging from large and high-powered models down to small and relatively low-powered models, and also to give representation to the products of each of the major auto-manufacturing countries. Estimates for 1970 of the country prices of each of the ten cars derived from the regression equations of Table 2.3 appear in the body of Table 2.5.[17] Of course, some of these cars were either larger or smaller than those actually purchased in quantity in particular countries. In some cases, as noted in the table, the car size is not in the middle 90 percent of the range of observation in the country; in other cases, the car is outside the range of observation altogether.

In comparing the automobile prices of the nonregression countries (Colombia, India, Iran, Kenya, and the Republic of Korea) with the others—specifically, with the United States and the United Kingdom—the cars used for price comparisons were the ones actually found in the five countries. Actual prices in the nonregression countries were compared with prices for equivalent U.S. or British automobiles as estimated from the U.S. or British regression equation.[18]

BINARY PRICE COMPARISONS. Three comparisons of each country's automobile prices with those of the United States are presented in Table 2.6. The

16. Consider two countries, one, say Italy, producing and consuming small cars and the other, say the United States, large ones. The only overlapping models available for price comparison, if any, are likely to be at opposite extremes of the spectrum of sizes in each country: in Italy the unusually large models and in the United States the unusually small models will enter into the price comparison. If scale economies are important, the atypically low level of production will lead to an unusually high price for the overlapping models in one or both countries. By introducing the volume of production for each model as a variable in the regression, this source of possible error in the price comparisons can be reduced.

17. The regressions were based upon data for the year 1969 except for Belgium, Malaysia, and the Netherlands (1970 data) and for the Philippines (1972 data). The regressions were adjusted using temporal automobile price indexes within the countries so that in Table 2.3 they all have a reference date of 1970. Temporal indexes were used to get 1973 prices where these were required in Chapters 4 and 5.

18. See *A System*, p. 115.

Table 2.3. Hedonic Automobile Regression Equations for Eleven Countries, 1970

(Dependent variable: Natural log of price in U.S. dollars)

Independent variables	Belgium	France	Germany, F.R.	Hungary	Italy	Japan
Displacement (cubic inches)	—	0.0049323 (0.0018971)	—	0.0062580 (0.0025032)	0.0092730 (0.0008134)	0.0065113 (0.0009866)
Horsepower (hundreds)	0.71011 (0.24716)	0.53095 (0.16089)	0.41348 (0.07384)	—	—	—
RPM (thousands)	−0.02879 (0.02064)	0.02901 (0.02918)	0.07552 (0.02360)	0.30624 (0.09430)	0.16187 (0.02158)	0.11559 (0.02819)
Number of cylinders	—	—	—	—	—	—
Weight (thousands of pounds)	0.27587 (0.14739)	—	0.31960 (0.06392)	—	—	0.25052 (0.54461)
Length (feet)	0.058193 (0.024674)	0.023749 (0.019792)	0.032820 (0.014269)	0.060470 (0.054973)	—	—
Width (feet)	—	—	—	—	0.08416 (0.05260)	—
Mean effective pressure [a]	—	—	—	—	0.0038115	—
Registration (thousands)	—	—	−0.00040986 (0.00021572)	—	−0.00079900 (0.00011580)	—
Hardtop	—	—	—	—	—	—
Constant [b]	5.99710 (0.28450)	6.28447 (0.20678)	5.80466 (0.17290)	5.15339 (0.73479)	5.03481 (0.21472)	5.81401 (0.19448)
Coefficient of determination ($\bar{R}^2$)	0.9447	0.9251	0.9612	0.8660	0.9910	0.9767
Standard error of estimate (SEE)	0.0593	0.0304	0.0295	0.0445	0.0144	0.0145
Reference year for regression	1970	1969	1969	1969	1969	1969
Number of observations [c]	26	38	59	11	22	28
Number of standard models used in comparing prices	7	8	9	7	7	5

first is the geometric mean of the price relatives of a set of standard cars using weights based upon the country's automobile expenditures, the second is the geometric mean based upon U.S. expenditure weights, and the third is the Fisher ideal index, the geometric mean of the first two.[19] The standard cars included in any particular binary comparison are the set of cars listed in Table 2.5 that are common to both the United States and the country being compared with the United States—that is, within the range of observation of both countries.[20]

MULTILATERAL PRICE COMPARISONS. Estimated prices have been entered in all of the cells of Table 2.5, although some of those prices refer to types of models not found in significant numbers in particular countries. In some cases (those noted as out of the range of observations), the estimated price was ignored because it refers to cars either too small or too large to have been actually included in the data used to estimate the regressions. Thus, for practical purposes, the automobile price table may be regarded as a

19. A number of different weighting schemes were investigated in the ICP's Phase I. The results of the alternatives were presented in Table 8.5 of *A System*, p. 113.

20. Note that comparisons of Table 2.6 are stated as PPPs. The prices used as inputs in the regressions in Table 2.3 and in the standard cars of Table 2.5 were denominated in U.S. dollars using exchange rates strictly as a matter of computational convenience.

Malaysia	Netherlands	Philippines	United Kingdom	United States	Independent variables
—	—	—	—	0.0002639 (0.0001147)	Displacement (cubic inches)
—	0.78852 (0.27190)	0.41096 (0.10526)	0.41833 (0.09729)	—	Horsepower (hundreds)
—	—	—	—	0.05158 (0.01322)	RPM (thousands)
−0.1141 (0.0681)	—	—	—	—	Number of cylinders
0.64380 (0.04313)	0.18345 (0.16677)	0.13918 (0.11094)	0.28207 (0.06560)	0.17937 (0.01573)	Weight (thousands of pounds)
—	0.070298 (0.028120)	—	—	—	Length (feet)
—	—	0.41750 (0.13352)	—	—	Width (feet)
—	—	—	—	0.0033664 (0.0005430)	Mean effective pressure [a]
—	—	—	−0.00085656 (0.00065889)	—	Registration (thousands)
—	—	—	—	0.059706 (0.010856)	Hardtop
7.06364 (0.27558)	5.90423 (0.22365)	5.50225 (0.55872)	6.77030 (0.08590)	6.53847 (0.09430)	Constant [b]
0.9528	0.8914	0.8546	0.8384	0.9401	Coefficient of determination ($\bar{R}^2$)
0.0325	0.0632	0.0787	0.0432	0.0176	Standard error of estimate (SEE)
1970	1970	1972	1969	1969	Reference year for regression
12	21	19	55	80	Number of observations [c]
6	7	8	9	4	Number of standard models used in comparing prices

—. Characteristic did not have a coefficient that was as large as its standard error.

Notes: Standard errors appear in parentheses below each regression coefficient. Exchange rates used in converting to U.S. dollars appear in Table 1.1, column 2.

a. Computed from the formula [(horsepower · number of cycles)÷(displacement · RPM)] · 198,000.

b. The constants of each regression equation have been adjusted: (1) to take account of differences between list and transaction prices; and (2) to make the reference year for all countries 1970.

c. Each automobile model is given a weight in a country regression that reflects its importance in the sales of that country.

tableau with holes wherever the note is made that the model is out of the range of observations. The country-product–dummy method (CPD), explained in Chapter 3, has been developed to estimate each country's price level relative to that of the United States for the many categories (like automobiles) for which identical specifications are not priced by all countries—that is, the price tableau has holes. The results of applying this method to automobiles appear in column 4 of Table 2.6 for the regression countries.[21]

Rents

The problem of standardization of quality is more thorny for housing services than for automobiles because dwelling units are more heterogeneous, both within and between countries. Furthermore, rents or house values are

21. Normally, it is not possible to incorporate weights that take account of the importance of an item in a country's overall spending because expenditure data are usually not available at the item level. Unit sales information is, however, available for each car, so it is possible to compute "double-weighted" CPD relative price estimates. See *A System*, pp. 63–65.

Table 2.4. Percentage Distribution of Total Automobile Sales in Eleven Countries by Weight and Horsepower

Horse-power \ Weight (pounds)	Below 1,401 (1)	1,401–1,700 (2)	1,701–2,000 (3)	2,001–2,300 (4)	2,301–2,600 (5)
1. Below 26	B 7.9 F 3.6 G 4.0 I 30.0 N 9.4 H 2.0				
2. 26–50	B 7.9 F 25.3 G 7.0 H 22.0 I 12.0 N 6.4 P 0.3 UK 9.0	B 29.9 F 10.8 G 8.0 H 24.0 I 12.0 N 35.3 P 19.2 UK 4.5	B 8.6 F 4.8 G 16.0 H 10.0 N 10.3 UK 2.2		
3. 51–75		B 2.8 F 6.0 G 9.0 I 18.0 J 43.5 M 36.0 N 3.1 UK 10.1 US 2.4	B 13.7 F 22.9 G 17.0 H 18.0 I 8.0 J 2.2 M 15.7 N 13.4 P 16.0 UK 29.2	B 13.9 F 13.2 G 7.0 H 16.0 I 8.0 N 11.3 P 5.1 UK 6.7 US 4.8	UK 1.1 M 5.7
4. 76–100			B 0.7 N 0.4 P 21.8 UK 13.5	B 4.4 F 3.6 G 5.0 H 2.0 I 10.0 J 34.8 M 7.0 N 4.1 P 23.3 UK 4.5 US 1.2	B 6.2 F 3.6 G 6.0 N 3.0 UK 1.1 M 10.5
5. 101–125			UK 1.1 US 1.2	B 1.3 F 1.2 G 6.0 J 9.8 N 1.1 P 1.3 UK 1.1	B 0.1 G 4.0 N 0.2 UK 2.2
6. 126–175					B 0.2 F 1.2 G 2.0 I 2.0 N 0.3 UK 1.1
7. 176–225					
8. Above 225					

B—Belgium
F—France
G—Germany, F.R.
H—Hungary
I—Italy
J—Japan
M—Malaysia
N—Netherlands
P—Philippines
UK—United Kingdom
US—United States

2,601–2,900 (6)	2,901–3,200 (7)	3,201–3,500 (8)	Above 3,500 (9)	Total	Weight (pounds)/Horse-power
				B 7.9 F 3.6 G 4.0 H 2.0 I 30.0 N 9.4	1. Below 26
				B 46.4 F 40.9 G 31.0 H 56.0 I 24.0 N 52.0 P 19.5 UK 15.7	2. 26–50
B 0.4 N 0.2	B 1.2 N 0.7 M 12.5			B 32.0 F 42.1 G 33.0 H 34.0 I 34.0 J 45.7 M 69.9 N 28.7 P 21.1 UK 47.1 US 7.2	3. 51–75
B 0.6 F 2.4 M 10.0 N 0.6 UK 4.5 US 1.2	H 6.0			B 11.9 F 9.6 G 11.0 H 8.0 I 10.0 J 34.8 M 27.5 N 8.1 P 45.1 UK 23.6 US 2.4	4. 76–100
B 0.2 F 1.2 J 9.8 M 2.7 N 0.2 UK 4.5 US 3.6	G 5.0 P 0.9			B 1.6 F 2.4 G 15.0 J 19.6 M 2.7 N 1.5 P 2.2 UK 8.9 US 4.8	5. 101–125
P 11.4 UK 1.1 US 1.2	G 2.0 P 0.7 US 9.6	UK 1.1 US 6.0	B 0.1 N 0.1 US 9.6	B 0.3 F 1.2 G 4.0 I 2.0 N 0.4 P 12.1 UK 3.3 US 26.4	6. 126–175
	G 1.0 UK 1.1 US 3.6	G 1.0 US 4.8	US 4.8	G 2.0 UK 1.1 US 13.2	7. 176–225
	US 1.2	US 4.8	B 0.02 N 0.03 US 39.8	B 0.02 N 0.03 US 45.8	8. Above 225

Table 2.5. Estimated Automobile Prices by Models for Eleven Countries, 1970

(U.S. dollars)

Cell [a]	Model	Belgium	France	Germany, F.R.	Hungary	Italy	Japan
2,1	Renault R4-40V	1,277	1,202	1,212	2,011	1,065	1,098 [b]
2,2	Fiat 850 Berlina	1,394	1,288	1,286	1,982	1,191	1,150 [b]
2,3	Volkswagen 1300	1,789	1,608	1,564	2,569	1,442	1,490 [b]
3,2	Escort 1100 DX 2D	1,697	1,591	1,605	3,128	1,550	1,476
3,3	Opel Kadett LS 45 PS	1,805	1,621	1,696	3,337	1,582	1,509
3,4	Peugeot 404 Berlina	2,436	1,936	2,095	3,377	1,794	1,905
4,4	Corona Mk II 1600 DX	2,701	2,311	2,274	4,009	2,228	2,032
5,5	Vauxhall Victor 2000 4D	3,214 [c]	2,841	2,674	5,317 [b]	2,794 [b]	2,594
6,6	American 6	4,587 [c]	4,961 [b]	2,949	5,630 [b]	5,180 [b]	4,254 [b]
7,7	Chevy II Nova V8	8,791 [c]	11,708 [b]	4,909 [c]	12,528 [b]	13,108 [b]	9,356 [b]

less uniform within a country, even for dwelling units of comparable quality, than are automobile prices. Nonetheless, using housing survey data and working with a number of objective variables that clearly are associated with housing quality—for example, size, facilities, and age—it has been possible to apply the hedonic regression technique to estimate for each country the parameters of a rent–quality relationship. About thirty-five specifications for standardized dwelling units were established as a basis for international comparisons. For each country the average rent was estimated from the country's own hedonic regression equations for a number of specifications. The precise number of specifications estimated ranged between seven and nineteen for the multilateral comparisons, but rather smaller numbers were priced for the binary comparisons.

Location is a variable that is important in the determination of rent levels in all sixteen countries. The ICP, however, has deliberately treated location as a price-increasing factor rather than as a quality variable adding to or subtracting from quantity. Although urban rents are universally higher than rural rents, the view adopted here, as in the Phase I report, is that the streams of housing services flowing from two identical dwelling units, one in the country and the other in the city, should be valued the same. Therefore, every housing specification selected for a country is priced at the national average rental for the specification.[22]

The hedonic equations obtained for the ten Phase I countries along with a description of the data underlying them appear in Chapter 9 of *A System*. Only information about the six new countries of Phase II will be given here.

Tables 2.7, 2.8, 2.9, and 2.10 set out the coefficients of the regression equations that describe the relationship between rent and housing characteristics in Iran, the Republic of Korea, Malaysia, and the Philippines. In the case of Belgium and the Netherlands, rents for dwelling units with selected characteristics were supplied directly by the Statistical Office of the European Communities on the basis of cross-tabulations of data collected for its own Common Market purchasing-power and product comparisons.

The sources of the survey data underlying the regressions are given in each table. The notes at the bottom of each table indicate the additional adjustments applied to the rent figures obtained from the regressions for the various specifications. The adjustments serve to make the final estimates (a) represent

---

22. For the rationale for this treatment of location, see *A System*, p. 118. This is an application of the "a potato is a potato" principle.

Malaysia	Nether-lands	Philip-pines	United Kingdom	United States	Cell [a]	Model
1,793 [b]	1,389	2,527 [c]	1,424	1,652 [b]	2,1	Renault R4-40V
1,916 [b]	1,505	2,491	1,529	1,824 [b]	2,2	Fiat 850 Berlina
2,371 [b]	1,923	3,235	1,750	1,794 [b]	2,3	Volkswagen 1300
2,131	1,903	3,327	1,699	1,854 [c]	3,2	Escort 1100 DX 2D
2,225	2,035	3,491	1,738	1,897 [c]	3,3	Opel Kadett LS 45 PS
3,240	2,604	4,102	2,146	2,043	3,4	Peugeot 404 Berlina
2,933	3,017	4,315	2,289	2,189	4,4	Corona Mk II 1600 DX
3,362	3,613 [c]	5,366	2,556	2,177	5,5	Vauxhall Victor 2000 4D
4,244	4,852 [c]	7,217	3,157	2,066 [d]	6,6	American 6
5,773 [b]	9,640 [c]	10,649 [b]	4,850 [c]	2,319 [d]	7,7	Chevy II Nova V8

Source: Prices are obtained from the application of the equations of Table 2.3 to the characteristics of the ten cars.

a. First figure applies to row number and second figure to column number in Table 2.4.

b. Out of range of observations.

c. Outside of middle 90 percent of country's range of observations.

d. U.S. prices for American 6 and Chevy II Nova V8 are lowered by 5.3 percent to reflect the larger average discount given for these cars in the United States.

mean rather than median estimates,[23] (b) refer to the country as a whole rather than to a narrower range of locations, and (c) refer to the standard reference year, 1970.

The principal problem encountered in estimating national average rentals arose from inadequate rural coverage of the surveys in a number of the countries. In some cases, only the urban rents for the selected specifications were available, and it was necessary to estimate rents for the rural sector for the same specifications on the basis of rural–urban rent relationships in other countries. The urban and rural rents were averaged to obtain the national rent with the use of appropriate weights derived from census materials. Where possible, the weighting factors were estimated separately for each specification according to the prevalence of the particular kind of dwelling unit in each area; in the case of Malaysia, however, the same weights were used for all specifications.

Estimates of rents for selected specifications of dwelling units for the six new Phase II countries are presented in Table 2.11.[24]

The main judgment that had to be made in pricing out individual specifications was with regard to what building materials and facilities corresponded to the three levels of construction defined in the ICP list of specifications: substandard (the first three specifications), intermediate (the next three), and standard (the rest). Generally, the inclusion in the regressions of some construction material variables with relatively low *t*-statistics was dictated by a concern for insuring better control over the groupings by construction quality. It must be admitted that the identification of the three distinct levels, particularly the intermediate level, was not entirely satisfactory for Iran among the new Phase II countries (nor for Colombia among the Phase I countries). Each particular country had its own problems. For example, in the Republic of Korea proper identification of total floor area was complicated by the omission in the rent survey of information about the area of the kitchen.

23. The adjustment is necessary because the log of rent is the dependent variable in the equations. The antilog of the mean value of the log of rent corresponds to the median rent when the distribution is lognormal. See *A System*, p. 123.

24. The specifications are defined in *A System*, pp. 143–45.

Table 2.6. Purchasing-Power Parities for Automobiles, 1970

| | | Binary comparisons | | | |
| | | Weighted arithmetic mean | | | |
Country	Unit of currency	U.S. weights (1)	Own weights (2)	Ideal Fisher (3)	Multilateral comparisons (4)
Belgium	B. franc	153.2	52.5	89.7	64.3
Colombia [a]	peso	—	—	31.6	37.94
France	franc	7.19	5.187	6.11	6.33
Germany, F.R.	DM	6.611	3.772	4.99	4.23
Hungary	forint	54.91	52.25	53.6	58.7
India [a]	rupee	—	—	9.17	10.78
Iran [a]	rial	168.8	125.3	145.4	121.8
Italy	lira	784.0	556.0	660.0	664.0
Japan	yen	416.0	334.0	373.0	375.0
Kenya [a]	shilling	—	—	7.64	9.23
Korea, Republic of [a]	won	—	—	697.0	761.0
Malaysia	M. dollar	5.017	4.336	4.664	4.68
Netherlands	guilder	12.09	4.18	7.11	5.13
Philippines	peso	20.11	13.63	16.56	14.66
United Kingdom	pound	0.758	0.429	0.570	0.490
United States	dollar	1.0	1.0	1.0	1.0

Note: The binary comparison entries are the main constituent parts of the "equipment" entries in Summary Binary Tables 5.1 to 5.15. The multilateral comparison entries in this table are repeated in Appendix Table 4.3, line 79.

a. Countries for which there were not enough observations to perform regression analysis. The entries in column 3 for these countries represent unweighted geometric means of price relatives for three or four models except for Iran for which the figure is a weighted mean based on two models.

The presence or absence of a kitchen was known, but its floor area, if present in the dwelling unit, was not included in the unit's size. Independent estimates were provided by the Korean Bureau of Statistics of the Economic Planning Board that gave a basis for estimating properly the relationship between rent and floor area.

RENT COMPARISONS: BINARY. The rents of five of the new Phase II countries—Belgium, Iran, Malaysia, Netherlands, and the Philippines—were compared directly with rents in the United States. The Republic of Korea, however, was compared directly with India and then indirectly via this bridge with the United States. For each of the five countries, the rent relatives for housing specifications common to both the country and the United States were averaged twice, once using expenditure weights of the country and once using expenditure weights of the United States. In addition, the Fisher ideal index, the geometric mean of the two, was calculated. These three comparisons appear in Table 2.12. For any particular country's comparisons, the number of specifications entering into each of the averages was typically less than the country's number of specifications for which rents appear in Table 2.11. Specifications were included only if there was an overlap in the 90 percent sense in the prevalence of dwelling units in the country and the United States.[25] The expenditure weights used in the averaging process were estimated from data on each country's housing stock as obtained from national censuses.

25. If housing specifications and associated proportions found in a country are arrayed by quality, a particular specification is regarded as eligible for inclusion in the binary comparisons only if dwelling units of that type lie within the middle 90 percent of the housing distribution.

Table 2.7. Iran: Coefficients of Regression Equation for Rents, 1974

(Dependent variable: Natural logarithm of rent in rials)

Independent variable	Coefficient	Standard error
Intercept	3.9004 [a]	0.1196
Facilities		
Water	0.3379 [a]	0.0526
Electricity	0.5308 [a]	0.0673
Telephone	0.3202 [a]	0.0845
Private kitchen	0.5701 [a]	0.0513
Private bath	0.4234 [a]	0.0691
None	0	—
Date of construction [b]		
Before 1930	0	—
1930	0.2798 [a]	0.1109
1940	0.1299	0.0923
1950	0.0413	0.0790
1960	0.2932 [a]	0.0771
1970	0.3814 [a]	0.1196
Size		
Log of area (square meters)	0.4206 [a]	0.0249
Location		
Tehran	0.7859 [a]	0.0553
Population 200,000–500,000	0.2027 [a]	0.0598
Population 50,000–200,000	0.2055 [a]	0.0653
Population less than 50,000	0	—

$\bar{R}^2 = 0.7666$
SEE $= 0.5343$

Notes: (1) Median-to-mean conversion factor: exp ($\frac{1}{2}$SEE^2) = 1.153. (2) Rural rent is estimated to be 43 percent of urban rents. Estimates of the proportions of rural and urban dwelling units varied with the housing specification. (3) Adjustment factor to shift reference to 1970: 0.698.

Source: Rent survey of 847 tenant-occupied dwellings in thirty-five cities conducted by the Central Bank of Iran for July 1974.

a. Statistically significant at the 0.05 level.

b. It is to be expected that the coefficients of the "date of construction" dummy variables would increase monotonicly with age. The possibility that dwelling units built just before World War II might have been built more sturdily than those before or after is suggested by the significant coefficient 0.2798. The statistically insignificant dummies for 1940 and 1950 were retained, the first because its *t*-statistic was greater than unity and the second because it seemed desirable to have all decades represented.

In the case of the Korean comparison, India was used as a bridge because there were so few overlapping specifications between the Republic of Korea and the United States. Using a bridge makes it impossible to construct either a pure Korea-weighted or U.S.-weighted index. But the index $\bar{P}_{K,I}{}^{(K)} \cdot \bar{P}_{I,US}{}^{(I)} = \bar{P}_{K,US}{}^{("K")}$ was taken to reflect more strongly Korean housing patterns, and $\bar{P}_{K,I}{}^{(I)} \cdot \bar{P}_{I,US}{}^{(US)} = \bar{P}_{K,US}{}^{("US")}$ was taken to reflect more strongly U.S. patterns.[26]

RENT COMPARISONS: MULTILATERAL. The tableau of rents presented in Table 2.11, along with the corresponding columns from Table 9.28 in *A*

26. $\bar{P}_{ij}{}^{(i)}$ is the expenditure-weighted average of $\left(\frac{P_{i\alpha}}{P_{j\alpha}}\right)$, $\alpha = 1, \dots, N_{ij}$, using the *i*th country's expenditures as weights; N_{ij} is the number of overlapping specifications in the *i*th and *j*th countries.

Table 2.8. Republic of Korea: Coefficients of Regression Equation for Rents, 1975

(Dependent variable: Natural logarithm of rent in won)

Independent variable [a]	Coefficient	Standard error
Intercept	6.6076 [a]	0.1402
Location		
Seoul or Pusan	0.2818 [a]	0.0197
Urban other than Seoul or Pusan	0	—
Type of payment		
Deposit	−0.4226 [a]	0.0182
Monthly payment	0	—
Wall construction		
Brick	0.0379	0.0896
Adobe	−0.0470	0.0922
Wood	−0.0660	0.0964
Other	0	—
Roof construction		
Tiles	0.0380	0.0272
Sheet	0.0043	0.0547
Ferroconcrete	0.0806 [a]	0.0363
Other	0	—
Facilities		
Piped water	0.1995 [a]	0.0250
Electricity	0.2785 [a]	0.0826
Toilet	0.0828 [a]	0.0193
Bath	0.0934 [a]	0.0272
None	0	—
Age		
Pre-1949	−0.0150	0.0298
1950–1969	−0.0844 [a]	0.0239
1970	0	—
Size		
Log of area (square meters)	0.6979 [a]	0.0173

$\bar{R}^2 = 0.6061$
SEE $= 0.3634$

Notes: (1) Median-to-mean conversion factor: exp $(\frac{1}{2}\text{SEE}^2) = 1.068$. (2) National average adjustment factor: variable depending upon the housing characteristics specification. (3) Adjustment factor to shift reference date to 1970: 0.671.

Source: Rent survey of 1972 dwelling units in May 1975 covering major urban areas including eleven cities conducted by the Bureau of Statistics, Economic Planning Board.

a. Statistically significant at the 0.05 level.

System for the ten Phase I countries,[27] constitutes the price input for multilateral rent comparisons among all sixteen Phase II countries. Because of the many missing entries—the consequences of many types of housing being absent from particular countries—the multilateral comparisons were handled by the same double-weighted CPD procedure used in the treatment of automobile comparisons.[28] The results of the multilateral comparisons appear in the last column of Table 2.12.

Capital Formation

The methods of selecting items and matching qualities in the price comparison work in the capital formation sectors follow closely those described in *A System.*[29] The following remarks are confined to an explanation of the

27. As noted above, the U.S. rents have been revised downward by approximately 7.5 percent.
28. See *A System,* pp. 63–65.
29. Ibid., Chapters 10 and 11.

Table 2.9. Malaysia: Coefficients of Regression Equation for Rents, 1973

(Dependent variable: Natural logarithm of rent in M. dollars)

Independent variable	Coefficient	Standard error
Intercept	—2.3513 [a]	0.2650
Type of house		
Detached house	0.3261 [a]	0.0756
Semidetached house	0.2421 [a]	0.0800
Row or terrace house	0.1066	0.0635
Flat in an apartment building	0.5357 [a]	0.1325
Flat in a housing block	—0.0758	0.1338
Flat in a shop, a house, or miscellaneous	0	—
Material of outer wall		
Brick	0.5452 [a]	0.1422
Concrete	0.4123 [a]	0.1679
Plank and brick	0.2051	0.1434
Plank	0.1200	0.1307
Zinc or miscellaneous	0	—
Material of roof		
Tiles	0.3134 [a]	0.0833
Cement	0.6340 [a]	0.1358
Asbestos sheet	0.1954 [a]	0.0943
Zinc	0.1783 [a]	0.0747
Thatch of palm leaves, or miscellaneous	0	—
Age of structure		
0–4 years	0.7277 [a]	0.1099
5–9 years	0.6278 [a]	0.0609
10–29 years	0.5154 [a]	0.0468
30 years or more	0	—
Facilities		
Neither water nor electricity	0	—
Water only	0.4241 [a]	0.1980
Electricity only	0.1162	0.1185
Water and electricity	0.5683 [a]	0.0963
Furnishings		
None	0.4847 [a]	0.1065
Furnished	0	—
Location, town size		
Population less than 7,670	0	—
Population 7,670–75,000	0.1814 [a]	0.0791
Population more than 75,000	0.3543 [a]	0.0818
Size		
Log of area (square meters)	0.4785 [a]	0.0375

$\bar{R}^2$=0.6079
SEE=0.5613

Notes: (1) Median-to-mean adjustment factor: exp (½SEE²)= 1.171. (2) National average rental adjustment factor=0.880 (factor is applied to rent estimate for "population less than 7,670"). (3) Adjustment factor to shift reference date to 1970: 0.981.

Source: Malaysia Department of Statistics, rent survey of 894 dwelling units, conducted in May 1974 but referring to June 1973, covering areas in four size categories ranging from urban-rural to metropolitan.

a. Statistically significant at the 0.05 level.

revisions in the original 1970 estimates and of the special features of the
Phase II data construction.

Construction

A number of revisions were made in the original 1970 cost estimates of
the Phase I countries. Most of these revisions were made because additional
information was received; less frequently, they were made to correct errors
or to revise methods of imputing PPPs for categories in which prices were
missing. Estimates for France, Italy, Japan, Kenya, the United Kingdom, and
the United States were altered. Usually, only one or two detailed categories
were affected, though the U.S. revisions were more extensive.

Of the six new Phase II countries, the Philippines furnished information on
costs of construction for both 1970 and 1973; Iran and the Republic of Korea
for 1973 only; and Belgium, the Netherlands, and Malaysia for 1970 only. In
each country, prices available for a particular reference year were extrapolated
to the other reference year on the basis of time-to-time indexes of construction costs. The extrapolation from 1970 to 1973 for most of the Phase I

**Table 2.10. Philippines: Coefficients of Regression
Equation for Rents, 1972**

(Dependent variable: Natural logarithm of rent in pesos)

Independent variable	Coefficient	Standard error
Intercept	1.5609[a]	0.3003
Rural versus urban		
Urban	1.0885[a]	0.0803
Rural	0	—
Size (square meters)		
15	0	—
25	0.3150[a]	0.0899
35	0.5874[a]	0.1032
45	0.7415[a]	0.1045
60	0.8695[a]	0.1114
75	1.0649[a]	0.1083
90	1.1210[a]	0.1341
More than 90[b]	0.9231[a]	0.1315
Age[c]		
Pre-1945	0	—
1945–54	0.0238	0.2242
1955–64	0.0540	0.2210
1965–72	0.2576	0.2234
Facilities		
None	0	—
Toilet only	0.2292	0.2076
Electricity only	0.3564	0.2429
Electricity and toilet	0.8864[a]	0.1945
Water and toilet	0.6458[a]	0.3763
Electricity and water	0.8777[a]	0.3881
All three	1.2809[a]	0.1971

$\bar{R}^2 = 0.8623$
SEE = 0.3164

Notes: (1) Median-to-mean adjustment factor: exp (½SEE²) =
1.051. (2) National average rental adjustment factor: Variable depending upon housing characteristic specification. (3) Adjustment
factor to shift reference date to 1970: 0.9163.
Source: Philippines National Census and Statistics Office, rent survey of dwellings in 1972.
a. Statistically significant at the 0.05 level.
b. The coefficient for "more than 90" is not significantly different
from that of "90."
c. In a previous tabulation, the data indicated that rents for
dwelling units built before 1942 were about the same as for those
built in 1942–44, the earliest time period represented in the survey.

countries and for Belgium and the Netherlands was carried out using the price deflators implicit in the current price and constant price expenditures provided in the updating worksheet for the various construction summary categories. That is, the extrapolation was carried out by the same method that was used for consumer goods.

For the Republic of Korea, an available construction cost index was used to adjust the 1973 figures to the 1970 reference date. For Iran, a specially prepared cost index based on wholesale price indexes for construction materials and on wage indexes for construction workers was used for the same purpose. In the case of the United States, a combination of building cost indexes, prepared for the ICP by the Boeckh Division of the American Appraisal Company, and implicit deflators from the U.S. national accounts were used in ways deemed appropriate for each detailed category.

For most of the countries, including Iran, Hungary, Japan, the Republic of Korea, the Philippines, the United Kingdom, and the United States, the coverage of the specifications was adequate to excellent, in terms of both the overall target number of specifications (thirty-nine) and their spread among the detailed construction categories.

For Belgium, France, the Federal Republic of Germany, Italy, and the Netherlands, estimated prices were available for eleven building and seven nonbuilding specifications. This is because the Statistical Office of the European Economic Communities followed the strategy of obtaining a relatively small number of carefully prepared estimates conforming to detailed specifications that had been agreed upon among the countries. The approach favored by the ICP relies upon abbreviated descriptions of buildings, usually about a page in length, and upon simplified descriptions of nonbuilding projects, indicating the major operations involved in them. Thus, a broad

Table 2.11. Rents in National Currencies for Various Housing Specifications Entering into Multilateral Comparisons, 1970: Belgium, Iran, Republic of Korea, Malaysia, Netherlands, Philippines

Specification [a]	Size [b]	Date	Facilities	Belgium (B. francs)	Iran (rials)	Korea, Republic of (won)	Malaysia (M. dollars)	Netherlands (guilders)	Philippines (pesos)
1	15	1930	None		104	1,591	2.52		5.70
2	25	1930	None		129	2,260	3.40		7.81
3	35	1930	None		149	2,849	4.18		10.25
4	15	1930	Electricity only		140	3,344	4.31		11.61
5	25	1930	Electricity only		173	4,751	7.71		15.91
6	35	1930	Electricity only		200	5,989	9.24		20.89
7	25	1950	Electricity only		220	4,751	12.91		16.54
8	35	1950	Electricity only		244	5,989	15.48		21.72
11	45	1930	All except heat		840		28.64		
12	60	1930	All except heat				65.76		
13	60	1910	Electricity only	1,037	678			45.0	
13A	25	1910	Electricity only	1,336	469	6,050	17.20	71.4	18.13
14	60	1910	Electricity, toilet only	1,707	838		28.64	91.2	
19	60	1950	All except heat	1,536				91.8	
20	75	1950	All except heat				85.74		
21	90	1950	All except heat		1,875		104.98		
24	60	1960	All except heat	1,685				109.8	
25	75	1960	All except heat		1,283		100.91		
26	90	1960	All except heat		1,385		110.09		
29	60	1950	All including heat	2,641				153.0	
34	60	1960	All including heat	2,983				172.8	

a. For an explanation of the specifications, see Irving B. Kravis, Zoltan Kenessey, Alan Heston, and Robert Summers, *A System of International Comparisons of Gross Product and Purchasing Power* (Baltimore: Johns Hopkins University Press, 1975), pp. 143-45.

b. Square meter of floor area.

Table 2.12. Purchasing-Power Parities for Rents, 1970

| | | Binary comparisons | | | |
| | | Weighted arithmetic mean | | | |
Country	Currency unit	U.S. weights (1)	Own weights (2)	Ideal Fisher (3)	Multilateral comparisons (4)
Belgium	B. franc	36.84	30.14	33.32	31.5
Colombia	peso	12.69	11.72	12.19	14.12
France	franc	3.35	3.15	3.25	3.18
Germany, F.R.	DM	2.61	2.46	2.53	2.60
Hungary	forint	11.67	8.57	10.01	9.4
India	rupee	1.92	1.86	1.89	1.90
Iran	rial	18.46	19.79	19.11	17.5
Italy	lira	322.0	334.0	328.0	321.0
Japan	yen	282.0	273.0	277.0	319.0
Kenya	shilling	7.48	5.55	6.44	5.98
Korea, Republic of	won	314.0	345.0	329.0	346.0
Malaysia	M. dollar	0.995	0.952	0.973	1.04
Netherlands	guilder	1.73	1.68	1.71	1.92
Philippines	peso	1.35	0.74	1.00	1.17
United Kingdom	pound	0.292	0.291	0.291	0.295

Note: The binary comparison entries are the main constituent parts of the "gross rents" entries in Summary Binary Tables 5.1 to 5.15. The mutilateral comparison entries in this table are repeated in Appendix Table 4.3, line 52.

description of a building or other construction project was provided, but the description was detailed enough to ensure that any project meeting the description would be at least roughly comparable to any other project meeting it. With this approach, it is more economical to gather each individual estimate and it is thus feasible to obtain costs for each of a large number of projects from alternative sources in each country. The approach of the EEC Statistical Office offers the benefit of careful estimates, but at the cost of having a reduced number of comparisons.

In terms of numbers of specifications compared, the other countries fell between these two groups. India and Colombia had good coverage of building specifications but only fair coverage of nonbuilding specifications, whereas Kenya had only fair coverage of building specifications but good coverage of nonbuilding specifications. Malaysia had the weakest coverage: it had less than a score of construction cost estimates for only four out of the fifteen detailed construction categories, and these accounted for only 40 percent of total construction expenditures.

In the aggregation of the detailed construction categories, revisions in expenditure data sometimes produced different PPPs for the overall construction aggregate from those reported in *A System,* even where there was little or no change in the PPPs for the component detailed categories. As noted above, this occurred where the PPPs for the different detailed categories were very different.

Producers' durables

The prices of producers' durable goods for Belgium and the Netherlands referred to 1970, whereas those for Iran had a 1973 reference date. The Republic of Korea, Malaysia, and the Philippines reported prices for both years, though the items covered in the two years were not always the same. In all six countries, 1973 prices were estimated from 1970 prices or 1970 prices were estimated from 1973 prices, depending upon the year for which data were available. Whenever possible the estimate was made by using an appropriate item or component from the wholesale price index. When this was not possible, deflators based on the updating worksheet were applied as described above in the section on expenditure data.[30]

The list of producers' durables used in the price comparison was substantially the same as that used in Phase I.[31] On the whole, the coverage provided by the new countries fell within the range of that provided in the earlier study by the original ten countries. The number of different kinds of producers' durable goods actually compared in Phase II ranged from twenty-four for Malaysia to fifty-five for the Philippines; for the original ten countries, the number ranged from fifteen for Japan to ninety-five for the United States. Generally, prices were compared for more than one variant of each kind of good. Coverage for the new Phase II countries in terms of categories was also reasonably satisfactory, though there were some categories in all six countries for which no price comparisons were available. Categories for which there were price comparisons accounted for 70 percent (Malaysia) to 90 percent (Belgium, India, and the Philippines) of expenditures on producers' durables. The missing categories for which prices were imputed are identified in Appendix Table 5.1.

The most important changes in producers' durables from the Phase I comparisons were for India and the United States. After Phase I was completed, the Indian Central Statistical Organisation furnished prices for some additional items, thus raising the number of items compared with the United States to forty-four from the earlier total of thirty-three. In addition, some previously estimated prices of a number of items were replaced by actual prices as reported by the Central Statistical Organisation.[32] This left only two categories (ICP 14.5 and ICP 17.2) for which the PPPs had to be imputed from PPPs for categories believed to have similar price relationships; together these categories accounted for less than 10 percent of the total investment in producers' durables in 1970. For the United States, some actual 1973 prices were obtained. For the most part, however, 1970 prices were adjusted to 1973 on the basis of appropriate wholesale price indexes. Less important revisions for Colombia, France, Japan, and Kenya involved the use of actual prices in lieu of imputations that had been made in Phase I.

As in Phase I, PPPs for the compensation of employees were obtained by comparing the compensation of government employees in about a score of jobs in four different categories differing mainly in educational requirements. The description of each job was taken from the International Standard Classification of Occupations.[33]

Government

For Belgium, Iran, Malaysia, the Netherlands, and all the Phase I countries except Colombia, the compensation for the jobs referred to 1970. The 1973 figures were estimated by applying deflators from the updating worksheet to the 1970 compensation figures in each of the four job categories. Colombia and the Republic of Korea supplied compensation figures for each job for both years.

Again as in Phase I, government purchases of commodities were allocated

30. Prices for India and Iran, reported on a calendar year basis, were adjusted to the fiscal years by the use of the appropriate implicit deflators.
31. See *A System*, p. 153.
32. The 1970 prices in many cases had been obtained by adjusting the 1967 reported prices using wholesale price changes.
33. *International Standard Classification of Occupations*, rev. 1968 (Geneva: International Labor Organization, 1969).

to thirteen industrial groupings based on the International Standard Industrial Classification of all Economic Activities (ISIC).[34]

Since no special price comparisons were made for government purchases of commodities, some assumptions had to be made about the PPPs for these groupings. The general approach was to use the most appropriate PPPs computed elsewhere in the study. In the binary comparisons, this was done by selecting on the basis of similarity in product composition one or more ICP categories for which PPPs were available and assigning those PPPs to the given grouping. To mention a simple example, the ISIC category food, beverages, and tobacco (ISIC Division 31), one of the groupings of government purchases, was assigned the PPP for the ICP category food, beverage, and tobacco (ICP 01). For ISIC groupings such as fabricated metal products (ISIC Division 38) for which several ICP categories had to be combined, the unweighted geometric mean was used.

For the multilateral comparisons, the method was a little more complicated. First, expenditures of each industrial grouping of government were distributed to the various ICP categories. For example, government expenditures on food, beverages, and tobacco were transferred to the appropriate consumption category (ICP 01), whereas government expenditures on wood and wood products were divided between furniture and fixtures in the consumption sector (ICP 04.11) and in the producers' durables sector (ICP 17.1). A Geary-Khamis calculation was then made to determine the values of each country's expenditure at international prices for each ICP category.[35] Following this, government commodity expenditures were reaggregated by taking from each ICP category the prorated share of government, thus yielding a total for government expenditure on commodities in international prices. Finally, the PPP for government expenditures on commodities was then obtained by dividing the ratio of each given country's government expenditure on commodities at international prices by the corresponding ratio for the United States.[36]

34. U.N. Statistical Office, *International Standard Industrial Classification of All Economic Activities,* Statistical Papers, Series M, No. 4, Rev. 2 (New York: United Nations, 1968).

35. The Geary-Khamis method is an aggregation method in which category international prices and country PPPs are estimated simultaneously from a system of linear equations. See Chapter 3 below and also *A System,* pp. 68–70.

36. That is $\frac{P_N Q_N}{\Pi Q_N} \div \frac{P_{US} Q_{US}}{\Pi Q_{US}} = \frac{P_N}{P_{US}} = \text{PPP}_N$, where the Ps are national prices, the Πs are international prices, and the Qs are quantities, all referring to commodities purchased by government, and N is a given country.

Appendix 1 to Chapter 2

The International Comparison Project: *updating worksheet*

Each country in Phase II of the International Comparison Project (ICP) was requested to provide detailed expenditure and price data for either 1970 or 1973. In addition, each country was asked to supply data on the ICP summary categories for both years. This latter information was supplied to the ICP staff on the following "updating worksheet":

UNITED NATIONS INTERNATIONAL COMPARISON PROJECT—PHASE II

Country ———————————— SCHEDULE FOR UPDATING Unit of Currency————————

Date of Completion———————— PHASE I RESULTS Constant Prices of Year————————

Expenditure on Gross Domestic Product at Current and Constant Market Prices, 1970, 1973

Line No.	Reference Code	Name of ICP Expenditure Category	At Current Prices		At Constant Prices	
			1970	1973	1970	1973
1	0	Final consumption expenditure of the population.........				
2	01	Food, beverages and tobacco				
3	01.1	Food				
4	01.10	Bread and cereals...............				
5	01.11	Meat				
6	01.12	Fish				
7	01.13	Milk, cheese, and eggs..........				
8	01.14	Oils and fats.................				
9	1.15–17	Fruits and vegetables				
10	01.19	Coffee, tea, and cocoa..........				
11	01.18, 01.20	Sugar and other foods..........				
12	01.3	Beverages				
13	01.4	Tobacco				
14	02	Clothing and footwear...............				
15	02.1	Clothing				
16	02.2	Footwear				
17	03	Gross rent, fuel and power..............				
18	03.1	Gross rents				
19	03.2	Fuel and power................				
20	04	House furnishings and operation..........				
21	04.1–4	Furnishings				
22	04.5	Household operation				
23	05	Medical care and health expenses...........				
24	06	Transport and communication............				
25	06.1	Personal transport equipment...........				
26	06.2	Operation of personal transport equipment..........				
27	06.3	Purchased transport services...........				
28	06.4	Communication				
29	07	Education, recreation, etc..........				
30	07.1–3	Recreation, etc...............				
31	07.4	Education				
32	08	Other goods and services...........				
33	08.1–2	Personal care				
34	08.3–4	Miscellaneous services				
35	1	Gross capital formation				
36	10–13	Construction				
37	10	Residential buildings				
38	11	Non-residential buildings				
39	12–13	Other construction, land improvement..............				
40	14–17	Producers' durables..........				
41	14	Transport equipment				
42	15	Non-electrical machinery, etc.......				
43	16	Electrical machinery, etc.......				
44	17	Other durables				
45	18	Increase in stocks				
46	19	Net exports of goods and services............				
47	2	Public final consumption expenditure...................				
48	20	Compensation of employees				
49	21	Expenditure on goods and services..................				
50	0–2	EXPENDITURE ON GROSS DOMESTIC PRODUCT AT MARKET PRICES				

GENERAL NOTE ON SCHEDULE FOR UPDATING PHASE I RESULTS

The classification of final expenditure in this table follows closely the classification recommended in the U.N. System of National Accounts (SNA). The detailed correspondence between the two schemes is given in the attached *Classification System* which has been prepared as one of the main working documents of the International Comparison Project. The code numbers shown in the second column of the table are those used for the individual categories of expenditure both in this *Classification System* and in the project generally.

The major differences between the two classifications arise from the transfer of certain types of expenditure from "government final consumption expenditure" as defined in SNA to "final consumption expenditure of the population" as defined for ICP. These transfers are designed to facilitate overall comparisons of final expenditure according to purpose and relate to general government expenditure on (i) medical and other health services, (ii) schools and other educational facilities, (iii) housing, and (iv) recreational and related cultural services. In the case of housing, a further difference from SNA definitions arises through the inclusion of housing subsidies in the category "gross rents" and in the aggregate "gross domestic product at market prices." These differences are indicated in detail in the footnotes in the *Classification System*.

Space is provided below for the presentation of any footnotes which may be required to the entries in the table or for any general note which the reporting country may wish to append to the table as a whole.

COUNTRY NOTES ON ENTRIES IN TABLE

Appendix 2 to
Chapter 2

The International
Comparison Project:
classification system

The classification of final expenditures follows closely the classifications suggested in the U.N. System of National Accounts (SNA; United Nations, *A System of National Accounts,* Studies in Methods, Series F, No. 2, Rev. 3 [New York: United Nations, 1968]). Some modifications have been necessary to meet the special requirements of the International Comparison Project; these are covered in footnotes (pages 65–67) indicated by letter superscripts. Actually, it has been necessary to develop a more detailed classification than that given in the SNA, but in this process, the list of items given in the SNA classifications has been used as a guide. For producers' durables, use has been made of the International Standard Industrial Classification (ISIC; United Nations, *International Standard Industrial Classification Statistical Papers,* Series M, No. 4, Rev. 2 [New York: United Nations, 1968]) in order to obtain more detailed product breakdowns.

The main categories and their code numbers are as follows:

0 Final Consumption Expenditure of the Population [a]
   01. Food, beverages, and tobacco
   02. Clothing and footwear
   03. Gross rent, fuel and power [b]
   04. Furniture, furnishings, household equipment, and operations
   05. Medical care and health expenses [c]
   06. Transport and communication
   07. Recreation, entertainment, education, and cultural services [d]
   08. Other goods and services [e]
1 Gross Capital Formation [f]
   10. Residential buildings [g]
   11. Nonresidential buildings [h]
   12. Other construction [i]
   13. Land improvement and plantation and orchard development [j]
   14. Transport equipment
   15. Nonelectrical machinery and equipment
   16. Electrical machinery and equipment
   17. Other durable furnishings and equipment
   18. Increase in stocks [k]
   19. Exports less imports of goods and services
2 Public Final Consumption Expenditure
   20. Compensation of employees
   21. Expenditure on commodities

The most disaggregated categories, which together account for the total GDP, constitute what is referred to in the text as the "detailed categories." The more aggregative "summary categories," which also account for the total GDP are in italics. (Two sets of footnotes are used. The first, using numerical superscripts following category numbers, refers to special groupings of categories in the summary tables in Chapters 4 and 5. The second, using letter superscripts following category titles, refers to more detailed explanations of the categories themselves.)

0 *Final Consumption Expenditure of the Population (CEP)*[a]
01.000 *Food, beverages, and tobacco*
  01.100 *Food*
    01.100 *Bread and cereals*
      01.101 Rice, glazed or polished but not otherwise worked (including broken rice)
      01.102 Maize; meal and flour of wheat, barley, and other cereals
      01.103 Bread and rolls

01.104 Biscuits, cake, and other bakery products; tarts and pies other than meat and fish tarts; farinaceous products stuffed with substances other than meat

01.105 Cereal preparations, preparations of flour, starch, or malt extract, used as infant food or for dietetic or culinary purposes

01.106 Macaroni, spaghetti, noodles, vermicelli, and similar products, whether cooked ready for consumption or not; rice cooked ready for consumption; malt, malt flour, malt extract, potato starch, sago, tapioca, and other starches; and the like

01.110 *Meat*

01.111 Fresh beef and veal

01.112 Fresh lamb and mutton

01.113 Fresh pork

01.114 Fresh poultry

01.115 Other fresh meat (sheep, goats, horses, game, edible offal, frog meat, and meat of marine mammals such as seals, walruses, and whales)

01.116 Frozen, chilled, dried, salted, smoked, canned meat, meat preparations, bacon, ham, and other dried, salted, or smoked meat and edible offals; meat extracts and meat juices; sausages, meat pies, meat soups in liquid, solid, or powder form, whether or not containing vegetables, spaghetti, rice, or the like; paste products filled with meat, such as canelloni, ravioli, and tortellini

01.120 *Fish*

01.121 Fresh or frozen fish and other sea food

01.122 Canned and preserved fish and other sea food and fish preparation; tinned fish soup, snails, fish pie

01.130 *Milk, cheese, and eggs*

01.131 Fresh milk

01.132 Milk products (evaporated, condensed, dried milk, cream, buttermilk, whey, yogurt, cheese, curd)

01.133 Eggs, treated eggs, egg products

01.140 *Oils and fats*

01.141 Butter

01.142 Margarine, edible oils, peanut butter, mayonnaise, other edible oils

01.143 Lard and other edible fat

01.150 [1] *Fresh fruits and vegetables* (other than potatoes and similar tubers)

01.151 Fresh fruits, tropical and subtropical (orange, tangerine, lemon, lime, grapefruit, banana, mango, pineapple, and the like)

01.152 Fresh fruits, other (apple, pear, cherry, grape, melon, plum, strawberry, and the like)

01.153 Fresh vegetables (beans, cabbages, carrots, cauliflowers, cucumbers, eggplants, garlic, ginger, onion, peas, pumpkins, squash, spinach, lettuce, tomatoes, edible seeds, herbs, lentils, pulses, mushrooms, rhubarb, truffles, and the like)

01.160 [1] *Fruits and vegetables other than fresh* (excluding potatoes and similar tubers)

01.161 Dried, frozen, preserved fruits, juices, fruit peel, nuts, and parts of plants preserved by sugar

01.162 Dried, frozen, preserved vegetables, vegetable juices, vegetable soups without meat or meat extract (or only traces)

1. In the summary tables, these categories are combined as Fruits and vegetables.

01.170 [1] *Potatoes, manioc, and other tubers* (potatoes, manioc, arrowroot, cassava, sweet potatoes, and other starchy roots; tinned and other products such as meal, flour, flakes, chips, except starches)

01.180 [2] *Sugar* (refined sugar and other products of refining beet and cane sugar, not including syrups)

01.190 *Coffee, tea and cocoa*

01.191 Coffee

01.192 Tea

01.193 Cocoa

01.200 [2] *Other foods*

01.201 Jam, preserves, marmalades, jellies, syrup, honey

01.202 Chocolate, sugar confectionery, ice cream

01.203 Salt, spices, vinegar, prepared baking powders, sauces, mixed condiments and mixed seasonings; yeast; substitutes for coffee, tea, and cocoa; and other food not elsewhere specified

01.300 *Beverages*

01.310 Nonalcoholic beverages (mineral waters and other soft drinks)

01.320 Alcoholic beverages

01.321 Spirits

01.322 Wine and cider (including cider with low alcohol content)

01.323 Beer (including beer with low alcohol content)

01.400 *Tobacco*

01.410 Cigarettes

01.420 Other (cigars, tobacco, snuff, and the like)

02.000 *Clothing and footwear*

02.100 *Clothing other than footwear, including repairs*

02.110 [3] Clothing materials

02.111 Woolen materials and materials of mixed fibres in which wool predominates by weight

02.112 Cotton materials and materials of mixed fibres in which cotton predominates by weight

02.113 Other materials, silk, synthetic fibres, flax, hemp, and the like; and materials of mixed fibres other than those classified above

02.120 [3] Outer clothing (coats, suits, trousers, shirts, blouses, skirts, dresses, sweaters, and the like, both ready-made and custom-tailored)

02.121 Men's (16 years and over)

02.122 Women's (16 years and over)

02.123 Boys' and girls' (15 years and under)

02.130 [3] Hosiery, underwear, and nightwear

02.131 Men's and boys'

02.132 Women's and girls'

02.150 [3] Other clothing (haberdashery, millinery, aprons, smocks, bibs, belts, gloves, and mittens other than rubber; handkerchiefs, except paper handkerchiefs; muffs, sleeve protectors, bathing suits, crash helmets, suspenders; accessories for making clothing such as buckles, buttons, fasteners, patterns, zippers, and the like)

02.160 [3] Rental of clothing, repairs to clothing other than footwear [1]

02.200 *Footwear, including repairs*

02.210 [4] Footwear (includes rubbers, sport shoes [other than boots and shoes with ice or roller skates attached, gaiters, spats, leggings, puttees])

02.211 Men's (16 years and over)

2. In the summary tables, these categories are combined as Spices, sweets, and sugar.
3. In the summary tables, these categories are combined as Clothing.
4. In the summary tables, these categories are combined as Footwear.

02.212 Women's (16 years and over)

02.213 Children's (15 years and under)

02.220 [4] Repairs to footwear (including shoe cleaning)

03.000 *Gross rent, fuel and power*

03.100 *Gross rents*

03.110 Gross rents (excluding indoor repair and upkeep.[ac] All gross rent in respect of dwellings, actual and imputed in the case of owner-occupied houses, including ground rents and taxes on the property. In general, house rent will be space rent, covering heating and plumbing facilities, lighting fixtures, fixed stoves, wash basins, and similar equipment that customarily is installed in the house before selling or letting. Also included are payments for garbage and sewage disposal. Rents paid for rooms in boardinghouses, but not in hotels, are included. Rents of secondary dwellings such as summer cottages, mountain chalets, and the like, also are included)

03.120 Expenditures of occupants of dwelling units on indoor repair and upkeep (indoor painting, wallpaper, decorating, and the like)[m]

03.200 *Fuel and power*

03.210 Electricity

03.220 Gas (natural and manufactured gas, including liquefied, petroleum gases [butane, propane, and the like])

03.230 Liquid fuels (heating and lighting oils)

03.240 Other fuels, water charges, and ice (coal, coke, briquettes, firewood, charcoal, peat, purchased heat, hot water, water charges, and ice)

04.000 *Furniture, furnishings, household equipment, and operation* [n]

04.100 [5] *Furniture, fixtures, carpets, and other floor coverings*

04.110 Furniture and fixtures (beds, chairs, tables, sofas, storage units, and hallboys; cribs, high chairs, playpens; door and dividing screens; sculptures, carvings, figurines, paintings, drawings, engravings, and other art objects; venetian blinds; fireplace equipment; other furniture and fixtures)

04.120 Floor coverings (carpets, large mats, and linoleum; other floor coverings)

04.200 [5] *Household textiles and other furnishings* (curtains, sheets, tablecloths and napkins, towels, tapestries, bedding mattresses, and other coverings, of all materials; furnishings such as ashtrays, candlesticks, and mirrors; awnings, counterpanes, and doormats; flags; garden umbrellas; garment and shoe bags, laundry hampers and bags, and shoe racks; mosquito nets; steamer and traveling rugs; wastepaper baskets and flower and plant boxes and pots)

04.300 [5] *Heating and cooking appliances, refrigerators, washing machines, and similar major household appliances, including fitting*

04.310 Refrigerators, freezers, and cooling appliances (refrigerators, food freezers, ice boxes, room air conditioners, and fans)

04.320 Washing appliances (dishwashers, other washing appliances)

04.330 Cooking appliances (cooking appliances, reflector ovens, camping stoves, and similar appliances, toasters, electric coffeemakers)

04.340 Heating appliances other than cooking (clothes drying and ironing appliances)

04.350 Cleaning appliances (electric floor-scrubbing, -waxing, and -polishing machines, vacuum cleaners, water-softening machines)

04.360 Other major household appliances (sewing and knitting ma-

---

5. In the summary tables, these categories are combined as Furniture and appliances.

chines, garden tractors, power-driven lawnmowers, nonportable safes, water pumps)

04.400 [6] *Glassware, tableware, and household utensils* (pottery, glassware, cutlery, silverware; hand kitchen and garden tools [not power driven]; all types of kitchen utensils; portable toilet and sanitary utensils for indoor use; electric bulbs, plugs, wire, cable, and switches; heating pads, saucepans, nonelectric coffeemakers; thermos bottles and flasks; watering cans, wheelbarrows, garden hose and sprinkling devices, lawnmowers [not power driven], and other garden appliances; portable money boxes and strong boxes; household scales; ladders; locksmith's wares)

04.500 *Household operation*

    04.510 [6] Nondurable household goods

        04.511 Household paper products

        04.512 Cleaning supplies (household soap, scourers, polishes, cleaning materials, shoe polish, mops, brooms and brushes, dyes for dyeing clothing and household textile furnishing; washers, insecticides, fungicides, and disinfectants)

        04.513 Others (matches, candles, lamp wicks, clothes hangers, clothespins, rope, string and twine, nails, nuts and bolts, screws, tacks, hooks, knobs, needles, pins, aluminum foil, and the like)

    04.520 [6] Domestic services (total compensation, including payments in kind to domestic servants, cleaners, and the like; includes payments in cash and in kind to babysitters, chauffeurs, gardeners, governesses, tutors, and the like)

    04.530 [6] Household services other than domestic (includes cleaning, dyeing, and laundering; hire of furniture, furnishings, and household equipment, including payments by subtenants for the use of furniture, and the like; service charges for insurance of household property against fire, theft, and other eventualities; payments for services such as chimney cleaning, window cleaning, snow removal, exterminating, disinfecting, and fumigating, and the like; also all repair of furniture, furnishings, and household equipment)

05.000 *Medical care and health expenses* [aa]

    05.100 [7] *Medical and pharmaceutical products* (includes medical and pharmaceutical products, whether directly purchased by consumers or by hospitals and independent practitioners, and the like, for use in the care of patients)

        05.110 Drugs and medical preparations (medicines, vitamins and vitamin preparations, cod and halibut liver oil)

        05.120 Medical supplies (clinical thermometers, hot-water bottles and ice bags; bandage materials, first-aid kits, elastic medical hosiery, and similar goods)

    05.200 [7] *Therapeutic appliances and equipment* (major appliances and equipment, whether directly purchased by consumers or by hospitals and independent practitioners, and the like, for use in the care of patients: eyeglasses; hearing aids; glass eyes, artificial limbs, orthopedic braces and supports; surgical belts, trusses, and supports; medical massage equipment and health lamps; wheelchairs and invalid carriages, motorized or not)

    05.300 [7] *Services of physicians, dentists, and nurses and related professional and semiprofessional personnel* (compensation of employed persons and net income of independent practitioners for services performed, both in and out of the hospital)

6. In the summary tables, these categories are combined as Supplies and operations.
7. In the summary tables, these categories are combined as Medical care.

05.310 Physicians

05.320 Dentists

05.330 Nurses, physiotherapists, technicians, midwives, and so forth

05.400 [7] *Current expenditures of hospitals, laboratories, clinics, and medical offices, not elsewhere classified*

05.410 Expenditure related to physical facilities

05.420 Personnel other than medical and related practitioners

05.430 Other

06.000 *Transport and communication*

06.100 *Personal transport equipment*

06.110 Passenger cars

06.120 Other

06.200 *Operation of personal transport equipment*

06.210 Tires, tubes, other parts and accessories

06.220 Repair charges

06.230 Gasoline, oils, and greases

06.231 Gasoline

06.232 Oils and greases

06.240 Other expenditures (parking and garaging; bridge, tunnel, ferry, and road tolls; driving lessons; hire of personal transport equipment, service charges on insurance of personal transport equipment)

06.300 *Purchased transport services*

06.310 [8] *Local transport* (fares on trains, buses and cabs; includes: local and long-distance water transport, moving and storage of household goods, service charges for special transport accident insurance)

06.320 [8] *Long-distance transport* (fares on transport; fees for transporting personal transportation equipment, for baggage transfer; storage and excess charges; tips to porters; service charges for baggage)

06.321 Rail

06.322 Bus

06.323 Air

06.440 *Communication*

06.410 Postal

06.420 Telephone and telegraph

07.000 *Recreation, entertainment, education, and cultural services*

07.100 [9] *Equipment and accessories, including repairs* [o]

07.110 Radios, television sets, and phonographs (radios, television sets, phonographs, tape recorders, radio transmitting and receiving sets for amateur radio stations, clock radios)

07.120 Major durables for recreational, entertainment, and cultural purposes (airplanes; boats and outboard motors; cameras, projection equipment, other photographic equipment, binoculars; microscopes and telescopes; pianos, organs, violins, cornets, and other major musical instruments; typewriters; power-driven equipment for woodworking, metalworking, and the like; horses; swimming pools that are not permanent fixtures)

07.130 Other recreational equipment and goods (semidurable and nondurable goods; harmonicas and other minor musical instruments; records; flowers; all sports equipment and supplies except sports clothing and footwear; camping equipment; films and other photographic supplies; used postage stamps for philatelic purposes; children's outdoor play

8. In the summary tables, these categories are combined as Purchased transport.

9. In the summary tables, these categories are combined as Recreation.

equipment; pets other than horses; feeding stuffs for pets; exercising equipment)

07.200 [9] *Entertainment, religious, recreational, and cultural services* (excluding hotels, restaurants, and cafes) [ad]

07.210 Public entertainment (private and public expenditures on places of public amusement and recreation, including theaters, cinemas, sports, museums, art galleries, historical monuments, botanical and zoological gardens, parks, ski facilities, and the like)

07.220 Other entertainment, religious, recreational and cultural services (expenditures on private entertainment such as hiring musicians, clowns, and the like, for private parties; bridge, dancing, and sports lessons; gambling; portrait and other services such as film developing and print processing furnished by photographers; hire of radio and television sets, airplanes, boats, horses, and other recreational equipment; veterinary and other services for pets; radio and television licenses where government broadcasting stations exist; religious activities)

07.300 [9] *Books, newspapers, magazines, and stationery* [p]

07.310 Books, newspapers, magazines, and other printed matter

07.320 Stationery supplies (ink, paper clips, pens, pencils; typewriter carbon and stencil paper; pencil sharpeners, paper punches, hand stamps and seals; typewriter ribbons; slide rules, drawing sets, and similar instruments)

07.400 [10] Education [ab]

07.410 Compensation of employees (total expenditure for personnel, whether paid by governments or institutions or directly by households)

07.411 Teachers for primary school

07.412 Teachers for secondary school

07.413 Teachers for colleges and universities

07.414 Other personnel (administration, clerical, and services)

07.420 [10] *Expenditures of educational institutions related to physical facilities*

07.430 [10] *Other expenditures of educational institutions*

07.431 Books, stationery, and related supplies

07.432 Other

08.000 *Other goods and services* [c]

08.100 [11] *Services of barber and beauty shops, baths, and the like*

08.200 [11] *Goods for personal care* [q]

08.210 Toilet articles and preparations (including shaving equipment; electric hair dryers and hair clippers, electric or not; permanent wave sets for home use; tooth and toilet brushes)

08.220 Personal effects (jewelry, watches, rings, and precious stones; travel goods, handbags, and similar goods; umbrellas, walking sticks and canes; pipes, lighters, tobacco pouches; pocket knives, sunglasses; clocks; baby carriages)

08.300 [12] *Expenditures in restaurants, cafes, and hotels*

08.310 Restaurants and cafes

08.320 Hotels and similar lodging places

08.400 [12] *Other services n.e.s.* (not elsewhere specified) [r] (service charges for life insurance and for insurance against civil responsibility for injuries to other persons or other persons' property not arising from the operation of personal transport equipment; actual charges for bank services; fees and

---

10. In the summary tables, these categories are combined as Education.
11. In the summary tables, these categories appear as Personal care.
12. In the summary tables, these categories appear as Miscellaneous services.

service charges for brokerage, investment counseling, household finance company loans and services of similar financial institutions; charges for money orders and other financial services provided by the post office; fees to tax consultants; administrative charges of private pension schemes. Fees for legal services and to employment agencies; dealers' margins on purchases from pawn-brokers; duplicating, blueprinting, photostating, addressing, mailing, and stenographic services; payments for copies of birth, death, and marriage certificates; charges for newspaper notices and advertisements; fees to house agents, and the like. Welfare services.[ae])

08.900 [13] *Net Expenditures of Residents Abroad*

1 Gross Capital Formation (GCF)

Construction (10.000 through 13.000)

10.000 *Residential buildings* (value of work put in place on the construction of buildings consisting wholly or primarily of dwellings, excluding the value of the land improvement, if this can be separately estimated; major alterations and improvements in residential buildings; and transfer and similar costs in respect of purchase of existing residential buildings. Includes the cost of external and internal painting of new buildings and of all permanent fixtures such as furnaces, fixed stoves, and central-heating, air-conditioning, and water-supply installations, as well as all equipment customarily installed before dwellings are occupied. Hotels, motels, and similar buildings operated on a purely transient basis are considered as nonresidential.)

   10.100 One- and two-dwelling buildings (detached, twin, and row houses, including prefabricated units)

   10.200 Multidwelling buildings (apartment buildings with three or more units)

11.000 *Nonresidential buildings* (value of work put in place on the construction of buildings and structures wholly or primarily for industrial or commercial use; major alterations and improvements in nonresidential buildings; and transfer and similar costs in respect of purchase of existing nonresidential buildings. Includes the construction of factories, warehouses, office buildings, stores, restaurants, hotels, farm buildings such as stables and barns, and buildings for religious, educational, recreational, and similar purposes; and the fixtures and nonmovable equipment that are an integral part of these structures.)

   11.100 Hotels and other nonhousekeeping units (including dormitories)

   11.200 Industrial buildings (factories, mines, and special buildings for utility industries such as power, communications, and transportation)

   11.300 Commercial buildings (stores, banks, warehouses, and garages)

   11.400 Office buildings

   11.500 Educational buildings (including day nurseries, laboratories, libraries, and museums)

   11.600 Hospital and institutional buildings

   11.700 Agricultural buildings (barns and storage facilities)

   11.800 Other buildings (including buildings for cultural, religious, sports, and social purposes)

12.000 *Other construction* (value of work put in place on new construction and major alterations and renewals of nonmilitary projects such as the permanent ways of railroads; roads, streets, sewers; bridges, viaducts, subways, and tunnels; harbors, piers, and other harbor facilities; car-parking facilities; airports; pipelines, oil wells, and mineshafts; canals and waterways; water-power projects, dams and dikes that are not part of irrigation and flood-

13. This category is normally combined with Other services.

control projects; aqueducts; drainage and sanitation projects; athletic fields, electric-transmission lines, gas mains and pipes, telephone and telegraph lines, and the like. Includes the cost of raising the surface of future building sites, leveling the sites, and laying out the necessary streets and sewers, but excludes groundwork within the building line, when a start is made on the actual construction, which should be included in residential or nonresidential buildings, as the case may be. Includes as well transfer and similar costs in respect of purchase of existing assets of this type)

    12.100 Roads, streets, and highways (including road bridges and tunnels)

    12.200 Transport (other than road) and utility lines (railroad ways; lines for telephone and power; pipes for gas, water, and sewer systems; airplane runways; canals; harbor facilities)

        12.210 Railroad ways

        12.220 Telephone and telegraph lines

        12.230 Power lines

        12.240 Pipelines for gas and oil, water, and sewer systems

        12.250 Other

    12.300 Other construction (including dams for power; petroleum and gas well drilling and exploration)

13.000 [14] *Land improvement and plantation and orchard developments* [s] (all land reclamation and land clearance, irrespective of whether it represents an addition to total land availability or not; irrigation and flood-control projects and dams and dikes that are part of these projects; forest clearance and afforestation; and transfer costs in connection with transactions in land, mineral and concessions, forests, fishing and concessions, and the like. Includes also planting and cultivation, until they yield products, of new orchards, rubber plantations, and other new holdings of fruit-bearing and sap-bearing plants that require more than a year to become productive)

Producers' Durables [t] (14.000 through 17.000)

14.000 *Transport equipment* [384]

    14.100 [15] *Railway vehicles* [3842] (locomotives of any type or gauge, and railway and tramway cars for freight and passenger service; specialized parts for locomotive, railroad, and tramway cars [3710, 3829, 3819])

        14.110 Locomotives

        14.120 Other

    14.200 [15] *Passenger cars* [3843] (complete passenger automobiles, commercial cars, taxis; specialized passenger automobile parts [3560] and accessories such as engines, brakes, clutches, axles, gears, transmissions, wheels, and frames)

    14.300 [15] *Trucks, buses, and trailers* [3843] (complete buses, trucks, and truck trailers, universal carriers, special-purpose motor vehicles [ambulances, fire trucks; trailer and pickup coaches; vehicle-drawn caravans; motorized sleighs]; specialized motor-vehicle parts and accessories, except automobile [3560], such as engines, brakes, clutches, axles, gears, transmissions, wheels, and frames)

    14.400 [15] *Aircraft* [3845] (airplanes, gliders, aircraft, and parts such as engines, propellers, pontoons, and undercarriages; space vehicles and specialized parts [3560])

    14.500 [15] *Ships and boats* [3841] (ships, barges, lighters, and boats, except rubber boats, specialized marine engine and ship parts [3560]; the conversion, alteration, and breaking up of ships [6100])

---

14. In the summary tables, this category is included with Other construction.
15. In the summary tables, these categories are combined as Transport equipment.

14.600 [15] *Other transport equipment* [3844, 3849] (motorcycles, scooters, bicycles, tricycles, pedicabs, and specialized parts such as motors, saddles, seat posts, frames, gears, and handlebars [3844]; transport equipment not elsewhere classified, such as animal-drawn wagons, carts, and sleighs, hand-drawn pushcarts, wheelbarrows, and baby carriages [3849])

15.000 *Nonelectrical machinery and equipment* [382]

15.100 [16] *Engines and turbines* [3821] (steam and gas engines and steam, gas, and hydraulic turbines; petrol, diesel, and other internal-combustion engines. Complete steam, gas, and hydraulic turbine-generator sets are classified as electrical industrial machinery and apparatus in category 16.100. Turbines or engines for a given type of transport equipment are classified in the appropriate transport-equipment category)

15.200 [16] *Agricultural machinery* [3822] (machinery and equipment for use in the preparation and maintenance of the soil, in planting and harvesting of the crop, in preparing crops for market on the farm, or in dairy farming and livestock raising; for use in performing other farm operations and processes such as planting, seeding, fertilizing, cultivating, harvesting; for example, ploughs, harrows, stalk cutters, milking machines, farm tractors, and the like)

    15.210 Tractors

    15.220 Other

15.300 [16] *Office machines* [3825] (office machines and equipment, such as calculating machines, adding machines, accounting machines; punch-card–system machines and equipment; digital and analog computers and associated electronic data-processing equipment and accessories; cash registers; typewriters; weighing machines except scientific apparatus for laboratories; duplicating machines except photocopying machines; and the like)

15.400 [16] *Metalworking machinery* [3823] (metalworking machinery such as lathes and machines for boring, drilling, milling, grinding, shearing, and shaping; drop forges and other forging machines; rolling mills, presses, and drawing machines; extruding, melting, and nonelectrical machines; and machine tools, dies, and jigs, including accessories for metalworking machines)

15.500 [16] *Construction, mining, and oil-field machinery* [3824] (cement-making and other heavy machinery and equipment used by construction industries; oil-refining machinery and equipment and heavy machinery and equipment used by mining industries)

15.600 [16] *Special industry machinery, not elsewhere specified* [3824, 3823] (special industrial machinery and equipment except metalworking machinery; for example, machinery used in the food, textile, paper, printing, chemical, and woodworking industries)

15.700 [16] *General industry machinery* [3829] (machinery and equipment, except electrical machinery, not elsewhere classified, such as pumps, air and gas compressors; blowers, air conditioning, and ventilating machinery; fire sprinklers; refrigerators and equipment; mechanical power-transmission equipment; lifting and hoisting machinery, cranes, elevators, moving stairways, industrial trucks, tractors, trailers, and stackers; sewing machines; industrial-process furnaces and ovens. Included are general-purpose parts of machinery such as ball and roller bearings, piston rings, valves; parts and accessories on a job or order basis)

15.800 [16] *Service industry machinery* [3829] (automatic merchandising

16. In the summary tables, these categories are combined as Nonelectrical machinery.

machines; washing, laundry, dry-cleaning, and pressing machines; cooking ranges and ovens; and the like)

16.000 *Electrical machinery and appliances* [383, 385]

16.100 [17] *Electrical transmission, distribution, and industrial apparatus* [3831] (electric motors; generators and complete turbine-generator and engine-generator sets; transformers; switchgear and switchboard apparatus; rectifiers; other electrical transmission and distribution equipment; electrical industrial-control devices such as motor starters and controllers, electronic timing and positioning devices, electromagnetic clutches and brakes; electrical welding apparatus; and the like)

16.200 [17] *Communications equipment* [3832] (radio and television receiving sets, sound reproducing and recording equipment, including public address systems, phonographs, dictating machines, and tape recorders; phonograph records and prerecorded magnetic tapes; wire and wireless telephone and telegraph equipment; radio and television transmitting, signaling, and detection equipment and apparatus; radar equipment and installations; parts and supplies specifically classified in this group; semiconductor and related sensitive semiconductor devices; fixed and variable electronic capacitors and condensers; radiographic, fluoroscopic, and other X-ray apparatus and tubes)

16.300 [17] *Other electrical equipment* [3839] (other electrical apparatus, accessories, and supplies not elsewhere classified, such as insulated wires and cables; storage and primary batteries, wet and dry; electric lamps and tubes; fixtures and lamp sockets and receptacles; snap switches, conductor connectors, and other current-carrying wiring devices; conduits and fittings; electrical insulators and insulation materials, except porcelain and glass insulators)

16.400 [17] *Instruments* [3851, 3852, 3853] (laboratory and scientific instruments and measuring and controlling equipment not elsewhere classified; cyclotrons, betatrons, and other accelerators; surgical, medical, and dental equipment, instruments, and supplies and orthopedic and prosthetic appliances [3851]; optical instruments and lenses, ophthalmic goods, photographic and photocopying equipment and supplies. Included are optical instruments for scientific and medical use [3852]; clocks and watches of all kinds; clock and watch parts and cases; and mechanisms for timing devices [3853].)

17.000 *Other durable furnishings and equipment*

17.100 [18] *Furniture and fixtures* [3320, 3812, 3851, 3901, 3902, 3909] (equipment, furnishings, and furniture used by businesses, governments, offices, hotels, boardinghouses, restaurants, hospitals, research institutions, schools, and other services)

17.200 [18] *Other durable goods* [3813, 3819, 3811] (all durable goods not elsewhere classified, such as containers, tanks, and nonelectrical hand tools)

18.000 *Increase in stocks*

18.100 [19] *Commodity stocks* (increase in value of materials and supplies, work in progress, and finished products and goods in the possession of industries; excludes standing timber and crops, but includes logs and harvested crops; excludes partially completed construction works)

18.200 [19] *Livestock, including breeding stock, dairy cattle, and the like* [k] (livestock raised for slaughter; all chicken and other fowl; value of additions to, less disposals of, breeding stocks, draught animals, dairy cattle, sheep, llamas, and the like, raised for wool clipping)

17. In the summary tables, these categories are combined as Electrical machinery.
18. In the summary tables, these categories are combined as Other durables.

19.000 [19] *Exports of goods and services less imports of goods and services* (merchandise exports, f.o.b. [free-on-board], and imports, c.i.f. [cost, insurance, and freight], include all transactions [sales and purchases] between the residents of a country and the rest of the world in commodities; include new and used ships and aircraft, though they may not cross the customs frontier of the country, and also electricity, gas, and water. Exclude such items as goods in direct transit through the country, goods not owned by residents for purposes of storage and transshipment only, tourists' and travelers' effects, and goods for exhibition or study, samples that are returnable or of no commercial value, returnable containers, and animals for racing or breeding. Data are net of the value of returned goods and in-transit losses. Exports and imports of services cover primarily freight, passenger, and other transport and communication services and insurance services; since merchandise imports are initially valued c.i.f. and may thus include payments of services to resident producers, such payments should be offset by a corresponding entry in exports of services.)

2 *Public Final Consumption Expenditure (PFC)*[u]

20.000 *Compensation of employees*

   20.100 [20] *Compensation of employees having first level of education* [v]

   20.200 [20] *Compensation of employees having second level of education* [v]

      20.210 Compensation of "blue collar" employees [w]

      20.220 Compensation of "white collar" employees [x]

   20.300 [20] *Compensation of employees having third level of education* [v]

21.000 *Expenditure on commodities*

[a] CEP (Final consumption expenditure of the population) is identical with "household final consumption expenditure" as defined by the SNA except for the following points:

  [aa] CEP *includes* certain expenditures on medical and other health services not included in household final consumption expenditure by the SNA. The expenditures to be included are defined in terms of SNA Tables 5.3 and 5.4 (SNA, pp. 87–89), as follows:

    [aaa] CEP *includes* government expenditures on "hospitals and clinics" and "individual health services" (items 4.2 and 4.3 in the SNA classification of the purposes of government—SNA Table 5.3). All expenditures of government on these items, which according to the SNA would be recorded as parts of "government final consumption expenditure," should be included in CEP.

    [aab] CEP *includes* expenditures of nonprofit bodies serving households—SNA Table 5.4. All expenditures of such nonprofit bodies on these items, which according to the SNA would be recorded as parts of "final consumption expenditure of nonprofit institutions serving households," should be included in CEP.

  [ab] CEP *includes* certain expenditures on schools and other educational facilities not included in household final consumption expenditure by the SNA. The expenditures to be included are defined in terms of SNA Tables 5.3 and 5.4, as follows:

    [aba] CEP *includes* government expenditures on "schools, universities, and other educational facilities" and "subsidiary services" (items 3.2 and 3.3 in SNA Table 5.3). The inclusion applies to all expenditures of government on these items, which according to the SNA would be recorded as parts of government final consumption expenditure.

    [abb] CEP *includes* expenditures of private nonprofit bodies on education (item 2 in SNA Table 5.4). The inclusion affects all expenditures of nonprofit bodies on this item, which according to the SNA would be recorded as parts of final consumption expenditure of nonprofit institutions serving households.

  [ac] CEP *includes* current expenditures of government for provision, assistance, or support of housing (for example, government expenditures to meet current costs of dwellings). Insofar as such expenditures of government constitute part of the compensation of employees in the government sector as income in kind, they are already included in household consumption expenditure (and therefore in CEP); and hence the inclusion of this item does not require additional rearrangement between house-

19. In the summary tables, these categories are included in Capital formation.

20. In the summary tables, these categories are combined as Compensation of government employees.

hold and government expenditures. However, government expenditure for provision, assistance, or support of housing *other* than that included in the compensation of employees of the government sector should be *included* in CEP and excluded from public final consumption expenditure.

[ad] CEP *includes* certain expenditures on recreational and related cultural services not included in household final consumption expenditure by the SNA. The expenditures to be *included* are the following:

> [ada] Expenditures on recreational and related cultural services and religion and services not elsewhere classified (items 7.1 and 7.2 in SNA Table 5.3), treated as part of final government consumption expenditure in the SNA.

> [adb] Expenditures on recreational and related cultural services and religious organizations (items 5 and 6 in SNA Table 5.4), treated as part of final consumption expenditure of nonprofit institutions serving households in the SNA.

[ae] CEP *includes* expenditures on welfare services by government and by nonprofit institutions serving households. The expenditures to be *included* are those described in item 5.2 of SNA Table 5.3 and item 4 of SNA Table 5.4.

[b] Includes government expenditures for housing, as described in note ([ae]), above.

[c] Includes certain expenditures of government and of nonprofit institutions serving households; see note ([aa]), above.

[d] Includes certain expenditures of government and of private nonprofit bodies on educational, recreational, and cultural services; see notes ([ab]) and ([ad]), above.

[e] Includes expenditures of government and of nonprofit institutions serving households on welfare services; see note ([ae]), above.

[f] "Gross capital formation" is identical with "gross capital formation" as defined by the United Nations, *System of National Accounts* (1968) except that it includes "exports of goods and services less imports of goods and services."

[g] For the definition of the scope of this category, see item 1 in Table 6.3 of the SNA (p. 114).

[h] For the definition of the scope of this category, see item 2 in Table 6.3 of the SNA (p. 114).

[i] For the definition of the scope of this category, see item 3 in Table 6.3 of the SNA (p. 114).

[j] For the definition of the scope of this category, see item 4 in Table 6.3 of the SNA (p. 114).

[k] Includes increase in breeding stocks, draught animals, dairy cattle, and the like, though these are in the SNA as part of gross fixed capital formation rather than as increase in stocks.

[l] In the SNA, custom tailoring and hire of clothing are included in the category "clothing other than footwear."

[m] Expenditures on indoor repair and upkeep are included in gross rents in the SNA.

[n] In the SNA, each subcategory of "furniture, furnishings, household equipment, and operation" includes a separate item for repair. The present classification combines all repairs within category 04. into the single subcategory 04.53.

[o] In the SNA, repairs are treated as a separate category rather than being added to each breakdown.

[p] Stationery is placed with miscellaneous goods in the SNA.

[q] Includes SNA categories "goods for personal care," "jewelry, watches, rings and precious stones," and "other personal goods."

[r] Membership dues in professional associations, included in this category by the SNA, here are classified with public final consumption expenditure. Also, the SNA separates financial services from other services, and both of them are included here.

[s] SNA separates "land improvement" and "plantation, orchard, and vineyard development."

[t] Bracketed numbers following categories refer to codes of the International Standard Industrial Classification; see U.N. Statistical Office, *International Standard Industrial Classification of All Economic Activities* (New York: United Nations, 1968). Descriptions, taken over with little or no modification, include some consumers' durables that should be excluded, insofar as they are purchased by the consumer. The ISIC codes are used solely to indicate the types of products included in each ICP category. Products used for current repairs rather than for additions or replacements to the stock of capital are excluded, in accordance with the rules of the SNA (see SNA paragraph 6:23).

[u] "Public final consumption expenditure" (PFC) is identical with "government final consumption expenditure," as defined by the SNA, except for the following points:

> [ua] PFC *includes*, in addition to the expenditures of government (that is, central government, state and local government, social security agencies, and the like) certain ex-

penditures of private nonprofit institutions serving households. The purposes for which expenditures are included are:

[uaa] Service charges on accident and health insurance (item 5.5 in SNA Table 6.1).

[uab] Membership dues in professional associations.

[uac] Research and scientific institutes (item 1 in SNA Table 5.4).

[uad] Professional, labor, and civic organizations (item 7 in SNA Table 5.4).

[ub] PFC *excludes* some expenditure classified as government final consumption expenditure in the SNA. The excluded categories are:

[uba] PFC *excludes* expenditures for provision, assistance, or support of housing (for example, government expenditures to meet current costs of dwellings) unless they are part of the compensation of employees in governments.

[ubb] Hospitals and clinics and individual health services (items 4.2 and 4.3 in the classification of the purposes of government, SNA Table 5.3). All expenditures of government on these items, which according to the SNA would be recorded as part of government final consumption expenditure, should be included in the final consumption expenditure of the population (CEP).

[ubc] PFC *excludes* expenditures on recreation and related cultural services and religion and services not elsewhere classified (items 7.1 and 7.2 in SNA Table 5.3). All expenditures of government on these items, which according to the SNA would be recorded as part of government final consumption expenditure, should be included in CEP.

[ubd] Schools, universities, and other educational facilities and subsidiary services (items 3.2 and 3.3 in SNA Table 5.3). All expenditures of government on these items, which according to the SNA would be recorded as part of government final consumption expenditures, should be included in CEP.

[ube] PFC *excludes* expenditures on welfare services (item 5.2 in SNA Table 5.3). All expenditures of government on this item, which according to the SNA would be recorded as part of government final consumption expenditures, should be included in CEP.

[v] The general definitions of the first, second, and third levels of education—as suggested by UNESCO—are as follows:

[va] The first level of education consists of schools such as elementary and primary schools "whose main function is to provide basic instruction in tools of learning."

[vb] The second level of education consists of schools such as middle, secondary, high, and vocational schools "which provide general or specialized instruction, or both, based upon at least four years previous instruction at the first level."

[vc] The third level of education consists of schools such as universities and higher professional schools, "which require, as a minimum condition of admission, completion of ten or more years of previous instruction at the first and second level or equivalent."

For the purposes of the present reporting, the three educational levels should be approximated in the following way: (1) first level, seven to nine years of completed education or less; (2) third level, more than twelve years of completed education; and (3) second level, years of completed education above the first level and under the third level. In case of lack of adequate data, the educational qualifications usually required for a given grade in government employment should be used for subdividing government employment (and the related PFC expenditures) according to the categories requested.

[w] Government employees at the second level of education whose occupations fall within the following ISCO (*International Standard Classification of Occupations*, rev., 1968 [Geneva: International Labor Organization, 1969] major groups can be considered as "blue collar" employees:

Major group number	Title
7/8/9	Production and related workers, transport equipment operators, and laborers
5	Service workers
6	Agricultural, animal husbandry, and forestry workers, fishermen, and hunters
10	Workers not classifiable by occupation

[x] Government employees at the second level of education whose occupations fall within the following ISCO major groups can be considered as "white collar" employees:

Major group number	Title
3	Clerical and related workers
2	Administrative and managerial workers
0/1	Professional, technical, and related workers
4	Sales workers

Chapter 3

A
Summary
of Methods

Binary Methods

THE METHODS USED IN PHASE II ARE, in the main, the same as those used in Phase I, as set forth in *A System,* Chapters 4 and 5.[1] Besides summarizing these methods, this chapter discusses the changes that have been made for Phase II. Some clarification is offered on one or two points, particularly in connection with certain properties of international prices. Also, an analysis of the consequences of alternative aggregation procedures, including changes arising from the addition of six new countries, is provided.

The basic material for producing the binary comparisons for each reference year consisted (mainly) of two sets of data for each country: per capita expenditures on each of the 153 detailed categories into which final expenditures on GDP were subdivided, and prices for from one to a score of items (or specifications) in each of these detailed categories. In addition, there were comparative quantity data for some categories.

The first step in making the binary comparisons was to average the price relatives or occasionally the quantity ratios relating to different specifications. Because expenditure data were not generally available below the detailed category level, the basic method of averaging was to use a simple, or un-weighted, geometric mean of the price relatives.[2] That is, for category i, the average relative price—the purchasing-power parity (PPP_{ij})—of the jth country relative to the nth country is given by equation 3.1:

$$(3.1) \qquad \left(\frac{P_j}{P_n}\right)_i = \prod_{\alpha=1}^{A} \left(\frac{P_{\alpha j}}{P_{\alpha n}}\right)_i^{1/A} ,$$

where $P_{\alpha j}$ is the price of the αth item in the jth country (stated in the jth country's currency unit), $P_{\alpha n}$ is the price of the αth good in the numéraire

1. Irving B. Kravis, Zoltan Kenessey, Alan Heston, and Robert Summers, *A System of International Comparisons of Gross Product and Purchasing Power* (Baltimore: Johns Hopkins University Press, 1975); referred to as *A System.*

2. For pragmatic considerations, usually turning on the availability of data rather than on matters of principle, each item was given equal weight within a detailed category. The price relatives for individual items, however, were weighted in a few categories in which there appeared to be wide differences in price relationships. These included: (1) rents, because price ratios vary significantly with the age and facilities of dwelling units from country to country; (2) potatoes, because the price ratios for yams differ substantially from those for potatoes; (3) passenger cars, because U.S. models become progressively cheaper relative to other countries as size and horsepower rise; (4) local transport, because price relatives for buses and taxis are quite different; (5) gasoline, oil, and grease, because relative prices for regular gasoline, premium gasoline, and motor oil differ; and (6) purchased meals, because price relatives for food and beverages vary widely. In some of these cases it was possible to obtain data from all or most countries for calculating weights, but even so it cannot be claimed that the weights are free of arbitrary elements. In other cases, similar weights for all countries were based on information available for a few countries. See *A System,* p. 52.

country (which in the present study is the United States), and A is the number of items within the category priced in both the jth and the nth countries.[3]

For a small number of categories, direct quantity indexes were obtained from available data on quantities. In most cases, however, indirect quantity indexes were derived by dividing category PPPs into category expenditure ratios and multiplying by 100. That is, $\left(\dfrac{Q_j}{Q_n}\right)_i = 100\left(\dfrac{E_j}{E_{US}}\right)_i / \text{PPP}_{ij}.$

The PPPs are subject mainly to sampling errors, but the indirect quantity indexes are also subject to some possible errors in the expenditure ratios. Unfortunately, certain categories are likely to be particularly susceptible to error. For example, substantial differences exist among the countries in their estimates of their distribution of footwear expenditures among men, women, and children. Some of this may reflect true differences in spending patterns, but a large part probably arises from country-to-country differences in the allocation of the footwear total to these categories. Incomparabilities in expenditure data are likely to be particularly great for residual categories such as "other major household appliances" (ICP 04.360) and "other services, n.e.s." (ICP 08.400), because it is unlikely that national income accountants in different countries assigned difficult-to-classify expenditures to these categories in identical ways.

In a few cases it was possible to make both direct quantity and direct price comparisons. But the product of the direct price and quantity indexes, each divided by 100, will not equal the expenditure ratio, because the indexes used do not meet the Fisher "factor-reversal test."[4] As a consequence, two choices are open. One possibility is to accept the discrepancy in order to obtain, as far as knowledge permits, the best price ratios and the best quantity ratios possible. A different course has, however, been followed: whichever direct ratio seems less trustworthy has been discarded and replaced by the one derived from the retained ratio (either the price ratio or the quantity ratio) and the expenditure ratio. Thus, in the main tables, in both the binary and the multilateral presentations, the product of the price and quantity ratios necessarily equals the expenditure ratio. Except for certain categories in which the quantity data lend themselves more readily to international comparisons than the price data, the price comparison was generally the one that was retained. This choice was made because price ratios for individual commodities are subject to less dispersion than quantity ratios, so the estimates derived from them are subject to smaller sampling errors.[5] The convenience of having consistent (in the factor-reversal sense) price and quantity ratios seemed to make it worthwhile to tolerate the small differences in the aggregate figures (for example, food, consumption, and GDP) that result when only one direct index is used.

The averaging process within each of the 153 detailed categories yields 153 PPPs and 153 quantity indexes for each of fifteen countries relative to the United States. (For convenience, the fifteen will be referred to as "partner countries.") In the binary comparison work, the 153 PPPs for each of the partner countries were averaged in two ways: using U.S. expenditure weights,

3. Reasons for using a geometric rather than an arithmetic mean and a discussion of the use of unweighted geometric means appear in *A System,* pp. 47–49.

4. The "factor-reversal test" is the requirement that, for any given item, category, or aggregate and for any given pair of countries, the product of the price ratio (or index) and the quantity ratio (or index) be equal to the expenditure ratio. See Irving Fisher, *The Making of Index Numbers* (Boston: Houghton Mifflin, 1922).

5. See *A System,* p. 19.

and using the partner country's expenditure weights. The formulas for the U.S.-weighted and partner-weighted indexes are:

$$(3.2) \qquad I_j{}^{(n)} = \sum_{i=1}^{m} \left(\frac{P_j}{P_n}\right)_i \cdot w_{in} \text{ and } I_j{}^{(j)} = \frac{1}{\sum_{i=1}^{m} \left(\frac{P_n}{P_j}\right)_i \cdot w_{ij}},$$

where index i runs over the m categories, n is the subscript for the United States (the numéraire country), and j is the subscript of the partner country. The weights are:

$$(3.3) \qquad w_{in} = \frac{e_{in}}{\sum_{i=1}^{153} e_{in}} \text{ and } w_{ij} = \frac{e_{ij}}{\sum_{i=1}^{153} e_{ij}},$$

where e_{ij} is per capita expenditure in the jth country, expressed in its own national currency, on the goods or services of the ith category.

The Fisher, or "ideal," index—that is, the geometric mean of the partner-weighted and U.S.-weighted indexes—is also presented. This index is not easy to justify in theoretical terms, but it is widely regarded as an evenhanded compromise between the index reflecting the consumption pattern of one partner and the index reflecting that of the other.

In a few cases, price comparisons were missing for particular detailed categories. An imputation was then made, by using the PPP for some other appropriately selected category.[6]

The binary comparisons described above have the advantages of familiarity and ease of interpretation. They have to the utmost degree what has come to be called "characteristicity." [7] This means that a comparison between any two countries is influenced only by the commodities, prices, and weights of the two countries. Data associated with all other countries are ignored. Such binary comparisons may be regarded as inefficient, however, in the sense that they fail to make use of all relevant price information. When all items are not priced in every country, knowledge of prices in other countries can be used to sharpen the comparison for any particular pair of countries.[8]

Furthermore, as will be discussed below, comparisons between two countries obtained as a ratio of the indexes of the two countries relative to the United States will not be the same as a direct comparison between the two countries, ignoring the United States. What is more, the comparison based upon the ratio of the indexes of the two countries will be different if a country other than the United States is used as a base. If what is wanted is a comparison involving a single pair of countries, all of this may not matter. Indeed, many questions relating to a particular pair of countries are best answered by a binary comparison between them.

But when a system of international comparisons involving many countries at once is sought, the lack of efficiency and dependence upon the choice of a base country are important deficiencies.

6. The extent of the need for imputations was described in Chapter 2 for the six new countries of Phase II. A discussion of this problem for the ten original Phase I countries may be found in the product chapters of *A System.* For further comment on the treatment of these cases, see *A System,* p. 50.

7. See Laszlo Drechsler, "Weighting of Index Numbers and Multilateral International Comparisons," *Review of Income and Wealth,* March 1973, pp. 17–34.

8. See a further discussion of this point in connection with multilateral methods in the section of Chapter 4 dealing with aggregation at the category level.

As the assessment of binary methods implies, the methods used to obtain a set of comparisons involving a number of countries should possess certain desired properties.

First, there should be GDPs and various subaggregate quantities for each country, denominated in a common currency, that are derived in a way that will treat all countries symmetrically. Though a particular country may be used as the standard of comparison, it should be regarded as a numéraire country only. That is, the final results should be *base-country invariant.* (This is a generalization of the Fisher "country-reversal test.")[9]

Second, the network of comparisons between pairs of countries should be transitive in the sense that, for comparisons of either prices or quantities, an index I_{jk} should be equal to I_{jl}/I_{kl} for any pair of countries, j and k, relative to any third country, l. This consistency property is the Fisher "circular test."[10]

Third, the final results inclusive of both detailed category and aggregate estimates should display "additive consistency." That is, it should be possible to produce quantities in value terms for each category such that the values for any category are directly comparable between countries; and the values for any country may be aggregated across categories to obtain any desired summary total (for example, consumption, capital formation, and so on).

Fourth, the basis for valuing a unit of one kind of good relative to a unit of another must be the working hypothesis that tastes are similar in all of the countries of the world. (This is analogous to the working hypothesis in national income accounting that the tastes of all individuals within a country are similar.) If differences in the proportions of GDP allocated to various categories of goods and services among countries can be explained (largely) in terms of economic variables defining country opportunities—primarily, prices and quantities—then the aggregation process should be based upon world tastes. Evidence bearing upon the plausibility of this conception of commonality of tastes is presented in Chapter 6.

The novel aspects of the ICP methodology that distinguish its multilateral comparisons from the conventional binary ones turn on aggregation procedures at two levels. The first deals with the treatment of prices of items to get detailed category prices, and the second deals with the treatment of detailed category prices to get prices for larger aggregations.

It might appear that the best way to obtain purchasing-power comparisons at the category level would be to work with an identical list of items in each country. This would in fact be satisfactory for a small homogeneous group of countries, but such a list is not adequate for a large number of possibly dissimilar countries.[11] If the ICP restricted its set of items to be priced to those

9. The "country-reversal test" is satisfied if, when country j is taken as the base country, the price or quantity index for countries j and k is the reciprocal of the index when country k is the base country. For example, $I_{j/k} \cdot I_{k/j} = 1$, where I is a price or quantity index.

10. Observe that this property would hold for binary comparisons if I_{jk} was *defined* to be equal to I_{jn}/I_{kn}.

11. Conceding that important differences in consumption among countries may exist at the item level is not necessarily inconsistent with the similarity-of-tastes viewpoint expressed above. A common affection for fruits could manifest itself in the form of a desire for peaches in some countries and pears in others.

in common consumption in every one of the countries, the result would be a greatly reduced list that probably would cover quite inadequately the full pattern of purchases in any one of the countries.

As a consequence, the ICP allowed the items priced for any given category to vary somewhat from country to country. This led to a tableau of prices for each category (with items on the row stubs and countries in the column headings) that in most cases had missing entries.[12] The preferred way of obtaining a base-country invariant PPP for each country relative to the United States—by computing the simple geometric mean of the ratios of a country's price to the U.S. price for all items in the category—could not be carried out for most categories because of the missing entries. Therefore, the ICP adopted the so-called country-product–dummy (CPD) method, a multiple regression procedure that in a systematic way allowed for the absence of price entries for particular items in particular countries. Specifically, a linear regression equation was formed in which the dependent variable was the natural logarithm of price. The independent variables consisted of two sets of dummy variables, one relating to the various countries (excluding the numéraire country) and the other relating to the various items. The regression coefficient of the dummy variable for each country was then interpreted as the logarithm of the purchasing-power parity of that country's currency relative to that of the numéraire country for the category.[13] The individual observations were frequency-weighted in such a way that the total importance of a country in the regression computation was the same whether many items were priced in the country or very few.[14] This was the way the weighting was done in Phase I. In the Phase II work, however, an additional weighting scheme was grafted on to allow for the relative importance of each country in the world. This will be discussed further in the next section in connection with "supercountries."

Apart from the following remarks about the CPD method, the reader is referred to the extensive discussion in *A System*.[15]

First, an intuitive understanding of the nature of the CPD method is conveyed by pointing out that, if there are no missing observations in the price tableau, the answer produced by the method for each country is simply the weighted geometric mean of the purchasing-power parities of the individual items.

Second, the CPD method may be thought of as a generalized bridge-country method. As usually employed, the bridge-country method links two countries to each other on the basis of the relationship of each to a third (base) country. For example, if prices in country j were found to be 20 percent higher based on one subset of vegetable prices than in country l, whereas prices in country k were found to be 15 percent higher than prices in country l based on a different subset of vegetable prices, the use of country l as the

12. The price tableau had no holes in only 15 out of 153 categories.

13. If, for a particular category, $\hat{\alpha}_j$ is the coefficient of the jth country's dummy variable, PPP_j for the category would be estimated as $\exp(\hat{\alpha}_j)$. To be fully consistent with the practice in estimating rents and automobile prices from hedonic regressions (see Chapter 2), since $\exp(\hat{\alpha}_j)$ is an estimate of the median of the sampling distribution of the PPP, it should be adjusted by the factor $\exp(\frac{1}{2}\hat{\alpha}^2)$. Omitting this adjustment factor does not distort the relative PPPs among all of the non-numéraire countries, but it does cause an overstatement of the PPPs relative to the numéraire country. The adjustment factor, however, will reduce to 1 for a complete tableau.

14. If n items were priced in a country, then each of the country's observations was given a weight of $1/n$.

15. See *A System*, pp. 55–65. See also Robert Summers, "International Comparisons with Incomplete Data," *Review of Income and Wealth*, March 1973, pp. 1–16.

bridge country would lead to the conclusion that prices in j were (approximately) 5 percent higher than prices in k. The CPD method takes advantage of all the information in the tableau in estimating the purchasing-power parity for each country. It uses all the possible bridge countries rather than just one.

Third, the method makes it unnecessary to compare each country's prices exclusively with those of the United States or any other particular base country. As long as at least two countries price a specification, prices for that specification can be usefully included.

Fourth, for reasons of computational convenience, a variant on the CPD method was applied to the twenty-two categories of producers' durables. For these categories each country's item price was expressed as a ratio of the U.S. price. The ratios were then regressed against just the fifteen country dummy variables.[16] This gives slightly different category PPPs from those obtained in the conventional way, but there is no obvious pattern in the differences. The differences disappear in categories with complete tableaus.

Fifth, a "double-weighted" CPD technique has been applied to situations in which no items have been priced in a particular country for an entire category. In the binary comparisons, the problems posed by missing prices for entire categories were met by imputing prices from other categories or by reassigning expenditures.[17] The application of the CPD method provides a less arbitrary, though still ad hoc, imputation that is useful for multilateral comparisons. The problem here is that there are holes in the matrix of category PPPs rather than the matrix of item prices. A CPD regression is applied to the entries that are present in the category PPP matrix. The weight applied to each PPP present is proportional to the product of the column expenditure proportions and the row quantity proportions. The column weights were adjusted to take account of supercountry weights described in a subsequent section. This hole-filling procedure was carried out more systematically in Phase II than in Phase I. It was applied separately to the sets of categories comprising construction, producers' durables, and the three-digit categories of consumption (for example, bread and cereals, meat, and fish). In addition, the double-weighting procedure was applied to a few select categories where it was deemed important that item expenditure weights be used.[18]

As in the binary procedures, a direct comparison of physical quantities was deemed more reliable than a price comparison for some categories, notably in health and education. In these instances, the PPP was obtained, as in the binary comparisons, by dividing the expenditure ratio (each country to the United States) by the quantity ratio (with the United States again as the base).

Aggregation of the categories

The method of aggregating the detailed categories in the multilateral comparisons turned basically on the establishment of a set of international prices for the various categories that were used to value the category quantities of each of the countries. The method of deriving these international prices was originally suggested by R. C. Geary and subsequently amplified by S. H. Khamis.[19] The Geary method as applied in the ICP work is based on the

16. There is a dummy variable for each country other than the numéraire country, but there are no item dummy variables in this version.

17. See *A System,* p. 63.

18. The two most important examples were automobiles (ICP 6.11) and rents (ICP 3.11). The other categories were local transport, potatoes, gasoline, and restaurants.

19. R. C. Geary, "A Note on Comparisons of Exchange Rates and Purchasing Power Between Countries," *Journal of the Royal Statistical Society,* vol. 21 (1958), pp. 97–

notion that there are two sets of unknowns, the overall purchasing powers of the currencies of the countries and the international prices of the detailed categories, the values of which can be found by establishing and solving a set of simultaneous equations. The international price for a category is simply the quantity-weighted average of the category prices observed in each country after they have all been made commensurate by being divided by their respective country PPPs. (Notice that introducing the PPPs makes the results invariant with respect to the currency units.) Computing the international prices is an easy matter if the PPPs are known. On the other hand, the PPP for a country is defined as the ratio of the country's GDP valued at its own prices to its GDP valued at international prices. The PPPs are easily computed if the international prices are known. Geary observed that it is possible to solve a set of equations, the number being equal to one less than the number of countries plus the number of categories, to get simultaneously all of the international prices and all of the PPPs. In the ICP application of the Geary-Khamis procedure, the inputs of the equation system are category numbers standing for prices for the various countries, obtained mainly by the CPD method, and for quantities, obtained for the most part by dividing the country domestic currency expenditures by the appropriate category PPPs.

Specifically, the Geary-Khamis equation system divides up into two subsets: the first, equation 3.4, defines m category international prices (Π_i) and the second, equation 3.5, defines the overall purchasing-power parities for n countries (PPP$_j$):

$$(3.4) \qquad \Pi_i = \sum_{j=1}^{n} \frac{p_{ij}}{\text{PPP}_j} \left[\frac{q_{ij}}{\sum_{j=1}^{n} q_{ij}} \right] \qquad i = 1, \ldots, m;$$

$$(3.5) \qquad \text{PPP}_j = \frac{\sum_{i=1}^{m} p_{ij} q_{ij}}{\sum_{i=1}^{m} \Pi_i q_{ij}} \qquad j = 1, \ldots, n.$$

Note the economic interpretations of the two subsystems: equation 3.4 says that the international price of the ith category is the quantity-weighted average of the purchasing-power–adjusted prices of the ith category in the n countries; and equation 3.5 says that the purchasing power of a country's currency is equal to the ratio of the cost of its total bill of goods at national prices to the cost at international prices.

Though the system as written consists of $(n+m)$ equations in $(n+m)$ unknowns, one of the equations is redundant. After suitable manipulation, the sum over i of equation 3.4 can be shown to be equal to the sum over j of equation 3.5—and the system is homogeneous. By dropping one equation and setting PPP$_n = 1$, a system of 168 linear equations in 168 unknowns (15 PPP$_j$s and 153 Π_is) is obtained.[20] Thus, the index j in equations 3.4 and 3.5 runs from 1 to $(n-1)$; that is, 1 to 15. The special block-diagonal struc-

99; and S. H. Khamis, "Some Problems Relating to International Comparability and Fluctuating of Production Volume Indicators," *Bulletin of International Statistical Institute*, vol. 42 (1967), pp. 213–320; "Properties and Conditions for the Existence of a New Type of Index Number," *Sankhya*, vol. 32 (1970), pp. 81–98; "A New System of Index Numbers for National and International Purposes," *Journal of the Royal Statistical Society*, vol. 135 (1972), pp. 96–121. For an early application of Geary's suggestion, see S. Kawakatsu, "International Average Prices and Comparisons of National Aggregate Production of Agriculture," *Review of Income and Wealth*, June 1970, pp. 173–84.

20. The system is actually linear in the Π_is and the reciprocals of the PPP$_j$s. Only fifteen PPP$_j$s are evaluated because the sixteenth country serves as the numéraire.

ture of the computational version of equations 3.4 and 3.5 makes the matrix inversion and solution of the system an easy rather than a formidable task.

The Geary method as originally propounded requires as inputs prices and physical quantities for the sets of goods and services to be covered. The ICP's data base, after the raw item prices were refined into category PPPs, comprised (1) a set of 153 prices for each of fifteen countries, denominated in national currency units and expressed relative to the U.S. dollar; and (2) a set of 153 expenditures for each of the sixteen countries, again denominated in national currency units.[21] The ICP's inputs into Geary-Khamis, then, are not quite those envisioned by Geary. The ICP uses a vector of 1's for the U.S. prices and the category PPPs as prices for the other countries. Instead of physical quantities, a set of "notional" quantities (Q_{ij}), is used; each is obtained as the ratio of expenditure to PPP. If the international prices and purchasing-power parities obtained using ICP inputs are denoted $\overline{\Pi}_i$ and $\overline{PPP}_j$ then their values are determined by the conditions of equations 3.6 and 3.7:

$$(3.6) \qquad \overline{\Pi}_i = \sum_{j=1} \frac{P_{ij}}{\overline{PPP}_j} \left[\frac{Q_{ij}}{\sum_{j=1} Q_{ij}} \right] \qquad\qquad i=1,\ldots,m;$$

$$(3.7) \qquad \overline{PPP}_j = \frac{\sum_{i=1}^{m} P_{ij}Q_{ij}}{\sum_{j=1}^{m} \overline{\Pi}_i Q_{ij}} \qquad\qquad j=1,\ldots,(n-1),$$

where $P_{ij}=p_{ij}/p_{i,US}$ and $Q_{ij}=\dfrac{p_{ij} \cdot q_{ij}}{p_{ij}/p_{i,US}}=q_{ij}p_{i,US}$. It is easy to show that $\overline{\Pi}_i = \Pi_i/p_{i,US}$ and $\overline{PPP}_j = PPP_j$. Thus, the ICP's PPP_j is indeed correct.

The fact that the ICP international price for each category $(\overline{\Pi}_i)$ deviates from the Geary concept (Π_i) by a factor equal to the U.S. price for that category would appear to be a source of concern. In view of the stress that was put upon the desirability of base-country invariance, it may seem surprising that the absolute values of the international prices used in ICP computations do not possess the property. It is clear that the $\overline{\Pi}$s are not base invariant because they are expressed relative to the prices of the numéraire country. This occurs because the CPD method produces for each category in each country PPPs that are expressed as values with the U.S. price equal to 1. Thus, if another country was used as the numéraire, then its price in each category would equal 1. The effect of this would be not only to change the whole level of the PPPs emerging from the CPD regressions but also to change their relative magnitudes. Since a different set of PPPs would be fed into the Geary-Khamis equations, it is to be expected that the international prices emerging from the solution of the equations would be different.

This poses the critical question: If the international prices themselves are not base-country invariant, how then can it be claimed that the GDP comparisons produced by valuing each country's quantities at international prices are base-country invariant?

The answer is that the international prices are never used alone. They are only used to value *notional* quantities that are themselves derived as the ratio of expenditures in national currency to PPPs. They appear only as part of terms of the form $\overline{\Pi}_i Q_{ij}$. Because this product is equal to $(\Pi_i/p_{i,US}) \cdot$

---

21. Actually, only 150 Π_i categories entered into the system of equations; three categories—those for net expenditures of residents abroad (ICP 08.900), increase in stocks (ICP 18.000), and exports minus imports (ICP 19.000)—were not included because the possibility that they may be negative makes a special treatment necessary. See *A System*, pp. 70–71.

$(q_{ij}p_{i,US}) = \overline{\Pi}_i q_{ij}$, the ICP real quantity values coming from Geary-Khamis are correct, even though the quantity input was notional rather than physical.

A further implication of this lack of independent economic significance of the ICP international prices is that they cannot be interpreted as reflections of the relative utilities of different categories of goods. Such an interpretation, inherent in Geary's formulation, is lost in the ICP because it has been necessary to move from a simple and concrete definition of price in terms of observable physical units to the abstraction of PPPs for categories of goods.

The fact that ICP international prices cannot be used by themselves does not mean that they do not facilitate international comparisons of price structure. The choice of the numéraire country does indeed determine the structure of the international prices; simultaneously, however, it determines in a precisely matching way the structure of each country's PPPs. Indeed, in Chapter 4 price structure comparisons based upon ICP international prices are presented.

Supercountries

The international price developed in the Geary system for a category is a quantity-weighted average of the individual country prices within the category. Without any adjustment of these quantity weights, the international prices (and therefore the estimates of per capita GDPs derived from them) would depend, fortuitously, on which countries happened to fall within the ICP set. The prices of each of the sixteen included countries—both in CPD and in Geary-Khamis—were therefore weighted in accordance with the degree to which each could be regarded as representative of the price structure of the various countries of the world as a whole. The sixteen countries were converted into "supercountries," each of which was assumed to have the same price and expenditure structure as a "representative" (ICP) country but to have a total GDP equal to the sum of the GDPs of all the countries included in the supercountry.

In the assignment procedure for the allocation of the countries not included in the ICP to the sixteen ICP countries, the countries of the world were arrayed by per capita GDP and then divided into five tiers.[22] Table 3.1 gives the per capita GDP class limits, the total GDP in billions of U.S. dollars in each tier, and the assignment of the total to the ICP countries in each tier. This assignment was done equally within tiers, except that each country received at least its own GDP. (This provision affected Germany in Tier 2.)

The five tiers presented in Table 3.1 differ from the three-tier system used in Phase I for two reasons: first, the wider range of low-income countries in the sample justifies separating Iran, Colombia, and Malaysia from India, Kenya, the Republic of Korea, and the Philippines; and, second, the equal

22. The basic source was the U.N. Statistical Office, *U.N. Yearbook of National Account Statistics, 1975,* vol. 3 (New York: United Nations), Table 1A. Data for some countries not included in this source (Bulgaria, the Peoples Republic of China, Czechoslovakia, Hungary, Poland, Romania, Taiwan, the U.S.S.R., and Yugoslavia) are from International Bank for Reconstruction and Development, *World Bank Atlas: Population, Per Capita Product and Growth Rates* (Washington: IBRD, 1975). Three points are worth noting in connection with the use of these data: (1) The GNP figures reported in the *World Bank Atlas* have been treated as though they referred to GDP because the distinction between the two concepts is of negligible importance in the present context. (2) Exchange-rate–converted GDPs are intentionally used for the supercountries rather than real (ICP-type) GDPs because the former kind of data constitute the appropriate input for the Geary-Khamis equations. (3) The 1970 GDP figures were used to form the supercountry weights for both 1970 and 1973. It should be mentioned also that an earlier version of the five-tier weights was used for the CPD calculations. The differences between the old and the new weights were deemed too small to warrant recalculation of the CPDs.

Table 3.1. Supercountry Gross Domestic Products for the Sixteen ICP Countries

(U.S. dollars)

Tier	Per capita GDP	Total GDP of tier (billions)	Supercountry GDP (billions)	
Tier 1	Above 3,500	1,074.6	United States	1,074.6
Tier 2	2,500–3,500	475.3	Belgium	143.8
			France	143.8
			Germany, F.R.	187.7
Tier 3	1,000–2,500	1,105.5	Hungary	221.1
			Italy	221.1
			Japan	221.1
			United Kingdom	221.1
			Netherlands	221.1
Tier 4	250–1,000	251.7	Colombia	83.9
			Malaysia	83.9
			Iran	83.9
Tier 5	Below 250	267.6	Kenya	66.9
			India	66.9
			Philippines	66.9
			Korea, Republic of	66.9

division in Phase I of the total income in each tier among the sample countries in the tier produced the anomalous situation that the United States received less weight as a supercountry than its own GDP would justify. If a three-tier system had been maintained, this anomaly would have been accentuated because more countries would have been in the top tier. With the five-tier arrangement, the United States is placed in a class by itself so that its weight equals its GDP. Although the assignment of countries to tiers is unavoidably arbitrary, limited investigations suggest that final GDP per capita comparisons are not highly sensitive to reasonable alternative choices.[23]

It should be emphasized that the Geary-Khamis method was applied to the prices and quantities of the supercountries only in order to estimate international prices. These international prices were then used to find relative GDPs and subcomponents for the various countries, and to express the quantities of each of the countries in "international" dollars.[24]

In this section an effort is made to assess the extent to which the Phase II results are sensitive to the methods that have been followed. First, the sources of the differences between the Phase I and the Phase II results for

Consequences of Alternative Procedures

23. The shift from Phase I to Phase II supercountry weights generally raised the indexes of real per capita GDP of partner countries by 2 to 3 percent relative to the United States (see Table 3.2, column 10). Other partitionings tried in Phase I, dealing with ten countries, were based on (1) a six-tier classification of countries according to income level, and (2) geographic regions. The three-tier method was chosen in Phase I on the grounds of simplicity; the more complicated classifications increased the number of cases in which arbitrary decisions had to be made about the assignment of countries to one supercountry or another. In any case, for the original ten countries, the maximum difference between per capita GDP as estimated by the selected partitioning method and the two other methods was only 6.3 percent. The average difference was around 3 or 4 percent.

24. An "international" dollar has the same purchasing power over GDP as a whole as a U.S. dollar, but its purchasing power over individual categories is different, being determined by the structure of international prices.

Table 3.2. Factors Accounting for Differences Between Phase I and Phase II Indexes of Gross Domestic Product per Capita, 1970

| | Real GDP per capita | | | Phase II figures as percent of Phase I | | |
| | | | | Reported GDP per capita in own currency | | |
Country	Phase I report (1)	Phase II report (2)	Real GDP per capita (3)=(2)÷(1)	Own change (4)	Relative to United States (5)	PPP (6)
Kenya	5.72	6.33	110.7	99.7	99.9	102.5
India	7.12	6.92	97.2	101.4	101.6	104.7
Colombia	15.9	18.1	113.8	104.0	104.2	98.8
Hungary	40.3	42.7	106.0	99.9	100.1	98.2
Italy	45.8	49.2	107.4	101.7	101.9	98.3
Japan	61.5	59.2	96.3	94.9	95.1	103.3
United Kingdom	60.3	63.5	105.3	102.4	102.6	102.0
France	75.0	73.2	97.6	95.7	95.9	99.6
Germany, F.R.	74.7	78.2	104.7	99.4	99.6	99.1
United States	100.0	100.0	100.0	99.8	100.0	100.0

the original ten countries are analyzed. (The exercise is included here out of convenience even though it turns more on data revisions than on methodological changes.) Second, the results of an alternative way of handling the 1973 data are considered. Finally, the results of alternative aggregation methods are compared and an assessment is made of the precision of the final Phase II measures of real per capita quantities.

Sources of change in the 1970 Phase II estimates

The Phase I and Phase II estimates for the nine original partner countries are shown in columns 1 and 2 of Table 3.2. Changes vary from a decline of around 4 percent in the case of Japan to an increase of 14 percent in the case of Colombia. Some of the revisions are attributable to data changes that were explained in Chapter 2. The effects of the revisions in expenditures on GDP are shown in column 5. The impact of the changes in prices is shown in column 6, and the overall result of data changes in column 7. The largest change because of data revision was for Japan, where a combination of a decline in the estimated GDP per capita of about 5 percent relative to the United States was associated with an upward revision of Japanese prices relative to U.S. prices of about 3 percent.

There are two major methodological sources of change between Phase I and Phase II: the shift from three tiers to five tiers in forming the super-country weights; and the inclusion of six more countries in the derivation of the average international prices. The effect of the former is to raise the indexes of most of the other countries relative to the United States by 2 or 3 percent. This is clearly the result of a substantial increase in U.S. weights made necessary for reasons already given. With respect to the second source, the addition of the six new countries generally has a very small impact on the indexes (see column 11) although the index for the Republic of Korea is raised by 5.5 percent on this account. This suggests that the use of super-country weights indeed fulfills the objective of making the multilateral results relatively independent of the collection of countries included.

In the final column of the table (column 12), the combined effect of the sometimes approximate measures of the various sources of changes is shown.

	1970 Real per capita GDP from ten-country Geary-Khamis (Phase II data)					
Change^a in per capita GDP because of data revisions (7)=(5)÷(6)	Three-tier weights (8)	Five-tier weights (9)	Change^a because of use of five rather than three tiers (10)=(9)÷(8)	Change^a because of inclusion of six or more countries (11)=(2)÷(9)	Change^a because of all factors (12)=(7)×(10)×(11)	Country
97.5	5.75	6.00	104.3	105.5	107.3	Kenya
97.0	6.57	6.78	103.2	102.1	102.2	India
105.5	17.2	17.5	101.7	103.4	110.9	Colombia
101.9	40.9	42.2	103.2	101.2	106.4	Hungary
103.7	47.8	49.2	102.9	100.0	106.7	Italy
92.1	57.3	59.0	103.0	100.3	95.1	Japan
100.6	61.4	62.7	102.1	101.3	104.0	United Kingdom
96.3	71.5	73.5	102.8	99.6	98.6	France
100.5	76.8	78.7	102.5	99.4	102.4	Germany, F.R.
100.0	100.0	100.0	100.0	100.0	100.0	United States

Sources: Column 1: Irving B. Kravis, Zoltan Kenessey, Alan Heston, and Robert Summers, *A System of International Comparisons of Gross Product and Purchasing Power* (Baltimore: Johns Hopkins University Press, 1975), p. 8. Column 2: Table 1.2. Column 4: Above, p. 31. Column 5: All entries in column 4 divided by U.S. entry. Column 6: Above, p. 33. Column 8: Computed using the following weights: for Tier 1 (the United States, the Federal Republic of Germany, and France), 515 each; for Tier 2 (the United Kingdom, Japan, Italy, and Hungary), 285 each; and for Tier 3 (Colombia, India, and Kenya), 183 each. Column 9: Computed using the following weights: for Tier 1 (the United States), 1,075; for Tier 2 (the Federal Republic of Germany and France), 238 each; for Tier 3 (the United Kingdom, Japan, Italy, and Hungary), 276 each; for Tier 4 (Colombia), 252; and for Tier 5 (Kenya and India), 134 each.

a. "Change" actually refers to later or revised index as a percentage of the index before the specified data or methodological alterations.

A comparison of these figures with the actual ratio of the Phase II to the Phase I estimates of real GDP per capita (column 3) shows to what degree the calculations have succeeded in accounting for the changed estimates. There is one notable failure: the calculations show a 2.2 percent rise for India, whereas a decline of 2.8 percent actually occurred. For the rest, the changes are reasonably well accounted for. For Hungary, Italy, Japan, the United Kingdom, and France, the correspondence between the two sets of figures is close. For the two countries with the largest change between Phase I and Phase II, 7.3 out of 10.7 percentage points change have been explained in the case of Kenya and 10.9 out of 13.8 percentage points change have been explained in the case of Colombia.

As explained in Chapter 2, the full set of price and expenditure information for all 153 detailed categories was available neither for 1970 nor for 1973. The data sets, it will be recalled, were filled out by extrapolating from the year for which the data were given at the level of the 153 detailed categories to the year for which they were given only at the level of the 36 summary categories. This was done by applying the implicit deflators and expenditures for the 36 summary categories that were available for both 1970 and 1973. Since the complete information was available in 1970 for more countries than was the case for 1973, the 1970 data set should be regarded as more reliable.

The extrapolations made it possible to take the PPPs and expenditures for the detailed categories as inputs for the Geary-Khamis equations for 1973,

An alternative approach to the 1973 estimates

even though such detailed information had not been provided by the countries in most of the cases. The alternative procedure would have been to base the Geary-Khamis calculations for 1973 on the 36 summary categories rather than on the 153 detailed categories. This procedure has the advantage of avoiding the synthesizing of detailed data where there were none actually available to the ICP, but it has the disadvantage of failing to make use of the detailed data that are available for some of the countries. The decision of the ICP to use the detailed categories was based on the view that distortions arising from the extrapolations of the detailed categories would be minimal and that the gain from using all of the information actually available was important.

The question that naturally arises, however, is how different would the results be if the summary categories had been used. In particular, it is worth asking how different the quantity relationships would be among the countries that provided summary data only for 1973 (Belgium, France, the Federal Republic of Germany, Hungary, Italy, Japan, Kenya, the Netherlands, and the United Kingdom) if a sixteen-country Geary-Khamis computation based on summary categories had been used instead of one based on the detailed categories. This matter is examined in Table 3.3. It can be seen that the 1973 results for all of these countries are substantially the same (within 1 percent) whether the Geary-Khamis computation is based on the 36 categories (column 2) or on the 153 categories (column 1). Larger differences, 3 or 4 percent, are found for several of the countries (Republic of Korea, Malaysia, and the Philippines) that provided detailed data for 1973. For the latter, there can be no doubt that the results based on the detailed data are to be preferred since they make more complete use of the available information. The margin of superiority for the column 1 figures on this account without

Table 3.3. Indexes of Real GDP per Capita, 1973: Results Based on Data of 153 Detailed Categories Compared with Results Based on Data of 36 Summary Categories

(United States=100)

Country	Based on data of		Ratio of summary-to-detailed results (3)= (2)÷(1)
	135 Detailed categories (1)	36 Summary categories (2)	
Kenya	6.12	6.16	1.007
India	6.37	6.30	0.989
Philippines	12.2	11.7	0.959
Korea, Republic of	14.6	14.0	0.959
Colombia	17.9	17.8	0.994
Malaysia	19.1	18.6	0.974
Iran	29.2	28.9	0.990
Hungary	45.1	44.8	0.993
Italy	47.0	46.8	0.996
Japan	64.0	63.9	0.998
United Kingdom	60.6	60.4	0.997
Netherlands	68.4	68.4	1.000
Belgium	75.3	74.7	0.992
France	76.1	75.7	0.995
Germany, F.R.	77.4	77.0	0.995
United States	100.0	100.0	1.000

Sources: Column 1: Table 1.2. Column 2: Obtained by special computation.

an offsetting disadvantage for the other group of countries confirms the choice of the method based on detailed categories.

Many alternative aggregation methods might, of course, have been used in the ICP work. As in Phase I, several methods that had been favored by one international body or another were examined in alternative calculations. A full description of these methods can be found in *A System*.[25] These included the widely used Fisher "ideal" index; the EKS method (named for its three independent discoverers, Elteto, Koves, and Szulz), which is a multilateral generalization of the Fisher index that has been used in Eastern Europe;[26] the van Yzeren method, which is based upon a complicated definition of sets of common market baskets and was employed in a comparison made by the European Coal and Steel Community;[27] and the Walsh index, which has been used in recent Latin American comparisons.[28]

The Geary-Khamis method was chosen by the ICP over the others for both economic and statistical reasons. On the economic side, the Geary-Khamis conception of a world price system with country and commodity influences accounting for observed prices corresponds directly to the view of the world that is implicit in the effort to make comparisons of price levels. As indicated above, the international prices that emerge from the ICP version of Geary-Khamis make it possible to achieve transitivity, additivity, and base-country invariance.

These advantages are, of course, purchased at a price. Like their binary counterparts, the EKS indexes exhibit a high degree of characteristicity that cannot be claimed for Geary-Khamis. The EKS method, applied to each pair of countries in turn, calls for the geometric mean of the direct Fisher index between the pairs of countries (weighted twice) and all the bridge-country comparisons. EKS seems rather mechanical compared to the Geary-Khamis approach and it has the further disadvantage of not producing additivity. The Walsh index, because of its use of expenditure weights, has the property of implying unitary price elasticities, but it is not certain that this comes closer to reality than the zero elasticities implied by quantity weights. There are, furthermore, certain conceptual problems in obtaining additivity with Walsh-type indexes.[29]

In Table 3.4 estimates based upon various aggregation methods are compared.[30] In addition, the table provides a judgment on the decree of accuracy of the Geary-Khamis estimates by supplementing the point estimates with

---

25. See *A System,* pp. 65–68.

26. The original publications describing these methods are not in English, but see Dreschler, "Weighting of Index Numbers in International Comparisons."

27. J. van Yzeren, "Three Methods of Comparing the Purchasing Power of Currencies," in Netherlands Central Bureau of Statistics, *Statistical Studies,* December 1956, pp. 3–34.

28. Correa M. Walsh, *The Measurement of General Exchange Values* (New York: Macmillan, 1910). See Richard Ruggles, "Price Indexes and International Price Comparisons," in *Ten Economic Studies in the Tradition of Irving Fisher* (New York: John Wiley, 1967), p. 200.

29. There are, in principle, two ways of obtaining a country's GDP expressed relative to a numéraire country: (1) by dividing its total expenditures by its PPP, and (2) by valuing each of its category quantities at the appropriate international price and then summing these values over all categories. The salient feature of Geary-Khamis is that it generates international prices and PPPs simultaneously in a way that insures these two totals will be equal. Although international prices could be obtained by inserting Walsh PPPs in equation 3.6 (or, for that matter, PPPs from any other method of aggregation), such international prices would not lead to a total valuation of category quantities that matches the PPP-derived GDP.

30. The estimates are based on the data of 150 categories. See footnote 21 on page 75.

Table 3.4. Estimates of per Capita Quantity Indexes for Gross Domestic Product, 1970: A Comparison of Alternative Estimating Methods, and Estimates of Degree of Accuracy

	Kenya	India	Korea, Republic of	Philip- pines	Colom- bia	Malaysia	Iran	Hungary
1. Methods [a]								
A. Geary-Khamis	6.33	6.92	12.1	12.0	18.1	19.1	20.3	42.7
B. Walsh	5.32	6.46	10.5	10.7	15.8	18.0	18.3	43.6
C. EKS	5.72	6.01	10.3	10.2	16.1	17.9	18.2	41.2
D. van Yzeren	5.73	6.02	10.3	10.2	16.1	17.9	18.2	41.2
E. Fisher ideal	5.99	6.00	10.0	10.2	16.3	17.4	18.6	41.6
F. Exchange-rate basis	2.99	2.07	3.86	5.39	7.24	8.10	8.37	21.6
2. Range of A, B, C, and D								
A. Low	5.32	6.01	10.3	10.2	15.8	17.9	18.2	41.2
B. High	6.33	6.92	12.1	12.0	18.1	19.1	20.3	43.6
C. High/Low	1.19	1.15	1.17	1.18	1.15	1.07	1.12	1.06
3. Geary-Khamis as a ratio of								
A. Exchange-rate basis [b]	2.12	3.35	3.11	2.25	2.50	2.36	2.42	1.97
B. Fisher ideal	1.11	1.17	1.26	1.21	1.11	1.13	1.16	1.05
4. Possible deviation of Geary-Khamis at 0.95 level (percent)	9.50	7.59	8.54	8.54	4.81	4.81	4.81	5.47
5. Confidence interval limits at 0.95 level								
A. Lower limit	5.73	6.39	11.07	10.98	17.23	18.18	19.32	40.36
B. Upper limit	6.93	7.45	13.13	13.02	18.97	20.02	21.28	45.04
6. Precision interval limits at 0.95 level								
A. Lower limit	4.82	5.55	9.43	9.37	15.00	17.03	17.35	38.94
B. Upper limit	6.93	7.45	13.13	13.02	18.97	20.02	21.28	45.98
7. Possible deviation taking account of aggregation differences (percent)	16.67	13.73	15.29	15.21	10.97	7.83	9.68	8.24

interval estimates. Line 2C shows that all of the alternative aggregation methods give virtually the same estimates as Geary-Khamis for the seven most affluent countries and almost the same for two of the next three. Line 3B indicates that to only a slightly lesser degree the same holds for the comparison of the Geary-Khamis with Fisher indexes. For this purpose, the Fisher indexes are based on the multilateral price inputs—that is, the CPD estimates of category prices. (The binary results, using binary methods for the price inputs as well as for aggregation, are compared with the Geary-Khamis results in Chapter 5.) The alternative methods definitely give lower estimates than Geary-Khamis, however, for the remaining low-income countries. Although these latter differences range up to as much as 19 percent for Kenya, it is noteworthy that the alternative to all of these methods, the comparison based upon the exchange rate (line 3A), is off for these same low-income countries by a much larger margin. This can be illustrated by the case of Kenya: the exchange-rate–based comparison with the United States is 2.99 instead of 6.33 as obtained by Geary-Khamis. Although the smallest of the alternative estimators, Walsh, is about 16 percent below Geary-Khamis, even this lower number is still more than 75 percent higher than the misleading exchange-rate–based value.

In the ICP Phase I work, an elaborate simulation exercise was carried out to estimate the degree of imprecision of the Geary-Khamis results. The category PPPs used as inputs to the various multilateral methods are *estimates* derived from CPD regressions. As such, they are subject to sampling error,

Italy	Japan	United Kingdom	Nether- lands	Belgium	France	Germany, F.R.		
							1.	Methods [a]
49.2	59.2	63.5	68.7	72.0	73.2	78.2		A. Geary-Khamis
49.9	58.4	65.7	68.0	69.7	73.4	76.2		B. Walsh
49.6	57.6	65.1	66.8	71.1	73.4	77.0		C. EKS
49.6	57.7	65.2	66.7	71.0	73.5	77.1		D. van Yzeren
49.9	58.2	64.5	67.4	70.7	71.7	76.3		E. Fisher ideal
36.0	39.8	45.7	50.8	55.1	58.2	64.1		F. Exchange-rate basis
							2.	Range of A, B, C, and D
49.2	57.7	63.5	66.7	69.7	73.2	76.2		A. Low
49.9	59.2	65.7	68.7	72.0	73.5	78.2		B. High
1.01	1.03	1.03	1.03	1.03	1.00	1.03		C. High/Low
							3.	Geary-Khamis as a ratio of
1.37	1.49	1.39	1.35	1.31	1.26	1.22		A. Exchange-rate basis [b]
0.99	1.05	1.01	1.05	1.08	1.02	1.06		B. Fisher ideal
							4.	Possible deviation of Geary-Khamis at 0.95
5.48	6.13	5.17	5.40	5.40	5.30	5.42		level (percent)
							5.	Confidence interval limits at 0.95 level
46.50	55.57	60.22	64.99	68.11	69.32	73.96		A. Lower limit
51.90	62.83	66.78	72.41	75.89	77.08	82.44		B. Upper limit
							6.	Precision interval limits at 0.95 level
46.50	54.14	60.22	63.12	65.96	69.32	72.03		A. Lower limit
52.61	62.83	69.09	72.41	75.89	77.43	82.44		B. Upper limit
							7.	Possible deviation taking account of aggregation
6.21	7.34	6.98	6.76	6.90	5.54	6.66		differences (percent)

Sources: Line 1F: Table 1.2, column 4. Line 4: *A System*, Table 5.8, line 4. Entries for non-Phase I countries are imputed as follows: the Republic of Korea and the Philippines equal the average of India and Kenya; Malaysia and Iran equal Colombia; the Netherlands and Belgium equal the average of France, the Federal Republic of Germany, and Italy. Line 5A: Line 1A entry times (1.0 − line 4 entry/100). Line 5B: Line 1A entry times (1.0 + line 4 entry/100). Line 6A: Minimum (lower limits of 0.95 confidence intervals of Geary-Khamis, Walsh, EKS, and van Yzeren methods) (line 2A entry times [1.0 − line 4 entry/100]). Line 6B: Maximum (upper limits of 0.95 confidence intervals of Geary-Khamis, Walsh, EKS, and van Yzeren methods) (line 2B entry times [1.0 + line 4 entry/100]). Line 7: ([6B − line 6A]/2) ÷ line 1A, converted to a percentage.

a. See text for a description of the methods. The methods of lines 1A through 1E are applied to category PPPS obtained mainly by the country-product-dummy method.

b. This is the same as the exchange-rate–deviation index appearing in Table 1.2, column 7.

and the simulation was designed to quantify the impact of that sampling error.[31] Line 4 of Table 3.4 contains the results of the exercise. The percentages recorded in this line indicate how much above and below the Geary-Khamis value the end points are for the 95 percent confidence intervals of the various countries. The confidence limits themselves appear in lines 5A and 5B. Not surprisingly, the width of these intervals tends to be greater, in percentage terms, for the less affluent countries.

After the effects on Geary-Khamis income comparisons of CPD sampling variation were estimated, admittedly in a loose way, an attempt was made to widen the confidence limits to allow somehow for the variations among methods shown in line 2. The following crude heuristic device was adopted: A "precision interval" for each country was defined such that its lower bound

31. See *A System*, pp. 77–79.

was the lower limit of the 0.95 confidence interval of the aggregation method yielding the smallest income comparison, and its upper bound was the upper limit of the confidence interval associated with the largest income comparison.[32] Even though the confidence intervals have a 0.95 probability interpretation, these precision intervals should not be regarded as more than rough indications of how accurate the individual income comparisons are. The resulting approximation of the uncertainty associated with the various countries is summarized in line 7. The entries there are one-half the width of the precision intervals expressed relative to the Geary-Khamis values. The numbers, ranging from 17 percent down to about 6 percent, indicate the authors' judgment of the band of uncertainty about the level of per capita GDP of each country relative to the United States.[33] (If the Geary-Khamis confidence intervals had been calculated for a probability of 0.99 [0.90] the precision intervals would have been one-sixth wider [one-half narrower].) A comparable set of calculations for 1973 indicates that the precision intervals for 1973 are of about the same width.

The reader should be reminded that these uncertainty estimates are to be regarded as minimum estimates of the true uncertainties because they assume that all item prices and expenditures reported to the ICP are exactly correct.[34]

32. The widths of the confidence intervals of all of the multilateral aggregations were about the same.

33. No clear guidance can be given on how to estimate the band of uncertainty for a comparison between two countries not including the United States. The band is certainly narrower than the difference between the ratio of the upper bound of the first to the lower bound of the second and the ratio of the lower bound of the first to the upper bound of the second.

34. The Geary-Khamis values in line 1 of Table 3.4 are based upon the five-tier supercountry weights of Table 3.1. The effect of shifting to five tiers from the three tiers of Phase I was quantified in Table 3.2. Here it is worth pointing out that, if the supercountry scheme was dropped entirely (that is, the supercountry weights were set uniformly at 1), the Geary-Khamis values would all go down and the differences between Geary-Khamis and the other aggregation methods would be reduced in size.

Chapter 4

Results of the Multilateral Comparisons

THE RESULTS OF THE MULTILATERAL COMPARISONS for sixteen countries in 1970 and in 1973 are presented and analyzed in this chapter. The analysis here is mainly of a descriptive character; a more analytical treatment is deferred until Chapter 6.

The basic expenditure, price, and quantity comparisons are presented in a series of ten tables, five for each reference year:

- Per capita expenditures in national currencies;
- Percentage distribution of per capita expenditures in national currencies;
- Purchasing-power parities per U.S. dollar;
- Real per capita quantities relative to the United States;
- Per capita quantities in international dollars.

Summary Multilateral Tables 4.1 to 4.5 follow this pattern of data presentation for 1970, each table giving the information for GDP, its three major components, and 34 summary categories. Summary Multilateral Tables 4.6 to 4.10 present the same information for 1973. There is also a set of five appendix tables for 1970 that are similar in numbering and content except that they provide the data for 153 detailed categories. As was stated earlier, the data in the detailed tables are presented in the spirit of offering worksheet materials for the convenience of the users who wish to achieve other kinds of aggregates than those provided in the tables. They are not presented as statistics of publishable quality.

In addition to these basic tables, there are a number of derived tables, Tables 4.11 to 4.19, that are designed to facilitate the analysis of the results. The first of these tables groups the sixteen countries into five per capita GDP classes as an aid in describing the way in which the composition of expenditures, the structure of prices, and relative quantities change as real income rises. Next, there are several tables that set out the expenditure, price, and quantity comparisons for "commodities" and "services," with all components of GDP assigned to one or the other, and for "traded" and "nontraded" goods, again with the two classifications being defined so that they exhaust GDP. Finally, the 1970 and 1973 results are extrapolated to other years with the aid of sectoral price indexes and expenditures of the individual countries.

Chapter 3 described the methods by which the ICP comparisons have been made. The key steps in the methodology are (1) the production of transitive, base-invariant PPPs at the detailed category level through the country-product–dummy method, and (2) the aggregation of category quantities by

An Explanation of the Tables

(*Text continues on page 114.*)

Summary Multilateral Table 4.1. Per Capita Expenditures in National Currencies, 1970

	Line numbers[a]	Kenya (shillings)	India (rupees)	Philippines (pesos)	Korea Republic of (won)	Colombia (pesos)	Malaysia (M.dollars)	Iran (rials)	Hungary (forints)
Consumption, ICP[b,c]	1–110	714.87	563.22	827.61	59780.	4657.59	786.43	18896.4	18783.8
Food, Beverage, and Tobacco	1– 39	349.36	375.38	467.52	33422.	1845.62	322.12	8819.5	6680.8
Food,	1– 33	317.21	350.95	412.27	28315.	1557.38	268.02	8375.4	5688.2
Bread and Cereals	1– 6	127.32	163.49	190.47	13634.	211.61	73.95	2574.0	742.0
Meat	7– 12	31.53	7.20	67.20	2851.	484.30	47.56	1580.7	1658.9
Fish	13– 14	7.68	5.74	71.32	1762.	28.96	40.20	68.9	43.7
Milk, Cheese, and Eggs	15– 17	42.74	33.51	19.79	1083.	216.81	25.46	1028.9	693.3
Oils and Fats	18– 20	11.57	39.55	8.24	379.	59.57	11.17	624.9	561.4
Fruits and Vegetables	21– 26	69.21	57.09	9.06	4878.	272.64	36.32	1473.6	997.5
Coffee, Tea, and Cocoa	27– 29	4.79	4.37	8.25	119.	84.60	5.15	360.9	229.6
Spices, Sweets, and Sugar	30– 33	22.37	40.00	37.93	3608.	198.88	28.20	663.4	761.8
Beverages	34– 37	22.44	6.79	30.90	2885.	195.97	18.57	87.0	701.4
Tobacco	38– 39	9.72	17.64	24.36	2222.	92.27	35.53	357.1	291.3
Clothing and Footwear	40– 51	28.03	38.65	48.25	6183.	449.66	39.01	1643.2	2173.8
Clothing	40– 47	22.88	35.15	41.98	5798.	343.00	34.22	1333.0	1737.3
Footwear	48– 51	5.15	3.49	6.27	385.	106.66	4.79	310.3	436.5
Gross Rent and Fuel	52– 57	73.56	41.69	83.18	4936.	437.17	90.42	3215.9	1433.2
Gross Rents	52– 53	62.33	22.65	57.75	2241.	387.90	72.93	2471.9	834.5
Fuel and Power	54– 57	11.22	19.04	25.43	2695.	49.27	17.50	744.0	598.6
House Furnishings and Operations	58– 71	44.25	16.39	47.70	1737.	321.14	43.87	857.1	1546.6
Furniture and Appliances	58– 66	8.70	3.70	23.98	970.	147.13	18.01	478.9	929.6
Supplies and Operation	67– 71	35.55	12.68	23.72	766.	174.00	25.86	378.2	617.0
Medical Care	72– 78	36.88	14.32	27.43	1705.	280.61	30.53	1001.6	1092.0
Transport and Communications	79– 91	52.03	28.80	20.54	3309.	465.79	113.94	837.4	1099.7
Equipment	79– 80	11.43	2.25	2.43	112.	65.35	23.93	287.3	345.8
Operation Costs	81– 84	6.50	2.76	2.81	5.	39.94	44.34	235.5	182.4
Purchased Transport	85– 89	32.68	21.83	14.33	2993.	336.88	39.87	279.8	503.8
Communications	90– 91	1.42	1.96	0.98	200.	23.62	5.80	34.9	67.7
Recreation and Education	92–103	84.08	28.39	66.35	5045.	378.04	89.00	1022.5	2085.7
Recreation	92– 98	29.10	4.98	12.87	2156.	177.45	37.80	370.1	1092.1
Education	99–103	54.98	23.41	53.48	2889.	200.58	51.20	652.4	993.6
Other Expenditures	104–109	46.68	19.62	66.65	3474.	479.59	57.56	1499.3	2672.1
Personal Care	104–106	5.79	5.97	20.23	1380.	82.36	23.30	628.3	431.9
Miscellaneous Services	107–109	40.89	13.65	46.42	2094.	397.23	34.25	871.0	2240.2
Capital Formation[d]	111–148	206.75	124.52	232.59	13504.	1286.0	278.25	7682.6	9892.6
Construction	111–124	98.93	70.62	62.04	12780.	721.14	102.18	3642.5	5795.0
Residential	111–112	33.23	17.64	24.75	2565.	197.08	27.87	1287.0	1525.5
Nonresidential Bldgs	113–120	25.09	18.66	22.37	4395.	36.78	32.10	1351.7	2440.7
Other Construction	121–124	40.61	34.32	14.93	5821.	487.27	42.21	1003.8	1828.7
Producers Durables	125–146	101.79	42.11	148.08	7168.	505.54	87.23	2153.9	3812.6
Transport Equipment	125–131	35.98	10.68	42.51	3137.	154.42	21.48	877.0	938.4
Nonelectrical Machinery	132–140	49.76	16.09	72.23	3187.	87.41	51.90	920.9	1986.9
Electrical Machinery	141–144	12.45	7.81	23.19	679.	238.68	10.98	274.1	407.3
Other Durables	145–146	3.60	7.53	10.15	165.	25.02	2.87	81.9	479.9
Government	149–153	102.33	58.54	62.26	6784.	415.55	129.15	4054.2	2412.2
Compensation	149–152	77.77	33.70	39.02	4237.	318.85	80.53	2448.9	623.9
Commodities	153	24.56	24.84	23.24	2547.	96.70	48.62	1605.3	1788.3
Gross Domestic Product	1–153	1023.95	746.27	1122.45	80067.	6359.07	1193.82	30633.1	31088.5
Aggregates									
ICP Concepts[e]									
Consumption (CEP)[b,c]	1–110	714.87	563.22	827.61	59780.	4657.59	786.43	18896.40	18783.8
Capital Formation (GCF)[d]	111–148	206.75	124.52	232.59	13504.	1286.00	278.60	7682.60	9892.6
Government (PFC)	149–153	102.33	58.54	62.26	6784.	415.55	129.15	4054.20	2412.2
Gross Domestic Product	1–153	1023.90	746.27	1122.45	80067.	6359.07	1193.82	30633.10	31088.5

Italy (lire)	Japan (yen)	United Kingdom (pounds)	Netherlands (guilders)	Belgium (B.francs)	France (francs)	Germany F.R. (DM)	United States (dollars)		Line numbers[a]
728771.	372907.	632.701	5539.86	85378.6	9809.39	6767.17	3270.65	Consumption, ICP[b,c]	1–110
278549.	120062.	186.977	1410.74	21896.6	2607.91	1526.31	564.33	Food, Beverage, and Tobacco	1– 39
231885.	97413.	111.455	1107.98	18501.7	2120.62	1249.02	447.07	Food,	1– 33
31327.	23473.	15.814	146.58	2310.2	297.32	224.60	49.50	Bread and Cereals	1– 6
75382.	11298.	32.727	290.18	7254.2	739.96	330.92	122.25	Meat	7– 12
8256.	18120.	3.836	30.24	637.3	106.89	19.72	16.00	Fish	13– 14
30768.	8282.	16.643	200.92	1874.9	300.57	142.16	71.79	Milk, Cheese, and Eggs	15– 17
14722.	1471.	4.809	50.27	1449.1	142.76	123.05	20.87	Oils and Fats	18– 20
54957.	21613.	19.831	217.11	2886.6	351.86	193.54	102.30	Fruits and Vegetables	21– 26
4845.	1658.	4.035	62.93	703.9	58.44	97.96	14.79	Coffee, Tea, and Cocoa	27– 29
11629.	11498.	13.761	109.75	1385.5	122.81	117.08	49.58	Spices, Sweets, and Sugar	30– 33
26519.	17776.	44.542	161.93	1799.4	351.53	171.54	64.57	Beverages	34– 37
20145.	4874.	30.980	140.83	1595.5	135.77	105.75	52.69	Tobacco	38– 39
64965.	33939.	49.333	526.40	6838.3	849.16	685.75	238.33	Clothing and Footwear	40– 51
53820.	31501.	40.544	450.19	5914.7	718.49	578.55	199.35	Clothing	40– 47
11144.	2438.	8.790	76.21	923.5	130.67	107.21	38.98	Footwear	48– 51
89769.	53567.	107.817	618.88	12285.5	1274.30	930.77	564.88	Gross Rent and Fuel	52– 57
68282.	43251.	80.890	423.87	8188.3	980.93	700.74	463.12	Gross Rents	52– 53
21487.	10316.	26.927	195.01	4097.2	293.36	230.02	101.76	Fuel and Power	54– 57
39937.	32393.	42.021	631.70	9155.2	776.38	797.41	239.23	House Furnishings and Operations	58– 71
23709.	21323.	25.018	427.01	4201.6	468.66	503.99	141.52	Furniture and Appliances	58– 66
16228.	11070.	17.003	204.68	4953.6	307.72	293.42	97.72	Supplies and Operation	67– 71
48155.	29620.	37.806	414.04	5335.8	953.99	588.19	316.67	Medical Care	72– 78
74394.	14647.	69.560	466.38	8098.8	978.10	743.07	443.92	Transport and Communications	79– 91
20071.	2880.	18.696	165.85	2647.3	248.30	185.52	151.53	Equipment	79– 80
34681.	3730.	26.351	180.20	3418.7	505.63	387.01	205.78	Operation Costs	81– 84
13269.	5255.	18.318	69.53	1429.4	176.60	127.25	30.43	Purchased Transport	85– 89
6373.	2782.	6.196	50.81	603.5	47.57	43.28	56.18	Communications	90– 91
83936.	44619.	87.446	894.40	10593.0	1184.54	829.05	498.80	Recreation and Education	92–103
39862.	16902.	44.002	380.74	3679.6	605.12	446.81	239.83	Recreation	92– 98
44074.	27717.	43.444	513.66	6913.5	579.42	382.24	258.97	Education	99–103
63660.	42803.	52.341	531.54	10636.6	1221.96	654.82	381.55	Other Expenditures	104–109
10883.	5312.	8.700	74.06	1425.7	210.16	93.82	91.21	Personal Care	104–106
52777.	37490.	43.642	457.48	9210.9	1011.80	561.01	290.34	Miscellaneous Services	107–109
255813.	277430.	185.536	2323.71	35010.7	4189.04	3448.87	852.78	Capital Formation[d]	111–148
144521.	135935.	78.044	1261.47	17136.5	2160.58	1594.46	496.55	Construction	111–124
75028.	49447.	29.593	462.62	6699.8	1065.61	569.66	172.96	Residential	111–112
44297.	56100.	35.861	521.10	5468.9	675.60	588.24	167.17	Nonresidential Bldgs	113–120
25196.	30389.	12.590	277.74	4967.8	419.38	436.55	156.30	Other Construction	121–124
85371.	103089.	91.084	1002.07	12549.9	1582.37	1391.19	334.36	Producers Durables	125–146
21934.	16671.	23.397	260.32	2433.3	254.40	322.62	84.79	Transport Equipment	125–131
32389.	35697.	40.778	465.85	5436.2	845.54	660.53	137.75	Nonelectrical Machinery	132–140
24748.	27135.	17.471	275.90	3549.3	423.08	355.66	79.30	Electrical Machinery	141–144
6299.	23587.	9.438	0.0	1131.1	59.35	52.38	32.53	Other Durables	145–146
95117.	33175.	96.236	929.39	10659.6	1428.82	985.97	666.13	Government	149–153
70257.	23919.	53.656	639.29	7232.3	985.64	693.65	338.72	Compensation	149–152
24860.	9256.	42.579	290.10	3427.4	443.18	292.32	327.41	Commodities	153
1079700.	683511.	914.469	8792.89	131047.5	15427.16	11201.92	4789.55	Gross Domestic Product	1–153
								Aggregates	
								ICP Concepts[e]	
728771.	372907.	632.701	85378.6	85378.6	9809.39	6767.17	3270.65	Consumption (CEP)[b,c]	1–110
255813.	277430.	185.536	2323.71	35010.7	4189.04	3448.87	852.78	Capital Formation (GCF)[d]	111–148
95117.	33175.	96.236	929.39	10659.6	1428.82	985.97	666.13	Government (PFC)	149–153
1079700.	683511.	914.469	8792.89	131047.5	15427.16	11201.92	4789.55	Gross Domestic Product	1–153

(Table continues on following page.)

Summary Multilateral Table 4.1 continued.

	Line numbers[a]	Kenya (shillings)	India (rupees)	Philippines (pesos)	Korea Republic of (won)	Colombia (pesos)	Malaysia (M.dollars)	Iran (rials)	Hungary (forints)
SNA Concepts[e]									
Consumption (PFCE)	1–110	663.80	550.52	794.33	57734.	4476.31	724.53	18039.13	16327.5
Capital Formation (GCF)	111–148	206.75	124.52	232.59	13504.	1286.01	278.25	7682.70	9892.6
Government (GFCE)	149–153	153.39	71.24	95.55	8830.	596.84	191.05	4911.64	4526.2
Gross Domestic Product	1–153	1023.95	746.28	1122.46	80068.	6359.18	1193.82	30633.40	30746.4

a. Line numbers refer to Appendix Tables 4.1–4.5 and show the detailed categories that are included in each aggregation.

b. Consumption, *ICP*, includes both household and government expenditures. The latter are shown separately in Table 2.1. Consumption, *SNA*, excludes these government expenditures.

c. The consumption aggregate (lines 1–110) includes net expenditure of residents abroad (line 110), not shown separately in these summary multilateral tables.

Summary Multilateral Table 4.2. Percentage Distribution of Expenditures in National Currencies, 1970

	Line numbers[a]	Kenya	India	Philippines	Korea Republic of	Colombia	Malaysia	Iran	Hungary
Consumption, ICP[b,c]	1–110	69.81	75.47	73.73	74.66	73.24	65.87	61.69	60.42
Food, Beverage, and Tobacco	1– 39	34.12	50.30	41.65	41.74	29.02	26.98	28.79	21.49
Food,	1– 33	30.98	47.03	36.73	35.36	24.49	22.45	27.34	18.30
Bread and Cereals	1– 6	12.43	21.91	16.97	17.03	3.33	6.19	8.40	2.39
Meat	7– 12	3.08	0.96	5.99	3.56	7.62	3.98	5.16	5.34
Fish	13– 14	0.75	0.77	6.35	2.20	0.46	3.37	0.22	0.14
Milk, Cheese, and Eggs	15– 17	4.17	4.49	1.76	1.35	3.41	2.13	3.36	2.23
Oils and Fats	18– 20	1.13	5.30	0.73	0.47	0.94	0.94	2.04	1.81
Fruits and Vegetables	21– 26	6.76	7.65	0.81	6.09	4.29	3.04	4.81	3.21
Coffee, Tea, and Cocoa	27– 29	0.47	0.59	0.73	0.15	1.33	0.43	1.18	0.74
Spices, Sweets, and Sugar	30– 33	2.18	5.36	3.38	4.51	3.13	2.36	2.17	2.45
Beverages	34– 37	2.19	0.91	2.75	3.60	3.08	1.56	0.28	2.26
Tobacco	38– 39	0.95	2.36	2.17	2.78	1.45	2.98	1.17	0.94
Clothing and Footwear	40– 51	2.74	5.18	4.30	7.72	7.07	3.27	5.36	6.99
Clothing	40– 47	2.23	4.71	3.74	7.24	5.39	2.87	4.35	5.59
Footwear	48– 51	0.50	0.47	0.56	0.48	1.68	0.40	1.01	1.40
Gross Rent and Fuel	52– 57	7.18	5.59	7.41	6.16	6.87	7.57	10.50	4.61
Gross Rents	52– 53	6.09	3.03	5.14	2.80	6.10	6.11	8.07	2.68
Fuel and Power	54– 57	1.10	2.55	2.27	3.37	0.77	1.47	2.43	1.93
House Furnishings and Operations	58– 71	4.32	2.20	4.25	2.17	5.05	3.67	2.80	4.97
Furniture and Appliances	58– 66	0.85	0.50	2.14	1.21	2.31	1.51	1.56	2.99
Supplies and Operation	67– 71	3.47	1.70	2.11	0.96	2.74	2.17	1.23	1.98
Medical Care	72– 78	3.60	1.92	2.44	2.13	4.41	2.56	3.27	3.51
Transport and Communications	79– 91	5.08	3.86	1.83	4.13	7.32	9.54	2.73	3.54
Equipment	79– 80	1.12	0.30	0.22	0.14	1.03	2.00	0.94	1.11
Operation Costs	81– 84	0.64	0.37	0.25	0.01	0.63	3.71	0.77	0.59
Purchased Transport	85– 89	3.19	2.93	1.28	3.74	5.30	3.34	0.91	1.62
Communications	90– 91	0.14	0.26	0.09	0.25	0.37	0.49	0.11	0.22
Recreation and Education	92–103	8.21	3.80	5.91	6.30	5.94	7.45	3.34	6.71
Recreation	92– 98	2.84	0.67	1.15	2.69	2.79	3.17	1.21	3.51
Education	99–103	5.37	3.14	4.76	3.61	3.15	4.29	2.13	3.20
Other Expenditures	104–109	4.56	2.63	5.94	4.34	7.54	4.82	4.89	8.60
Personal Care	104–106	0.57	0.80	1.80	1.72	1.30	1.95	2.05	1.39
Miscellaneous Services	107–109	3.99	1.83	4.14	2.62	6.25	2.87	2.84	7.21

Italy (lire)	Japan (yen)	United Kingdom (pounds)	Netherlands (guilders)	Belgium (B.francs)	France (francs)	Germany F.R. (DM)	United States (dollars)		Line numbers[a]
								SNA Concepts[e]	
680066.	348793.	555.060	5019.02	76155.0	9178.78	6321.75	2955.20	Consumption (PFCE)	1–110
255814.	277430.	185.537	2323.71	35020.8	4189.05	3448.87	852.79	Capital Formation (GCF)	111–148
143816.	56179.	168.408	1450.26	19753.9	2055.02	1423.12	979.14	Government (GFCE)	149–153
1079693.	682401.	909.005	8793.02	130920.1	15422.87	11193.75	4787.13	Gross Domestic Product	1–153

d. The capital formation aggregate (lines 111–148) includes increase in stocks (line 147) and net exports (line 148) not shown separately in these summary multilateral tables.

e. Letters in parentheses are: *CEP*, consumption expenditures of the population; *GCF*, gross capital formation; *PFC*, public final consumption expenditure; *PFCE*, private final consumption expenditure; *GFCE*, government final consumption expenditure. See Glossary for definitions.

Italy	Japan	United Kingdom	Netherlands	Belgium	France	Germany F.R.	United States		Line numbers[a]
67.50	54.56	69.19	63.00	65.15	63.59	60.41	68.29	Consumption, ICP[b,c]	1–110
25.80	17.57	20.45	16.04	16.71	16.90	13.63	11.78	Food, Beverage, and Tobacco	1– 39
21.48	14.25	12.19	12.60	14.12	13.75	11.15	9.33	Food,	1– 33
2.90	3.43	1.73	1.67	1.76	1.93	2.01	1.03	Bread and Cereals	1– 6
6.98	1.65	3.58	3.30	5.54	4.80	2.95	2.55	Meat	7– 12
0.76	2.65	0.42	0.34	0.49	0.69	0.18	0.33	Fish	13– 14
2.85	1.21	1.82	2.29	1.43	1.95	1.27	1.50	Milk, Cheese, and Eggs	15– 17
1.36	0.22	0.53	0.57	1.11	0.93	1.10	0.44	Oils and Fats	18– 20
5.09	3.16	2.17	2.47	2.20	2.28	1.73	2.14	Fruits and Vegetables	21– 26
0.45	0.24	0.44	0.72	0.54	0.38	0.87	0.31	Coffee, Tea, and Cocoa	27– 29
1.08	1.68	1.50	1.25	1.06	0.80	1.05	1.04	Spices, Sweets, and Sugar	30– 33
2.46	2.60	4.87	1.84	1.37	2.28	1.53	1.35	Beverages	34– 37
1.87	0.71	3.39	1.60	1.22	0.88	0.94	1.10	Tobacco	38– 39
6.02	4.97	5.39	5.99	5.22	5.50	6.12	4.98	Clothing and Footwear	40– 51
4.98	4.61	4.43	5.12	4.51	4.66	5.16	4.16	Clothing	40– 47
1.03	0.36	0.96	0.87	0.70	0.85	0.96	0.81	Footwear	48– 51
8.31	7.84	11.79	7.04	9.37	8.26	8.31	11.79	Gross Rent and Fuel	52– 57
6.32	6.33	8.85	4.82	6.25	6.36	6.26	9.67	Gross Rents	52– 53
1.99	1.51	2.94	2.22	3.13	1.90	2.05	2.12	Fuel and Power	54– 57
3.70	4.74	4.60	7.18	6.99	5.03	7.12	4.99	House Furnishings and Operations	58– 71
2.20	3.12	2.74	4.86	3.21	3.04	4.50	2.95	Furniture and Appliances	58– 66
1.50	1.62	1.86	2.33	3.78	1.99	2.62	2.04	Supplies and Operation	67– 71
4.46	4.33	4.13	4.71	4.07	6.18	5.25	6.61	Medical Care	72– 78
6.89	2.14	7.61	5.30	6.18	6.34	6.63	9.27	Transport and Communications	79– 91
1.86	0.42	2.04	1.89	2.02	1.61	1.66	3.16	Equipment	79– 80
3.21	0.55	2.88	2.05	2.61	3.28	3.45	4.30	Operation Costs	81– 84
1.23	0.77	2.00	0.79	1.09	1.14	1.14	0.64	Purchased Transport	85– 89
0.59	0.41	0.68	0.58	0.46	0.31	0.39	1.17	Communications	90– 91
7.77	6.53	9.56	10.17	8.08	7.68	7.40	10.41	Recreation and Education	92–103
3.69	2.47	4.81	4.33	2.81	3.92	3.99	5.01	Recreation	92– 98
4.08	4.06	4.75	5.84	5.28	3.76	3.41	5.41	Education	99–103
5.90	6.26	5.72	6.05	8.12	7.92	5.85	7.97	Other Expenditures	104–109
1.01	0.78	0.95	0.84	1.09	1.36	0.84	1.90	Personal Care	104–106
4.89	5.48	4.77	5.20	7.03	6.56	5.01	6.06	Miscellaneous Services	107–109

(Table continues on following page.)

Summary Multilateral Table 4.2 continued.

	Line numbers[a]	Kenya	India	Philippines	Korea Republic of	Colombia	Malaysia	Iran	Hungary
Capital Formation[d]	111–148	20.19	16.69	20.72	16.87	20.22	23.31	25.08	31.82
Construction	111–124	9.66	9.46	5.53	15.96	11.34	8.56	11.89	18.64
Residential	111–112	3.25	2.36	2.20	3.20	3.10	2.33	4.20	4.91
Nonresidential Bldgs	113–120	2.45	2.50	1.99	5.49	0.58	2.69	4.41	7.85
Other Construction	121–124	3.97	4.60	1.33	7.27	7.66	3.54	3.28	5.88
Producers Durables	125–146	9.94	5.64	13.19	8.95	7.95	7.31	7.03	12.26
Transport Equipment	125–131	3.51	1.43	3.79	3.92	2.43	1.80	2.86	3.02
Nonelectrical Machinery	132–140	4.86	2.16	6.43	3.98	1.37	4.35	3.01	6.39
Electrical Machinery	141–144	1.22	1.05	2.07	0.85	3.75	0.92	0.89	1.31
Other Durables	145–146	0.35	1.01	0.90	0.21	0.39	0.24	0.27	1.54
Government	149–153	9.99	7.84	5.55	8.47	6.53	10.82	13.23	7.76
Compensation	149–152	7.60	4.52	3.48	5.29	5.01	6.75	7.99	2.01
Commodities	153	2.40	3.33	2.07	3.18	1.52	4.07	5.24	5.75
Gross Domestic Product	1–153	100.00	100.00	100.00	100.00	100.00	100.00	100.00	100.00
Aggregates									
ICP Concepts[e]									
Consumption (CEP)[b,c]	1–110	69.8	75.5	73.7	74.7	73.2	65.9	61.7	60.4
Capital Formation (GCF)[d]	111–148	20.2	16.7	20.7	16.9	20.2	23.3	25.1	31.8
Government (PFC)	149–153	10.0	7.8	5.5	8.5	6.5	10.8	13.2	7.8
Gross Domestic Product	1–153	100.0	100.0	100.0	100.0	100.0	100.0	100.0	100.0
SNA Concepts[e]									
Consumption (PFCE)	1–110	64.8	73.8	70.8	72.1	70.4	60.7	58.9	53.1
Capital Formation (GCF)	111–148	20.2	16.7	20.7	16.9	20.2	23.3	25.1	32.2
Government (GFCE)	149–153	15.0	9.5	8.5	11.0	9.4	16.0	16.0	14.7
Gross Domestic Product	1–153	100.0	100.0	100.0	100.0	100.0	100.0	100.0	100.0

a. Line numbers refer to Appendix Tables 4.1–4.5 and show the detailed categories that are included in each aggregation.

b. Consumption, *ICP*, includes both household and government expenditures. The latter are shown separately in Table 2.1. Consumption, *SNA*, excludes these government expenditures.

c. The consumption aggregate (lines 1–110) includes net expenditure of residents abroad (line 110), not shown separately in these summary multilateral tables.

Summary Multilateral Table 4.3. Purchasing-Power Parties per U.S. Dollar, 1970

	Line numbers[a]	Kenya (shillings)	India (rupees)	Philippines (pesos)	Korea Republic of (won)	Colombia (pesos)	Malaysia (M.dollars)	Iran (rials)	Hungary (forints)
Consumption, ICP[b,c]	1–110	3.42	2.40	1.86	143.	7.5	1.30	29.1	13.9
Food, Beverage, and Tobacco	1–39	4.07	3.56	2.72	203.	9.2	1.62	44.8	19.4
Food,	1–33	3.94	3.52	2.83	191.	9.7	1.52	45.5	20.9
Bread and Cereals	1–6	3.18	2.47	2.30	134.	9.1	1.05	31.6	10.4
Meat	7–12	3.99	3.95	2.09	240.	10.4	2.04	53.4	29.9
Fish	13–14	3.21	1.20	2.84	158.	13.4	1.13	44.0	12.0
Milk, Cheese, and Eggs	15–17	4.50	3.47	4.24	256.	10.3	1.85	29.6	16.9
Oils and Fats	18–20	6.49	6.68	3.47	374.	15.2	1.89	93.4	25.9
Fruits and Vegetables	21–26	2.88	3.42	2.73	177.	8.1	1.39	42.1	16.7
Coffee, Tea, and Cocoa	27–29	5.42	5.34	6.40	1009.	11.9	3.70	130.9	100.0
Spices, Sweets, and Sugar	30–33	5.32	5.26	3.60	255.	8.0	1.78	64.5	27.4
Beverages	34–37	8.84	9.99	1.76	450.	11.5	2.34	53.9	18.9
Tobacco	38–39	4.72	4.33	3.04	250.	3.0	2.51	38.5	8.2

Italy	Japan	United Kingdom	Netherlands	Belgium	France	Germany F.R.	United States		Line numbers[a]
23.69	40.59	20.29	26.43	26.72	27.15	30.79	17.81	Capital Formation[d]	111–148
13.39	19.89	8.53	14.35	13.08	14.01	14.23	10.36	Construction	111–124
6.95	7.23	3.24	5.26	5.11	6.91	5.09	3.61	Residential	111–112
4.10	8.21	3.92	5.93	4.17	4.38	5.25	3.49	Nonresidential Bldgs	113–120
2.33	4.45	1.38	3.16	3.79	2.72	3.90	3.26	Other Construction	121–124
7.91	15.08	9.96	11.40	9.58	10.26	12.42	6.98	Producers Durables	125–146
2.03	2.44	2.56	2.96	1.86	1.65	2.88	1.77	Transport Equipment	125–131
3.00	5.22	4.46	5.30	4.15	5.48	5.90	2.88	Nonelectrical Machinery	132–140
2.29	3.97	1.91	3.14	2.71	2.74	3.18	1.66	Electrical Machinery	141–144
0.58	3.45	1.03	0.0	0.86	0.38	0.47	0.68	Other Durables	145–146
8.81	4.85	10.52	10.57	8.13	9.26	8.80	13.91	Government	149–153
6.51	3.50	5.87	7.27	5.52	6.39	6.19	7.07	Compensation	149–152
2.30	1.35	4.66	3.30	2.62	2.87	2.61	6.84	Commodities	153
100.00	100.00	100.00	100.00	100.00	100.00	100.00	100.00	Gross Domestic Product	1–153
								Aggregates	
								ICP Concepts[e]	
67.5	54.6	69.2	63.0	65.2	63.6	60.4	68.3	Consumption (CEP)[b,c]	1–110
23.7	40.6	20.3	26.4	26.7	27.2	30.8	17.8	Capital Formation(GCF)[d]	111–148
8.8	4.9	10.5	10.6	8.1	9.3	8.8	13.9	Government (PFC)	149–153
100.0	100.0	100.0	100.0	100.0	100.0	100.0	100.0	Gross Domestic Product	1–153
								SNA Concepts[e]	
63.0	51.1	61.1	57.1	58.2	59.5	56.5	61.7	Consumption (PFCE)	1–110
23.7	40.7	20.4	26.4	26.7	27.2	30.8	17.8	Capital Formation (GCF)	1–110
13.3	8.2	18.5	16.5	15.1	13.3	12.7	20.5	Government (GFCE)	149–153
100.0	100.0	100.0	100.0	100.0	100.0	100.0	100.0	Gross Domestic Product	1–153

d. The capital formation aggregate (lines 111–148) includes increase in stocks (line 147) and net exports (line 148) not shown separately in these summary multilateral tables.

e. Letters in parentheses are: *CEP*, consumption expenditures of the population; *GCF*, gross capital formation; *PFC*, public final consumption expenditure; *PFCE*, private final consumption expenditure; *GFCE*, government final consumption expenditure. See Glossary for definitions.

Italy (lire)	Japan (yen)	United Kingdom (pounds)	Netherlands (guilders)	Belgium (B.francs)	France (francs)	Germany F.R. (DM)	United States (dollars)		Line numbers[a]
466.	231.	0.309	2.69	37.4	4.55	3.20	1.00	Consumption, ICP[b,c]	1–110
597.	336.	0.367	3.04	43.9	4.81	3.77	1.00	Food, Beverage, and Tobacco	1– 39
609.	358.	0.296	3.28	47.1	5.10	4.01	1.00	Food,	1– 33
474.	244.	0.196	2.76	39.9	4.91	3.53	1.00	Bread and Cereals	1– 6
665.	463.	0.302	3.78	52.9	5.35	4.17	1.00	Meat	7– 12
588.	345.	0.384	2.55	49.4	4.93	3.43	1.00	Fish	13– 14
607.	279.	0.294	2.62	35.7	3.89	2.86	1.00	Milk, Cheese, and Eggs	15– 17
628.	348.	0.275	3.33	53.7	6.02	4.49	1.00	Oils and Fats	18– 20
500.	399.	0.340	3.06	39.4	4.57	3.83	1.00	Fruits and Vegetables	21– 26
1742.	446.	0.317	5.55	90.1	8.07	9.97	1.00	Coffee, Tea, and Cocoa	27– 29
748.	357.	0.361	3.71	52.4	6.24	4.40	1.00	Spices, Sweets, and Sugar	30– 33
501.	288.	0.514	2.27	33.4	3.85	2.52	1.00	Beverages	34– 37
623.	208.	0.657	2.49	30.0	3.87	4.24	1.00	Tobacco	38– 39

(Table continues on following page.)

Summary Multilateral Table 4.3 continued.

	Line numbers[a]	Kenya (shillings)	India (rupees)	Philippines (pesos)	Korea Republic of (won)	Colombia (pesos)	Malaysia (M.dollars)	Iran (rials)	Hungary (forints)
Clothing and Footwear	40– 51	3.95	3.16	1.85	169.	10.4	0.96	29.3	22.0
Clothing	40– 47	4.52	3.21	1.90	182.	11.4	1.00	34.4	22.7
Footwear	48– 51	2.32	3.17	1.59	90.	7.4	0.76	16.1	18.7
Gross Rent and Fuel	52– 57	5.08	2.26	1.60	179.	12.3	1.31	22.3	10.2
Gross Rents	52– 53	5.89	1.53	1.14	318.	13.7	1.08	17.4	8.8
Fuel and Power	54– 47	3.28	5.44	6.35	181.	7.1	3.20	69.8	15.6
House Furnishings and Operations	58– 71	4.32	2.26	2.27	136.	7.2	1.32	27.9	22.5
Furniture and Appliances	58– 66	6.13	3.63	2.50	269.	13.2	1.46	25.9	24.1
Supplies and Operation	67– 71	3.32	1.68	1.89	71.	4.4	1.08	31.3	19.8
Medical Care	72– 78	1.66	0.74	1.33	42.	5.1	0.52	21.3	4.7
Transport and Communications	79– 91	5.50	3.29	2.24	169.	7.5	2.33	31.7	23.4
Equipment	79– 80	9.15	8.12	13.49	739.	37.6	4.51	112.7	41.4
Operation Costs	81– 84	3.33	2.94	4.16	377.	6.6	2.75	35.3	22.4
Purchased Transport	85– 89	4.83	2.85	1.54	146.	5.0	1.45	15.7	18.3
Communications	90– 91	3.06	1.36	1.95	71.	2.8	1.30	14.9	7.8
Recreation and Education	92–103	2.37	0.79	0.84	77.	4.9	1.02	21.4	7.8
Recreation	92– 98	5.11	2.37	2.24	123.	12.2	1.67	48.7	9.1
Education	99–103	1.47	0.53	0.56	50.	2.5	0.66	12.9	6.4
Other Expenditures	104–109	2.78	1.59	1.51	112.	6.5	1.26	20.1	12.3
Personal Care	104–106	4.05	3.77	1.60	104.	10.5	1.70	29.1	14.2
Miscellaneous Services	107–109	2.54	1.23	1.50	129.1	5.8	1.10	16.7	11.6
Capital Formation[d]	111–148	5.13	2.77	3.55	173.	8.2	1.43	38.4	21.2
Construction	111–124	3.93	1.65	1.65	135.	4.9	0.72	21.9	16.2
Residential	111–112	3.23	1.71	1.81	105.	4.3	0.67	17.2	16.6
Nonresidential Bldgs	113–120	3.67	1.82	2.43	152.	4.4	0.73	23.2	18.2
Other Construction	121–124	4.91	1.44	0.96	134.	4.6	0.72	32.8	13.9
Producers Durables	125–146	7.26	7.64	6.96	323.	21.6	3.04	76.1	30.1
Transport Equipment	125–131	7.64	8.10	11.03	515.	20.2	3.86	89.4	32.1
Nonelectrical Machinery	132–140	7.65	7.43	6.70	301.	25.3	2.91	78.0	31.7
Electrical Machinery	141–144	7.16	7.88	6.39	213.	21.6	3.42	75.5	21.7
Other Durables	145–146	6.02	6.89	3.04	82.	18.0	1.46	37.8	30.3
Government	149–153	1.79	1.07	0.93	76.	4.6	1.16	34.5	11.9
Compensation	149–152	1.20	0.61	0.57	48.	3.2	0.89	29.8	5.6
Commodities	153	3.97	2.51	1.98	143.	9.2	1.42	36.5	18.9
Gross Domestic Product	1–153	3.38	2.25	1.95	138.	7.3	1.30	31.5	15.2
Aggregates									
ICP Concepts[e]									
Consumption (CEP)[b,c]	1–110	3.42	2.40	1.86	143.	7.53	1.30	29.1	13.9
Capital Formation (GCF)[d]	111–148	5.13	2.77	3.55	173.	8.22	1.43	38.4	21.2
Government (PFC)	149–153	1.79	1.07	4.92	76.	4.64	1.16	34.5	11.9
Gross Domestic Product	1–153	3.34	2.23	1.95	138.	7.32	1.30	31.5	15.2
SNA Concepts[e]									
Consumption (PFCE)	1–110	3.42	2.40	1.86	143.	7.53	1.30	29.1	13.9
Capital Formation (GCF)	111–148	5.12	2.78	3.55	173.	8.22	1.43	38.4	21.2
Government (GFCE)	149–153	2.16	1.23	1.14	87.	5.34	1.20	34.0	12.5
Gross Domestic Product	1–153	3.38	2.25	1.95	138.	7.32	1.30	31.5	15.2

a. Line numbers refer to Appendix Tables 4.1–4.5 and show the detailed categories that are included in each aggregation.

b. Consumption, *ICP*, includes both household and government expenditures. The latter are shown separately in Table 2.1. Consumption, *SNA*, excludes these government expenditures.

c. The consumption aggregate (lines 1–110) includes net expenditure of residents abroad (line 110), not shown separately in these summary multilateral tables.

Italy (lire)	Japan (yen)	United Kingdom (pounds)	Netherlands (guilders)	Belgium (B.francs)	France (francs)	Germany F.R. (DM)	United States (dollars)		Line numbers[a]
547.	208.	0.321	2.95	46.4	6.27	3.82	1.00	Clothing and Footwear	40– 51
554.	213.	0.341	3.03	47.9	6.45	3.96	1.00	Clothing	40– 47
505.	191.	0.236	2.56	38.8	5.36	3.14	1.00	Footwear	48– 51
384.	327.	0.334	2.19	38.8	3.93	2.95	1.00	Gross Rent and Fuel	52– 57
315.	307.	0.311	1.96	31.3	3.30	2.58	1.00	Gross Rents	52– 53
827.	407.	0.439	3.18	73.5	7.62	4.72	1.00	Fuel and Power	54– 57
494.	274.	0.361	2.87	38.9	4.92	3.16	1.00	House Furnishings and Operations	58– 71
563.	329.	0.409	3.39	47.4	5.88	3.83	1.00	Furniture and Appliances	58– 66
396.	200.	0.291	2.12	29.7	3.68	2.29	1.00	Supplies and Operation	67– 71
196.	79.	0.152	1.35	21.8	2.50	1.75	1.00	Medical Care	72– 78
638.	306.	0.395	3.84	60.8	6.82	4.39	1.00	Transport and Communications	79– 91
655.	400.	0.490	5.05	63.9	6.27	4.14	1.00	Equipment	79– 80
730.	437.	0.368	3.78	64.4	7.70	4.96	1.00	Operation Costs	81– 84
481.	197.	0.388	3.27	52.0	6.03	4.10	1.00	Purchased Transport	85– 89
420.	228.	0.208	1.95	44.4	4.58	2.23	1.00	Communications	90– 91
430.	220.	0.255	3.15	30.9	4.72	2.96	1.00	Recreation and Education	92–103
576.	272.	0.294	2.93	44.8	4.80	3.27	1.00	Recreation	92– 98
309.	169.	0.214	3.23	21.8	4.78	2.68	1.00	Education	99–103
502.	147.	0.293	2.42	27.8	4.38	2.90	1.00	Other Expenditures	104–109
579.	264.	0.269	3.33	45.3	5.67	3.79	1.00	Personal Care	104–106
474.	132.	0.293	2.22	25.1	4.04	2.68	1.00	Miscellaneous Services	107–109
453.	286.	0.298	2.69	41.6	4.40	2.80	1.00	Capital Formation[d]	111–148
369.	260.	0.240	1.92	33.1	3.79	2.22	1.00	Construction	111–124
426.	248.	0.196	1.90	36.4	4.58	2.53	1.00	Residential	111–112
371.	326.	0.313	2.35	35.3	3.82	2.31	1.00	Nonresidential Bldgs	113–120
266.	203.	0.239	1.46	26.0	2.63	1.84	1.00	Other Construction	121–124
539.	317.	0.376	3.96	54.2	5.04	3.53	1.00	Producers Durables	125–146
658.	345.	0.487	5.35	69.7	5.39	3.90	1.00	Transport Equipment	125–131
521.	297.	0.364	3.60	50.0	5.11	3.48	1.00	Nonelectrical Machinery	132–140
443.	325.	0.355	3.61	46.0	4.39	3.21	1.00	Electrical Machinery	141–144
679.	272.	0.260	0.00	60.5	5.47	4.25	1.00	Other Durables	145–146
498.	201.	0.273	2.93	39.7	4.25	3.29	1.00	Government	149–153
430.	148.	0.218	2.53	31.3	3.58	2.92	1.00	Compensation	149–152
471.	282.	0.322	2.93	46.7	4.39	3.08	1.00	Commodities	153
458.	241.	0.301	2.67	38.0	4.40	2.99	1.00	Gross Domestic Product	1–153
								Aggregates	
								ICP Concepts[e]	
466.	231.	0.309	2.69	37.4	4.55	3.20	1.00	Consumption (CEP)[b,c]	1–110
453.	286.	0.298	2.69	41.6	4.40	2.80	1.00	Capital Formation (GCF)[d]	111–148
498.	201.	0.273	2.93	39.7	4.25	3.29	1.00	Government (PFC)	149–153
458.	241.	0.301	2.67	38.0	4.40	2.99	1.00	Gross Domestic Product	1–153
								SNA Concepts[e]	
466.	231.	0.309	2.69	37.4	4.55	3.20	1.00	Consumption (PFCE)	1–110
453.	286.	0.298	2.69	41.6	4.40	2.80	1.00	Capital Formation (GCF)	111–148
484.	211.	0.284	2.82	37.7	4.36	3.26	1.00	Government (GFCE)	149–153
458.	241.	0.301	2.67	38.0	4.40	2.99	1.00	Gross Domestic Product	1–153

d. The capital formation aggregate (lines 111–148) includes increase in stocks (line 147) and net exports (line 148) not shown separately in these summary multilateral tables.

e. Letters in parentheses are: *CEP*, consumption expenditures of the population; *GCF*, gross capital formation; *PFC*, public final consumption expenditure; *PFCE*, private final consumption expenditure; *GFCE*, government final consumption expenditure. See Glossary for definitions.

Summary Multilateral Table 4.4. Quantities per Capita, 1970 (U.S.=100)

	Line numbers[a]	Kenya	India	Philippines	Korea Republic of	Colombia	Malaysia	Iran	Hungary
Consumption, ICP[b,c]	1–110	6.4	7.2	13.6	12.7	18.9	18.5	19.8	41.3
Food, Beverage, and Tobacco	1– 39	15.2	18.7	30.5	29.2	35.6	35.3	34.9	61.1
Food,	1– 33	18.0	22.3	32.6	33.2	36.0	39.3	41.2	60.9
Bread and Cereals	1– 6	80.8	134.0	167.4	205.5	47.2	142.4	164.8	143.5
Meat	7– 12	6.5	1.5	26.3	9.7	38.2	19.0	24.2	45.4
Fish	13– 14	15.0	29.9	157.0	69.5	13.5	222.9	9.8	22.7
Milk, Cheese, and Eggs	15– 17	13.2	13.5	6.5	5.9	29.2	19.2	48.3	57.3
Oils and Fats	18– 20	8.6	28.4	11.4	4.9	18.8	28.4	32.1	103.8
Fruits and Vegetables	21– 26	23.5	16.3	3.2	27.0	32.9	25.5	34.2	58.5
Coffee, Tea, and Cocoa	27– 29	6.0	5.5	8.7	0.8	48.0	9.4	18.6	15.5
Spices, Sweets, and Sugar	30– 33	8.5	15.3	21.3	28.5	44.6	32.0	20.8	56.0
Beverages	34– 37	3.9	1.1	27.2	9.9	26.3	12.3	2.5	57.5
Tobacco	38– 39	3.9	7.7	15.2	16.9	44.1	26.8	17.6	67.6
Clothing and Footwear	40– 51	3.0	5.1	10.9	15.3	18.1	17.0	23.6	41.4
Clothing	40– 47	2.5	5.5	11.1	16.0	15.1	17.1	19.4	38.4
Footwear	48– 51	5.7	2.8	10.1	10.9	37.1	16.2	49.5	59.8
Gross Rent and Fuel	52– 57	2.6	3.3	9.2	4.9	6.3	12.2	25.5	24.8
Gross Rents	52– 53	2.3	3.2	11.0	1.5	6.1	14.6	30.7	20.4
Fuel and Power	54– 57	3.4	3.4	3.9	14.7	6.8	5.4	10.5	37.6
House Furnishings and Operations	58– 71	4.3	3.0	8.8	5.3	18.5	13.9	12.8	28.8
Furniture and Appliances	58– 66	1.0	0.7	6.8	2.5	7.9	8.7	13.1	27.3
Supplies and Operation	67– 71	11.0	7.7	12.9	11.0	40.2	24.5	12.3	31.8
Medical Care	72– 78	7.0	6.1	6.5	12.7	17.3	18.5	14.9	72.7
Transport and Communications	79– 91	2.1	2.0	2.1	4.4	13.9	11.0	6.0	10.6
Equipment	79– 80	0.8	0.2	0.1	0.1	1.1	3.5	1.7	5.5
Operation Costs	81– 84	0.9	0.5	0.3	0.0	3.0	7.8	3.2	4.0
Purchased Transport	85– 89	22.2	25.2	30.6	67.3	184.8	90.6	58.6	90.4
Communications	90– 91	0.8	2.6	0.9	5.0	15.2	7.9	4.2	15.5
Recreation and Education	92–103	7.1	7.2	15.9	13.2	15.6	17.5	9.6	53.9
Recreation	92– 98	2.4	0.9	2.4	7.3	6.1	9.4	3.2	50.2
Education	99–103	14.5	17.1	37.0	22.3	30.5	30.1	19.5	59.8
Other Expenditures	104–109	4.4	3.2	11.6	8.1	19.2	12.0	19.6	57.0
Personal Care	104–106	1.6	1.7	13.9	14.5	8.6	15.0	23.7	33.4
Miscellaneous Services	107–109	5.5	3.8	10.6	5.6	23.5	10.7	17.9	66.5
Capital Formation[d]	111–148	4.7	5.3	7.7	9.1	18.3	22.8	23.5	54.6
Construction	111–124	5.1	8.6	7.6	19.1	29.8	28.6	33.6	71.9
Residential	111–112	6.0	6.0	7.9	14.1	26.3	24.0	43.4	53.2
Nonresidential Bldgs	113–120	4.1	6.1	5.5	17.3	4.9	26.4	34.9	80.2
Other Construction	121–124	5.3	15.3	9.9	27.8	67.7	37.3	19.6	83.9
Producers Durables	125–146	4.2	1.6	6.4	6.6	7.0	8.6	8.5	37.9
Transport Equipment	125–131	5.6	1.6	4.5	7.2	9.0	6.6	11.6	34.5
Nonelectrical Machinery	132–140	4.7	1.6	7.8	7.7	2.5	13.0	8.6	45.5
Electrical Machinery	141–144	2.2	1.2	4.6	4.0	13.9	4.0	4.6	23.7
Other Durables	145–146	1.8	3.4	10.3	6.2	4.3	6.0	6.7	48.7
Government	149–153	8.6	8.2	10.1	13.4	13.4	16.8	17.6	30.5
Compensation	149–152	19.1	16.3	20.3	26.0	29.5	26.6	24.2	33.2
Commodities	153	1.9	3.0	3.6	5.4	3.2	10.5	13.4	28.9
Gross Domestic Product	1–153	6.3	6.9	12.0	12.1	18.1	19.1	20.3	42.7
Aggregates ICP Concepts[e]									
Consumption (CEP)[b,c]	1–110	6.4	7.2	13.6	12.7	18.9	18.5	19.8	41.3
Capital Formation (GCF)[d]	111–148	4.7	5.3	7.7	9.1	18.3	22.8	23.5	54.6
Government (PFC)	149–153	8.6	8.2	10.1	13.4	13.4	16.8	1.6	30.5
Gross Domestic Product	1–153	6.3	6.9	12.0	12.1	18.1	19.1	20.3	42.7

Italy	Japan	United Kingdom	Netherlands	Belgium	France	Germany F.R.	United States		Line numbers[a]
47.9	49.3	62.5	62.9	69.8	65.9	64.7	100.0	Consumption, ICP[b,c]	1–110
82.7	63.4	90.3	82.2	88.5	96.2	71.7	100.0	Food, Beverage, and Tobacco	1– 39
85.1	60.9	84.3	75.6	87.8	93.1	69.6	100.0	Food,	1– 33
133.6	194.1	162.7	107.2	117.1	122.2	128.5	100.0	Bread and Cereals	1– 6
92.7	20.0	88.7	62.8	112.1	113.2	64.9	100.0	Meat	7– 12
87.7	328.1	62.4	74.2	80.6	135.5	36.0	100.0	Fish	13– 14
70.6	41.4	78.9	106.7	73.2	107.7	69.2	100.0	Milk, Cheese, and Eggs	15– 17
112.3	20.3	83.9	72.4	129.4	113.7	131.3	100.0	Oils and Fats	18– 20
107.4	53.0	57.0	69.3	71.7	75.2	49.4	100.0	Fruits and Vegetables	21– 26
18.8	25.2	86.0	76.6	52.8	49.0	66.4	100.0	Coffee, Tea, and Cocoa	27– 29
31.4	64.9	76.8	59.7	53.3	39.7	53.7	100.0	Spices, Sweets, and Sugar	30– 33
82.0	95.7	134.3	110.5	83.5	141.3	105.4	100.0	Beverages	34– 37
61.4	44.5	89.5	107.3	101.1	66.5	47.3	100.0	Tobacco	38– 39
49.8	68.5	64.5	74.8	61.8	56.8	75.2	100.0	Clothing and Footwear	40– 51
48.7	74.2	59.6	74.6	61.9	55.9	73.3	100.0	Clothing	40– 47
56.6	32.8	95.5	76.2	61.1	62.5	87.7	100.0	Footwear	48– 51
41.4	29.0	57.2	50.1	56.1	57.5	55.9	100.0	Gross Rent and Fuel	52– 57
46.8	30.4	56.1	46.7	56.5	64.2	58.7	100.0	Gross Rents	52– 53
25.5	24.9	60.3	60.2	54.8	37.9	47.9	100.0	Fuel and Power	54– 57
33.8	49.4	48.7	92.1	98.4	65.9	105.5	100.0	House Furnishings and Operations	58– 71
29.7	45.8	43.3	88.9	62.7	56.3	92.9	100.0	Furniture and Appliances	58– 66
41.9	56.8	59.8	98.7	171.0	85.5	131.2	100.0	Supplies and Operation	67– 71
77.6	119.1	78.6	97.1	77.4	120.7	106.3	100.0	Medical Care	72– 78
26.3	10.8	39.7	27.3	30.0	32.3	38.2	100.0	Transport and Communications	79– 91
20.2	4.8	25.2	21.7	27.4	26.1	29.6	100.0	Equipment	79– 80
23.1	4.1	34.8	23.2	25.8	31.9	37.9	100.0	Operation Costs	81– 84
90.7	87.7	155.3	69.9	90.3	96.3	102.0	100.0	Purchased Transport	85– 89
27.0	21.7	52.9	46.5	24.2	18.5	34.6	100.0	Communications	90– 91
39.1	40.6	68.7	57.0	68.8	50.3	56.2	100.0	Recreation and Education	92–103
28.9	25.9	62.4	54.2	34.2	52.6	56.9	100.0	Recreation	92– 98
55.1	63.4	78.5	61.4	122.5	46.8	55.2	100.0	Education	99–103
33.3	76.2	46.8	57.7	100.3	73.2	59.2	100.0	Other Expenditures	104–109
20.6	22.1	35.5	24.4	34.5	40.7	27.2	100.0	Personal Care	104–106
38.3	97.9	51.3	71.0	126.6	86.2	72.1	100.0	Miscellaneous Services	107–109
66.2	113.7	73.0	101.2	98.8	111.8	144.5	100.0	Capital Formation[d]	111–148
79.0	105.3	65.4	132.6	104.4	114.7	144.6	100.0	Construction	111–124
101.9	115.4	87.5	140.9	106.3	134.5	130.4	100.0	Residential	111–112
71.5	102.9	68.6	132.6	92.7	105.9	152.3	100.0	Nonresidential Bldgs	113–120
60.6	95.9	33.6	122.1	117.8	102.2	151.8	100.0	Other Construction	121–124
47.3	97.1	72.5	75.7	69.3	93.9	117.9	100.0	Producers Durables	125–146
39.3	57.0	56.6	57.4	41.2	55.7	97.5	100.0	Transport Equipment	125–131
45.2	87.2	81.4	94.0	78.9	120.0	137.9	100.0	Nonelectrical Machinery	132–140
70.4	105.4	62.1	96.4	95.3	121.7	139.8	100.0	Electrical Machinery	141–144
28.5	267.0	111.7	0.0	57.5	33.3	37.9	100.0	Other Durables	145–146
28.6	24.8	52.9	47.6	40.3	50.5	45.1	100.0	Government	149–153
48.3	47.8	72.6	74.7	68.3	81.2	70.2	100.0	Compensation	149–152
16.1	10.0	40.4	30.3	22.4	30.9	29.0	100.0	Commodities	153
49.2	59.2	63.5	68.7	72.0	73.2	78.2	100.0	Gross Domestic Product	1–153
								Aggregates ICP Concepts[e]	
47.9	49.3	62.5	62.9	69.8	65.9	64.7	100.0	Consumption (CEP)[b,c]	1–110
66.2	113.7	73.0	101.2	98.8	111.8	144.5	100.0	Capital Formation (GCF)[d]	111–148
28.6	24.8	52.9	47.6	40.3	50.5	45.1	100.0	Government (PFC)	149–153
49.2	59.2	63.5	68.7	72.0	73.2	78.2	100.0	Gross Domestic Product	1–153

(Table continues on following page.)

Summary Multilateral Table 4.4 continued.

	Line numbers[a]	Kenya	India	Philippines	Korea Republic of	Colombia	Malaysia	Iran	Hungary
SNA Concepts[e]									
Consumption (PFCE)	1–110	6.6	7.8	14.6	13.6	20.1	18.8	21.0	39.7
Capital Formation (GCF)	111–148	4.7	5.3	7.7	9.1	18.3	22.8	23.5	54.6
Government (GFCE)	149–153	7.3	5.9	8.6	10.3	11.4	16.2	14.7	36.9
Gross Domestic Product	1–153	6.3	6.9	12.0	12.1	18.2	19.1	20.3	42.2

a. Line numbers refer to Appendix Tables 4.1–4.5 and show the detailed categories that are included in each aggregation.

b. Consumption, *ICP*, includes both household and government expenditures. The latter are shown separately in Table 2.1. Consumption, *SNA*, excludes these government expenditures.

c. The consumption aggregate (lines 1–110) includes net expenditure of residents abroad (line 110), not shown separately in these summary multilateral tables.

Summary Multilateral Table 4.5. Quantities per Capita Valued at International Prices, 1970

	Line numbers[a]	Kenya	India	Philippines	Korea Republic of	Colombia	Malaysia	Iran	Hungary
Consumption, ICP[b,c]	1–110	208.7	234.0	444.5	415.8	617.1	602.1	646.9	1347.0
Food, Beverage, and Tobacco	1–39	108.7	133.6	217.8	208.9	254.2	251.9	249.0	436.7
Food,	1–33	103.2	128.1	186.9	190.7	206.4	225.8	236.3	349.8
Bread and Cereals	1–6	40.1	66.4	83.0	101.9	23.4	70.6	81.7	71.2
Meat	7–12	10.6	2.4	43.1	16.0	62.7	31.2	39.8	74.5
Fish	13–14	2.8	5.5	28.9	12.8	2.5	41.0	1.8	4.2
Milk, Cheese, and Eggs	15–17	11.0	11.2	5.4	4.9	24.2	15.9	40.1	47.5
Oils and Fats	18–20	3.0	10.0	4.0	1.7	6.6	10.0	11.3	36.7
Fruits and Vegetables	21–26	27.6	19.2	3.8	31.8	38.7	30.1	40.3	68.8
Coffee, Tea, and Cocoa	27–29	1.8	1.7	2.7	0.2	14.8	2.9	5.7	4.8
Spices, Sweets, and Sugar	30–33	6.4	11.5	16.0	21.4	33.5	24.0	15.6	42.1
Beverages	34–37	3.1	0.8	21.5	7.9	20.8	9.7	2.0	45.6
Tobacco	38–39	2.4	4.7	9.3	10.3	26.9	16.4	10.7	41.3
Clothing and Footwear	40–51	7.9	13.7	29.2	40.8	48.2	45.3	62.8	110.3
Clothing	40–47	5.8	12.7	25.5	36.8	34.6	39.4	44.7	88.4
Footwear	48–51	2.1	1.0	3.7	4.0	13.6	5.9	18.1	21.9
Gross Rent and Fuel	52–57	14.1	17.9	50.5	26.8	34.7	67.2	140.3	136.5
Gross Rents	52–53	9.4	13.1	45.0	6.2	25.1	59.7	125.6	83.7
Fuel and Power	54–57	4.7	4.8	5.5	20.6	9.6	7.5	14.7	52.8
House Furnishings and Operations	58–71	11.1	7.9	22.8	13.9	48.1	36.1	33.3	74.6
Furniture and Appliances	58–66	1.7	1.3	11.8	4.4	13.7	15.2	22.7	47.4
Supplies and Operation	67–71	9.4	6.6	11.0	9.4	34.4	20.9	10.6	27.2
Medical Care	72–78	12.4	10.8	11.5	22.3	30.3	32.5	26.1	127.7
Transport and Communications	79–91	11.6	10.7	11.2	23.9	75.7	59.8	32.4	57.5
Equipment	79–80	1.7	0.4	0.2	0.2	2.4	7.3	3.5	11.5
Operation Costs	81–84	2.4	1.2	0.8	0.0	7.6	20.0	8.3	10.1
Purchased Transport	85–89	7.0	8.0	9.7	21.3	58.6	28.7	18.6	28.7
Communications	90–91	0.4	1.2	0.4	2.4	7.1	3.7	2.0	7.2
Recreation and Education	92–103	28.3	28.7	63.3	52.4	62.1	69.6	38.0	214.5
Recreation	92–98	5.7	2.1	5.8	17.7	14.7	22.8	7.7	121.5
Education	99–103	22.5	26.6	57.5	34.6	47.4	46.8	30.3	93.0
Other Expenditures	104–109	14.6	10.7	38.4	27.0	63.8	39.7	65.0	189.2
Personal Care	104–106	1.5	1.6	13.2	13.8	8.2	14.3	22.5	31.7
Miscellaneous Services	107–109	13.1	9.1	25.2	13.2	55.7	25.4	42.5	157.6

Italy	Japan	United Kingdom	Netherlands	Belgium	France	Germany F.R.	United States		Line numbers[a]
								SNA Concepts[e]	
49.4	51.1	60.7	63.0	68.9	68.2	66.9	100.0	Consumption (PFCE)	1–110
66.2	113.7	73.0	101.2	98.8	111.8	144.5	100.0	Capital Formation (GCF)	111–148
30.3	27.2	60.5	52.6	53.5	48.2	44.6	100.0	Government (GCF)	149–153
49.2	59.1	63.1	68.7	72.0	73.2	78.2	100.0	Gross Domestic product	1–153

d. The capital formation aggregate (lines 111–148) includes increase in stocks (line 147) and net exports (line 148) not shown separately in these summary multilateral tables.

e. Letters in parentheses are: *CEP,* consumption expenditures of the population; *GCF,* gross capital formation; *PFC,* public final consumption expenditure; *PFCE,* private final consumption expenditure; *GFCE,* government final consumption expenditure. See Glossary for definitions.

Italy	Japan	United Kingdom	Netherlands	Belgium	France	Germany F.R.	United States		Line numbers[a]
1560.5	1608.7	2038.5	2050.6	2276.1	2148.8	2111.2	3261.2	Consumption, ICP[b,c]	1–110
591.0	452.8	645.2	586.9	631.9	686.8	512.0	714.2	Food, Beverage, and Tobacco	1– 39
488.6	349.8	484.1	434.0	504.0	534.3	399.6	574.0	Food,	1– 33
66.2	96.2	80.7	53.2	58.1	60.6	63.7	49.6	Bread and Cereals	1– 6
152.1	32.7	145.5	103.0	183.9	185.7	106.4	164.0	Meat	7– 12
16.2	60.4	11.5	13.7	14.9	25.0	6.6	18.4	Fish	13– 14
58.6	34.4	65.5	88.5	60.8	89.4	57.4	83.0	Milk, Cheese, and Eggs	15– 17
39.7	7.2	29.7	25.6	45.8	40.2	46.5	35.4	Oils and Fats	18– 20
126.4	62.4	67.2	81.6	84.4	88.5	58.2	117.7	Fruits and Vegetables	21– 26
5.8	7.7	26.4	23.5	16.2	15.0	20.4	30.7	Coffee, Tea, and Cocoa	27– 29
23.6	48.8	57.7	44.9	40.1	29.8	40.4	75.1	Spices, Sweets, and Sugar	30– 33
64.9	75.8	106.4	87.5	66.2	112.0	83.5	79.2	Beverages	34– 37
37.5	27.1	54.6	65.4	61.7	40.6	28.9	61.0	Tobacco	38– 39
132.7	182.6	171.9	199.5	164.8	151.5	200.6	266.6	Clothing and Footwear	40– 51
112.0	170.6	137.0	171.6	142.4	128.6	168.5	230.0	Clothing	40– 47
20.7	12.0	34.9	27.9	22.4	22.9	32.1	36.6	Footwear	48– 51
227.5	159.5	314.3	275.5	308.2	315.9	307.4	549.6	Gross Rent and Fuel	52– 57
191.7	124.5	229.8	191.1	231.4	262.8	240.3	409.4	Gross Rents	52– 53
35.8	34.9	84.5	84.4	76.8	53.1	67.1	140.1	Fuel and Power	54– 57
87.6	128.3	126.4	239.1	255.2	171.0	273.8	259.5	House Furnishings and Operations	58– 71
51.7	79.8	75.3	154.7	109.1	97.9	161.7	174.0	Furniture and Appliances	58– 66
35.9	48.5	51.1	84.4	146.2	73.1	112.2	85.5	Supplies and Operation	67– 71
136.2	209.1	138.1	170.5	135.9	212.0	186.7	175.6	Medical Care	72– 78
142.7	58.5	215.6	148.5	163.0	175.5	207.3	543.2	Transport and Communications	79– 91
42.3	9.9	52.7	45.4	57.2	54.7	61.8	209.1	Equipment	79– 80
59.0	10.6	88.9	59.2	65.9	81.6	96.9	255.5	Operation Costs	81– 84
28.8	27.8	49.2	22.2	28.6	30.5	32.3	31.7	Purchased Transport	85– 89
12.7	10.2	24.8	21.8	11.3	8.7	16.2	46.9	Communications	90– 91
155.6	161.4	273.2	226.6	273.4	200.0	223.6	397.6	Recreation and Education	92–103
69.9	62.7	151.0	131.1	82.9	127.3	137.7	242.1	Recreation	92– 98
85.7	98.7	122.1	95.5	190.5	72.7	85.8	155.5	Education	99–103
110.4	253.0	155.3	191.3	332.8	242.8	196.6	331.9	Other Expenditures	104–109
19.6	21.0	33.7	23.2	32.8	38.6	25.8	94.9	Personal Care	104–106
90.8	232.0	121.6	168.2	300.1	204.3	170.8	237.0	Miscellaneous Services	107–109

(Table continues on following page.)

Summary Multilateral Table 4.5 continued.

	Line numbers[a]	Kenya	India	Philippines	Korea Republic of	Colombia	Malaysia	Iran	Hungary
Capital Formation[d]	111–148	45.1	50.1	73.2	87.0	174.7	216.9	223.7	520.4
Construction	111–124	21.9	37.2	32.7	82.6	128.5	123.6	145.0	310.6
Residential	111–112	8.9	8.9	11.8	21.1	39.2	35.7	64.6	79.2
Nonresidential Bldgs	113–120	6.7	10.0	9.0	28.2	8.1	43.0	56.9	130.7
Other Construction	121–124	6.4	18.3	11.9	33.3	81.3	44.8	23.5	100.7
Producers Durables	125–146	20.7	8.1	31.3	32.7	34.5	42.3	41.7	186.6
Transport Equipment	125–131	8.2	2.3	6.7	10.6	13.3	9.6	17.0	50.7
Nonelectrical Machinery	132–140	9.5	3.2	15.7	15.4	5.0	26.0	17.2	91.2
Electrical Machinery	141–144	2.3	1.3	4.8	4.2	14.5	4.2	4.8	24.6
Other Durables	145–146	0.8	1.4	4.2	2.6	1.8	2.5	2.8	20.1
Government	149–153	49.5	47.2	58.2	77.4	77.4	96.4	101.5	175.8
Compensation	149–152	42.9	36.6	45.6	58.3	66.1	59.7	54.4	74.5
Commodities	153	6.6	10.6	12.6	19.1	11.3	36.8	47.2	101.3
Gross Domestic Product	1–153	303.3	331.3	575.9	580.2	869.2	915.4	972.1	2043.2
Aggregates									
ICP Concepts[e]									
Consumption (CEP)[b,c]	1–110	208.7	234.0	444.5	415.8	617.1	602.1	646.9	1,347.0
Capital Formation (GCF)[d]	111–148	45.1	50.1	73.2	87.0	174.7	216.9	223.7	520.4
Government (PFC)	149–153	49.5	47.2	58.2	77.4	77.4	96.4	101.5	175.8
Gross Domestic Product	1–153	303.3	331.3	575.9	580.2	869.2	915.4	972.1	2,043.2
SNA Concepts[e]									
Consumption (PFCE)	1–110	193.8	228.7	426.6	401.6	593.1	554.7	617.5	1,170.9
Capital Formation (GCF)	111–148	45.1	50.1	73.2	87.0	174.7	216.9	223.7	520.4
Government (GFCE)	149–153	64.4	52.5	76.1	91.6	101.4	143.8	130.9	327.4
Gross Domestic Product	1–153	303.3	331.3	575.9	580.2	869.2	915.4	972.1	2,018.6

a. Line numbers refer to Appendix Tables 4.1–4.5 and show the detailed categories that are included in each aggregation.

b. Consumption, *ICP*, includes both household and government expenditures. The latter are shown separately in Table 2.1. Consumption, *SNA*, excludes these government expenditures.

c. The consumption aggregate (lines 1–110) includes net expenditure of residents abroad (line 110), not shown separately in these summary multilateral tables.

Summary Multilateral Table 4.6. Per Capita Expenditures in National Currencies, 1973

	Line numbers[a]	Kenya (shillings)	India (rupees)	Philippines (pesos)	Korea Republic of (won)	Colombia (pesos)	Malaysia (M.dollars)	Iran (rials)	Hungary (forints)
Consumption, ICP[b,c]	1–110	853.96	758.56	1255.36	101570.	7474.37	951.64	28876.0	22922.7
Food, Beverage, and Tobacco	1–39	407.25	509.51	741.64	56766.	2955.37	389.78	11908.5	7841.7
Food,	1–33	370.28	479.34	667.60	47827.	2513.73	324.32	11340.6	6461.7
Bread and Cereals	1–6	156.78	218.38	308.48	24797.	377.64	89.47	3508.1	766.1
Meat	7–12	34.92	10.49	108.84	4223.	880.31	57.57	2264.4	1809.9
Fish	13–14	9.05	7.50	115.51	3070.	53.11	48.65	115.0	58.4
Milk, Cheese, and Eggs	15–17	43.06	44.81	32.05	1847.	315.47	30.80	1189.4	859.0
Oils and Fats	18–20	14.26	53.23	13.35	512.	92.27	13.52	941.5	536.2
Fruits and Vegetables	21–26	86.27	79.73	14.69	7258.	445.47	43.96	2042.6	1212.6
Coffee, Tea, and Cocoa	27–29	5.29	5.55	13.35	250.	116.62	6.22	446.4	282.6
Spices, Sweets, and Sugar	30–33	20.66	59.64	61.43	5870.	232.84	34.13	833.3	937.0
Beverages	34–37	26.22	7.08	44.41	4789.	319.69	22.47	100.8	1001.2
Tobacco	38–39	10.75	23.09	29.53	4151.	121.96	43.00	467.0	378.8

Italy	Japan	United Kingdom	Netherlands	Belgium	France	Germany F.R.	United States		Line numbers[a]
630.7	1083.8	695.9	964.5	941.0	1064.8	1376.4	952.8	Capital Formation[d]	111–148
341.0	454.6	282.4	572.4	450.8	495.5	624.5	431.8	Construction	111–124
151.8	171.9	130.3	209.9	158.3	200.3	194.2	148.9	Residential	111–112
116.5	167.7	111.7	216.0	151.1	172.6	248.1	162.9	Nonresidential Bldgs	113–120
72.8	115.1	40.4	146.5	141.4	122.6	182.3	120.0	Other Construction	121–124
233.1	478.3	356.8	372.8	341.3	462.5	580.5	492.5	Producers Durables	125–146
57.7	83.7	83.1	84.2	60.5	81.7	143.2	146.8	Transport Equipment	125–131
90.5	174.8	163.1	188.4	158.1	240.6	276.5	200.4	Nonelectrical Machinery	132–140
73.1	109.5	64.5	100.1	99.0	126.4	145.2	103.9	Electrical Machinery	141–144
11.8	110.3	46.1	0.0	23.7	13.8	15.6	41.3	Other Durables	145–146
164.9	142.5	304.7	274.1	232.1	290.6	259.3	575.6	Government	149–153
108.3	107.2	162.9	167.7	153.3	182.3	157.6	224.4	Compensation	149–152
56.6	35.3	141.8	106.4	78.8	108.3	101.7	351.1	Commodities	153
2356.1	2834.9	3039.1	3289.1	3449.2	3504.2	3746.9	4789.5	Gross Domestic Product	1–153
								Aggregates	
								ICP Concepts[e]	
1,560.5	1,608.7	2,038.5	2,050.6	2,276.1	2,148.8	2,111.2	3,261.2	Consumption (CEP)[b,c]	1–110
630.7	1,083.8	695.9	964.5	941.0	1,064.8	1,376.4	952.8	Capital Formation (GCF)[d]	111–148
164.9	142.5	304.7	274.1	232.1	290.6	259.3	575.6	Government (PFC)	149–153
2,356.1	2,834.9	3,039.1	3,289.1	3,449.2	3,504.2	3,746.9	4,789.5	Gross Domestic Product	1–153
								SNA Concepts[e]	
1,456.2	1,504.7	1,788.3	1,857.8	2,030.2	2,010.6	1,972.2	2,946.7	Consumption (PFCE)	1–110
630.7	1,083.8	695.9	964.5	941.0	1,064.8	1,376.4	952.8	Capital Formation (GCF)	111–148
269.2	241.7	537.2	466.9	474.5	427.8	395.7	887.7	Government (GFCE)	149–153
2,356.1	2,830.1	3,021.4	3,289.1	3,445.7	3,503.2	3,744.3	4,787.1	Gross Domestic Production	1–153

d. The capital formation aggregate (lines 111–148) includes increase in stocks (line 147) and net exports (line 148) not shown separately in these summary multilateral tables.

e. Letters in parentheses are: CEP, consumption expenditures of the population; GCF, gross capital formation; PFC, public final consumption expenditure; PFCE, private final consumption expenditure; GFCE, government final consumption expenditure. See Glossary for definitions.

Italy (lire)	Japan (yen)	United Kingdom (pounds)	Netherlands (guilders)	Belgium (B.francs)	France (francs)	Germany F.R. (DM)	United States (dollars)		Line numbers[a]
1013091.	556310.	905.543	7583.77	118944.7	13602.78	9100.98	4210.62	Consumption, ICP[b,c]	1–110
364139.	167913.	246.430	1863.84	27718.4	3411.18	1890.67	671.52	Food, Beverage, and Tobacco	1–39
305315.	135131.	146.626	1437.50	23120.0	2774.00	1542.85	536.26	Food,	1–33
38192.	27838.	19.404	180.06	2756.7	383.29	277.44	61.64	Bread and Cereals	1–6
110599.	18647.	45.876	384.60	9120.5	969.06	408.79	149.85	Meat	7–12
10308.	26621.	5.516	37.20	951.5	148.67	24.36	20.22	Fish	13–14
41741.	10135.	22.885	263.39	2436.7	407.86	175.59	79.79	Milk, Cheese, and Eggs	15–17
19924.	2027.	5.552	69.20	1556.9	171.61	152.00	23.99	Oils and Fats	18–20
65305.	31487.	26.330	281.32	3808.2	468.06	239.04	120.11	Fruits and Vegetables	21–26
5698.	2433.	4.248	82.59	780.3	65.97	120.99	17.67	Coffee, Tea, and Cocoa	27–29
13549.	15945.	16.815	139.14	1709.2	159.49	144.63	62.99	Spices, Sweets, and Sugar	30–33
34620.	26492.	65.084	247.77	2516.5	473.97	215.30	72.84	Beverages	34–37
24203.	6290.	34.720	178.57	2081.9	163.21	132.53	62.42	Tobacco	38–39

(Table continues on following page.)

Summary Multilateral Table 4.6 continued.

	Line numbers[a]	Kenya (shillings)	India (rupees)	Philippines (pesos)	Korea Republic of (won)	Colombia (pesos)	Malaysia (M.dollars)	Iran (rials)	Hungary (forints)
Clothing and Footwear	40– 51	37.74	54.74	80.93	11244.	789.87	47.20	1983.5	2526.7
Clothing	40– 47	28.27	50.62	70.41	10418.	596.53	41.41	1565.2	2069.6
Footwear	48– 51	9.47	4.12	10.52	825.	193.33	5.79	418.3	457.1
Gross Rent and Fuel	52– 57	104.77	50.80	115.45	7464.	714.00	109.43	5203.1	1685.9
Gross Rents	52– 53	90.95	27.42	80.28	3375.	577.69	88.25	4092.0	987.8
Fuel and Power	54– 57	13.83	23.38	35.17	4089.	136.31	21.18	1111.1	698.1
House Furnishings and Operations	58– 71	54.05	19.53	77.59	3080.	651.64	53.09	1738.8	1967.6
Furniture and Appliances	58– 66	13.47	4.90	40.78	1819.	232.04	21.79	878.6	1175.0
Supplies and Operation	67– 71	40.58	14.63	36.81	1260.	419.60	31.30	860.2	792.6
Medical Care	72– 78	38.94	19.14	38.07	3376.	364.04	36.94	1530.1	1358.5
Transport and Communications	79– 91	59.36	44.02	24.47	5801.	689.38	137.88	2039.5	1605.2
Equipment	79– 80	12.55	3.67	2.89	249.	90.67	28.96	866.0	567.5
Operation Costs	81– 84	7.18	4.71	3.35	10.	55.20	53.66	455.0	359.2
Purchased Transport	85– 89	37.84	33.16	17.07	5183.	508.18	48.24	638.1	575.3
Communications	90– 91	1.79	2.47	1.16	358.	35.33	7.02	80.5	103.3
Recreation and Education	92–103	96.07	35.14	90.63	7976.	707.69	107.71	2500.6	2674.0
Recreation	92– 98	38.35	7.00	15.92	3263.	316.22	45.75	723.4	1344.8
Education	99–103	57.72	28.13	74.70	4713.	391.47	61.96	1777.3	1329.2
Other Expenditures	104–109	55.77	25.71	86.60	7237.	602.49	69.63	1972.0	3263.2
Personal Care	104–106	7.08	8.38	28.36	3299.	102.44	28.21	599.0	570.5
Miscellaneous Services	107–109	48.69	17.33	58.24	3937.	500.04	41.42	1372.9	2692.7
Capital Formation[d]	111–148	311.83	167.49	399.90	33149.	2324.62	410.43	25377.2	14118.5
Construction	111–124	154.82	79.87	110.87	19286.	1109.38	150.72	7106.0	7137.5
Residential	111–112	36.60	19.99	34.86	4467.	345.56	41.11	2406.9	2153.4
Nonresidential Bldgs	113–120	31.75	7.76	34.47	7507.	71.11	47.34	2894.0	2767.5
Other Construction	121–124	86.47	52.12	41.54	7312.	692.71	62.27	1805.2	2216.5
Producers Durables	125–146	136.04	65.10	203.35	15013.	707.87	128.65	4463.5	4646.7
Transport Equipment	125–131	36.07	12.59	54.59	6044.	183.96	31.69	1133.4	1019.7
Nonelectrical Machinery	132–140	78.24	22.65	101.80	7185.	137.73	76.53	2266.8	2642.0
Electrical Machinery	141–144	19.55	15.16	31.36	1301.	349.51	16.19	773.6	459.4
Other Durables	145–146	2.18	14.69	15.60	483.	36.67	4.24	289.7	525.6
Government	149–153	125.36	73.57	95.40	11028.	688.36	184.14	8522.8	2757.5
Compensation	149–152	95.26	43.90	42.39	6206.	543.38	114.82	3677.2	720.3
Commodities	153	30.10	29.66	53.01	4822.	144.98	69.32	4845.6	2037.2
Gross Domestic Product	1–153	1291.14	999.61	1750.66	145746.	10487.27	1546.21	62775.9	39798.7
Aggregates									
ICP Concepts[e]									
Consumption (CEP)[b,c]	1–110	853.96	758.56	1255.36	101570.	7474.37	951.64	28876.00	22922.7
Capital Formation (G CF)[d]	111–148	311.83	167.49	399.90	33149.	2324.62	410.43	25377.20	14118.5
Government (PFC)	149–153	125.36	73.57	95.40	11028.	688.36	184.14	8522.80	2757.5
Gross Domestic Product	1–153	1291.14	999.61	1750.66	145746.	10487.27	1546.21	62775.90	39798.7
SNA Concepts[e]									
Consumption (PFCE)	1–110	800.23	742.51	1204.37	98375.	7151.40	876.75	26930.84	19813.2
Capital Formation (GCF)	111–148	311.83	167.49	399.90	33149.	2324.62	410.43	25377.30	14118.6
Government (GFCE)	149–153	179.09	69.64	146.40	14224.	1011.43	259.05	10468.02	5461.8
Gross Domestic Product	1–153	1291.14	999.63	1750.67	145750.	10487.46	1546.21	62776.20	39393.6

a. Line numbers refer to Appendix Tables 4.1–4.5 and show the detailed categories that are included in each aggregation.

b. Consumption, *ICP*, includes both household and government expenditures. The latter are shown separately in Table 2.1. Consumption, *SNA*, excludes these government expenditures.

c. The consumption aggregate (lines 1–110) includes net expenditure of residents abroad (line 110), not shown separately in these summary multilateral tables.

Italy (lire)	Japan (yen)	United Kingdom (pounds)	Netherlands (guilders)	Belgium (B.francs)	France (francs)	Germany F.R. (DM)	United States (dollars)		Line numbers[a]
87838.	53113.	69.297	673.36	9496.8	1064.99	878.64	299.03	Clothing and Footwear	40– 51
71264.	49728.	57.354	580.36	8218.2	893.88	754.73	250.54	Clothing	40– 47
16574.	3385.	11.942	93.01	1278.6	171.11	123.91	48.48	Footwear	48– 51
131012.	81071.	154.820	909.30	15622.5	1799.21	1273.02	730.16	Gross Rent and Fuel	52– 57
103642.	66712.	120.939	645.83	10236.7	1389.78	917.72	595.67	Gross Rents	52– 53
27370.	14359.	33.881	263.47	5385.7	409.44	355.31	134.49	Fuel and Power	54– 57
58042.	48417.	60.907	756.62	14505.8	1092.04	1051.87	308.72	House Furnishings and Operations	58– 71
34888.	31755.	37.879	518.38	7069.1	679.17	664.81	190.86	Furniture and Appliances	58– 66
23154.	16662.	23.027	238.24	7436.7	412.87	387.06	117.86	Supplies and Operation	67– 71
75340.	44561.	54.284	690.48	7859.4	1421.56	908.91	433.93	Medical Care	72– 78
106394.	24999.	111.192	680.73	11731.4	1397.97	981.90	611.80	Transport and Communications	79– 91
30869.	5854.	36.558	209.08	4032.8	410.57	213.39	236.83	Equipment	79– 80
50191.	6802.	38.486	288.69	5204.5	687.38	543.34	263.91	Operation Costs	81– 84
15718.	6916.	25.652	92.19	1652.3	227.55	155.40	35.18	Purchased Transport	85– 89
9616.	5427.	10.496	90.77	841.9	72.47	69.76	75.88	Communications	90– 91
115478.	66020.	132.720	1282.66	16042.6	1694.86	1165.21	655.22	Recreation and Education	92–103
52338.	22549.	65.512	547.62	5775.8	867.50	596.47	310.36	Recreation	92– 98
63140.	43471.	67.208	735.04	10266.8	827.35	568.75	344.86	Education	99–103
92351.	66941.	75.866	716.44	14664.9	1727.22	862.60	475.51	Other Expenditures	104–109
14296.	8362.	12.031	86.24	2108.7	302.70	132.06	108.46	Personal Care	104–106
78055.	58579.	63.834	630.21	12556.2	1424.51	730.54	367.05	Miscellaneous Services	107–109
308852.	406660.	234.630	3402.75	45314.1	5780.79	4266.69	1215.39	Capital Formation[d]	111–148
174141.	232753.	118.922	1676.64	23022.0	2951.14	2102.74	697.45	Construction	111–124
90985.	89705.	48.376	789.43	8812.1	1489.05	901.90	301.71	Residential	111–112
54017.	90473.	51.196	562.28	8383.9	892.46	684.48	212.43	Nonresidential Bldgs	113–120
29139.	52576.	19.350	324.93	5826.1	569.63	516.36	183.31	Other Construction	121–124
134910.	140721.	128.508	1203.79	15998.9	2229.00	1585.22	446.67	Producers Durables	125–146
30887.	21913.	37.772	363.76	3335.7	390.96	368.23	132.14	Transport Equipment	125–131
53777.	45811.	49.875	530.51	7074.0	1153.92	751.53	174.08	Nonelectrical Machinery	132–140
38936.	35941.	21.367	279.32	3726.0	594.46	404.66	100.04	Electrical Machinery	141–144
11309.	37056.	19.493	30.21	1863.1	89.66	60.79	40.41	Other Durables	145–146
149882.	54477.	138.451	1318.38	15723.6	1890.93	1422.73	766.26	Government	149–153
104717.	34103.	79.240	959.00	11087.9	1372.99	1050.03	412.20	Compensation	149–152
45165.	20374.	59.211	359.37	4635.7	517.94	372.70	354.06	Commodities	153
1471802.	1017446.	1278.619	12304.84	179981.2	21274.44	14790.33	6192.20	Gross Domestic Product	1–153
								Aggregates	
								ICP Concepts[e]	
1013091.	556310.	905.543	7583.77	118944.7	13602.78	9100.98	4210.62	Consumption (CEP)[b,c]	1–110
308852.	406660.	234.630	3402.75	45314.1	5780.79	4266.69	1215.39	Capital Formation (GCF)[d]	111–148
149882.	54477.	138.451	1318.38	15723.6	1890.93	1422.73	766.26	Government (PFC)	149–153
1471802.	1017446.	1278.619	12304.84	179981.2	21274.44	14790.33	6192.20	Gross Domestic Product	1–153
								SNA Concepts[e]	
942374.	518839.	789.824	6834.95	105304.5	12697.69	8432.79	3771.66	Consumption (PFCE)	1–110
308852.	406659.	234.630	3402.75	45314.2	5780.82	4266.70	1215.39	Capital Formation (GCF)	111–148
220592.	90238.	245.984	2067.26	29202.6	2769.72	2080.07	1202.05	Government (GFCE)	149–153
1471815.	1015735.	1270.438	12304.98	179821.5	21268.25	14779.59	6189.13	Gross Domestic Product	1–153

d. The capital formation aggregate (lines 111–148) includes increase in stocks (line 147) and net exports (line 148) not shown separately in these summary multilateral tables.

e. Letters in parentheses are: *CEP*, consumption expenditures of the population; *GCF*, gross capital formation; *PFC*, public final consumption expenditure; *PFCE*, private final consumption expenditure; *GFCE*, government final consumption expenditure. See Glossary for definitions.

Summary Multilateral Table 4.7. Percentage Distribution of Expenditures in National Currencies, 1973

	Line numbers[a]	Kenya	India	Philippines	Korea Republic of	Colombia	Malaysia	Iran	Hungary
Consumption, ICP[b,c]	1–110	66.14	75.89	71.71	69.69	71.27	61.55	46.00	57.60
Food, Beverage, and Tobacco	1– 39	31.54	50.97	42.36	38.95	28.18	25.21	18.97	19.70
Food,	1– 33	28.68	47.95	38.14	32.82	23.97	20.98	18.07	16.24
Bread and Cereals	1– 6	12.14	21.85	17.62	17.01	3.60	5.79	5.59	1.92
Meat	7– 12	2.70	1.05	6.22	2.90	8.39	3.72	3.61	4.55
Fish	13– 14	0.70	0.75	6.60	2.11	0.51	3.15	0.18	0.15
Milk, Cheese, and Eggs	15– 17	3.34	4.48	1.83	1.27	3.01	1.99	1.89	2.16
Oils and Fats	18– 20	1.10	5.32	0.76	0.35	0.88	0.87	1.50	1.35
Fruits and Vegetables	21– 26	6.68	7.98	0.84	4.98	4.25	2.84	3.25	3.05
Coffee, Tea, and Cocoa	27– 29	0.41	0.56	0.76	0.17	1.11	0.40	0.71	0.71
Spices, Sweets, and Sugar	30– 33	1.60	5.97	3.51	4.03	2.22	2.21	1.33	2.35
Beverages	34– 37	2.03	0.71	2.54	3.29	3.05	1.45	0.16	2.52
Tobacco	38– 39	0.83	2.31	1.69	2.85	1.16	2.78	0.74	0.95
Clothing and Footwear	40– 51	2.92	5.48	4.62	7.71	7.53	3.05	3.16	6.35
Clothing	40– 47	2.19	5.06	4.02	7.15	5.69	2.68	2.49	5.20
Footwear	48– 51	0.73	0.41	0.60	0.57	1.84	0.37	0.67	1.15
Gross Rent and Fuel	52– 57	8.11	5.08	6.59	5.12	6.81	7.08	8.29	4.24
Gross Rents	52– 53	7.04	2.74	4.59	2.32	5.51	5.71	6.52	2.48
Fuel and Power	54– 57	1.07	2.34	2.01	2.81	1.30	1.37	1.77	1.75
House Furnishings and Operations	58– 71	4.19	1.95	4.43	2.11	6.21	3.43	2.77	4.94
Furniture and Appliances	58– 66	1.04	0.49	2.33	1.25	2.21	1.41	1.40	2.95
Supplies and Operation	67– 71	3.14	1.46	2.10	0.86	4.00	2.02	1.37	1.99
Medical Care	72– 78	3.02	1.91	2.17	2.32	3.47	2.39	2.44	3.41
Transport and Communications	79– 91	4.60	4.40	1.40	3.98	6.57	8.92	3.25	4.03
Equipment	79– 80	0.97	0.37	0.17	0.17	0.86	1.87	1.38	1.43
Operation Costs	81– 84	0.56	0.47	0.19	0.01	0.53	3.47	0.72	0.90
Purchased Transport	85– 89	2.93	3.32	0.97	3.56	4.85	3.12	1.02	1.45
Communications	90– 91	0.14	0.25	0.07	0.25	0.34	0.45	0.13	0.26
Recreation and Education	92–103	7.44	3.51	5.18	5.47	6.75	6.97	3.98	6.72
Recreation	92– 98	2.97	0.70	0.91	2.24	3.02	2.96	1.15	3.38
Education	99–103	4.47	2.81	4.27	3.23	3.73	4.01	2.83	3.34
Other Expenditures	104–109	4.32	2.57	4.95	4.97	5.74	4.50	3.14	8.20
Personal Care	104–106	0.55	0.84	1.62	2.26	0.98	1.82	0.95	1.43
Miscellaneous Services	107–109	3.77	1.73	3.33	2.70	4.77	2.68	2.19	6.77
Capital Formation[d]	111–148	24.15	16.76	22.84	22.74	22.17	26.54	40.43	35.47
Construction	111–124	11.99	7.99	6.33	13.23	10.58	9.75	11.32	17.93
Residential	111–112	2.83	2.00	1.99	3.06	3.29	2.66	3.83	5.41
Nonresidential Bldgs	113–120	2.46	0.78	1.97	5.15	0.68	3.06	4.61	6.95
Other Construction	121–124	6.70	5.21	2.37	5.02	6.61	4.03	2.88	5.57
Producers Durables	125–146	10.54	6.51	11.62	10.30	6.75	8.32	7.11	11.68
Transport Equipment	125–131	2.79	1.26	3.12	4.15	1.75	2.05	1.81	2.56
Nonelectrical Machinery	132–140	6.06	2.27	5.82	4.93	1.31	4.95	3.61	6.64
Electrical Machinery	141–144	1.51	1.52	1.79	0.89	3.33	1.05	1.23	1.15
Other Durables	145–146	0.17	1.47	0.89	0.33	0.35	0.27	0.46	1.32
Government	149–153	9.71	7.36	5.45	7.57	6.56	11.91	13.58	6.93
Compensation	149–152	7.38	4.39	2.42	4.26	5.18	7.43	5.86	1.81
Commodities	153	2.33	2.97	3.03	3.31	1.38	4.48	7.72	5.12
Gross Domestic Product	1–153	100.00	100.00	100.00	100.00	100.00	100.00	100.00	100.00
Aggregates									
ICP Concepts[e]									
Consumption (CEP)[b,c]	1–110	66.1	75.9	71.7	69.7	71.3	61.5	46.0	57.6
Capital Formation (GCF)[d]	111–148	24.2	16.8	22.8	22.7	22.2	26.5	40.4	35.5
Government (PFC)	149–153	9.7	7.4	5.4	7.6	6.6	11.9	13.6	6.9
Gross Domestic Product	1–153	100.0	100.0	100.0	100.0	100.0	100.0	100.0	100.0

Italy	Japan	United Kingdom	Netherlands	Belgium	France	Germany F.R.	United States		Line numbers[a]
68.83	54.68	70.82	61.63	66.09	63.94	61.53	68.00	Consumption, ICP[b,c]	1–110
24.74	16.50	19.27	15.15	15.40	16.03	12.78	10.84	Food, Beverage, and Tobacco	1– 39
20.74	13.28	11.47	11.68	12.85	13.04	10.43	8.66	Food,	1– 33
2.59	2.74	1.52	1.46	1.53	1.80	1.88	1.00	Bread and Cereals	1– 6
7.51	1.83	3.59	3.13	5.07	4.56	2.76	2.42	Meat	7– 12
0.70	2.62	0.43	0.30	0.53	0.70	0.16	0.33	Fish	13– 14
2.84	1.00	1.79	2.14	1.35	1.92	1.19	1.29	Milk, Cheese, and Eggs	15– 17
1.35	0.20	0.43	0.56	0.87	0.81	1.03	0.39	Oils and Fats	18– 20
4.44	3.09	2.06	2.29	2.12	2.20	1.62	1.94	Fruits and Vegetables	21– 26
0.39	0.24	0.33	0.67	0.43	0.31	0.82	0.29	Coffee, Tea, and Cocoa	27– 29
0.92	1.57	1.32	1.13	0.95	0.75	0.98	1.02	Spices, Sweets, and Sugar	30– 33
2.35	2.60	5.09	2.01	1.40	2.23	1.46	1.18	Beverages	34– 37
1.64	0.62	2.72	1.45	1.16	0.77	0.90	1.01	Tobacco	38– 39
5.97	5.22	5.42	5.47	5.28	5.01	5.94	4.83	Clothing and Footwear	40– 51
4.84	4.89	4.49	4.72	4.57	4.20	5.10	4.05	Clothing	40– 47
1.13	0.33	0.93	0.76	0.71	0.80	0.84	0.78	Footwear	48– 51
8.90	7.97	12.11	7.39	8.68	8.46	8.61	11.79	Gross Rent and Fuel	52– 57
7.04	6.56	9.46	5.25	5.69	6.53	6.20	9.62	Gross Rents	52– 53
1.86	1.41	2.65	2.14	2.99	1.92	2.40	2.17	Fuel and Power	54– 57
3.94	4.76	4.76	6.15	8.06	5.13	7.11	4.99	House Furnishings and Operations	58– 71
2.37	3.12	2.96	4.21	3.93	3.19	4.49	3.08	Furniture and Appliances	58– 66
1.57	1.64	1.80	1.94	4.13	1.94	2.62	1.90	Supplies and Operation	67– 71
5.12	4.38	4.25	5.61	4.37	6.68	6.15	7.01	Medical Care	72– 78
7.23	2.46	8.70	5.53	6.52	6.57	6.64	9.88	Transport and Communications	79– 91
2.10	0.58	2.86	1.70	2.24	1.93	1.44	3.82	Equipment	79– 80
3.41	0.67	3.01	2.35	2.89	3.23	3.67	4.26	Operation Costs	81– 84
1.07	0.68	2.01	0.75	0.92	1.07	1.05	0.57	Purchased Transport	85– 89
0.65	0.53	0.82	0.74	0.47	0.34	0.47	1.23	Communications	90– 91
7.85	6.49	10.38	10.42	8.91	7.97	7.88	10.58	Recreation and Education	92–103
3.56	2.22	5.12	4.45	3.21	4.08	4.03	5.01	Recreation	92– 98
4.29	4.27	5.26	5.97	5.70	3.89	3.85	5.57	Education	99–103
6.27	6.58	5.93	5.82	8.15	8.12	5.83	7.68	Other Expenditures	104–109
0.97	0.82	0.94	0.70	1.17	1.42	0.89	1.75	Personal Care	104–106
5.30	5.76	4.99	5.12	6.98	6.70	4.94	5.93	Miscellaneous Services	107–109
20.98	39.97	18.35	27.65	25.18	27.17	28.85	19.63	Capital Formation[d]	111–148
11.83	22.88	9.30	13.63	12.79	13.87	14.22	11.26	Construction	111–124
6.18	8.82	3.78	6.42	4.90	7.00	6.10	4.87	Residential	111–112
3.67	8.89	4.00	4.57	4.66	4.19	4.63	3.43	Nonresidential Bldgs	113–120
1.98	5.17	1.51	2.64	3.24	2.68	3.49	2.96	Other Construction	121–124
9.17	13.83	10.05	9.78	8.89	10.48	10.72	7.21	Producers Durables	125–146
2.10	2.15	2.95	2.96	1.85	1.84	2.49	2.13	Transport Equipment	125–131
3.65	4.50	3.90	4.31	3.93	5.42	5.08	2.81	Nonelectrical Machinery	132–140
2.65	3.53	1.67	2.27	2.07	2.79	2.74	1.62	Electrical Machinery	141–144
0.77	3.64	1.52	0.25	1.04	0.42	0.41	0.65	Other Durables	145–146
10.18	5.35	10.83	10.71	8.74	8.89	9.62	12.37	Government	149–153
7.11	3.35	6.20	7.79	6.16	6.45	7.10	6.66	Compensation	149–152
3.07	2.00	4.63	2.92	2.58	2.43	2.52	5.72	Commodities	153
100.00	100.00	100.00	100.00	100.00	100.00	100.00	100.00	Gross Domestic Product	1–153
								Aggregates ICP Concepts[e]	
68.8	54.7	70.8	61.6	66.1	63.9	61.5	68.0	Consumption (CEP)[b,c]	1–110
21.0	40.0	18.4	27.7	25.2	27.2	28.8	19.6	Capital Formation (GCF)[d]	111–148
10.2	5.4	10.8	10.7	8.7	8.9	9.6	12.4	Government (PFC)	149–153
100.0	100.0	100.0	100.0	100.0	100.0	100.0	100.0	Gross Domestic Product	1–153

(Table continues on following page.)

Summary Multilateral Table 4.7 continued.

	Line numbers[a]	Kenya	India	Philippines	Korea Republic of	Colombia	Malaysia	Iran	Hungary
SNA Concepts[e]									
Consumption (PFCE)	1–110	62.0	74.3	68.8	67.5	68.2	56.7	42.9	50.3
Capital Formation (GCF)	111–148	24.2	16.8	22.8	22.7	22.2	26.5	40.4	35.8
Government (GFCE)	149–153	13.9	9.0	8.4	9.8	9.6	16.8	16.7	13.9
Gross Domestic Product	1–153	100.0	100.0	100.0	100.0	100.0	100.0	100.0	100.0

a. Line numbers refer to Appendix Tables 4.1–4.5 and show the detailed categories that are included in each aggregation.

b. Consumption, *ICP*, includes both household and government expenditures. The latter are shown separately in Table 2.1. Consumption, *SNA*, excludes these government expenditures.

c. The consumption aggregate (lines 1–110) includes net expenditure of residents abroad (line 110), not shown separately in these summary multilateral tables.

Summary Multilateral Table 4.8. Purchasing-Power Parities per U.S. Dollar, 1973

	Line numbers[a]	Kenya (shillings)	India (rupees)	Philippines (pesos)	Korea Republic of (won)	Colombia (pesos)	Malaysia (M.dollars)	Iran (rials)	Hungary (forints)
Consumption, ICP[b,c]	1–110	3.31	2.81	2.20	164.	9.6	1.29	29.7	13.0
Food, Beverage, and Tobacco	1– 39	3.74	4.24	3.34	235.	13.5	1.58	46.3	18.2
Food,	1– 33	3.62	4.22	3.58	225.	14.0	1.49	47.2	18.8
Bread and Cereals	1– 6	3.11	2.87	2.91	167.	12.5	0.99	31.7	9.0
Meat	7– 12	3.10	4.10	2.54	266.	14.8	1.86	55.8	22.7
Fish	13– 14	2.86	1.11	3.26	127.	17.0	1.09	63.4	9.2
Milk, Cheese, and Eggs	15– 17	3.74	4.17	5.42	276.	14.4	1.80	32.4	16.8
Oils and Fats	18– 20	6.49	8.27	3.79	437.	21.0	1.66	109.9	22.7
Fruits and Vegetables	21– 26	2.69	4.55	3.97	219.	10.4	1.36	38.9	15.7
Coffee, Tea, and Cocoa	27– 29	5.29	5.56	7.53	978.	17.1	3.56	135.1	83.8
Spices, Sweets, and Sugar	30– 33	4.96	8.12	5.63	359.	15.7	2.26	72.3	31.0
Beverages	34– 37	8.74	8.53	1.84	472.	17.1	2.37	49.7	20.4
Tobacco	38– 39	4.61	5.14	2.96	236.	6.1	2.39	37.3	9.6
Clothing and Footwear	40– 51	4.29	3.56	2.36	176.	13.8	1.04	29.3	20.6
Clothing	40– 47	4.49	3.64	2.46	187.	15.3	1.11	33.8	21.0
Footwear	48– 51	3.51	3.20	1.83	108.	9.9	0.68	18.1	18.3
Gross Rent and Fuel	52– 57	6.09	2.55	1.80	200.	13.1	1.29	21.3	9.6
Gross Rents	52– 53	7.20	1.70	1.32	352.	16.9	1.10	17.7	8.8
Fuel and Power	54– 57	3.27	6.21	6.50	180.	7.6	2.89	54.1	12.4
House Furnishings and Operations	58– 71	4.74	2.74	2.99	158.	9.4	1.47	34.7	20.6
Furniture and Appliances	58– 66	7.78	4.63	3.41	273.	17.6	1.64	34.2	21.4
Supplies and Operation	67– 71	3.49	2.00	2.38	85.	6.3	1.19	32.7	18.8
Medical Care	72– 78	1.48	0.76	1.46	52.	6.0	0.53	20.0	4.5
Transport and Communications	79– 91	5.51	4.76	2.26	204.	8.1	2.21	35.6	22.4
Equipment	79– 80	8.77	8.81	14.26	881.	39.2	4.81	114.4	39.1
Operation Costs	81– 84	3.43	4.54	4.56	423.	7.1	2.71	36.3	21.8
Purchased Transport	85– 89	4.77	4.30	1.52	184.	6.5	1.30	16.1	16.0
Communications	90– 91	3.18	1.34	2.01	55.	2.8	1.13	19.9	6.8
Recreation and Education	92–103	2.29	0.81	0.87	99.	5.3	1.05	26.6	7.5
Recreation	92– 98	6.01	2.67	2.45	149.	14.3	1.79	39.1	9.0
Education	99–103	1.27	0.52	0.57	66.	2.8	0.65	18.7	5.9
Other Expenditures	104–109	2.68	1.91	1.72	133.	8.2	1.23	20.5	11.3
Personal Care	104–106	4.33	4.80	2.06	133.	14.0	1.66	30.5	13.3
Miscellaneous Services	107–109	2.43	1.43	1.62	152.	7.3	1.08	17.8	10.7

Italy	Japan	United Kingdom	Netherlands	Belgium	France	Germany F.R.	United States		Line numbers[a]
								SNA Concepts[e]	
64.0	51.1	62.2	55.5	58.6	59.7	57.1	60.9	Consumption (PFCE)	1–110
21.0	40.0	18.5	27.7	25.2	27.2	26.9	19.6	Capital Formation (GCF)	111–148
15.0	8.9	19.4	16.8	16.2	13.1	14.1	19.4	Government (GFCE)	149–153
100.0	100.0	100.0	100.0	100.0	100.0	100.0	100.0	Gross Domestic Product	1–153

d. The capital formation aggregate (lines 111–148) includes increase in stocks (line 147) and net exports (line 148) not shown separately in these summary multilateral tables.

e. Letters in parentheses are: *CEP*, consumption expenditures of the population; *GCF*, gross capital formation; *PFC*, public final consumption expenditure; *PFCE*, private final consumption expenditure; *GFCE*, government final consumption expenditure. See Glossary for definitions.

Italy (lire)	Japan (yen)	United Kingdom (pounds)	Netherlands (guilders)	Belgium (B.francs)	France (francs)	Germany F.R. (DM)	United States (dollars)		Line numbers[a]
508.	247.	0.346	2.98	37.8	4.76	3.38	1.00	Consumption, ICP[b,c]	1–110
629.	348.	0.403	3.10	43.8	5.07	3.79	1.00	Food, Beverage, and Tobacco	1– 39
643.	379.	0.337	3.36	46.8	5.35	3.99	1.00	Food,	1– 33
472.	230.	0.226	2.93	41.8	5.22	3.58	1.00	Bread and Cereals	1– 6
669.	482.	0.348	3.78	48.7	5.25	3.79	1.00	Meat	7– 12
577.	369.	0.482	2.69	47.2	4.96	2.96	1.00	Fish	13– 14
656.	301.	0.321	2.69	37.9	4.22	2.84	1.00	Milk, Cheese, and Eggs	15– 17
642.	351.	0.288	3.23	50.1	5.97	4.50	1.00	Oils and Fats	18– 20
525.	382.	0.339	2.86	37.1	4.72	3.54	1.00	Fruits and Vegetables	21– 26
1683.	501.	0.337	5.53	81.7	7.19	10.23	1.00	Coffee, Tea, and Cocoa	27– 29
889.	491.	0.457	4.73	63.2	7.91	5.78	1.00	Spices, Sweets, and Sugar	30– 33
572.	283.	0.523	2.41	33.3	4.22	2.60	1.00	Beverages	34– 37
577.	195.	0.650	2.38	32.1	4.03	4.66	1.00	Tobacco	38– 39
585.	261.	0.346	3.26	45.7	6.36	4.01	1.00	Clothing and Footwear	40– 51
577.	267.	0.366	3.29	46.4	6.42	4.08	1.00	Clothing	40– 47
611.	231.	0.263	3.22	42.7	6.00	3.64	1.00	Footwear	48– 51
439.	347.	0.397	2.58	38.3	4.01	3.11	1.00	Gross Rent and Fuel	52– 57
389.	338.	0.388	2.50	32.0	3.47	2.70	1.00	Gross Rents	52– 53
725.	379.	0.441	3.02	63.5	7.25	5.01	1.00	Fuel and Power	54– 57
539.	269.	0.396	3.14	42.5	5.09	3.28	1.00	House Furnishings and Operations	58– 71
609.	319.	0.433	3.64	50.5	5.94	3.93	1.00	Furniture and Appliances	58– 66
430.	197.	0.333	2.35	32.7	3.86	2.39	1.00	Supplies and Operation	67– 71
219.	84.	0.170	1.81	23.1	2.69	2.25	1.00	Medical Care	72– 78
730.	339.	0.457	4.59	69.4	7.34	5.02	1.00	Transport and Communications	79– 91
792.	393.	0.537	5.87	68.9	7.02	4.57	1.00	Equipment	79– 80
820.	497.	0.430	4.67	78.4	8.14	5.91	1.00	Operation Costs	81– 84
491.	222.	0.465	4.12	55.7	6.58	4.48	1.00	Purchased Transport	85– 89
485.	209.	0.234	2.26	49.0	4.66	2.26	1.00	Communications	90– 91
499.	255.	0.284	3.66	33.6	5.10	3.15	1.00	Recreation and Education	92–103
665.	314.	0.328	3.48	48.8	5.27	3.43	1.00	Recreation	92– 98
359.	193.	0.237	3.67	23.3	5.10	2.89	1.00	Education	99–103
566.	162.	0.322	2.57	25.0	4.57	2.99	1.00	Other Expenditures	104–109
651.	316.	0.286	3.51	50.1	5.69	4.70	1.00	Personal Care	104–106
537.	144.	0.324	2.38	22.0	4.26	2.69	1.00	Miscellaneous Services	107–109

(Table continues on following page.)

Summary Multilateral Table 4.8 continued.

	Line numbers[a]	Kenya (shillings)	India (rupees)	Philippines (pesos)	Korea Republic of (won)	Colombia (pesos)	Malaysia (M.dollars)	Iran (rials)	Hungary (forints)
Capital Formation[d]	111–148	5.90	3.18	4.01	199.	11.0	1.45	44.7	19.7
Construction	111–124	4.19	1.67	1.75	133.	5.8	0.76	21.4	14.2
Residential	111–112	2.00	1.68	1.97	108.	5.2	0.70	17.7	14.3
Nonresidential Bldgs	113–120	3.48	1.83	2.71	147.	5.4	0.76	22.0	16.0
Other Construction	121–124	5.21	1.49	1.16	137.	5.6	0.78	31.1	12.2
Producers Durables	125–146	9.84	8.96	8.43	387.	32.5	2.88	74.4	29.5
Transport Equipment	125–131	10.21	8.53	12.89	535.	28.6	4.05	83.9	32.4
Nonelectrical Machinery	132–140	10.10	9.44	8.35	388.	38.0	2.89	81.2	30.6
Electrical Machinery	141–144	9.41	8.68	6.83	239.	31.4	2.10	77.1	21.2
Other Durables	145–146	8.63	7.76	4.51	156.	26.2	1.56	32.4	28.6
Government	149–153	1.68	0.93	1.06	91.	6.3	1.17	34.0	9.8
Compensation	149–152	1.13	0.52	0.51	58.	4.8	0.89	28.6	4.5
Commodities	153	3.81	2.60	2.63	160.	7.9	1.52	40.5	16.4
Gross Domestic Product	1–153	3.41	2.53	2.32	161.	9.5	1.31	34.7	14.3
Aggregates									
ICP Concepts[e]									
Consumption (CEP)[b,c]	1–110	3.31	2.81	2.20	164.	9.58	1.29	29.7	13.0
Capital Formation (GCF)[d]	111–148	5.90	3.18	4.01	199.	10.95	1.45	44.7	19.7
Government (PFC)	149–153	1.68	0.93	1.06	91.	6.27	1.17	34.0	9.8
Gross Domestic Product	1–153	3.41	2.53	2.32	161.	9.48	1.31	34.7	14.3
SNA Concepts[e]									
Consumption (PFCE)	1–110	3.31	2.81	2.20	164.	9.58	1.29	29.7	13.0
Capital Formation (GCF)	111–148	5.89	3.18	4.01	199.	10.95	1.45	44.7	19.7
Government (GFCE)	149–153	2.04	1.12	1.33	105.	7.21	1.22	34.1	11.0
Gross Domestic Product	1–153	3.41	2.53	2.32	161.	9.48	1.31	34.7	14.3

. a. Line numbers refer to Appendix Tables 4.1–4.5 and show the detailed categories that are included in each aggregation.

b. Consumption, *ICP*, includes both household and government expenditures. The latter are shown separately in Table 2.1. Consumption, *SNA*, excludes these government expenditures.

c. The consumption aggregate (lines 1–110) includes net expenditure of residents abroad (line 110), not shown separately in these summary multilateral tables.

Summary Multilateral Table 4.9. Quantities per Capita, 1973 (U.S.=100)

	Line numbers[a]	Kenya	India	Philippines	Korea Republic of	Colombia	Malaysia	Iran	Hungary
Consumption, ICP[b,c]	1–110	6.1	6.4	13.5	14.7	18.5	17.5	23.1	42.0
Food, Beverage, and Tobacco	1– 39	16.2	17.9	33.1	36.0	32.5	36.7	38.3	64.3
Food,	1– 33	19.1	21.2	34.8	39.7	33.5	40.5	44.8	64.0
Bread and Cereals	1– 6	81.8	123.3	172.3	240.8	49.0	147.2	179.3	138.3
Meat	7– 12	7.5	1.7	28.6	10.6	39.8	20.6	27.1	53.2
Fish	13– 14	15.6	33.5	175.1	119.2	15.4	220.6	9.0	31.5
Milk, Cheese, and Eggs	15– 17	14.4	13.5	7.4	8.4	27.4	21.4	46.0	63.9
Oils and Fats	18– 20	9.2	26.8	14.7	4.9	18.3	33.9	35.7	98.7
Fruits and Vegetables	21– 26	26.7	14.6	3.1	27.5	35.8	26.9	43.7	64.5
Coffee, Tea, and Cocoa	27– 29	5.7	5.7	10.0	1.4	38.6	9.9	18.7	19.1
Spices, Sweets, and Sugar	30– 33	6.6	11.7	17.3	25.9	23.6	24.0	18.3	48.0
Beverages	34– 37	4.1	1.1	33.2	13.9	25.7	13.0	2.8	67.4
Tobacco	38– 39	3.7	7.2	16.0	28.2	31.9	28.8	20.1	63.3

Italy (lire)	Japan (yen)	United Kingdom (pounds)	Netherlands (guilders)	Belgium (B.francs)	France (francs)	Germany F.R. (DM)	United States (dollars)		Line numbers[a]
493.	297.	0.343	2.77	41.3	4.33	2.70	1.00	Capital Formation[d]	111–148
381.	278.	0.279	2.01	32.5	3.63	2.19	1.00	Construction	111–124
435.	267.	0.234	2.04	35.5	4.31	2.49	1.00	Residential	111–112
390.	349.	0.349	2.33	34.1	3.63	2.20	1.00	Nonresidential Bldgs	113–120
268.	217.	0.294	1.58	27.0	2.56	1.79	1.00	Other Construction	121–124
645.	309.	0.439	4.22	57.2	5.20	3.53	1.00	Producers Durables	125–146
807.	339.	0.549	5.73	70.6	6.03	3.97	1.00	Transport Equipment	125–131
619.	292.	0.415	3.70	52.5	5.21	3.45	1.00	Nonelectrical Machinery	132–140
515.	298.	0.400	3.75	48.6	4.39	3.14	1.00	Electrical Machinery	141–144
802.	273.	0.361	6.68	69.8	5.82	4.36	1.00	Other Durables	145–146
552.	232.	0.306	3.29	43.4	4.21	3.37	1.00	Government	149–153
485.	176.	0.259	2.87	34.9	3.62	3.25	1.00	Compensation	149–152
542.	301.	0.347	3.18	50.0	4.17	2.72	1.00	Commodities	153
505.	257.	0.341	2.91	38.6	4.52	3.09	1.00	Gross Domestic Product	1–153
								Aggregates	
								ICP Concepts[e]	
508.	247.	0.346	2.98	37.8	4.76	3.38	1.00	Consumption (CEP)[b,c]	1–110
493.	297.	0.343	2.77	41.3	4.32	2.70	1.00	Capital Formation (GCF)[d]	111–148
552.	232.	0.306	3.29	43.4	4.21	3.37	1.00	Government (PFC)	149–153
505.	257.	0.341	2.91	38.6	4.52	3.09	1.00	Gross Domestic Product	149–153
								SNA Concepts[e]	
508.	247.	0.346	2.98	37.8	4.76	3.38	1.00	Consumption (PFCE)	1–110
493.	297.	0.343	2.77	41.3	4.32	2.70	1.00	Capital Formation (GCF)	111–148
539.	237.	0.320	3.16	39.6	4.43	3.40	1.00	Government (GFCE)	149–153
505.	257.	0.341	2.91	38.6	4.52	3.09	1.00	Gross Domestic Product	1–153

d. The capital formation aggregate (lines 111–148) includes increase in stocks (line 147) and net exports (line 148) not shown separately in these summary multilateral tables.

e. Letters in parentheses are: *CEP*, consumption expenditures of the population; *GCF*, gross capital formation; *PFC*, public final consumption expenditure; *PFCE*, private final consumption expenditure; *GFCE*, government final consumption expenditure. See Glossary for definitions.

Italy	Japan	United Kingdom	Netherlands	Belgium	France	Germany F.R.	United States		Line numbers[a]
47.4	53.5	62.2	60.3	74.8	67.9	63.9	100.0	Consumption, ICP[b,c]	1–110
86.2	71.8	91.0	89.5	94.3	100.2	74.3	100.0	Food, Beverage, and Tobacco	1– 39
88.5	66.5	81.2	79.7	92.1	96.7	72.1	100.0	Food,	1– 33
131.4	196.3	139.3	99.8	107.1	119.1	125.7	100.0	Bread and Cereals	1– 6
110.3	25.8	88.1	67.9	124.9	123.1	71.9	100.0	Meat	7– 12
88.3	356.8	56.6	68.5	99.7	148.2	40.7	100.0	Fish	13– 14
79.8	42.2	89.2	122.6	80.5	121.2	77.5	100.0	Milk, Cheese, and Eggs	15– 17
129.4	24.0	80.3	89.2	129.6	119.8	140.9	100.0	Oils and Fats	18– 20
103.5	68.6	64.6	82.0	85.5	82.5	56.2	100.0	Fruits and Vegetables	21– 26
19.2	27.5	71.4	84.5	54.1	51.9	66.9	100.0	Coffee, Tea, and Cocoa	27– 29
24.2	51.6	58.4	46.7	42.9	32.0	39.7	100.0	Spices, Sweets, and Sugar	30– 33
83.0	128.7	170.7	141.0	103.6	154.2	113.8	100.0	Beverages	34– 37
67.2	51.7	85.6	120.2	104.0	64.9	45.6	100.0	Tobacco	38– 39

(Table continues on following page.)

Summary Multilateral Table 4.9 continued.

	Line numbers[a]	Kenya	India	Philippines	Korea Republic of	Colombia	Malaysia	Iran	Hungary
Clothing and Footwear	40– 51	2.9	5.1	11.5	21.3	19.1	15.2	22.6	41.0
Clothing	40– 47	2.5	5.5	11.4	22.2	15.6	14.8	18.5	39.3
Footwear	48– 51	5.6	2.7	11.9	15.7	40.4	17.5	47.6	51.6
Gross Rent and Fuel	52– 57	2.4	2.7	8.8	5.1	7.4	11.6	33.4	24.1
Gross Rents	52– 53	2.1	2.7	10.2	1.6	5.7	13.5	38.8	18.9
Fuel and Power	54– 47	3.1	2.8	4.0	16.9	13.3	5.5	15.3	41.9
House Furnishings and Operations	58– 71	3.7	2.3	8.4	6.3	22.4	11.7	16.2	30.9
Furniture and Appliances	58– 66	0.9	0.6	6.3	3.5	6.9	7.0	13.5	28.7
Supplies and Operation	67– 71	9.9	6.2	13.1	12.6	56.8	22.2	22.3	35.9
Medical Care	72– 78	6.1	5.8	6.0	14.8	13.9	16.0	17.6	68.8
Transport and Communications	79– 91	1.8	1.5	1.8	4.6	13.8	10.2	9.4	11.7
Equipment	79– 80	0.6	0.2	0.1	0.1	1.0	2.5	3.2	6.1
Operation Costs	81– 84	0.8	0.4	0.3	0.0	2.9	7.5	4.7	6.2
Purchased Transport	85– 89	22.5	21.9	32.0	79.9	221.7	105.6	112.8	96.3
Communications	90– 91	0.7	2.4	0.8	8.7	16.9	8.2	5.3	20.1
Recreation and Education	92–103	6.4	6.6	15.9	12.3	20.3	15.7	14.3	54.8
Recreation	92– 98	2.1	0.8	2.1	7.1	7.1	8.2	6.0	48.3
Education	99–103	13.2	15.6	37.7	20.6	41.0	27.5	27.5	65.0
Other Expenditures	104–109	4.4	2.8	10.6	11.4	15.4	11.9	20.2	60.6
Personal Care	104–106	1.5	1.6	12.7	22.9	6.8	15.6	18.1	39.5
Miscellaneous Services	107–109	5.5	3.3	9.8	7.0	18.7	10.5	21.0	68.6
Capital Formation[d]	111–148	4.4	4.3	8.2	13.7	17.5	23.3	46.7	59.0
Construction	111–124	5.3	6.8	9.1	20.8	27.5	28.4	47.6	72.1
Residential	111–112	4.0	4.0	5.9	13.7	22.1	19.5	45.1	49.8
Nonresidential Bldgs	113–120	4.3	2.0	6.0	24.0	6.2	29.2	61.9	81.6
Other Construction	121–124	9.1	19.1	19.5	29.2	67.8	43.7	31.6	99.3
Producers Durables	125–146	3.1	1.6	5.4	8.7	4.9	10.0	13.4	35.3
Transport Equipment	125–131	2.7	1.1	3.2	8.5	4.9	5.9	10.2	23.8
Nonelectrical Machinery	132–140	4.4	1.4	7.0	10.6	2.1	15.2	16.0	49.6
Electrical Machinery	141–144	2.1	1.7	4.6	5.4	11.1	7.7	10.0	21.6
Other Durables	145–146	0.6	4.7	8.6	7.7	3.5	6.7	22.1	45.4
Government	149–153	9.8	10.3	11.7	15.8	14.3	20.5	32.7	36.6
Compensation	149–152	20.4	20.4	20.3	26.2	27.3	31.4	31.2	38.6
Commodities	153	2.2	3.2	5.7	8.5	5.2	12.9	33.8	35.1
Gross Domestic Product	1–153	6.1	6.4	12.2	14.6	17.9	19.1	29.2	45.1
Aggregates									
ICP Concepts[e]									
Consumption (CEP)[b,c]	1–110	6.1	6.4	13.5	14.7	18.5	17.5	23.1	42.0
Capital Formation (GCF)[d]	111–148	4.4	4.3	8.2	13.7	17.5	23.3	46.7	59.0
Government (PFC)	149–153	9.8	10.3	11.7	15.8	14.3	20.5	32.7	36.6
Gross Domestic Product	1–153	6.1	6.4	12.2	14.6	17.9	19.1	29.2	45.1
SNA Concepts[e]									
Consumption (PFCE)	1–110	6.4	7.0	14.5	15.9	19.8	18.0	24.1	40.5
Capital Formation (GCF)	111–148	4.4	4.3	8.2	13.7	17.5	23.3	46.7	59.0
Government (GFCE)	149–153	7.3	6.7	9.1	11.2	11.7	17.6	25.5	41.1
Gross Domestic Product	1–153	6.1	6.4	12.2	14.6	17.9	19.1	29.2	44.6

a. Line numbers refer to Detailed Multilateral Tables 4.21–4.25 and show the detailed categories included in each aggregation.
b. Expenditures for lines 1 through 109 include both household and government expenditures. The latter are shown separately in Table 2.9. Consumption (SNA) excludes these government expenditures.
c. The consumption aggregate (lines 1 through 109) includes net expenditure of residents abroad, not shown separately in this table.

Italy	Japan	United Kingdom	Netherlands	Belgium	France	Germany F.R.	United States		Line numbers[a]
50.2	68.1	66.9	69.0	69.5	56.0	73.3	100.0	Clothing and Footwear	40– 51
49.3	74.4	62.5	70.5	70.8	55.5	73.8	100.0	Clothing	40– 47
55.9	30.3	93.8	59.6	61.8	58.8	70.2	100.0	Footwear	48– 51
40.9	32.0	53.4	48.3	55.9	61.5	56.1	100.0	Gross Rent and Fuel	52– 57
44.7	33.1	52.3	43.4	53.7	67.3	57.1	100.0	Gross Rents	52– 53
28.1	28.1	57.1	64.9	63.1	42.0	52.8	100.0	Fuel and Power	54– 57
34.9	58.3	49.9	78.1	110.5	69.5	103.9	100.0	House Furnishings and Operations	58– 71
30.0	52.1	45.9	74.6	73.3	59.9	88.7	100.0	Furniture and Appliances	58– 66
45.7	71.9	58.7	85.9	192.8	90.7	137.7	100.0	Supplies and Operation	67– 71
79.3	122.7	73.4	88.0	78.4	121.7	93.1	100.0	Medical Care	72– 78
23.8	12.1	39.7	24.2	27.6	31.1	32.0	100.0	Transport and Communications	79– 91
16.5	6.3	28.7	15.0	24.7	24.7	19.7	100.0	Equipment	79– 80
23.2	5.2	33.9	23.4	25.2	32.0	34.9	100.0	Operation Costs	81– 84
90.9	88.4	156.8	63.6	84.4	98.3	98.6	100.0	Purchased Transport	85– 89
26.1	34.2	59.2	52.9	22.7	20.5	40.7	100.0	Communications	90– 91
35.3	39.5	71.3	53.5	72.9	50.7	56.4	100.0	Recreation and Education	92–103
25.4	23.1	64.4	50.6	38.1	53.0	56.0	100.0	Recreation	92– 98
51.0	65.2	82.2	58.0	127.7	47.0	57.1	100.0	Education	99–103
34.3	86.8	49.6	58.5	123.6	79.5	60.7	100.0	Other Expenditures	104–109
20.3	24.4	38.8	22.7	38.8	49.1	25.9	100.0	Personal Care	104–106
39.6	110.5	53.7	72.1	155.8	91.1	73.9	100.0	Miscellaneous Services	107–109
51.5	112.7	56.3	101.2	90.2	110.0	130.0	100.0	Capital Formation[d]	111–148
65.6	119.8	61.1	119.4	101.7	116.6	137.8	100.0	Construction	111–124
69.4	111.4	68.5	128.0	82.2	114.6	120.1	100.0	Residential	111–112
65.1	122.1	69.1	113.7	115.6	115.7	146.6	100.0	Nonresidential Bldgs	113–120
59.4	132.0	35.9	111.9	117.6	121.5	157.6	100.0	Other Construction	121–124
46.8	102.0	65.5	63.9	62.6	96.0	100.6	100.0	Producers Durables	125–146
29.0	48.9	52.1	48.0	35.8	49.1	70.3	100.0	Transport Equipment	125–131
49.9	90.2	69.0	82.5	77.4	127.3	125.3	100.0	Nonelectrical Machinery	132–140
75.5	120.4	53.4	74.5	76.6	135.4	128.7	100.0	Electrical Machinery	141–144
34.9	336.4	133.6	11.2	66.1	38.1	34.5	100.0	Other Durables	145–146
35.4	30.7	59.0	52.2	47.2	58.6	55.1	100.0	Government	149–153
52.3	47.1	74.2	81.1	77.1	91.9	78.3	100.0	Compensation	149–152
23.5	19.1	48.2	31.9	26.2	35.1	38.7	100.0	Commodities	153
47.0	64.0	60.6	68.4	75.3	76.1	77.4	100.0	Gross Domestic Product	1–153
								Aggregates	
								ICP Concepts[e]	
47.4	53.5	62.2	60.3	74.8	67.9	63.9	100.0	Consumption (CEP)[b,c]	1–110
51.5	112.7	56.3	101.2	90.2	110.0	130.0	100.0	Capital Formation (GCF)[d]	111–148
35.4	30.7	59.0	52.2	47.2	58.6	55.1	100.0	Government (PFC)	149–153
47.0	64.0	60.6	68.4	75.3	76.1	77.4	100.0	Gross Domestic Product	1–153
								SNA Concepts[e]	
49.2	55.7	60.6	60.7	73.9	70.7	66.1	100.0	Consumption (PFCE)	1fl110
51.5	112.7	56.3	101.2	90.2	110.0	130.0	100.0	Capital Formation (GCF)	111–148
34.0	31.7	64.0	54.4	61.3	52.4	50.9	100.0	Government (GFCE)	149–153
47.1	63.9	60.2	68.4	75.3	76.1	77.4	100.0	Gross Domestic Product	1–153

d. The capital formation aggregate (lines 110 through 147) include increase in stocks (line 147) and net exports (line 148). See Table 5.34 for these items.

e. The ideal of the Fisher index is the geometric mean of the indexes with weights of the United States and of the United Kingdom.

f. Letters in parentheses are (CEP), consumption expenditure of the population; (GCF), gross capital formation; (PFC), public final consumption expenditure; (PFCE), private final consumption expenditure; and (GFCE), government final consumption expenditure. For definitions, see the Glossary.

Summary Multilateral Table 4.10. Quantities per Capita Valued at International Prices, 1973

	Line numbers[a]	Kenya	India	Philippines	Korea Republic of	Colombia	Malaysia	Iran	Hungary
Consumption, ICP[b,c]	1–110	258.2	270.1	569.4	618.3	780.0	736.0	972.4	1766.6
Food, Beverage, and Tobacco	1– 39	138.7	153.0	282.9	307.6	277.9	313.5	327.8	549.9
Food,	1– 33	132.4	146.9	241.6	275.0	232.1	281.3	311.0	444.0
Bread and Cereals	1– 6	51.7	77.9	108.8	152.1	30.9	93.0	113.3	87.3
Meat	7– 12	14.3	3.3	54.5	20.2	75.8	39.3	51.6	101.4
Fish	13– 14	3.4	7.3	38.1	25.9	3.4	48.0	2.0	6.8
Milk, Cheese, and Eggs	15– 17	13.6	12.7	7.0	7.9	25.9	20.2	43.5	60.4
Oils and Fats	18– 20	3.7	10.9	5.9	2.0	7.4	13.7	14.5	40.0
Fruits and Vegetables	21– 26	36.2	19.7	4.2	37.2	48.4	36.4	59.1	87.2
Coffee, Tea, and Cocoa	27– 29	2.0	2.0	3.5	0.5	13.6	3.5	6.6	6.7
Spices, Sweets, and Sugar	30– 33	7.4	13.1	19.5	29.2	26.6	27.1	20.6	54.1
Beverages	34– 37	3.7	1.0	30.0	12.6	23.2	11.8	2.5	60.9
Tobacco	38– 39	2.7	5.1	11.4	20.0	22.6	20.5	14.3	45.0
Clothing and Footwear	40– 51	10.0	17.4	38.9	72.2	64.7	51.5	76.6	139.0
Clothing	40– 47	7.3	16.1	33.2	64.7	45.3	43.1	53.8	114.2
Footwear	48– 51	2.7	1.3	5.7	7.5	19.4	8.4	22.8	24.7
Gross Rent and Fuel	52– 57	16.9	19.6	63.2	36.7	53.5	83.5	240.1	173.3
Gross Rents	52– 53	11.8	15.0	56.6	8.9	31.7	74.5	215.0	104.4
Fuel and Power	54– 57	5.2	4.6	6.6	27.8	21.8	9.0	25.1	68.9
House Furnishings and Operations	58– 71	12.5	7.8	28.4	21.4	75.8	39.6	54.9	104.8
Furniture and Appliances	58– 66	2.1	1.3	14.6	8.2	16.1	16.2	31.4	67.0
Supplies and Operation	67– 71	10.4	6.5	13.8	13.2	59.8	23.4	23.5	37.7
Medical Care	72– 78	15.4	14.8	15.3	37.7	35.3	40.7	44.7	174.7
Transport and Communications	79– 91	13.1	11.2	13.1	34.4	102.6	75.5	69.4	86.7
Equipment	79– 80	1.9	0.6	0.3	0.4	3.1	8.0	10.1	19.4
Operation Costs	81– 84	2.6	1.3	0.9	0.0	9.6	24.6	15.6	20.5
Purchased Transport	85– 89	8.1	7.9	11.5	28.7	79.6	37.9	40.5	34.6
Communications	90– 91	0.5	1.5	0.5	5.3	10.3	5.0	3.2	12.2
Recreation and Education	92–103	33.5	34.5	83.5	64.5	106.3	82.3	75.1	287.0
Recreation	92– 98	6.6	2.7	6.7	22.6	22.8	26.3	19.1	154.6
Education	99–103	26.9	31.8	76.8	41.9	83.5	56.0	56.0	132.4
Other Expenditures	104–109	18.2	11.8	44.0	47.3	63.8	49.3	83.8	251.4
Personal Care	104–106	1.7	1.8	14.5	26.1	7.7	17.9	20.7	45.1
Miscellaneous Services	107–109	16.4	9.9	29.6	21.2	56.1	31.4	63.1	206.3
Capital Formation[d]	111–148	58.5	58.3	110.2	184.1	234.6	313.2	627.8	792.3
Construction	111–124	31.4	40.6	53.9	123.2	162.8	168.5	282.3	427.5
Residential	111–112	10.3	10.1	14.9	34.9	56.3	49.6	114.9	126.7
Nonresidential Bldgs	113–120	8.6	4.0	11.9	47.9	12.4	58.2	123.5	162.8
Other Construction	121–124	12.6	26.6	27.1	40.5	94.2	60.7	43.9	137.9
Producers Durables	125–146	20.6	10.8	36.0	57.9	32.5	66.8	89.5	235.1
Transport Equipment	125–131	5.9	2.5	7.1	18.8	10.7	13.1	22.5	52.5
Nonelectrical Machinery	132–140	11.7	3.6	18.4	28.0	5.5	40.1	42.2	130.3
Electrical Machinery	141–144	2.7	2.3	6.0	7.1	14.5	10.1	13.1	28.2
Other Durables	145–146	0.3	2.5	4.5	4.1	1.8	3.6	11.7	24.1
Government	149–153	62.4	66.1	75.1	101.2	91.7	131.3	209.2	233.8
Compensation	149–152	54.1	54.0	53.8	69.2	72.3	82.9	82.6	102.1
Commodities	153	8.4	12.1	21.3	32.0	19.4	48.3	126.6	131.8
Gross Domestic Product	1–153	379.1	394.5	754.8	903.5	1106.3	1180.5	1809.4	2792.7
Aggregates									
ICP Concepts[e]									
Consumption (CEP)[b,c]	1–110	258.2	270.1	569.4	618.3	780.0	736.0	972.4	1766.6
Capital Formation (GCF)[d]	111–148	58.5	58.3	110.2	184.1	234.6	313.2	627.8	792.3
Government (PFC)	149–153	62.4	66.1	75.1	101.2	91.7	131.3	209.2	233.8
Gross Domestic Product	1–153	379.1	394.5	754.8	903.5	1106.3	1180.5	1809.4	2792.7

Italy (lire)	Japan (yen)	United Kingdom (pounds)	Netherlands (guilders)	Belgium (B.francs)	France (francs)	Germany F.R. (DM)	United States (dollars)		Line numbers[a]
1994.5	2251.8	2617.6	2540.3	3149.4	2857.0	2691.7	4209.3	Consumption, ICP[b,c]	1–110
736.9	613.9	778.3	765.4	806.3	856.4	635.2	855.0	Food, Beverage, and Tobacco	1– 39
614.2	461.0	563.3	552.7	638.8	671.0	500.0	693.6	Food,	1– 33
83.0	124.0	88.0	63.1	67.6	75.2	79.4	63.2	Bread and Cereals	1– 6
210.2	49.2	167.8	129.4	237.9	234.5	137.0	190.5	Meat	7– 12
19.2	77.6	12.3	14.9	21.7	32.2	8.9	21.8	Fish	13– 14
75.4	39.9	84.4	115.9	76.1	114.6	73.3	94.5	Milk, Cheese, and Eggs	15– 17
52.4	9.7	32.5	36.1	52.5	48.5	57.1	40.5	Oils and Fats	18– 20
140.0	92.8	87.3	110.8	115.6	111.6	76.1	135.2	Fruits and Vegetables	21– 26
6.8	9.7	25.2	29.8	19.1	18.3	23.6	35.2	Coffee, Tea, and Cocoa	27– 29
27.3	58.1	65.8	52.6	48.4	36.1	44.7	112.7	Spices, Sweets, and Sugar	30– 33
75.0	116.2	154.2	127.3	93.6	139.3	102.8	90.3	Beverages	34– 37
47.7	36.7	60.8	85.4	73.9	46.2	32.4	71.1	Tobacco	38– 39
170.3	230.9	226.7	233.8	235.5	189.8	248.3	338.9	Clothing and Footwear	40– 51
143.4	216.4	181.7	205.2	205.9	161.6	214.7	290.9	Clothing	40– 47
26.8	14.5	45.0	28.6	29.6	28.2	33.6	47.9	Footwear	48– 51
293.8	229.8	383.5	346.9	401.3	441.7	402.8	718.2	Gross Rent and Fuel	52– 57
247.7	183.6	289.8	240.2	297.7	372.7	316.1	553.9	Gross Rents	52– 53
46.1	46.2	93.7	106.7	103.7	69.0	86.7	164.3	Fuel and Power	54– 57
118.1	197.2	168.8	264.3	374.0	235.1	351.8	338.5	House Furnishings and Operations	58– 71
70.0	121.5	107.0	173.9	171.0	139.6	206.9	233.2	Furniture and Appliances	58– 66
48.1	75.7	61.8	90.4	203.0	95.5	144.9	105.3	Supplies and Operation	67– 71
201.5	311.4	186.3	223.5	199.0	309.1	236.3	253.9	Medical Care	72– 78
176.7	89.5	294.7	179.6	204.8	230.9	236.9	741.4	Transport and Communications	79– 91
52.1	19.9	90.9	47.6	78.2	78.1	62.4	316.4	Equipment	79– 80
76.1	17.0	111.3	76.9	82.5	105.0	114.4	328.1	Operation Costs	81– 84
32.7	31.7	56.3	22.8	30.3	35.3	35.4	35.9	Purchased Transport	85– 89
15.9	20.9	36.0	32.2	13.8	12.5	24.8	60.9	Communications	90– 91
185.0	206.7	373.5	280.3	382.1	265.5	295.5	523.9	Recreation and Education	92–103
81.2	74.0	206.1	162.2	122.1	169.8	179.4	320.3	Recreation	92– 98
103.8	132.7	167.3	118.1	260.0	95.7	116.2	203.6	Education	99–103
142.3	360.4	205.9	242.9	512.9	329.9	251.8	414.9	Other Expenditures	104–109
23.1	27.8	44.2	25.9	44.3	56.0	29.6	114.1	Personal Care	104–106
119.2	332.5	161.7	217.0	468.6	273.9	222.2	300.8	Miscellaneous Services	107–109
691.8	1513.8	755.7	1359.6	1211.3	1477.4	1746.7	1343.3	Capital Formation[d]	111–148
389.0	710.6	362.2	708.1	603.1	691.4	817.2	592.9	Construction	111–124
176.6	283.7	174.5	326.0	209.3	291.8	305.8	254.6	Residential	111–112
129.9	243.5	137.8	226.7	230.6	230.8	292.5	199.4	Nonresidential Bldgs	113–120
82.5	183.4	49.9	155.4	163.3	168.8	218.9	138.9	Other Construction	121–124
312.1	680.3	436.7	425.8	417.2	639.6	670.5	666.6	Producers Durables	125–146
63.8	107.6	114.7	105.8	78.7	108.0	154.7	220.2	Transport Equipment	125–131
131.3	237.1	181.5	216.8	203.5	334.8	329.6	263.0	Nonelectrical Machinery	132–140
98.5	157.1	69.7	97.2	99.8	176.5	167.9	130.4	Electrical Machinery	141–144
18.5	178.4	70.9	5.9	35.1	20.2	18.3	53.0	Other Durables	145–146
226.7	196.2	377.1	334.2	302.2	374.8	352.5	639.7	Government	149–153
138.4	124.5	196.2	214.5	203.9	243.1	207.2	264.5	Compensation	149–152
88.3	71.7	180.9	119.7	98.3	131.6	145.3	375.2	Commodities	153
2913.0	3961.8	3750.5	4234.0	4662.8	4709.2	4790.9	6192.2	Gross Domestic Product	1–153
								Aggregates ICP Concepts[e]	
1994.5	2251.8	2617.6	2540.3	3149.4	2857.0	2691.7	4209.3	Consumption (CEP)[b,c]	1–110
691.8	1513.8	755.7	1359.6	1211.3	1477.4	1746.7	1343.3	Capital Formation (GCF)[d]	111–148
226.7	3961.8	377.1	334.2	302.2	374.8	352.5	639.7	Government (PFC)	149–153
2913.0	3961.8	3750.5	4234.0	4662.8	4709.2	4790.9	6192.2	Gross Domestic Product	1–153

(Table continues on following page.)

Summary Multilateral Table 4.10 continued.

	Line numbers[a]	Kenya	India	Philippines	Korea Republic of	Colombia	Malaysia	Iran	Hungary
SNA Concepts[e]									
Consumption (PFCE)	1–110	242.0	264.4	546.3	598.8	746.3	678.1	906.9	1527.0
Capital Formation (GCF)	111–148	58.5	58.3	110.2	184.1	234.6	313.2	627.8	792.3
Government (GFCE)	149–153	78.6	71.8	98.2	120.7	125.4	189.2	274.7	442.2
Gross Domestic Product	1–153	379.1	394.5	754.8	903.5	1106.3	1180.5	1809.4	2761.5

a. Line numbers refer to Appendix Tables 4.1–4.5 and show the detailed categories that are included in each aggregation.

b. Consumption, *ICP*, includes both household and government expenditures. The latter are shown separately in Table 2.1. Consumption, *SNA*, excludes these government expenditures.

c. The consumption aggregate (lines 1–110) includes net expenditure of residents abroad (line 110), not shown separately in these summary multilateral tables.

Italy	Japan	United Kingdom	Netherlands	Belgium	France	Germany F.R.	United States		Line numbers[a]
								SNA Concepts[e]	
1855.3	2100.1	2283.1	2289.5	2788.2	2666.9	2494.1	3770.5	Consumption (PFCE)	1–110
691.8	1513.8	755.7	1359.6	1211.3	1477.4	1746.7	1343.3	Capital Formation (GCF)	111–148
365.9	541.0	687.9	585.0	659.1	563.6	546.9	1075.4	Government (GFCE)	149–153
2913.0	3954.9	3726.8	4234.0	4658.5	4707.9	4787.7	6189.0	Gross Domestic Product	1–153

d. The capital formation aggregate (lines 111–148) includes increase in stocks (line 147) and net exports (line 148) not shown separately in these summary multilateral tables.

e. Letters in parentheses are: CEP, consumption expenditures of the population; GCF, gross capital formation; PFC, public final consumption expenditure; PFCE, private final consumption expenditure; GFCE, government final consumption expenditure. See Glossary for definitions.

means of the Geary-Khamis formulas, which also incorporate transitive and base-invariant properties. The methods may be illuminated further by setting out the mechanical operations by which some of the tables are derived from others. The explanation will be given in terms of the 1970 set of data, but it applies equally to the 1973 data set.

The starting point for the preparation of the tables was the PPPs for the detailed categories. Most of these were obtained by means of the CPD method outlined in Chapter 3. The PPPs for the detailed categories set out in Appendix Table 4.3 are expressed in terms of national currency units per U.S. dollar, but, as was brought out in the presentation of the method, the United States serves simply as a numéraire country in this procedure. The relative purchasing powers would be the same if another country had been chosen for this role.

Once the PPPs are in hand, the quantity comparisons for the detailed categories are obtained by dividing the PPPs into corresponding expenditure ratios.[1] That is, for each category and for each country the ratio of the country's expenditure on the category to the United States's expenditure, each taken from Appendix Table 4.1, is divided by the country's PPP for the category as obtained from Appendix Table 4.3. For example, the French quantity index for bread was obtained by dividing the ratio of French to U.S. expenditures on bread ($136.95 \div 25.80 = 5.308$) by the PPP for bread (2.52). The result ($5.308 \div 2.52 = 2.11$) is entered (multiplied by 100 to place it in percentage form) in Appendix Table 4.4. Each row of this table shows the real quantity for a detailed category as a percentage of the U.S. quantity.

The next step is to combine the PPPs and the quantity comparisons for these detailed categories into the desired levels of aggregation ("rice," "bread," and so on, into "bread and cereals"; then "bread and cereals," "meat," and so on into "food"; and so on to "consumption" and "GDP").

The procedures used to produce the aggregations in Summary Multilateral Tables 4.3 and 4.4 are based on the Geary-Khamis method described in Chapter 3. The inputs for the estimation of the Geary-Khamis equations are the expenditures of Appendix Table 4.1 rescaled by the supercountry weights and the PPPs of Appendix Table 4.3. A set of "notional" Qs is obtained by dividing the PPPs into expenditures for each detailed category in each country, the expenditures being denominated in each country's own national currency. (The quotes around *notional* are meant to indicate that these are not strictly quantities but rather values of quantities at U.S. prices.[2] These notional quantities are not shown in the tables because they represent only intermediate data.) The notional quantity for French bread (54.3), for example, was obtained by dividing the French expenditure on bread (136.95 francs) from Appendix Table 4.1 by the PPP for bread (2.52) from Appendix Table 4.3.

The international prices for the detailed categories obtained as part of the solution of the Geary-Khamis equations are entered in the right-most column of Appendix Table 4.3. This set of prices can be used to value each country's quantities. For example, the international price of bread is 0.63. Since the

---

1. For a given category: $\dfrac{Q_j}{Q_{US}} = \dfrac{P_j Q_j}{P_{US} Q_{US}} \div \dfrac{P_j}{P_{US}}$, where P represents price, Q represents quantity, and the subscripts represent the United States and any one of the fifteen partner countries.

2. For a given category: $\dfrac{P_j Q_j}{\text{PPP}_j{}^{US}} = \dfrac{P_j Q_j}{P_j / P_{US}} = Q_j P_{US}$. It may be noted that for purposes of the multilateral comparisons, each detailed category is treated as a single commodity with a price, quantity, and expenditure for each country.

quantities are notional, as described above, in the French bread illustration, the notional quantity 54.3 is multiplied by the international price of bread (0.63) to obtain the value of French bread consumption at international prices. This turns out to be 34.2 and is entered in Appendix Table 4.5.

Appendix Table 4.5 is in a form that makes it possible to aggregate real quantities simply by addition over any particular selection of categories. This is because the quantities for the detailed categories have been made commensurate from row to row as well as from column to column by valuing them at international prices. This simple additivity is the key to the derivation of the summary tables, particularly Summary Multilateral Table 4.4 and, indirectly, Summary Multilateral Table 4.3.

Before turning to the summary tables, attention may be called to Appendix Table 4.4. The relationships along any row of this table are identical to those along the corresponding row of Appendix Table 4.5: that is, relative quantities among the different countries for any given category are the same in both tables. The figures are expressed with the United States equal to 100 in Appendix Table 4.4 to facilitate comparisons with the United States.

To explain the PPP and quantity comparisons in the summary tables, it is convenient to start with Summary Multilateral Table 4.5. The values in this table are aggregates obtained by summing appropriate entries within columns of Appendix Table 4.5. The "line numbers" column gives the lines over which the aggregation takes place. For example, an entry in residential construction in Summary Multilateral Table 4.5 is the sum of the entries for the same country in line 111, one- and two-dwelling buildings, and line 112, multidwelling buildings, of Appendix Table 4.5. Specifically, India's entry for residential construction (8.9) is the sum of India's line 111 (4.7) and line 112 (4.2) entries in Appendix Table 4.5. The values are in terms of "international dollars" (I$), which have the same purchasing power over total U.S. GDP as a U.S. dollar (US$). For subaggregates and for the detailed categories, however, the purchasing power of an international dollar differs from that of a U.S. dollar because it depends upon the structure of average international prices rather than upon the U.S. relative price structure.

Because the aggregations of Summary Multilateral Table 4.5 are summations at international prices of the quantities of a given set of goods consumed by the different countries, they may be recast in index number form. This has been done with the United States taken as 100 in Summary Multilateral Table 4.4. For example, the expenditure of the United Kingdom on meat at international prices comes to I$143.8, whereas that of the United States is I$186.7 (Summary Multilateral Table 4.5). The ratio between the two is 0.770, which is entered in percentage form in Summary Multilateral Table 4.4. Particularly noteworthy are the lines that contain country comparisons with the United States at the level of consumption, capital formation, government, and GDP. These aggregates may also be found along with the corresponding SNA aggregates at the bottom of the table.

The PPPs for the aggregated categories are obtained by dividing the quantity ratios in Summary Multilateral Table 4.4 into expenditure ratios taken from Summary Multilateral Table 4.1. For example, when the United Kingdom–United States expenditure ratio for meat (32.727÷122.5) is divided by the quantity ratio (0.887), the result is a PPP of 0.302 pounds per dollar, which is entered in Summary Multilateral Table 4.3.[3]

3. The explanation given in the text is in rather mechanical terms, being intended to guide the reader through the tables. In principle, the PPP_j for category i for country j is taken relative to international prices, and then this ratio is divided by the numéraire country (United States) PPP relative to the international price.

Comparisons of the Structure of Expenditures, Prices, and Quantities for Five Groups of Countries

The results of the comparisons at the level of GDP and its three major components have already been discussed in Chapter 1. This section will focus on the more salient features of the comparisons at a lower level of aggregation—namely, the summary categories. Attention is concentrated on the search for patterns associated with the large differences in real per capita GDP that exist among these sixteen countries; for the most part, each reader is left to study differences among individual countries according to his own interest.

It will have been noticed that as a means of facilitating the perusal of the data, the countries are arrayed in columns from left to right in order of ascending 1970 real GDP per capita in all of the basic tables in this chapter (Summary Multilateral Tables 4.1 to 4.10 and Appendix Tables 4.1 to 4.5).

In order to make the data still more manageable for discussion purposes, some of the aggregations and summary categories from the basic tables have been selected and have been presented as averages for five groups of countries classified according to real per capita GDP. The grouping of countries inevitably has an arbitrary element even though an effort was made to draw the dividing lines at points where there were gaps between the real per capita GDPs of countries with successive ranks. The groupings, which are the same for 1970 and 1973, are as follows:

Group	Real GDP per capita (United States = 100)	Countries
I	less than 15 percent	Kenya India Philippines Korea, Republic of
II	15–35 percent	Colombia Malaysia Iran
III	35–65 percent	Hungary Italy Japan United Kingdom
IV	65–80 percent	Netherlands Belgium France Germany, F.R.
V	more than 80 percent	United States

In Table 4.11 the percentage distribution in own currency for each of the five groups of countries is examined. The figures are simple averages of the countries included in each group. (The same procedure will be followed in the subsequent tables in which data for the five groups are presented. In this case they are simple averages of the numbers in Summary Multilateral Table 4.2 for 1970 and Summary Multilateral Table 4.7 for 1973.)

One of the most striking aspects of these data is the sharp decline in the proportion of GDP that is accounted for by expenditures on food. The food share in both years drops from about 37 percent for Group I to 9 percent or less for Group V. A substantial part of this is accounted for by the decline in the relative importance of expenditures on breads and cereals, particularly in the transition from the very lowest group to the next lowest; in both years expenditures on bread and cereals accounted for about 17 percent of GDP per capita for Group I, only 5 or 6 percent for Group II, and less than 3 percent for the other groups. A tendency for declines is evident

**Table 4.11. Average Percentage Distribution of Expenditures in National
Currencies for Groups of Countries Classified by Real
per Capita GDP, 1970 and 1973**

Category	Line numbers [a]	Group I	Group II	Group III	Group IV	Group V
1970						
Consumption, ICP	1–110	73.4	66.9	62.9	63.0	68.3
Food	1–33	37.5	24.8	16.6	12.9	9.3
Bread and cereals	1–6	17.1	6.0	2.6	1.8	1.0
Meat	7–12	3.4	5.6	4.4	4.1	2.6
Fish	13–14	2.5	1.3	1.0	0.4	0.3
Milk, cheese, and eggs	15–17	2.9	3.0	2.0	1.7	1.5
Oils and fats	18–20	1.9	1.3	1.0	0.9	0.4
Fruits and vegetables	21–26	5.3	4.0	3.4	2.2	2.1
Clothing and footwear	40–51	5.0	5.2	5.8	5.7	5.0
Clothing	40–47	4.5	4.2	4.9	4.9	4.2
Footwear	48–51	0.5	1.0	0.9	0.8	0.8
Gross rents and fuel	52–57	6.6	8.3	8.1	8.2	11.8
Gross rents	52–53	4.3	6.8	6.0	5.9	9.7
House furnishings and operations	58–71	3.2	3.8	4.5	6.6	5.0
Medical care	72–78	2.5	3.4	4.1	5.1	6.6
Transport and communications	79–91	3.7	6.5	5.0	6.1	9.3
Equipment	79–80	0.4	1.3	1.4	1.8	3.2
Purchased transport	85–89	2.8	3.2	1.4	1.0	0.6
Recreation and education	92–103	6.1	5.6	7.6	8.3	10.4
Recreation	92–98	1.8	2.4	3.6	3.8	5.0
Education	99–103	4.2	3.2	4.0	4.6	5.4
Capital formation	111–148	18.6	22.9	29.1	27.8	17.8
Construction	111–124	10.2	10.6	15.1	13.9	10.4
Producers' durables	125–146	9.4	7.4	11.3	10.9	7.0
Government	149–153	8.0	10.2	8.0	9.2	13.9
Compensation	149–152	5.2	6.6	4.5	6.3	7.1
Commodities	153–153	2.7	3.6	3.5	2.8	6.8
Gross domestic product	1–153	100.0	100.0	100.0	100.0	100.0
1973						
Consumption, ICP	1–110	70.9	59.6	63.0	63.3	68.0
Food	1–33	36.9	21.0	15.4	12.0	8.7
Bread and cereals	1–6	17.2	5.0	2.2	1.7	1.0
Meat	7–12	3.2	5.2	4.4	3.9	2.4
Fish	13–14	2.5	1.3	1.0	0.4	0.3
Milk, cheese, and eggs	15–17	2.7	2.3	1.9	1.6	1.3
Oils and fats	18–20	1.9	1.1	0.8	0.8	0.4
Fruits and vegetables	21–26	5.1	3.4	3.2	2.1	1.9
Clothing and footwear	40–51	5.2	4.6	5.7	5.4	4.8
Clothing	40–47	4.6	3.6	4.9	4.6	4.1
Footwear	48–51	0.6	1.0	0.9	0.8	0.8
Gross rents and fuel	52–57	6.2	7.4	8.3	8.3	11.8
Gross rents	52–53	4.2	5.9	6.4	5.9	9.6
House furnishings and operations	58–71	3.2	4.1	4.6	6.6	5.0
Medical care	72–78	2.4	2.8	4.3	5.7	7.0
Transport and communications	79–91	3.6	6.2	5.6	6.3	9.9
Equipment	79–80	0.4	1.4	1.7	1.8	3.8
Purchased transport	85–89	2.7	3.0	1.3	0.9	0.6
Recreation and education	92–103	5.4	5.9	7.9	8.8	10.6
Recreation	92–98	1.7	2.4	3.6	3.9	5.0
Education	99–103	3.7	3.5	4.3	4.9	5.6
Capital formation	111–148	21.6	29.7	28.7	27.2	19.6
Construction	111–124	9.9	10.5	15.5	13.6	11.3
Producers' durables	125–146	9.7	7.4	11.2	10.0	7.2
Government	149–153	7.5	10.7	8.3	9.5	12.4
Compensation	149–152	4.6	6.2	4.6	6.9	6.7
Commodities	153–153	2.9	4.5	3.7	2.6	5.7
Gross domestic product	1–153	100.0	100.0	100.0	100.0	100.0

Note: For countries included in each group, see page 116.
Source: Summary Multilateral Tables 4.2 and 4.7.
a. Line numbers refer to the Detailed Multilateral Tables and show the detailed categories that are included in each aggregation.

also for the other food components; however, the share accounted for by meat rises from Group I to Group II. The falling food shares for the higher income levels is offset by steady increases in shares for medical care, personal transport equipment, and recreation, and by less regular increases in other categories.

Underlying these differences in expenditures are differences in both prices and quantities. The behavior of the quantities (that is, averages of the real per capita quantity indexes with the United States equal to 100, from Summary Multilateral Tables 4.4 and 4.9) is shown for each of the five groups in Table 4.12. The figures tend to rise steadily from one GDP group to another for many more categories than the figures in Table 4.11. This only reflects the fact that higher incomes tend to spill over into spending on all kinds of final products. There are, to be sure, some occasional declines in average real quantities between one group and the next higher one, but these tend to be exceptional and often reflect the particular circumstances of a given country. For example, the high per capita consumption of fish in Group III relative to Groups IV and V results almost entirely from the very large fish consumption of one Group III country—Japan. The Philippines (Group I) and Malaysia (Group II) are also big fish consumers (see Summary Multilateral Tables 4.4 and 4.8). Geography, particularly long coast lines, rather than real per capita income explains these consumption levels.

For food as a whole, per capita quantity averages range from 27 percent of the U.S. average for Group I to 82 percent for Group IV in 1970, and from 29 percent for Group I to 85 percent for Group IV in 1973. Aside from fish, to which reference has already been made, the only food categories for which figures in excess of 100 are found in Table 4.12, indicating that the per capita quantity is larger than in the United States, are breads and cereals (all groups in both years), oils and fats (Group IV in both years), and, marginally, milk, cheese, and eggs (Group IV in 1973).

Outside of the food categories, the instances in which indexes exceed 100 include medical care (Group IV in 1970), purchased transport (Groups II and III in both years), and construction (Group IV in both years).

In Table 4.13 price levels for each category and country are compared with those of the United States. The figures in the table are derived by dividing the PPPs of Summary Multilateral Tables 4.3 and 4.8 by the appropriate exchange rates. In 1970, price levels for GDP as a whole and for consumption in its entirety were about 40 percent of U.S. price levels in Groups I and II, about 65 percent in Group III, and between 75 and 80 percent in Group IV. The products constituting capital formation are more expensive in the lower- and middle-income countries (Groups I–III) than the goods making up GDP as a whole.

For GDP as a whole, the price levels of Group I compared with the United States remained the same in 1973; prices rose, however, for Group II to 48 percent of the U.S. price level, for Group III to around 80 percent, and for Group IV to a point slightly above U.S. prices. These changes reflect a combination of relative (to the United States) internal rates of inflation and exchange-rate changes. For Group I relative inflation pushed the indexes up despite currency depreciations; for the other groups, particularly Groups III and IV, substantial appreciations accounted for most of the change.

For the most part, the individual categories follow the price patterns described above for GDP as a whole, but there are some notable deviations. A few categories are characterized by much smaller differences between the lowest and the highest price groups than the twofold to threefold price spread

Table 4.12. Average Quantities per Capita for Groups of Countries Classified by Real per Capita GDP, 1970 and 1973

(United States = 100)

Category	Line numbers [a]	Group I	Group II	Group III	Group IV	Group V
1970						
Consumption, ICP	1–110	10.0	19.1	50.3	65.8	100.0
Food	1–33	26.5	38.8	72.8	81.5	100.0
Bread and cereals	1–6	146.9	118.1	158.5	118.8	100.0
Meat	7–12	11.0	27.1	61.7	88.2	100.0
Fish	13–14	67.8	82.1	125.2	81.6	100.0
Milk, cheese, and eggs	15–17	9.8	32.2	62.0	89.2	100.0
Oils and fats	18–20	13.3	26.4	80.1	111.7	100.0
Fruits and vegetables	21–26	17.5	30.9	69.0	66.4	100.0
Clothing and footwear	40–51	8.6	19.6	56.0	67.1	100.0
Clothing	40–47	8.8	17.2	55.2	66.4	100.0
Footwear	48–51	7.4	34.3	61.2	71.9	100.0
Gross rents and fuel	52–57	5.0	14.7	38.1	54.9	100.0
Gross rents	52–53	4.5	17.1	38.4	56.5	100.0
House furnishings and operations	58–71	5.3	15.1	40.2	90.5	100.0
Medical care	72–78	8.1	16.9	87.0	100.4	100.0
Transport and communications	79–91	2.6	10.3	21.8	31.9	100.0
Equipment	79–80	0.3	2.1	13.9	26.2	100.0
Purchased transport	85–89	36.3	111.3	106.0	89.6	100.0
Recreation and education	92–103	10.8	14.2	50.6	58.1	100.0
Recreation	92–98	3.2	6.2	41.8	49.5	100.0
Education	99–103	22.7	26.7	64.2	71.5	100.0
Capital formation	111–148	6.7	21.5	76.9	114.1	100.0
Construction	111–124	10.1	30.7	80.4	124.1	100.0
Producers' durables	125–146	4.7	8.0	63.7	89.2	100.0
Government	149–153	10.1	15.9	34.2	45.9	100.0
Compensation	149–152	20.4	26.8	50.5	73.6	100.0
Commodities	153–153	3.5	9.0	23.8	28.1	100.0
Gross domestic product	1–153	9.3	19.2	53.6	73.0	100.0
1973						
Consumption, ICP	1–110	10.2	19.7	51.3	66.7	100.0
Food	1–33	28.7	39.6	75.0	85.1	100.0
Bread and cereals	1–6	154.5	125.2	151.3	112.9	100.0
Meat	7–12	12.1	29.2	69.3	96.9	100.0
Fish	13–14	85.8	81.7	133.3	89.3	100.0
Milk, cheese, and eggs	15–17	10.9	31.6	68.8	100.4	100.0
Oils and fats	18–20	13.9	29.3	83.1	119.9	100.0
Fruits and vegetables	21–26	18.0	35.5	75.3	76.5	100.0
Clothing and footwear	40–51	10.2	19.0	56.5	66.9	100.0
Clothing	40–47	10.4	16.3	56.4	67.6	100.0
Footwear	48–51	9.0	35.2	57.9	62.6	100.0
Gross rents and fuel	52–57	4.8	17.5	37.6	55.4	100.0
Gross rents	52–53	4.1	19.3	37.3	55.4	100.0
House furnishings and operations	58–71	5.2	16.8	43.5	90.5	100.0
Medical care	72–78	8.2	15.8	86.0	95.3	100.0
Transport and communications	79–91	2.4	11.1	21.8	28.7	100.0
Equipment	79–80	0.3	2.2	14.4	21.0	100.0
Purchased transport	85–89	39.1	146.7	108.1	86.2	100.0
Recreation and education	92–103	10.3	16.8	50.2	58.4	100.0
Recreation	92–98	3.0	7.1	40.3	49.4	100.0
Education	99–103	21.8	32.0	65.8	72.4	100.0
Capital formation	111–148	7.6	29.2	69.9	107.8	100.0
Construction	111–124	10.5	34.5	79.6	118.9	100.0
Producers' durables	125–146	4.7	9.4	62.4	80.8	100.0
Government	149–153	11.9	22.5	40.4	53.3	100.0
Compensation	149–152	21.8	30.0	53.1	82.1	100.0
Commodities	153–153	4.9	17.3	31.5	33.0	100.0
Gross domestic product	1–153	9.8	22.1	54.2	74.3	100.0

Note: For countries included in each group, see page 116.
Source: Summary Multilateral Tables 4.4 and 4.9.
a. Line numbers refer to the Detailed Multilateral Tables and show the detailed categories that are included in each aggregation.

**Table 4.13. Average Price Indexes for Groups of Countries Classified
by Real per Capita GDP, 1970 and 1973**

(United States=100)

Category	Line numbers [a]	Group I	Group II	Group III	Group IV	Group V
1970						
Consumption ICP	1–110	39.1	40.5	64.8	79.9	100.0
Food	1–33	52.6	53.9	84.4	96.9	100.0
Bread and cereals	1–6	39.6	41.6	56.4	85.6	100.0
Meat	7–12	55.0	64.2	101.8	105.6	100.0
Fish	13–14	39.7	55.8	80.6	88.3	100.0
Milk, cheese, and eggs	15–17	65.4	51.7	75.3	73.3	100.0
Oils and fats	18–20	89.4	88.8	87.4	108.0	100.0
Fruits and vegetables	21–26	46.9	48.1	82.0	87.9	100.0
Clothing and footwear	40–51	45.6	42.1	73.9	98.3	100.0
Clothing	40–47	49.0	46.6	76.3	101.4	100.0
Footwear	48–51	32.5	28.6	63.2	83.0	100.0
Gross rents and fuel	52–57	46.4	46.2	66.6	72.6	100.0
Gross rents	52–53	56.0	44.1	60.0	61.9	100.0
House furnishings and operations	58–71	43.0	39.6	79.2	83.3	100.0
Medical care	72–78	17.1	24.2	26.4	43.5	100.0
Transport and communications	79–91	53.1	52.7	90.0	118.1	100.0
Equipment	79–80	174.2	166.2	117.9	123.8	100.0
Purchased transport	85–89	44.5	33.4	71.4	104.1	100.0
Recreation and education	92–103	20.5	29.2	54.3	78.9	100.0
Recreation	92–98	44.9	61.4	67.1	87.0	100.0
Education	99–103	13.2	17.4	42.2	73.3	100.0
Capital formation	111–148	55.8	47.2	73.6	78.6	100.0
Construction	111–124	36.9	26.2	60.8	62.3	100.0
Producers' durables	125–146	105.5	105.2	91.3	101.6	100.0
Government	149–153	19.7	36.0	60.1	82.0	100.0
Compensation	149–152	12.5	28.5	45.1	69.4	100.0
Commodities	153–153	42.0	48.0	73.5	84.7	100.0
Gross domestic product	1–153	38.5	41.2	65.8	78.0	100.0
1973						
Consumption ICP	1–110	39.3	45.5	78.9	109.2	100.0
Food	1–33	53.9	62.8	102.2	127.5	100.0
Bread and cereals	1–6	41.6	46.4	64.3	115.7	100.0
Meat	7–12	50.4	73.1	117.4	130.0	100.0
Fish	13–14	33.8	69.5	97.5	109.9	100.0
Milk, cheese, and eggs	15–17	64.2	60.5	92.6	98.6	100.0
Oils and fats	18–20	91.3	105.4	100.5	136.6	100.0
Fruits and vegetables	21–26	52.7	51.9	94.3	109.0	100.0
Clothing and footwear	40–51	46.6	47.8	91.2	131.7	100.0
Clothing	40–47	48.6	53.0	93.1	133.4	100.0
Footwear	48–51	36.4	31.9	82.1	123.9	100.0
Gross rents and fuel	52–57	49.2	46.3	84.7	99.2	100.0
Gross rents	52–53	58.1	47.3	80.5	87.6	100.0
House furnishings and operations	58–71	46.7	50.1	93.0	114.6	100.0
Medical care	72–78	16.4	25.4	32.1	67.1	100.0
Transport and communications	79–91	56.2	58.8	113.2	173.8	100.0
Equipment	79–80	167.7	176.0	142.8	178.9	100.0
Purchased transport	85–89	48.1	34.6	87.3	151.4	100.0
Recreation and education	92–103	20.2	34.6	69.8	112.4	100.0
Recreation	92–98	48.5	63.5	86.6	124.2	100.0
Education	99–103	12.5	21.9	53.7	103.5	100.0
Capital formation	111–148	58.6	56.8	89.5	100.8	100.0
Construction	111–124	35.2	28.9	73.4	79.6	100.0
Producers' durables	125–146	119.5	120.8	112.9	136.7	100.0
Government	149–153	18.6	41.2	73.7	112.5	100.0
Compensation	149–152	11.2	32.7	57.4	98.8	100.0
Commodities	153–153	41.8	51.5	88.8	109.3	100.0
Gross domestic product	1–153	39.0	48.0	80.6	105.0	100.0

Note: For countries included in each group, see page 116.
Source: Summary Multilateral Tables 4.3 and 4.8.
a. Line numbers refer to the Detailed Multilateral Tables and show the detailed categories that are included in each aggregation.

for overall GDP per capita.[4] Producers' durable goods exhibit the smallest international price differences, as might be expected from the high proportion of the production of these goods that enters international trade. This is true both in 1970, when the prices for producers' durables in Groups I to IV were either lower than or only slightly above U.S. prices, and in 1973, when they were 13 percent to 37 percent higher. Oils and fats, which were among the most expensive categories outside the United States, also exhibited relatively small price spreads.

Personal transport equipment, however, occupies the position of the highest price category in the low-income countries, probably reflecting high taxes in some countries, high-cost local production in others, and a combination of the two in still others. At the other extreme, labor-intensive categories such as the compensation of government employees and medical care tend to be very low in price in the low-income countries. It may be noted that construction, unlike producers' durables, tends to follow the same price pattern as GDP as a whole.

A different standard for assessing price structures is employed in Table 4.14. In this table, the percent distribution of expenditures in national currencies in Summary Multilateral Tables 4.2 and 4.7 is divided by the share of each category in expenditures in international dollars (the calculation of the share of international dollars being based on the data in Summary Multilateral Tables 4.5 and 4.10). The ratio computed in this way for each country is averaged to obtain the group figures shown in the table. For example, the 1970 entry of 1.07 for meat for Group I is an average of the ratios for Kenya, India, the Philippines, and the Republic of Korea. To carry the illustration one step further, the ratio for Korea was 1.30, which was derived by dividing the share of meat in GDP at national prices, 3.6 (Summary Multilateral Table 4.2), by the share of meat in GDP valued at international prices, 2.76 (calculated from Summary Multilateral Table 4.5).[5]

The significance of the ratio is brought out by examining its formula, which is:

$$(4.1) \qquad R_{ij} = \frac{P_{ij}Q_{ij}/\sum_{i=1}^{m} P_{ij}Q_{ij}}{\Pi_i Q_{ij}/\sum_{i=1}^{m} \Pi_i Q_{ij}},$$

where P_{ij} and Q_{ij} are the domestic price and quantity of the ith category in the jth country, and Π is the international price. It can be seen that R_{ij} is a measure of the relative price of each category in each country in comparison with the relative international price of the category. The R_{ij}s thus provide a means of comparing the price structures of different countries.

The value of R_{ij} for GDP as a whole is 1 (both the numerator and the denominator would be 1 for all of GDP.[6] Consequently, a value of more than

4. For GDP the 1970 spread is $\frac{\text{Group V}}{\text{Group I}} = \frac{100.0}{38.5} = 2.6$; for 1973 it is $\frac{\text{Group IV}}{\text{Group I}} = \frac{105.0}{39.0} = 2.7$.

5. Appendix Table 4.6 gives the relative price structures of the individual countries.

6. Benjamin B. King of the World Bank, who suggested the use of this ratio to show relative prices, has called attention to the fact that equation 4.1 is equivalent to

$$\frac{P_{ij}}{\Pi_i} \cdot \frac{1}{PPP_j}.$$

In this form, it is the ratio of national prices (deflated by the PPP for GDP as a whole) to international prices. King has also pointed out that the ratio of the expression 4.1 for country j to the same expression for the United States will be equal to the ratio of country j's PPP for category i to its PPP for GDP as a whole.

Table 4.14. Average Relation of National Price Structures to International Price Structures for Groups of Countries Classified by Real per Capita GDP, 1970 and 1973

Category	Line numbers [a]	Group I	Group II	Group III	Group IV	Group V
1970						
Consumption ICP	1–110	1.02	0.99	0.98	1.03	1.00
Food	1–33	1.08	1.02	1.01	0.97	0.78
Bread and cereals	1–6	1.05	1.01	0.85	1.09	0.99
Meat	7–12	1.07	1.16	1.18	1.01	0.74
Fish	13–14	0.88	1.18	1.04	0.98	0.86
Milk, cheese, and eggs	15–17	1.49	1.09	0.99	0.81	0.87
Oils and fats	18–20	1.39	1.28	0.81	0.82	0.60
Fruits and vegetables	21–26	1.10	1.02	1.08	0.98	0.87
Clothing and footwear	40–51	1.06	0.92	1.02	1.12	0.89
Clothing	40–47	1.10	0.99	1.02	1.12	0.87
Footwear	48–51	0.96	0.75	1.04	1.13	1.06
Gross rents and fuel	52–57	1.19	1.16	1.02	0.95	1.03
Gross rents	52–53	1.50	1.22	1.01	0.90	1.13
House furnishings and operations	58–71	1.02	0.89	1.13	0.98	0.92
Medical care	72–78	0.81	1.07	0.71	1.00	1.80
Transport and communications	79–91	1.12	1.04	1.13	1.24	0.82
Equipment	79–80	3.72	2.95	1.35	1.16	0.72
Purchased transport	85–89	1.09	0.78	1.05	1.28	0.97
Recreation and education	92–103	0.64	0.89	1.01	1.27	1.25
Recreation	92–98	1.15	1.48	0.98	1.11	0.99
Education	99–103	0.55	0.70	1.04	1.57	1.67
Capital formation	111–148	1.30	1.03	1.02	0.90	0.90
Construction	111–124	1.07	0.73	1.08	0.92	1.15
Producers' durables	125–146	1.94	1.74	0.97	0.89	0.68
Government	149–153	0.59	1.01	1.04	1.22	1.16
Compensation	149–152	0.48	1.04	1.00	1.34	1.51
Commodities	153–153	1.01	1.09	1.05	1.01	0.93
Gross domestic product	1–153	1.00	1.00	1.00	1.00	1.00
1973						
Consumption ICP	1–110	1.01	0.95	0.97	1.04	1.00
Food	1–33	1.09	1.02	0.98	0.94	0.77
Bread and cereals	1–6	1.06	0.97	0.76	1.07	0.98
Meat	7–12	1.03	1.20	1.14	0.97	0.79
Fish	13–14	0.81	1.35	1.08	0.97	0.94
Milk, cheese, and eggs	15–17	1.44	1.08	0.97	0.79	0.85
Oils and fats	18–20	1.40	1.31	0.75	0.77	0.60
Fruits and vegetables	21–26	1.25	0.96	1.03	0.92	0.89
Clothing and footwear	40–51	1.05	0.91	1.02	1.11	0.88
Clothing	40–47	1.07	0.99	1.02	1.09	0.86
Footwear	48–51	0.94	0.70	1.05	1.19	1.01
Gross rents and fuel	52–57	1.22	1.01	1.03	0.96	1.02
Gross rents	52–53	1.49	1.13	1.03	0.90	1.08
House furnishings and operations	58–71	1.08	0.95	1.08	1.00	0.91
Medical care	72–78	0.72	0.92	0.67	1.09	1.71
Transport and communications	79–91	1.18	0.98	1.17	1.37	0.83
Equipment	79–80	3.12	2.77	1.39	1.28	0.75
Purchased transport	85–89	1.20	0.70	1.08	1.41	0.98
Recreation and education	92–103	0.62	0.89	1.04	1.34	1.25
Recreation	92–98	1.16	1.29	1.00	1.15	0.97
Education	99–103	0.52	0.75	1.09	1.67	1.69
Capital formation	111–148	1.34	1.07	1.02	0.87	0.90
Construction	111–124	1.02	0.71	1.07	0.90	1.18
Producers' durables	125–146	2.09	1.74	0.98	0.88	0.67
Government	149–153	0.56	1.01	1.07	1.28	1.20
Compensation	149–152	0.43	1.04	1.06	1.46	1.56
Commodities	153–153	1.01	1.00	1.04	0.99	0.94
Gross domestic product	1–153	1.00	1.00	1.00	1.00	1.00

Note: For countries included in each group, see page 116.
Source: Summary Multilateral Tables 4.5 and 4.10.
a. Line numbers refer to the Detailed Multilateral Tables and show the detailed categories that are included in each aggregation.

1.00 for a given country in a given category indicates that, relative to the relationship of the country's prices to international prices for its GDP as a whole, its prices for that particular category are high. A figure below 1.00, on the other hand, indicates a category is cheap in the country's structure of relative prices compared with the world structure of relative prices.

In the lowest-income countries (Groups I and II) in both years, the most expensive items in the relative price structure compared with the world relative price structure are personal transport equipment and producers' durable goods. Other items that tend to be relatively high in price are milk, cheese, and eggs; oils and fats; housing space (that is, gross rents); and recreation.

In the highest-income countries (Groups IV and V), on the other hand, education and the compensation of government employees are among the most expensive categories. In the United States both of these categories are topped by medical care. Within capital formation, construction is cheap relative to producers' durables in the two lowest-income groups and is more expensive in the other three groups.

A further exploration of R_{ij} appears in Chapter 6.

Thus far, the results of the ICP have been analyzed in terms of the familiar functional classification of final expenditures (that is, food, clothing, and so forth). For some analytical purposes, it is useful to distinguish between commodities and services and between traded and nontraded goods. Accordingly, in this section the summary categories are aggregated to obtain expenditure, quantity, and price comparisons for commodities and services and for traded and nontraded goods. "Services" are defined to include categories in which expenditures are entirely on personnel (for example, domestic services, teachers, and government employees), repairs of various kinds (footwear, auto), rents, public transport and communication, public entertainment, and household services. All the other categories of GDP are regarded as "commodities." Services and one important commodity sector—construction—constitute nontraded goods; all other categories are placed in the traded classification.

The distribution of expenditures between services and commodities and between traded and nontraded goods is shown in Table 4.15, in terms of expenditures both at national prices and at international prices. Once again, the countries are ranked by order of increasing real per capita GDP, and averages are provided for five groups of countries in order to see more easily the structural changes associated with rising income levels.

An often-expressed generalization holds that the expenditures on services tend to rise as per capita incomes increases. Does this hold true on a cross-section basis for the sixteen ICP countries?

In terms of each country's own prices, the share of services in GDP (column 2) does tend to be positively associated with per capita GDP, ranging from an average of 22.5 percent in 1970 for the lowest-income countries (Group I) to 39.6 percent for the United States (Group V). When international prices are used, however, the share of services in GDP (column 7) of the low-income countries expands and that of the high-income countries contracts. Thus, in these terms, the share declines from 33 percent for Groups I and II to 26 percent for Group IV and 28 percent for the United States. Similar relationships prevail for 1973.

The differences in price structures producing these alternatives sets of results are set out in Table 4.16. Here the shares in expenditures at national prices are divided by the shares at international prices. As explained earlier, the result gives the ratio of the national prices for the category relative to the

Comparisons for Commodities and Services and for Traded and Nontraded Goods

Table 4.15. Division of Expenditures between Commodities and Services and between Traded and Nontraded Goods, 1970 and 1973

(Percentage)

Country	National prices Com-modities (1)	Ser-vices (2)	Traded goods (3)	Non-traded goods (4)	GDP (5)	International prices Com-modities (6)	Ser-vices (7)	Traded goods (8)	Non-traded goods (9)
				1970					
Group I	77.5	22.5	67.3	32.7	100.0	66.1	33.9	56.6	43.4
Kenya	69.6	30.4	60.0	40.1	100.0	63.0	37.0	55.8	44.2
India	82.8	17.1	73.4	26.6	100.0	67.0	33.0	55.8	44.2
Philippines	79.0	21.0	73.4	26.6	100.0	64.7	35.3	59.0	41.0
Korea, Republic of	78.5	21.5	62.5	37.5	100.0	69.8	30.2	55.6	44.4
Group II	71.1	28.9	60.5	39.5	100.0	67.0	33.0	52.6	47.4
Colombia	67.6	32.4	56.2	43.7	100.0	62.7	37.3	47.9	52.1
Malaysia	72.2	27.8	63.6	36.3	100.0	70.6	29.4	57.1	42.9
Iran	73.5	26.5	61.6	38.4	100.0	67.6	32.4	52.7	47.3
Group III	73.7	26.3	58.3	41.7	100.0	71.5	28.5	57.5	42.5
Hungary	79.3	20.7	60.6	39.3	100.0	68.6	31.4	53.4	46.6
Italy	71.7	28.2	57.0	43.0	100.0	71.9	28.1	56.5	43.5
Japan	76.8	23.2	57.1	42.9	100.0	74.4	25.6	58.5	41.5
United Kingdom	67.0	33.0	58.4	41.7	100.0	71.0	29.0	61.6	38.4
Group IV	70.3	29.6	56.6	43.3	100.0	73.5	26.5	58.3	41.7
Netherlands	71.1	28.8	57.3	42.6	100.0	75.4	24.6	58.4	41.6
Belgium	68.3	31.6	55.7	44.3	100.0	68.3	31.7	55.6	44.4
France	69.6	30.4	55.4	44.6	100.0	74.0	26.0	59.7	40.3
Germany, F.R.	72.1	27.8	58.0	41.9	100.0	76.3	23.7	59.7	40.3
Group V									
United States	60.4	39.6	50.5	49.5	100.0	71.9	28.1	63.3	36.7
				1973					
Group I	79.5	20.5	69.4	30.6	100.0	67.6	32.4	57.6	42.4
Kenya	70.6	29.4	58.6	41.4	100.0	63.7	36.3	55.4	44.6
India	83.3	16.6	75.3	24.7	100.0	65.2	34.8	54.9	45.1
Philippines	82.4	17.7	76.0	24.0	100.0	66.4	33.6	59.3	40.7
Korea, Republic of	81.7	18.3	67.5	32.5	100.0	75.0	25.0	61.0	39.0
Group II	73.8	26.1	63.3	36.6	100.0	68.1	31.9	53.3	46.7
Colombia	69.4	30.6	58.8	41.1	100.0	61.7	38.3	47.0	53.0
Malaysia	72.8	27.1	63.1	36.8	100.0	70.8	29.2	56.6	43.4
Iran	79.3	20.7	68.0	32.0	100.0	71.8	28.2	56.2	43.8
Group III	72.7	27.3	57.0	43.0	100.0	70.9	29.1	56.6	43.4
Hungary	80.2	19.8	62.3	37.7	100.0	69.4	30.6	54.1	45.9
Italy	69.3	30.6	56.3	43.6	100.0	70.4	29.6	56.0	44.0
Japan	76.1	23.9	53.5	46.4	100.0	74.1	25.9	56.5	43.5
United Kingdom	65.0	35.0	55.7	44.3	100.0	69.7	30.3	60.0	40.0
Group IV	69.0	31.0	55.7	44.3	100.0	72.8	27.2	57.8	42.2
Netherlands	70.0	30.0	56.4	43.6	100.0	75.9	24.1	59.3	40.7
Belgium	67.4	32.6	55.3	44.7	100.0	66.9	33.1	54.6	45.4
France	68.7	31.3	54.8	43.2	100.0	73.3	26.7	58.6	41.4
Germany, F.R.	69.9	30.0	56.3	43.6	100.0	75.2	24.8	58.8	41.2
Group V									
United States	60.9	39.0	50.1	49.9	100.0	72.1	27.9	62.9	37.1

Table 4.16. Relation of the National Price Structure to the International Price Structure, 1970 and 1973 [a]

	1970					1973				
Country	Com-modities (1)	Ser-vices (2)	Traded goods (3)	Non-traded goods (4)	GDP (5)	Com-modities (6)	Ser-vices (7)	Traded goods (8)	Non-traded goods (9)	GDP (10)
Group I	1.17	0.66	1.19	0.75	1.00	1.18	0.63	1.20	0.72	1.00
Kenya	1.10	0.82	1.08	0.91	1.00	1.11	0.81	1.06	0.93	1.00
India	1.24	0.52	1.32	0.60	1.00	1.28	0.48	1.37	0.55	1.00
Philippines	1.22	0.59	1.24	0.65	1.00	1.24	0.53	1.28	0.59	1.00
Korea, Republic of	1.12	0.71	1.12	0.84	1.00	1.09	0.73	1.11	0.83	1.00
Group II	1.06	0.88	1.15	0.83	1.00	1.08	0.82	1.19	0.78	1.00
Colombia	1.08	0.87	1.17	0.84	1.00	1.12	0.80	1.25	0.78	1.00
Malaysia	1.02	0.95	1.11	0.85	1.00	1.03	0.93	1.11	0.85	1.00
Iran	1.09	0.82	1.17	0.81	1.00	1.10	0.73	1.21	0.73	1.00
Group III	1.03	0.92	1.01	0.98	1.00	1.03	0.94	1.01	0.99	1.00
Hungary	1.16	0.66	1.13	0.84	1.00	1.16	0.65	1.15	0.82	1.00
Italy	1.00	1.00	1.01	0.99	1.00	0.98	1.03	1.01	0.99	1.00
Japan	1.03	0.91	0.98	1.03	1.00	1.03	0.92	0.95	1.07	1.00
United Kingdom	0.94	1.14	0.95	1.09	1.00	0.93	1.16	0.93	1.11	1.00
Group IV	0.96	1.12	0.97	1.04	1.00	0.95	1.14	0.96	1.05	1.00
Netherlands	0.94	1.17	0.98	1.02	1.00	0.92	1.24	0.95	1.07	1.00
Belgium	1.00	1.00	1.00	1.00	1.00	1.01	0.98	1.01	0.98	1.00
France	0.94	1.17	0.93	1.11	1.00	0.94	1.17	0.94	1.09	1.00
Germany, F.R.	0.94	1.17	0.97	1.04	1.00	0.93	1.21	0.96	1.06	1.00
Group V United States	0.84	1.41	0.80	1.35	1.00	0.84	1.40	0.80	1.35	1.00

Source: Table 4.15.

a. Ratio of the share of each component in GDP in national prices to its share in international prices.

average international price, with this ratio being taken relative to the corresponding ratio for GDP as a whole. It is therefore a measure of each country's—in this case, each group's—own price structure relative to an international price structure, with the figures being normalized around a ratio of 1 for GDP as a whole.[7]

The price of services in this double relative sense rises with per capita income; in 1970 it is 0.66 for Group I countries and 1.41 for the United States, and in 1973 it is 0.63 for Group I countries and 1.40 for the United States. The relative price of commodities moves in the opposite direction; it is 1.17 in 1970 and 1.18 in 1973 for Group I countries and 0.84 in both years for the United States. The rise in relative prices for services is an important factor pushing up the share of expenditures on services in terms of own currency.

The addition of construction to the service categories to form the aggregate of nontraded goods narrows the difference between relative prices for low- and high-income countries, but not by much. Relative prices for nontraded goods rise in both years from approximately 0.75 for Group I to approximately 1.35 for the United States. The relative prices of traded goods on the other hand decline in both years from around 1.20 to 0.80 for the two extreme income groups.

A similar story emerges in columns 6 to 10 of Table 4.17, in which the

7. Note, however, that equation 4.1 indicates that each country's ratio of its own to international prices for GDP as a whole is weighted by its own quantities.

Table 4.17. Quantity and Price Indexes per Capita for Commodities and Services and for Traded and Nontraded Goods, 1970 and 1973

(United States = 100)

Country	Quantity ratios					Price indexes				
	Com-modities (1)	Ser-vices (2)	Traded goods (3)	Non-traded goods (4)	GDP (5)	Com-modities (6)	Ser-vices (7)	Traded goods (8)	Non-traded goods (9)	GDP (10)
1970										
Group I	8.6	11.1	8.4	11.0	9.3	53.1	18.7	56.5	22.1	38.5
Kenya	5.6	8.3	5.6	7.6	6.3	62.2	27.6	63.7	31.7	47.3
India	6.5	8.1	6.1	8.3	6.9	44.2	11.1	49.6	13.4	30.0
Philippines	10.8	15.1	11.2	13.4	12.0	46.7	13.6	50.2	15.4	32.1
Korea, Republic of	11.8	13.0	10.6	14.7	12.1	59.5	22.5	62.7	27.8	44.5
Group II	17.9	22.5	15.9	24.8	19.2	52.1	25.6	59.5	25.4	41.2
Colombia	15.8	24.1	13.7	25.8	18.1	51.2	24.5	58.8	24.8	39.9
Malaysia	18.8	20.0	17.2	22.4	19.1	51.6	28.4	59.2	26.6	42.3
Iran	19.1	23.4	18.9	26.2	20.3	53.4	24.0	60.5	24.8	41.3
Group III	53.5	54.0	49.1	61.5	53.6	80.1	44.3	83.3	48.6	65.8
Hungary	40.7	47.6	36.0	54.2	42.7	69.8	23.8	72.3	31.7	50.7
Italy	49.2	49.1	43.8	58.4	49.2	86.8	52.1	92.6	53.4	73.1
Japan	61.3	53.9	54.6	67.0	59.2	82.8	43.2	82.5	51.5	67.3
United Kingdom	62.7	65.5	61.7	66.4	63.5	81.0	58.2	85.7	57.9	72.1
Group IV	74.7	68.7	67.3	82.9	73.0	89.0	62.5	95.1	60.2	78.0
Netherlands	72.0	60.1	63.3	78.0	68.7	83.1	61.4	91.2	56.0	73.9
Belgium	68.5	81.1	63.2	87.3	72.0	91.2	54.2	96.2	56.5	76.5
France	75.4	67.6	69.0	80.4	73.2	89.2	66.0	92.7	65.2	79.6
Germany, F.R.	83.0	66.0	73.7	86.0	78.2	92.4	68.2	100.1	63.2	82.0
Group V										
United States	100.0	100.0	100.0	100.0	100.0	100.0	100.0	100.0	100.0	100.0
1973										
Group I	9.4	10.9	9.1	11.0	9.8	53.9	18.4	58.1	21.7	39.0
Kenya	5.4	8.0	5.4	7.4	6.1	63.8	28.2	64.6	33.5	48.6
India	5.8	7.9	5.6	7.8	6.4	49.5	11.2	56.4	13.3	32.7
Philippines	11.2	14.7	11.5	13.4	12.2	50.3	12.9	55.2	15.0	34.3
Korea, Republic of	15.2	13.1	14.1	15.3	14.6	52.1	21.2	56.2	25.1	40.5
Group II	21.1	24.6	18.9	27.4	22.0	61.4	28.3	71.5	28.1	48.0
Colombia	15.3	24.5	13.4	25.5	17.9	52.9	22.7	62.6	23.0	39.8
Malaysia	18.7	19.9	17.1	22.3	19.1	65.2	35.6	75.2	33.8	53.6
Iran	29.1	29.5	26.1	34.5	29.2	65.9	26.5	76.7	27.4	50.5
Group III	53.4	56.1	49.0	63.0	54.2	96.7	55.5	100.7	60.8	80.6
Hungary	43.4	49.5	38.8	55.8	45.1	79.2	26.8	83.8	35.4	58.0
Italy	45.9	49.9	41.9	55.8	47.0	101.0	64.1	109.5	63.9	86.7
Japan	65.8	59.3	57.4	75.1	64.0	114.6	62.2	112.3	74.8	94.4
United Kingdom	58.5	65.8	57.8	65.3	60.6	92.2	69.0	97.4	68.9	83.6
Group IV	75.0	72.4	68.3	84.5	74.3	117.7	86.9	127.0	82.2	105.0
Netherlands	72.0	59.0	64.4	75.1	68.4	113.3	92.6	124.3	82.7	104.0
Belgium	69.8	89.4	65.4	92.1	75.3	118.0	69.8	125.8	72.6	99.0
France	77.3	72.7	70.8	84.9	76.1	112.4	85.1	119.1	82.3	101.4
Germany, F.R.	80.7	68.7	72.4	85.9	77.4	127.0	100.1	138.8	91.1	115.5
Group V										
United States	100.0	100.0	100.0	100.0	100.0	100.0	100.0	100.0	100.0	100.0

prices of services and of nontraded goods are compared with the U.S. relative price structure rather than the international structure. The prices of services (column 7) rise from 19 percent of the U.S. prices for Group I in 1970 to 62 percent for Group IV, and nontraded goods (column 9) rise from 22 percent to 60 percent. A similar progression occurs with a larger upward thrust in 1973. In both years the prices of commodities (column 6) and of traded goods (column 8) are also positively associated with income levels. Even the Group I prices, however, are more than half of the U.S. levels for commodities and traded goods (compared to the less than one-fourth level for services and nontraded goods). Thus, the dispersion of price levels is smaller for commodities than for services and for traded goods than for nontraded goods. Also, the depreciation of the U.S. dollar leads to 1973 commodity and traded goods prices for Group IV countries that are higher than U.S. prices, and the same is true for some Group III countries.

In view of these sharp differences in price relationships for commodities versus services and for traded versus nontraded goods, it is of interest to note that the lower-income countries tend to absorb slightly larger quantities of services than of commodities relative to the higher-income countries. In 1970, for example, the Group I countries had an average quantity index for services (column 2) of 11.1 and an average quantity index for commodities (column 1) of 8.6; the corresponding indexes for the Group IV countries were 68.7 and 74.7. (The Group II averages also had a larger quantity index for services, but the Group III quantity indexes for services and commodities are about equal.) There is also some tendency for the quantity indexes for nontraded goods to be higher for the low-income countries relative to their indexes for traded goods, but the progression toward lower ratios of nontraded to traded goods quantity indexes as per capita incomes rise is hardly an even one. Even in terms of the group averages, the nontraded-to-traded quantity index ratio in both years rises from Group I to Group II, although it falls from Group II to Group III and (slightly) from Group III to Group IV.

Thus, the positive association between the share of services in expenditures and per capita income that has been so widely commented upon reflects, if this cross-section sample of sixteen countries is typical, mainly a tendency for services to become more expensive as income rises rather than a tendency toward the consumption of relatively greater quantities of services. Services do increase with rising income but, if their prices did not rise, the service share would remain constant or even diminish (compare columns 2 and 5 of Table 4.17). The sharp rise in service prices (column 7 of Table 4.17) inhibits the increase in their consumption, but not so much that their share of expenditures does not rise.

The relationships outlined above may be explained in terms of the productivity differential model described in Chapter 1 and treated at greater length elsewhere.[8] Briefly, the argument runs as follows: (1) International competition makes the prices of traded goods equal in all countries. (2) Wages in each country's traded goods industries will depend upon the productivity of its labor in those industries. (3) The wages established in each country's traded goods industries will prevail in its nontraded goods industries as well. (4) Productivity differentials are smaller in nontraded goods industries than in traded goods industries. (5) It follows that nontraded goods, of which services are a major component, will be relatively cheap in low-

8. Irving B. Kravis, Alan Heston, and Robert Summers, "Real GDP Per Capita for More than One Hundred Countries," *Economic Journal* 88, no. 350 (June 1978), pp. 1–29.

income countries. That is, low wages of low-income countries, established by their low productivity in traded goods production, extend to the nontraded goods industries in which relatively better productivity produces low prices.

Approximations to Real GDP per Capita for Other Years

Although it has taken a great deal of work to produce the comparisons for the sixteen countries for two reference years, these comparisons represent only a small part of what is needed for most practical and analytical purposes. What is required is a set of comprehensive annual comparisons covering all or at least a high proportion of the countries of the world.

The expansion of the system to a large number of countries by the present methods will at best take a long time, and it is not at all certain that the resources will be available to do the job. Even with the most optimistic appraisal of the future for ICP-type work, it is unrealistic to believe that the methods described in Chapter 3 can be applied to every country; some just will be unable to supply the requisite data, and others will not be willing to do the work.

The question that arises now and that will persist for the foreseeable future is whether the experience and data of the ICP can be used to produce better estimates of real GDP per capita than exchange-rate conversions for countries for which benchmark ICP estimates are not available. There will be a better basis for answering this question at the end of Phase III when comparisons for approximately thirty countries will be available. It is already clear from the data of the sixteen Phase II countries that pairs of countries with not too similar per capita incomes can better be compared using adjustment factors based upon ICP data than by means of exchange-rate conversions. Work under way on methods of using ICP data to aid in obtaining at least rough approximations of real GDP per capita for non-ICP countries is reported upon elsewhere.[9]

The other need—to keep the estimates up to date for the countries that have been included in the system, is somewhat easier to meet—and it is treated in this section. The need for annual comparisons can be satisfied in a reasonably satisfactory manner because, once there is a benchmark estimate for a country, its own time-to-time data, in conjunction with corresponding data for the base country, may be used to adjust the comparison to other years.

Some methodological problems

Two main methodological decisions must be made, one relating to the choice between alternative concepts of aggregate output or income that should be employed and the other concerning the degree of disaggregation employed in the extrapolations of the estimates for benchmark years to other years. The conceptual problem is treated first, assuming for the moment that the extrapolations are performed at the aggregate GDP level (that is, with no disaggregating).

The quantity change in the per capita GDP in constant prices of each partner country relative to the base country appears to provide the most straightforward method of extrapolation. The index of a country's real GDP per capita Q_{jt} (with the United States equal to 100) in the benchmark year may be extrapolated to any year t from a base year 0 by applying the formula:

$$(4.2) \qquad Q_{jt} = Q_{j0} \cdot \frac{G_{jt}/G_{j0}}{G_{US,t}/G_{US,0}},$$

where G = GDP per capita in constant prices of the jth country in the tth year.

9. See ibid.

This was the formula used in *A System* to compare the 1970 ICP results with extrapolations of the Gilbert and Kravis 1950 estimates for France, the Federal Republic of Germany, Italy, and the United Kingdom.[10] Since the formula holds all the prices of the benchmark year constant, including the prices of exports and imports, changes in a country's terms of trade cannot influence the measured change in the country's real GDP. The formula therefore yields an extrapolation of relative real output *produced*. If the aim is to measure the relative *real income* at the disposal of the country in each year, it is necessary to take into account the extent to which that income is larger or smaller because the country obtains a different quantity of imports per unit of exports.[11] For many countries trade is a small fraction of GDP and/or changes in the terms of trade over short periods are small. In such cases, ignoring terms of trade considerations would not give a misleading measure of the change in real income. The years since 1970, however, and especially those beginning in 1973 have seen sufficiently large changes in international price relationships so that the real per capita incomes of some countries, particularly oil exporters, rose relative to their production of goods and services. By the same token, perhaps as important, higher import prices of some commodities made the real incomes of other countries lower than what the constant price GDP figures indicate.

Since the ICP focuses on the comparisons of income rather than product, where a distinction exists between the two,[12] it was necessary to devise a method of extrapolation that takes account of the impact on real income of changes in the terms of trade.

The portion of GDP representing "domestic absorption"—that is, expenditures on GDP minus the net foreign balance (exports minus imports)—can be extrapolated from a benchmark year to a given year by a formula directly analogous to equation 4.2. For most countries both the expenditure data and the necessary price series are available for the extrapolation of real domestic absorption from one year to the next.

The difficult problem lies in the handling of the net foreign balance. There is no wholly satisfactory way to incorporate the effects on real income of changes in the terms of trade. This is because there are no uniquely appropriate price indexes for the deflation of the net foreign balance that will measure its contribution to real income.[13] Results based on two alternative approaches are presented here, although others were included in experimental work.[14]

10. See Irving B. Kravis, Zoltan Kenessey, Alan Heston, and Robert Summers, *A System of International Comparisons of Gross Product and Purchasing Power* (Baltimore: Johns Hopkins University Press, 1975), pp. 8–9; referred to as *A System*. The Gilbert and Kravis 1950 estimates are found in M. Gilbert and Kravis, *An International Comparison of National Products and the Purchasing Power of Currencies* (Paris: Organization for European Economic Development, 1954).

11. The authors were reminded of the distinction between the two approaches by Jack Hibbert of the United Kingdom's Central Statistical Office. See Jack Hibbert, "International Comparisons on the Basis of Purchasing Power Parities," *Economic Trends,* No. 265 (November 1975), especially Appendix II.

12. See *A System,* p. 20 f.

13. For a summary of alternative methods in the intertemporal context, see R. C. Geary, "Introduction to Part I: Problems in the Deflation of National Accounts," in *Studies in Social and Financial Accounting,* ed. Phyllis Deane (London: Bowes and Bowes, 1961).

14. An additional alternative considered seriously but not offered in the text is to gauge the contribution to real income of the net foreign balance in terms of domestic opportunity cost. This would call for the use of price indexes for domestically absorbed GDP for the foreign balance as well. In the ICP context this solution has the dis-

Of the two procedures tried, the one closest in spirit to the ICP practice for benchmark years involves the use of the international price for the net foreign balance for the benchmark years. The average international price for an expenditure category, it will be recalled from Chapter 3, is used to evaluate the quantity absorbed by each country in the category. The quantities obtained are notional quantities, obtained by dividing expenditures in own currency by the purchasing-power parity of the country for the category. In the case of the net foreign balance the exchange rate is taken as the purchasing-power parity.

It may be noted that for all categories of expenditure other than the net foreign balance, the international prices of the benchmark year are used implicitly to evaluate the quantities of the year for which the extrapolation is being made. This is the case because, as can be seen from formula 4.2, the benchmark international dollar totals are extrapolated to the new year on the basis of real quantity changes.

For the net foreign balance, however, there is no satisfactory estimate for each country of the real quantity change. What must be found is a way to apply the international price of the benchmark year directly to the net foreign balance of the new year. The difficulty is that the net foreign balance will be affected by price changes between the benchmark year and the extrapolation year. If there has been a sharp inflation, for example, the difference between exports and imports for a surplus country will be a larger magnitude than if the price had remained unchanged, all other things, including the physical volume of exports and imports, being equal. If the inflation were worldwide, it would not be offset by the division of exchange rates. A way must therefore be found to deflate the net foreign balance of the extrapolation year to prices of the benchmark year. There are two choices. One is to find some world average rate of inflation for exports and imports, and the other is to use the price change of exports and imports in the numéraire country. The latter option has been chosen because it is more consistent with the character of the international price used in the ICP. As explained in Chapter 3, each ICP international price is expressed relative to the corresponding U.S. category price. When a country's notional quantity for a category is valued at the appropriate international price, the U.S. price element in the notional quantity cancels out the U.S. price element in the international price. This preserves the original spirit of the Geary equations. In order to avoid the difficulties inherent in the separate deflation of exports and imports, the average of the U.S. export and import implicit deflators has been used.

The formulas for this approach to extrapolation, which will be referred to as the "international price" method, are:

$$(4.3) \qquad DA_{jt}{}^{\Pi} = DA_{j0}{}^{\Pi} \cdot \frac{DA_{jt}{}^{dk}}{DA_{j0}{}^{dk}},$$

where $DA_{j0}{}^{\Pi} = \dfrac{X_{j0}{}^{dc} - M_{j0}{}^{dc}}{ER_{j0}} \cdot \Pi_{NFB,\ 0}$;

$$(4.4) \qquad NFB_{jt}{}^{\Pi} = \Pi_{NFB,0} \cdot \frac{X_{jt}{}^{dc} - M_{jt}{}^{dc}}{ER_{jt}} \Big/ \frac{P_{US,t}{}^{XM}}{P_{US,0}{}^{XM}},$$

where $DA_{jt}{}^{\Pi} =$ per capita domestic absorption expressed in international prices in the jth country in the tth year;

---

advantage that it is inconsistent with the ICP's use of exchange rates in the benchmark years as the PPP for net foreign claims. The ICP rationale is that the investigation of PPPs is based on the fundamental assumption that each sector has its own PPP and that no sector can be assessed in terms of opportunity costs based on others. The reductio ad absurdum of the denial of individual PPPs for each sector would allow a comparison based upon the PPP of any single arbitrarily selected category.

$DA_{jt}{}^{dk}$ = per capita domestic absorption, expressed in its own constant prices in the jth country in the tth year;

$NFB_{jt}{}^{II}$ = per capita net foreign balance (exports minus imports), expressed in international prices, in the jth country in the tth year;

$\Pi_{NFB,0}$ = the international price of the net foreign balance in the benchmark year;

$X_{jt}{}^{dc}$ = per capita exports, expressed in current domestic currency prices, of the jth country in the tth year;

$M_{jt}{}^{dc}$ = per capita imports, expressed in current domestic currency prices, of the jth country in the tth year;

ER_{jt} = exchange rate (local currency units per dollar) of the jth country in the tth year;

$P_{US,t}{}^{XM}$ = the average of the implicit deflators for U.S. exports and imports in the tth year.

The total per capita GDP in international dollars of country j for the year t may be obtained by adding $DA_j{}^{II}$ to $NFB_j{}^{II}$ for the extrapolation year t. The international dollar GDP for the numéraire country is obtained in the same way and is used as the base for the calculation of the sought-after index number of real GDP per capita.

The alternative procedure is to deflate a positive foreign balance by an index of the country's import price (which shows how the real ability to command goods abroad changed) and a negative balance by the country's export prices (which shows how much the country would have to give up to pay the external debt incurred). The formulas for this approach, which will be referred to as the "net deflation" method, appear in the following equations:

$$(4.5) \qquad Q_{jt} = Q_{j0} \cdot \frac{F_{jt}}{F_{US,t}},$$

$$(4.6) \qquad F_{jt} = \frac{\dfrac{DA_{jt}{}^{dc}}{P_{jt}{}^{DA}/P_{j0}{}^{DA}} + \dfrac{X_{jt}{}^{dc} - M_{jt}{}^{dc}}{P_{jt}{}^{xm}/P_{j0}{}^{xm}}}{\text{GDP}_{j0}{}^{dc}},$$

where $DA_{jt}{}^{dc}$ = per capita domestic absorption expressed in current domestic currency prices for the jth country in the tth year;

$\text{GDP}_{jt}{}^{dc}$ = per capita GDP in current domestic currency prices for the jth country in the tth year;

$P_{jt}{}^{DA}$ = price index for domestic absorption for the jth country in the tth year;

$P_{jt}{}^{xm}$ = the price index for imports when X>M and for exports when X<M, for the jth country in the tth year;

F_{jt} = change in the jth country's income between the base and t^{th} years.

and the other symbols have the same meanings as before.

These two methods are used in Table 4.18 to extrapolate the 1970 ICP results for per capita GDP to 1973. The extrapolations in columns 2 and 3 may then be compared with the actual ICP results for 1973 (in column 1). In most of the fourteen cases for which comparisons can be made, the international price method produces a 1973 estimate that is marginally closer to the 1973 actual (compare columns 5 and 6). The only large difference is for Iran, a country with a very large 1973 net foreign balance; here the international price method comes much closer than the net deflation method.

As a matter of information, extrapolations assuming constant terms of trade (using formula 4.2) are also shown in Table 4.18 (column 4). It can be seen that these extrapolations are substantially short of the mark for Iran, Kenya, the Philippines, and Colombia, and they are somewhat less so for

Table 4.18. Results of Alternative Methods of Estimating 1973 Real per Capita GDP Compared with Actual ICP Figures

Country	1973 ICP actual (1)	1970 ICP actual extrapolated to 1973			Ratios of 1973 estimates to 1973 actuals			Net foreign balance as percent of GDP (international dollars)	
		Allowing for changes in terms of trade		Constant terms of trade (4)	(5)= (2)÷(1)	(6)= (3)÷(1)	(7)= (4)÷(1)	1970 (8)	1973 (9)
		International price method (2)	Net deflation method (3)						
Kenya	6.12	5.90	6.16	5.53	0.964	0.997	0.904	−1.22	−0.79
India	6.37	—	—	5.90	—	—	—	−0.30	−0.20
Philippines	12.2	11.5	11.7	11.1	0.943	0.961	0.909	−0.23	1.22
Korea, Republic of	14.6	13.9	14.2	13.8	0.952	0.969	0.945	−6.65	−1.72
Colombia	17.9	18.2	18.3	16.6	1.017	1.022	0.927	−0.98	0.95
Malaysia	19.1	20.6	20.5	20.6	1.079	1.073	1.079	2.81	3.57
Iran	29.2	26.9	25.7	24.6	0.921	0.880	0.843	3.62	15.39
Hungary	45.1	44.6	45.7	46.2	0.989	1.013	1.024	−2.18	3.13
Italy	47.0	47.1	47.2	47.5	1.002	1.004	1.010	0.63	−2.51
Japan	64.0	64.5	64.3	64.1	1.008	1.005	1.002	1.32	0.02
United Kingdom	60.6	62.3	62.2	63.6	1.028	1.026	1.050	0.99	−2.49
Netherlands	68.4	69.5	68.6	67.1	1.016	1.003	0.981	−1.99	3.87
Belgium	75.3	75.2	74.3	76.0	0.999	0.987	1.009	2.75	2.89
France	76.1	76.0	75.8	74.4	0.999	0.996	0.978	0.71	0.93
Germany, F.R.	77.4	77.8	77.0	76.9	1.005	0.995	0.994	2.35	4.35
United States	100.0	100.0	100.0	100.0	1.000	1.000	1.000	0.31	0.09

Sources: Column 1: Table 1.2. Column 2: Formulas 4.3 and 4.4. Column 3: Formulas 4.5 and 4.6. Column 4: Formula 4.2. Column 8: Appendix Table 4.5. Column 9: Corresponding 1973 table to Appendix Table 4.5 (not published).

the Republic of Korea. The explanation may lie in an improvement in the terms of trade for primary exporters between 1970 and 1973.[15] This does not, however, explain the case of the Republic of Korea for which the largest part of exports are basic and miscellaneous manufactures.[16]

Because of the greater consistency of the international price approach with ICP methods and in view of the (admittedly limited) empirical evidence in its favor found in Table 4.18, this method has been adopted for the extrapolation of ICP indexes from benchmark years to other years.

It has been assumed thus far that the extrapolations are made at a highly aggregated level—that is, for GDP as a whole. Extrapolations at this level have the effect of adjusting the partner country's quantities using its own price weights while adjusting the base country's quantities using *its* price weights. Thus, the more extensive the changes in price structure between the given year and the benchmark year, the further removed are the results from the ideal, which would be to value the relative quantities of the different countries at current international prices. This objection would be diminished

15. It seems likely that such an improvement occurred, although actual export or import price indexes are available to measure changes in the terms of trade for only a few countries. The United Nations reports an 80 percent rise in export prices for primary commodities between 1970 and 1973 and a 34 percent rise in unit values for manufactured exports. See United Nations, *Monthly Bulletin of Statistics,* September 1976, p. xx. The unit values are unreliable measures of price change, but their bias is likely to be upwards. See I. B. Kravis and R. E. Lipsey, *Price Competitiveness in World Trade* (New York: National Bureau of Economic Research, 1971), pp. 4–5 and 17.

16. SITC sections 6 and 8, respectively. See United Nations, *Standard International Trade Classification, Revised,* Statistical Papers, No. 34 (New York: United Nations, 1961).

if the extrapolation were carried out at a very detailed level. At the extreme, one could imagine that each individual price could be extrapolated from the benchmark year to each given year; in this case it would be possible, at least as far as the price requirements are concerned, to make a full benchmark comparison for each year.

Since it is not feasible to obtain such detailed data annually for a large number of countries, a compromise has to be found between this extreme degree of disaggregation and the opposite end of the spectrum represented by extrapolations based on GDP as a whole. The updating worksheet, already referred to and appended to Chapter 2, has been developed with this need in mind; it provides the necessary data in the form of current and constant price expenditures for each of the 36 summary categories. These data can be used to make extrapolations of the PPPS for each of the summary categories. The new PPPS and the expenditures for all the included countries for each of the summary categories, except the net foreign balance, may then be used as inputs for a Geary-Khamis calculation that will value each country's quantities at current international prices. As in the full-scale benchmark comparisons, the net foreign balance will be treated by taking the current year exchange rate as the PPP, and a supercountry-weighted international price will be calculated and used to value the notional quantities. This procedure will ensure the measurement of real income rather than real product. Of course, the use of 36 summary categories will not produce identical results to those obtained from 153 detailed categories, but the experiment reported in Chapter 3 (see Table 3.3) gives hope that the differences will not be great.

For the present, however, the extrapolations have been carried out at the aggregative level, simply on grounds of expediency. It is planned to ask ICP countries to provide the constant and current price expenditures for a 36-category breakdown of GDP in future years.

The results of applying the international price method are represented by the annual approximations to real GDP per capita for the sixteen Phase II countries for the period 1965–75 presented in Table 4.19.

Where the benchmark indexes are available, they are the ones entered in the table. Thus, the figures for 1970 and 1973 are the ICP results reported in Table 1.2 and in Summary Multilateral Tables 4.4 and 4.9 For 1967 the

Approximations for 1965–75

Table 4.19. Approximate Indexes of Real GDP per Capita, 1965–75

Country	1965	1966	1967	1968	1969	1970	1971	1972	1973	1974	1975
Kenya	5.18	5.47	5.64	5.62	5.77	6.33	6.44	6.19	6.12	6.23	6.09
India	—	—	6.93	—	—	6.92	—	—	6.37	—	—
Philippines	12.9	12.6	13.0	12.6	12.4	12.0	11.9	12.0	12.2	13.1	13.9
Korea, Republic of	9.8	10.2	10.8	11.0	11.8	12.1	13.2	13.3	14.6	15.9	16.9
Colombia	19.5	19.6	18.8	18.1	17.7	18.1	18.3	18.1	17.9	19.4	19.8
Malaysia	22.0	21.3	20.7	19.2	19.1	19.1	18.7	18.0	19.1	21.8	19.9
Iran	17.8	18.2	19.5	19.6	19.4	20.3	22.2	23.1	29.2	36.7	40.8
Hungary	33.4	34.4	37.6	37.1	39.0	42.7	45.5	44.4	45.1	49.6	—
Italy	47.7	47.7	49.9	48.6	47.9	49.2	48.0	46.9	47.0	47.7	47.1
Japan	42.7	44.4	48.3	51.8	54.4	59.2	61.4	62.9	64.0	63.2	65.1
United Kingdom	63.3	61.6	61.9	61.5	61.2	63.5	63.4	61.7	60.6	60.5	62.0
Netherlands	69.9	68.0	69.8	68.9	67.7	68.7	69.1	68.8	68.4	70.3	70.5
Belgium	73.1	71.5	72.8	69.4	69.6	72.0	72.9	74.0	75.3	79.2	78.3
France	73.5	73.4	75.4	72.3	72.3	73.2	75.4	76.2	76.1	78.6	79.5
Germany, F.R.	80.8	78.6	76.9	75.4	75.6	78.2	78.7	77.7	77.4	78.9	79.2
United States	100.0	100.0	100.0	100.0	100.0	100.0	100.0	100.0	100.0	100.0	100.0

— Not available.

entries for Hungary, India, Japan, Kenya, and the United Kingdom are taken from Table 1.3; they represent the results of the Phase I 1967 benchmark estimates with minor adjustments owing to subsequent revisions in each country's estimates of its GDP and in that of the U.S. GDP.

All other figures in the table are derived by extrapolations or interpolations from these basic data.

The 1974 and 1975 extrapolations were based on 1973 as the benchmark year. For Hungary, India, Japan, Kenya, and the United Kingdom, the benchmark year for the 1965 and 1966 extrapolations was 1967. For 1968 and 1969 for these five countries, two extrapolations were made, one forward from 1967 and the other backward from 1970. The 1968 figures shown in the table are averages in which the extrapolations based on 1967 are given a weight of two and the extrapolations based on 1970 a weight of one. The 1969 figures are also averages of the two sets of extrapolations, with the weights reversed. For the other countries, 1970 was the benchmark year for 1965–69 inclusive. The 1971 and 1972 figures for all countries were based on averages of extrapolations forward from 1970 and backward from 1973; here too, the extrapolations from the nearer year were given a weight of two and the extrapolations from the farther year a weight of one.

The figures indicate some substantial changes in the relative fortunes of different nations. More than half of the countries gained ground on the United States: Iran gained most spectacularly, especially in the last few years; the Republic of Korea, Hungary, and Japan gained substantially; and Belgium and France gained moderately and mainly in the 1970s. Kenya's indexes for the 1970s are above those for the 1960s. Aside from India, the other countries—the Philippines, Malaysia, Italy, the United Kingdom, the Netherlands, and the Federal Republic of Germany—remained in about the same relative positions during the decade. India declined relative to the United States in the last of the three years for which data are available. Since the underlying indexes are base-country invariant, any country other than the United States could be taken as the standard of comparison. Iran, the Republic of Korea, Hungary, and Japan would, of course, still emerge as large gainers relative to the Philippines, Malaysia, Italy, the United Kingdom, the Netherlands, the Federal Republic of Germany, and the United States.

This appendix amplifies the multilateral comparisons across all sixteen ICP countries for 1970. Appendix Tables 4.1 through 4.5 extend the information in Summary Multilateral Tables 4.1 through 4.5, respectively, by presenting the data at the level of what are referred to in the text as "detailed categories," or the lowest level of aggregation. For a full discussion of the appendix, see the section in this chapter headed "An Explanation of the Tables."

Appendix 1 to Chapter 4

Detailed Multilateral Tables

			Kenya (shillings)	India (rupees)	Philippines (pesos)	Korea Republic of (won)	Colombia (pesos)	Malaysia (M.dollars)	Iran (rials)	Hungary (forints)
1.	1.101	Rice	1.83	83.98	134.85	9712.	68.17	54.46	839.4	51.4
2.	1.102	Meal and other cereals	117.62	77.31	25.14	2607.	56.27	5.60	1039.5	179.7
3.	1.103	Bread	4.83	0.16	16.19	449.	40.86	3.14	577.3	300.8
4.	1.104	Biscuits, cakes, and the like	2.05	1.02	5.91	414.	14.67	5.29	83.0	96.6
5.	1.105	Cereal preparations	0.84	0.00	2.09	0.	14.77	1.62	27.8	81.0
6.	1.106	Macaroni and spaghetti	0.15	1.01	6.28	452.	16.86	3.84	7.1	32.5
7.	1.111	Fresh beef and veal	22.78	0.74	11.96	1695.	347.28	1.17	176.3	81.8
8.	1.112	Fresh lamb and mutton	2.78	0.99	0.00	0.	5.73	0.90	1154.1	17.1
9.	1.113	Fresh pork	0.55	0.50	31.32	676.	29.25	22.86	0.0	712.4
10.	1.114	Fresh poultry	0.97	1.92	17.34	326.	31.58	20.69	213.9	399.9
11.	1.115	Other fresh meat	2.43	3.03	3.90	142.	28.33	0.00	28.5	48.8
12.	1.116	Frozen and salted meat	2.01	0.03	2.69	11.	42.13	1.94	8.0	398.8
13.	1.121	Fresh and frozen fish	6.67	3.21	52.42	926.	10.45	31.11	61.7	29.1
14.	1.122	Canned fish	1.01	2.53	18.90	836.	18.51	9.10	7.2	14.6
15.	1.131	Fresh milk	38.27	23.48	11.82	74.	119.14	2.24	129.0	272.0
16.	1.132	Milk products	4.14	7.66	1.21	197.	44.85	12.19	681.2	129.3
17.	1.133	Eggs and egg products	0.34	2.36	6.77	812.	52.82	11.02	218.7	292.1
18.	1.141	Butter	5.57	1.62	0.46	21.	10.64	0.82	151.0	88.4
19.	1.142	Margerine and edible oil	4.84	29.67	1.01	192.	44.70	10.36	276.8	36.9
20.	1.143	Lard and edible fat	1.17	8.25	6.77	165.	4.23	0.00	197.0	436.1
21.	1.151	Fresh tropical fruits	13.48	16.08	1.69	5.	90.91	13.39	225.0	102.7
22.	1.152	Other fresh fruits	0.33	3.52	0.45	802.	3.98	4.81	490.1	323.1
23.	1.153	Fresh vegetables	20.04	15.23	4.65	2265.	61.18	11.82	476.1	283.6
24.	1.161	Fruit other than fresh	0.11	2.41	0.08	94.	4.28	1.08	69.6	52.0
25.	1.162	Vegetables other than fresh	3.67	15.72	0.04	0.	55.83	3.75	89.7	55.6
26.	1.170	Tubers, including potatoes	31.58	4.14	2.17	1713.	56.46	1.47	123.1	180.5
27.	1.191	Coffee	0.98	1.10	6.84	92.	49.71	3.59	0.5	206.7
28.	1.192	Tea	3.55	3.27	0.44	15.	1.17	1.49	359.5	11.6
29.	1.193	Cocoa	0.26	0.00	0.97	12.	33.72	0.07	0.9	11.3
30.	1.180	Sugar	13.69	26.06	15.70	419.	126.72	17.87	548.4	227.8
31.	1.201	Jam, syrup, and honey	2.73	3.49	4.48	55.	14.97	0.27	26.2	6.1
32.	1.202	Chocolate and ice cream	1.99	1.26	3.45	1.	8.79	3.19	20.3	359.1
33.	1.203	Salt, spices, and sauces	3.96	9.18	14.31	3133.	48.40	6.87	68.6	168.9
34.	1.310	Nonalcoholic beverages	5.95	0.44	9.18	272.	31.83	4.16	35.7	36.3
35.	1.321	Spirits	2.08	5.70	10.89	1796.	101.41	5.02	9.3	183.0
36.	1.322	Wine and cider	0.48	0.11	2.96	67.	35.52	1.16	23.4	357.1
37.	1.323	Beer	13.93	0.55	7.86	750.	27.21	8.22	18.6	125.0
38.	1.410	Cigarettes	9.52	5.82	20.36	2222.	69.48	32.71	269.5	286.8
39.	1.420	Cigars, tobacco, and snuff	0.20	11.82	3.99	0.	22.79	2.82	87.6	4.4
40.	2.110	Clothing materials	5.41	30.47	25.13	2152.	35.08	19.69	375.4	168.0
41.	2.121	Men's clothing	8.06	0.32	4.27	1762.	123.57	3.76	385.9	416.6
42.	2.122	Women's clothing	4.67	0.45	2.56	789.	55.73	3.01	281.3	353.1
43.	2.123	Boys' and girls' clothing	2.41	0.05	0.93	197.	37.61	0.75	43.5	224.1
44.	2.131	Men's and boys' underwear	0.56	0.69	1.20	378.	19.87	1.54	39.0	137.9
45.	2.132	Women's and girls' underwear	0.48	0.69	1.23	360.	34.55	1.03	65.4	140.7
46.	2.150	Haberdashery and millinery	0.67	1.44	5.94	136.	25.46	4.43	141.6	224.4
47.	2.160	Clothing rental and repair	0.63	1.06	0.71	23.	11.13	0.00	0.8	72.5
48.	2.211	Men's footwear	3.38	1.38	2.60	123.	40.23	1.92	137.6	141.8
49.	2.212	Women's footwear	0.84	1.38	1.88	107.	31.83	1.92	135.9	188.8
50.	2.213	Children's footwear	0.65	0.70	1.05	153.	27.41	0.95	11.1	67.2
51.	2.220	Footwear, repairs	0.27	0.03	0.74	2.	7.19	0.00	25.7	38.7
52.	3.110	Rents	62.13	20.62	51.97	2184.	346.21	65.08	2233.1	663.0
53.	3.120	Indoor repair and upkeep	0.20	2.02	5.77	57.	41.69	7.84	238.8	171.6
54.	3.210	Electricity	1.46	1.24	5.87	677.	24.30	8.79	177.4	160.7
55.	3.220	Gas	0.11	0.23	2.01	0.	8.26	1.49	43.2	83.9

Italy (lire)	Japan (yen)	United Kingdom (pounds)	Netherlands (guilders)	Belgium (B.francs)	France (francs)	Germany F.R. (DM)	United States (dollars)			
744.	14806.	0.108	3.22	36.7	4.33	4.80	1.90	1.	1.101	Rice
1692.	241.	0.738	10.59	110.0	12.13	40.02	9.78	2.	1.102	Meal and other cereals
14750.	1393.	6.862	67.61	1224.9	136.95	116.49	25.80	3.	1.103	Bread
5887.	5395.	6.628	58.63	821.5	126.57	48.39	8.06	4.	1.104	Biscuits, cakes, and the like
134.	146.	1.171	2.84	43.9	1.73	2.37	2.48	5.	1.105	Cereal preparations
8120.	1492.	0.306	3.68	73.2	15.60	12.53	1.48	6.	1.106	Macaroni and spaghetti
38820.	2540.	8.483	121.87	2480.9	278.69	68.69	44.88	7.	1.111	Fresh beef and veal
1530.	44.	4.503	0.00	0.0	22.93	0.00	1.36	8.	1.112	Fresh lamb and mutton
6482.	3636.	2.035	78.82	912.7	78.49	95.58	25.07	9.	1.113	Fresh pork
9978.	1819.	2.918	14.50	791.4	88.20	18.52	14.81	10.	1.114	Fresh poultry
4517.	675.	1.279	4.37	301.8	101.44	5.38	2.04	11.	1.115	Other fresh meat
14055.	2583.	13.509	70.61	2767.5	170.22	142.75	34.08	12.	1.116	Frozen and salted meat
5548.	9262.	2.468	24.79	377.0	74.28	7.17	8.91	13.	1.121	Fresh and frozen fish
2708.	8858.	1.369	5.45	260.4	32.62	12.55	7.09	14.	1.122	Canned fish
8636.	3934.	9.024	92.63	807.4	81.29	51.38	33.55	15.	1.131	Fresh milk
15963.	874.	3.710	77.74	700.6	165.41	44.20	25.09	16.	1.132	Milk products
6168.	3475.	3.909	30.54	366.9	53.87	46.58	13.15	17.	1.133	Eggs and egg products
3408.	217.	3.080	10.05	968.5	105.32	79.44	4.20	18.	1.141	Butter
11314.	1242.	1.153	40.21	480.6	37.44	43.61	15.08	19.	1.142	Margerine and edible oil
0.	13.	0.576	0.00	0.0	0.00	0.00	1.59	20.	1.143	Lard and edible fat
7281.	3650.	1.801	42.59	503.5	46.13	23.89	6.10	21.	1.151	Fresh tropical fruits
13161.	3772.	2.540	28.47	610.1	78.20	35.85	11.68	22.	1.152	Other fresh fruits
24924.	8603.	4.917	58.79	957.4	132.14	37.03	25.19	23.	1.153	Fresh vegetables
3781.	823.	2.179	22.79	113.5	14.08	22.70	15.90	24.	1.161	Fruit other than fresh
2590.	3678.	3.890	40.75	241.2	43.00	44.20	36.58	25.	1.162	Vegetables other than fresh
3220.	1087.	4.503	23.71	461.0	38.31	29.86	6.85	26.	1.170	Tubers, including potatoes
4502.	366.	1.099	47.12	679.7	49.44	84.22	12.41	27.	1.191	Coffee
196.	1131.	2.828	10.90	8.1	2.70	6.56	2.00	28.	1.192	Tea
147.	161.	0.108	4.91	16.2	6.30	7.17	0.38	29.	1.193	Cocoa
3928.	1277.	2.323	26.02	275.7	28.90	41.22	15.68	30.	1.180	Sugar
878.	1988.	1.189	7.21	108.7	14.46	11.95	9.54	31.	1.201	Jam, syrup, and honey
4445.	1850.	9.204	60.63	942.9	68.62	60.33	16.44	32.	1.202	Chocolate and ice cream
2378.	6384.	1.045	15.89	58.1	10.83	3.58	7.92	33.	1.203	Salt, spices, and sauces
2797.	2140.	3.242	53.26	373.4	30.37	20.18	11.27	34.	1.310	Nonalcoholic beverages
4135.	1240.	11.455	50.42	560.3	44.26	46.66	14.01	35.	1.321	Spirits
16908.	9534.	5.421	29.32	373.4	255.19	39.74	5.33	36.	1.322	Wine and cider
2678.	4861.	24.424	28.93	492.2	21.71	64.96	33.97	37.	1.323	Beer
18858.	4866.	27.089	81.81	1201.9	116.37	95.42	46.73	38.	1.410	Cigarettes
1288.	8.	3.890	59.02	393.7	19.40	10.34	5.96	39.	1.420	Cigars, tobacco, and snuff
5891.	10149.	1.315	29.01	537.0	30.51	28.28	3.04	40.	2.110	Clothing materials
12874.	5430.	7.691	123.64	1279.0	218.02	132.18	52.07	41.	2.121	Men's clothing
6692.	6472.	12.770	151.19	1010.4	167.97	150.63	68.35	42.	2.122	Women's clothing
5380.	2508.	2.522	7.21	508.8	25.45	48.57	20.86	43.	2.123	Boys' and girls' clothing
13164.	1967.	4.089	41.06	466.4	68.72	44.88	3.12	44.	2.131	Men's and boys' underwear
5820.	1630.	5.494	71.99	1279.1	130.63	110.06	17.44	45.	2.132	Women's and girls' underwear
1381.	1914.	5.800	21.26	268.6	64.47	55.94	14.36	46.	2.150	Haberdashery and millinery
2618.	1431.	0.865	4.83	565.4	12.72	8.00	20.10	47.	2.160	Clothing rental and repair
4993.	902.	2.576	23.87	310.2	40.54	21.22	14.78	48.	2.211	Men's footwear
2026.	952.	3.548	31.62	372.2	48.79	29.20	17.72	49.	2.212	Women's footwear
2967.	521.	1.927	14.27	110.3	32.26	34.49	5.24	50.	2.213	Children's footwear
1159.	64.	0.738	6.45	130.9	9.08	22.29	1.24	51.	2.220	Footwear, repairs
66882.	41297.	67.345	326.71	7435.4	829.60	659.27	420.98	52.	3.110	Rents
1400.	1954.	13.545	97.16	752.9	151.33	41.47	42.14	53.	3.120	Indoor repair and upkeep
9663.	4768.	11.924	74.29	1061.9	96.55	98.24	48.17	54.	3.210	Electricity
5540.	3054.	6.970	58.48	792.5	80.78	38.32	27.29	55.	3.220	Gas

(Table continues on following page.)

			Kenya (shillings)	India (rupees)	Philippines (pesos)	Korea Republic of (won)	Colombia (pesos)	Malaysia (M.dollars)	Iran (rials)	Hungary (forints)
56.	3.230	Liquid fuels	1.41	5.62	6.66	91.	12.39	2.80	293.6	45.6
57.	3.240	Other fuels and ice	8.25	11.96	10.88	1926.	4.32	4.42	229.7	308.4
58.	4.110	Furniture and fixtures	4.01	0.82	4.28	72.	74.59	4.26	39.1	377.0
59.	4.120	Floor coverings	0.66	0.33	0.09	0.	4.76	0.57	258.3	54.6
60.	4.200	Household textiles and the like	2.57	0.51	8.89	103.	27.26	7.17	67.8	213.8
61.	4.310	Refrigerators and freezers	0.40	0.57	3.99	222.	5.64	2.10	61.9	90.2
62.	4.320	Washing appliances	0.05	0.00	0.56	0.	6.71	0.13	9.3	43.5
63.	4.330	Cooking appliances	0.41	0.03	3.22	24.	14.63	0.90	18.6	79.6
64.	4.340	Heating appliances	0.37	0.05	0.30	102.	3.11	0.20	11.5	39.2
65.	4.350	Cleaning appliances	0.06	0.00	0.47	9.	6.95	0.18	1.5	15.8
66.	4.360	Other household appliances	0.16	1.40	2.19	438.	3.50	2.49	10.8	15.9
67.	4.400	Household utensils	4.53	5.14	4.60	191.	10.01	7.56	112.8	205.5
68.	4.510	Nondurable household goods	21.13	2.71	11.68	268.	66.91	11.01	191.2	232.7
69.	4.520	Domestic services	8.31	2.01	5.41	77.	79.35	7.17	52.5	36.7
70.	4.530	Household services	1.49	2.12	0.88	136.	17.74	0.00	18.0	24.4
71.	4.600	House furnishing repairs	0.10	0.70	1.15	94.	0.00	0.13	3.7	117.8
72.	5.110	Drugs and medical preparations	7.17	8.92	7.79	514.	69.87	9.73	473.3	329.8
73.	5.120	Medical supplies	0.56	0.84	0.63	98.	0.00	0.65	5.4	85.9
74.	5.200	Therapeutic equipment	0.09	0.21	0.93	20.	9.09	0.75	18.2	0.0
75.	5.310	Physicians' services	5.13	1.10	5.55	380.	98.35	8.18	190.1	108.0
76.	5.320	Dentists' services	0.41	0.01	1.51	44.	21.43	1.74	32.0	8.4
77.	5.330	Nurses' services	5.45	1.62	6.76	207.	8.55	4.32	48.5	113.8
78.	5.410	Hospitals	18.07	1.63	4.26	444.	73.32	5.15	234.1	446.0
79.	6.110	Personal automobiles	11.32	0.95	2.33	108.	65.16	22.14	262.1	254.2
80.	6.120	Other personal transport	0.12	1.30	0.09	5.	0.19	1.79	25.2	91.7
81.	6.210	Tires, tubes, and accessories	2.22	0.20	0.59	1.	7.19	11.31	38.1	48.1
82.	6.220	Automobile repairs	2.23	0.86	0.19	0.	12.73	3.83	72.4	55.1
83.	6.230	Gasoline, oil, and grease	1.18	1.55	1.27	2.	9.82	27.21	77.2	72.0
84.	6.240	Parking, tolls, and the like	0.87	0.16	0.77	1.	10.20	1.99	47.7	7.3
85.	6.310	Local transport	2.28	3.37	2.82	1160.	114.43	10.22	122.8	147.0
86.	6.321	Rail transport	1.42	3.61	0.26	527.	60.50	1.02	25.5	141.2
87.	6.322	Bus transport	13.45	11.60	2.83	1183.	12.24	18.38	92.2	162.5
88.	6.323	Air transport	15.31	0.08	1.85	17.	149.71	8.53	31.7	24.2
89.	6.330	Miscellaneous transport	0.23	3.18	6.57	106.	0.00	1.71	7.6	28.9
90.	6.410	Postal communication	0.41	0.81	0.33	93.	1.94	1.92	5.1	37.2
91.	6.420	Telephone and telegraph	1.01	1.15	0.65	107.	21.67	3.88	29.8	30.5
92.	7.110	Radios, televisions, and phonographs	3.81	1.23	3.72	403.	44.61	9.10	95.3	253.3
93.	7.120	Major durable recreational equipment	5.52	0.16	1.49	29.	5.73	2.84	9.9	9.7
94.	7.130	Other recreational equipment	3.78	0.26	0.86	53.	12.54	1.72	35.2	84.8
95.	7.210	Public entertainment	5.69	0.40	3.59	14.	71.77	10.40	30.4	236.3
96.	7.230	Other recreational and cultural activities	4.12	1.83	1.36	922.	13.90	6.35	134.4	248.3
97.	7.310	Books, papers, and magazines	6.09	0.87	1.67	528.	26.97	6.05	35.0	194.7
98.	7.320	Stationery	0.09	0.21	0.18	207.	1.94	1.33	29.8	65.1
99.	7.411	First- and second- level teachers	40.67	16.62	31.99	1798.	122.25	44.67	503.6	510.0
100.	7.412	College teachers	2.26	3.10	8.40	263.	32.70	1.42	91.4	52.5
101.	7.420	Physical facilities for education	5.81	1.19	7.18	265.	13.95	2.42	33.4	272.5
102.	7.431	Educational books and supplies	2.39	1.17	3.03	208.	12.00	0.97	8.6	28.2
103.	7.432	Other educational expenditures	3.85	1.33	2.87	355.	19.68	1.72	15.4	130.4
104.	8.100	Barber and beauty shops	0.46	1.14	4.57	1088.	15.11	3.00	531.7	94.3
105.	8.210	Toilet articles	2.66	2.41	7.83	146.	50.73	10.15	48.3	135.0
106.	8.220	Other personal care goods	2.66	2.42	7.83	146.	16.52	10.14	48.3	202.6
107.	8.310	Restaurants and cafes	14.02	2.58	22.64	1445.	172.98	18.84	510.4	1725.3
108.	8.320	Hotels and lodging	14.71	2.58	0.39	135.	12.93	9.27	64.6	64.5
109.	8.400	Other services	12.16	8.48	23.39	514.	211.32	6.15	296.1	450.4
110.	8.900	Net expenditures of residents abroad	0.00	0.00	0.00	-30.	0.00	0.00	0.0	0.0

Italy (lire)	Japan (yen)	United Kingdom (pounds)	Netherlands (guilders)	Belgium (B.francs)	France (francs)	Germany F.R. (DM)	United States (dollars)			
4460.	986.	1.117	38.99	871.7	55.70	41.35	16.77	56.	3.230	Liquid fuels
1824.	1508.	6.916	23.25	1371.1	60.33	52.12	9.52	57.	3.240	Other fuels and ice
10777.	5228.	6.412	135.00	2389.9	205.79	206.64	56.34	58.	4.110	Furniture and fixtures
1001.	2022.	5.205	63.78	302.9	26.20	44.19	17.23	59.	4.120	Floor coverings
5004.	2137.	5.115	83.42	456.7	83.26	122.24	34.18	60.	4.200	Household textiles and the like
1079.	4167.	1.495	24.56	126.2	26.20	18.93	7.64	61.	4.310	Refrigerators and freezers
2540.	1942.	1.945	40.52	168.3	47.71	40.99	6.41	62.	4.320	Washing appliances
1463.	775.	1.729	12.89	218.9	28.07	14.99	5.08	63.	4.330	Cooking appliances
846.	2103.	1.621	36.84	437.7	20.58	15.78	0.51	64.	4.340	Heating appliances
384.	921.	1.153	7.37	42.1	14.02	14.99	2.05	65.	4.350	Cleaning appliances
615.	2029.	0.342	22.64	58.8	16.84	25.24	12.08	66.	4.360	Other household appliances
4003.	6043.	6.988	93.25	2019.8	81.39	115.96	18.36	67.	4.400	Household utensils
4830.	1948.	4.575	71.83	1705.7	164.86	130.93	41.85	68.	4.510	Nondurable household goods
0.	363.	2.125	0.00	0.0	0.00	0.00	24.66	69.	4.520	Domestic services
7395.	2527.	2.702	39.60	1228.1	61.47	46.53	4.58	70.	4.530	Household services
0.	189.	0.612	0.00	0.0	0.00	0.00	8.25	71.	4.600	House furnishing repairs
20870.	9782.	6.646	127.24	1384.5	400.02	181.32	59.87	72.	5.110	Drugs and medical preparations
143.	9914.	1.171	3.91	62.7	7.94	18.35	7.92	73.	5.120	Medical supplies
324.	296.	1.927	37.45	156.0	22.63	48.39	12.01	74.	5.200	Therapeutic equipment
13660.	1760.	5.421	152.19	2131.6	289.60	186.56	75.03	75.	5.310	Physicians' services
6057.	379.	1.801	65.46	160.8	160.76	69.45	27.07	76.	5.320	Dentists' services
1616.	1555.	9.042	7.37	762.7	33.13	42.03	11.06	77.	5.330	Nurses' services
5485.	5934.	11.798	20.41	677.5	39.91	42.09	123.71	78.	5.410	Hospitals
19158.	2004.	17.579	143.36	2522.8	229.60	175.80	135.66	79.	6.110	Personal automobiles
913.	875.	1.117	22.49	124.5	18.69	9.73	15.87	80.	6.120	Other personal transport
2633.	138.	3.872	42.36	641.0	74.71	46.45	22.39	81.	6.210	Tires, tubes, and accessories
6996.	882.	3.656	33.77	663.9	159.86	93.54	47.81	82.	6.220	Automobile repairs
19937.	1842.	12.284	70.76	1770.4	192.02	201.24	107.37	83.	6.230	Gasoline, oil, and grease
5116.	868.	6.538	33.31	343.4	79.04	45.79	28.22	84.	6.240	Parking, tolls, and the like
6167.	3589.	9.870	22.95	418.6	66.48	31.51	12.30	85.	6.310	Local transport
4120.	1104.	2.594	30.24	562.3	49.64	64.81	0.90	86.	6.321	Rail transport
2598.	295.	0.504	10.90	345.9	51.55	28.19	2.42	87.	6.322	Bus transport
384.	119.	3.476	5.45	102.6	8.94	2.74	10.57	88.	6.323	Air transport
0.	148.	1.873	0.00	0.0	0.00	0.00	4.23	89.	6.330	Miscellaneous transport
2467.	356.	2.125	16.19	198.8	20.27	27.42	7.08	90.	6.410	Postal communication
3906.	2427.	4.071	34.61	404.8	27.30	15.86	49.10	91.	6.420	Telephone and telegraph
5408.	3546.	2.972	80.05	764.8	113.20	48.80	42.97	92.	7.110	Radios, televisions, and phonographs
209.	557.	1.549	13.66	80.5	28.70	36.32	25.62	93.	7.120	Major durable recreational equipment
6517.	2471.	10.195	126.09	1119.2	151.49	176.24	46.34	94.	7.130	Other recreational equipment
11299.	5848.	6.376	36.91	306.0	34.29	28.19	38.07	95.	7.210	Public entertainment
3258.	1328.	13.437	25.79	660.2	49.44	55.32	46.59	96.	7.230	Other recreational and cultural activities
11299.	2624.	7.673	76.90	652.3	145.89	74.82	30.53	97.	7.310	Books, papers, and magazines
1873.	527.	1.801	21.34	96.6	82.12	27.11	9.70	98.	7.320	Stationery
35794.	15012.	25.991	360.48	5114.4	473.33	260.89	176.26	99.	7.411	First- and second- level teachers
4245.	4342.	6.178	46.89	747.9	70.10	52.23	45.04	100.	7.412	College teachers
2367.	3614.	5.530	77.44	721.7	27.34	49.17	26.72	101.	7.420	Physical facilities for education
403.	1092.	2.071	14.43	137.4	4.20	2.29	3.19	102.	7.431	Educational books and supplies
1265.	3657.	3.674	14.43	192.0	4.45	17.66	7.75	103.	7.432	Other educational expenditures
3902.	2041.	2.720	12.28	765.9	45.72	25.11	19.39	104.	8.100	Barber and beauty shops
3142.	2577.	2.882	30.93	330.0	74.00	30.92	35.65	105.	8.210	Toilet articles
3839.	694.	3.098	30.85	329.9	90.45	37.79	36.17	106.	8.220	Other personal care goods
34283.	14511.	15.742	184.65	8099.7	693.09	343.31	156.49	107.	8.310	Restaurants and cafes
16148.	5628.	10.050	118.42	477.6	276.99	151.33	9.68	108.	8.320	Hotels and lodging
2346.	17352.	17.849	154.41	633.6	41.72	66.36	124.16	109.	8.400	Other services
-14592.	1258.	-0.594	45.82	539.4	-36.83	11.87	22.95	110.	8.900	Net expenditures of residents abroad

(Table continues on following page.)

Appendix Table 4.1 continued.

			Kenya (shillings)	India (rupees)	Philippines (pesos)	Korea Republic of (won)	Colombia (pesos)	Malaysia (M.dollars)	Iran (rials)	Hungary (forints)
111.	10.100	One- and two-dwelling buildings	28.90	8.82	10.89	2192.	174.59	13.94	934.3	730.2
112.	10.200	Multidwelling buildings	4.33	8.82	13.86	372.	22.50	13.94	352.8	795.4
113.	11.100	Hotels	0.63	0.73	0.47	138.	1.12	1.61	78.6	106.5
114.	11.200	Industrial buildings	11.79	1.67	1.68	925.	11.76	8.10	600.3	1029.8
115.	11.300	Commercial buildings	2.33	4.45	10.09	1112.	3.69	6.05	70.1	163.4
116.	11.400	Office buildings	3.01	1.84	2.46	402.	7.39	6.05	216.8	176.6
117.	11.500	Educational buildings	2.96	1.12	5.35	219.	3.45	4.20	47.6	140.5
118.	11.600	Hospital buildings	3.02	0.71	1.19	680.	1.31	2.87	21.6	49.0
119.	11.700	Agricultural buildings	0.60	6.59	1.01	332.	6.75	1.61	231.4	725.0
120.	11.800	Other buildings	0.75	1.56	0.13	587.	1.31	1.61	85.4	49.9
121.	12.100	Roads, streets, and highways	12.10	4.25	10.06	1474.	147.18	4.84	309.0	286.8
122.	12.200	Transport and utility lines	9.14	12.30	4.17	1284.	122.69	15.97	346.3	925.9
123.	12.300	Other construction	14.57	8.78	0.33	2974.	85.67	3.51	348.4	485.3
124.	13.000	Land improvement	4.79	8.99	0.36	88.	131.73	17.89	0.0	130.7
125.	14.110	Locomotives	3.01	0.38	0.46	165.	0.15	0.05	0.8	71.9
126.	14.120	Other railway vehicles	5.33	0.83	0.05	143.	2.04	0.00	17.0	149.7
127.	14.200	Passenger automobiles	11.01	0.37	19.16	858.	42.27	4.73	252.9	61.2
128.	14.300	Trucks, busses, and trailers	12.62	6.88	14.63	1025.	60.06	10.76	234.5	389.1
129.	14.400	Aircraft	2.92	0.25	1.41	205.	19.39	0.00	52.3	28.9
130.	14.500	Ships and boats	0.50	0.74	5.70	681.	29.06	4.89	70.9	16.0
131.	14.600	Other transport equipment	0.58	1.24	1.11	60.	1.46	1.06	248.5	221.7
132.	15.100	Engines and turbines	2.88	1.48	10.69	403.	3.89	4.42	136.2	80.4
133.	15.210	Tractors	3.17	0.84	5.25	0.	3.74	4.40	23.9	124.7
134.	15.220	Others agricultural machinery	4.48	0.16	1.33	75.	5.20	0.65	119.4	183.9
135.	15.300	Office machinery	2.47	0.26	4.33	90.	5.20	2.17	20.7	119.5
136.	15.400	Metalworking machinery	1.53	1.51	2.09	301.	9.91	2.41	87.5	199.5
137.	15.500	Construction and mining machinery	6.28	1.01	12.78	182.	13.95	11.73	31.7	210.0
138.	15.600	Special industrial machinery	13.48	2.75	9.32	852.	19.14	12.37	308.0	776.9
139.	15.700	General industrial machinery	12.73	7.50	21.02	1065.	25.41	11.13	132.4	254.1
140.	15.800	Service industrial machinery	2.74	0.57	5.42	219.	0.97	2.63	61.1	38.0
141.	16.100	Electrical transmission equipment	5.34	3.47	5.24	325.	67.25	3.96	115.9	81.3
142.	16.200	Communications equipment	3.80	3.36	8.17	121.	44.02	4.46	33.5	110.4
143.	16.300	Other electrical equipment	1.45	0.61	7.66	212.	82.85	0.02	66.7	21.3
144.	16.400	Instruments	1.86	0.37	2.13	21.	44.56	2.55	58.0	194.3
145.	17.100	Furniture and fixtures	0.98	0.27	1.72	85.	13.80	2.61	41.2	435.0
146.	17.200	Other durable goods	2.62	7.26	8.43	80.	11.22	0.26	40.7	44.9
147.	18.000	Increase in stocks	23.85	16.65	27.79	1671.	165.60	35.22	65.8	1192.1
148.	19.000	Exports minuus imports	-17.81	-4.86	-5.32	-8115.	-106.27	53.62	1820.4	-907.0
149.	20.100	Unskilled blue collar	38.47	11.42	4.00	170.	62.24	4.74	1111.8	220.2
150.	20.210	Skilled blue collar	2.72	0.93	1.78	269.	13.75	2.09	341.9	12.5
151.	20.220	White collar	10.52	12.82	23.98	3096.	83.82	28.52	409.9	205.3
152.	20.300	Professional	26.07	8.53	9.26	702.	159.04	45.18	585.3	185.9
153.	21.000	Commodities of government	24.56	24.84	23.24	2547.	96.70	48.62	1605.3	1788.3

Appendix Table 4.2. Percentage Distribution of Expenditures in National Currencies, 1970

			Kenya	India	Philippines	Korea Republic of	Colombia	Malaysia	Iran	Hungary
1.	1.101	Rice	0.18	11.25	12.01	12.13	1.07	4.56	2.74	0.17
2.	1.102	Meal and other cereals	11.49	10.36	2.24	3.26	0.88	0.47	3.39	0.58
3.	1.103	Bread	0.47	0.02	1.44	0.56	0.64	0.26	1.88	0.97
4.	1.104	Biscuits, cakes, and the like	0.20	0.14	0.53	0.52	0.23	0.44	0.27	0.31
5.	1.105	Cereal preparations	0.08	0.0	0.19	0.0	0.23	0.14	0.09	0.26

Italy (lire)	Japan (yen)	United Kingdom (pounds)	Netherlands (guilders)	Belgium (B.francs)	France (francs)	Germany F.R. (DM)	United States (dollars)			
56286.	33700.	20.173	115.50	741.4	346.60	140.20	103.01	111.	10.100	One- and two-dwelling buildings
18742.	15746.	9.420	347.12	5958.4	719.01	429.46	69.96	112.	10.200	Multidwelling buildings
1834.	3005.	0.630	7.60	94.9	19.42	24.17	6.63	113.	11.100	Hotels
19361.	9543.	13.491	136.61	3013.5	122.20	223.30	34.19	114.	11.200	Industrial buildings
2751.	9545.	4.575	83.96	691.7	97.93	67.14	29.97	115.	11.300	Commercial buildings
7700.	10557.	3.080	45.74	361.9	102.93	83.96	19.27	116.	11.400	Office buildings
3668.	6619.	5.980	114.43	281.4	110.48	99.04	31.62	117.	11.500	Educational buildings
2566.	2307.	2.936	87.80	68.4	36.83	47.01	16.66	118.	11.600	Hospital buildings
4584.	1615.	1.621	38.14	804.3	75.32	33.57	7.52	119.	11.700	Agricultural buildings
1834.	12909.	3.548	6.83	152.8	110.48	10.06	21.31	120.	11.800	Other buildings
9502.	8073.	5.818	107.37	2491.9	108.61	176.31	53.98	121.	12.100	Roads, streets, and highways
9193.	9484.	3.440	115.89	2417.7	281.37	226.68	88.73	122.	12.200	Transport and utility lines
731.	12540.	1.819	15.58	25.2	19.38	25.18	13.59	123.	12.300	Other construction
5770.	292.	1.513	38.91	33.0	10.03	8.39	0.00	124.	13.000	Land improvement
518.	403.	0.180	3.07	52.2	10.08	2.13	2.41	125.	14.110	Locomotives
529.	46.	0.306	4.60	93.4	15.60	10.37	5.82	126.	14.120	Other railway vehicles
8474.	5880.	7.835	75.98	730.7	83.12	108.46	26.26	127.	14.200	Passenger automobiles
8485.	7360.	0.811	83.35	816.2	121.82	117.58	32.38	128.	14.300	Trucks, busses, and trailers
1504.	187.	2.323	33.69	438.5	7.50	24.40	11.68	129.	14.400	Aircraft
1616.	2023.	7.331	58.63	302.4	15.40	59.19	4.13	130.	14.500	Ships and boats
809.	771.	4.611	1.00	0.0	0.87	0.49	2.11	131.	14.600	Other transport equipment
1032.	1562.	0.108	10.05	63.9	11.54	6.45	6.23	132.	15.100	Engines and turbines
1964.	309.	0.865	17.04	319.3	59.58	22.13	7.20	133.	15.210	Tractors
2583.	1445.	1.279	17.04	309.4	100.67	29.46	11.74	134.	15.220	Others agricultural machinery
2971.	4154.	2.900	40.29	395.1	129.68	101.10	23.93	135.	15.300	Office machinery
4881.	5643.	4.089	26.09	305.5	59.86	77.51	17.25	136.	15.400	Metalworking machinery
2920.	3560.	4.287	60.48	1064.5	170.95	84.88	19.32	137.	15.500	Construction and mining machinery
7179.	9372.	7.079	91.86	873.0	199.00	124.67	18.98	138.	15.600	Special industrial machinery
7568.	8858.	19.651	162.70	1892.4	95.39	191.87	20.15	139.	15.700	General industrial machinery
1291.	793.	0.522	40.29	213.0	18.87	22.46	12.94	140.	15.800	Service industrial machinery
11327.	9443.	6.124	87.34	885.3	156.06	117.18	16.83	141.	16.100	Electrical transmission equipment
4448.	9865.	8.033	70.53	852.6	106.82	116.01	36.40	142.	16.200	Communications equipment
4886.	2717.	1.693	29.78	926.9	30.18	25.54	7.13	143.	16.300	Other electrical equipment
4087.	5110.	1.621	88.26	884.5	130.04	96.93	18.94	144.	16.400	Instruments
2078.	15371.	7.709	0.00	545.7	22.22	26.17	15.68	145.	17.100	Furniture and fixtures
4221.	8215.	1.729	0.00	585.4	37.13	26.22	16.84	146.	17.200	Other durable goods
19642.	29315.	7.925	220.11	2129.4	353.02	245.66	12.02	147.	18.000	Increase in stocks
6280.	9092.	8.483	-159.94	3195.0	93.07	217.56	9.97	148.	19.000	Exports minuus imports
20703.	5813.	23.613	45.20	1931.3	36.71	44.96	68.14	149.	20.100	Unskilled blue collar
9120.	11481.	2.918	50.65	472.6	217.83	125.52	48.17	150.	20.210	Skilled blue collar
34588.	2822.	18.642	401.53	3431.2	416.23	438.47	127.62	151.	20.220	White collar
5846.	3804.	8.483	141.90	1397.1	314.87	84.70	94.80	152.	20.300	Professional
24860.	9256.	42.579	290.10	3427.4	443.18	292.32	327.41	153.	21.000	Commodities of government

Italy	Japan	United Kingdom	Netherlands	Belgium	France	Germany F.R.	United States			
0.07	2.17	0.01	0.04	0.03	0.03	0.04	0.04	1.	1.101	Rice
0.16	0.04	0.08	0.12	0.08	0.08	0.36	0.20	2.	1.102	Meal and other cereals
1.37	0.20	0.75	0.77	0.93	0.89	1.04	0.54	3.	1.103	Bread
0.55	0.79	0.72	0.67	0.63	0.82	0.43	0.17	4.	1.104	Biscuits, cakes, and the like
0.01	0.02	0.13	0.03	0.03	0.01	0.02	0.05	5.	1.105	Cereal preparations

(Table continues on following page.)

			Kenya	India	Philippines	Korea Republic of	Colombia	Malaysia	Iran	Hungary
6.	1.106	Macaroni and spaghetti	0.01	0.14	0.56	0.56	0.27	0.32	0.02	0.10
7.	1.111	Fresh beef and veal	2.22	0.10	1.07	2.12	5.46	0.10	0.58	0.26
8.	1.112	Fresh lamb and mutton	0.27	0.13	0.07	0.0	0.09	0.07	3.77	0.06
9.	1.113	Fresh pork	0.05	0.07	2.79	0.84	0.46	1.91	0.0	2.29
10.	1.114	Fresh poultry	0.09	0.26	1.54	0.41	0.50	1.73	0.70	1.29
11.	1.115	Other fresh meat	0.24	0.41	0.35	0.18	0.45	0.0	0.09	0.16
12.	1.116	Frozen and salted meat	0.20	0.00	0.24	0.01	0.66	0.16	0.03	1.28
13.	1.121	Fresh and frozen fish	0.65	0.43	4.67	1.16	0.16	2.61	0.20	0.09
14.	1.122	Canned fish	0.10	0.34	1.68	1.04	0.29	0.76	0.02	0.05
15.	1.131	Fresh milk	3.74	3.15	1.05	0.09	1.87	0.19	0.42	0.87
16.	1.132	Milk products	0.40	1.03	0.11	0.25	0.71	1.02	2.22	0.42
17.	1.133	Eggs and egg products	0.03	0.32	0.60	1.01	0.83	0.92	0.71	0.94
18.	1.141	Butter	0.54	0.22	0.04	0.03	0.17	0.07	0.49	0.28
19.	1.142	Margerine and edible oil	0.47	3.98	0.09	0.24	0.70	0.87	0.90	0.12
20.	1.143	Lard and edible fat	0.11	1.11	0.60	0.21	0.07	0.0	0.64	1.40
21.	1.151	Fresh tropical fruits	1.32	2.15	0.15	0.01	1.43	1.12	0.73	0.33
22.	1.152	Other fresh fruits	0.03	0.47	0.04	1.00	0.06	0.40	1.60	1.04
23.	1.153	Fresh vegetables	1.96	2.04	0.41	2.83	0.96	0.99	1.55	0.91
24.	1.161	Fruit other than fresh	0.01	0.32	0.01	0.12	0.07	0.09	0.23	0.17
25.	1.162	Vegetables other than fresh	0.36	2.11	0.00	0.0	0.88	0.31	0.29	0.18
26.	1.170	Tubers, including potatoes	3.08	0.55	0.19	2.14	0.89	0.12	0.40	0.58
27.	1.191	Coffee	0.10	0.15	0.61	0.12	0.78	0.30	0.00	0.66
28.	1.192	Tea	0.35	0.44	0.04	0.02	0.02	0.12	1.17	0.04
29.	1.193	Cocoa	0.03	0.00	0.09	0.01	0.53	0.01	0.00	0.04
30.	1.180	Sugar	1.34	3.49	1.40	0.52	1.99	1.50	1.79	0.73
31.	1.201	Jam, syrup, and honey	0.27	0.47	0.40	0.07	0.24	0.02	0.09	0.02
32.	1.202	Chocolate and ice cream	0.19	0.17	0.31	0.00	0.14	0.27	0.07	1.16
33.	1.203	Salt, spices, and sauces	0.39	1.23	1.27	3.91	0.76	0.58	0.22	0.54
34.	1.310	Nonalcoholic beverages	0.58	0.06	0.82	0.34	0.50	0.35	0.12	0.12
35.	1.321	Spirits	0.20	0.76	0.97	2.24	1.59	0.42	0.03	0.59
36.	1.322	Wine and cider	0.05	0.01	0.26	0.08	0.56	0.10	0.08	1.15
37.	1.323	Beer	1.36	0.07	0.70	0.94	0.43	0.69	0.06	0.40
38.	1.410	Cigarettes	0.93	0.78	1.81	2.78	1.09	2.74	0.88	0.92
39.	1.420	Cigars, tobacco, and snuff	0.02	1.58	0.36	0.0	0.36	0.24	0.29	0.01
40.	2.110	Clothing materials	0.53	4.08	2.24	2.69	0.55	1.65	1.23	0.54
41.	2.121	Men's clothing	0.79	0.04	0.38	2.20	1.94	0.32	1.26	1.34
42.	2.122	Women's clothing	0.46	0.06	0.23	0.98	0.88	0.25	0.92	1.14
43.	2.123	Boys' and girls' clothing	0.24	0.01	0.08	0.25	0.59	0.06	0.14	0.72
44.	2.131	Men's and boys' underwear	0.05	0.09	0.11	0.47	0.31	0.13	0.13	0.44
45.	2.132	Women's and girls' underwear	0.05	0.09	0.11	0.45	0.54	0.09	0.21	0.45
46.	2.150	Haberdashery and millinery	0.07	0.19	0.53	0.17	0.40	0.37	0.46	0.72
47.	2.160	Clothing rental and repair	0.06	0.14	0.06	0.03	0.17	0.0	0.00	0.23
48.	2.211	Men's footwear	0.33	0.19	0.23	0.15	0.63	0.16	0.45	0.46
49.	2.212	Women's footwear	0.08	0.19	0.17	0.13	0.50	0.16	0.44	0.61
50.	2.213	Children's footwear	0.06	0.09	0.09	0.19	0.43	0.08	0.04	0.22
51.	2.220	Footwear, repairs	0.03	0.00	0.07	0.00	0.11	0.0	0.08	0.12
52.	3.110	Rents	6.07	2.76	4.63	2.73	5.44	5.45	7.29	2.13
53.	3.120	Indoor repair and upkeep	0.02	0.27	0.51	0.07	0.66	0.66	0.78	0.55
54.	3.210	Electricity	0.14	0.17	0.52	0.85	0.38	0.74	0.58	0.52
55.	3.220	Gas	0.01	0.03	0.18	0.0	0.13	0.12	0.14	0.27
56.	3.230	Liquid fuels	0.14	0.75	0.59	0.11	0.19	0.23	0.96	0.15
57.	3.240	Other fuels and ice	0.81	1.60	0.97	2.41	0.07	0.37	0.75	0.99
58.	4.110	Furniture and fixtures	0.39	0.11	0.38	0.09	1.17	0.36	0.13	1.21
59.	4.120	Floor coverings	0.06	0.04	0.01	0.0	0.07	0.05	0.84	0.18
60.	4.200	Household textiles and the like	0.25	0.07	0.79	0.13	0.43	0.60	0.22	0.69

Italy	Japan	United Kingdom	Netherlands	Belgium	France	Germany F.R.	United States			
0.75	0.22	0.03	0.04	0.06	0.10	0.11	0.03	6.	1.106	Macaroni and spaghetti
3.60	0.37	0.93	1.39	1.89	1.81	0.61	0.94	7.	1.111	Fresh beef and veal
0.14	0.01	0.49	0.0	0.0	0.15	0.0	0.03	8.	1.112	Fresh lamb and mutton
0.60	0.53	0.22	0.90	0.70	0.51	0.85	0.52	9.	1.113	Fresh pork
0.92	0.27	0.32	0.16	0.60	0.57	0.17	0.31	10.	1.114	Fresh poultry
0.42	0.10	0.14	0.05	0.23	0.66	0.05	0.04	11.	1.115	Other fresh meat
1.30	0.38	1.48	0.80	2.11	1.10	1.27	0.71	12.	1.116	Frozen and salted meat
0.51	1.36	0.27	0.28	0.29	0.48	0.06	0.19	13.	1.121	Fresh and frozen fish
0.25	1.30	0.15	0.06	0.20	0.21	0.11	0.15	14.	1.122	Canned fish
0.80	0.58	0.99	1.05	0.62	0.53	0.46	0.70	15.	1.131	Fresh milk
1.48	0.13	0.41	0.88	0.53	1.07	0.39	0.52	16.	1.132	Milk products
0.57	0.51	0.43	0.35	0.28	0.35	0.42	0.27	17.	1.133	Eggs and egg products
0.32	0.03	0.34	0.11	0.74	0.68	0.71	0.09	18.	1.141	Butter
1.05	0.18	0.13	0.46	0.37	0.24	0.39	0.31	19.	1.142	Margerine and edible oil
0.0	0.00	0.06	0.0	0.0	0.0	0.0	0.03	20.	1.143	Lard and edible fat
0.67	0.53	0.20	0.48	0.38	0.30	0.21	0.13	21.	1.151	Fresh tropical fruits
1.22	0.55	0.28	0.32	0.47	0.51	0.32	0.24	22.	1.152	Other fresh fruits
2.31	1.26	0.54	0.67	0.73	0.86	0.33	0.53	23.	1.153	Fresh vegetables
0.35	0.12	0.24	0.26	0.09	0.09	0.20	0.33	24.	1.161	Fruit other than fresh
0.24	0.54	0.43	0.46	0.18	0.28	0.39	0.76	25.	1.162	Vegetables other than fresh
0.30	0.16	0.49	0.27	0.35	0.25	0.27	0.14	26.	1.170	Tubers, including potatoes
0.42	0.05	0.12	0.54	0.52	0.32	0.75	0.26	27.	1.191	Coffee
0.02	0.17	0.31	0.12	0.01	0.02	0.06	0.04	28.	1.192	Tea
0.01	0.02	0.01	0.06	0.01	0.04	0.06	0.01	29.	1.193	Cocoa
0.36	0.19	0.25	0.30	0.21	0.19	0.37	0.33	30.	1.180	Sugar
0.08	0.29	0.13	0.08	0.08	0.09	0.11	0.20	31.	1.201	Jam, syrup, and honey
0.41	0.27	1.01	0.69	0.72	0.44	0.54	0.34	32.	1.202	Chocolate and ice cream
0.22	0.93	0.11	0.18	0.04	0.07	0.03	0.17	33.	1.203	Salt, spices, and sauces
0.26	0.31	0.35	0.61	0.28	0.20	0.18	0.24	34.	1.310	Nonalcoholic beverages
0.38	0.18	1.25	0.57	0.43	0.29	0.42	0.29	35.	1.321	Spirits
1.57	1.39	0.59	0.33	0.28	1.65	0.35	0.11	36.	1.322	Wine and cider
0.25	0.71	2.67	0.33	0.38	0.14	0.58	0.71	37.	1.323	Beer
1.75	0.71	2.96	0.93	0.92	0.75	0.85	0.98	38.	1.410	Cigarettes
0.12	0.00	0.43	0.67	0.30	0.13	0.09	0.12	39.	1.420	Cigars, tobacco, and snuff
0.55	1.48	0.14	0.33	0.41	0.20	0.25	0.06	40.	2.110	Clothing materials
1.19	0.79	0.84	1.41	0.98	1.41	1.18	1.09	41.	2.121	Men's clothing
0.62	0.95	1.40	1.72	0.77	1.09	1.34	1.43	42.	2.122	Women's clothing
0.50	0.37	0.28	0.08	0.39	0.16	0.43	0.44	43.	2.123	Boys' and girls' clothing
1.22	0.29	0.45	0.47	0.36	0.45	0.40	0.07	44.	2.131	Men's and boys' underwear
0.54	0.24	0.60	0.82	0.98	0.85	0.98	0.36	45.	2.132	Women's and girls' underwear
0.13	0.28	0.63	0.24	0.20	0.42	0.50	0.30	46.	2.150	Haberdashery and millinery
0.24	0.21	0.09	0.05	0.43	0.08	0.07	0.42	47.	2.160	Clothing rental and repair
0.46	0.13	0.28	0.27	0.24	0.26	0.19	0.31	48.	2.211	Men's footwear
0.19	0.14	0.39	0.36	0.28	0.32	0.26	0.37	49.	2.212	Women's footwear
0.27	0.08	0.21	0.16	0.08	0.21	0.31	0.11	50.	2.213	Children's footwear
0.11	0.01	0.08	0.07	0.10	0.06	0.20	0.03	51.	2.220	Footwear, repairs
6.19	6.04	7.36	3.72	5.67	5.38	5.89	8.79	52.	3.110	Rents
0.13	0.29	1.48	1.10	0.57	0.98	0.37	0.88	53.	3.120	Indoor repair and upkeep
0.89	0.70	1.30	0.84	0.81	0.63	0.88	1.01	54.	3.210	Electricity
0.51	0.45	0.76	0.67	0.60	0.52	0.34	0.57	55.	3.220	Gas
0.41	0.14	0.12	0.44	0.67	0.36	0.37	0.35	56.	3.230	Liquid fuels
0.17	0.22	0.76	0.26	1.05	0.39	0.47	0.20	57.	3.240	Other fuels and ice
1.00	0.76	0.70	1.54	1.82	1.33	1.84	1.18	58.	4.110	Furniture and fixtures
0.09	0.30	0.57	0.73	0.23	0.17	0.39	0.36	59.	4.120	Floor coverings
0.46	0.31	0.56	0.95	0.35	0.54	1.09	0.71	60.	4.200	Household textiles and the like

(Table continues on following page.)

			Kenya	India	Philippines	Korea Republic of	Colombia	Malaysia	Iran	Hungary
61.	4.310	Refrigerators and freezers	0.04	0.08	0.36	0.28	0.09	0.18	0.20	0.29
62.	4.320	Washing appliances	0.01	0.0	0.05	0.0	0.11	0.01	0.03	0.14
63.	4.330	Cooking appliances	0.04	0.00	0.29	0.03	0.23	0.08	0.06	0.26
64.	4.340	Heating appliances	0.04	0.01	0.03	0.13	0.05	0.02	0.04	0.13
65.	4.350	Cleaning appliances	0.01	0.0	0.04	0.01	0.11	0.02	0.00	0.05
66.	4.360	Other household appliances	0.02	0.19	0.20	0.55	0.06	0.21	0.04	0.05
67.	4.400	Household utensils	0.44	0.69	0.41	0.24	0.16	0.63	0.37	0.66
68.	4.510	Nondurable household goods	2.06	0.36	1.04	0.34	1.05	0.92	0.62	0.75
69.	4.520	Domestic services	0.81	0.27	0.48	0.10	1.25	0.60	0.17	0.12
70.	4.530	Household services	0.15	0.28	0.08	0.17	0.28	0.0	0.06	0.08
71.	4.600	House furnishing repairs	0.01	0.09	0.10	0.12	0.08	0.01	0.01	0.38
72.	5.110	Drugs and medical preparations	0.70	1.20	0.69	0.64	1.10	0.82	1.55	1.06
73.	5.120	Medical supplies	0.05	0.11	0.06	0.12	0.00	0.05	0.02	0.28
74.	5.200	Therapeutic equipment	0.01	0.03	0.08	0.03	0.14	0.06	0.06	0.0
75.	5.310	Physicians' services	0.50	0.15	0.49	0.47	1.55	0.69	0.62	0.35
76.	5.320	Dentists' services	0.04	0.00	0.13	0.05	0.34	0.15	0.10	0.03
77.	5.330	Nurses' services	0.53	0.22	0.60	0.26	0.13	0.36	0.16	0.37
78.	5.410	Hospitals	1.76	0.22	0.38	0.55	1.15	0.43	0.76	1.43
79.	6.110	Personal automobiles	1.11	0.13	0.21	0.13	1.02	1.85	0.86	0.82
80.	6.120	Other personal transport	0.01	0.17	0.01	0.01	0.00	0.15	0.08	0.29
81.	6.210	Tires, tubes, and accessories	0.22	0.03	0.05	0.00	0.11	0.95	0.12	0.15
82.	6.220	Automobile repairs	0.22	0.11	0.02	0.00	0.20	0.32	0.24	0.18
83.	6.230	Gasoline, oil, and grease	0.12	0.21	0.11	0.00	0.15	2.28	0.25	0.23
84.	6.240	Parking, tolls, and the like	0.09	0.02	0.07	0.00	0.16	0.17	0.16	0.02
85.	6.310	Local transport	0.22	0.45	0.25	1.45	1.80	0.86	0.40	0.47
86.	6.321	Rail transport	0.14	0.48	0.02	0.66	0.95	0.09	0.08	0.45
87.	6.322	Bus transport	1.31	1.55	0.25	1.48	0.19	1.54	0.30	0.52
88.	6.323	Air transport	1.49	0.01	0.16	0.02	2.35	0.71	0.10	0.08
89.	6.330	Miscellaneous transport	0.02	0.43	0.59	0.13	0.05	0.14	0.02	0.09
90.	6.410	Postal communication	0.04	0.11	0.03	0.12	0.03	0.16	0.02	0.12
91.	6.420	Telephone and telegraph	0.10	0.15	0.06	0.13	0.34	0.32	0.10	0.10
92.	7.110	Radios, televisions, and phonographs	0.37	0.16	0.33	0.50	0.70	0.76	0.31	0.81
93.	7.120	Major durable recreational equipment	0.54	0.02	0.13	0.04	0.09	0.24	0.03	0.03
94.	7.130	Other recreational equipment	0.37	0.04	0.08	0.07	0.20	0.14	0.11	0.27
95.	7.210	Public entertainment	0.56	0.05	0.32	0.02	1.13	0.87	0.10	0.76
96.	7.230	Other recreational and cultural activities	0.40	0.25	0.12	1.15	0.22	0.53	0.44	0.80
97.	7.310	Books, papers, and magazines	0.60	0.12	0.15	0.66	0.42	0.51	0.11	0.63
98.	7.320	Stationery	0.01	0.03	0.02	0.26	0.03	0.11	0.10	0.21
99.	7.411	First- and second- level teachers	3.97	2.23	2.85	2.25	1.92	3.74	1.64	1.64
100.	7.412	College teachers	0.22	0.41	0.75	0.33	0.51	0.12	0.30	0.17
101.	7.420	Physical facilities for education	0.57	0.16	0.64	0.33	0.22	0.20	0.11	0.88
102.	7.431	Educational books and supplies	0.23	0.16	0.27	0.26	0.19	0.08	0.03	0.09
103.	7.432	Other educational expenditures	0.38	0.18	0.26	0.44	0.31	0.14	0.05	0.42
104.	8.100	Barber and beauty shops	0.05	0.15	0.41	1.36	0.24	0.25	1.74	0.30
105.	8.210	Toilet articles	0.26	0.32	0.70	0.18	0.80	0.85	0.16	0.43
106.	8.220	Other personal care goods	0.26	0.32	0.70	0.18	0.26	0.85	0.16	0.65
107.	8.310	Restaurants and cafes	1.37	0.35	2.02	1.80	2.72	1.58	1.67	5.55
108.	8.320	Hotels and lodging	1.44	0.35	0.03	0.17	0.20	0.78	0.21	0.21
109.	8.400	Other services	1.19	1.14	2.08	0.64	3.32	0.52	0.97	1.45
110.	8.900	Net expenditures of residents abroad	0.0	0.0	0.08	-0.04	0.02	0.0	0.0	0.0

Italy	Japan	United Kingdom	Netherlands	Belgium	France	Germany F.R.	United States			
0.10	0.61	0.16	0.28	0.10	0.17	0.17	0.16	61.	4.310	Refrigerators and freezers
0.24	0.28	0.21	0.46	0.13	0.31	0.37	0.13	62.	4.320	Washing appliances
0.14	0.11	0.19	0.15	0.17	0.18	0.13	0.11	63.	4.330	Cooking appliances
0.08	0.31	0.18	0.42	0.33	0.13	0.14	0.01	64.	4.340	Heating appliances
0.04	0.13	0.13	0.08	0.03	0.09	0.13	0.04	65.	4.350	Cleaning appliances
0.06	0.30	0.04	0.26	0.04	0.11	0.23	0.25	66.	4.360	Other household appliances
0.37	0.88	0.76	1.06	1.54	0.53	1.04	0.38	67.	4.400	Household utensils
0.45	0.28	0.50	0.82	1.30	1.07	1.17	0.87	68.	4.510	Nondurable household goods
0.0	0.05	0.23	0.0	0.0	0.0	0.0	0.51	69.	4.520	Domestic services
0.68	0.37	0.30	0.45	0.94	0.40	0.42	0.10	70.	4.530	Household services
0.0	0.03	0.07	0.0	0.0	0.0	0.0	0.17	71.	4.600	House furnishing repairs
1.93	1.43	0.73	1.45	1.06	2.59	1.62	1.25	72.	5.110	Drugs and medical preparations
0.01	1.45	0.13	0.04	0.05	0.05	0.16	0.17	73.	5.120	Medical supplies
0.03	0.04	0.21	0.43	0.12	0.15	0.43	0.25	74.	5.200	Therapeutic equipment
1.27	0.26	0.59	1.73	1.63	1.88	1.67	1.57	75.	5.310	Physicians' services
0.56	0.06	0.20	0.74	0.12	1.04	0.62	0.57	76.	5.320	Dentists' services
0.15	0.23	0.99	0.08	0.58	0.21	0.38	0.23	77.	5.330	Nurses' services
0.51	0.87	1.29	0.23	0.52	0.26	0.38	2.58	78.	5.410	Hospitals
1.77	0.29	1.92	1.63	1.93	1.49	1.57	2.83	79.	6.110	Personal automobiles
0.08	0.13	0.12	0.26	0.09	0.12	0.09	0.33	80.	6.120	Other personal transport
0.24	0.02	0.42	0.48	0.49	0.48	0.41	0.47	81.	6.210	Tires, tubes, and accessories
0.65	0.13	0.40	0.38	0.51	1.04	0.84	1.00	82.	6.220	Automobile repairs
1.85	0.27	1.34	0.80	1.35	1.24	1.80	2.24	83.	6.230	Gasoline, oil, and grease
0.47	0.13	0.71	0.38	0.26	0.51	0.41	0.59	84.	6.240	Parking, tolls, and the like
0.57	0.53	1.08	0.26	0.32	0.43	0.28	0.26	85.	6.310	Local transport
0.38	0.16	0.28	0.34	0.43	0.32	0.58	0.02	86.	6.321	Rail transport
0.24	0.04	0.06	0.12	0.26	0.33	0.25	0.05	87.	6.322	Bus transport
0.04	0.02	0.38	0.06	0.08	0.06	0.02	0.22	88.	6.323	Air transport
0.0	0.02	0.20	0.0	0.0	0.0	0.0	0.09	89.	6.330	Miscellaneous transport
0.23	0.05	0.23	0.18	0.15	0.13	0.24	0.15	90.	6.410	Postal communication
0.36	0.36	0.45	0.39	0.31	0.18	0.14	1.03	91.	6.420	Telephone and telegraph
0.50	0.52	0.32	0.91	0.58	0.73	0.44	0.90	92.	7.110	Radios, televisions, and phonographs
0.02	0.08	0.17	0.16	0.06	0.19	0.32	0.54	93.	7.120	Major durable recreational equipment
0.60	0.36	1.11	1.43	0.85	0.98	1.57	0.97	94.	7.130	Other recreational equipment
1.05	0.86	0.70	0.42	0.23	0.22	0.25	0.79	95.	7.210	Public entertainment
0.30	0.19	1.47	0.29	0.50	0.32	0.49	0.97	96.	7.230	Other recreational and cultural activities
1.05	0.38	0.84	0.87	0.50	0.95	0.67	0.64	97.	7.310	Books, papers, and magazines
0.17	0.08	0.20	0.24	0.07	0.53	0.24	0.20	98.	7.320	Stationery
3.32	2.20	2.84	4.10	3.90	3.07	2.33	3.68	99.	7.411	First- and second- level teachers
0.39	0.64	0.68	0.53	0.57	0.45	0.47	0.94	100.	7.412	College teachers
0.22	0.53	0.60	0.88	0.55	0.18	0.44	0.56	101.	7.420	Physical facilities for education
0.04	0.16	0.23	0.16	0.10	0.03	0.02	0.07	102.	7.431	Educational books and supplies
0.12	0.54	0.40	0.16	0.15	0.03	0.16	0.16	103.	7.432	Other educational expenditures
0.36	0.30	0.30	0.14	0.58	0.30	0.22	0.40	104.	8.100	Barber and beauty shops
0.29	0.38	0.32	0.35	0.25	0.48	0.28	0.74	105.	8.210	Toilet articles
0.36	0.10	0.34	0.35	0.25	0.59	0.34	0.76	106.	8.220	Other personal care goods
3.18	2.12	1.72	2.10	6.18	4.49	3.06	3.27	107.	8.310	Restaurants and cafes
1.50	0.82	1.10	1.35	0.36	1.80	1.35	0.20	108.	8.320	Hotels and lodging
0.22	2.54	1.95	1.76	0.48	0.27	0.59	2.59	109.	8.400	Other services
-1.35	0.18	-0.06	0.52	0.41	-0.24	0.11	0.48	110.	8.900	Net expenditures of residents abroad

(Table continues on following page.)

145

			Kenya	India	Philippines	Korea Republic of	Colombia	Malaysia	Iran	Hungary
111.	10.100	One- and two-dwelling buildings	2.82	1.18	0.97	2.74	2.75	1.17	3.05	2.35
112.	10.200	Multidwelling buildings	0.42	1.18	1.23	0.47	0.35	1.17	1.15	2.56
113.	11.100	Hotels	0.06	0.10	0.04	0.17	0.02	0.13	0.26	0.34
114.	11.200	Industrial buildings	1.15	0.22	0.15	1.16	0.18	0.68	1.96	3.31
115.	11.300	Commercial buildings	0.23	0.60	0.90	1.39	0.06	0.51	0.23	0.53
116.	11.400	Office buildings	0.29	0.25	0.22	0.50	0.12	0.51	0.71	0.57
117.	11.500	Educational buildings	0.29	0.15	0.48	0.27	0.05	0.35	0.16	0.45
118.	11.600	Hospital buildings	0.29	0.09	0.11	0.85	0.02	0.24	0.07	0.16
119.	11.700	Agricultural buildings	0.06	0.88	0.09	0.41	0.11	0.13	0.76	2.33
120.	11.800	Other buildings	0.07	0.21	0.01	0.73	0.02	0.13	0.28	0.16
121.	12.100	Roads, streets, and highways	1.18	0.57	0.90	1.84	2.31	0.41	1.01	0.92
122.	12.200	Transport and utility lines	0.89	1.65	0.37	1.60	1.93	1.34	1.13	2.98
123.	12.300	Other construction	1.42	1.18	0.03	3.71	1.35	0.29	1.14	1.56
124.	13.000	Land improvement	0.47	1.21	0.03	0.11	2.07	1.50	0.0	0.42
125.	14.110	Locomotives	0.29	0.05	0.04	0.21	0.00	0.00	0.00	0.23
126.	14.120	Other railway vehicles	0.52	0.11	0.00	0.18	0.03	0.0	0.06	0.48
127.	14.200	Passenger automobiles	1.08	0.05	1.71	1.07	0.66	0.40	0.83	0.20
128.	14.300	Trucks, busses, and trailers	1.23	0.92	1.30	1.28	0.94	0.90	0.77	1.25
129.	14.400	Aircraft	0.28	0.03	0.13	0.26	0.30	0.0	0.17	0.09
130.	14.500	Ships and boats	0.05	0.10	0.51	0.85	0.46	0.41	0.23	0.05
131.	14.600	Other transport equipment	0.06	0.17	0.10	0.08	0.02	0.09	0.81	0.71
132.	15.100	Engines and turbines	0.28	0.20	0.95	0.50	0.06	0.37	0.44	0.26
133.	15.210	Tractors	0.31	0.11	0.47	0.0	0.06	0.37	0.08	0.40
134.	15.220	Others agricultural machinery	0.44	0.02	0.12	0.09	0.08	0.05	0.39	0.59
135.	15.300	Office machinery	0.24	0.03	0.39	0.11	0.08	0.18	0.07	0.38
136.	15.400	Metalworking machinery	0.15	0.20	0.19	0.38	0.16	0.20	0.29	0.64
137.	15.500	Construction and mining machinery	0.61	0.14	1.14	0.23	0.22	0.98	0.10	0.68
138.	15.600	Special industrial machinery	1.32	0.37	0.83	1.06	0.30	1.04	1.01	2.50
139.	15.700	General industrial machinery	1.24	1.01	1.87	1.33	0.40	0.93	0.43	0.82
140.	15.800	Service industrial machinery	0.27	0.08	0.48	0.27	0.02	0.22	0.20	0.12
141.	16.100	Electrical transmission equipment	0.52	0.46	0.47	0.41	1.06	0.33	0.38	0.26
142.	16.200	Communications equipment	0.37	0.45	0.73	0.15	0.69	0.37	0.11	0.36
143.	16.300	Other electrical equipment	0.14	0.08	0.68	0.26	1.30	0.00	0.22	0.07
144.	16.400	Instruments	0.18	0.05	0.19	0.03	0.70	0.21	0.19	0.62
145.	17.100	Furniture and fixtures	0.10	0.04	0.15	0.11	0.22	0.22	0.13	1.40
146.	17.200	Other durable goods	0.26	0.97	0.75	0.10	0.18	0.02	0.13	0.14
147.	18.000	Increase in stocks	2.33	2.23	2.48	2.09	2.60	2.95	0.21	3.83
148.	19.000	Exports minuus imports	-1.74	-0.65	-0.47	-10.13	-1.67	4.49	5.94	-2.92
149.	20.100	Unskilled blue collar	3.76	1.53	0.36	0.21	0.98	0.40	3.63	0.71
150.	20.210	Skilled blue collar	0.27	0.12	0.16	0.34	0.22	0.17	1.12	0.04
151.	20.220	White collar	1.03	1.72	2.14	3.87	1.32	2.39	1.34	0.66
152.	20.300	Professional	2.55	1.14	0.83	0.88	2.50	3.78	1.91	0.60
153.	21.000	Commodities of government	2.40	3.33	2.07	3.18	1.52	4.07	5.24	5.75

Appendix Table 4.3. Purchasing-Power Parities per U.S. Dollar and International Prices, 1970

			Kenya (shillings)	India (rupees)	Philippines (pesos)	Korea Republic of (won)	Colombia (pesos)	Malaysia (M.dollars)	Iran (rials)	Hungary (forints)
1.	1.101	Rice	4.11	4.51	3.33	252.	11.6	1.62	69.1	51.7
2.	1.102	Meal and other cereals	4.84	3.34	6.27	150.	12.0	1.48	42.0	16.6
3.	1.103	Bread	2.42	2.50	3.39	163.	11.1	1.13	16.0	5.0
4.	1.104	Biscuits, cakes, and the like	1.00	8.63	6.35	473.	21.0	6.48	57.2	22.1
5.	1.105	Cereal preparations	9.48	2.97	6.14	174.	19.2	4.05	52.0	11.6

Italy	Japan	United Kingdom	Netherlands	Belgium	France	Germany F.R.	United States			
5.21	4.93	2.21	1.31	0.57	2.25	1.25	2.15	111.	10.100	One- and two-dwelling buildings
1.74	2.30	1.03	3.95	4.55	4.66	3.83	1.46	112.	10.200	Multidwelling buildings
0.17	0.44	0.07	0.09	0.07	0.13	0.22	0.14	113.	11.100	Hotels
1.79	1.40	1.48	1.55	2.30	0.79	1.99	0.71	114.	11.200	Industrial buildings
0.25	1.40	0.50	0.95	0.53	0.63	0.60	0.63	115.	11.300	Commercial buildings
0.71	1.54	0.34	0.52	0.28	0.67	0.75	0.40	116.	11.400	Office buildings
0.34	0.97	0.65	1.30	0.21	0.72	0.88	0.66	117.	11.500	Educational buildings
0.24	0.34	0.32	1.00	0.05	0.24	0.42	0.35	118.	11.600	Hospital buildings
0.42	0.24	0.18	0.43	0.61	0.49	0.30	0.16	119.	11.700	Agricultural buildings
0.17	1.89	0.39	0.08	0.12	0.72	0.09	0.44	120.	11.800	Other buildings
0.88	1.18	0.64	1.22	1.90	0.70	1.57	1.13	121.	12.100	Roads, streets, and highways
0.85	1.39	0.38	1.32	1.84	1.82	2.02	1.85	122.	12.200	Transport and utility lines
0.07	1.83	0.20	0.18	0.02	0.13	0.22	0.28	123.	12.300	Other construction
0.53	0.04	0.17	0.44	0.03	0.06	0.07	0.0	124.	13.000	Land improvement
0.05	0.06	0.02	0.03	0.04	0.07	0.02	0.05	125.	14.110	Locomotives
0.05	0.01	0.03	0.05	0.07	0.10	0.09	0.12	126.	14.120	Other railway vehicles
0.78	0.86	0.86	0.86	0.56	0.54	0.97	0.55	127.	14.200	Passenger automobiles
0.79	1.08	0.09	0.95	0.62	0.79	1.05	0.68	128.	14.300	Trucks, busses, and trailers
0.14	0.03	0.25	0.38	0.33	0.05	0.22	0.24	129.	14.400	Aircraft
0.15	0.30	0.80	0.67	0.23	0.10	0.53	0.09	130.	14.500	Ships and boats
0.07	0.11	0.50	0.01	0.0	0.01	0.00	0.04	131.	14.600	Other transport equipment
0.10	0.23	0.01	0.11	0.05	0.07	0.06	0.13	132.	15.100	Engines and turbines
0.18	0.05	0.09	0.19	0.24	0.39	0.20	0.15	133.	15.210	Tractors
0.24	0.21	0.14	0.19	0.24	0.65	0.26	0.25	134.	15.220	Others agricultural machinery
0.28	0.61	0.32	0.46	0.30	0.84	0.90	0.50	135.	15.300	Office machinery
0.45	0.83	0.45	0.30	0.23	0.39	0.69	0.36	136.	15.400	Metalworking machinery
0.27	0.52	0.47	0.69	0.81	1.11	0.76	0.40	137.	15.500	Construction and mining machinery
0.66	1.37	0.77	1.04	0.67	1.29	1.11	0.40	138.	15.600	Special industrial machinery
0.70	1.30	2.15	1.85	1.44	0.62	1.71	0.42	139.	15.700	General industrial machinery
0.12	0.12	0.06	0.46	0.16	0.12	0.20	0.27	140.	15.800	Service industrial machinery
1.05	1.38	0.67	0.99	0.68	1.01	1.05	0.35	141.	16.100	Electrical transmission equipment
0.41	1.44	0.88	0.80	0.65	0.69	1.04	0.76	142.	16.200	Communications equipment
0.45	0.40	0.19	0.34	0.71	0.20	0.23	0.15	143.	16.300	Other electrical equipment
0.38	0.75	0.18	1.00	0.67	0.84	0.87	0.40	144.	16.400	Instruments
0.19	2.25	0.84	0.0	0.42	0.14	0.23	0.33	145.	17.100	Furniture and fixtures
0.39	1.20	0.19	0.0	0.45	0.24	0.23	0.35	146.	17.200	Other durable goods
1.82	4.29	0.87	2.50	1.62	2.29	2.19	0.25	147.	18.000	Increase in stocks
0.58	1.33	0.93	-1.82	2.44	0.60	1.94	0.21	148.	19.000	Exports minuus imports
1.92	0.85	2.58	0.51	1.47	0.24	0.40	1.42	149.	20.100	Unskilled blue collar
0.84	1.68	0.32	0.58	0.36	1.41	1.12	1.01	150.	20.210	Skilled blue collar
3.20	0.41	2.04	4.57	2.62	2.70	3.91	2.66	151.	20.220	White collar
0.54	0.56	0.93	1.61	1.07	2.04	0.76	1.98	152.	20.300	Professional
2.30	1.35	4.66	3.30	2.62	2.87	2.61	6.84	153.	21.000	Commodities of government

Italy (lire)	Japan (yen)	United Kingdom (pounds)	Netherlands (guilders)	Belgium (B.francs)	France (francs)	Germany F.R. (DM)	United States (dollars)			
589.	441.	0.390	4.38	69.8	4.81	5.21	1.76	1.	1.101	Rice
1209.	242.	0.248	6.05	81.7	9.64	7.61	1.44	2.	1.102	Meal and other cereals
304.	180.	0.145	1.50	20.0	2.52	2.03	0.63	3.	1.103	Bread
854.	305.	0.233	4.37	71.8	9.75	4.00	1.41	4.	1.104	Biscuits, cakes, and the like
1055.	477.	0.275	3.50	62.3	7.68	4.23	1.20	5.	1.105	Cereal preparations

(Table continues on following page.)

			Kenya (shillings)	India (rupees)	Philippines (pesos)	Korea Republic of (won)	Colombia (pesos)	Malaysia (M.dollars)	Iran (rials)	Hungary (forints)
6.	1.106	Macaroni and spaghetti	9.89	9.17	5.53	79.	8.5	1.55	47.2	19.1
7.	1.111	Fresh beef and veal	3.56	2.78	1.94	232.	9.3	1.52	54.6	37.7
8.	1.112	Fresh lamb and mutton	4.19	3.84	1.98	224.	5.6	2.21	57.1	10.0
9.	1.113	Fresh pork	6.32	2.02	1.86	204.	8.9	1.69	57.5	45.7
10.	1.114	Fresh poultry	4.75	7.11	3.15	324.	19.5	3.56	91.2	33.1
11.	1.115	Other fresh meat	3.30	3.90	2.54	243.	8.3	1.86	38.7	13.5
12.	1.116	Frozen and salted meat	5.90	4.35	3.91	338.	12.0	3.31	66.3	23.2
13.	1.121	Fresh and frozen fish	2.88	1.21	2.70	160.	10.0	1.56	41.7	8.7
14.	1.122	Canned fish	12.09	1.19	3.31	157.	15.4	0.58	81.1	51.1
15.	1.131	Fresh milk	4.18	2.86	5.22	391.	7.9	5.05	65.5	12.0
16.	1.132	Milk products	4.78	5.20	3.42	326.	14.9	1.78	21.7	15.8
17.	1.133	Eggs and egg products	5.64	5.34	4.03	306.	17.4	2.04	66.9	31.1
18.	1.141	Butter	4.48	4.01	5.22	104.	15.6	2.49	99.6	26.2
19.	1.142	Margerine and edible oil	8.07	7.62	5.26	436.	13.9	1.81	90.4	31.5
20.	1.143	Lard and edible fat	10.84	7.52	5.09	643.	36.0	2.44	129.4	39.1
21.	1.151	Fresh tropical fruits	2.26	2.81	1.89	1233.	3.8	0.76	68.6	46.8
22.	1.152	Other fresh fruits	15.73	3.58	1.80	170.	21.4	2.38	38.4	11.1
23.	1.153	Fresh vegetables	1.74	1.41	2.06	130.	6.8	1.18	18.0	7.3
24.	1.161	Fruit other than fresh	4.48	5.81	4.67	391.	21.1	2.76	38.8	57.4
25.	1.162	Vegetables other than fresh	5.29	6.51	4.94	344.	27.9	2.83	44.4	30.2
26.	1.170	Tubers, including potatoes	1.83	3.37	1.40	82.	7.6	0.79	31.0	13.0
27.	1.191	Coffee	7.71	10.46	6.62	1032.	11.3	4.53	147.1	113.1
28.	1.192	Tea	2.88	2.72	6.52	615.	18.9	1.67	76.7	52.1
29.	1.193	Cocoa	8.70	15.22	5.63	1245.	11.9	3.54	108.4	45.2
30.	1.180	Sugar	5.44	7.32	3.40	519.	10.1	2.02	82.9	33.4
31.	1.201	Jam, syrup, and honey	3.54	8.64	3.81	474.	14.3	3.13	102.3	18.1
32.	1.202	Chocolate and ice cream	21.06	6.58	5.41	954.	12.4	4.04	60.0	31.2
33.	1.203	Salt, spices, and sauces	5.11	1.92	2.51	143.	5.1	0.92	21.3	14.7
34.	1.310	Nonalcoholic beverages	15.33	5.32	4.59	722.	9.9	2.81	59.2	23.9
35.	1.321	Spirits	5.76	9.60	0.94	458.	9.0	1.72	43.3	24.2
36.	1.322	Wine and cider	18.28	12.28	1.49	58.	27.5	2.13	47.0	13.9
37.	1.323	Beer	8.21	9.97	2.37	505.	8.3	2.61	53.6	17.2
38.	1.410	Cigarettes	4.85	8.12	3.12	258.	3.4	2.56	41.1	8.3
39.	1.420	Cigars, tobacco, and snuff	4.17	2.72	2.35	167.	7.6	2.26	26.6	16.6
40.	2.110	Clothing materials	6.84	5.78	4.37	365.	18.5	1.70	78.9	50.4
41.	2.121	Men's clothing	4.52	3.13	1.40	144.	9.8	1.11	20.3	22.4
42.	2.122	Women's clothing	6.95	3.41	1.13	260.	16.7	0.98	68.4	25.9
43.	2.123	Boys' and girls' clothing	3.04	2.46	1.80	278.	12.3	1.09	47.2	21.8
44.	2.131	Men's and boys' underwear	8.23	1.81	2.17	166.	12.8	1.33	35.7	26.4
45.	2.132	Women's and girls' underwear	4.16	5.69	1.46	167.	13.8	1.45	40.5	24.8
46.	2.150	Haberdashery and millinery	3.38	4.09	1.59	117.	8.0	0.91	27.7	18.6
47.	2.160	Clothing rental and repair	3.10	1.27	0.37	110.	5.9	0.44	11.1	9.2
48.	2.211	Men's footwear	2.75	3.08	2.53	117.	7.0	0.98	24.6	22.6
49.	2.212	Women's footwear	1.71	3.56	0.00	241.	6.6	0.88	11.4	19.3
50.	2.213	Children's footwear	1.74	2.61	1.21	48.	7.1	0.39	19.9	11.6
51.	2.220	Footwear, repairs	4.01	3.53	2.53	122.	6.3	0.65	19.9	16.9
52.	3.110	Rents	5.98	1.90	1.17	346.	14.1	1.04	17.5	9.4
53.	3.120	Indoor repair and upkeep	3.21	0.45	0.84	76.	10.2	1.66	16.0	6.3
54.	3.210	Electricity	9.27	7.39	3.16	448.	7.2	4.31	99.4	30.4
55.	3.220	Gas	9.98	6.66	8.71	206.	5.3	3.75	60.2	18.2
56.	3.230	Liquid fuels	17.17	12.96	12.13	383.	10.7	3.62	59.0	41.9
57.	3.240	Other fuels and ice	1.78	2.90	5.47	100.	4.3	1.37	57.9	7.8
58.	4.110	Furniture and fixtures	4.51	4.08	1.87	103.	9.5	0.76	31.2	21.2
59.	4.120	Floor coverings	8.58	1.56	2.97	179.	9.9	1.21	15.0	28.7
60.	4.200	Household textiles and the like	7.63	2.52	1.72	288.	13.2	1.47	51.3	28.1

Italy (lire)	Japan (yen)	United Kingdom (pounds)	Netherlands (guilders)	Belgium (B.francs)	France (francs)	Germany F.R. (DM)	United States (dollars)			
401.	294.	0.384	4.04	54.3	3.79	3.23	1.07	6.	1.106	Macaroni and spaghetti
621.	608.	0.236	4.06	53.3	4.75	3.97	1.22	7.	1.111	Fresh beef and veal
616.	433.	0.314	3.54	49.8	5.16	4.03	1.51	8.	1.112	Fresh lamb and mutton
661.	447.	0.347	3.23	44.9	4.78	3.66	1.37	9.	1.113	Fresh pork
868.	461.	0.361	4.66	67.0	6.84	5.42	1.79	10.	1.114	Fresh poultry
501.	400.	0.274	2.88	46.2	5.19	3.89	1.17	11.	1.115	Other fresh meat
658.	455.	0.336	3.56	50.8	5.63	4.41	1.29	12.	1.116	Frozen and salted meat
576.	294.	0.340	2.40	43.4	4.43	2.83	1.15	13.	1.121	Fresh and frozen fish
613.	422.	0.501	3.52	61.8	6.61	3.91	1.16	14.	1.122	Canned fish
512.	375.	0.365	2.18	29.4	3.08	2.31	1.09	15.	1.131	Fresh milk
623.	345.	0.172	2.93	37.2	3.79	3.24	1.05	16.	1.132	Milk products
707.	261.	0.376	3.26	50.7	5.54	3.76	1.53	17.	1.133	Eggs and egg products
904.	411.	0.217	3.82	55.0	6.17	4.00	1.39	18.	1.141	Butter
549.	365.	0.328	3.07	37.9	3.82	3.88	1.68	19.	1.142	Margerine and edible oil
769.	563.	0.386	4.21	76.8	8.86	6.07	2.70	20.	1.143	Lard and edible fat
658.	452.	0.354	3.30	57.3	5.83	3.80	0.99	21.	1.151	Fresh tropical fruits
273.	370.	0.369	1.47	26.6	2.92	2.15	0.87	22.	1.152	Other fresh fruits
294.	205.	0.211	1.69	24.7	2.61	1.83	0.69	23.	1.153	Fresh vegetables
989.	381.	0.348	3.00	62.3	8.43	5.02	1.40	24.	1.161	Fruit other than fresh
951.	521.	0.360	5.02	81.4	8.65	6.60	1.56	25.	1.162	Vegetables other than fresh
448.	322.	0.228	2.42	15.5	2.29	3.26	0.73	26.	1.170	Tubers, including potatoes
1879.	709.	0.368	6.53	96.3	8.79	11.03	2.23	27.	1.191	Coffee
1087.	224.	0.180	2.55	52.6	6.49	8.55	1.22	28.	1.192	Tea
1145.	663.	0.293	3.75	88.4	5.40	4.99	1.72	29.	1.193	Cocoa
888.	504.	0.288	4.13	55.3	4.77	4.54	1.78	30.	1.180	Sugar
567.	380.	0.196	2.77	44.0	5.02	3.51	1.34	31.	1.201	Jam, syrup, and honey
1059.	539.	0.472	4.50	59.3	8.80	5.48	1.66	32.	1.202	Chocolate and ice cream
323.	183.	0.330	1.84	36.4	4.35	2.39	0.90	33.	1.203	Salt, spices, and sauces
556.	370.	0.382	2.59	29.9	3.22	3.09	1.32	34.	1.310	Nonalcoholic beverages
386.	235.	0.370	1.63	33.0	3.34	2.01	1.09	35.	1.321	Spirits
449.	221.	0.833	3.52	35.8	3.42	3.32	1.01	36.	1.322	Wine and cider
408.	333.	0.572	2.05	30.8	2.96	2.23	1.29	37.	1.323	Beer
638.	214.	0.656	3.88	34.0	4.21	4.70	1.19	38.	1.410	Cigarettes
512.	139.	0.638	1.30	16.9	2.26	1.97	0.89	39.	1.420	Cigars, tobacco, and snuff
1057.	329.	0.334	5.66	86.8	10.53	6.57	2.04	40.	2.110	Clothing materials
510.	251.	0.324	2.32	40.8	5.32	3.05	1.04	41.	2.121	Men's clothing
806.	233.	0.444	3.73	62.3	9.13	4.65	1.29	42.	2.122	Women's clothing
479.	284.	0.299	3.06	35.3	5.02	4.39	1.16	43.	2.123	Boys' and girls' clothing
597.	259.	0.437	3.63	58.0	6.02	4.87	1.34	44.	2.131	Men's and boys' underwear
746.	256.	0.353	3.88	66.3	8.84	5.01	1.37	45.	2.132	Women's and girls' underwear
461.	209.	0.273	2.55	44.4	5.23	3.50	1.01	46.	2.150	Haberdashery and millinery
257.	94.	0.326	2.34	25.4	3.98	4.60	0.72	47.	2.160	Clothing rental and repair
616.	192.	0.234	2.66	37.2	5.64	3.48	1.05	48.	2.211	Men's footwear
478.	205.	0.259	2.51	41.7	5.75	2.86	0.90	49.	2.212	Women's footwear
449.	168.	0.185	2.42	37.6	4.12	3.03	0.78	50.	2.213	Children's footwear
311.	112.	0.220	2.21	34.4	5.00	2.55	0.87	51.	2.220	Footwear, repairs
321.	319.	0.295	1.92	31.5	3.18	2.60	0.90	52.	3.110	Rents
224.	175.	0.415	1.91	28.9	3.95	2.45	0.76	53.	3.120	Indoor repair and upkeep
759.	307.	0.333	2.96.	81.9	7.69	4.19	1.32	54.	3.210	Electricity
1324.	1188.	0.850	3.44	93.6	9.51	7.71	1.53	55.	3.220	Gas
645.	414.	0.408	2.87	51.4	5.61	3.33	1.53	56.	3.230	Liquid fuels
878.	208.	0.319	5.11	62.4	6.89	5.17	0.94	57.	3.240	Other fuels and ice
506.	296.	0.545	2.63	41.4	5.04	2.99	1.10	58.	4.110	Furniture and fixtures
668.	313.	0.305	3.80	51.8	5.88	3.70	0.99	59.	4.120	Floor coverings
813.	363.	0.290	4.42	73.1	7.28	6.22	1.30	60.	4.200	Household textiles and the like

(Table continues on following page.)

			Kenya (shillings)	India (rupees)	Philippines (pesos)	Korea Republic of (won)	Colombia (pesos)	Malaysia (M.dollars)	Iran (rials)	Hungary (forints)
61.	4.310	Refrigerators and freezers	10.03	14.17	10.15	980.	28.2	4.46	104.8	49.4
62.	4.320	Washing appliances	5.87	3.29	2.85	257.	60.6	1.56	134.1	29.5
63.	4.330	Cooking appliances	11.39	5.69	6.18	310.	18.5	2.70	44.0	13.7
64.	4.340	Heating appliances	6.81	4.53	9.55	374.	30.3	4.43	107.0	34.3
65.	4.350	Cleaning appliances	7.10	3.98	3.44	310.	64.0	1.89	28.1	32.8
66.	4.360	Other household appliances	14.31	4.28	4.70	287.	47.1	5.56	26.1	24.4
67.	4.400	Household utensils	3.39	4.64	4.41	84.	7.6	0.83	37.8	22.7
68.	4.510	Nondurable household goods	6.27	7.50	3.50	231.	11.3	1.90	44.0	30.2
69.	4.520	Domestic services	0.67	0.24	0.35	29.	0.0	0.42	9.5	9.3
70.	4.530	Household services	4.05	1.11	1.24	137.	5.8	1.62	30.8	14.6
71.	4.600	House furnishing repairs	1.34	0.45	0.74	11.	1.6	0.63	14.5	9.5
72.	5.110	Drugs and medical preparations	3.64	3.06	2.76	75.	20.3	1.40	30.2	12.0
73.	5.120	Medical supplies	4.63	2.47	1.65	126.	9.9	0.94	22.7	21.5
74.	5.200	Therapeutic equipment	1.83	0.67	1.86	88.	12.6	0.46	22.5	5.7
75.	5.310	Physicians' services	0.98	0.13	1.18	20.	4.9	0.79	14.7	1.3
76.	5.320	Dentists' services	1.13	0.01	1.83	14.	3.3	1.32	11.6	0.7
77.	5.330	Nurses' services	3.14	4.70	13.88	147.	4.5	1.69	86.6	13.5
78.	5.410	Hospitals	1.04	0.20	0.26	84.	2.3	0.10	25.6	3.5
79.	6.110	Personal automobiles	9.23	10.78	14.66	761.	37.9	4.68	121.8	58.7
80.	6.120	Other personal transport	8.76	6.35	4.50	463.	31.5	3.10	61.6	21.2
81.	6.210	Tires, tubes, and accessories	10.91	8.24	5.35	405.	15.1	2.16	75.2	26.5
82.	6.220	Automobile repairs	1.56	1.09	2.22	211.	5.0	1.25	21.4	14.8
83.	6.230	Gasoline, oil, and grease	8.84	11.48	3.37	961.	6.8	4.34	59.8	37.7
84.	6.240	Parking, tolls, and the like	1.29	0.97	8.82	119.	3.3	1.24	15.3	4.4
85.	6.310	Local transport	1.90	1.23	0.63	66.	2.4	1.14	6.6	7.9
86.	6.321	Rail transport	3.16	2.20	2.00	75.	3.7	1.23	18.0	11.9
87.	6.322	Bus transport	2.62	2.01	1.08	137.	3.7	0.83	10.1	15.0
88.	6.323	Air transport	11.22	8.26	2.73	166.	11.7	2.56	92.7	28.3
89.	6.330	Miscellaneous transport	7.84	4.80	2.33	241.	9.8	2.11	22.8	35.1
90.	6.410	Postal communication	4.39	1.56	2.37	164.	7.0	1.85	98.4	11.3
91.	6.420	Telephone and telegraph	2.75	1.28	1.81	48.	2.6	1.15	12.9	5.9
92.	7.110	Radios, televisions, and phonographs	11.58	7.54	7.80	301.	26.5	2.66	110.7	40.2
93.	7.120	Major durable recreational equipment	8.19	2.49	4.11	294.	23.4	1.73	142.4	19.7
94.	7.130	Other recreational equipment	7.56	5.77	3.84	119.	23.8	2.58	37.3	26.4
95.	7.210	Public entertainment	1.66	2.29	0.81	77.	5.5	0.62	13.1	3.8
96.	7.230	Other recreational and cultural activities	2.57	0.86	0.63	50.	7.2	2.79	39.0	2.5
97.	7.310	Books, papers, and magazines	6.22	2.67	2.79	207.	10.4	1.93	39.2	13.1
98.	7.320	Stationery	15.65	2.42	4.34	113.	11.0	1.28	33.4	50.8
99.	7.411	First- and second- level teachers	0.92	0.33	0.31	29.	1.5	0.46	8.2	3.0
100.	7.412	College teachers	4.48	0.77	0.77	63.	4.6	0.95	31.8	4.3
101.	7.420	Physical facilities for education	6.20	4.29	3.61	198.	8.6	2.51	49.5	18.1
102.	7.431	Educational books and supplies	6.55	2.41	2.84	171.	11.5	1.84	38.6	12.8
103.	7.432	Other educational expenditures	4.46	3.85	4.48	294.	11.6	2.11	51.0	23.7
104.	8.100	Barber and beauty shops	2.45	1.32	0.40	40.	4.1	0.39	12.3	3.4
105.	8.210	Toilet articles	10.72	5.24	2.67	201.	14.8	3.10	32.3	12.7
106.	8.220	Other personal care goods	2.88	4.02	1.97	129.	8.2	1.72	25.8	34.7
107.	8.310	Restaurants and cafes	2.71	3.26	3.51	206.	9.2	2.50	15.5	14.4
108.	8.320	Hotels and lodging	4.01	3.81	3.43	107.	8.1	0.63	36.9	16.8
109.	8.400	Other services	1.61	0.71	0.80	61.	3.7	0.83	19.6	7.1
110.	8.900	Net expenditures of residents abroad	7.14	7.50	6.07	310.	18.4	3.08	76.4	30.0

Italy (lire)	Japan (yen)	United Kingdom (pounds)	Netherlands (guilders)	Belgium (B.francs)	France (francs)	Germany F.R. (DM)	United States (dollars)			
420.	677.	0.949	2.69	37.6	4.84	2.64	1.77	61.	4.310	Refrigerators and freezers
591.	293.	0.448	4.97	77.6	9.13	5.22	1.48	62.	4.320	Washing appliances
416.	217.	0.357	2.86	46.3	6.01	4.18	1.19	63.	4.330	Cooking appliances
798.	436.	0.691	4.89	55.1	7.82	4.00	1.84	64.	4.340	Heating appliances
898.	427.	0.821	4.75	70.2	7.57	4.79	1.75	65.	4.350	Cleaning appliances
769.	325.	0.643	4.45	57.2	7.90	4.86	1.42	66.	4.360	Other household appliances
333.	228.	0.364	2.10	30.5	3.66	2.45	0.96	67.	4.400	Household utensils
554.	283.	0.343	3.01	38.0	4.92	2.92	1.24	68.	4.510	Nondurable household goods
98.	136.	0.185	0.55	7.4	0.91	0.55	0.28	69.	4.520	Domestic services
571.	208.	0.265	3.51	48.2	6.42	4.51	1.04	70.	4.530	Household services
212.	84.	0.134	1.09	14.7	1.73	1.04	0.49	71.	4.600	House furnishing repairs
409.	140.	0.155	2.04	26.3	2.86	3.45	0.86	72.	5.110	Drugs and medical preparations
167.	195.	0.212	2.01	34.0	3.85	2.49	0.89	73.	5.120	Medical supplies
549.	70.	0.174	1.50	20.2	3.52	2.53	0.73	74.	5.200	Therapeutic equipment
246.	34.	0.097	2.69	31.2	4.82	2.34	0.51	75.	5.310	Physicians' services
224.	21.	0.130	4.93	18.7	7.46	2.60	0.66	76.	5.320	Dentists' services
812.	260.	1.630	1.29	258.3	5.81	6.91	1.53	77.	5.330	Nurses' services
37.	32.	0.080	0.12	5.0	0.36	0.23	0.28	78.	5.410	Hospitals
664.	375.	0.490	5.13	64.3	6.33	4.24	1.39	79.	6.110	Personal automobiles
549.	445.	0.532	4.43	62.3	5.73	3.09	1.27	80.	6.120	Other personal transport
509.	305.	0.242	3.79	56.3	6.19	4.85	1.23	81.	6.210	Tires, tubes, and accessories
608.	339.	0.161	4.18	59.6	9.36	5.34	1.05	82.	6.220	Automobile repairs
1373.	562.	0.641	5.79	83.6	10.66	5.86	1.47	83.	6.230	Gasoline, oil, and grease
191.	249.	0.272	1.26	27.0	2.53	2.01	0.72	84.	6.240	Parking, tolls, and the like
296.	101.	0.214	1.95	29.7	3.40	2.56	0.52	85.	6.310	Local transport
255.	117.	0.283	1.87	35.9	3.22	2.62	0.69	86.	6.321	Rail transport
333.	144.	0.236	2.05	33.4	5.18	2.68	0.77	87.	6.322	Bus transport
619.	235.	0.369	8.84	61.0	6.19	4.40	1.57	88.	6.323	Air transport
873.	330.	0.997	5.06	117.4	11.74	8.14	1.50	89.	6.330	Miscellaneous transport
459.	258.	0.271	2.09	29.3	3.67	1.96	0.89	90.	6.410	Postal communication
409.	224.	0.189	1.92	63.2	6.03	3.47	0.83	91.	6.420	Telephone and telegraph
894.	207.	0.608	4.97	76.4	9.39	4.34	1.50	92.	7.110	Radios, televisions, and phonographs
716.	216.	0.396	4.15	53.8	6.53	3.55	1.17	93.	7.120	Major durable recreational equipment
634.	276.	0.441	4.09	55.0	5.99	4.01	1.26	94.	7.130	Other recreational equipment
370.	361.	0.104	0.97	16.8	2.41	1.35	0.56	95.	7.210	Public entertainment
444.	172.	0.330	2.10	30.0	3.78	2.93	0.57	96.	7.230	Other recreational and cultural activities
548.	369.	0.167	3.05	45.2	4.25	3.45	1.02	97.	7.310	Books, papers, and magazines
376.	269.	0.342	2.19	33.9	3.94	3.18	1.05	98.	7.320	Stationery
224.	118.	0.165	3.45	33.1	3.53	1.98	0.44	99.	7.411	First- and second- level teachers
400.	231.	0.530	4.15	5.2	7.80	5.98	0.69	100.	7.412	College teachers
643.	341.	0.409	3.08	54.8	6.17	3.98	1.24	101.	7.420	Physical facilities for education
532.	335.	0.168	2.96	43.9	4.13	3.35	1.05	102.	7.431	Educational books and supplies
631.	377.	0.336	3.61	52.8	5.67	4.18	1.39	103.	7.432	Other educational expenditures
237.	135.	0.113	1.39	17.0	2.51	1.74	0.43	104.	8.100	Barber and beauty shops
723.	301.	0.365	3.51	54.3	5.57	3.92	1.22	105.	8.210	Toilet articles
631.	202.	0.266	4.25	54.6	7.38	4.51	1.19	106.	8.220	Other personal care goods
619.	110.	0.386	2.07	28.4	5.18	3.40	0.94	107.	8.310	Restaurants and cafes
430.	267.	0.285	2.69	26.9	3.54	2.35	0.91	108.	8.320	Hotels and lodging
345.	127.	0.227	2.27	28.9	3.99	2.53	0.65	109.	8.400	Other services
627.	358.	0.417	3.62	49.7	5.53	3.65	1.00	110.	8.900	Net expenditures of residents abroad

(Table continues on following page.)

			Kenya (shillings)	India (rupees)	Philippines (pesos)	Korea Republic of (won)	Colombia (pesos)	Malaysia (M.dollars)	Iran (rials)	Hungary (forints)
111.	10.100	One- and two-dwelling buildings	3.31	1.71	1.84	112.	4.6	0.70	15.9	17.1
112.	10.200	Multidwelling buildings	3.64	1.66	1.71	92.	3.0	0.63	24.7	15.6
113.	11.100	Hotels	4.89	1.74	2.23	180.	3.9	0.66	37.2	16.0
114.	11.200	Industrial buildings	5.04	2.57	3.49	157.	6.7	0.87	25.5	22.0
115.	11.300	Commercial buildings	3.71	1.84	3.49	158.	4.3	0.81	33.2	19.7
116.	11.400	Office buildings	2.59	1.59	1.83	178.	2.8	0.69	16.2	12.7
117.	11.500	Educational buildings	2.66	1.79	1.51	139.	2.8	0.47	18.1	14.4
118.	11.600	Hospital buildings	3.19	1.38	1.66	176.	4.9	0.69	17.1	11.8
119.	11.700	Agricultural buildings	1.97	2.29	4.02	106.	7.1	1.00	35.3	22.8
120.	11.800	Other buildings	4.29	1.70	1.00	153.	5.3	0.74	21.0	17.9
121.	12.100	Roads, streets, and highways	3.24	1.62	0.69	133.	4.3	0.56	53.3	16.9
122.	12.200	Transport and utility lines	4.56	1.28	3.63	147.	4.4	0.79	36.0	14.8
123.	12.300	Other construction	9.20	1.40	3.19	132.	4.3	0.61	22.5	12.1
124.	13.000	Land improvement	3.61	1.37	1.81	47.	4.3	0.60	17.5	9.7
125.	14.110	Locomotives	6.84	8.35	11.68	274.	16.5	6.01	82.9	62.2
126.	14.120	Other railway vehicles	9.46	7.61	11.67	275.	22.6	3.66	82.9	42.5
127.	14.200	Passenger automobiles	8.92	10.20	14.08	761.	50.3	4.68	121.4	76.1
128.	14.300	Trucks, busses, and trailers	6.99	9.62	10.14	519.	31.6	3.51	163.1	27.8
129.	14.400	Aircraft	7.75	9.52	9.32	487.	28.1	3.31	77.8	35.2
130.	14.500	Ships and boats	5.49	3.52	9.54	519.	5.6	3.66	89.9	16.9
131.	14.600	Other transport equipment	7.99	5.89	3.54	236.	34.3	2.88	51.6	27.9
132.	15.100	Engines and turbines	8.21	11.17	10.72	497.	28.0	2.79	89.6	45.8
133.	15.210	Tractors	6.82	5.24	7.98	342.	19.5	2.65	44.2	30.7
134.	15.220	Others agricultural machinery	9.56	5.92	9.74	1042.	33.7	2.65	143.4	23.0
135.	15.300	Office machinery	9.98	6.43	6.66	407.	43.0	2.38	99.0	45.1
136.	15.400	Metalworking machinery	4.48	5.04	4.71	109.	13.8	5.28	44.3	29.0
137.	15.500	Construction and mining machinery	9.41	10.78	9.37	387.	31.3	3.55	91.7	27.5
138.	15.600	Special industrial machinery	6.64	5.89	6.40	316.	21.6	3.02	105.7	34.7
139.	15.700	General industrial machinery	7.54	7.67	4.61	284.	27.9	2.80	41.9	28.6
140.	15.800	Service industrial machinery	11.09	7.77	11.24	527.	36.5	3.02	185.6	38.7
141.	16.100	Electrical transmission equipment	5.41	7.80	8.90	198.	30.4	3.32	75.3	21.8
142.	16.200	Communications equipment	11.94	9.74	6.28	543.	23.7	3.55	75.3	15.8
143.	16.300	Other electrical equipment	4.84	7.31	5.05	143.	13.2	0.66	46.9	27.1
144.	16.400	Instruments	7.29	2.59	5.53	97.	24.9	3.32	101.1	25.6
145.	17.100	Furniture and fixtures	5.91	5.77	2.45	39.	18.8	1.15	43.9	23.9
146.	17.200	Other durable goods	6.64	8.07	3.58	417.	16.7	2.59	34.0	51.2
147.	18.000	Increase in stocks	4.41	3.31	3.03	186.	9.4	1.60	40.5	20.2
148.	19.000	Exports minuus imports	7.14	7.50	6.07	310.	18.4	3.08	76.4	30.0
149.	20.100	Unskilled blue collar	0.48	0.34	0.54	36.	1.9	0.36	17.0	4.4
150.	20.210	Skilled blue collar	1.18	0.37	0.47	41.	2.4	0.33	22.9	5.0
151.	20.220	White collar	1.91	0.56	0.56	49.	2.8	0.79	35.1	5.3
152.	20.300	Professional	4.26	1.21	0.65	57.	4.7	1.48	47.2	5.9
153.	21.000	Commodities of government	3.97	2.51	1.98	143.	9.2	1.42	36.5	18.9

Appendix Table 4.4. Quantities per Capita, 1970 (U.S.=100)

			Kenya	India	Philippines	Korea Republic of	Colombia	Malaysia	Iran	Hungary
1.	1.101	Rice	23.4	980.4	2132.4	2028.4	310.5	1768.5	639.7	52.3
2.	1.102	Meal and other cereals	248.7	236.7	41.0	177.6	47.9	38.8	247.3	110.7
3.	1.103	Bread	7.7	0.2	18.5	10.7	14.2	10.7	139.9	231.3
4.	1.104	Biscuits, cakes, and the like	25.4	1.5	11.5	10.9	8.3	10.1	18.0	54.2
5.	1.105	Cereal preparations	3.6	0.0	13.7	0.0	30.9	16.1	21.1	281.0

Italy (lire)	Japan (yen)	United Kingdom (pounds)	Netherlands (guilders)	Belgium (B.francs)	France (francs)	Germany F.R. (DM)	United States (dollars)			
500.	257.	0.195	3.06	52.9	5.79	3.00	0.91	111.	10.100	One- and two-dwelling buildings
299.	237.	0.205	1.57	32.5	3.90	2.10	0.79	112.	10.200	Multidwelling buildings
229.	286.	0.403	1.63	25.4	1.97	1.39	0.85	113.	11.100	Hotels
413.	575.	0.391	2.42	36.7	4.04	2.43	1.10	114.	11.200	Industrial buildings
256.	449.	0.342	1.70	30.2	2.47	1.65	0.95	115.	11.300	Commercial buildings
327.	288.	0.260	2.17	36.2	3.46	2.03	0.83	116.	11.400	Office buildings
450.	213.	0.316	3.65	56.2	6.32	3.53	0.97	117.	11.500	Educational buildings
396.	179.	0.244	1.78	32.1	3.74	2.13	0.81	118.	11.600	Hospital buildings
543.	654.	0.246	4.21	62.9	5.00	4.35	1.29	119.	11.700	Agricultural buildings
428.	280.	0.265	1.93	34.8	4.04	2.31	0.00	120.	11.800	Other buildings
228.	286.	0.256	1.20	27.0	2.76	1.86	0.74	121.	12.100	Roads, streets, and highways
278.	170.	0.163	1.58	25.7	2.64	2.01	0.79	122.	12.200	Transport and utility lines
83.	195.	0.313	1.27	16.9	1.83	0.89	0.77	123.	12.300	Other construction
374.	165.	0.355	1.75	38.5	4.00	2.20	0.61	124.	13.000	Land improvement
986.	372.	0.463	5.69	113.1	8.93	4.96	2.02	125.	14.110	Locomotives
1328.	386.	0.481	5.69	113.1	9.22	3.83	1.87	126.	14.120	Other railway vehicles
788.	376.	0.575	4.61	54.0	4.82	4.76	1.85	127.	14.200	Passenger automobiles
575.	351.	0.438	5.69	76.6	5.79	3.85	1.73	128.	14.300	Trucks, busses, and trailers
661.	350.	0.435	4.41	67.8	4.92	3.35	1.48	129.	14.400	Aircraft
405.	261.	0.335	5.69	76.6	3.83	2.60	1.38	130.	14.500	Ships and boats
821.	278.	0.530	4.71	45.0	5.49	4.11	1.70	131.	14.600	Other transport equipment
646.	395.	0.308	3.79	52.0	6.29	4.33	2.16	132.	15.100	Engines and turbines
557.	311.	0.323	3.63	50.1	4.89	3.41	1.49	133.	15.210	Tractors
868.	316.	0.380	4.23	62.7	5.39	3.90	1.46	134.	15.220	Others agricultural machinery
670.	337.	0.431	3.96	49.5	5.58	3.68	1.36	135.	15.300	Office machinery
301.	410.	0.298	3.40	44.0	2.78	2.66	1.15	136.	15.400	Metalworking machinery
803.	286.	0.365	5.37	71.2	7.74	5.60	1.69	137.	15.500	Construction and mining machinery
519.	217.	0.366	3.02	44.6	4.76	3.18	1.45	138.	15.600	Special industrial machinery
423.	292.	0.314	2.93	39.6	3.59	2.57	1.26	139.	15.700	General industrial machinery
523.	354.	0.441	4.74	56.3	8.99	6.80	1.64	140.	15.800	Service industrial machinery
401.	262.	0.327	2.96	41.9	3.61	2.83	1.19	141.	16.100	Electrical transmission equipment
591.	353.	0.542	6.39	111.0	5.46	3.67	1.46	142.	16.200	Communications equipment
272.	302.	0.216	3.85	28.5	3.60	2.97	1.12	143.	16.300	Other electrical equipment
577.	388.	0.165	2.63	40.3	4.22	2.89	1.20	144.	16.400	Instruments
569.	224.	0.202	3.85	46.1	4.24	3.71	1.03	145.	17.100	Furniture and fixtures
786.	312.	0.389	6.40	75.9	6.62	4.67	1.49	146.	17.200	Other durable goods
541.	297.	0.341	2.99	45.4	4.95	3.39	1.15	147.	18.000	Increase in stocks
627.	358.	0.417	3.62	49.7	5.53	3.65	1.48	148.	19.000	Exports minuus imports
348.	142.	0.153	2.43	24.8	3.24	2.77	0.40	149.	20.100	Unskilled blue collar
341.	118.	0.145	1.87	20.7	3.08	2.45	0.64	150.	20.210	Skilled blue collar
396.	124.	0.201	2.51	28.6	4.05	2.92	0.66	151.	20.220	White collar
513.	244.	0.274	3.27	42.5	4.20	3.72	0.87	152.	20.300	Professional
471.	282.	0.322	2.93	46.7	4.39	3.08	1.07	153.	21.000	Commodities of government

Italy	Japan	United Kingdom	Netherlands	Belgium	France	Germany F.R.	United States			
66.4	1769.7	14.6	38.8	27.7	47.5	48.6	100.0	1.	1.101	Rice
14.3	10.2	30.5	17.9	13.8	12.9	53.8	100.0	2.	1.102	Meal and other cereals
187.9	30.1	182.9	175.3	226.7	211.0	222.3	100.0	3.	1.103	Bread
85.5	219.3	353.7	166.7	142.1	161.0	120.2	100.0	4.	1.104	Biscuits, cakes, and the like
5.1	12.3	171.3	32.7	28.4	9.1	22.6	100.0	5.	1.105	Cereal preparations

(Table continues on following page.)

			Kenya	India	Philippines	Korea Republic of	Colombia	Malaysia	Iran	Hungary
6.	1.106	Macaroni and spaghetti	1.0	7.4	76.6	384.0	133.7	166.6	10.1	114.8
7.	1.111	Fresh beef and veal	14.3	0.6	13.8	16.3	83.2	1.7	7.2	4.8
8.	1.112	Fresh lamb and mutton	49.0	19.0	0.0	0.0	75.4	29.8	1490.3	114.9
9.	1.113	Fresh pork	0.3	1.0	67.2	13.2	13.1	53.9	0.0	62.2
10.	1.114	Fresh poultry	1.4	1.8	37.2	6.8	10.9	39.2	15.8	81.7
11.	1.115	Other fresh meat	36.1	38.1	75.3	28.7	167.7	0.0	36.1	177.3
12.	1.116	Frozen and salted meat	1.0	0.0	2.0	0.1	9.5	1.7	0.4	50.5
13.	1.121	Fresh and frozen fish	26.0	29.7	218.2	65.0	10.7	223.8	16.6	37.7
14.	1.122	Canned fish	1.2	30.1	80.5	75.1	16.9	221.7	1.3	4.0
15.	1.131	Fresh milk	27.3	24.5	6.7	0.6	45.0	1.3	5.9	67.4
16.	1.132	Milk products	3.5	5.9	1.4	2.4	12.0	27.3	125.0	32.6
17.	1.133	Eggs and egg products	0.5	3.4	12.8	20.2	23.1	41.0	24.9	71.4
18.	1.141	Butter	29.6	9.6	2.1	4.9	16.2	7.8	36.1	80.3
19.	1.142	Margerine and edible oil	4.0	25.8	1.3	2.9	21.4	37.9	20.3	7.8
20.	1.143	Lard and edible fat	6.8	69.0	83.6	16.1	7.2	0.0	95.7	701.6
21.	1.151	Fresh tropical fruits	98.0	94.0	14.6	0.1	390.0	287.3	53.8	36.0
22.	1.152	Other fresh fruits	0.2	8.4	2.1	40.5	1.6	17.3	109.2	249.8
23.	1.153	Fresh vegetables	45.8	42.8	9.0	69.1	35.5	39.9	99.6	155.1
24.	1.161	Fruit other than fresh	0.2	2.6	0.1	1.5	1.3	2.5	11.3	5.7
25.	1.162	Vegetables other than fresh	1.9	6.6	0.0	0.0	5.5	3.6	5.5	5.0
26.	1.170	Tubers, including potatoes	252.2	17.9	22.6	306.9	107.8	27.2	58.0	202.4
27.	1.191	Coffee	1.0	0.8	8.3	0.7	35.6	6.4	0.0	14.7
28.	1.192	Tea	61.7	60.2	3.3	1.2	3.1	44.7	234.1	11.1
29.	1.193	Cocoa	8.0	0.1	45.1	2.5	742.2	5.0	2.3	65.7
30.	1.180	Sugar	16.0	22.7	29.4	5.1	80.2	56.6	42.2	43.5
31.	1.201	Jam, syrup, and honey	8.1	4.2	12.3	1.2	11.0	0.9	2.7	3.5
32.	1.202	Chocolate and ice cream	0.6	1.2	3.9	0.0	4.3	4.8	2.0	70.1
33.	1.203	Salt, spices, and sauces	9.8	60.5	71.9	277.7	118.9	94.7	40.6	145.1
34.	1.310	Nonalcoholic beverages	3.4	0.7	17.7	3.3	28.5	13.1	5.3	13.5
35.	1.321	Spirits	2.6	4.2	82.7	28.0	72.5	20.9	1.5	54.1
36.	1.322	Wine and cider	0.5	0.2	37.3	21.8	24.3	10.3	9.3	481.3
37.	1.323	Beer	5.0	0.2	9.8	4.4	9.7	9.3	1.0	21.4
38.	1.410	Cigarettes	4.2	1.5	14.0	18.5	43.5	27.4	14.0	73.6
39.	1.420	Cigars, tobacco, and snuff	0.8	73.1	28.6	0.0	50.4	21.0	55.2	4.5
40.	2.110	Clothing materials	26.0	173.3	188.9	194.1	62.3	381.1	156.4	109.7
41.	2.121	Men's clothing	3.4	0.2	5.9	23.5	24.3	6.5	36.4	35.8
42.	2.122	Women's clothing	1.0	0.2	3.3	4.4	4.9	4.5	6.0	19.9
43.	2.123	Boys' and girls' clothing	3.8	0.1	2.5	3.4	14.6	3.3	4.4	49.4
44.	2.131	Men's and boys' underwear	2.2	12.2	17.8	73.2	50.0	37.2	35.1	167.7
45.	2.132	Women's and girls' underwear	0.7	0.7	4.8	12.4	14.3	4.1	9.3	32.6
46.	2.150	Haberdashery and millinery	1.4	2.5	26.0	8.1	19.8	34.0	35.5	84.0
47.	2.160	Clothing rental and repair	1.0	4.2	9.6	1.1	9.4	0.0	0.4	39.4
48.	2.211	Men's footwear	8.3	3.0	7.0	7.2	34.1	13.3	37.8	42.5
49.	2.212	Women's footwear	2.8	2.2	10.6	2.5	27.0	12.3	67.1	55.1
50.	2.213	Children's footwear	7.2	5.1	16.6	60.3	73.4	46.3	10.7	110.5
51.	2.220	Footwear, repairs	5.5	0.8	23.4	1.4	91.9	0.0	104.1	184.7
52.	3.110	Rents	2.5	2.6	10.5	1.5	5.8	14.9	30.3	16.7
53.	3.120	Indoor repair and upkeep	0.2	10.6	16.4	1.8	9.7	11.2	35.4	64.3
54.	3.210	Electricity	0.3	0.3	3.9	3.1	7.0	4.2	3.7	11.0
55.	3.220	Gas	0.0	0.1	0.8	0.0	5.7	1.5	2.6	16.9
56.	3.230	Liquid fuels	0.5	2.6	3.3	1.4	6.9	4.6	29.2	6.5
57.	3.240	Other fuels and ice	48.7	43.4	20.9	203.2	10.5	34.0	41.7	413.6
58.	4.110	Furniture and fixtures	1.6	0.4	4.1	1.2	13.9	10.0	2.2	31.5
59.	4.120	Floor coverings	0.4	1.2	0.2	0.0	2.8	2.7	99.8	11.0
60.	4.200	Household textiles and the like	1.0	0.6	15.1	1.0	6.0	14.2	3.9	22.3

Italy	Japan	United Kingdom	Netherlands	Belgium	France	Germany F.R.	United States			
1363.8	341.8	53.8	61.4	91.0	277.6	261.3	100.0	6.	1.106	Macaroni and spaghetti
139.2	9.3	80.1	66.9	103.8	130.8	38.5	100.0	7.	1.111	Fresh beef and veal
183.0	7.5	1057.6	0.0	0.0	327.5	0.0	100.0	8.	1.112	Fresh lamb and mutton
39.1	32.4	23.4	97.4	81.2	65.5	104.3	100.0	9.	1.113	Fresh pork
77.6	26.6	54.6	21.0	79.7	87.1	23.1	100.0	10.	1.114	Fresh poultry
441.7	82.8	228.6	74.4	320.1	957.4	67.7	100.0	11.	1.115	Other fresh meat
62.7	16.7	118.0	58.2	160.0	88.7	95.0	100.0	12.	1.116	Frozen and salted meat
108.0	353.3	81.4	116.1	97.6	188.3	28.5	100.0	13.	1.121	Fresh and frozen fish
62.3	296.5	38.6	21.8	59.5	69.6	45.3	100.0	14.	1.122	Canned fish
50.3	31.2	73.7	126.7	81.8	78.6	66.2	100.0	15.	1.131	Fresh milk
102.1	10.1	86.1	105.9	75.2	173.8	54.5	100.0	16.	1.132	Milk products
66.3	101.1	79.0	71.3	55.1	73.9	94.1	100.0	17.	1.133	Eggs and egg products
89.8	12.6	338.0	62.7	419.5	407.0	472.6	100.0	18.	1.141	Butter
136.6	25.3	23.3	87.0	84.1	65.0	74.5	100.0	19.	1.142	Margerine and edible oil
0.0	1.4	93.8	0.0	0.0	0.0	0.0	100.0	20.	1.143	Lard and edible fat
181.5	132.8	83.5	211.9	144.3	129.8	103.1	100.0	21.	1.151	Fresh tropical fruits
412.4	87.3	58.9	166.2	196.6	229.5	143.0	100.0	22.	1.152	Other fresh fruits
336.8	166.4	92.6	138.3	154.2	201.4	80.3	100.0	23.	1.153	Fresh vegetables
24.0	13.6	39.4	35.9	11.5	10.5	28.4	100.0	24.	1.161	Fruit other than fresh
7.4	19.3	29.6	22.2	8.1	13.6	18.3	100.0	25.	1.162	Vegetables other than fresh
105.1	49.2	289.0	143.4	434.3	244.5	133.9	100.0	26.	1.170	Tubers, including potatoes
19.3	4.2	24.1	58.2	56.9	45.4	61.5	100.0	27.	1.191	Coffee
9.0	252.8	785.0	214.0	7.7	20.8	38.4	100.0	28.	1.192	Tea
33.8	63.8	96.8	344.0	48.1	306.4	377.9	100.0	29.	1.193	Cocoa
28.2	16.2	51.4	40.1	31.8	38.7	57.9	100.0	30.	1.180	Sugar
16.2	54.8	63.6	27.3	25.9	30.2	35.7	100.0	31.	1.201	Jam, syrup, and honey
25.5	20.9	118.7	82.0	96.8	47.4	66.9	100.0	32.	1.202	Chocolate and ice cream
93.0	441.8	40.0	109.1	20.2	31.4	18.9	100.0	33.	1.203	Salt, spices, and sauces
44.7	51.3	75.3	182.9	111.1	83.7	58.0	100.0	34.	1.310	Nonalcoholic beverages
76.6	37.7	221.0	221.0	121.2	94.5	166.1	100.0	35.	1.321	Spirits
706.9	808.0	122.1	156.3	196.0	1401.7	224.8	100.0	36.	1.322	Wine and cider
19.3	43.0	125.7	41.5	47.1	21.6	85.7	100.0	37.	1.323	Beer
63.2	48.6	88.3	45.1	73.6	59.2	43.4	100.0	38.	1.410	Cigarettes
42.2	0.9	102.3	762.0	390.9	144.0	88.3	100.0	39.	1.420	Cigars, tobacco, and snuff
183.3	1013.3	129.4	168.6	203.5	95.3	141.5	100.0	40.	2.110	Clothing materials
48.5	41.6	45.6	102.5	60.3	78.7	83.3	100.0	41.	2.121	Men's clothing
12.1	40.7	42.1	59.3	23.7	26.9	47.4	100.0	42.	2.122	Women's clothing
53.8	42.3	40.5	11.3	69.1	24.3	53.0	100.0	43.	2.123	Boys' and girls' clothing
707.2	243.3	299.9	362.9	257.8	366.0	295.4	100.0	44.	2.131	Men's and boys' underwear
44.7	36.5	89.2	106.3	110.6	84.7	125.9	100.0	45.	2.132	Women's and girls' underwear
20.8	63.7	148.2	58.0	42.2	85.9	111.3	100.0	46.	2.150	Haberdashery and millinery
50.7	76.1	13.2	10.3	110.7	15.9	8.6	100.0	47.	2.160	Clothing rental and repair
54.9	31.8	74.4	60.6	56.5	48.6	41.3	100.0	48.	2.211	Men's footwear
23.9	26.2	77.4	71.2	50.4	47.8	57.7	100.0	49.	2.212	Women's footwear
126.1	59.3	199.3	112.9	56.1	149.7	217.1	100.0	50.	2.213	Children's footwear
300.4	45.8	270.7	235.5	307.0	146.4	705.9	100.0	51.	2.220	Footwear, repairs
49.6	30.8	54.3	40.4	56.1	61.9	60.3	100.0	52.	3.110	Rents
14.8	26.5	77.5	120.9	61.8	90.8	40.3	100.0	53.	3.120	Indoor repair and upkeep
26.4	32.2	74.3	52.1	26.9	26.1	48.7	100.0	54.	3.210	Electricity
15.3	9.4	30.1	62.3	31.0	31.1	18.2	100.0	55.	3.220	Gas
41.2	14.2	16.3	81.1	101.2	59.2	74.0	100.0	56.	3.230	Liquid fuels
21.8	76.1	227.8	47.8	230.9	92.0	105.8	100.0	57.	3.240	Other fuels and ice
37.8	31.3	20.9	91.1	102.6	72.4	122.5	100.0	58.	4.110	Furniture and fixtures
8.7	37.5	99.0	97.4	34.0	25.8	69.3	100.0	59.	4.120	Floor coverings
18.0	17.2	51.5	55.2	18.3	33.5	57.5	100.0	60.	4.200	Household textiles and the like

(Table continues on following page.)

			Kenya	India	Philippines	Korea Republic of	Colombia	Malaysia	Iran	Hungary
61.	4.310	Refrigerators and freezers	0.5	0.5	5.1	3.0	2.6	6.2	7.7	23.9
62.	4.320	Washing appliances	0.1	0.0	3.1	0.0	1.7	1.3	1.1	23.1
63.	4.330	Cooking appliances	0.7	0.1	10.3	1.5	15.6	6.6	8.2	114.9
64.	4.340	Heating appliances	10.8	2.1	6.1	53.9	20.2	9.0	20.9	225.2
65.	4.350	Cleaning appliances	0.4	0.0	6.7	1.4	5.2	4.7	2.6	23.4
66.	4.360	Other household appliances	0.1	2.7	3.9	12.6	0.6	3.7	3.4	5.4
67.	4.400	Household utensils	7.3	6.0	5.7	12.4	7.2	49.4	16.3	49.3
68.	4.510	Nondurable household goods	8.0	0.9	8.0	2.8	14.1	13.9	10.4	18.4
69.	4.520	Domestic services	50.2	34.0	62.7	10.6	327.1	70.1	22.3	16.0
70.	4.530	Household services	8.0	41.5	15.5	21.7	66.6	0.0	12.7	36.4
71.	4.600	House furnishing repairs	0.9	18.9	18.8	99.7	0.0	2.4	3.1	149.6
72.	5.110	Drugs and medical preparations	3.3	4.9	4.7	11.5	5.8	11.6	26.2	45.8
73.	5.120	Medical supplies	1.5	4.3	4.9	9.8	0.0	8.8	3.0	50.4
74.	5.200	Therapeutic equipment	0.4	2.6	4.2	1.9	6.0	13.5	6.7	0.0
75.	5.310	Physicians' services	7.0	11.3	6.3	25.6	27.0	13.9	17.2	114.8
76.	5.320	Dentists' services	1.3	3.0	3.1	11.3	24.1	4.9	10.2	43.3
77.	5.330	Nurses' services	15.7	3.1	4.4	12.7	17.2	23.1	5.1	76.2
78.	5.410	Hospitals	14.1	6.6	13.2	4.3	26.3	41.6	7.4	101.9
79.	6.110	Personal automobiles	0.9	0.1	0.1	0.1	1.3	3.5	1.6	3.2
80.	6.120	Other personal transport	0.1	1.3	0.1	0.1	0.0	3.6	2.6	27.3
81.	6.210	Tires, tubes, and accessories	0.9	0.1	0.5	0.0	2.1	23.4	2.3	8.1
82.	6.220	Automobile repairs	3.0	1.6	0.2	0.0	5.3	6.4	7.1	7.8
83.	6.230	Gasoline, oil, and grease	0.1	0.1	0.4	0.0	1.3	5.8	1.2	1.8
84.	6.240	Parking, tolls, and the like	2.4	0.6	0.3	0.0	10.9	5.7	11.0	5.8
85.	6.310	Local transport	9.7	22.2	36.5	142.7	391.5	73.1	152.3	152.0
86.	6.321	Rail transport	49.8	181.9	14.3	779.0	1823.1	92.0	148.7	1313.0
87.	6.322	Bus transport	211.9	238.7	107.9	357.2	136.3	918.9	375.7	447.4
88.	6.323	Air transport	12.9	0.1	6.4	1.0	120.5	31.6	3.2	8.1
89.	6.330	Miscellaneous transport	0.7	15.7	66.8	10.4	0.0	19.2	7.9	19.5
90.	6.410	Postal communication	1.3	7.3	1.9	8.0	3.9	14.7	0.7	46.8
91.	6.420	Telephone and telegraph	0.8	1.8	0.7	4.6	17.0	6.9	4.7	10.6
92.	7.110	Radios, televisions, and phonographs	0.8	0.4	1.1	3.1	3.9	8.0	2.0	14.7
93.	7.120	Major durable recreational equipment	2.6	0.3	1.4	0.4	1.0	6.4	0.3	1.9
94.	7.130	Other recreational equipment	1.1	0.1	0.5	1.0	1.1	1.4	2.0	6.9
95.	7.210	Public entertainment	9.0	0.5	11.6	0.5	34.3	43.9	6.1	162.9
96.	7.230	Other recreational and cultural activities	3.4	4.6	4.6	39.4	4.2	4.9	7.4	211.4
97.	7.310	Books, papers, and magazines	3.2	1.1	2.0	8.4	8.5	10.2	2.9	48.9
98.	7.320	Stationery	0.1	0.9	0.4	18.8	1.8	10.7	9.2	13.2
99.	7.411	First- and second- level teachers	25.1	29.0	58.7	35.1	47.7	55.3	34.7	72.3
100.	7.412	College teachers	1.1	8.9	24.3	9.2	15.9	3.3	6.4	27.0
101.	7.420	Physical facilities for education	3.5	1.0	7.4	5.0	6.1	3.6	2.5	56.5
102.	7.431	Educational books and supplies	11.4	15.2	33.5	38.1	32.7	16.5	7.0	68.9
103.	7.432	Other educational expenditures	11.1	4.5	8.3	15.6	21.9	10.5	3.8	71.0
104.	8.100	Barber and beauty shops	1.0	4.5	58.7	139.8	19.1	39.7	223.5	142.2
105.	8.210	Toilet articles	0.7	1.3	8.2	2.0	9.6	9.2	4.2	29.8
106.	8.220	Other personal care goods	2.6	1.7	11.0	3.1	5.6	16.3	5.2	16.1
107.	8.310	Restaurants and cafes	3.3	0.5	4.1	4.5	12.0	4.8	21.1	76.4
108.	8.320	Hotels and lodging	37.9	7.0	1.2	13.0	16.5	153.1	18.1	39.7
109.	8.400	Other services	6.1	9.6	23.6	6.8	45.4	6.0	12.2	51.2
110.	8.900	Net expenditures of residents abroad	0.0	0.0	0.0	-0.4	0.0	0.0	0.0	0.0

Italy	Japan	United Kingdom	Netherlands	Belgium	France	Germany F.R.	United States			
33.6	80.6	20.6	119.6	44.0	70.8	94.0	100.0	61.	4.310	Refrigerators and freezers
67.0	103.3	67.8	127.3	33.9	81.5	122.5	100.0	62.	4.320	Washing appliances
69.2	70.2	95.4	88.8	93.2	92.0	70.6	100.0	63.	4.330	Cooking appliances
209.0	949.4	462.2	1483.9	1564.8	518.5	776.3	100.0	64.	4.340	Heating appliances
20.8	105.0	68.3	75.5	29.2	90.2	152.2	100.0	65.	4.350	Cleaning appliances
6.6	51.6	4.4	42.1	8.5	17.7	43.0	100.0	66.	4.360	Other household appliances
65.4	144.2	104.5	242.3	360.7	121.3	258.3	100.0	67.	4.400	Household utensils
20.8	16.5	31.9	57.1	107.2	80.0	107.0	100.0	68.	4.510	Nondurable household goods
0.0	10.8	46.6	0.0	0.0	0.0	0.0	100.0	69.	4.520	Domestic services
282.4	264.5	222.8	246.3	556.5	208.9	225.3	100.0	70.	4.530	Household services
0.0	27.4	55.3	0.0	0.0	0.0	0.0	100.0	71.	4.600	House furnishing repairs
85.1	116.7	71.6	104.3	87.9	233.6	87.7	100.0	72.	5.110	Drugs and medical preparations
10.9	641.8	69.9	24.6	23.3	26.0	93.0	100.0	73.	5.120	Medical supplies
4.9	35.1	92.4	208.6	64.5	53.6	159.4	100.0	74.	5.200	Therapeutic equipment
73.9	68.1	74.6	75.3	90.9	80.1	106.4	100.0	75.	5.310	Physicians' services
99.9	67.5	51.2	49.1	31.7	79.6	98.8	100.0	76.	5.320	Dentists' services
18.0	54.1	50.2	51.8	26.7	51.6	55.0	100.0	77.	5.330	Nurses' services
119.4	152.3	119.3	143.4	109.0	90.6	151.2	100.0	78.	5.410	Hospitals
21.3	3.9	26.5	20.6	28.9	26.7	30.6	100.0	79.	6.110	Personal automobiles
10.5	12.4	13.2	32.0	12.6	20.5	19.8	100.0	80.	6.120	Other personal transport
23.1	2.0	71.6	49.9	50.9	53.9	42.8	100.0	81.	6.210	Tires, tubes, and accessories
24.1	5.4	47.5	16.9	23.3	35.7	36.6	100.0	82.	6.220	Automobile repairs
13.5	3.1	17.9	11.4	19.7	16.8	32.0	100.0	83.	6.230	Gasoline, oil, and grease
95.1	12.4	85.3	94.0	45.1	110.9	80.8	100.0	84.	6.240	Parking, tolls, and the like
169.2	288.3	374.5	95.6	114.7	158.9	100.1	100.0	85.	6.310	Local transport
1789.5	1048.1	1015.2	1789.3	1737.2	1706.4	2739.1	100.0	86.	6.321	Rail transport
322.1	84.6	88.2	219.3	428.4	410.9	434.1	100.0	87.	6.322	Bus transport
5.9	4.8	89.1	5.8	15.9	13.7	5.9	100.0	88.	6.323	Air transport
0.0	10.6	44.4	0.0	0.0	0.0	0.0	100.0	89.	6.330	Miscellaneous transport
76.0	19.5	110.9	109.7	95.8	78.1	197.5	100.0	90.	6.410	Postal communication
19.4	22.0	43.9	36.7	13.1	9.2	9.3	100.0	91.	6.420	Telephone and telegraph
14.1	39.8	11.4	37.5	23.3	28.1	26.1	100.0	92.	7.110	Radios, televisions, and phonographs
1.1	10.1	15.3	12.9	5.8	17.2	39.9	100.0	93.	7.120	Major durable recreational equipment
22.2	19.3	49.9	66.5	43.9	54.6	94.9	100.0	94.	7.130	Other recreational equipment
80.2	42.5	161.4	100.0	47.9	37.5	54.7	100.0	95.	7.210	Public entertainment
15.7	16.6	87.5	26.4	47.2	28.1	40.5	100.0	96.	7.230	Other recreational and cultural activities
67.6	23.3	150.4	82.6	47.3	112.3	71.0	100.0	97.	7.310	Books, papers, and magazines
51.3	20.2	54.3	100.4	29.4	214.6	87.7	100.0	98.	7.320	Stationery
90.8	71.9	89.4	59.3	87.6	76.0	74.8	100.0	99.	7.411	First- and second- level teachers
23.5	41.7	25.9	25.1	317.2	20.0	19.4	100.0	100.	7.412	College teachers
13.8	39.7	50.6	94.1	49.3	16.6	46.2	100.0	101.	7.420	Physical facilities for education
23.7	102.2	386.4	152.8	98.2	31.8	21.4	100.0	102.	7.431	Educational books and supplies
25.9	125.3	141.1	51.6	46.9	10.1	54.6	100.0	103.	7.432	Other educational expenditures
85.0	77.8	123.7	45.4	220.0	93.9	74.5	100.0	104.	8.100	Barber and beauty shops
12.2	24.0	22.1	24.7	17.0	37.3	22.1	100.0	105.	8.210	Toilet articles
16.8	9.5	32.2	20.1	16.7	33.9	23.2	100.0	106.	8.220	Other personal care goods
35.4	84.2	26.0	56.9	182.6	85.5	64.5	100.0	107.	8.310	Restaurants and cafes
387.8	217.9	364.1	454.7	183.3	808.5	665.1	100.0	108.	8.320	Hotels and lodging
5.5	110.0	63.4	54.8	17.7	8.4	21.2	100.0	109.	8.400	Other services
-101.4	15.3	-6.2	55.2	47.3	-29.0	14.2	100.0	110.	8.900	Net expenditures of residents abroad

(Table continues on following page.)

			Kenya	India	Philippines	Korea Republic of	Colombia	Malaysia	Iran	Hungary
111.	10.100	One- and two-dwelling buildings	8.5	5.0	5.7	19.1	37.1	19.4	57.0	41.5
112.	10.200	Multidwelling buildings	1.7	7.6	11.6	5.8	8.1	31.7	20.4	72.9
113.	11.100	Hotels	1.9	6.3	3.2	11.6	4.3	36.6	31.9	94.6
114.	11.200	Industrial buildings	6.8	1.9	1.4	17.3	5.1	27.2	68.8	131.1
115.	11.300	Commercial buildings	2.1	8.1	9.7	23.4	2.9	25.0	7.0	27.7
116.	11.400	Office buildings	6.0	6.0	7.0	11.7	13.7	45.5	69.6	72.0
117.	11.500	Educational buildings	3.5	2.0	11.2	5.0	3.9	28.4	8.3	30.9
118.	11.600	Hospital buildings	5.7	3.1	4.3	23.2	1.6	25.1	7.6	24.9
119.	11.700	Agricultural buildings	4.1	38.3	3.3	41.6	12.6	21.3	87.2	423.0
120.	11.800	Other buildings	0.8	4.3	0.3	18.0	1.2	10.2	19.0	13.1
121.	12.100	Roads, streets, and highways	6.9	4.9	27.1	20.5	64.1	16.0	10.7	31.5
122.	12.200	Transport and utility lines	2.3	10.9	1.3	9.9	31.3	22.7	10.6	70.6
123.	12.300	Other construction	11.7	46.2	0.8	165.3	145.2	42.2	114.1	295.4
124.	13.000	Land improvement	0.5	1.2	0.0	0.1	2.1	1.5	0.0	0.4
125.	14.110	Locomotives	18.3	1.9	1.6	25.0	0.4	0.3	0.4	48.0
126.	14.120	Other railway vehicles	9.7	1.9	0.1	9.0	1.6	0.0	3.5	60.5
127.	14.200	Passenger automobiles	4.7	0.1	5.2	4.3	3.2	3.8	7.9	3.1
128.	14.300	Trucks, busses, and trailers	5.6	2.2	4.5	6.1	5.9	9.5	4.4	43.3
129.	14.400	Aircraft	3.2	0.2	1.3	3.6	5.9	0.0	5.8	7.0
130.	14.500	Ships and boats	2.2	5.1	14.4	31.7	125.4	32.3	19.1	22.9
131.	14.600	Other transport equipment	3.4	10.0	14.8	12.2	2.0	17.4	228.3	376.8
132.	15.100	Engines and turbines	5.6	2.1	16.0	13.0	2.2	25.4	24.4	28.1
133.	15.210	Tractors	6.5	2.2	9.1	0.0	2.7	23.0	7.5	56.4
134.	15.220	Others agricultural machinery	4.0	0.2	1.2	0.6	1.4	2.1	7.1	68.0
135.	15.300	Office machinery	1.0	0.2	2.7	0.9	0.5	3.8	0.9	11.1
136.	15.400	Metalworking machinery	2.0	1.7	2.6	16.0	4.2	2.6	11.5	39.9
137.	15.500	Construction and mining machinery	3.5	0.5	7.1	2.4	2.3	17.1	1.8	39.5
138.	15.600	Special industrial machinery	10.7	2.5	7.7	14.2	4.7	21.6	15.4	118.0
139.	15.700	General industrial machinery	8.4	4.9	22.6	18.6	4.5	19.7	15.7	44.1
140.	15.800	Service industrial machinery	1.9	0.6	3.7	3.2	0.2	6.7	2.5	7.6
141.	16.100	Electrical transmission equipment	5.9	2.6	3.5	9.7	13.1	7.1	9.1	22.2
142.	16.200	Communications equipment	0.9	0.9	3.6	0.6	5.1	3.4	1.2	19.2
143.	16.300	Other electrical equipment	4.2	1.2	21.3	20.8	88.0	0.4	19.9	11.0
144.	16.400	Instruments	1.3	0.8	2.0	1.1	9.4	4.1	3.0	40.1
145.	17.100	Furniture and fixtures	1.1	0.3	4.5	14.0	4.7	14.5	6.0	116.0
146.	17.200	Other durable goods	2.3	5.3	14.0	1.1	4.0	0.6	7.1	5.2
147.	18.000	Increase in stocks	45.0	41.9	76.2	74.7	146.7	183.1	13.5	491.3
148.	19.000	Exports minuus imports	-25.0	-6.5	-8.8	-262.2	-58.1	174.6	239.0	-303.2
149.	20.100	Unskilled blue collar	118.0	49.6	10.9	7.0	48.7	19.4	95.7	73.8
150.	20.210	Skilled blue collar	4.8	5.3	7.8	13.6	11.7	13.1	31.0	5.1
151.	20.220	White collar	4.3	18.1	33.3	49.5	23.6	28.4	9.2	30.3
152.	20.300	Professional	6.5	7.4	14.9	13.1	35.6	32.1	13.1	33.0
153.	21.000	Commodities of government	1.9	3.0	3.6	5.4	3.2	10.5	13.4	28.9

Appendix Table 4.5. Quantities per Capita Valued at International Prices, 1970

			Kenya	India	Philippines	Korea Republic of	Colombia	Malaysia	Iran	Hungary
1.	1.101	Rice	0.783	32.773	71.282	67.807	10.380	59.119	21.383	1.749
2.	1.102	Meal and other cereals	35.011	33.334	5.770	25.003	6.745	5.462	34.819	15.591
3.	1.103	Bread	1.253	0.039	3.000	1.733	2.308	1.740	22.656	37.478
4.	1.104	Biscuits, cakes, and the like	2.899	0.168	1.315	1.239	0.944	1.155	2.051	6.172
5.	1.105	Cereal preparations	0.106	0.0	0.409	0.0	0.920	0.479	0.629	8.365

Italy	Japan	United Kingdom	Netherlands	Belgium	France	Germany F.R.	United States			
109.3	127.5	100.4	36.7	13.6	58.1	34.1	100.0	111.	10.100	One- and two-dwelling buildings
89.5	95.2	65.7	316.6	262.5	263.2	292.7	100.0	112.	10.200	Multidwelling buildings
120.9	158.4	23.6	70.4	56.5	149.0	262.2	100.0	113.	11.100	Hotels
137.1	48.5	100.8	165.0	240.5	88.5	268.3	100.0	114.	11.200	Industrial buildings
35.8	71.0	44.7	165.0	76.4	132.2	135.4	100.0	115.	11.300	Commercial buildings
122.3	190.0	61.5	109.3	52.0	154.6	214.9	100.0	116.	11.400	Office buildings
25.8	98.2	59.8	99.3	15.8	55.3	88.9	100.0	117.	11.500	Educational buildings
38.9	77.4	72.3	295.8	12.8	59.1	132.4	100.0	118.	11.600	Hospital buildings
112.4	32.8	87.6	120.4	170.2	167.1	102.6	100.0	119.	11.700	Agricultural buildings
20.1	216.3	62.7	16.6	20.6	128.2	20.5	100.0	120.	11.800	Other buildings
77.2	52.3	42.1	165.5	165.2	72.9	175.3	100.0	121.	12.100	Roads, streets, and highways
37.3	62.9	23.8	82.7	106.0	120.2	126.9	100.0	122.	12.200	Transport and utility lines
64.7	473.8	42.8	90.5	11.0	78.1	207.5	100.0	123.	12.300	Other construction
0.5	0.0	0.2	0.4	0.0	0.1	0.1	100.0	124.	13.000	Land improvement
21.8	45.1	16.2	22.4	19.2	46.9	17.8	100.0	125.	14.110	Locomotives
6.9	2.1	10.9	13.9	14.2	29.1	46.6	100.0	126.	14.120	Other railway vehicles
40.9	59.5	51.8	62.7	50.6	65.6	86.8	100.0	127.	14.200	Passenger automobiles
45.6	64.7	5.7	45.2	32.9	65.0	94.2	100.0	128.	14.300	Trucks, busses, and trailers
19.5	4.6	45.7	65.4	55.4	13.1	62.3	100.0	129.	14.400	Aircraft
96.5	187.7	529.3	249.2	95.6	97.2	551.0	100.0	130.	14.500	Ships and boats
46.7	131.8	412.2	10.0	0.0	7.5	5.7	100.0	131.	14.600	Other transport equipment
25.6	63.5	5.6	42.6	19.7	29.5	23.9	100.0	132.	15.100	Engines and turbines
49.0	13.8	37.1	65.1	88.6	169.3	90.2	100.0	133.	15.210	Tractors
25.3	38.9	28.7	34.3	42.0	159.1	64.4	100.0	134.	15.220	Others agricultural machinery
18.5	51.5	28.1	42.5	33.4	97.2	114.8	100.0	135.	15.300	Office machinery
94.1	79.7	79.4	44.6	39.4	125.0	168.9	100.0	136.	15.400	Metalworking machinery
18.8	64.4	60.7	58.3	77.4	114.3	78.4	100.0	137.	15.500	Construction and mining machinery
72.9	227.9	101.8	160.2	103.1	220.3	206.5	100.0	138.	15.600	Special industrial machinery
88.9	150.4	310.3	276.0	237.1	131.7	370.0	100.0	139.	15.700	General industrial machinery
19.1	17.3	9.1	65.7	29.2	16.2	25.5	100.0	140.	15.800	Service industrial machinery
167.7	213.8	111.4	175.5	125.7	257.3	245.8	100.0	141.	16.100	Electrical transmission equipment
20.7	76.8	40.7	30.3	20.9	53.7	86.9	100.0	142.	16.200	Communications equipment
252.2	126.2	109.9	108.6	456.4	117.7	120.9	100.0	143.	16.300	Other electrical equipment
37.4	69.6	51.9	177.0	116.0	162.6	177.0	100.0	144.	16.400	Instruments
23.3	438.4	243.7	0.0	75.6	33.4	45.0	100.0	145.	17.100	Furniture and fixtures
31.9	156.1	26.4	0.0	45.8	33.3	33.3	100.0	146.	17.200	Other durable goods
302.3	821.4	193.2	612.6	390.3	593.7	603.2	100.0	147.	18.000	Increase in stocks
100.4	254.6	203.8	-443.5	645.3	168.8	598.3	100.0	148.	19.000	Exports minuus imports
87.4	60.0	226.6	27.4	114.3	16.6	23.8	100.0	149.	20.100	Unskilled blue collar
55.6	201.8	41.8	56.2	47.4	146.7	106.6	100.0	150.	20.210	Skilled blue collar
68.4	17.9	72.6	125.6	94.0	80.4	117.6	100.0	151.	20.220	White collar
12.0	16.5	32.7	45.8	34.7	79.1	24.0	100.0	152.	20.300	Professional
16.1	10.0	40.4	30.3	22.4	30.9	29.0	100.0	153.	21.000	Commodities of government

Italy	Japan	United Kingdom	Netherlands	Belgium	France	Germany F.R.	United States			
2.221	59.160	0.487	1.297	0.926	1.586	1.623	3.343	1.	1.101	Rice
2.015	1.432	4.295	2.519	1.939	1.811	7.574	14.080	2.	1.102	Meal and other cereals
30.434	4.870	29.634	28.402	36.718	34.184	36.014	16.200	3.	1.103	Bread
9.745	24.994	40.315	18.994	16.192	18.354	13.699	11.397	4.	1.104	Biscuits, cakes, and the like
0.152	0.366	5.101	0.973	0.844	0.270	0.672	2.977	5.	1.105	Cereal preparations

(Table continues on following page.)

159

			Kenya	India	Philippines	Korea Republic of	Colombia	Malaysia	Iran	Hungary
6.	1.106	Macaroni and spaghetti	0.017	0.118	1.217	6.097	2.122	2.645	0.161	1.822
7.	1.111	Fresh beef and veal	7.808	0.325	7.528	8.911	45.537	0.942	3.939	2.650
8.	1.112	Fresh lamb and mutton	1.006	0.391	0.028	0.0	1.548	0.612	30.595	2.359
9.	1.113	Fresh pork	0.119	0.336	23.018	4.519	4.479	18.491	0.0	21.327
10.	1.114	Fresh poultry	0.367	0.484	9.871	1.807	2.904	10.417	4.206	21.693
11.	1.115	Other fresh meat	0.858	0.905	1.791	0.681	3.989	0.0	0.859	4.217
12.	1.116	Frozen and salted meat	0.440	0.008	0.888	0.043	4.195	0.759	0.156	22.247
13.	1.121	Fresh and frozen fish	2.659	3.042	22.318	6.643	1.093	22.886	1.698	3.853
14.	1.122	Canned fish	0.096	2.463	6.597	6.152	1.387	18.162	0.103	0.330
15.	1.131	Fresh milk	9.969	8.947	2.463	0.206	16.442	0.483	2.145	24.608
16.	1.132	Milk products	0.911	1.548	0.372	0.636	3.156	7.192	32.980	8.599
17.	1.133	Eggs and egg products	0.091	0.676	2.563	4.049	4.637	8.237	4.992	14.334
18.	1.141	Butter	1.733	0.564	0.123	0.287	0.949	0.458	2.114	4.699
19.	1.142	Margerine and edible oil	1.003	6.523	0.323	0.739	5.392	9.578	5.129	1.962
20.	1.143	Lard and edible fat	0.291	2.957	3.585	0.692	0.308	0.0	4.103	30.084
21.	1.151	Fresh tropical fruits	5.931	5.691	0.884	0.004	23.609	17.388	3.258	2.178
22.	1.152	Other fresh fruits	0.018	0.854	0.217	4.112	0.162	1.756	11.098	25.385
23.	1.153	Fresh vegetables	7.992	7.458	1.563	12.042	6.184	6.957	▾17.370	27.038
24.	1.161	Fruit other than fresh	0.035	0.579	0.023	0.335	0.284	0.545	2.510	1.267
25.	1.162	Vegetables other than fresh	1.078	3.754	0.011	0.0	3.114	2.063	3.140	2.868
26.	1.170	Tubers, including potatoes	12.566	0.894	1.126	15.291	5.373	1.358	2.890	10.086
27.	1.191	Coffee	0.282	0.233	2.302	0.199	9.828	1.767	0.007	4.071
28.	1.192	Tea	1.503	1.468	0.082	0.030	0.075	1.089	5.707	0.271
29.	1.193	Cocoa	0.052	0.000	0.295	0.016	4.856	0.033	0.015	0.430
30.	1.180	Sugar	4.485	6.349	8.230	1.440	22.431	15.824	11.800	12.168
31.	1.201	Jam, syrup, and honey	1.030	0.540	1.570	0.155	1.403	0.115	0.342	0.450
32.	1.202	Chocolate and ice cream	0.157	0.319	1.059	0.002	1.176	1.309	0.552	19.120
33.	1.203	Salt, spices, and sauces	0.700	4.320	5.132	19.830	8.491	6.766	2.899	10.361
34.	1.310	Nonalcoholic beverages	0.513	0.108	2.640	0.498	4.244	1.955	0.796	2.005
35.	1.321	Spirits	0.394	0.646	12.625	4.275	11.062	3.192	0.235	8.253
36.	1.322	Wine and cider	0.026	0.009	2.013	1.178	1.309	0.554	0.505	25.975
37.	1.323	Beer	2.181	0.070	4.264	1.911	4.218	4.047	0.445	9.355
38.	1.410	Cigarettes	2.340	0.854	7.775	10.291	24.264	15.260	7.811	41.016
39.	1.420	Cigars, tobacco, and snuff	0.043	3.866	1.511	0.0	2.664	1.109	2.922	0.238
40.	2.110	Clothing materials	1.608	10.722	11.691	12.009	3.858	23.585	9.678	6.787
41.	2.121	Men's clothing	1.860	0.106	3.178	12.751	13.173	3.551	19.781	19.412
42.	2.122	Women's clothing	0.867	0.169	2.932	3.908	4.315	3.975	5.305	17.579
43.	2.123	Boys' and girls' clothing	0.916	0.022	0.598	0.820	3.529	0.796	1.068	11.930
44.	2.131	Men's and boys' underwear	0.091	0.509	0.744	3.063	2.090	1.555	1.467	7.011
45.	2.132	Women's and girls' underwear	0.158	0.166	1.149	2.970	3.424	0.974	2.218	7.793
46.	2.150	Haberdashery and millinery	0.200	0.355	3.764	1.173	2.867	4.929	5.153	12.178
47.	2.160	Clothing rental and repair	0.146	0.603	1.396	0.153	1.371	0.0	0.054	5.726
48.	2.211	Men's footwear	1.284	0.469	1.077	1.106	5.272	2.058	5.845	6.563
49.	2.212	Women's footwear	0.445	0.349	1.699	0.399	4.313	1.955	10.707	8.799
50.	2.213	Children's footwear	0.296	0.209	0.683	2.479	3.016	1.901	0.439	4.541
51.	2.220	Footwear, repairs	0.059	0.008	0.252	0.015	0.989	0.0	1.120	1.987
52.	3.110	Rents	9.316	9.717	39.724	5.653	21.974	56.104	114.228	63.091
53.	3.120	Indoor repair and upkeep	0.048	3.412	5.255	0.572	3.124	3.597	11.352	20.617
54.	3.210	Electricity	0.207	0.221	2.455	2.000	4.472	2.693	2.361	6.992
55.	3.220	Gas	0.017	0.053	0.354	0.0	2.370	0.611	1.102	7.070
56.	3.230	Liquid fuels	0.125	0.664	0.841	0.362	1.779	1.183	7.491	1.665
57.	3.240	Other fuels and ice	4.363	3.882	1.871	18.192	0.936	3.042	3.729	37.025
58.	4.110	Furniture and fixtures	0.972	0.219	2.503	0.761	8.558	6.155	1.373	19.428
59.	4.120	Floor coverings	0.076	0.212	0.031	0.0	0.477	`0.467	17.092	1.891
60.	4.200	Household textiles and the like	0.439	0.263	6.721	0.467	2.688	6.342	1.724	9.913

Italy	Japan	United Kingdom	Netherlands	Belgium	France	Germany F.R.	United States			
21.653	5.426	0.854	0.975	1.445	4.407	4.149	1.588	6.	1.106	Macaroni and spaghetti
76.189	5.097	43.856	36.618	56.806	71.556	21.090	54.721	7.	1.111	Fresh beef and veal
3.756	0.155	21.713	0.0	0.0	6.723	0.0	2.053	8.	1.112	Fresh lamb and mutton
13.399	11.107	8.015	33.367	27.817	22.464	35.735	34.275	9.	1.113	Fresh pork
20.626	7.075	14.501	5.583	21.183	23.135	6.126	26.566	10.	1.114	Fresh poultry
10.505	1.969	5.437	1.770	7.614	22.770	1.609	2.378	11.	1.115	Other fresh meat
27.590	7.333	51.960	25.633	70.449	39.046	41.815	44.031	12.	1.116	Frozen and salted meat
11.049	36.141	8.328	11.871	9.980	19.257	2.913	10.228	13.	1.121	Fresh and frozen fish
5.104	24.282	3.158	1.788	4.873	5.703	3.713	8.190	14.	1.122	Canned fish
18.365	11.404	26.910	46.271	29.893	28.706	24.178	36.523	15.	1.131	Fresh milk
26.935	2.663	22.723	27.945	19.829	45.847	14.365	26.377	16.	1.132	Milk products
13.323	20.298	15.859	14.314	11.060	14.838	18.901	20.083	17.	1.133	Eggs and egg products
5.257	0.735	19.773	3.669	24.542	23.810	27.652	5.850	18.	1.141	Butter
34.486	6.383	5.886	21.963	21.235	16.409	18.806	25.247	19.	1.142	Margerine and edible oil
0.0	0.060	4.021	0.0	0.0	0.0	0.0	4.288	20.	1.143	Lard and edible fat
10.984	8.041	5.055	12.824	8.733	7.854	6.238	6.053	21.	1.151	Fresh tropical fruits
41.907	8.872	5.989	16.890	19.984	23.323	14.535	10.162	22.	1.152	Other fresh fruits
58.735	29.023	16.144	24.124	26.886	35.119	14.009	17.438	23.	1.153	Fresh vegetables
5.341	3.018	8.753	7.970	2.546	2.334	6.319	22.223	24.	1.161	Fruit other than fresh
4.237	10.986	16.820	12.628	4.610	7.726	10.415	56.870	25.	1.162	Vegetables other than fresh
5.237	2.454	14.402	7.147	21.643	12.183	6.671	4.983	26.	1.170	Tubers, including potatoes
5.338	1.151	6.651	16.081	15.728	12.533	17.005	27.635	27.	1.191	Coffee
0.219	6.163	19.138	5.217	0.188	0.507	0.935	2.438	28.	1.192	Tea
0.221	0.417	0.633	2.251	0.315	2.004	2.473	0.654	29.	1.193	Cocoa
7.896	4.521	14.374	11.227	8.895	10.817	16.189	27.967	30.	1.180	Sugar
2.069	6.988	8.110	3.476	3.301	3.848	4.555	12.744	31.	1.201	Jam, syrup, and honey
6.963	5.702	32.383	22.381	26.413	12.938	18.262	27.291	32.	1.202	Chocolate and ice cream
6.638	31.545	2.859	7.792	1.441	2.244	1.352	7.141	33.	1.203	Salt, spices, and sauces
6.653	7.636	11.213	27.233	16.534	12.460	8.634	14.888	34.	1.310	Nonalcoholic beverages
11.681	5.754	33.721	33.715	18.493	14.418	25.341	15.258	35.	1.321	Spirits
38.155	43.609	6.591	8.437	10.578	75.656	12.135	5.397	36.	1.322	Wine and cider
8.439	18.794	54.900	18.129	20.586	9.430	37.421	43.682	37.	1.323	Beer
35.242	27.091	49.223	25.141	41.009	32.963	24.213	55.727	38.	1.410	Cigarettes
2.233	0.049	5.412	40.304	20.674	7.617	4.668	5.289	39.	1.420	Cigars, tobacco, and snuff
11.343	62.703	8.007	10.434	12.591	5.899	8.754	6.188	40.	2.110	Clothing materials
26.321	22.598	24.769	55.647	32.729	42.728	45.210	54.295	41.	2.121	Men's clothing
10.711	35.914	37.134	52.276	20.945	23.754	41.820	88.206	42.	2.122	Women's clothing
12.996	10.211	9.773	2.728	16.691	5.869	12.807	24.157	43.	2.123	Boys' and girls' clothing
29.569	10.173	12.540	15.176	10.781	15.303	12.351	4.181	44.	2.131	Men's and boys' underwear
10.711	8.741	21.359	25.456	26.475	20.273	30.142	23.938	45.	2.132	Women's and girls' underwear
3.022	9.237	21.484	8.409	6.113	12.452	16.141	14.496	46.	2.150	Haberdashery and millinery
7.363	11.042	1.917	1.491	16.079	2.308	1.255	14.520	47.	2.160	Clothing rental and repair
8.481	4.909	11.502	9.368	8.731	7.512	6.382	15.461	48.	2.211	Men's footwear
3.820	4.176	12.347	11.366	8.037	7.635	9.211	15.959	49.	2.212	Women's footwear
5.179	2.434	8.189	4.637	2.303	6.149	8.917	4.108	50.	2.213	Children's footwear
3.231	0.493	2.912	2.533	3.301	1.574	7.591	1.075	51.	2.220	Footwear, repairs
187.001	116.067	204.924	152.365	211.603	233.690	227.435	377.394	52.	3.110	Rents
4.745	8.479	24.849	38.741	19.817	29.109	12.902	32.052	53.	3.120	Indoor repair and upkeep
16.822	20.502	47.346	33.208	17.142	16.606	31.018	63.683	54.	3.210	Electricity
6.416	3.944	12.582	26.079	12.985	13.028	7.620	41.858	55.	3.220	Gas
10.577	3.648	4.183	20.803	25.969	15.191	18.973	25.656	56.	3.230	Liquid fuels
1.953	6.812	20.395	4.276	20.670	8.235	9.473	8.951	57.	3.240	Other fuels and ice
23.331	19.313	12.878	56.149	63.267	44.668	75.553	61.666	58.	4.110	Furniture and fixtures
1.488	6.413	16.952	16.668	5.814	4.424	11.863	17.120	59.	4.120	Floor coverings
8.025	7.676	22.950	24.594	8.148	14.912	25.617	44.541	60.	4.200	Household textiles and the like

(Table continues on following page.)

Appendix Table 4.5 continued.

			Kenya	India	Philippines	Korea Republic of	Colombia	Malaysia	Iran	Hungary
61.	4.310	Refrigerators and freezers	0.070	0.071	0.695	0.400	0.354	0.832	1.045	3.227
62.	4.320	Washing appliances	0.013	0.0	0.289	0.0	0.164	0.119	0.102	2.186
63.	4.330	Cooking appliances	0.043	0.007	0.619	0.092	0.939	0.398	0.493	6.931
64.	4.340	Heating appliances	0.101	0.019	0.057	0.502	0.188	0.084	0.195	2.097
65.	4.350	Cleaning appliances	0.016	0.0	0.240	0.052	0.187	0.170	0.095	0.842
66.	4.360	Other household appliances	0.016	0.464	0.660	2.159	0.105	0.634	0.587	0.919
67.	4.400	Household utensils	1.288	1.069	1.007	2.193	1.272	8.751	2.878	8.738
68.	4.510	Nondurable household goods	4.191	0.449	4.154	1.446	7.341	7.221	5.402	9.574
69.	4.520	Domestic services	3.470	2.349	4.335	0.735	22.625	4.849	1.546	1.109
70.	4.530	Household services	0.381	1.972	0.739	1.030	3.166	0.0	0.606	1.730
71.	4.600	House furnishing repairs	0.037	0.762	0.761	4.028	0.066	0.098	0.127	6.047
72.	5.110	Drugs and medical preparations	1.690	2.497	2.417	5.899	2.954	5.946	13.437	23.485
73.	5.120	Medical supplies	0.108	0.303	0.342	0.687	0.054	0.623	0.213	3.549
74.	5.200	Therapeutic equipment	0.038	0.227	0.366	0.169	0.528	1.187	0.594	0.0
75.	5.310	Physicians' services	2.680	4.351	2.412	9.862	10.386	5.327	6.607	44.152
76.	5.320	Dentists' services	0.238	0.543	0.548	2.034	4.312	0.874	1.827	7.770
77.	5.330	Nurses' services	2.661	0.529	0.747	2.153	2.919	3.914	0.858	12.926
78.	5.410	Hospitals	4.938	2.304	4.627	1.495	9.242	14.628	2.601	35.814
79.	6.110	Personal automobiles	1.708	0.123	0.221	0.197	2.393	6.595	2.999	6.032
80.	6.120	Other personal transport	0.017	0.259	0.027	0.013	0.008	0.733	0.518	5.497
81.	6.210	Tires, tubes, and accessories	0.250	0.029	0.135	0.003	0.585	6.438	0.623	2.228
82.	6.220	Automobile repairs	1.490	0.821	0.088	0.002	2.649	3.198	3.539	3.900
83.	6.230	Gasoline, oil, and grease	0.196	0.199	0.553	0.003	2.129	9.220	1.897	2.806
84.	6.240	Parking, tolls, and the like	0.487	0.116	0.062	0.008	2.203	1.148	2.234	1.172
85.	6.310	Local transport	0.617	1.407	2.316	9.047	24.817	4.636	9.652	9.636
86.	6.321	Rail transport	0.308	1.126	0.088	4.822	11.286	0.569	0.920	8.128
87.	6.322	Bus transport	3.941	4.439	2.007	6.642	2.534	17.086	6.985	8.319
88.	6.323	Air transport	2.138	0.014	1.063	0.159	19.975	5.229	0.537	1.341
89.	6.330	Miscellaneous transport	0.043	0.991	4.222	0.655	0.075	1.212	0.500	1.232
90.	6.410	Postal communication	0.083	0.459	0.122	0.505	0.246	0.928	0.046	2.944
91.	6.420	Telephone and telegraph	0.304	0.744	0.297	1.848	6.890	2.783	1.912	4.302
92.	7.110	Radios, televisions, and phonographs	0.494	0.244	0.716	2.015	2.527	5.128	1.292	9.448
93.	7.120	Major durable recreational equipment	0.788	0.076	0.424	0.116	0.286	1.924	0.081	0.574
94.	7.130	Other recreational equipment	0.631	0.058	0.284	0.563	0.666	0.844	1.193	4.056
95.	7.210	Public entertainment	1.920	0.099	2.486	0.100	7.333	9.388	1.302	34.810
96.	7.230	Other recreational and cultural activities	0.912	1.217	1.228	10.432	1.100	1.294	1.960	56.032
97.	7.310	Books, papers, and magazines	0.997	0.334	0.608	2.602	2.638	3.187	0.909	15.193
98.	7.320	Stationery	0.006	0.092	0.044	1.907	0.184	1.083	0.934	1.339
99.	7.411	First- and second- level teachers	19.453	22.499	45.506	27.167	36.987	42.874	26.883	56.067
100.	7.412	College teachers	0.346	2.756	7.502	2.850	4.917	1.025	1.970	8.326
101.	7.420	Physical facilities for education	1.159	0.342	2.460	1.658	2.006	1.188	0.834	18.658
102.	7.431	Educational books and supplies	0.382	0.508	1.118	1.275	1.092	0.553	0.233	2.302
103.	7.432	Other educational expenditures	1.200	0.480	0.890	1.677	2.358	1.133	0.412	7.645
104.	8.100	Barber and beauty shops	0.080	0.368	4.834	11.514	1.572	3.271	18.410	11.710
105.	8.210	Toilet articles	0.303	0.562	3.580	0.888	4.187	3.994	1.825	12.989
106.	8.220	Other personal care goods	1.103	0.717	4.738	1.352	2.406	7.015	2.229	6.959
107.	8.310	Restaurants and cafes	4.889	0.748	6.098	6.630	17.704	7.102	31.149	112.879
108.	8.320	Hotels and lodging	3.339	0.618	0.104	1.146	1.450	13.486	1.592	3.493
109.	8.400	Other services	4.902	7.695	19.011	5.463	36.521	4.804	9.797	41.217
110.	8.900	Net expenditures of residents abroad	0.0	0.0	0.011	-0.098	0.021	0.0	0.0	0.0

Italy	Japan	United Kingdom	Netherlands	Belgium	France	Germany F.R.	United States			
4.543	10.887	2.785	16.168	5.945	9.565	12.701	13.516	61.	4.310	Refrigerators and freezers
6.357	9.793	6.426	12.073	3.211	7.731	11.621	9.483	62.	4.320	Washing appliances
4.177	4.237	5.755	5.359	5.625	5.552	4.258	6.034	63.	4.330	Cooking appliances
1.946	8.842	4.305	13.819	14.572	4.829	7.230	0.931	64.	4.340	Heating appliances
0.748	3.776	2.455	2.716	1.050	3.241	5.473	3.595	65.	4.350	Cleaning appliances
1.132	8.824	0.754	7.198	1.457	3.019	7.352	17.094	66.	4.360	Other household appliances
11.588	25.532	18.504	42.900	63.860	21.475	45.737	17.707	67.	4.400	Household utensils
10.853	8.574	16.598	29.746	55.849	41.684	55.707	52.075	68.	4.510	Nondurable household goods
0.0	0.747	3.222	0.0	0.0	0.0	0.0	6.918	69.	4.520	Domestic services
13.424	12.572	10.588	11.707	26.450	9.929	10.709	4.753	70.	4.530	Household services
0.0	1.108	2.235	0.0	0.0	0.0	0.0	4.042	71.	4.600	House furnishing repairs
43.675	59.842	36.731	53.487	45.100	119.810	45.007	51.294	72.	5.110	Drugs and medical preparations
0.765	45.231	4.923	1.731	1.640	1.833	6.554	7.047	73.	5.120	Medical supplies
0.434	3.096	8.143	18.392	5.685	4.726	14.048	8.815	74.	5.200	Therapeutic equipment
28.409	26.176	28.668	28.961	34.966	30.806	40.916	38.454	75.	5.310	Physicians' services
17.914	12.099	9.179	8.796	5.681	14.269	17.714	17.927	76.	5.320	Dentists' services
3.052	9.171	8.506	8.790	4.527	8.747	9.329	16.958	77.	5.330	Nurses' services
41.956	53.502	41.922	50.364	38.290	31.834	53.111	35.133	78.	5.410	Hospitals
40.178	7.445	50.026	38.941	54.668	50.527	57.843	189.019	79.	6.110	Personal automobiles
2.110	2.497	2.661	6.436	2.536	4.136	3.989	20.129	80.	6.120	Other personal transport
6.357	0.555	19.678	13.727	13.982	14.829	11.771	27.496	81.	6.210	Tires, tubes, and accessories
12.051	2.722	23.787	8.459	11.666	17.864	18.317	50.028	82.	6.220	Automobile repairs
21.333	4.820	28.162	17.973	31.116	26.458	50.428	157.752	83.	6.230	Gasoline, oil, and grease
19.246	2.502	17.259	19.017	9.121	22.433	16.343	20.237	84.	6.240	Parking, tolls, and the like
10.724	18.277	23.743	6.059	7.273	10.076	6.345	6.340	85.	6.310	Local transport
11.078	6.488	6.284	11.076	10.754	10.563	16.956	0.619	86.	6.321	Rail transport
5.990	1.574	1.639	4.078	7.965	7.640	8.072	1.859	87.	6.322	Bus transport
0.972	0.790	14.760	0.967	2.636	2.266	0.974	16.572	88.	6.323	Air transport
0.0	0.672	2.808	0.0	0.0	0.0	0.0	6.319	89.	6.330	Miscellaneous transport
4.784	1.226	6.979	6.908	6.033	4.918	12.432	6.295	90.	6.410	Postal communication
7.882	8.938	17.813	14.874	5.295	3.742	3.780	40.561	91.	6.420	Telephone and telegraph
9.074	25.662	7.340	24.149	15.022	18.097	16.857	64.482	92.	7.110	Radios, televisions, and phonographs
0.341	3.019	4.575	3.854	1.753	5.147	11.974	29.990	93.	7.120	Major durable recreational equipment
12.970	11.284	29.167	38.883	25.691	31.914	55.520	58.504	94.	7.130	Other recreational equipment
17.142	9.092	34.496	21.359	10.225	8.004	11.687	21.368	95.	7.210	Public entertainment
4.169	4.397	23.186	6.985	12.516	7.434	10.732	26.500	96.	7.230	Other recreational and cultural activities
21.018	7.243	46.766	25.694	14.713	34.925	22.079	31.098	97.	7.310	Books, papers, and magazines
5.200	2.046	5.506	10.176	2.980	21.752	8.892	10.136	98.	7.320	Stationery
70.334	55.742	69.302	45.994	67.924	58.933	57.962	77.497	99.	7.411	First- and second- level teachers
7.269	12.882	7.995	7.745	97.927	6.163	5.989	30.872	100.	7.412	College teachers
4.550	13.119	16.724	31.079	16.297	5.483	15.266	33.034	101.	7.420	Physical facilities for education
0.792	3.416	12.912	5.107	3.281	1.063	0.716	3.342	102.	7.431	Educational books and supplies
2.786	13.497	15.204	5.556	5.054	1.091	5.877	10.772	103.	7.432	Other educational expenditures
6.997	6.404	10.192	3.742	18.122	7.735	6.135	8.236	104.	8.100	Barber and beauty shops
5.305	10.467	9.639	10.765	7.419	16.219	9.638	43.526	105.	8.210	Toilet articles
7.258	4.098	13.871	8.655	7.209	14.620	9.992	43.124	106.	8.220	Other personal care goods
52.254	124.361	38.474	84.041	269.723	126.271	95.221	147.739	107.	8.310	Restaurants and cafes
34.162	19.191	32.078	40.052	16.151	71.224	58.587	8.809	108.	8.320	Hotels and lodging
4.406	88.468	51.019	44.079	14.205	6.769	17.027	80.447	109.	8.400	Other services
-23.267	3.513	-1.424	12.669	10.863	-6.662	3.256	22.955	110.	8.900	Net expenditures of residents abroad

(Table continues on following page.)

163

			Kenya	India	Philippines	Korea Republic of	Colombia	Malaysia	Iran	Hungary
111.	10.100	One- and two-dwelling buildings	7.926	4.679	5.367	17.830	34.687	18.154	53.277	38.735
112.	10.200	Multidwelling buildings	0.944	4.219	6.424	3.223	4.491	17.589	11.327	40.428
113.	11.100	Hotels	0.110	0.358	0.180	0.653	0.242	2.071	1.804	5.351
114.	11.200	Industrial buildings	2.566	0.713	0.529	6.482	1.927	10.196	25.823	49.208
115.	11.300	Commercial buildings	0.597	2.293	2.748	6.667	0.818	7.117	2.005	7.875
116.	11.400	Office buildings	0.967	0.962	1.116	1.874	2.192	7.294	11.146	11.545
117.	11.500	Educational buildings	1.084	0.607	3.446	1.526	1.190	8.735	2.563	9.513
118.	11.600	Hospital buildings	0.764	0.415	0.578	3.130	0.217	3.375	1.022	3.354
119.	11.700	Agricultural buildings	0.395	3.718	0.324	4.044	1.225	2.072	8.470	41.105
120.	11.800	Other buildings	0.175	0.919	0.066	3.823	0.248	2.159	4.051	2.776
121.	12.100	Roads, streets, and highways	2.753	1.933	10.785	8.137	25.494	6.362	4.268	12.525
122.	12.200	Transport and utility lines	1.581	7.591	0.906	6.900	21.879	15.875	7.376	49.315
123.	12.300	Other construction	1.211	4.799	0.079	17.180	15.086	4.384	11.856	30.700
124.	13.000	Land improvement	0.806	3.991	0.120	1.132	18.815	18.184	0.0	8.160
125.	14.110	Locomotives	0.890	0.091	0.079	1.220	0.018	0.016	0.019	2.339
126.	14.120	Other railway vehicles	1.055	0.204	0.008	0.975	0.169	0.0	0.385	6.589
127.	14.200	Passenger automobiles	2.278	0.068	2.512	2.079	1.551	1.864	3.846	1.483
128.	14.300	Trucks, busses, and trailers	3.126	1.237	2.499	3.417	3.286	5.301	2.488	24.237
129.	14.400	Aircraft	0.558	0.039	0.224	0.625	1.022	0.0	0.995	1.219
130.	14.500	Ships and boats	0.125	0.290	0.823	1.807	7.144	1.840	1.087	1.302
131.	14.600	Other transport equipment	0.123	0.357	0.531	0.435	0.072	0.625	8.172	13.489
132.	15.100	Engines and turbines	0.757	0.286	2.151	1.747	0.289	3.417	3.280	3.782
133.	15.210	Tractors	0.691	0.238	0.978	0.0	0.285	2.468	0.805	6.039
134.	15.220	Others agricultural machinery	0.685	0.041	0.199	0.105	0.232	0.361	1.215	11.651
135.	15.300	Office machinery	0.337	0.054	0.885	0.301	0.161	1.235	0.284	3.601
136.	15.400	Metalworking machinery	0.390	0.344	0.509	3.159	0.822	0.522	2.262	7.876
137.	15.500	Construction and mining machinery	1.128	0.159	2.305	0.792	0.752	5.584	0.584	12.910
138.	15.600	Special industrial machinery	2.945	0.677	2.112	3.915	1.285	5.942	4.229	32.513
139.	15.700	General industrial machinery	2.126	1.232	5.747	4.718	1.148	5.010	3.978	11.207
140.	15.800	Service industrial machinery	0.406	0.120	0.792	0.683	0.044	1.430	0.541	1.615
141.	16.100	Electrical transmission equipment	1.173	0.528	0.699	1.947	2.626	1.416	1.828	4.432
142.	16.200	Communications equipment	0.465	0.504	1.900	0.326	2.710	1.834	0.650	10.207
143.	16.300	Other electrical equipment	0.335	0.093	1.694	1.653	7.005	0.033	1.588	0.878
144.	16.400	Instruments	0.306	0.172	0.463	0.259	2.145	0.922	0.689	9.122
145.	17.100	Furniture and fixtures	0.172	0.049	0.725	2.274	0.759	2.349	0.972	18.816
146.	17.200	Other durable goods	0.587	1.340	3.510	0.286	1.003	0.149	1.780	1.304
147.	18.000	Increase in stocks	6.217	5.783	10.527	10.314	20.259	25.286	1.870	67.836
148.	19.000	Exports minuus imports	-3.681	-0.957	-1.295	-38.595	-8.549	25.705	35.188	-44.635
149.	20.100	Unskilled blue collar	32.471	13.665	3.004	1.918	13.414	5.339	26.353	20.311
150.	20.210	Skilled blue collar	1.474	1.621	2.403	4.193	3.617	4.034	9.558	1.583
151.	20.220	White collar	3.615	15.140	27.875	41.419	19.730	23.772	7.659	25.338
152.	20.300	Professional	5.327	6.143	12.314	10.801	29.346	26.509	10.789	27.221
153.	21.000	Commodities of government	6.632	10.605	12.569	19.080	11.288	36.789	47.153	101.317

Italy	Japan	United Kingdom	Netherlands	Belgium	France	Germany F.R.	United States			
102.118	119.101	93.836	34.253	12.713	54.329	31.821	93.441	111.	10.100	One- and two-dwelling buildings
49.641	52.790	36.434	175.600	145.598	146.020	162.379	55.472	112.	10.200	Multidwelling buildings
6.841	8.961	1.336	3.980	3.195	8.429	14.831	5.656	113.	11.100	Hotels
51.461	18.227	37.860	61.941	90.288	33.232	100.744	37.544	114.	11.200	Industrial buildings
10.194	20.208	12.715	46.963	21.751	37.629	38.541	28.460	115.	11.300	Commercial buildings
19.590	30.445	9.850	17.512	8.326	24.778	34.433	16.024	116.	11.400	Office buildings
7.929	30.212	18.393	30.537	4.876	17.019	27.337	30.764	117.	11.500	Educational buildings
5.245	10.426	9.738	39.858	1.722	7.968	17.843	13.473	118.	11.600	Hospital buildings
10.924	3.192	8.509	11.702	16.543	16.233	9.972	9.717	119.	11.700	Agricultural buildings
4.275	45.997	13.341	3.533	4.388	27.269	4.353	21.267	120.	11.800	Other buildings
30.666	20.792	16.713	65.769	65.636	28.966	69.673	39.742	121.	12.100	Roads, streets, and highways
26.037	43.967	16.632	57.838	74.105	84.013	88.703	69.895	122.	12.200	Transport and utility lines
6.721	49.243	4.446	9.405	1.144	8.112	21.562	10.393	123.	12.300	Other construction
9.356	1.078	2.590	13.538	0.520	1.520	2.312	0.0	124.	13.000	Land improvement
1.063	2.196	0.787	1.092	0.934	2.285	0.869	4.870	125.	14.110	Locomotives
0.746	0.224	1.191	1.514	1.545	3.166	5.069	10.886	126.	14.120	Other railway vehicles
19.837	28.839	25.120	30.395	24.534	31.811	42.057	48.457	127.	14.200	Passenger automobiles
25.537	36.251	3.206	25.346	18.451	36.394	52.796	56.027	128.	14.300	Trucks, busses, and trailers
3.373	0.793	7.907	11.323	9.584	2.262	10.786	17.308	129.	14.400	Aircraft
5.497	10.694	30.152	14.198	5.443	5.539	31.389	5.697	130.	14.500	Ships and boats
1.672	4.718	14.758	0.359	0.0	0.268	0.205	3.580	131.	14.600	Other transport equipment
3.446	8.531	0.756	5.722	2.651	3.960	3.212	13.445	132.	15.100	Engines and turbines
5.249	1.482	3.979	6.976	9.493	18.141	9.663	10.713	133.	15.210	Tractors
4.342	6.665	4.911	5.881	7.202	27.270	11.031	17.138	134.	15.220	Others agricultural machinery
6.027	16.742	9.140	13.830	10.851	31.614	37.327	32.524	135.	15.300	Office machinery
18.592	15.746	15.693	8.800	7.783	24.684	33.359	19.753	136.	15.400	Metalworking machinery
6.144	21.042	19.821	19.035	25.281	37.335	25.595	32.651	137.	15.500	Construction and mining machinery
20.084	62.767	28.049	44.110	28.410	60.679	56.889	27.543	138.	15.600	Special industrial machinery
22.566	38.173	78.793	70.077	60.204	33.443	93.946	25.389	139.	15.700	General industrial machinery
4.065	3.684	1.946	13.983	6.226	3.453	5.433	21.286	140.	15.800	Service industrial machinery
33.550	42.763	22.279	35.097	25.141	51.455	49.162	20.002	141.	16.100	Electrical transmission equipment
10.993	40.858	21.668	16.139	11.128	28.588	46.222	53.190	142.	16.200	Communications equipment
20.081	10.050	8.747	8.646	36.337	9.368	9.626	7.962	143.	16.300	Other electrical equipment
8.502	15.816	11.789	40.245	26.373	36.970	40.232	22.733	144.	16.400	Instruments
3.778	71.107	39.530	0.0	12.256	5.415	7.292	16.219	145.	17.100	Furniture and fixtures
7.993	39.144	6.615	0.0	11.491	8.357	8.351	25.079	146.	17.200	Other durable goods
41.743	113.402	26.680	84.574	53.887	81.962	83.277	13.806	147.	18.000	Increase in stocks
14.785	37.479	30.007	-65.292	94.997	24.852	88.087	14.722	148.	19.000	Exports minuus imports
24.067	16.514	62.377	7.529	31.460	4.573	6.565	27.528	149.	20.100	Unskilled blue collar
17.125	62.185	12.869	17.309	14.602	45.195	32.836	30.807	150.	20.210	Skilled blue collar
57.201	14.933	60.697	105.040	78.619	67.275	98.378	83.628	151.	20.220	White collar
9.911	13.575	26.955	37.804	28.629	65.232	19.814	82.462	152.	20.300	Professional
56.578	35.261	141.772	106.371	78.796	108.327	101.731	351.141	153.	21.000	Commodities of government

This appendix amplifies the information presented in Table 4.14 by giving the relative price structures for the sixteen individual ICP countries. In Appendix Table 4.6, the percentage distribution of expenditures in national prices is expressed relative to the distribution in international prices. This provides a measure of the way category prices in a country differ from the average of international prices as discussed in the text.

Appendix 2 to Chapter 4

Relative Price Structures of the Phase II Countries

**Appendix Table 4.6. Ratios of Percentage Distribution of Expenditures in National Prices
to Expenditures at International Prices, 1970 and 1973**

1970

	Line numbers[a]	Kenya	India	Philippines	Korea Republic of	Colombia	Malaysia	Iran	Hungary
Consumption, ICP[b,c]	1–110	1.01	1.07	0.96	1.04	1.03	1.00	0.93	0.92
Food, Beverage, and Tobacco	1– 39	0.95	1.25	1.10	1.16	0.99	0.98	1.12	1.01
Food,	1– 33	0.91	1.22	1.13	1.08	1.03	0.91	1.12	1.07
Bread and Cereals	1– 6	0.94	1.09	1.18	0.97	1.24	0.80	1.00	0.69
Meat	7– 12	0.88	1.33	0.80	1.29	1.06	1.17	1.26	1.46
Fish	13– 14	0.81	0.46	1.27	1.00	1.60	0.75	1.19	0.68
Milk, Cheese, and Eggs	15– 17	1.15	1.33	1.88	1.60	1.22	1.23	0.81	0.96
Oils and Fats	18– 20	1.14	1.76	1.05	1.60	1.24	0.86	1.75	1.01
Fruits and Vegetables	21– 26	0.74	1.32	1.23	1.11	0.96	0.92	1.16	0.95
Coffee, Tea, and Cocoa	27– 29	0.79	1.15	1.56	4.35	0.78	1.36	2.01	3.15
Spices Sweets, and Sugar	30– 33	1.03	1.54	1.22	1.22	0.81	0.90	1.35	1.19
Beverages	34– 37	2.14	3.77	0.74	2.64	1.29	1.47	1.36	1.01
Tobacco	38– 39	1.20	1.66	1.34	1.57	0.47	1.66	1.06	0.47
Clothing and Footwear	40– 51	1.05	1.25	0.85	1.10	1.27	0.66	0.83	1.29
Clothing	40– 47	1.17	1.23	0.84	1.14	1.35	0.67	0.95	1.29
Footwear	48– 51	0.72	1.56	0.87	0.70	1.07	0.62	0.54	1.31
Gross Rent and Fuel	52– 57	1.54	1.03	0.85	1.33	1.72	1.03	0.73	0.69
Gross Rents	52– 53	1.96	0.77	0.66	2.62	2.11	0.94	0.62	0.65
Fuel and Power	54– 57	0.71	1.76	2.38	0.95	0.70	1.79	1.61	0.75
House Furnishings and Operations	58– 71	1.18	0.92	1.07	0.91	0.91	0.93	0.82	1.36
Furniture and Appliances	58– 66	1.52	1.27	1.04	1.60	1.47	0.91	0.67	1.29
Supplies and Operation	67– 71	1.12	0.85	1.10	0.59	0.69	0.95	1.13	1.49
Medical Care	72– 78	0.88	0.59	1.22	0.55	1.27	0.72	1.22	0.56
Transport and Communications	79– 91	1.33	1.20	0.94	1.00	0.84	1.46	0.82	1.26
Equipment	79– 80	2.00	2.48	6.33	4.06	3.73	2.51	2.61	1.97
Operation Costs	81– 84	0.81	1.02	1.80	0.00	0.72	1.70	0.90	1.19
Purchased Transport	85– 89	1.38	1.21	0.76	1.02	0.79	1.07	0.48	1.15
Communications	90– 91	1.06	0.72	1.30	0.60	0.45	1.21	0.53	0.62
Recreation and Education	92–103	0.88	0.44	0.54	0.70	0.83	0.98	0.85	0.64
Recreation	92– 98	1.51	1.06	1.14	0.88	1.65	1.27	1.53	0.59
Education	99–103	0.72	0.39	0.48	0.61	0.58	0.84	0.68	0.70
Other Expenditures	104–109	0.95	0.81	0.89	0.93	1.03	1.11	0.73	0.93
Personal Care	104–106	1.15	1.66	0.79	0.72	1.38	1.25	0.89	0.90
Miscellaneous Services	107–109	0.92	0.67	0.95	1.15	0.98	1.03	0.65	0.93
Capital Formation[d]	111–148	1.36	1.10	1.63	1.13	1.01	0.98	1.09	1.25
Construction	111–124	1.34	0.84	0.97	1.12	0.77	0.63	0.80	1.23
Residential	111–112	1.11	0.88	1.07	0.88	0.69	0.60	0.63	1.27
Nonresidential Bldgs	113–120	1.11	0.83	1.27	1.13	0.62	0.57	0.75	1.23
Other Construction	121–124	1.88	0.83	0.64	1.27	0.82	0.72	1.36	1.19
Producers Durables	125–146	1.46	2.31	2.43	1.59	2.00	1.58	1.64	1.34
Transport Equipment	125–131	1.30	2.06	3.26	2.15	1.59	1.72	1.64	1.22
Nonelectrical Machinery	132–140	1.55	2.24	2.36	1.50	2.38	1.53	1.70	1.43
Electrical Machinery	141–144	1.61	2.68	2.48	1.17	2.25	2.01	1.80	1.09
Other Durables	145–146	1.33	2.39	1.23	0.47	1.88	0.88	0.94	1.57
Increase in stocks	147	1.14	1.28	1.36	1.18	1.12	1.07	1.09	1.15
Exports minus imports	148	1.43	2.25	2.09	1.52	1.70	1.60	1.64	1.34
Government	149–153	0.61	0.55	0.55	0.63	0.73	1.03	1.27	0.90
Compensation	149–152	0.54	0.41	0.44	0.53	0.66	1.03	1.43	0.55
Commodities	153	1.10	1.04	0.95	0.97	1.17	1.01	1.08	1.16
Gross Domestic Product	1–153	1.00	1.00	1.00	1.00	1.00	1.00	1.00	1.00

1970

Italy	Japan	United Kingdom	Netherlands	Belgium	France	Germany F.R.	United States		Line numbers[a]
1.02	0.96	1.03	1.01	0.99	1.04	1.07	1.00	Consumption, ICP[b,c]	1–110
1.03	1.10	0.96	0.90	0.91	0.86	1.00	0.79	Food, Beverage, and Tobacco	1– 39
1.04	1.15	0.77	0.95	0.97	0.90	1.05	0.78	Food,	1– 33
1.03	1.01	0.65	1.03	1.04	1.12	1.18	0.99	Bread and Cereals	1– 6
1.08	1.43	0.75	1.05	1.04	0.91	1.04	0.74	Meat	7– 12
1.11	1.24	1.11	0.82	1.13	0.97	1.02	0.86	Fish	13– 14
1.15	1.00	0.84	0.85	0.81	0.76	0.83	0.87	Milk, Cheese, and Eggs	15– 17
0.81	0.87	0.54	0.73	0.84	0.81	0.89	0.60	Oils and Fats	18– 20
0.95	1.44	0.98	1.00	0.90	0.90	1.11	0.87	Fruits and Vegetables	21– 26
1.83	0.88	0.51	1.01	1.15	0.89	1.60	0.48	Coffee, Tea, and Cocoa	27– 29
1.08	0.98	0.79	0.92	0.91	0.94	0.97	0.66	Spices Sweets, and Sugar	30– 33
0.89	0.97	1.39	0.69	0.71	0.71	0.69	0.82	Beverages	34– 37
1.17	0.74	1.89	0.80	0.68	0.76	1.22	0.86	Tobacco	38– 39
1.07	0.77	0.95	0.99	1.09	1.27	1.14	0.89	Clothing and Footwear	40– 51
1.05	0.77	0.98	0.98	1.09	1.27	1.15	0.87	Clothing	40– 47
1.17	0.85	0.84	1.03	1.08	1.30	1.12	1.06	Footwear	48– 51
0.86	1.39	1.14	0.84	1.05	0.92	1.01	1.03	Gross Rent and Fuel	52– 57
0.78	1.44	1.17	0.83	0.93	0.85	0.98	1.13	Gross Rents	52– 53
1.31	1.23	1.06	0.87	1.41	1.25	1.14	0.72	Fuel and Power	54– 57
								House Furnishings and	
1.00	1.05	1.11	0.99	0.94	1.03	0.97	0.92	Operations	58– 71
1.00	1.11	1.11	1.03	1.01	1.09	1.04	0.81	Furniture and Appliances	58– 66
0.98	0.95	1.11	0.91	0.89	0.95	0.87	1.14	Supplies and Operation	67– 71
0.77	0.59	0.91	0.91	1.03	1.02	1.05	1.80	Medical Care	72– 78
1.14	1.04	1.07	1.17	1.31	1.27	1.20	0.82	Transport and Communications	79– 91
1.04	1.20	1.18	1.37	1.22	1.03	1.01	0.72	Equipment	79– 80
1.28	1.47	0.98	1.14	1.37	1.41	1.33	0.81	Operation Costs	81– 84
1.01	0.79	1.24	1.17	1.31	1.31	1.32	0.97	Purchased Transport	85– 89
1.09	1.14	0.83	0.88	1.40	1.25	0.90	1.19	Communications	90– 91
1.18	1.15	1.06	1.48	1.02	1.35	1.24	1.25	Recreation and Education	92–103
1.24	1.12	0.97	1.09	1.17	1.08	1.09	0.99	Recreation	92– 98
1.12	1.17	1.18	2.01	0.96	1.81	1.49	1.67	Education	99–103
1.26	0.70	1.12	1.04	0.84	1.14	1.11	1.15	Other Expenditures	104–109
1.21	1.05	0.86	1.19	1.15	1.23	1.22	0.96	Personal Care	104–106
1.27	0.67	1.19	1.02	0.81	1.13	1.10	1.22	Miscellaneous Services	107–109
0.88	1.06	0.89	0.90	0.98	0.89	0.84	0.90	Capital Formation[d]	111–148
0.93	1.24	0.92	0.82	1.00	0.99	0.85	1.15	Construction	111–124
1.08	1.19	0.76	0.82	1.11	1.21	0.98	1.16	Residential	111–112
0.83	1.39	1.07	0.90	0.95	0.89	0.79	1.03	Nonresidential Bldgs	113–120
0.75	1.10	1.04	0.71	0.92	0.78	0.80	1.30	Other Construction	121–124
0.80	0.89	0.85	1.01	0.97	0.78	0.80	0.68	Producers Durables	125–146
0.83	0.83	0.94	1.16	1.06	0.71	0.75	0.58	Transport Equipment	125–131
0.78	0.85	0.83	0.93	0.91	0.80	0.80	0.69	Nonelectrical Machinery	132–140
0.74	1.03	0.90	1.03	0.94	0.76	0.82	0.77	Electrical Machinery	141–144
1.16	0.89	0.68	0.00	1.25	0.96	1.13	0.79	Other Durables	145–146
1.03	1.07	0.99	0.97	1.04	0.98	0.99	0.87	Increase in stocks	147
0.92	1.01	0.94	0.92	0.89	0.85	0.83	0.68	Exports minus imports	148
1.26	0.96	1.05	1.27	1.21	1.12	1.27	1.16	Government	149–153
1.42	0.93	1.10	1.43	1.24	1.23	1.47	1.51	Compensation	149–152
0.96	1.08	1.00	1.02	1.15	0.93	0.96	0.93	Commodities	153
1.00	1.00	1.00	1.00	1.00	1.00	1.00	1.00	Gross Domestic Product	1–153

Appendix Table 4.6. continued.

1973

	Line numbers[a]	Kenya	India	Philippines	Korea Republic of	Colombia	Malaysia	Iran	Hungary
Consumption, ICP[b,c]	1–110	0.97	1.11	0.95	1.02	1.01	0.99	0.86	0.91
Food, Beverage, and Tobacco	1– 39	0.86	1.31	1.13	1.14	1.12	0.95	1.05	1.00
Food,	1– 33	0.82	1.29	1.19	1.08	1.14	0.88	1.05	1.02
Bread and Cereals	1– 6	0.89	1.11	1.22	1.01	1.29	0.73	0.89	0.61
Meat	7– 12	0.72	1.26	0.86	1.30	1.22	1.12	1.27	1.25
Fish	13– 14	0.78	0.41	1.31	0.74	1.66	0.77	1.63	0.62
Milk, Cheese, and Eggs	15– 17	0.93	1.39	1.97	1.45	1.29	1.16	0.79	1.00
Oils and Fats	18– 20	1.13	1.93	0.97	1.58	1.32	0.75	1.87	0.94
Fruits and Vegetables	21– 26	0.70	1.60	1.51	1.21	0.97	0.92	1.00	0.98
Coffee, Tea, and Cocoa	27– 29	0.78	1.10	1.64	3.07	0.90	1.35	1.95	2.96
Spices Sweets, and Sugar	30– 33	0.82	1.80	1.36	1.25	0.92	0.96	1.17	1.21
Beverages	34– 37	2.08	2.80	0.64	2.36	1.45	1.45	1.16	1.16
Tobacco	38– 39	1.17	1.79	1.12	1.29	0.57	1.60	0.94	0.59
Clothing and Footwear	40– 51	1.11	1.24	0.90	0.96	1.29	0.70	0.75	1.28
Clothing	40– 47	1.14	1.24	0.91	1.00	1.39	0.73	0.84	1.27
Footwear	48– 51	1.02	1.24	0.79	0.69	1.05	0.52	0.53	1.30
Gross Rent and Fuel	52– 57	1.82	1.02	0.79	1.26	1.41	1.00	0.62	0.68
Gross Rents	52– 53	2.26	0.72	0.61	2.36	1.92	0.90	0.55	0.66
Fuel and Power	54– 57	0.78	2.01	2.30	0.91	0.66	1.80	1.28	0.71
House Furnishings and Operations	58– 71	1.27	0.99	1.18	0.89	0.91	1.02	0.91	1.32
Furniture and Appliances	58– 66	1.88	1.49	1.20	1.38	1.52	1.03	0.81	1.23
Supplies and Operation	67– 71	1.14	0.89	1.15	0.59	0.74	1.02	1.05	1.47
Medical Care	72– 78	0.74	0.51	1.07	0.56	1.09	0.69	0.99	0.55
Transport and Communications	79– 91	1.33	1.55	0.81	1.05	0.71	1.39	0.85	1.30
Equipment	79– 80	1.94	2.43	4.28	3.84	3.07	2.76	2.47	2.06
Operation Costs	81– 84	0.82	1.43	1.59	0.00	0.61	1.67	0.84	1.23
Purchased Transport	85– 89	1.37	1.66	0.64	1.12	0.67	0.97	0.46	1.17
Communications	90– 91	1.06	0.66	1.06	0.43	0.37	1.06	0.74	0.60
Recreation and Education	92–103	0.84	0.40	0.47	0.77	0.70	1.00	0.96	0.65
Recreation	92– 98	1.71	1.02	1.03	0.90	1.47	1.33	1.09	0.61
Education	99–103	0.63	0.35	0.42	0.70	0.49	0.85	0.91	0.70
Other Expenditures	104–109	0.90	0.86	0.85	0.95	1.00	1.08	0.68	0.91
Personal Care	104–106	1.23	1.84	0.84	0.78	1.41	1.20	0.83	0.89
Miscellaneous Services	107–109	0.87	0.69	0.85	1.15	0.94	1.01	0.63	0.92
Capital Formation[d]	111–148	1.57	1.13	1.56	1.12	1.05	1.00	1.17	1.25
Construction	111–124	1.45	0.78	0.89	0.97	0.72	0.68	0.73	1.17
Residential	111–112	1.04	0.78	1.01	0.79	0.65	0.63	0.60	1.19
Nonresidential Bldgs	113–120	1.08	0.77	1.25	0.97	0.61	0.62	0.68	1.19
Other Construction	121–124	2.02	0.77	0.66	1.12	0.78	0.78	1.19	1.13
Producers Durables	125–146	1.94	2.38	2.44	1.61	2.30	1.47	1.44	1.39
Transport Equipment	125–131	1.79	1.99	3.32	1.99	1.81	1.85	1.46	1.36
Nonelectrical Machinery	132–140	1.96	2.49	2.39	1.59	2.64	1.46	1.55	1.42
Electrical Machinery	141–144	2.12	2.61	2.25	1.13	2.54	1.23	1.70	1.14
Other Durables	145–146	2.15	2.32	1.49	0.73	2.15	0.89	0.71	1.53
Increase in stocks	147	1.16	1.42	1.48	1.21	1.16	1.11	1.11	1.14
Exports minus imports	148	1.57	2.32	2.24	1.89	1.93	1.43	1.52	1.32
Government	149–153	0.59	0.44	0.55	0.68	0.79	1.07	1.17	0.83
Compensation	149–152	0.52	0.32	0.34	0.56	0.79	1.06	1.28	0.50
Commodities	153	1.05	0.97	1.07	0.93	0.79	1.09	1.10	1.08
Gross Domestic Product	1–153	1.00	1.00	1.00	1.00	1.00	1.00	1.00	1.00

1973

Italy	Japan	United Kingdom	Netherlands	Belgium	France	Germany F.R.	United States		Line numbers[a]
1.01	0.96	1.01	1.03	0.98	1.05	1.10	1.00	Consumption, ICP[b,c]	1–110
0.98	1.06	0.93	0.84	0.89	0.88	0.96	0.79	Food, Beverage, and Tobacco	1– 39
0.98	1.14	0.76	0.89	0.94	0.92	1.00	0.77	Food,	1– 33
0.91	0.88	0.65	0.98	1.06	1.13	1.13	0.98	Bread and Cereals	1– 6
1.04	1.47	0.80	1.02	0.99	0.92	0.97	0.79	Meat	7– 12
1.06	1.34	1.31	0.85	1.14	1.02	0.86	0.94	Fish	13– 14
1.10	0.99	0.80	0.78	0.83	0.79	0.78	0.85	Milk, Cheese, and Eggs	15– 17
0.75	0.82	0.50	0.66	0.77	0.79	0.86	0.60	Oils and Fats	18– 20
0.92	1.32	0.88	0.88	0.86	0.93	1.02	0.89	Fruits and Vegetables	21– 26
1.67	0.98	0.49	0.95	1.05	0.80	1.66	0.51	Coffee, Tea, and Cocoa	27– 29
0.98	1.07	0.75	0.91	0.92	0.98	1.05	0.56	Spices Sweets, and Sugar	30– 33
0.91	0.89	1.24	0.67	0.70	0.75	0.68	0.81	Beverages	34– 37
1.00	0.67	1.68	0.72	0.73	0.78	1.33	0.88	Tobacco	38– 39
1.02	0.90	0.90	0.99	1.05	1.24	1.15	0.88	Clothing and Footwear	40– 51
0.98	0.90	0.93	0.97	1.03	1.22	1.14	0.86	Clothing	40– 47
1.23	0.90	0.78	1.13	1.12	1.34	1.20	1.01	Footwear	48– 51
0.88	1.37	1.18	0.90	1.01	0.90	1.02	1.02	Gross Rent and Fuel	52– 57
0.83	1.42	1.22	0.93	0.89	0.83	0.94	1.08	Gross Rents	52– 53
1.18	1.21	1.06	0.85	1.34	1.31	1.33	0.82	Fuel and Power	54– 57
								House Furnishings and Operations	58– 71
0.97	0.96	1.06	0.99	1.00	1.03	0.97	0.91		
0.99	1.02	1.04	1.03	1.07	1.08	1.04	0.82	Furniture and Appliances	58– 66
0.95	0.86	1.09	0.91	0.95	0.96	0.87	1.12	Supplies and Operation	67– 71
0.74	0.56	0.86	1.06	1.02	1.02	1.25	1.71	Medical Care	72– 78
1.19	1.09	1.11	1.30	1.48	1.34	1.34	0.83	Transport and Communications	79– 91
1.17	1.15	1.18	1.51	1.34	1.16	1.11	0.75	Equipment	79– 80
1.31	1.56	1.01	1.29	1.63	1.45	1.54	0.80	Operation Costs	81– 84
0.95	0.85	1.34	1.39	1.42	1.43	1.42	0.98	Purchased Transport	85– 89
1.19	1.00	0.85	0.97	1.59	1.28	0.91	1.25	Communications	90– 91
1.24	1.24	1.04	1.57	1.09	1.41	1.28	1.25	Recreation and Education	92–103
1.28	1.19	0.93	1.16	1.23	1.13	1.08	0.97	Recreation	92– 98
1.20	1.27	1.18	2.14	1.02	1.91	1.59	1.69	Education	99–103
1.28	0.72	1.08	1.01	0.74	1.16	1.11	1.15	Other Expenditures	104–109
1.22	1.17	0.80	1.14	1.23	1.19	1.44	0.95	Personal Care	104–106
1.30	0.69	1.16	1.00	0.69	1.15	1.07	1.22	Miscellaneous Services	107–109
0.88	1.05	0.91	0.86	0.97	0.87	0.79	0.90	Capital Formation[d]	111–148
0.89	1.28	0.96	0.81	0.99	0.94	0.83	1.18	Construction	111–124
1.02	1.23	0.81	0.83	1.09	1.13	0.96	1.18	Residential	111–112
0.82	1.45	1.09	0.85	0.94	0.85	0.76	1.07	Nonresidential Bldgs	113–120
0.70	1.12	1.13	0.72	0.93	0.75	0.76	1.32	Other Construction	121–124
0.86	0.81	0.86	0.97	0.99	0.77	0.77	0.67	Producers Durables	125–146
0.96	0.79	0.96	1.18	1.10	0.80	0.77	0.60	Transport Equipment	125–131
0.81	0.75	0.81	0.84	0.90	0.76	0.74	0.66	Nonelectrical Machinery	132–140
0.78	0.89	0.90	0.99	0.97	0.74	0.78	0.77	Electrical Machinery	141–144
1.21	0.81	0.80	1.79	1.38	0.98	1.07	0.76	Other Durables	145–146
1.01	1.05	0.96	0.95	1.04	0.97	0.97	0.85	Increase in stocks	147
0.88	0.88	0.92	0.74	0.78	0.75	0.66	0.78	Exports minus imports	148
1.31	1.08	1.08	1.36	1.35	1.12	1.31	1.20	Government	149–153
1.50	1.07	1.19	1.54	1.41	1.25	1.64	1.56	Compensation	149–152
1.01	1.11	0.96	1.03	1.22	0.87	0.83	0.94	Commodities	153
1.00	1.00	1.00	1.00	1.00	1.00	1.00	1.00	Gross Domestic Product	1–153

Chapter 5

Results of the Binary Comparisons

IN THIS CHAPTER the results of the binary comparisons are presented and compared with the results of the multilateral comparisons. There are, to start with, two sets of summary tables. The first set, Summary Binary Tables 5.1 to 5.15, show "original country" binary comparisons [1] between the United States and each of fifteen other ("partner") countries for 1970, and the second set, Summary Binary Tables 5.16 to 5.30, give the analogous comparisons for 1973. In both sets there is a separate table for the comparison of each country with the United States, and the tables are arranged in alphabetical order with respect to countries. Per capita expenditures in national currencies, purchasing-power parities (PPPs), and per capita quantity ratios, with the United States as 100, are shown for GDP, its three major components, and thirty-four summary categories.[2]

An appendix table at the end of the chapter gives the 1970 PPPs for the 153 detailed categories. Each country's 1970 expenditures for these categories may be found in Appendix Table 4.1 of the immediately preceding chapter. Once again the reader is reminded that the data for the detailed categories are provided despite the fact that they do not meet the ordinary standards of publication. The purpose is to make them available for the use of statisticians and economists who wish to aggregate the data in ways different from those chosen here.

Aside from giving the basic tables that contain the binary results, the chapter is concerned mainly with comparing these results with the multilateral results presented in Chapters 1 and 4. From a substantive point of view, the broad conclusions about price and quantity structures that were observed in the multilateral results are found in the binary comparisons also. In both sets of data, for example, capital formation of the Federal Republic of Germany is a much higher percent of that of the United States than is German consumption. There are, however, some not-so-trivial differences—mainly with respect to relative quantity levels. The 1970 per capita income of the Republic of Korea, for example, is 9.6 percent of that of the United States according to the binary (Fisher) index and 12.1 percent according to the multilateral (Geary-Khamis) index. The reasons for such differences are discussed and the case for preferring the multilateral results is presented.

---

1. That is, comparisons based on the data of the two countries and no others; in contradistinction to "bridge country" binary comparisons. See Glossary.

2. Two categories, "increase in stocks" (ICP 18) and "exports less imports" (ICP 19) are not shown separately. They are, however, included in the capital formation total and may be found individually in the appendix tables.

GDP Comparisons

The summary binary tables contain three sets of PPPs. The first set is aggregated from the PPPs for 153 detailed categories with the use of U.S. expenditure weights. The second set is aggregated from the same materials using the partner country's own weights. The third set is the geometric mean of the first two (the Fisher, or ideal, index).

There are also three sets of per capita quantity indexes, each based on the United States as 100. These indexes are usually derived by dividing the PPPs into the expenditure ratio (other country to United States) on each row of the tables. Division of the expenditure ratio by the U.S.-weighted PPP yields own-weighted quantity indexes, whereas the division of the expenditure ratio by the own-weighted PPP yields U.S.-weighted quantity indexes.

The results yielded by the binary comparisons of per capita GDP—own-weighted, U.S.-weighted, and ideal indexes—have been culled from the summary tables and placed alongside the exchange-rate–converted indexes and multilateral indexes in Table 5.31. To facilitate comparisons with results in Chapters 1 and 4, the countries are arrayed here and in ensuing tables in order of rising per capita GDP in 1970 in terms of international dollars (see column 5 of Table 5.31 for the index and column 6 of Table 1.2 for the international dollar figures).

Depending on which set of these alternative quantity indexes (columns 1 to 5) is examined, the range of 1970 per capita GDPs that can be observed varies from 2 percent to 64 percent of that of the United States (the exchange-rate–derived indexes) for the other fifteen countries, to a range as high as 8 percent to 81 percent (the U.S.-weighted indexes). The differences are quite substantial, especially for the low-income countries. Which set of results should be believed?

The exchange-rate conversions (column 1) may be ruled out for reasons already given in Chapter 1: exchange rates do not necessarily reflect the relative purchasing powers of currencies. The lack of a necessary or even a close relationship is dramatically illustrated by the rise in the index for the Federal Republic of Germany from 64 percent of the U.S. index in 1970 to 89 percent in 1973, a rise that the method produces despite the fact that U.S. real GDP per capita actually increased slightly more than the German GDP between the two years.[3] One of these indexes *must* be far off the mark, and the results of the indexes in the other columns suggest that both are.

In considering the relationships among the other indexes, it is useful to recall that they are all based on the same raw data inputs, consisting mainly of expenditures and of comparative prices for the detailed categories. The differences among them must therefore be because of aggregation techniques. The most important difference in aggregation methods in this context turns on the prices used to value the quantities. In the binary indexes, U.S. prices and each partner country's own prices are used in turn, and the ideal index is then computed as the geometric mean of these two results. In the multilateral approach, average international prices, derived by weighting each country's prices by the GDP of the supercountry which it represents, are used to value the quantities.[4]

It is not surprising that own prices produce the lowest indexes among the binary and multilateral sets. The structure of each country's quantities adapts to its own price structure: expensive commodities are consumed in relatively small amounts, and cheap ones are consumed in relatively large amounts.

(Text continues on page 219.)

3. See page 11. It would not be difficult to find other examples.
4. See Chapter 3.

Summary Binary Table 5.1. Belgium and United States: Expenditures per Capita, Purchasing-Power Parities, and Quantity per Capita, 1970

Category	Line numbers[a]	Expenditure per capita Belgium (B. francs)	Expenditure per capita United States (dollars)	Purchasing-power parities (B. franc/dollar) U.S. weight	Purchasing-power parities (B. franc/dollar) Belgium weight	Purchasing-power parities (B. franc/dollar) Ideal[b]	Quantity per capita (United States=100) U.S. weight	Quantity per capita (United States=100) Belgium weight	Quantity per capita (United States=100) Ideal[b]
Consumption, ICP[c,d]	1–110	85378.7	3270.65	48.1	35.0	41.0	74.6	54.3	63.6
Food, Beverage, and Tobacco	1– 39	21896.6	564.33	47.3	39.9	43.4	97.3	82.0	89.3
Food,	1– 33	18501.7	447.07	51.7	42.9	47.1	96.5	80.0	87.8
Bread and Cereals	1– 6	2310.2	49.50	46.6	33.8	39.7	137.9	100.2	117.5
Meat	7– 12	7254.3	122.25	51.2	50.8	51.0	116.9	115.8	116.4
Fish	13– 14	637.3	16.00	65.0	57.7	61.3	69.0	61.2	65.0
Milk, Cheese, and Eggs	15– 17	1874.9	71.79	35.5	34.5	35.0	75.8	73.6	74.7
Oils and Fats	18– 20	1449.1	20.87	45.6	49.5	47.5	140.4	152.3	146.2
Fruits and Vegetables	21– 26	2886.6	102.30	54.8	30.6	40.9	92.2	51.5	68.9
Coffee, Tea, and Cocoa	27– 29	703.9	14.79	90.7	95.7	93.2	49.7	52.5	51.1
Spices, Sweets, and Sugar	30– 33	1385.5	49.58	62.1	58.3	60.1	47.9	45.0	46.5
Beverages	34– 37	1799.4	64.57	30.9	31.2	31.1	89.2	90.0	89.6
Tobacco	38– 39	1595.5	52.69	29.9	26.6	28.2	113.9	101.4	107.5
Clothing and Footwear	40– 51	6838.3	238.33	46.7	42.7	44.6	67.2	61.5	64.3
Clothing	40– 47	5914.7	199.35	48.4	43.7	46.0	67.9	61.3	64.5
Footwear	48– 51	923.5	38.98	37.8	37.3	37.5	63.5	62.7	63.1
Gross Rent and Fuel	52– 57	12285.5	564.88	43.1	36.4	39.6	59.8	50.4	54.9
Gross Rents	52– 53	8188.3	463.12	36.0	29.8	32.8	59.2	49.2	54.0
Fuel and Power	54– 57	4097.2	101.76	75.7	64.7	70.0	62.2	53.2	57.5
House Furnishings and Operations	58– 71	9155.2	239.23	45.5	40.8	43.1	93.9	84.2	88.9
Furniture and Appliances	58– 66	4201.6	141.52	52.1	44.1	48.0	67.3	57.0	61.9
Supplies and Operation	67– 71	4953.6	97.72	35.8	38.3	37.0	132.4	141.4	136.8
Medical Care	72– 78	5335.8	316.67	27.2	19.2	22.9	87.5	62.0	73.6
Transport and Communications	79– 91	8098.8	443.92	92.2	50.3	68.1	36.3	19.8	26.8
Equipment	79– 80	2647.3	151.53	143.6	52.8	87.1	33.1	12.2	20.1
Operation Costs	81– 84	3418.7	205.78	69.5	60.5	64.8	27.5	23.9	25.6
Purchased Transport	85– 89	1429.4	30.43	42.7	34.2	38.2	137.2	110.1	122.9
Communications	90– 91	603.5	56.18	64.1	47.5	55.2	22.6	16.8	19.5
Recreation and Education	92–103	10593.0	498.80	37.3	25.4	30.8	83.7	57.0	69.0
Recreation	92– 98	3679.6	239.83	43.8	37.7	40.6	40.7	35.1	37.8
Education	99–103	6913.5	258.97	31.3	21.6	26.0	123.4	85.4	102.6
Other Expenditures	104–109	10636.6	381.55	38.9	35.4	37.1	78.8	71.7	75.1
Personal Care	104–106	1425.7	91.21	48.5	27.1	36.3	57.6	32.2	43.1
Miscellaneous Services	107–109	9210.9	290.34	35.9	37.1	36.5	85.5	88.4	86.9
Capital Formation[e]	111–148	35010.7	852.78	47.9	39.2	43.3	104.8	85.8	94.8
Construction	111–124	17136.5	496.44	36.2	32.1	34.1	107.6	95.3	101.3
Residential	111–112	6699.8	172.96	41.0	32.7	36.6	118.5	94.5	105.8
Nonresidential Bldgs	113–120	5468.9	167.17	41.1	38.4	39.7	85.1	79.6	82.3
Other Construction	121–124	4967.8	156.30	25.8	26.5	26.2	119.7	123.2	121.5
Producers Durables	125–146	12549.9	334.36	64.8	51.6	57.9	72.7	57.9	64.9
Transport Equipment	125–131	2433.3	84.79	78.5	76.3	77.4	37.6	36.5	37.1
Nonelectrical Machinery	132–140	5436.2	137.75	53.2	51.0	52.1	77.3	74.2	75.7
Electrical Machinery	141–144	3549.3	79.30	71.6	41.6	54.6	107.6	62.5	82.0
Other Durables	145–146	1131.1	32.53	61.9	58.4	60.1	59.5	56.2	57.9
Government	149–153	10659.6	666.13	39.4	32.1	35.5	49.9	40.7	45.0
Compensation	149–152	7232.3	338.73	30.1	29.1	29.6	73.4	70.9	72.2
Commodities	153	3427.4	327.41	48.9	41.1	44.8	25.5	21.4	23.4
Gross Domestic Product	1–153	131047.6	4789.55	46.8	35.8	40.9	76.5	58.4	66.9

Summary Binary Table 5.1 continued.

Category	Line numbers	Expenditure per capita		Purchasing-power parities (B. franc/dollar)			Quantity per capita (United States = 100)		
		Belgium (B. francs)	United States (dollars)	U.S. weight	Belgium weight	Ideal[e]	U.S. weight	Belgium weight	Ideal[e]
Aggregates									
ICP Concepts[f]									
Consumption (CEP)[c,d]	1–110	85378.7	3270.65	48.1	35.0	41.0	74.6	54.3	63.6
Capital Formation (GCF)[e]	111–148	35010.7	852.78	47.9	39.2	43.3	104.8	85.8	94.8
Government (PFC)	149–153	10659.6	666.13	39.4	32.1	35.5	49.9	40.7	45.0
Gross Domestic Product	1–153	131047.6	4789.55	46.8	35.8	40.9	76.5	58.4	66.9
SNA Concepts[f]									
Consumption (PFCE)	1–110	76155.1	2955.19	49.9	38.7	43.9	66.6	51.7	58.6
Capital Formation (GCF)	111–148	35010.7	852.78	47.9	39.2	43.3	104.8	85.8	94.8
Government (GFCE)	149–153	19753.9	979.14	36.7	24.7	30.1	81.6	55.0	67.0
Gross Domestic Product	1–153	130917.9	4787.10	46.8	35.8	40.9	76.5	58.4	66.8

Note: See end of Summary Binary Table 5.30 for notes.
Exchange rate: BF49.656 = US$1.00.

Summary Binary Table 5.2. Colombia and United States: Expenditures per Capita, Purchasing-Power Parities, and Quantity per Capita, 1970

Category	Line numbers[a]	Expenditure per capita		Purchasing-power parities (peso/dollar)			Quantity per capita (United States = 100)		
		Colombia (pesos)	United States (dollars)	U.S. weight	Colombia weight	Ideal[b]	U.S. weight	Colombia weight	Ideal[b]
Consumption, ICP[c,d]	1–110	4657.6	3270.65	11.2	6.0	8.2	23.7	12.7	17.4
Food, Beverage, and Tobacco	1– 39	1845.6	564.33	13.0	8.8	10.7	37.0	25.1	30.5
Food,	1– 33	1557.4	447.07	14.6	9.4	11.7	36.9	23.9	29.7
Bread and Cereals	1– 6	211.6	49.50	15.0	13.2	14.1	32.3	28.5	30.3
Meat	7– 12	484.3	122.25	11.7	10.2	10.9	38.8	33.9	36.3
Fish	13– 14	29.0	16.00	14.5	15.0	14.7	12.0	12.5	12.3
Milk, Cheese, and Eggs	15– 17	216.8	71.79	11.9	10.1	11.0	29.8	25.3	27.4
Oils and Fats	18– 20	59.6	20.87	18.9	17.6	18.2	16.2	15.1	15.7
Fruits and Vegetables	21– 26	272.6	102.30	21.0	6.0	11.2	44.7	12.7	23.8
Coffee, Tea, and Cocoa	27– 29	84.6	14.79	12.4	11.7	12.0	49.0	46.0	47.5
Spices, Sweets, and Sugar	30– 33	198.9	49.58	10.7	9.2	9.9	43.7	37.4	40.4
Beverages	34– 37	196.0	64.57	9.9	10.3	10.1	29.5	30.7	30.1
Tobacco	38– 39	92.3	52.69	3.9	3.7	3.8	47.3	45.1	46.2
Clothing and Footwear	40– 51	449.7	238.33	11.3	10.0	10.6	18.9	16.7	17.7
Clothing	40– 47	343.0	199.35	12.1	11.5	11.8	15.0	14.2	14.6
Footwear	48– 51	106.7	38.98	7.0	7.1	7.0	38.8	38.9	38.8
Gross Rent and Fuel	52– 57	437.2	564.88	11.3	10.3	10.8	7.5	6.9	7.2
Gross Rents	52– 53	387.9	463.12	12.2	11.0	11.6	7.6	6.9	7.2
Fuel and Power	54– 57	49.3	101.76	7.0	7.0	7.0	6.9	6.9	6.9

(Table continues on following page.)

Summary Binary Table 5.2 continued.

Category	Line numbers[a]	Expenditure per capita		Purchasing-power parities (peso/dollar)			Quantity per capita (United States=100)		
		Colombia (pesos)	United States (dollars)	U.S. weight	Colombia weight	Ideal[b]	U.S. weight	Colombia weight	Ideal[b]
House Furnishings and Operations	58– 71	321.1	239.23	15.0	3.2	6.9	42.0	8.9	19.4
Furniture and Appliances	58– 66	147.1	141.52	19.7	14.0	16.6	7.4	5.3	6.3
Supplies and Operation	67– 71	174.0	97.72	8.2	1.9	4.0	92.2	21.6	44.6
Medical Care	72– 78	280.6	316.67	5.7	4.2	4.9	21.1	15.4	18.1
Transport and Communications	79– 91	465.8	443.92	14.9	4.7	8.4	22.3	7.0	12.5
Equipment	79– 80	65.4	151.53	31.5	31.6	31.6	1.4	1.4	1.4
Operation Costs	81– 84	39.9	205.78	7.1	5.2	6.1	3.8	2.7	3.2
Purchased Transport	85– 89	336.9	30.43	6.7	4.2	5.3	265.6	166.4	210.2
Communications	90– 91	23.6	56.18	3.2	2.7	2.9	15.3	13.3	14.3
Recreation and Education	92–103	378.0	498.80	9.7	3.2	5.6	23.8	7.8	13.6
Recreation	92– 98	177.5	239.83	16.6	7.8	11.4	9.5	4.5	6.5
Education	99–103	200.6	258.97	3.3	2.1	2.6	37.0	23.5	29.5
Other Expenditures	104–109	479.6	381.55	7.9	5.0	6.3	24.9	15.9	19.9
Personal Care	104–106	82.4	91.21	9.9	9.1	9.5	9.9	9.1	9.5
Miscellaneous Services	107–109	397.2	290.34	7.3	4.6	5.8	29.6	18.8	23.6
Capital Formation[e]	111–148	1286.0	852.78	13.9	6.5	9.5	23.1	10.9	15.8
Construction	111–124	721.1	496.44	4.3	4.4	4.4	33.1	33.7	33.4
Residential	111–112	197.1	172.96	4.3	4.5	4.4	25.4	26.5	25.9
Nonresidential Bldgs	113–120	36.8	167.17	4.2	4.0	4.1	5.5	5.2	5.3
Other Construction	121–124	487.3	156.30	4.4	4.4	4.4	71.0	71.2	71.1
Producers Durables	125–146	505.5	334.36	27.9	23.2	25.5	6.5	5.4	5.9
Transport Equipment	125–131	154.4	84.79	30.8	31.7	31.2	5.7	5.9	5.8
Nonelectrical Machinery	132–140	87.4	137.75	30.4	25.5	27.8	2.5	2.1	2.3
Electrical Machinery	141–144	238.7	79.30	24.6	19.7	22.0	15.3	12.2	13.7
Other Durables	145–146	25.0	32.53	18.4	18.4	18.4	4.2	4.2	4.2
Government	149–153	415.5	666.13	8.3	3.6	5.5	17.3	7.5	11.4
Compensation	149–152	318.9	338.73	3.1	3.1	3.1	30.3	30.5	30.4
Commodities	153	96.7	327.41	13.6	8.0	10.4	3.7	2.2	2.8
Gross Domestic Product	1–153	6359.1	4789.55	11.3	5.8	8.1	22.7	11.8	16.3
Aggregates									
ICP Concepts[f]									
Consumption (CEP)[c,d]	1–110	4657.6	3270.65	11.2	6.0	8.2	23.7	12.7	17.4
Capital Formation (GCF)[e]	111–148	1286.0	852.78	13.9	6.5	9.5	23.1	10.9	15.8
Government (PFC)	149–153	415.5	666.13	8.3	3.6	5.5	17.3	7.5	11.4
Gross Domestic Product	1–153	6359.1	4789.55	11.3	5.8	8.1	22.7	11.8	16.3
SNA Concepts[f]									
Consumption (PFCE)	1–110	4476.3	2955.19	12.0	6.4	8.8	23.6	12.7	17.3
Capital Formation (GCF)	111–148	1286.0	852.78	13.9	6.5	9.5	23.1	10.9	15.8
Government (GFCE)	149–153	596.8	979.14	7.0	3.1	4.6	19.9	8.7	13.2
Gross Domestic Product	1–153	6359.1	4787.10	11.3	5.8	8.1	22.7	11.8	16.4

Note: See end of Summary Binary Table 5.30 for notes.
Exchange rate: Col$18.352 = US$1.00.

Summary Binary Table 5.3. France and United States: Expenditures per Capita, Purchasing-Power Parities, and Quantity per Capita, 1970

Category	Line numbers[a]	Expenditure per capita France (francs)	Expenditure per capita United States (dollars)	Purchasing-power parities (franc/dollar) U.S. weight	Purchasing-power parities France weight	Purchasing-power parities Ideal[b]	Quantity per capita (United States = 100) U.S. weight	Quantity per capita France weight	Quantity per capita Ideal[b]
Consumption, ICP[c,d]	1–110	9809.38	3270.65	5.08	4.17	4.60	71.9	59.0	65.1
Food, Beverage, and Tobacco	1– 39	2607.91	564.33	5.14	4.24	4.67	109.0	90.0	99.1
Food,	1– 33	2120.62	447.07	5.61	4.55	5.05	104.3	84.6	93.9
Bread and Cereals	1– 6	297.32	49.50	5.24	4.06	4.61	147.9	114.6	130.2
Meat	7– 12	739.96	122.25	5.27	5.08	5.17	119.3	114.9	117.0
Fish	13– 14	106.89	16.00	7.20	6.23	6.70	107.2	92.8	99.7
Milk, Cheese, and Eggs	15– 17	300.57	71.79	3.73	3.70	3.72	113.1	112.2	112.6
Oils and Fats	18– 20	142.76	20.87	4.81	5.47	5.13	125.1	142.1	133.3
Fruits and Vegetables	21– 26	351.86	102.30	6.14	3.60	4.70	95.6	56.0	73.2
Coffee, Tea, and Cocoa	27– 29	58.44	14.79	8.48	8.19	8.33	48.3	46.6	47.4
Spices, Sweets, and Sugar	30– 33	122.81	49.58	7.38	6.96	7.17	35.6	33.6	34.6
Beverages	34– 37	351.53	64.57	3.10	3.18	3.14	171.0	175.4	173.2
Tobacco	38– 39	135.77	52.69	3.62	3.50	3.56	73.6	71.1	72.4
Clothing and Footwear	40– 51	849.16	238.33	6.50	6.33	6.41	56.3	54.8	55.5
Clothing	40– 47	718.49	199.35	6.74	6.68	6.71	54.0	53.5	53.7
Footwear	48– 51	130.67	38.98	5.29	4.93	5.10	68.0	63.4	65.7
Gross Rent and Fuel	52– 57	1274.30	564.88	4.11	3.63	3.86	62.2	54.9	58.5
Gross Rents	52– 53	980.93	463.12	3.34	3.17	3.25	66.9	63.4	65.1
Fuel and Power	54– 57	293.36	101.76	7.58	7.08	7.33	40.7	38.0	39.4
House Furnishings and Operations	58– 71	776.38	239.23	5.37	5.42	5.40	59.9	60.4	60.1
Furniture and Appliances	58– 66	468.66	141.52	5.95	5.60	5.77	59.1	55.7	57.3
Supplies and Operation	67– 71	307.72	97.72	4.54	5.16	4.84	61.0	69.4	65.1
Medical Care	72– 78	953.99	316.67	2.97	2.72	2.84	110.8	101.6	106.1
Transport and Communications	79– 91	978.10	443.92	7.58	5.25	6.31	42.0	29.1	34.9
Equipment	79– 80	248.30	151.53	7.03	5.22	6.05	31.4	23.3	27.1
Operation Costs	81– 84	505.63	205.78	8.78	6.10	7.32	40.3	28.0	33.6
Purchased Transport	85– 89	176.60	30.43	4.76	3.82	4.26	152.0	121.9	136.1
Communications	90– 91	47.57	56.18	6.23	4.89	5.52	17.3	13.6	15.3
Recreation and Education	92–103	1184.54	498.80	4.82	4.15	4.47	57.2	49.3	53.1
Recreation	92– 98	605.12	239.83	5.04	4.48	4.75	56.3	50.1	53.1
Education	99–103	579.42	258.97	4.61	3.86	4.22	58.0	48.5	53.0
Other Expenditures	104–109	1221.96	381.55	4.55	4.20	4.37	76.3	70.3	73.3
Personal Care	104–106	210.16	91.21	5.31	4.71	5.00	48.9	43.4	46.1
Miscellaneous Services	107–109	1011.80	290.34	4.32	4.10	4.21	84.9	80.7	82.8
Capital Formation[e]	111–148	4189.04	852.78	4.46	4.11	4.28	119.5	110.3	114.8
Construction	111–124	2160.59	496.44	3.84	3.64	3.74	119.4	113.4	116.4
Residential	111–112	1065.61	172.96	4.62	4.15	4.38	148.4	133.3	140.7
Nonresidential Bldgs	113–120	675.60	167.17	4.19	3.79	3.98	106.5	96.6	101.4
Other Construction	121–124	419.38	156.30	2.60	2.65	2.63	101.2	103.2	102.2
Producers Durables	125–146	1582.37	334.36	5.30	4.79	5.04	98.7	89.3	93.9
Transport Equipment	125–131	254.40	84.79	5.62	5.50	5.56	54.5	53.4	53.9
Nonelectrical Machinery	132–140	845.54	137.75	5.45	5.05	5.25	121.6	112.6	117.0
Electrical Machinery	141–144	423.08	79.30	4.48	3.98	4.23	134.0	119.0	126.3
Other Durables	145–146	59.35	32.53	5.81	5.88	5.85	31.0	31.4	31.2
Government	149–153	1428.82	666.13	4.33	3.96	4.14	54.2	49.5	51.8
Compensation	149–152	985.64	338.73	3.80	3.76	3.78	77.4	76.6	77.0
Commodities	153	443.18	327.41	4.88	4.50	4.69	30.1	27.7	28.9
Gross Domestic Product	1–153	15427.15	4789.55	4.87	4.13	4.49	77.9	66.2	71.8

(Table continues on following page.)

Summary Binary Table 5.3 continued.

Category	Line numbers	Expenditure per capita		Purchasing-power parities (franc/dollar)			Quantity per capita (United States = 100)		
		France (francs)	United States (dollars)	U.S. weight	France weight	Ideal[e]	U.S. weight	France weight	Ideal[e]
Aggregates									
ICP Concepts[f]									
Consumption (CEP)[c,d]	1–110	9809.38	3270.65	5.08	4.17	4.60	71.9	59.0	65.1
Capital Formation (GCF)[e]	111–148	4189.04	852.78	4.46	4.11	4.28	119.5	110.3	114.8
Government (PFC)	149–153	1428.82	666.13	4.33	3.96	4.14	54.2	49.5	51.8
Gross Domestic Product	1–153	15427.15	4789.55	4.87	4.13	4.49	77.9	66.2	71.8
SNA Concepts[f]									
Consumption (PFCE)	1–110	9178.69	2955.19	5.21	4.22	4.69	73.6	59.7	66.3
Capital Formation (GCF)	111–148	4189.04	852.78	4.46	4.11	4.28	119.5	110.3	114.8
Government (GFCE)	149–153	2055.01	979.14	4.20	3.85	4.02	54.5	50.0	52.2
Gross Domestic Product	1–153	15422.64	4787.10	4.87	4.14	4.49	77.9	66.2	71.8

Note: See end of Summary Binary Table 5.30 for notes.
Exchange rate: F5.5289 = US$1.00.

Summary Binary Table 5.4. Federal Republic of Germany and United States: Expenditures per Capita, Purchasing-Power Parities, and Quantity per Capita, 1970

Category	Line numbers[a]	Expenditure per capita		Purchasing-power parities (DM/dollar)			Quantity per capita (United States = 100)		
		Germany F.R. (DM)	United States (dollars)	U.S. weight	Germany weight	Ideal[b]	U.S. weight	Germany weight	Ideal[b]
Consumption, ICP[c,d]	1–110	6767.16	3270.65	3.56	2.99	3.26	69.1	58.1	63.4
Food, Beverage, and Tobacco	1– 39	1526.31	564.33	4.00	3.56	3.77	76.0	67.6	71.6
Food,	1– 33	1249.02	447.07	4.24	3.78	4.00	73.9	65.9	69.8
Bread and Cereals	1– 6	224.60	49.50	3.90	3.32	3.60	136.8	116.3	126.1
Meat	7– 12	330.92	122.25	3.90	3.81	3.85	71.1	69.5	70.3
Fish	13– 14	19.72	16.00	4.29	4.44	4.36	27.8	28.7	28.2
Milk, Cheese, and Eggs	15– 17	142.16	71.79	2.82	2.88	2.85	68.7	70.1	69.4
Oils and Fats	18– 20	123.05	20.87	4.23	4.08	4.16	144.6	139.3	141.9
Fruits and Vegetables	21– 26	193.54	102.30	4.49	3.34	3.87	56.7	42.2	48.9
Coffee, Tea, and Cocoa	27– 29	97.96	14.79	10.66	10.05	10.35	65.9	62.2	64.0
Spices, Sweets, and Sugar	30– 33	117.08	49.58	5.01	4.87	4.94	48.5	47.1	47.8
Beverages	34– 37	171.54	64.57	2.39	2.42	2.41	109.6	111.2	110.4
Tobacco	38– 39	105.75	52.69	3.98	3.84	3.91	52.3	50.5	51.4
Clothing and Footwear	40– 51	685.75	238.33	3.92	3.89	3.90	74.0	73.4	73.7
Clothing	40– 47	578.55	199.35	4.10	4.19	4.14	69.3	70.9	70.1
Footwear	48– 51	107.21	38.98	3.01	2.81	2.91	97.8	91.5	94.6
Gross Rent and Fuel	52– 57	930.77	564.88	3.02	2.75	2.88	59.9	54.6	57.2
Gross Rents	52– 53	700.74	463.12	2.59	2.45	2.52	61.6	58.4	60.0
Fuel and Power	54– 57	230.02	101.76	4.97	4.36	4.65	51.8	45.5	48.6

Summary Binary Table 5.4 continued.

Category	Line numbers[a]	Expenditure per capita		Purchasing-power parities (DM/dollar)			Quantity per capita (United States = 100)		
		Germany F.R. (DM)	United States (dollars)	U.S. weight	Germany weight	Ideal[b]	U.S. weight	Germany weight	Ideal[b]
House Furnishings and Operations	58– 71	797.41	239.23	3.63	3.45	3.54	96.7	91.9	94.2
Furniture and Appliances	58– 66	503.99	141.52	4.13	3.77	3.95	94.5	86.1	90.2
Supplies and Operation	67– 71	293.42	97.72	2.89	3.01	2.95	99.8	103.7	101.8
Medical Care	72– 78	588.19	316.67	1.95	1.56	1.75	118.7	95.0	106.2
Transport and Communications	79– 91	743.07	443.92	5.49	3.79	4.56	44.2	30.5	36.7
Equipment	79– 80	185.52	151.53	6.24	3.72	4.82	32.9	19.6	25.4
Operation Costs	81– 84	387.01	205.78	5.79	4.85	5.30	38.8	32.5	35.5
Purchased Transport	85– 89	127.25	30.43	3.32	2.64	2.96	158.2	125.9	141.1
Communications	90– 91	43.28	56.18	3.56	2.36	2.90	32.6	21.6	26.6
Recreation and Education	92–103	829.05	498.80	3.00	2.72	2.86	61.1	55.3	58.1
Recreation	92– 98	446.81	239.83	3.08	3.08	3.08	60.6	60.4	60.5
Education	99–103	382.24	258.97	2.93	2.39	2.65	61.6	50.3	55.7
Other Expenditures	104–109	654.82	381.55	3.25	3.16	3.21	54.3	52.7	53.5
Personal Care	104–106	93.82	91.21	3.56	3.04	3.29	33.8	28.9	31.3
Miscellaneous Services	107–109	561.01	290.34	3.16	3.18	3.17	60.7	61.2	61.0
Capital Formation[e]	111–148	3448.87	852.78	3.11	2.72	2.91	148.8	130.0	139.1
Construction	111–124	1594.46	496.44	2.46	2.13	2.29	150.5	130.8	140.3
Residential	111–112	569.66	172.96	2.96	2.28	2.59	144.7	111.3	126.9
Nonresidential Bldgs	113–120	588.24	167.17	2.54	2.35	2.44	149.8	138.7	144.2
Other Construction	121–124	436.55	156.30	1.81	1.77	1.79	157.5	154.1	155.8
Producers Durables	125–146	1391.19	334.36	4.04	3.57	3.80	116.7	103.0	109.6
Transport Equipment	125–131	322.62	84.79	4.79	4.86	4.82	78.3	79.5	78.9
Nonelectrical Machinery	132–140	660.53	137.75	3.95	3.40	3.67	141.0	121.3	130.8
Electrical Machinery	141–144	355.66	79.30	3.19	3.02	3.10	148.7	140.6	144.6
Other Durables	145–146	52.38	32.53	4.53	4.53	4.53	35.6	35.5	35.5
Government	149–153	985.97	666.13	3.28	2.92	3.09	50.7	45.2	47.9
Compensation	149–152	693.65	338.73	3.04	2.85	2.94	71.9	67.5	69.6
Commodities	153	292.32	327.41	3.52	3.10	3.31	28.8	25.3	27.0
Gross Domestic Product	1–153	11201.91	4789.55	3.44	2.90	3.16	80.8	68.0	74.1
Aggregates									
ICP Concepts[f]									
Consumption (CEP)[c,d]	1–110	6767.16	3270.65	3.56	2.99	3.26	69.1	58.1	63.4
Capital Formation (GCF)[e]	111–148	3448.87	852.78	3.11	2.72	2.91	148.8	130.0	139.1
Government (PFC)	149–153	985.97	666.13	3.28	2.92	3.09	50.7	45.2	47.9
Gross Domestic Product	1–153	11201.91	4789.55	3.44	2.90	3.16	80.8	68.0	74.1
SNA Concepts[f]									
Consumption (PFCE)	1–110	6321.69	2955.19	3.67	3.21	3.43	66.7	58.3	62.4
Capital Formation (GCF)	111–148	3448.87	852.78	3.11	2.72	2.91	148.8	130.0	139.1
Government (GFCE)	149–153	1423.12	979.14	3.05	2.28	2.63	63.8	47.7	55.2
Gross Domestic Product	1–153	11193.56	4787.10	3.44	2.90	3.16	80.7	67.9	74.1

Note: See end of Summary Binary Table 5.30 for notes.
Exchange rate: DM3.6465 = US$1.00.

Summary Binary Table 5.5. Hungary and United States: Expenditures per Capita, Purchasing-Power Parities, and Quantity per Capita, 1970

Category	Line numbers[a]	Expenditure per capita		Purchasing-power parities (forint/dollar)			Quantity per capita (United States = 100)		
		Hungary (forint)	United States (dollars)	U.S. weight	Hungary weight	Ideal[b]	U.S. weight	Hungary weight	Ideal[b]
Consumption, ICP[c,d]	1–110	18783.7	3270.65	19.4	11.6	15.0	49.5	29.6	38.3
Food, Beverage, and Tobacco	1– 39	6680.8	564.33	27.0	17.6	21.8	67.1	43.8	54.2
Food,	1– 33	5688.2	447.07	30.1	18.5	23.6	68.9	42.2	53.9
Bread and Cereals	1– 6	742.0	49.50	12.5	8.4	10.3	178.4	119.7	146.2
Meat	7– 12	1658.9	122.25	35.9	33.7	34.8	40.2	37.8	39.0
Fish	13– 14	43.7	16.00	40.7	20.3	28.7	13.5	6.7	9.5
Milk, Cheese, and Eggs	15– 17	693.3	71.79	16.7	17.1	16.9	56.5	57.8	57.1
Oils and Fats	18– 20	561.4	20.87	29.0	35.5	32.1	75.8	92.8	83.9
Fruits and Vegetables	21– 26	997.5	102.30	30.4	12.5	19.5	78.1	32.1	50.0
Coffee, Tea, and Cocoa	27– 29	229.6	14.79	105.2	101.6	103.4	15.3	14.8	15.0
Spices, Sweets, and Sugar	30– 33	761.8	49.58	27.1	25.5	26.3	60.2	56.6	58.4
Beverages	34– 37	701.4	64.57	19.7	19.5	19.6	55.6	55.2	55.4
Tobacco	38– 39	291.3	52.69	9.5	8.4	8.9	65.8	58.2	61.9
Clothing and Footwear	40– 51	2173.8	238.33	22.3	21.7	22.0	42.0	40.9	41.5
Clothing	40– 47	1737.3	199.35	22.9	22.9	22.9	38.1	38.1	38.1
Footwear	48– 51	436.5	38.98	19.3	18.0	18.6	62.1	58.2	60.1
Gross Rent and Fuel	52– 57	1433.2	564.88	14.1	9.0	11.3	28.0	18.0	22.5
Gross Rents	52– 53	834.5	463.12	11.2	8.0	9.5	22.4	16.1	19.0
Fuel and Power	54– 57	598.6	101.76	27.3	11.0	17.3	53.6	21.5	34.0
House Furnishings and Operations	58– 71	1546.6	239.23	24.9	21.5	23.2	30.1	25.9	27.9
Furniture and Appliances	58– 66	929.6	141.52	26.1	24.8	25.4	26.5	25.2	25.8
Supplies and Operation	67– 71	617.0	97.72	23.2	17.9	20.4	35.3	27.2	31.0
Medical Care	72– 78	1092.0	316.67	4.9	4.1	4.5	84.4	70.2	77.0
Transport and Communications	79– 91	1099.7	443.92	32.0	15.4	22.2	16.1	7.8	11.2
Equipment	79– 80	345.8	151.53	51.3	37.3	43.7	6.1	4.4	5.2
Operation Costs	81– 84	182.4	205.78	27.2	19.4	23.0	4.6	3.3	3.9
Purchased Transport	85– 89	503.8	30.43	16.0	11.6	13.6	142.9	103.4	121.6
Communications	90– 91	67.7	56.18	5.8	7.2	6.5	16.7	20.8	18.7
Recreation and Education	92–103	2085.7	498.80	13.6	5.9	9.0	70.3	30.8	46.6
Recreation	92– 98	1092.1	239.83	20.1	5.8	10.8	78.5	22.6	42.1
Education	99–103	993.6	258.97	7.5	6.1	6.8	62.8	51.3	56.8
Other Expenditures	104–109	2672.1	381.55	15.0	12.1	13.4	57.9	46.8	52.1
Personal Care	104–106	431.9	91.21	20.2	10.1	14.3	46.9	23.5	33.2
Miscellaneous Services	107–109	2240.2	290.34	13.3	12.6	12.9	61.3	58.0	59.6
Capital Formation[e]	111–148	9892.6	852.78	24.3	19.3	21.6	60.2	47.7	53.6
Construction	111–124	5795.0	496.44	16.7	16.5	16.6	70.6	69.9	70.2
Residential	111–112	1525.5	172.96	16.6	16.2	16.4	54.6	53.1	53.9
Nonresidential Bldgs	113–120	2440.7	167.17	17.5	19.7	18.5	74.3	83.5	78.7
Other Construction	121–124	1828.7	156.30	16.0	13.9	14.9	84.4	73.2	78.6
Producers Durables	125–146	3812.6	334.36	35.4	31.7	33.5	36.0	32.2	34.0
Transport Equipment	125–131	938.4	84.79	45.2	35.7	40.2	31.0	24.5	27.5
Nonelectrical Machinery	132–140	1986.9	137.75	35.9	34.0	34.9	42.4	40.2	41.3
Electrical Machinery	141–144	407.4	79.30	22.6	22.9	22.8	22.4	22.7	22.6
Other Durables	145–146	479.9	32.53	38.9	26.9	32.3	54.9	37.9	45.7
Government	149–153	2412.2	666.13	13.0	10.9	11.9	33.2	27.9	30.4
Compensation	149–152	623.9	338.73	5.4	5.2	5.3	35.1	34.4	34.8
Commodities	153	1788.3	327.41	20.9	17.5	19.1	31.1	26.2	28.6
Gross Domestic Product	1–153	31088.5	4789.55	19.4	13.2	16.0	49.1	33.5	40.6

Summary Binary Table 5.5 continued.

Category	Line numbers[a]	Expenditure per capita		Purchasing-power parities (forint/dollar)			Quantity per capita (United States = 100)		
		Hungary (forint)	United States (dollars)	U.S. weight	Hungary weight	Ideal[b]	U.S. weight	Hungary weight	Ideal[b]
Aggregates									
ICP Concepts[f]									
Consumption (CEP)[c,d]	1–110	18783.7	3270.65	19.4	11.6	15.0	49.5	29.6	38.3
Capital Formation (GCF)[e]	111–148	9892.6	852.78	24.3	19.3	21.6	60.2	47.7	53.6
Government (PFC)	149–153	2412.2	666.13	13.0	10.9	11.9	33.2	27.9	30.4
Gross Domestic Product	1–153	31088.5	4789.55	19.4	13.2	16.0	49.1	33.5	40.6
SNA Concepts[f]									
Consumption (PFCE)	1–110	16327.4	2955.19	20.7	14.6	17.4	37.8	26.7	31.7
Capital Formation (GCF)	111–148	9892.6	852.78	24.3	19.3	21.6	60.2	47.7	53.6
Government (GFCE)	149–153	4526.2	979.14	11.0	6.6	8.5	70.0	42.0	54.2
Gross Domestic Product	1–153	30746.1	4787.10	19.4	13.3	16.0	48.3	33.2	40.0

Note: See end of Summary Binary Table 5.30 for notes.
Exchange rate: Ft30.0 = US$1.00.

Summary Binary Table 5.6. India and United States: Expenditures per Capita, Purchasing-Power Parities, and Quantity per Capita, 1970

Category	Line numbers[a]	Expenditure per capita		Purchasing-power parities (rupee/dollar)			Quantity per capita (United States = 100)		
		India (rupees)	United States (dollars)	U.S. weight	India weight	Ideal[b]	U.S. weight	India weight	Ideal[b]
Consumption, ICP[c,d]	1–110	563.23	3270.65	3.85	2.17	2.89	7.9	4.5	6.0
Food, Beverage, and Tobacco	1– 39	375.38	564.33	5.57	3.54	4.44	18.8	11.9	15.0
Food,	1– 33	350.95	447.07	4.71	3.51	4.07	22.3	16.7	19.3
Bread and Cereals	1– 6	163.49	49.50	4.24	3.58	3.89	92.4	78.0	84.9
Meat	7– 12	7.20	122.25	4.12	4.27	4.19	1.4	1.4	1.4
Fish	13– 14	5.74	16.00	4.40	2.12	3.06	16.9	8.2	11.7
Milk, Cheese, and Eggs	15– 17	33.51	71.79	4.00	3.29	3.63	14.2	11.7	12.9
Oils and Fats	18– 20	39.55	20.87	5.79	4.27	4.97	44.4	32.7	38.1
Fruits and Vegetables	21– 26	57.09	102.30	4.35	2.70	3.43	20.6	12.8	16.3
Coffee, Tea, and Cocoa	27– 29	4.37	14.79	9.55	3.33	5.64	8.9	3.1	5.2
Spices, Sweets, and Sugar	30– 33	40.00	49.58	6.60	5.08	5.79	15.9	12.2	13.9
Beverages	34– 37	6.79	64.57	10.00	9.73	9.86	1.1	1.1	1.1
Tobacco	38– 39	17.64	52.69	7.49	3.26	4.94	10.3	4.5	6.8
Clothing and Footwear	40– 51	38.65	238.33	3.59	5.26	4.34	3.1	4.5	3.7
Clothing	40– 47	35.15	199.35	3.55	5.51	4.42	3.2	5.0	4.0
Footwear	48– 51	3.49	38.98	3.81	3.60	3.70	2.5	2.4	2.4
Gross Rent and Fuel	52– 57	41.69	564.88	2.80	2.10	2.43	3.5	2.6	3.0
Gross Rents	52– 53	22.65	463.12	1.79	1.46	1.62	3.4	2.7	3.0
Fuel and Power	54– 57	19.04	101.76	7.40	4.41	5.71	4.2	2.5	3.3

(Table continues on following page.)

Summary Binary Table 5.6 continued.

Category	Line numbers[a]	Expenditure per capita		Purchasing-power parities (rupee/dollar)			Quantity per capita (United States=100)		
		India (rupees)	United States (dollars)	U.S. weight	India weight	Ideal[b]	U.S. weight	India weight	Ideal[b]
House Furnishings and Operations	58– 71	16.39	239.23	4.22	1.16	2.21	5.9	1.6	3.1
Furniture and Appliances	58– 66	3.70	141.52	4.34	4.16	4.25	0.6	0.6	0.6
Supplies and Operation	67– 71	12.68	97.72	4.04	0.96	1.97	13.6	3.2	6.6
Medical Care	72– 78	14.34	316.67	0.97	0.68	0.81	6.7	4.7	5.6
Transport and Communications	79– 91	28.80	443.92	6.85	1.92	3.63	3.4	0.9	1.8
Equipment	79– 80	2.25	151.53	8.87	7.30	8.05	0.2	0.2	0.2
Operation Costs	81– 84	2.76	205.78	7.40	2.75	4.51	0.5	0.2	0.3
Purchased Transport	85– 89	21.83	30.43	3.44	1.79	2.48	40.1	20.8	28.9
Communications	90– 91	1.96	56.18	1.20	1.33	1.26	2.6	2.9	2.8
Recreation and Education	92–103	28.39	498.80	2.70	0.48	1.14	11.9	2.1	5.0
Recreation	92– 98	4.98	239.83	4.34	1.64	2.67	1.3	0.5	0.8
Education	99–103	23.41	258.97	1.19	0.42	0.70	21.7	7.6	12.8
Other Expenditures	104–109	19.62	381.55	2.97	1.20	1.89	4.3	1.7	2.7
Personal Care	104–106	5.97	91.21	3.90	3.10	3.48	2.1	1.7	1.9
Miscellaneous Services	107–109	13.65	290.34	2.68	0.95	1.59	5.0	1.8	3.0
Capital Formation[e]	111–148	124.52	852.78	4.14	2.27	3.06	6.4	3.5	4.8
Construction	111–124	70.62	496.44	1.71	1.57	1.64	9.1	8.3	8.7
Residential	111–112	17.64	172.96	1.61	1.62	1.62	6.3	6.3	6.3
Nonresidential Bldgs	113–120	18.66	167.17	1.92	1.78	1.85	6.3	5.8	6.0
Other Construction	121–124	34.32	156.30	1.59	1.45	1.52	15.1	13.8	14.5
Producers Durables	125–146	42.11	334.36	7.62	7.16	7.39	1.8	1.7	1.7
Transport Equipment	125–131	10.68	84.79	9.11	8.68	8.89	1.5	1.4	1.4
Nonelectrical Machinery	132–140	16.09	137.75	7.33	7.32	7.32	1.6	1.6	1.6
Electrical Machinery	141–144	7.81	79.30	7.51	7.84	7.67	1.3	1.3	1.3
Other Durables	145–146	7.53	32.53	5.19	5.19	5.19	4.5	4.5	4.5
Government	149–153	58.54	666.13	2.35	0.74	1.32	11.9	3.7	6.7
Compensation	149–152	33.70	338.73	0.67	0.51	0.58	19.7	14.9	17.1
Commodities	153	24.84	327.41	4.08	1.96	2.83	3.9	1.9	2.7
Gross Domestic Product	1–153	746.28	4789.55	3.69	1.90	2.65	8.2	4.2	5.9
Aggregates									
ICP Concepts[f]									
Consumption (CEP)[c,d]	1–110	563.23	3270.65	3.85	2.17	2.89	7.9	4.5	6.0
Capital Formation (GCF)[e]	111–148	124.52	852.78	4.14	2.27	3.06	6.4	3.5	4.8
Government (PFC)	149–153	58.54	666.13	2.35	0.74	1.32	11.9	3.7	6.7
Gross Domestic Product	1–153	746.28	4789.55	3.69	1.90	2.65	8.2	4.2	5.9
SNA Concepts[f]									
Consumption (PFCE)	1–110	550.53	2955.19	4.13	2.46	3.19	7.6	4.5	5.8
Capital Formation (GCF)	111–148	124.52	852.78	4.14	2.27	3.06	6.4	3.5	4.8
Government (GFCE)	149–153	71.25	979.14	1.99	0.62	1.11	11.7	3.7	6.5
Gross Domestic Product	1–153	746.28	4787.10	3.69	1.90	2.65	8.2	4.2	5.9

Note: See end of Summary Binary Table 5.30 for notes.
Exchange rate: Rs7.499 = US$1.00.

Summary Binary Table 5.7. Iran and United States: Expenditures per Capita, Purchasing-Power Parities, and Quantity per Capita, 1970

Category	Line numbers[a]	Expenditure per capita Iran (rials)	United States (dollars)	PPP U.S. weight	PPP Iran weight	PPP Ideal[b]	Qty U.S. weight	Qty Iran weight	Qty Ideal[b]
Consumption, ICP[c,d]	1–110	18896.4	3270.65	44.3	27.6	35.0	20.9	13.0	16.5
Food, Beverage, and Tobacco	1– 39	8819.5	564.33	54.9	39.2	46.4	39.8	28.5	33.7
Food,	1– 33	8375.4	447.07	56.8	39.0	47.1	48.1	33.0	39.8
Bread and Cereals	1– 6	2574.0	49.50	36.5	40.7	38.5	127.8	142.4	134.9
Meat	7– 12	1580.7	122.25	64.2	69.5	66.8	18.6	20.1	19.4
Fish	13– 14	68.9	16.00	67.6	31.7	46.3	13.6	6.4	9.3
Milk, Cheese, and Eggs	15– 17	1028.9	71.79	47.3	18.5	29.6	77.4	30.3	48.4
Oils and Fats	18– 20	624.9	20.87	94.4	82.7	88.3	36.2	31.7	33.9
Fruits and Vegetables	21– 26	1473.6	102.30	35.9	30.3	33.0	47.6	40.1	43.7
Coffee, Tea, and Cocoa	27– 29	360.9	14.79	136.9	76.9	102.6	31.7	17.8	23.8
Spices, Sweets, and Sugar	30– 33	663.4	49.58	72.7	65.0	68.8	20.6	18.4	19.5
Beverages	34– 37	87.0	64.57	50.9	52.9	51.9	2.5	2.6	2.6
Tobacco	38– 39	357.1	52.69	43.2	43.2	43.2	15.7	15.7	15.7
Clothing and Footwear	40– 51	1643.2	238.33	40.7	28.6	34.1	24.1	16.9	20.2
Clothing	40– 47	1333.0	199.35	45.3	35.8	40.3	18.7	14.8	16.6
Footwear	48– 51	310.3	38.98	17.6	15.4	16.5	51.7	45.2	48.4
Gross Rent and Fuel	52– 57	3215.9	564.88	29.2	23.1	26.0	24.7	19.5	21.9
Gross Rents	52– 53	2471.9	463.12	18.2	19.2	18.7	27.7	29.4	28.5
Fuel and Power	54– 57	744.0	101.76	79.3	68.1	73.5	10.7	9.2	9.9
House Furnishings and Operations	58– 71	857.1	239.23	41.1	26.9	33.2	13.3	8.7	10.8
Furniture and Appliances	58– 66	478.9	141.52	47.0	23.4	33.2	14.4	7.2	10.2
Supplies and Operation	67– 71	378.2	97.72	32.5	33.0	32.7	11.7	11.9	11.8
Medical Care	72– 78	1001.6	316.67	25.5	25.1	25.3	12.6	12.4	12.5
Transport and Communications	79– 91	837.4	443.92	71.1	19.3	37.0	9.8	2.7	5.1
Equipment	79– 80	287.3	151.53	129.5	152.1	140.3	1.2	1.5	1.4
Operation Costs	81– 84	235.5	205.78	45.7	26.6	34.9	4.3	2.5	3.3
Purchased Transport	85– 89	279.8	30.43	39.8	9.2	19.2	99.6	23.1	48.0
Communications	90– 91	34.9	56.18	23.5	14.7	18.6	4.2	2.6	3.3
Recreation and Education	92–103	1022.5	498.80	38.4	13.6	22.8	15.1	5.3	9.0
Recreation	92– 98	370.1	239.83	59.5	38.1	47.6	4.1	2.6	3.2
Education	99–103	652.4	258.97	18.8	10.0	13.7	25.3	13.4	18.4
Other Expenditures	104–109	1499.3	381.55	45.5	20.5	30.5	19.2	8.6	12.9
Personal Care	104–106	628.3	91.21	31.1	14.1	20.9	48.9	22.1	32.9
Miscellaneous Services	107–109	871.0	290.34	50.0	30.6	39.1	9.8	6.0	7.7
Capital Formation[e]	111–148	7682.6	852.78	55.2	36.0	44.6	25.0	16.3	20.2
Construction	111–124	3642.6	496.44	28.2	22.6	25.3	32.4	26.0	29.0
Residential	111–112	1287.0	172.96	18.6	17.1	17.8	43.6	40.0	41.7
Nonresidential Bldgs	113–120	1351.7	167.17	24.1	24.3	24.2	33.3	33.6	33.4
Other Construction	121–124	1003.8	156.30	43.3	33.6	38.1	19.1	14.8	16.9
Producers Durables	125–146	2153.9	334.36	94.8	80.6	87.4	8.0	6.8	7.4
Transport Equipment	125–131	877.0	84.79	131.9	91.1	109.6	11.3	7.8	9.4
Nonelectrical Machinery	132–140	920.9	137.75	94.3	83.8	88.9	8.0	7.1	7.5
Electrical Machinery	141–144	274.1	79.30	78.9	68.9	73.7	5.0	4.4	4.7
Other Durables	145–146	81.9	32.53	38.8	38.4	38.6	6.6	6.5	6.5
Government	149–153	4054.2	666.13	40.8	26.6	33.0	22.8	14.9	18.5
Compensation	149–152	2448.9	338.73	32.8	23.4	27.7	30.9	22.1	26.1
Commodities	153	1605.3	327.41	49.1	33.8	40.8	14.5	10.0	12.0
Gross Domestic Product	1–153	30633.1	4789.55	45.7	29.2	36.5	21.9	14.0	17.5

(Table continues on following page.)

Summary Binary Table 5.7 continued.

Category	Line numbers[a]	Expenditure per capita		Purchasing-power parities (rial/dollar)			Quantity per capita (United States=100)		
		Iran (rials)	United States (dollars)	U.S. weight	Iran weight	Ideal[b]	U.S. weight	Iran weight	Ideal[b]
Aggregates									
ICP Concepts[f]									
Consumption (CEP)[c,d]	1–110	18896.4	3270.65	44.3	27.6	35.0	20.9	13.0	16.5
Capital Formation (GCF)[e]	111–148	7682.6	852.78	55.2	36.0	44.6	25.0	16.3	20.2
Government (PFC)	149–153	4054.2	666.13	40.8	26.6	33.0	22.8	14.9	18.5
Gross Domestic Product	1–153	30633.1	4789.55	45.7	29.2	36.5	21.9	14.0	17.5
SNA Concepts[f]									
Consumption (PFCE)	1–110	18038.9	2955.19	46.9	29.5	37.2	20.7	13.0	16.4
Capital Formation (GCF)	111–148	7682.6	852.78	55.2	36.0	44.6	25.0	16.3	20.2
Government (GFCE)	149–153	4911.6	979.14	34.0	21.8	27.2	23.1	14.8	18.4
Gross Domestic Product	1–153	30633.1	4787.10	45.8	29.2	36.5	21.9	14.0	17.5

Note: See end of Summary Binary Table 5.30 for notes.
Exchange rate: Rls76.38 = US$1.00.

Summary Binary Table 5.8. Italy and United States: Expenditures per Capita, Purchasing-Power Parities, and Quantity per Capita, 1970

Category	Line numbers[a]	Expenditure per capita		Purchasing-power parities (lira/dollar)			Quantity per capita (United States=100)		
		Italy (lire)	United States (dollars)	U.S. weight	Italy weight	Ideal[b]	U.S. weight	Italy weight	Ideal[b]
Consumption, ICP[c,d]	1–110	728770.	3270.65	531.	407.	465.	54.8	42.0	48.0
Food, Beverage, and Tobacco	1– 39	278549.	564.33	661.	508.	579.	97.1	74.7	85.2
Food,	1– 33	231885.	447.07	703.	515.	601.	100.8	73.8	86.2
Bread and Cereals	1– 6	31327.	49.50	534.	394.	458.	160.7	118.6	138.0
Meat	7– 12	75382.	122.25	643.	613.	628.	100.6	96.0	98.3
Fish	13– 14	8256.	16.00	766.	732.	749.	70.5	67.4	68.9
Milk, Cheese, and Eggs	15– 17	30768.	71.79	579.	592.	585.	72.4	74.0	73.2
Oils and Fats	18– 20	14722.	20.87	686.	647.	667.	109.0	102.8	105.8
Fruits and Vegetables	21– 26	54957.	102.30	693.	375.	510.	143.3	77.5	105.4
Coffee, Tea, and Cocoa	27– 29	4845.	14.79	1772.	1811.	1791.	18.1	18.5	18.3
Spices, Sweets, and Sugar	30– 33	11629.	49.58	889.	911.	900.	25.8	26.4	26.1
Beverages	34– 37	26519.	64.57	441.	427.	434.	96.2	93.2	94.7
Tobacco	38– 39	20145.	52.69	570.	571.	570.	67.0	67.1	67.1
Clothing and Footwear	40– 51	64965.	238.33	586.	532.	558.	51.2	46.5	48.8
Clothing	40– 47	53820.	199.35	602.	546.	573.	49.4	44.9	47.1
Footwear	48– 51	11144.	38.98	505.	474.	490.	60.3	56.6	58.4
Gross Rent and Fuel	52– 57	89769.	564.88	409.	384.	396.	41.4	38.8	40.1
Gross Rents	52– 53	68282.	463.12	312.	330.	321.	44.7	47.3	46.0
Fuel and Power	54– 57	21487.	101.76	855.	797.	826.	26.5	24.7	25.6

Summary Binary Table 5.8 continued.

Category	Line numbers[a]	Expenditure per capita Italy (lire)	Expenditure per capita United States (dollars)	Purchasing-power parities (lira/dollar) U.S. weight	Purchasing-power parities (lira/dollar) Italy weight	Purchasing-power parities (lira/dollar) Ideal[b]	Quantity per capita (United States=100) U.S. weight	Quantity per capita (United States=100) Italy weight	Quantity per capita (United States=100) Ideal[b]
House Furnishings and Operations	58– 71	39937.	239.23	536.	510.	523.	32.7	31.2	31.9
Furniture and Appliances	58– 66	23709.	141.52	593.	513.	551.	32.7	28.3	30.4
Supplies and Operation	67– 71	16228.	97.72	453.	507.	479.	32.7	36.6	34.6
Medical Care	72– 78	48155.	316.67	225.	168.	195.	90.3	67.5	78.0
Transport and Communications	79– 91	74394.	443.92	804.	477.	620.	35.1	20.8	27.0
Equipment	79– 80	20071.	151.53	759.	555.	649.	23.9	17.5	20.4
Operation Costs	81– 84	34681.	205.78	991.	576.	756.	29.2	17.0	22.3
Purchased Transport	85– 89	13269.	30.43	427.	293.	354.	148.9	102.1	123.3
Communications	90– 91	6373.	56.18	449.	450.	450.	25.2	25.3	25.2
Recreation and Education	92–103	83936.	498.80	438.	313.	370.	53.7	38.4	45.4
Recreation	92– 98	39862.	239.83	565.	439.	498.	37.8	29.4	33.4
Education	99–103	44074.	258.97	321.	249.	282.	68.4	53.1	60.3
Other Expenditures	104–109	63660.	381.55	530.	515.	523.	32.4	31.5	31.9
Personal Care	104–106	10883.	91.21	628.	429.	519.	27.8	19.0	23.0
Miscellaneous Services	107–109	52777.	290.34	500.	537.	518.	33.8	36.4	35.1
Capital Formation[e]	111–148	255813.	852.78	461.	410.	435.	73.1	65.1	69.0
Construction	111–124	144521.	496.44	333.	353.	343.	82.4	87.5	84.9
Residential	111–112	75028.	172.96	385.	395.	390.	109.8	112.8	111.3
Nonresidential Bldgs	113–120	44297.	167.17	373.	378.	375.	70.2	71.0	70.6
Other Construction	121–124	25196.	156.30	232.	248.	240.	65.1	69.6	67.3
Producers Durables	125–146	85371.	334.36	640.	521.	577.	49.0	39.9	44.2
Transport Equipment	125–131	21934.	84.79	819.	795.	807.	32.5	31.6	32.1
Nonelectrical Machinery	132–140	32389.	137.75	583.	488.	533.	48.2	40.3	44.1
Electrical Machinery	141–144	24748.	79.30	506.	402.	451.	77.6	61.7	69.2
Other Durables	145–146	6299.	32.53	741.	753.	747.	25.7	26.1	25.9
Government	149–153	95117.	666.13	463.	396.	428.	36.1	30.8	33.4
Compensation	149–152	70257.	338.73	403.	384.	393.	54.1	51.5	52.8
Commodities	153	24860.	327.41	526.	434.	478.	17.5	14.4	15.9
Gross Domestic Product	1–153	1079700.	4789.55	509.	407.	455.	55.5	44.3	49.6
Aggregates									
ICP Concepts[f]									
Consumption (CEP)[c,d]	1–110	728770.	3270.65	531.	407.	465.	54.8	42.0	48.0
Capital Formation (GCF)[e]	111–148	255813.	852.78	461.	410.	435.	73.1	65.1	69.0
Government (PFC)	149–153	95117.	666.13	463.	396.	428.	36.1	30.8	33.4
Gross Domestic Product	1–153	1079700.	4789.55	509.	407.	455.	55.5	44.3	49.6
SNA Concepts[f]									
Consumption (PFCE)	1–110	680071.	2955.19	555.	448.	499.	51.4	41.4	46.2
Capital Formation (GCF)	111–148	255813.	852.78	461.	410.	435.	73.1	65.1	69.0
Government (GFCE)	149–153	143817.	979.14	411.	280.	339.	52.4	35.8	43.3
Gross Domestic Product	1–153	1079700.	4787.10	509.	407.	455.	55.5	44.3	49.6

Note: See end of Summary Binary Table 5.30 for notes.
Exchange rate: Lit627.16 = US$1.00.

Summary Binary Table 5.9. Japan and United States: Expenditures per Capita, Purchasing-Power Parities, and Quantity per Capita, 1970

Category	Line numbers[a]	Expenditure per capita		Purchasing-power parities (yen/dollar)			Quantity per capita (United States = 100)		
		Japan (yen)	United States (dollars)	U.S. weight	Japan weight	Ideal[b]	U.S. weight	Japan weight	Ideal[b]
Consumption, ICP[c,d]	1–110	372907.	3270.65	285.	211.	245.	54.1	40.1	46.6
Food, Beverage, and Tobacco	1– 39	120062.	564.33	387.	312.	348.	68.1	54.9	61.2
Food,	1– 33	97413.	447.07	419.	324.	368.	67.2	52.0	59.1
Bread and Cereals	1– 6	23473.	49.50	270.	365.	314.	130.0	175.4	151.0
Meat	7– 12	11298.	122.25	495.	474.	484.	19.5	18.7	19.1
Fish	13– 14	18120.	16.00	331.	320.	325.	354.3	341.8	348.0
Milk, Cheese, and Eggs	15– 17	8282.	71.79	365.	319.	341.	36.1	31.6	33.8
Oils and Fats	18– 20	1471.	20.87	416.	394.	405.	17.9	17.0	17.4
Fruits and Vegetables	21– 26	21613.	102.30	400.	308.	351.	68.6	52.8	60.2
Coffee, Tea, and Cocoa	27– 29	1658.	14.79	637.	291.	430.	38.6	17.6	26.0
Spices, Sweets, and Sugar	30– 33	11498.	49.58	459.	230.	325.	100.8	50.5	71.4
Beverages	34– 37	17776.	64.57	316.	292.	304.	94.1	87.2	90.6
Tobacco	38– 39	4874.	52.69	208.	208.	208.	44.5	44.5	44.5
Clothing and Footwear	40– 51	33939.	238.33	225.	253.	238.	56.4	63.4	59.8
Clothing	40– 47	31501.	199.35	232.	260.	246.	60.7	68.2	64.3
Footwear	48– 51	2438.	38.98	189.	182.	185.	34.4	33.2	33.8
Gross Rent and Fuel	52– 57	53567.	564.88	333.	284.	307.	33.4	28.5	30.9
Gross Rents	52– 53	43251.	463.12	274.	268.	271.	34.9	34.1	34.5
Fuel and Power	54– 57	10316.	101.76	603.	377.	476.	26.9	16.8	21.3
House Furnishings and Operations	58– 71	32393.	239.23	318.	297.	307.	45.6	42.6	44.1
Furniture and Appliances	58– 66	21323.	141.52	369.	370.	369.	40.8	40.9	40.8
Supplies and Operation	67– 71	11070.	97.72	244.	215.	229.	52.6	46.5	49.4
Medical Care	72– 78	29620.	316.67	68.	77.	73.	121.0	137.4	128.9
Transport and Communications	79– 91	14647.	443.92	406.	196.	282.	16.8	8.1	11.7
Equipment	79– 80	2880.	151.53	418.	360.	388.	5.3	4.5	4.9
Operation Costs	81– 84	3730.	205.78	466.	441.	453.	4.1	3.9	4.0
Purchased Transport	85– 89	5255.	30.43	160.	108.	131.	159.9	108.0	131.4
Communications	90– 91	2782.	56.18	291.	290.	291.	17.1	17.0	17.0
Recreation and Education	92–103	44619.	498.80	222.	189.	205.	47.3	40.4	43.7
Recreation	92– 98	16902.	239.83	267.	281.	274.	25.1	26.4	25.8
Education	99–103	27717.	258.97	180.	158.	168.	67.8	59.5	63.5
Other Expenditures	104–109	42803.	381.55	194.	167.	180.	67.0	57.9	62.3
Personal Care	104–106	5312.	91.21	209.	188.	198.	30.9	27.9	29.4
Miscellaneous Services	107–109	37490.	290.34	189.	165.	176.	78.4	68.4	73.2
Capital Formation[e]	111–148	277430.	852.78	300.	284.	292.	114.5	108.4	111.4
Construction	111–124	135935.	496.44	274.	257.	265.	106.5	100.1	103.3
Residential	111–112	49447.	172.96	250.	252.	251.	113.5	114.4	114.0
Nonresidential Bldgs	113–120	56100.	167.17	355.	308.	331.	109.1	94.4	101.5
Other Construction	121–124	30389.	156.30	212.	202.	207.	96.1	91.6	93.8
Producers Durables	125–146	103089.	334.36	337.	324.	330.	95.2	91.6	93.4
Transport Equipment	125–131	16671.	84.79	374.	374.	374.	52.5	52.5	52.5
Nonelectrical Machinery	132–140	35697.	137.75	306.	289.	297.	89.7	84.8	87.2
Electrical Machinery	141–144	27135.	79.30	356.	351.	353.	97.5	96.2	96.9
Other Durables	145–146	23587.	32.53	323.	323.	323.	224.5	224.5	224.5
Government	149–153	33175.	666.13	228.	153.	187.	32.5	21.9	26.7
Compensation	149–152	23919.	338.73	160.	136.	147.	52.1	44.1	47.9
Commodities	153	9256.	327.41	297.	230.	261.	12.3	9.5	10.8
Gross Domestic Product	1–153	683511.	4789.55	279.	231.	254.	61.9	51.1	56.2

Summary Binary Table 5.9 continued.

Category	Line numbers[a]	Expenditure per capita		Purchasing-power parities (yen/dollar)			Quantity per capita (United States=100)		
		Japan (yen)	United States (dollars)	U.S. weight	Japan weight	Ideal[b]	U.S. weight	Japan weight	Ideal[b]
Aggregates									
ICP Concepts[f]									
Consumption (CEP)[c,d]	1–110	372907.	3270.65	285.	211.	245.	54.1	40.1	46.6
Capital Formation (GCF)[e]	111–148	277430.	852.78	300.	284.	292.	114.5	108.4	111.4
Government (PFC)	149–153	33175.	666.13	228.	153.	187.	32.5	21.9	26.7
Gross Domestic Product	1–153	683511.	4789.55	279.	231.	254.	61.9	51.1	56.2
SNA Concepts[f]									
Consumption (PFCE)	1–110	348794.	2955.19	298.	224.	258.	52.7	39.6	45.7
Capital Formation (GCF)	111–148	277430.	852.78	300.	284.	292.	114.5	108.4	111.4
Government (GFCE)	149–153	56179.	979.14	205.	132.	165.	43.4	27.9	34.8
Gross Domestic Product	1–153	682402.	4787.10	279.	231.	254.	61.8	51.0	56.2

Note: See end of Summary Binary Table 5.30 for notes.

Exchange rate: ¥358.15 = US$1.00.

Summary Binary Table 5.10. Kenya and United States: Expenditures per Capita, Purchasing-Power Parities, and Quantity per Capita, 1970

Category	Line numbers[a]	Expenditure per capita		Purchasing-power parities (shilling/dollar)			Quantity per capita (United States=100)		
		Kenya (shillings)	United States (dollars)	U.S. weight	Kenya weight	Ideal[b]	U.S. weight	Kenya weight	Ideal[b]
Consumption, ICP[c,d]	1–110	714.86	3270.65	5.45	2.81	3.91	7.8	4.0	5.6
Food, Beverage, and Tobacco	1– 39	349.36	564.33	6.37	3.49	4.71	17.7	9.7	13.1
Food,	1– 33	317.21	447.07	6.24	3.32	4.55	21.3	11.4	15.6
Bread and Cereals	1– 6	127.32	49.50	3.70	4.39	4.03	58.6	69.4	63.8
Meat	7– 12	31.53	122.25	4.77	3.32	3.98	7.8	5.4	6.5
Fish	13– 14	7.68	16.00	7.44	4.49	5.78	10.7	6.4	8.3
Milk, Cheese, and Eggs	15– 17	42.74	71.79	5.10	4.28	4.67	13.9	11.7	12.7
Oils and Fats	18– 20	11.57	20.87	8.05	6.09	7.00	9.1	6.9	7.9
Fruits and Vegetables	21– 26	69.21	102.30	5.52	1.83	3.18	37.0	12.3	21.3
Coffee, Tea, and Cocoa	27– 29	4.79	14.79	7.01	3.44	4.91	9.4	4.6	6.6
Spices, Sweets, and Sugar	30– 33	22.37	49.58	14.12	5.49	8.81	8.2	3.2	5.1
Beverages	34– 37	22.44	64.57	9.01	9.10	9.05	3.8	3.9	3.8
Tobacco	38– 39	9.72	52.69	4.29	4.34	4.31	4.3	4.3	4.3
Clothing and Footwear	40– 51	28.03	238.33	4.93	4.27	4.59	2.8	2.4	2.6
Clothing	40– 47	22.88	199.35	5.47	5.23	5.34	2.2	2.1	2.1
Footwear	48– 51	5.15	38.98	2.19	2.35	2.27	5.6	6.0	5.8
Gross Rent and Fuel	52– 57	73.56	564.88	7.52	4.47	5.80	2.9	1.7	2.2
Gross Rents	52– 53	62.33	463.12	7.09	5.54	6.26	2.4	1.9	2.1
Fuel and Power	54– 57	11.22	101.76	9.52	2.16	4.53	5.1	1.2	2.4

(Table continues on following page.)

Summary Binary Table 5.10 continued.

Category	Line numbers[a]	Expenditure per capita		Purchasing-power parities (shilling/dollar)			Quantity per capita (United States=100)		
		Kenya (shillings)	United States (dollars)	U.S. weight	Kenya weight	Ideal[b]	U.S. weight	Kenya weight	Ideal[b]
House Furnishings and Operations	58– 71	44.25	239.23	6.27	2.41	3.89	7.7	2.9	4.8
Furniture and Appliances	58– 66	8.70	141.52	7.59	5.94	6.71	1.0	0.8	0.9
Supplies and Operation	67– 71	35.55	97.72	4.36	2.10	3.03	17.3	8.3	12.0
Medical Care	72– 78	36.88	316.67	1.62	1.36	1.48	8.6	7.2	7.8
Transport and Communications	79– 91	52.03	443.92	6.88	4.31	5.45	2.7	1.7	2.2
Equipment	79– 80	11.43	151.53	7.74	7.65	7.70	1.0	1.0	1.0
Operation Costs	81– 84	6.50	205.78	7.53	3.31	4.99	1.0	0.4	0.6
Purchased Transport	85– 89	32.68	30.43	5.55	4.01	4.72	26.8	19.3	22.8
Communications	90– 91	1.42	56.18	2.93	3.05	2.99	0.8	0.9	0.8
Recreation and Education	92–103	84.08	498.80	4.42	1.50	2.58	11.2	3.8	6.5
Recreation	92– 98	29.10	239.83	6.52	3.46	4.75	3.5	1.9	2.6
Education	99–103	54.98	258.97	2.48	1.16	1.69	18.4	8.6	12.5
Other Expenditures	104–109	46.68	381.55	3.55	2.68	3.08	4.6	3.5	4.0
Personal Care	104–106	5.79	91.21	6.10	5.93	6.01	1.1	1.0	1.1
Miscellaneous Services	107–109	40.89	290.34	2.74	2.49	2.61	5.7	5.1	5.4
Capital Formation[e]	111–148	206.75	852.78	5.65	5.01	5.32	4.8	4.3	4.6
Construction	111–124	98.93	496.44	3.98	4.10	4.04	4.9	5.0	4.9
Residential	111–112	33.23	172.96	3.45	3.37	3.41	5.7	5.6	5.6
Nonresidential Bldgs	113–120	25.09	167.17	3.58	3.70	3.64	4.1	4.2	4.1
Other Construction	121–124	40.61	156.30	4.99	5.43	5.21	4.8	5.2	5.0
Producers Durables	125–146	101.79	334.36	8.03	7.51	7.77	4.1	3.8	3.9
Transport Equipment	125–131	35.98	84.79	7.67	7.69	7.68	5.5	5.5	5.5
Nonelectrical Machinery	132–140	49.76	137.75	8.21	7.70	7.95	4.7	4.4	4.5
Electrical Machinery	141–144	12.45	79.30	8.82	6.74	7.71	2.3	1.8	2.0
Other Durables	145–146	3.60	32.53	6.25	6.40	6.33	1.7	1.8	1.7
Government	149–153	102.33	666.13	4.27	1.06	2.13	14.4	3.6	7.2
Compensation	149–152	77.77	338.73	2.18	0.87	1.38	26.3	10.5	16.7
Commodities	153	24.56	327.41	6.43	3.53	4.76	2.1	1.2	1.6
Gross Domestic Product	1–153	1023.95	4789.55	5.32	2.62	3.73	8.2	4.0	5.7
Aggregates									
ICP Concepts[f]									
Consumption (CEP)[c,d]	1–110	714.86	3270.65	5.45	2.81	3.91	7.8	4.0	5.6
Capital Formation (GCF)[e]	111–148	206.75	852.78	5.65	5.01	5.32	4.8	4.3	4.6
Government (PFC)	149–153	102.33	666.13	4.27	1.06	2.13	14.4	3.6	7.2
Gross Domestic Product	1–153	1023.95	4789.55	5.32	2.62	3.73	8.2	4.0	5.7
SNA Concepts[f]									
Consumption (PFCE)	1–110	663.81	2955.19	5.80	3.16	4.28	7.1	3.9	5.2
Capital Formation (GCF)	111–148	206.75	852.78	5.65	5.01	5.32	4.8	4.3	4.6
Government (GFCE)	149–153	153.39	979.14	3.58	1.09	1.98	14.3	4.4	7.9
Gross Domestic Product	1–153	1023.95	4787.10	5.32	2.62	3.73	8.2	4.0	5.7

Note: See end of Summary Binary Table 5.30 for notes.
Exchange rate: KSh7.1429 = US$1.00.

Summary Binary Table 5.11. Republic of Korea and United States: Expenditures per Capita, Purchasing-Power Parities, and Quantity per Capita, 1970

Category	Line numbers[a]	Expenditure per capita — Korea Republic of (won)	Expenditure per capita — United States (dollars)	Purchasing-power parities (won/dollar) U.S. weight	Purchasing-power parities (won/dollar) Korea Republic of weight	Purchasing-power parities (won/dollar) Ideal[b]	Quantity per capita (United States=100) U.S. weight	Quantity per capita (United States=100) Korea Republic of weight	Quantity per capita (United States=100) Ideal[b]
Consumption, ICP[c,d]	1–110	59780.	3270.65	266.	134.	189.	13.6	6.9	9.7
Food, Beverage, and Tobacco	1– 39	33422.	564.33	358.	191.	261.	31.0	16.6	22.7
Food,	1– 33	28315.	447.07	349.	177.	248.	35.8	18.2	25.5
Bread and Cereals	1– 6	13634.	49.50	242.	195.	217.	141.4	113.7	126.8
Meat	7– 12	2851.	122.25	262.	236.	249.	9.9	8.9	9.4
Fish	13– 14	1762.	16.00	148.	148.	148.	74.3	74.3	74.3
Milk, Cheese, and Eggs	15– 17	1083.	71.79	355.	316.	335.	4.8	4.3	4.5
Oils and Fats	18– 20	379.	20.87	323.	383.	352.	4.7	5.6	5.2
Fruits and Vegetables	21– 26	4878.	102.30	289.	122.	188.	39.0	16.5	25.4
Coffee, Tea, and Cocoa	27– 29	119.	14.79	983.	966.	974.	0.8	0.8	0.8
Spices, Sweets, and Sugar	30– 33	3608.	49.58	668.	165.	332.	44.1	10.9	21.9
Beverages	34– 37	2885.	64.57	492.	440.	466.	10.1	9.1	9.6
Tobacco	38– 39	2222.	52.69	271.	271.	271.	15.6	15.6	15.6
Clothing and Footwear	40– 51	6183.	238.33	203.	214.	208.	12.1	12.8	12.5
Clothing	40– 47	5798.	199.35	209.	238.	223.	12.2	13.9	13.1
Footwear	48– 51	385.	38.98	174.	85.	122.	11.6	5.7	8.1
Gross Rent and Fuel	52– 57	4936.	564.88	322.	374.	347.	2.3	2.7	2.5
Gross Rents	52– 53	2241.	463.12	291.	308.	299.	1.6	1.7	1.6
Fuel and Power	54– 57	2695.	101.76	467.	455.	461.	5.8	5.7	5.7
House Furnishings and Operations	58– 71	1737.	239.23	226.	81.	135.	9.0	3.2	5.4
Furniture and Appliances	58– 66	970.	141.52	289.	413.	346.	1.7	2.4	2.0
Supplies and Operation	67– 71	766.	97.72	134.	40.	73.	19.6	5.9	10.7
Medical Care	72– 78	1705.	316.67	65.	47.	55.	11.5	8.3	9.8
Transport and Communications	79– 91	3309.	443.92	524.	88.	215.	8.4	1.4	3.5
Equipment	79– 80	112.	151.53	672.	683.	678.	0.1	0.1	0.1
Operation Costs	81– 84	5.	205.78	601.	294.	420.	0.0	0.0	0.0
Purchased Transport	85– 89	2993.	30.43	115.	87.	100.	113.2	85.5	98.4
Communications	90– 91	200.	56.18	62.	71.	66.	5.0	5.8	5.4
Recreation and Education	92–103	5045.	498.80	117.	58.	82.	17.6	8.6	12.3
Recreation	92– 98	2156.	239.83	162.	116.	137.	7.7	5.5	6.5
Education	99–103	2889.	258.97	76.	42.	56.	26.7	14.6	19.8
Other Expenditures	104–109	3474.	381.55	168.	76.	113.	12.0	5.4	8.1
Personal Care	104–106	1380.	91.21	138.	47.	81.	31.9	11.0	18.7
Miscellaneous Services	107–109	2094.	290.34	178.	125.	149.	5.8	4.1	4.8
Capital Formation[e]	111–148	13504.	852.78	255.	139.	188.	11.4	6.2	8.4
Construction	111–124	12780.	496.44	137.	138.	138.	18.6	18.8	18.7
Residential	111–112	2565.	172.96	109.	115.	112.	12.8	13.6	13.2
Nonresidential Bldgs	113–120	4395.	167.17	161.	163.	162.	16.2	16.4	16.3
Other Construction	121–124	5821.	156.30	142.	135.	138.	27.6	26.3	26.9
Producers Durables	125–146	7168.	334.36	426.	317.	367.	6.8	5.0	5.8
Transport Equipment	125–131	3137.	84.79	553.	512.	532.	7.2	6.7	7.0
Nonelectrical Machinery	132–140	3187.	137.75	441.	285.	354.	8.1	5.2	6.5
Electrical Machinery	141–144	679.	79.30	342.	235.	284.	3.6	2.5	3.0
Other Durables	145–146	165.	32.53	235.	69.	127.	7.4	2.2	4.0
Government	149–153	6784.	666.13	151.	64.	98.	16.0	6.7	10.4
Compensation	149–152	4237.	338.73	47.	49.	48.	25.6	26.5	26.0
Commodities	153	2547.	327.41	258.	130.	184.	6.0	3.0	4.2
Gross Domestic Product	1–153	80067.	4789.55	248.	123.	175.	13.6	6.7	9.6

(Table continues on following page.)

Summary Binary Table 5.11 continued.

Category	Line numbers[a]	Expenditure per capita Korea Republic of (won)	United States (dollars)	Purchasing-power parities (won/dollar) U.S. weight	Korea Republic of weight	Ideal[b]	Quantity per capita (United States=100) U.S. weight	Korea Republic of weight	Ideal[b]
Aggregates									
ICP Concepts[f]									
Consumption (CEP)[c,d]	1–110	59780.	3270.65	266.	134.	189.	13.6	6.9	9.7
Capital Formation (GCF)[e]	111–148	13504.	852.78	255.	139.	188.	11.4	6.2	8.4
Government (PFC)	149–153	6784.	666.13	151.	64.	98.	16.0	6.7	10.4
Gross Domestic Product	1–153	80067.	4789.55	248.	123.	175.	13.6	6.7	9.6
SNA Concepts[f]									
Consumption (PFCE)	1–110	57735.	2955.19	287.	147.	205.	13.3	6.8	9.5
Capital Formation (GCF)	111–148	13504.	852.78	255.	139.	188.	11.4	6.2	8.4
Government (GFCE)	149–153	8829.	979.14	124.	55.	83.	16.3	7.2	10.9
Gross Domestic Product	1–153	80067.	4787.10	248.	123.	175.	13.6	6.7	9.6

Note: See end of Summary Binary Table 5.30 for notes.
Exchange rate: W310.42 = US$1.00.

Summary Binary Table 5.12. Malaysia and United States: Expenditures per Capita, Purchasing-Power Parities, and Quantity per Capita, 1970

Category	Line numbers[a]	Expenditure per capita Malaysia (M. dollars)	United States (dollars)	Purchasing-power parities (M. dollar/dollar) U.S. weight	Malaysia weight	Ideal[b]	Quantity per capita (United States=100) U.S. weight	Malaysia weight	Ideal[b]
Consumption, ICP[c,d]	1–110	786.43	3270.65	1.93	1.23	1.54	19.6	12.5	15.6
Food, Beverage, and Tobacco	1–39	322.12	564.33	2.52	1.78	2.12	32.0	22.6	26.9
Food,	1–33	268.02	447.07	2.54	1.69	2.07	35.5	23.6	29.0
Bread and Cereals	1–6	73.95	49.50	2.52	1.68	2.06	88.8	59.3	72.6
Meat	7–12	47.56	122.25	2.27	2.40	2.33	16.2	17.2	16.7
Fish	13–14	40.20	16.00	1.31	1.37	1.34	183.0	191.3	187.1
Milk, Cheese, and Eggs	15–17	25.46	71.79	3.43	2.16	2.72	16.4	10.3	13.0
Oils and Fats	18–20	11.17	20.87	2.13	2.09	2.11	25.6	25.1	25.3
Fruits and Vegetables	21–26	36.32	102.30	2.20	1.18	1.61	30.0	16.1	22.0
Coffee, Tea, and Cocoa	27–29	5.15	14.79	4.12	3.02	3.53	11.5	8.4	9.9
Spices, Sweets, and Sugar	30–33	28.20	49.58	2.70	1.76	2.18	32.4	21.0	26.1
Beverages	34–37	18.57	64.57	2.34	2.25	2.30	12.8	12.3	12.5
Tobacco	38–39	35.53	52.69	2.63	2.64	2.63	25.6	25.7	25.6
Clothing and Footwear	40–51	39.01	238.33	0.97	1.27	1.11	12.9	16.8	14.7
Clothing	40–47	34.22	199.35	1.00	1.42	1.19	12.1	17.1	14.4
Footwear	48–51	4.79	38.98	0.82	0.72	0.77	17.1	14.9	15.9
Gross Rent and Fuel	52–57	90.42	564.88	1.59	1.17	1.37	13.6	10.1	11.7
Gross Rents	52–53	72.93	463.12	1.07	1.00	1.04	15.7	14.7	15.2
Fuel and Power	54–57	17.50	101.76	3.94	4.01	3.98	4.3	4.4	4.3

Summary Binary Table 5.12 continued.

Category	Line numbers[a]	Expenditure per capita		Purchasing-power parities (M. dollar/dollar)			Quantity per capita (United States = 100)		
		Malaysia (M. dollars)	United States (dollars)	U.S. weight	Malaysia weight	Ideal[b]	U.S. weight	Malaysia weight	Ideal[b]
House Furnishings and Operations	58– 71	43.87	239.23	1.81	1.45	1.62	12.7	10.1	11.3
Furniture and Appliances	58– 66	18.01	141.52	1.93	1.46	1.68	8.7	6.6	7.6
Supplies and Operation	67– 71	25.86	97.72	1.65	1.44	1.54	18.3	16.0	17.1
Medical Care	72– 78	30.53	316.67	0.79	0.42	0.58	23.1	12.1	16.7
Transport and Communications	79– 91	113.94	443.92	3.21	1.61	2.27	15.9	8.0	11.3
Equipment	79– 80	23.93	151.53	4.82	4.21	4.50	3.8	3.3	3.5
Operation Costs	81– 84	44.34	205.78	2.78	1.87	2.28	11.5	7.8	9.4
Purchased Transport	85– 89	39.87	30.43	1.65	1.08	1.33	121.5	79.4	98.2
Communications	90– 91	5.80	56.18	1.28	1.35	1.31	7.6	8.1	7.9
Recreation and Education	92–103	89.00	498.80	1.39	0.67	0.97	26.7	12.8	18.5
Recreation	92– 98	37.80	239.83	1.99	1.20	1.54	13.2	7.9	10.2
Education	99–103	51.20	258.97	0.84	0.50	0.65	39.2	23.4	30.3
Other Expenditures	104–109	57.56	381.55	2.29	1.24	1.69	12.2	6.6	8.9
Personal Care	104–106	23.30	91.21	2.00	1.40	1.67	18.2	12.8	15.3
Miscellaneous Services	107–109	34.25	290.34	2.38	1.15	1.66	10.2	5.0	7.1
Capital Formation[e]	111–148	278.25	852.78	1.64	1.27	1.44	25.7	20.0	22.7
Construction	111–124	102.18	496.44	0.69	0.68	0.69	30.1	29.9	30.0
Residential	111–112	27.87	172.96	0.62	0.63	0.63	25.8	25.8	25.8
Nonresidential Bldgs	113–120	32.10	167.17	0.57	0.59	0.58	32.3	33.6	33.0
Other Construction	121–124	42.21	156.30	0.88	0.83	0.86	32.5	30.6	31.5
Producers Durables	125–146	87.23	334.36	2.98	2.78	2.88	9.4	8.8	9.1
Transport Equipment	125–131	21.48	84.79	3.76	3.60	3.68	7.0	6.7	6.9
Nonelectrical Machinery	132–140	51.90	137.75	3.10	2.96	3.03	12.7	12.2	12.4
Electrical Machinery	141–144	10.98	79.30	2.38	1.98	2.17	7.0	5.8	6.4
Other Durables	145–146	2.87	32.53	1.90	1.21	1.52	7.3	4.7	5.8
Government	149–153	129.15	666.13	1.37	1.04	1.19	18.6	14.2	16.2
Compensation	149–152	80.53	338.73	0.83	0.93	0.88	25.5	28.6	27.0
Commodities	153	48.62	327.41	1.93	1.29	1.58	11.5	7.7	9.4
Gross Domestic Product	1–153	1193.82	4789.55	1.80	1.21	1.48	20.6	13.9	16.9
Aggregates									
ICP Concepts[f]									
Consumption (CEP)[c,d]	1–110	786.43	3270.65	1.93	1.23	1.54	19.6	12.5	15.6
Capital Formation (GCF)[e]	111–148	278.25	852.78	1.64	1.27	1.44	25.7	20.0	22.7
Government (PFC)	149–153	129.15	666.13	1.37	1.04	1.19	18.6	14.2	16.2
Gross Domestic Product	1–153	1193.82	4789.55	1.80	1.21	1.48	20.6	13.9	16.9
SNA Concepts[f]									
Consumption (PFCE)	1–110	724.53	2955.19	2.04	1.44	1.72	17.0	12.0	14.3
Capital Formation (GCF)	111–148	278.25	852.78	1.64	1.27	1.44	25.7	20.0	22.7
Government (GFCE)	149–153	191.05	979.14	1.21	0.73	0.94	26.9	16.2	20.8
Gross Domestic Product	1–153	1193.82	4787.10	1.80	1.21	1.48	20.6	13.9	16.9

Note: See end of Summary Binary Table 5.30 for notes.

Exchange rate: M$3.0797 = US$1.00.

Summary Binary Table 5.13. Netherlands and United States: Expenditures per Capita, Purchasing-Power Parities, and Quantity per Capita, 1970

Category	Line numbers[a]	Expenditure per capita — Netherlands (guilders)	Expenditure per capita — United States (dollars)	Purchasing-power parities (guilder/dollar) — U.S. weight	Purchasing-power parities — Netherlands weight	Purchasing-power parities — Ideal[b]	Quantity per capita (United States=100) — U.S. weight	Quantity per capita — Netherlands weight	Quantity per capita — Ideal[b]
Consumption, ICP[c,d]	1–110	5539.84	3270.65	3.27	2.47	2.84	68.6	51.8	59.6
Food, Beverage, and Tobacco	1– 39	1410.74	564.33	3.30	2.73	3.00	91.5	75.9	83.3
Food,	1– 33	1107.98	447.07	3.47	2.97	3.21	83.4	71.3	77.1
Bread and Cereals	1– 6	146.58	49.50	2.98	2.43	2.69	121.8	99.4	110.1
Meat	7– 12	290.18	122.25	3.54	3.32	3.42	71.6	67.1	69.3
Fish	13– 14	30.24	16.00	3.66	2.82	3.21	67.0	51.6	58.8
Milk, Cheese, and Eggs	15– 17	200.92	71.79	2.53	2.46	2.50	113.7	110.5	112.1
Oils and Fats	18– 20	50.27	20.87	3.56	3.41	3.48	70.6	67.7	69.1
Fruits and Vegetables	21– 26	217.11	102.30	3.55	2.71	3.10	78.2	59.7	68.4
Coffee, Tea, and Cocoa	27– 29	62.93	14.79	5.98	4.95	5.44	86.0	71.1	78.2
Spices, Sweets, and Sugar	30– 33	109.75	49.58	4.17	4.34	4.25	51.0	53.1	52.1
Beverages	34– 37	161.93	64.57	2.10	2.09	2.09	120.2	119.3	119.8
Tobacco	38– 39	140.83	52.69	3.24	2.14	2.63	124.9	82.4	101.4
Clothing and Footwear	40– 51	526.40	238.33	2.86	2.94	2.90	75.2	77.1	76.2
Clothing	40– 47	450.19	199.35	2.94	3.05	3.00	74.0	76.7	75.4
Footwear	48– 51	76.21	38.98	2.46	2.41	2.43	81.2	79.5	80.4
Gross Rent and Fuel	52– 57	618.88	564.88	2.00	2.00	2.00	54.8	54.8	54.8
Gross Rents	52– 53	423.87	463.12	1.74	1.71	1.72	53.7	52.7	53.2
Fuel and Power	54– 57	195.01	101.76	3.19	3.19	3.19	60.2	60.1	60.1
House Furnishings and Operations	58– 71	631.70	239.23	3.11	3.12	3.12	84.6	84.8	84.7
Furniture and Appliances	58– 66	427.01	141.52	3.44	3.39	3.41	89.1	87.6	88.4
Supplies and Operation	67– 71	204.68	97.72	2.63	2.69	2.66	78.0	79.5	78.7
Medical Care	72– 78	414.04	316.67	1.68	1.21	1.42	108.0	78.0	91.8
Transport and Communications	79– 91	466.38	443.92	6.67	2.94	4.43	35.7	15.7	23.7
Equipment	79– 80	165.85	151.53	11.28	4.20	6.88	26.0	9.7	15.9
Operation Costs	81– 84	180.20	205.78	4.84	2.96	3.78	29.6	18.1	23.1
Purchased Transport	85– 89	69.53	30.43	4.56	2.06	3.06	111.1	50.1	74.6
Communications	90– 91	50.81	56.18	2.10	2.09	2.09	43.3	43.1	43.2
Recreation and Education	92–103	894.40	498.80	3.27	2.94	3.11	60.9	54.8	57.7
Recreation	92– 98	380.74	239.83	2.96	2.51	2.73	63.4	53.5	58.3
Education	99–103	513.66	258.97	3.56	3.38	3.47	58.6	55.7	57.1
Other Expenditures	104–109	531.54	381.55	2.83	2.43	2.63	57.2	49.2	53.1
Personal Care	104–106	74.06	91.21	3.25	2.96	3.10	27.5	25.0	26.2
Miscellaneous Services	107–109	457.48	290.34	2.70	2.37	2.53	66.6	58.3	62.3
Capital Formation[e]	111–148	2323.71	852.78	3.13	2.37	2.72	115.2	87.0	100.1
Construction	111–124	1261.47	496.44	2.08	1.84	1.95	138.3	122.3	130.0
Residential	111–112	462.62	172.96	2.25	1.71	1.96	156.4	119.0	136.4
Nonresidential Bldgs	113–120	521.10	167.17	2.60	2.49	2.54	125.2	119.9	122.6
Other Construction	121–124	277.74	156.30	1.33	1.34	1.34	132.2	133.5	132.8
Producers Durables	125–146	998.39	334.36	4.66	3.85	4.24	77.5	64.1	70.5
Transport Equipment	125–131	260.32	84.79	5.71	5.65	5.68	54.3	53.8	54.1
Nonelectrical Machinery	132–140	465.85	137.75	3.97	3.60	3.78	93.9	85.3	89.5
Electrical Machinery	141–144	275.90	79.30	4.49	3.26	3.83	106.7	77.5	90.9
Other Durables	145–146	-3.68	32.53	5.31	5.46	5.38	-2.1	-2.1	2.1
Government	149–153	929.39	666.13	3.03	2.60	2.80	53.7	46.1	49.7
Compensation	149–152	639.29	338.73	2.76	2.59	2.68	72.8	68.4	70.5
Commodities	153	290.10	327.41	3.31	2.61	2.94	34.0	26.8	30.2
Gross Domestic Product	1–153	8792.87	4789.55	3.21	2.45	2.81	74.8	57.1	65.4

Summary Binary Table 5.13 continued.

Category	Line numbers	Expenditure per capita — Netherlands (guilders)	Expenditure per capita — United States (dollars)	Purchasing-power parities (guilder/dollar) — U.S. weight	Netherlands weight	Ideal[b]	Quantity per capita (United States=100) — U.S. weight	Netherlands weight	Ideal[b]
Aggregates									
ICP Concepts[f]									
Consumption (CEP)[c,d]	1–110	5539.84	3270.65	3.27	2.47	2.84	68.6	51.8	59.6
Capital Formation (GCF)[e]	111–148	2323.71	852.78	3.13	2.37	2.72	115.2	87.0	100.1
Government (PFC)	149–153	929.39	666.13	3.03	2.60	2.80	53.7	46.1	49.7
Gross Domestic Product	1–153	8792.87	4789.55	3.21	2.45	2.81	74.8	57.1	65.4
SNA Concepts[f]									
Consumption (PFCE)	1–110	5018.98	2955.19	3.30	2.44	2.84	69.6	51.4	59.8
Capital Formation (GCF)	111–148	2323.71	852.78	3.13	2.37	2.72	115.2	87.0	100.1
Government (GFCE)	149–153	1450.27	979.14	3.02	2.67	2.84	55.4	49.1	52.2
Gross Domestic Product	1–153	8792.87	4787.10	3.21	2.45	2.81	74.8	57.1	65.4

Note: See end of Summary Binary Table 5.30 for notes.
Exchange rate: f3.6166 = US$1.00.

Summary Binary Table 5.14. Philippines and United States: Expenditures per Capita, Purchasing-Power Parities, and Quantity per Capita, 1970

Category	Line numbers[a]	Expenditure per capita — Philippines (pesos)	United States (dollars)	Purchasing-power parities (peso/dollar) — U.S. weight	Philippines weight	Ideal[b]	Quantity per capita (United States=100) — U.S. weight	Philippines weight	Ideal[b]
Consumption, ICP[c,d]	1–110	827.61	3270.65	3.35	1.59	2.31	15.9	7.5	11.0
Food, Beverage, and Tobacco	1–39	467.52	564.33	3.61	2.98	3.28	27.8	22.9	25.3
Food,	1–33	412.27	447.07	3.85	3.15	3.48	29.3	24.0	26.5
Bread and Cereals	1–6	190.47	49.50	5.21	3.65	4.36	105.5	73.8	88.3
Meat	7–12	67.20	122.25	2.67	2.31	2.48	23.8	20.6	22.2
Fish	13–14	71.32	16.00	2.93	2.78	2.85	160.4	152.1	156.2
Milk, Cheese, and Eggs	15–17	19.79	71.79	4.53	4.63	4.58	5.9	6.1	6.0
Oils and Fats	18–20	8.24	20.87	6.21	6.12	6.17	6.5	6.4	6.4
Fruits and Vegetables	21–26	9.06	102.30	3.32	1.95	2.55	4.5	2.7	3.5
Coffee, Tea, and Cocoa	27–29	8.25	14.79	6.65	6.55	6.60	8.5	8.4	8.4
Spices, Sweets, and Sugar	30–33	37.93	49.58	3.97	3.09	3.50	24.8	19.3	21.9
Beverages	34–37	30.90	64.57	2.46	1.70	2.05	28.1	19.5	23.4
Tobacco	38–39	24.36	52.69	3.04	3.04	3.04	15.2	15.2	15.2
Clothing and Footwear	40–51	48.25	238.33	1.38	2.20	1.74	9.2	14.7	11.6
Clothing	40–47	41.98	199.35	1.34	2.36	1.77	8.9	15.8	11.9
Footwear	48–51	6.27	38.98	1.58	1.53	1.55	10.5	10.2	10.4
Gross Rent and Fuel	52–57	83.18	564.88	2.12	1.02	1.47	14.5	6.9	10.0
Gross Rents	52–53	57.75	463.12	1.29	0.74	0.98	16.8	9.6	12.7
Fuel and Power	54–57	25.43	101.76	5.91	6.21	6.06	4.0	4.2	4.1

(Table continues on following page.)

Summary Binary Table 5.14 continued.

Category	Line numbers[a]	Expenditure per capita		Purchasing-power parities (peso/dollar)			Quantity per capita (United States=100)		
		Philippines (pesos)	United States (dollars)	U.S. weight	Philippines weight	Ideal[b]	U.S. weight	Philippines weight	Ideal[b]
House Furnishings and Operations	58– 71	47.70	239.23	3.40	1.55	2.29	12.9	5.9	8.7
Furniture and Appliances	58– 66	23.98	141.52	3.86	2.65	3.19	6.4	4.4	5.3
Supplies and Operation	67– 71	23.72	97.72	2.73	1.09	1.73	22.2	8.9	14.1
Medical Care	72– 78	27.43	316.67	1.80	1.08	1.39	8.0	4.8	6.2
Transport and Communications	79– 91	20.54	443.92	8.66	1.20	3.22	3.9	0.5	1.4
Equipment	79– 80	2.43	151.53	18.47	12.62	15.27	0.1	0.1	0.1
Operation Costs	81– 84	2.81	205.78	4.33	4.35	4.34	0.3	0.3	0.3
Purchased Transport	85– 89	14.33	30.43	1.53	0.91	1.18	52.0	30.8	40.0
Communications	90– 91	0.98	56.18	1.91	2.01	1.96	0.9	0.9	0.9
Recreation and Education	92–103	66.35	498.80	2.11	0.52	1.05	25.4	6.3	12.7
Recreation	92– 98	12.87	239.83	3.36	1.56	2.29	3.4	1.6	2.3
Education	99–103	53.48	258.97	0.95	0.45	0.65	45.8	21.8	31.6
Other Expenditures	104–109	66.65	381.55	2.57	1.10	1.68	15.8	6.8	10.4
Personal Care	104–106	20.23	91.21	1.98	1.08	1.46	20.5	11.2	15.2
Miscellaneous Services	107–109	46.42	290.34	2.76	1.11	1.75	14.4	5.8	9.1
Capital Formation[e]	111–148	232.59	852.78	4.49	3.25	3.82	8.4	6.1	7.1
Construction	111–124	62.04	496.44	2.27	1.57	1.89	8.0	5.5	6.6
Residential	111–112	24.75	172.96	1.79	1.76	1.77	8.1	8.0	8.1
Nonresidential Bldgs	113–120	22.37	167.17	2.52	2.35	2.44	5.7	5.3	5.5
Other Construction	121–124	14.93	156.30	2.55	0.93	1.54	10.3	3.7	6.2
Producers Durables	125–146	148.08	334.36	7.73	6.88	7.29	6.4	5.7	6.1
Transport Equipment	125–131	42.51	84.79	11.76	11.66	11.71	4.3	4.3	4.3
Nonelectrical Machinery	132–140	72.23	137.75	7.05	6.55	6.79	8.0	7.4	7.7
Electrical Machinery	141–144	23.19	79.30	6.49	6.01	6.24	4.9	4.5	4.7
Other Durables	145–146	10.15	32.53	3.13	3.38	3.25	9.2	10.0	9.6
Government	149–153	62.26	666.13	2.20	0.72	1.26	13.0	4.2	7.4
Compensation	149–152	39.02	338.73	0.57	0.57	0.57	20.1	20.2	20.2
Commodities	153	23.24	327.41	3.88	1.25	2.20	5.7	1.8	3.2
Gross Domestic Product	1–153	1122.45	4789.55	3.39	1.65	2.37	14.2	6.9	9.9
Aggregates									
ICP Concepts[f]									
Consumption (CEP)[c,d]	1–110	827.61	3270.65	3.35	1.59	2.31	15.9	7.5	11.0
Capital Formation (GCF)[e]	111–148	232.59	852.78	4.49	3.25	3.82	8.4	6.1	7.1
Government (PFC)	149–153	62.26	666.13	2.20	0.72	1.26	13.0	4.2	7.4
Gross Domestic Product	1–153	1122.45	4789.55	3.39	1.65	2.37	14.2	6.9	9.9
SNA Concepts[f]									
Consumption (PFCE)	1–110	794.32	2955.19	3.58	1.85	2.57	14.5	7.5	10.4
Capital Formation (GCF)	111–148	232.59	852.78	4.49	3.25	3.82	8.4	6.1	7.1
Government (GFCE)	149–153	95.55	979.14	1.88	0.54	1.00	18.2	5.2	9.7
Gross Domestic Product	1–153	1122.45	4787.10	3.39	1.65	2.37	14.2	6.9	9.9

Note: See end of Summary Binary Table 5.30 for notes.
Exchange rate: ₱6.0652 = US$1.00.

Summary Binary Table 5.15. United Kingdom and United States: Expenditures per Capita, Purchasing-Power Parities, and Quantity per Capita, 1970

Category	Line numbers[a]	Expenditure per capita — United Kingdom (pounds)	Expenditure per capita — United States (dollars)	Purchasing-power parities (pound/dollar) — U.S. weight	Purchasing-power parities (pound/dollar) — United Kingdom weight	Purchasing-power parities (pound/dollar) — Ideal[b]	Quantity per capita (United States=100) — U.S. weight	Quantity per capita (United States=100) — United Kingdom weight	Quantity per capita (United States=100) — Ideal[b]
Consumption, ICP[c,d]	1–110	632.700	3270.65	0.349	0.282	0.314	68.5	55.4	61.6
Food, Beverage, and Tobacco	1– 39	186.977	564.33	0.381	0.362	0.372	91.5	87.0	89.2
Food,	1– 33	111.455	447.07	0.324	0.288	0.305	86.5	77.1	81.7
Bread and Cereals	1– 6	15.814	49.50	0.257	0.233	0.245	137.0	124.2	130.4
Meat	7– 12	32.727	122.25	0.290	0.270	0.280	99.3	92.3	95.7
Fish	13– 14	3.836	16.00	0.377	0.325	0.350	73.9	63.6	68.6
Milk, Cheese, and Eggs	15– 17	16.643	71.79	0.315	0.319	0.317	72.7	73.6	73.1
Oils and Fats	18– 20	4.809	20.87	0.383	0.265	0.319	87.1	60.1	72.3
Fruits and Vegetables	21– 26	19.831	102.30	0.351	0.313	0.331	61.9	55.3	58.5
Coffee, Tea, and Cocoa	27– 29	4.035	14.79	0.341	0.212	0.269	128.9	79.9	101.5
Spices, Sweets, and Sugar	30– 33	13.761	49.58	0.381	0.416	0.398	66.7	72.8	69.7
Beverages	34– 37	44.542	64.57	0.522	0.525	0.524	131.3	132.1	131.7
Tobacco	38– 39	30.980	52.69	0.695	0.696	0.695	84.5	84.6	84.5
Clothing and Footwear	40– 51	49.334	238.33	0.344	0.321	0.332	64.5	60.1	62.3
Clothing	40– 47	40.544	199.35	0.368	0.359	0.364	56.6	55.3	55.9
Footwear	48– 51	8.790	38.98	0.224	0.215	0.219	104.9	100.7	102.8
Gross Rent and Fuel	52– 57	107.817	564.88	0.333	0.317	0.325	60.3	57.4	58.8
Gross Rents	52– 53	80.890	463.12	0.298	0.300	0.299	58.2	58.6	58.4
Fuel and Power	54– 57	26.927	101.76	0.492	0.379	0.432	69.9	53.8	61.3
House Furnishings and Operations	58– 71	42.021	239.23	0.388	0.345	0.366	50.9	45.3	48.0
Furniture and Appliances	58– 66	25.018	141.52	0.439	0.391	0.414	45.2	40.3	42.7
Supplies and Operation	67– 71	17.003	97.72	0.314	0.294	0.304	59.1	55.4	57.3
Medical Care	72– 78	37.806	316.67	0.165	0.135	0.149	88.5	72.4	80.0
Transport and Communications	79– 91	69.560	443.92	0.520	0.319	0.407	49.1	30.1	38.5
Equipment	79– 80	18.696	151.53	0.733	0.434	0.564	28.5	16.8	21.9
Operation Costs	81– 84	26.351	205.78	0.471	0.342	0.401	37.5	27.2	31.9
Purchased Transport	85– 89	18.318	30.43	0.390	0.269	0.324	223.7	154.3	185.8
Communications	90– 91	6.196	56.18	0.197	0.209	0.203	52.9	55.9	54.4
Recreation and Education	92–103	87.446	498.80	0.305	0.217	0.257	80.9	57.4	68.1
Recreation	92– 98	44.002	239.83	0.351	0.224	0.281	81.8	52.3	65.4
Education	99–103	43.444	258.97	0.263	0.210	0.235	80.0	63.7	71.4
Other Expenditures	104–109	52.341	381.55	0.315	0.250	0.281	54.9	43.5	48.9
Personal Care	104–106	8.700	91.21	0.274	0.205	0.237	46.6	34.8	40.2
Miscellaneous Services	107–109	43.642	290.34	0.328	0.262	0.293	57.5	45.9	51.3
Capital Formation[e]	111–148	185.537	852.78	0.318	0.298	0.308	72.9	68.5	70.7
Construction	111–124	78.044	496.44	0.245	0.248	0.247	63.5	64.1	63.8
Residential	111–112	29.593	172.96	0.201	0.196	0.198	87.2	85.3	86.3
Nonresidential Bldgs	113–120	35.861	167.17	0.319	0.322	0.320	66.7	67.2	67.0
Other Construction	121–124	12.590	156.30	0.216	0.239	0.227	33.7	37.3	35.4
Producers Durables	125–146	91.084	334.36	0.419	0.354	0.385	77.0	65.0	70.8
Transport Equipment	125–131	23.397	84.79	0.647	0.624	0.635	44.2	42.7	43.5
Nonelectrical Machinery	132–140	40.778	137.75	0.355	0.338	0.347	87.6	83.3	85.4
Electrical Machinery	141–144	17.471	79.30	0.372	0.322	0.346	68.5	59.3	63.7
Other Durables	145–146	9.438	32.53	0.210	0.210	0.210	138.2	138.2	138.2
Government	149–153	96.236	666.13	0.272	0.224	0.247	64.6	53.2	58.6
Compensation	149–152	53.656	338.73	0.204	0.178	0.191	89.1	77.8	83.3
Commodities	153	42.579	327.41	0.342	0.332	0.337	39.2	38.0	38.6
Gross Domestic Product	1–153	914.467	4789.55	0.333	0.278	0.304	68.8	57.3	62.8

(Table continues on following page.)

Summary Binary Table 5.15 continued.

Category	Line numbers[a]	Expenditure per capita		Purchasing-power parities (pound/dollar)			Quantity per capita (United States = 100)		
		United Kingdom (pounds)	United States (dollars)	U.S. weight	United Kingdom weight	Ideal[b]	U.S. weight	United Kingdom weight	Ideal[b]
Aggregates									
ICP Concepts[f]									
Consumption (CEP)[c,d]	1–110	632.700	3270.65	0.349	0.282	0.314	68.5	55.4	61.6
Capital Formation (GCF)[e]	111–148	185.537	852.78	0.318	0.298	0.308	72.9	68.5	70.7
Government (PFC)	149–153	96.236	666.13	0.272	0.224	0.247	64.6	53.2	58.6
Gross Domestic Product	1–153	914.467	4789.55	0.333	0.278	0.304	68.8	57.3	62.8
SNA Concepts[f]									
Consumption (PFCE)	1–110	555.054	2955.19	0.364	0.315	0.338	59.7	51.6	55.5
Capital Formation (GCF)	111–148	185.537	852.78	0.318	0.298	0.308	72.9	68.5	70.7
Government (GFCE)	149–153	168.408	979.14	0.253	0.189	0.219	90.8	67.9	78.5
Gross Domestic Product	1–153	908.991	4787.10	0.333	0.278	0.304	68.4	57.0	62.4

Note: See end of Summary Binary Table 5.30 for notes.

Exchange rate: £.0.4174 = US$1.00.

Summary Binary Table 5.16. Belgium and United States: Expenditures per Capita, Purchasing-Power Parities, and Quantity per Capita, 1973

Category	Line numbers[a]	Expenditure per capita		Purchasing-power parities (B. francs/dollar)			Quantity per capita (United States = 100)		
		Belgium (B. francs)	United States (dollars)	U.S. weight	United Kingdom weight	Ideal[b]	U.S. weight	Belgium weight	Ideal[b]
Consumption, ICP[c,d]	1–110	118944.4	4210.62	52.2	35.5	43.0	79.6	54.1	65.6
Food, Beverage, and Tobacco	1–39	27718.4	671.52	47.5	38.9	43.0	106.2	86.9	96.1
Food,	1–33	23120.0	536.26	51.4	41.1	45.9	104.9	83.9	93.8
Bread and Cereals	1–6	2756.7	61.64	46.9	34.7	40.3	129.1	95.3	110.9
Meat	7–12	9120.5	149.85	48.1	47.2	47.6	129.1	126.6	127.8
Fish	13–14	951.5	20.22	58.2	53.6	55.9	87.8	80.9	84.3
Milk, Cheese, and Eggs	15–17	2436.7	79.79	37.8	36.8	37.3	83.0	80.7	81.8
Oils and Fats	18–20	1556.9	23.99	41.3	48.4	44.7	134.2	157.1	145.2
Fruits and Vegetables	21–26	3808.2	120.11	50.7	27.5	37.3	115.4	62.6	85.0
Coffee, Tea, and Cocoa	27–29	780.3	17.67	82.8	87.5	85.1	50.4	53.3	51.9
Spices, Sweets, and Sugar	30–33	1709.2	62.99	74.8	65.7	70.1	41.3	36.3	38.7
Beverages	34–37	2516.5	72.84	31.7	32.3	32.0	107.0	108.8	107.9
Tobacco	38–39	2081.9	62.42	32.5	28.6	30.5	116.5	102.7	109.4
Clothing and Footwear	40–51	9496.8	299.03	45.7	42.7	44.1	74.4	69.5	71.9
Clothing	40–47	8218.2	250.54	46.1	42.7	44.3	76.9	71.2	74.0
Footwear	48–51	1278.6	48.48	43.8	42.7	43.2	61.8	60.2	61.0
Gross Rent and Fuel	52–57	15622.5	730.16	42.2	36.3	39.1	58.9	50.7	54.7
Gross Rents	52–53	10236.7	595.67	36.7	30.5	33.4	56.4	46.8	51.4
Fuel and Power	54–57	5385.7	134.49	66.3	57.3	61.7	69.9	60.4	64.9

Summary Binary Table 5.16 continued.

Category	Line numbers[a]	Expenditure per capita Belgium (B. francs)	Expenditure per capita United States (dollars)	Purchasing-power parities (B. franc/dollar) U.S. weight	Purchasing-power parities Belgium weight	Purchasing-power parities Ideal[b]	Quantity per capita (United States = 100) U.S. weight	Quantity per capita Belgium weight	Quantity per capita Ideal[b]
House Furnishings and Operations	58– 71	14505.8	308.72	49.9	44.7	47.3	105.1	94.1	99.4
Furniture and Appliances	58– 66	7069.1	190.86	56.8	48.5	52.5	76.4	65.2	70.6
Supplies and Operation	67– 71	7436.7	117.86	38.9	41.7	40.2	151.5	162.3	156.8
Medical Care	72– 78	7859.4	433.93	27.9	20.3	23.8	89.1	65.0	76.1
Transport and Communications	79– 91	11731.4	611.80	108.5	57.7	79.1	33.2	17.7	24.2
Equipment	79– 80	4032.8	236.83	156.9	59.1	96.3	28.8	10.9	17.7
Operation Costs	81– 84	5204.5	263.91	84.0	73.2	78.4	27.0	23.5	25.2
Purchased Transport	85– 89	1652.3	35.18	47.6	34.4	40.4	136.6	98.8	116.1
Communications	90– 91	841.9	75.88	71.5	52.8	61.4	21.0	15.5	18.1
Recreation and Education	92–103	16042.6	655.22	46.6	27.6	35.8	88.8	52.5	68.3
Recreation	92– 98	5775.8	310.36	49.0	41.0	44.8	45.4	38.0	41.5
Education	99–103	10266.8	344.86	44.5	23.3	32.2	127.8	66.9	92.5
Other Expenditures	104–109	14664.9	475.51	38.1	32.2	35.0	95.9	81.0	88.1
Personal Care	104–106	2108.7	108.46	54.1	28.4	39.2	68.4	35.9	49.6
Miscellaneous Services	107–109	12556.2	367.05	33.3	32.9	33.1	104.0	102.6	103.3
Capital Formation[e]	111–148	45314.1	1215.39	49.1	39.3	43.9	94.8	75.9	84.9
Construction	111–124	23022.0	697.45	36.0	32.5	34.2	101.5	91.8	96.5
Residential	111–112	8812.1	301.71	40.1	33.0	36.4	88.4	72.8	80.2
Nonresidential Bldgs	113–120	8383.9	212.43	39.0	37.7	38.4	104.6	101.2	102.9
Other Construction	121–124	5826.1	183.31	25.6	26.6	26.1	119.4	124.2	121.8
Producers Durables	125–146	15998.9	446.67	68.3	55.8	61.7	64.2	52.4	58.0
Transport Equipment	125–131	3335.7	132.14	79.3	77.8	78.6	32.4	31.8	32.1
Nonelectrical Machinery	132–140	7074.0	174.08	56.9	54.0	55.4	75.2	71.4	73.3
Electrical Machinery	141–144	3726.0	100.04	72.7	43.7	56.3	85.3	51.3	66.1
Other Durables	145–146	1863.1	40.41	70.7	67.6	69.1	68.2	65.3	66.7
Government	149–153	15723.6	766.26	42.8	35.1	38.7	58.5	47.9	53.0
Compensation	149–152	11087.9	412.20	33.2	32.0	32.6	83.9	81.0	82.4
Commodities	153	4635.7	354.06	53.9	45.2	49.4	28.9	24.3	26.5
Gross Domestic Product	1–153	179980.9	6192.20	50.4	36.3	42.8	80.0	57.6	67.9
Aggregates									
ICP Concepts[f]									
Consumption (CEP)[c,d]	1–110	118944.4	4210.62	52.2	35.5	43.0	79.6	54.1	65.6
Capital Formation (GCF)[e]	111–148	45314.1	1215.39	49.1	39.3	43.9	94.8	75.9	84.9
Government (PFC)	149–153	15723.6	766.26	42.8	35.1	38.7	58.5	47.9	53.0
Gross Domestic Product	1–153	179980.9	6192.20	50.4	36.3	42.8	80.0	57.6	67.9
SNA Concepts[f]									
Consumption (PFCE)	1–110	105303.8	3771.67	53.7	39.1	45.8	71.4	52.0	61.0
Capital Formation (GCF)	111–148	45314.1	1215.39	49.1	39.3	43.9	94.8	75.9	84.9
Government (GFCE)	149–153	29202.6	1202.06	41.7	26.5	33.3	91.6	58.3	73.1
Gross Domestic Product	1–153	179818.9	6189.04	50.4	36.3	42.8	79.9	57.6	67.9

Note: See end of Summary Binary Table 5.30 for notes.
Exchange rate: BF38.977 = US$1.00.

Summary Binary Table 5.17. Colombia and United States: Expenditures per Capita, Purchasing-Power Parities, and Quantity per Capita, 1973

Category	Line numbers[a]	Expenditure per capita		Purchasing-power parities (peso/dollar)			Quantity per capita (United States=100)		
		Colombia (pesos)	United States (dollars)	U.S. weight	Colombia weight	Ideal[b]	U.S. weight	Colombia weight	Ideal[b]
Consumption, ICP[c,d]	1–110	7474.3	4210.62	14.2	6.8	9.8	26.3	12.5	18.1
Food, Beverage, and Tobacco	1– 39	2955.4	671.52	18.5	13.0	15.5	33.8	23.7	28.3
Food,	1– 33	2513.7	536.26	20.3	13.6	16.6	34.5	23.1	28.2
Bread and Cereals	1– 6	377.6	61.64	22.5	19.6	21.0	31.3	27.2	29.2
Meat	7– 12	880.3	149.85	17.1	15.0	16.0	39.3	34.3	36.7
Fish	13– 14	53.1	20.22	17.8	19.1	18.5	13.7	14.7	14.2
Milk, Cheese, and Eggs	15– 17	315.5	79.79	16.9	14.2	15.5	27.9	23.4	25.5
Oils and Fats	18– 20	92.3	23.99	25.3	24.4	24.8	15.8	15.2	15.5
Fruits and Vegetables	21– 26	445.5	120.11	25.8	7.6	14.0	48.6	14.4	26.4
Coffee, Tea, and Cocoa	27– 29	116.6	17.67	15.3	18.2	16.7	36.3	43.1	39.5
Spices, Sweets, and Sugar	30– 33	232.8	62.99	20.1	17.4	18.7	21.2	18.4	19.8
Beverages	34– 37	319.7	72.84	16.2	15.5	15.8	28.3	27.2	27.7
Tobacco	38– 39	122.0	62.42	6.0	5.7	5.9	34.1	32.6	33.4
Clothing and Footwear	40– 51	789.9	299.03	15.6	13.6	14.6	19.4	17.0	18.2
Clothing	40– 47	596.5	250.54	16.7	15.7	16.2	15.2	14.2	14.7
Footwear	48– 51	193.3	48.48	9.6	9.6	9.6	41.4	41.6	41.5
Gross Rent and Fuel	52– 57	714.0	730.16	13.7	11.9	12.8	8.2	7.1	7.7
Gross Rents	52– 53	577.7	595.67	15.1	13.6	14.4	7.1	6.4	6.8
Fuel and Power	54– 57	136.3	134.49	7.7	7.6	7.7	13.3	13.2	13.2
House Furnishings and Operations	58– 71	651.6	308.72	22.2	3.1	8.3	69.0	9.5	25.6
Furniture and Appliances	58– 66	232.0	190.86	28.9	19.1	23.5	6.4	4.2	5.2
Supplies and Operation	67– 71	419.6	117.86	11.4	2.1	4.9	170.3	31.3	73.0
Medical Care	72– 78	364.0	433.93	6.8	4.8	5.7	17.4	12.4	14.7
Transport and Communications	79– 91	689.4	611.80	16.8	4.6	8.8	24.4	6.7	12.8
Equipment	79– 80	90.7	236.83	33.1	33.2	33.1	1.2	1.2	1.2
Operation Costs	81– 84	55.2	263.91	7.3	5.2	6.2	4.0	2.9	3.4
Purchased Transport	85– 89	508.2	35.18	7.3	4.1	5.5	349.4	198.2	263.2
Communications	90– 91	35.3	75.88	3.1	2.7	2.9	17.0	14.9	16.0
Recreation and Education	92–103	707.7	655.22	11.1	3.4	6.1	31.8	9.8	17.6
Recreation	92– 98	316.2	310.36	19.7	9.0	13.3	11.3	5.2	7.6
Education	99–103	391.5	344.86	3.4	2.3	2.8	50.2	33.8	41.2
Other Expenditures	104–109	602.5	475.51	9.8	5.2	7.1	24.3	13.0	17.8
Personal Care	104–106	102.4	108.46	12.9	11.4	12.1	8.3	7.3	7.8
Miscellaneous Services	107–109	500.0	367.05	8.8	4.7	6.4	29.1	15.4	21.2
Capital Formation[e]	111–148	2324.6	1215.39	19.5	8.7	13.1	21.9	9.8	14.7
Construction	111–124	1109.4	697.45	5.1	5.2	5.1	30.6	31.3	31.0
Residential	111–112	345.6	301.71	5.1	5.3	5.2	21.7	22.4	22.0
Nonresidential Bldgs	113–120	71.1	212.43	5.0	4.9	5.0	6.8	6.7	6.7
Other Construction	121–124	692.7	183.31	5.1	5.2	5.1	73.0	74.2	73.6
Producers Durables	125–146	707.9	446.67	42.2	33.9	37.8	4.7	3.8	4.2
Transport Equipment	125–131	184.0	132.14	45.9	46.1	46.0	3.0	3.0	3.0
Nonelectrical Machinery	132–140	137.7	174.08	46.3	38.5	42.2	2.1	1.7	1.9
Electrical Machinery	141–144	349.5	100.04	36.1	29.2	32.5	12.0	9.7	10.8
Other Durables	145–146	36.7	40.41	27.1	27.1	27.1	3.4	3.3	3.4
Government	149–153	688.4	766.26	6.4	2.8	4.2	31.6	14.1	21.2
Compensation	149–152	543.4	412.20	2.5	2.5	2.5	53.3	53.3	53.3
Commodities	153	145.0	354.06	10.9	6.3	8.3	6.5	3.8	4.9
Gross Domestic Product	1–153	10487.2	6192.20	14.3	6.5	9.6	26.1	11.9	17.6

Summary Binary Table 5.17 continued.

Category	Line numbers[a]	Expenditure per capita		Purchasing-power parities (peso/dollar)			Quantity per capita (United States = 100)		
		Colombia (pesos)	United States (dollars)	U.S. weight	Colombia weight	Ideal[b]	U.S. weight	Colombia weight	Ideal[b]
Aggregates									
ICP Concepts[f]									
Consumption (CEP)[c,d]	1–110	7474.3	4210.62	14.2	6.8	9.8	26.3	12.5	18.1
Capital Formation (GCF)[e]	111–148	2324.6	1215.39	19.5	8.7	13.1	21.9	9.8	14.7
Government (PFC)	149–153	688.4	766.26	6.4	2.8	4.2	31.6	14.1	21.2
Gross Domestic Product	1–153	10487.2	6192.20	14.3	6.5	9.6	26.1	11.9	17.6
SNA Concepts[f]									
Consumption (PFCE)	1–110	7151.3	3771.67	15.2	7.4	10.6	25.7	12.4	17.9
Capital Formation (GCF)	111–148	2324.6	1215.39	19.5	8.7	13.1	21.9	9.8	14.7
Government (GFCE)	149–153	1011.4	1202.06	5.9	2.7	4.0	31.5	14.3	21.2
Gross Domestic Product	1–153	10487.2	6189.04	14.3	6.5	9.6	26.1	11.9	17.6

Note: See end of Summary Binary Table 5.30 for notes.
Exchange rate: Col$23.813 = US$1.00.

Summary Binary Table 5.18. France and United States: Expenditures per Capita, Purchasing-Power Parities, and Quantity per Capita, 1973

Category	Line numbers[a]	Expenditure per capita		Purchasing-power parities (franc/dollar)			Quantity per capita (United States = 100)		
		France (francs)	United States (dollars)	U.S. weight	France weight	Ideal[b]	U.S. weight	France weight	Ideal[b]
Consumption, ICP[c,d]	1–110	13602.75	4210.62	5.33	4.38	4.83	73.7	60.6	66.9
Food, Beverage, and Tobacco	1– 39	3411.18	671.52	5.44	4.51	4.95	112.6	93.4	102.6
Food,	1– 33	2774.00	536.26	5.89	4.67	5.24	110.8	87.8	98.6
Bread and Cereals	1– 6	383.29	61.64	5.40	4.26	4.79	146.0	115.2	129.7
Meat	7– 12	969.06	149.85	5.22	5.08	5.15	127.4	123.9	125.6
Fish	13– 14	148.67	20.22	6.76	6.04	6.39	121.7	108.7	115.0
Milk, Cheese, and Eggs	15– 17	407.86	79.79	4.09	4.05	4.07	126.1	125.1	125.6
Oils and Fats	18– 20	171.61	23.99	4.59	5.72	5.13	125.0	155.8	139.6
Fruits and Vegetables	21– 26	468.06	120.11	6.12	3.59	4.69	108.6	63.6	83.2
Coffee, Tea, and Cocoa	27– 29	65.97	17.67	7.73	7.45	7.59	50.1	48.3	49.2
Spices, Sweets, and Sugar	30– 33	159.49	62.99	9.50	8.61	9.05	29.4	26.7	28.0
Beverages	34– 37	473.97	72.84	3.53	4.04	3.77	161.1	184.4	172.4
Tobacco	38– 39	163.21	62.42	3.78	3.64	3.71	71.9	69.2	70.5
Clothing and Footwear	40– 51	1064.99	299.03	6.47	6.45	6.46	55.3	55.1	55.2
Clothing	40– 47	893.88	250.54	6.54	6.56	6.55	54.4	54.5	54.5
Footwear	48– 51	171.11	48.48	6.09	5.89	5.99	59.9	58.0	58.9
Gross Rent and Fuel	52– 57	1799.21	730.16	4.21	3.77	3.98	65.4	58.6	61.9
Gross Rents	52– 53	1389.78	595.67	3.51	3.33	3.42	70.1	66.5	68.3
Fuel and Power	54– 57	409.44	134.49	7.29	6.87	7.08	44.3	41.8	43.0

(Table continues on following page.)

Summary Binary Table 5.18 continued.

Category	Line numbers[a]	Expenditure per capita		Purchasing-power parities (franc/dollar)			Quantity per capita (United States=100)		
		France (francs)	United States (dollars)	U.S. weight	France weight	Ideal[b]	U.S. weight	France weight	Ideal[b]
House Furnishings and Operations	58– 71	1092.04	308.72	5.61	5.59	5.60	63.2	63.1	63.2
Furniture and Appliances	58– 66	679.17	190.86	6.14	5.78	5.96	61.5	57.9	59.7
Supplies and Operation	67– 71	412.87	117.86	4.74	5.31	5.02	66.0	73.8	69.8
Medical Care	72– 78	1421.56	433.93	3.02	2.95	2.98	111.1	108.6	109.8
Transport and Communications	79– 91	1397.97	611.80	8.17	5.60	6.76	40.8	28.0	33.8
Equipment	79– 80	410.57	236.83	7.84	5.87	6.79	29.5	22.1	25.5
Operation Costs	81– 84	687.38	263.91	9.35	6.43	7.75	40.5	27.9	33.6
Purchased Transport	85– 89	227.55	35.18	5.31	3.89	4.55	166.1	121.8	142.2
Communications	90– 91	72.47	75.88	6.41	5.02	5.67	19.0	14.9	16.8
Recreation and Education	92–103	1694.86	655.22	5.22	4.46	4.82	58.0	49.5	53.6
Recreation	92– 98	867.50	310.36	5.65	4.88	5.25	57.3	49.5	53.3
Education	99–103	827.35	344.86	4.84	4.09	4.45	58.7	49.6	53.9
Other Expenditures	104–109	1727.22	475.51	4.64	4.32	4.48	84.1	78.2	81.1
Personal Care	104–106	302.70	108.46	5.18	4.45	4.80	62.8	53.8	58.1
Miscellaneous Services	107–109	1424.51	367.05	4.48	4.29	4.39	90.4	86.6	88.5
Capital Formation[e]	111–148	5780.79	1215.39	4.52	4.09	4.30	116.2	105.2	110.6
Construction	111–124	2951.14	697.45	3.74	3.55	3.64	119.3	113.2	116.2
Residential	111–112	1489.05	301.71	4.38	4.01	4.19	123.1	112.8	117.8
Nonresidential Bldgs	113–120	892.46	212.43	3.85	3.69	3.77	113.8	109.1	111.4
Other Construction	121–124	569.63	183.31	2.56	2.60	2.58	119.5	121.6	120.5
Producers Durables	125–146	2229.00	446.67	5.54	4.94	5.23	101.1	90.0	95.4
Transport Equipment	125–131	390.96	132.14	6.10	6.07	6.09	48.7	48.5	48.6
Nonelectrical Machinery	132–140	1153.92	174.08	5.58	5.13	5.35	129.2	118.7	123.9
Electrical Machinery	141–144	594.46	100.04	4.47	4.02	4.24	148.0	133.0	140.3
Other Durables	145–146	89.66	40.41	6.21	6.33	6.27	35.1	35.7	35.4
Government	149–153	1890.93	766.26	4.40	4.02	4.21	61.3	56.1	58.7
Compensation	149–152	1372.99	412.20	3.88	3.84	3.86	86.7	85.8	86.2
Commodities	153	517.94	354.06	4.99	4.60	4.79	31.8	29.3	30.5
Gross Domestic Product	1–153	21274.41	6192.20	5.05	4.27	4.64	80.5	68.0	74.0
Aggregates									
ICP Concepts[f]									
Consumption (CEP)[c,d]	1–110	13602.75	4210.62	5.33	4.38	4.83	73.7	60.6	66.9
Capital Formation (GCF)[e]	111–148	5780.79	1215.39	4.52	4.09	4.30	116.2	105.2	110.6
Government (PFC)	149–153	1890.93	766.26	4.40	4.02	4.21	61.3	56.1	58.7
Gross Domestic Product	1–153	21274.41	6192.20	5.05	4.27	4.64	80.5	68.0	74.0
SNA Concepts[f]									
Consumption (PFCE)	1–110	12697.59	3771.67	5.47	4.43	4.92	76.0	61.6	68.4
Capital Formation (GCF)	111–148	5780.79	1215.39	4.52	4.09	4.30	116.2	105.2	110.6
Government (GFCE)	149–153	2789.72	1202.06	4.31	3.94	4.12	58.8	53.9	56.3
Gross Domestic Product	1–153	21268.03	6189.04	5.05	4.27	4.64	80.5	68.0	74.0

Note: See end of Summary Binary Table 5.30 for notes.
Exchange rate: F4.454 = US$1.00.

Summary Binary Table 5.19. Federal Republic of Germany and United States: Expenditures per Capita, Purchasing-Power Parities, and Quantity per Capita, 1973

Category	Line numbers[a]	Expenditure per capita — Germany, F.R. (DM)	Expenditure per capita — United States (dollars)	Purchasing-power parities (DM/dollar) — U.S. weight	Purchasing-power parities (DM/dollar) — Germany, F.R. weight	Purchasing-power parities (DM/dollar) — Ideal[b]	Quantity per capita (United States=100) — U.S. weight	Quantity per capita (United States=100) — Germany, F.R. weight	Quantity per capita (United States=100) — Ideal[b]
Consumption, ICP[c,d]	1–110	9100.95	4210.62	3.83	3.17	3.48	68.1	56.5	62.0
Food, Beverage, and Tobacco	1– 39	1890.67	671.52	4.05	3.54	3.78	79.6	69.6	74.4
Food,	1– 33	1542.85	536.26	4.21	3.68	3.94	78.2	68.3	73.1
Bread and Cereals	1– 6	277.44	61.64	3.81	3.31	3.55	136.0	118.0	126.7
Meat	7– 12	408.79	149.85	3.54	3.49	3.52	78.1	77.0	77.5
Fish	13– 14	24.36	20.22	3.55	3.81	3.67	31.7	34.0	32.8
Milk, Cheese, and Eggs	15– 17	175.59	79.79	2.83	2.85	2.84	77.2	77.7	77.5
Oils and Fats	18– 20	152.00	23.99	4.19	4.30	4.24	147.3	151.3	149.3
Fruits and Vegetables	21– 26	239.04	120.11	3.99	2.98	3.45	66.8	49.8	57.7
Coffee, Tea, and Cocoa	27– 29	120.99	17.67	11.17	10.52	10.84	65.1	61.3	63.2
Spices, Sweets, and Sugar	30– 33	144.63	62.99	6.64	6.18	6.41	37.2	34.6	35.8
Beverages	34– 37	215.30	72.84	2.53	2.57	2.55	115.2	116.8	116.0
Tobacco	38– 39	132.53	62.42	4.38	4.21	4.30	50.4	48.5	49.4
Clothing and Footwear	40– 51	878.64	299.03	4.02	4.10	4.06	71.7	73.1	72.4
Clothing	40– 47	754.73	250.54	4.09	4.22	4.15	71.4	73.7	72.5
Footwear	48– 51	123.91	48.48	3.68	3.47	3.58	73.6	69.4	71.4
Gross Rent and Fuel	52– 57	1273.02	730.16	3.18	2.94	3.06	59.3	54.9	57.1
Gross Rents	52– 53	917.72	595.67	2.71	2.56	2.63	60.1	56.9	58.5
Fuel and Power	54– 57	355.31	134.49	5.27	4.72	4.99	56.0	50.2	53.0
House Furnishings and Operations	58– 71	1051.87	308.72	3.81	3.60	3.71	94.6	89.4	91.9
Furniture and Appliances	58– 66	664.81	190.86	4.32	3.95	4.13	88.1	80.6	84.3
Supplies and Operation	67– 71	387.06	117.86	2.99	3.13	3.06	104.9	109.9	107.4
Medical Care	72– 78	908.90	433.93	2.53	2.00	2.25	104.5	82.7	93.0
Transport and Communications	79– 91	981.90	611.80	6.18	4.18	5.09	38.4	26.0	31.6
Equipment	79– 80	213.39	236.83	6.78	4.13	5.29	21.8	13.3	17.0
Operation Costs	81– 84	543.34	263.91	6.69	5.59	6.11	36.9	30.8	33.7
Purchased Transport	85– 89	155.40	35.18	3.77	2.72	3.20	162.1	117.2	137.9
Communications	90– 91	69.76	75.88	3.67	2.43	2.99	37.8	25.0	30.8
Recreation and Education	92–103	1165.21	655.22	3.19	2.84	3.01	62.5	55.8	59.0
Recreation	92– 98	596.47	310.36	3.26	3.19	3.22	60.2	59.0	59.6
Education	99–103	568.75	344.86	3.13	2.55	2.83	64.6	52.7	58.4
Other Expenditures	104–109	862.60	475.51	3.48	3.28	3.37	55.4	52.2	53.8
Personal Care	104–106	132.06	108.46	4.36	3.57	3.95	34.1	27.9	30.8
Miscellaneous Services	107–109	730.54	367.05	3.21	3.23	3.22	61.7	61.9	61.8
Capital Formation[e]	111–148	4266.69	1215.39	3.18	2.61	2.88	134.5	110.6	122.0
Construction	111–124	2102.74	697.45	2.45	2.13	2.28	141.9	123.3	132.2
Residential	111–112	901.90	301.71	2.93	2.31	2.60	129.2	102.0	114.8
Nonresidential Bldgs	113–120	684.48	212.43	2.33	2.28	2.31	141.4	138.0	139.7
Other Construction	121–124	516.36	183.31	1.78	1.73	1.75	163.2	158.5	160.8
Producers Durables	125–146	1585.22	446.67	4.16	3.57	3.86	99.4	85.3	92.0
Transport Equipment	125–131	368.23	132.14	5.09	5.05	5.07	55.1	54.8	55.0
Nonelectrical Machinery	132–140	751.53	174.08	3.94	3.38	3.65	127.6	109.6	118.2
Electrical Machinery	141–144	404.66	100.04	3.12	2.98	3.05	135.7	129.6	132.6
Other Durables	145–146	60.79	40.41	4.68	4.68	4.68	32.2	32.2	32.2
Government	149–153	1422.73	766.26	3.65	3.26	3.45	57.0	50.8	53.8
Compensation	149–152	1050.03	412.20	3.40	3.19	3.29	79.8	74.9	77.3
Commodities	153	372.70	354.06	3.95	3.47	3.70	30.3	26.7	28.4
Gross Domestic Product	1–153	14790.30	6192.20	3.68	2.99	3.32	79.8	65.0	72.0

(Table continues on following page.)

Summary Binary Table 5.19 continued.

Category	Line numbers[a]	Expenditure per capita		Purchasing-power parities (DM/dollar)			Quantity per capita (United States=100)		
		Germany F.R. (DM)	United States (dollars)	U.S. weight	Germany weight	Ideal[b]	U.S. weight	Germany weight	Ideal[b]
Aggregates									
ICP Concepts[f]									
Consumption (CEP)[c,d]	1–110	9100.95	4210.62	3.83	3.17	3.48	68.1	56.5	62.0
Capital Formation (GCF)[e]	111–148	4266.69	1215.39	3.18	2.61	2.88	134.5	110.6	122.0
Government (PFC)	149–153	1422.73	766.26	3.65	3.26	3.45	57.0	50.8	53.8
Gross Domestic Product	1–153	14790.30	6192.20	3.68	2.99	3.32	79.8	65.0	72.0
SNA Concepts[f]									
Consumption (PFCE)	1–110	8432.71	3771.67	3.93	3.39	3.65	66.0	56.9	61.3
Capital Formation (GCF)	111–148	4266.69	1215.39	3.18	2.61	2.88	134.5	110.6	122.0
Government (GFCE)	149–153	2080.07	1202.06	3.40	2.56	2.95	67.5	50.9	58.6
Gross Domestic Product	1–153	14779.37	6189.04	3.68	2.99	3.32	79.8	64.9	72.0

Note: See end of Summary Binary Table 5.30 for notes.
Exchange rate: DM2.6725 = US$1.00.

Summary Binary Table 5.20. Hungary and United States: Expenditures per Capita, Purchasing-Power Parities, and Quantity per Capita, 1973

Category	Line numbers[a]	Expenditure per capita		Purchasing-power parities (forint/dollar)			Quantity per capita (United States=100)		
		Hungary (forint)	United States (dollars)	U.S. weight	Hungary weight	Ideal[b]	U.S. weight	Hungary weight	Ideal[b]
Consumption, ICP[c,d]	1–110	22922.6	4210.62	17.9	10.8	13.9	50.5	30.4	39.1
Food, Beverage, and Tobacco	1– 39	7841.7	671.52	23.9	16.5	19.9	70.9	48.8	58.8
Food,	1– 33	6461.7	536.26	25.7	16.4	20.5	73.5	46.8	58.7
Bread and Cereals	1– 6	766.1	61.64	10.3	7.2	8.6	173.2	120.8	144.6
Meat	7– 12	1809.9	149.85	26.3	24.6	25.4	49.1	45.9	47.5
Fish	13– 14	58.4	20.22	27.6	15.0	20.3	19.2	10.5	14.2
Milk, Cheese, and Eggs	15– 17	859.0	79.79	16.7	17.1	16.9	63.0	64.4	63.7
Oils and Fats	18– 20	536.2	23.99	25.6	31.7	28.5	70.5	87.3	78.5
Fruits and Vegetables	21– 26	1212.6	120.11	27.7	11.4	17.8	88.5	36.4	56.8
Coffee, Tea, and Cocoa	27– 29	282.6	17.67	89.9	86.9	88.4	18.4	17.8	18.1
Spices, Sweets, and Sugar	30– 33	937.0	62.99	28.7	28.2	28.4	52.7	51.9	52.3
Beverages	34– 37	1001.2	72.84	21.5	23.3	22.4	59.1	64.0	61.5
Tobacco	38– 39	378.8	62.42	11.0	9.8	10.4	61.6	55.0	58.2
Clothing and Footwear	40– 51	2526.7	299.03	20.6	20.5	20.6	41.2	41.0	41.1
Clothing	40– 47	2069.6	250.54	21.0	21.3	21.2	38.8	39.3	39.0
Footwear	48– 51	457.1	48.48	18.6	17.7	18.1	53.4	50.6	52.0
Gross Rent and Fuel	52– 57	1685.9	730.16	13.1	8.3	10.5	27.7	17.6	22.1
Gross Rents	52– 53	987.8	595.67	11.2	8.1	9.5	20.5	14.8	17.4
Fuel and Power	54– 57	698.1	134.49	21.4	8.8	13.7	59.2	24.2	37.9

Summary Binary Table 5.20 continued.

Category	Line numbers[a]	Expenditure per capita		Purchasing-power parities (forint/dollar)			Quantity per capita (United States = 100)		
		Hungary (forint)	United States (dollars)	U.S. weight	Hungary weight	Ideal[b]	U.S. weight	Hungary weight	Ideal[b]
House Furnishings and Operations	58– 71	1967.6	308.72	22.7	18.9	20.7	33.8	28.1	30.8
Furniture and Appliances	58– 66	1175.0	190.86	22.8	21.3	22.0	28.9	27.0	27.9
Supplies and Operation	67– 71	792.6	117.86	22.4	16.1	19.0	41.7	30.0	35.4
Medical Care	72– 78	1358.5	433.93	5.1	3.9	4.5	79.7	61.8	70.2
Transport and Communications	79– 91	1605.2	611.80	30.7	14.7	21.2	17.9	8.6	12.4
Equipment	79– 80	567.5	236.83	47.1	35.0	40.6	6.8	5.1	5.9
Operation Costs	81– 84	359.2	263.91	25.5	18.6	21.8	7.3	5.3	6.3
Purchased Transport	85– 89	575.3	35.18	14.3	10.0	12.0	163.6	114.1	136.6
Communications	90– 91	103.3	75.88	5.0	6.3	5.6	21.7	27.1	24.2
Recreation and Education	92–103	2674.0	655.22	13.2	5.7	8.7	71.7	30.9	47.1
Recreation	92– 98	1344.8	310.36	20.1	5.6	10.6	77.1	21.6	40.8
Education	99–103	1329.2	344.86	7.0	5.8	6.3	66.9	55.2	60.8
Other Expenditures	104–109	3263.2	475.51	13.7	11.1	12.3	61.8	50.1	55.6
Personal Care	104–106	570.5	108.46	19.0	9.1	13.2	57.7	27.7	40.0
Miscellaneous Services	107–109	2692.7	367.05	12.1	11.6	11.9	63.0	60.4	61.7
Capital Formation[e]	111–148	14118.5	1215.39	22.6	18.5	20.5	62.7	51.4	56.7
Construction	111–124	7137.5	697.45	14.5	14.2	14.4	72.0	70.5	71.3
Residential	111–112	2153.4	301.71	14.4	14.1	14.2	50.8	49.7	50.2
Nonresidential Bldgs	113–120	2767.6	212.43	15.2	16.9	16.1	77.0	85.6	81.2
Other Construction	121–124	2216.5	183.31	13.9	11.9	12.9	101.2	86.9	93.7
Producers Durables	125–146	4646.7	446.67	35.2	31.2	33.1	33.4	29.5	31.4
Transport Equipment	125–131	1019.7	132.14	45.4	36.4	40.6	21.2	17.0	19.0
Nonelectrical Machinery	132–140	2642.0	174.08	34.9	33.2	34.1	45.7	43.5	44.5
Electrical Machinery	141–144	459.4	100.04	22.4	22.5	22.5	20.4	20.5	20.5
Other Durables	145–146	525.6	40.41	35.1	24.7	29.5	52.6	37.0	44.1
Government	149–153	2757.5	766.26	10.0	8.7	9.3	41.4	36.0	38.6
Compensation	149–152	720.3	412.20	4.3	4.2	4.2	41.7	40.8	41.3
Commodities	153	2037.2	354.06	16.7	14.0	15.3	41.1	34.5	37.6
Gross Domestic Product	1–153	39798.7	6192.20	17.9	12.4	14.9	51.7	36.0	43.1
Aggregates									
ICP Concepts[f]									
Consumption (CEP)[c,d]	1–110	22922.6	4210.62	17.9	10.8	13.9	50.5	30.4	39.1
Capital Formation (GCF)[e]	111–148	14118.5	1215.39	22.6	18.5	20.5	62.7	51.4	56.7
Government (PFC)	149–153	2757.5	766.26	10.0	8.7	9.3	41.4	36.0	38.6
Gross Domestic Product	1–153	39798.7	6192.20	17.9	12.4	14.9	51.7	36.0	43.1
SNA Concepts[f]									
Consumption (PFCE)	1–110	19813.1	3771.67	19.2	13.6	16.2	38.7	27.3	32.5
Capital Formation (GCF)	111–148	14118.5	1215.39	22.6	18.5	20.5	62.7	51.4	56.7
Government (GFCE)	149–153	5461.8	1202.06	8.9	5.8	7.2	77.8	51.3	63.2
Gross Domestic Product	1–153	39393.4	6189.04	17.9	12.5	14.9	51.0	35.6	42.6

Note: See end of Summary Binary Table 5.30 for notes.

Exchange rate: Ft24.59 = US$1.00.

Summary Binary Table 5.21. India and United States: Expenditures per Capita, Purchasing-Power Parities, and Quantity per Capita, 1973

Category	Line numbers[a]	Expenditure per capita India (rupees)	Expenditure per capita United States (dollars)	Purchasing-power parities (rupee/dollar) U.S. weight	Purchasing-power parities (rupee/dollar) India weight	Purchasing-power parities (rupee/dollar) Ideal[b]	Quantity per capita (United States=100) U.S. weight	Quantity per capita (United States=100) India weight	Quantity per capita (United States=100) Ideal[b]
Consumption, ICP[c,d]	1–110	758.56	4210.62	4.52	2.56	3.40	7.0	4.0	5.3
Food, Beverage, and Tobacco	1– 39	509.51	671.52	6.56	4.50	5.43	16.9	11.6	14.0
Food,	1– 33	479.34	536.26	5.74	4.50	5.08	19.9	15.6	17.6
Bread and Cereals	1– 6	218.38	61.64	5.64	4.60	5.09	77.1	62.8	69.6
Meat	7– 12	10.49	149.85	4.22	4.47	4.34	1.6	1.7	1.6
Fish	13– 14	7.50	20.22	3.70	1.94	2.68	19.2	10.0	13.9
Milk, Cheese, and Eggs	15– 17	44.81	79.79	4.84	3.97	4.38	14.2	11.6	12.8
Oils and Fats	18– 20	53.23	23.99	7.67	4.94	6.16	44.9	28.9	36.0
Fruits and Vegetables	21– 26	79.73	120.11	5.60	3.73	4.57	17.8	11.8	14.5
Coffee, Tea, and Cocoa	27– 29	5.55	17.67	10.07	3.20	5.67	9.8	3.1	5.5
Spices, Sweets, and Sugar	30– 33	59.64	62.99	9.60	7.75	8.62	12.2	9.9	11.0
Beverages	34– 37	7.08	72.84	10.35	8.40	9.32	1.2	0.9	1.0
Tobacco	38– 39	23.09	62.42	9.13	3.94	5.99	9.4	4.1	6.2
Clothing and Footwear	40– 51	54.74	299.03	4.10	6.43	5.14	2.8	4.5	3.6
Clothing	40– 47	50.62	250.54	4.12	6.85	5.31	2.9	4.9	3.8
Footwear	48– 51	4.12	48.48	4.02	3.67	3.84	2.3	2.1	2.2
Gross Rent and Fuel	52– 57	50.80	730.16	3.09	2.35	2.69	3.0	2.2	2.6
Gross Rents	52– 53	27.42	595.67	1.99	1.62	1.79	2.8	2.3	2.6
Fuel and Power	54– 57	23.38	134.49	7.99	4.98	6.31	3.5	2.2	2.8
House Furnishings and Operations	58– 71	19.53	308.72	5.01	1.19	2.45	5.3	1.3	2.6
Furniture and Appliances	58– 66	4.90	190.86	5.25	5.15	5.20	0.5	0.5	0.5
Supplies and Operation	67– 71	14.63	117.86	4.63	0.95	2.10	13.1	2.7	5.9
Medical Care	72– 78	19.14	433.93	0.92	0.64	0.76	6.9	4.8	5.8
Transport and Communications	79– 91	44.02	611.80	8.98	2.70	4.92	2.7	0.8	1.5
Equipment	79– 80	3.67	236.83	9.48	7.79	8.59	0.2	0.2	0.2
Operation Costs	81– 84	4.71	263.91	11.22	4.23	6.89	0.4	0.2	0.3
Purchased Transport	85– 89	33.16	35.18	5.53	2.59	3.78	36.5	17.1	24.9
Communications	90– 91	2.47	75.88	1.19	1.30	1.25	2.5	2.7	2.6
Recreation and Education	92–103	35.14	655.22	2.93	0.49	1.20	10.9	1.8	4.5
Recreation	92– 98	7.00	310.36	4.71	1.97	3.05	1.1	0.5	0.7
Education	99–103	28.13	344.86	1.32	0.41	0.74	19.8	6.2	11.0
Other Expenditures	104–109	25.71	475.51	3.35	1.43	2.19	3.8	1.6	2.5
Personal Care	104–106	8.38	108.46	4.78	3.91	4.33	2.0	1.6	1.8
Miscellaneous Services	107–109	17.33	367.05	2.92	1.10	1.79	4.3	1.6	2.6
Capital Formation[e]	111–148	167.49	1215.39	4.59	2.44	3.35	5.6	3.0	4.1
Construction	111–124	79.87	697.45	1.64	1.46	1.54	7.8	7.0	7.4
Residential	111–112	19.99	301.71	1.59	1.61	1.60	4.1	4.2	4.1
Nonresidential Bldgs	113–120	7.76	212.43	1.89	1.82	1.85	2.0	1.9	2.0
Other Construction	121–124	52.12	183.31	1.41	1.37	1.39	20.7	20.1	20.4
Producers Durables	125–146	65.10	446.67	8.96	7.98	8.46	1.8	1.6	1.7
Transport Equipment	125–131	12.59	132.14	9.97	9.42	9.69	1.0	1.0	1.0
Nonelectrical Machinery	132–140	22.65	174.08	9.50	9.43	9.47	1.4	1.4	1.4
Electrical Machinery	141–144	15.16	100.04	8.09	8.71	8.39	1.7	1.9	1.8
Other Durables	145–146	14.69	40.41	5.48	5.48	5.48	6.6	6.6	6.6
Government	149–153	73.57	766.26	1.87	0.60	1.06	16.0	5.1	9.0
Compensation	149–152	43.90	412.20	0.56	0.42	0.48	25.3	19.1	22.0
Commodities	153	29.66	354.06	3.41	1.64	2.36	5.1	2.5	3.5
Gross Domestic Product	1–153	999.61	6192.20	4.21	2.05	2.94	7.9	3.8	5.5

Summary Binary Table 5.21 continued.

Category	Line numbers[a]	Expenditure per capita		Purchasing-power parities (rupee/dollar)			Quantity per capita (United States = 100)		
		India (rupees)	United States (dollars)	U.S. weight	India weight	Ideal[b]	U.S. weight	India weight	Ideal[b]
Aggregates									
ICP Concepts[f]									
Consumption (CEP)[c,d]	1–110	758.56	4210.62	4.52	2.56	3.40	7.0	4.0	5.3
Capital Formation (GCF)[e]	111–148	167.49	1215.39	4.59	2.44	3.35	5.6	3.0	4.1
Government (PFC)	149–153	73.57	766.26	1.87	0.60	1.06	16.0	5.1	9.0
Gross Domestic Product	1–153	999.61	6192.20	4.21	2.05	2.94	7.9	3.8	5.5
SNA Concepts[f]									
Consumption (PFCE)	1–110	742.49	3771.67	4.89	2.97	3.81	6.6	4.0	5.2
Capital Formation (GCF)	111–148	167.49	1215.39	4.59	2.44	3.35	5.6	3.0	4.1
Government (GFCE)	149–153	89.64	1202.06	1.69	0.53	0.95	14.0	4.4	7.9
Gross Domestic Product	1–153	999.61	6189.04	4.21	2.05	2.94	7.9	3.8	5.5

Note: See end of Summary Binary Table 5.30 for notes.
Exchange rate: Rs7.742 = US$1.00.

Summary Binary Table 5.22. Iran and United States: Expenditures per Capita, Purchasing-Power Parities, and Quantity per Capita, 1973

Category	Line numbers[a]	Expenditure per capita		Purchasing-power parities (rial/dollar)			Quantity per capita (United States = 100)		
		Iran (rials)	United States (dollars)	U.S. weight	Iran weight	Ideal[b]	U.S. weight	Iran weight	Ideal[b]
Consumption, ICP[c,d]	1–110	28875.9	4210.62	47.7	27.8	36.4	24.6	14.4	18.8
Food, Beverage, and Tobacco	1– 39	11908.5	671.52	58.3	37.1	46.5	47.8	30.4	38.1
Food,	1– 33	11340.6	536.26	61.7	36.9	47.7	57.4	34.2	44.3
Bread and Cereals	1– 6	3508.1	61.64	36.9	30.9	33.8	184.1	154.2	168.5
Meat	7– 12	2264.4	149.85	63.8	69.0	66.3	21.9	23.7	22.8
Fish	13– 14	115.0	20.22	89.7	44.3	63.0	12.8	6.3	9.0
Milk, Cheese, and Eggs	15– 17	1189.4	79.79	44.8	21.6	31.1	69.0	33.3	47.9
Oils and Fats	18– 20	941.5	23.99	108.4	99.1	103.7	39.6	36.2	37.9
Fruits and Vegetables	21– 26	2042.6	120.11	43.3	26.5	33.8	64.3	39.3	50.2
Coffee, Tea, and Cocoa	27– 29	446.4	17.67	133.3	75.0	100.0	33.7	19.0	25.3
Spices, Sweets, and Sugar	30– 33	833.3	62.99	91.0	76.5	83.4	17.3	14.5	15.9
Beverages	34– 37	100.8	72.84	47.3	46.0	46.7	3.0	2.9	3.0
Tobacco	38– 39	467.0	62.42	41.4	41.4	41.4	18.1	18.1	18.1
Clothing and Footwear	40– 51	1983.5	299.03	32.6	28.3	30.4	23.4	20.3	21.8
Clothing	40– 47	1565.2	250.54	35.0	34.4	34.7	18.2	17.9	18.0
Footwear	48– 51	418.3	48.48	20.7	17.0	18.8	50.6	41.7	46.0
Gross Rent and Fuel	52– 57	5203.1	730.16	28.9	24.5	26.6	29.1	24.7	26.8
Gross Rents	52– 53	4092.0	595.67	19.8	21.2	20.5	32.4	34.6	33.5
Fuel and Power	54– 57	1111.1	134.49	68.9	58.7	63.6	14.1	12.0	13.0

(Table continues on following page.)

Summary Binary Table 5.22 continued.

Category	Line numbers[a]	Expenditure per capita		Purchasing-power parities (rial/dollar)			Quantity per capita (United States = 100)		
		Iran (rials)	United States (dollars)	U.S. weight	Iran weight	Ideal[b]	U.S. weight	Iran weight	Ideal[b]
House Furnishings and Operations	58– 71	1738.8	308.72	45.6	33.7	39.2	16.7	12.4	14.4
Furniture and Appliances	58– 66	878.6	190.86	51.4	33.5	41.5	13.8	9.0	11.1
Supplies and Operation	67– 71	860.2	117.86	36.2	34.0	35.1	21.4	20.1	20.8
Medical Care	72– 78	1530.1	433.93	25.4	23.3	24.3	15.1	13.9	14.5
Transport and Communications	79– 91	2039.5	611.80	89.5	20.4	42.8	16.3	3.7	7.8
Equipment	79– 80	866.0	236.83	166.1	130.4	147.2	2.8	2.2	2.5
Operation Costs	81– 84	455.0	263.91	44.7	30.7	37.1	5.6	3.9	4.7
Purchased Transport	85– 89	638.1	35.18	44.2	8.6	19.5	211.1	41.0	93.1
Communications	90– 91	80.5	75.88	26.8	19.6	23.0	5.4	4.0	4.6
Recreation and Education	92–103	2500.6	655.22	43.3	18.9	28.6	20.2	8.8	13.3
Recreation	92– 98	723.4	310.36	67.8	25.0	41.2	9.3	3.4	5.7
Education	99–103	1777.3	344.86	21.3	17.2	19.2	29.9	24.2	26.9
Other Expenditures	104–109	1972.0	475.51	43.7	23.2	31.9	17.9	9.5	13.0
Personal Care	104–106	599.0	108.46	32.0	17.6	23.7	31.4	17.3	23.3
Miscellaneous Services	107–109	1372.9	367.05	47.2	27.0	35.7	13.9	7.9	10.5
Capital Formation[e]	111–148	25377.2	1215.39	58.8	44.3	51.0	47.2	35.5	40.9
Construction	111–124	7106.0	697.45	28.2	21.4	24.5	47.7	36.1	41.5
Residential	111–112	2406.9	301.71	19.1	17.5	18.3	45.6	41.8	43.6
Nonresidential Bldgs	113–120	2894.0	212.43	25.1	21.3	23.1	64.1	54.3	59.0
Other Construction	121–124	1805.2	183.31	46.9	30.5	37.8	32.3	21.0	26.0
Producers Durables	125–146	4463.5	446.67	106.9	82.4	93.9	12.1	9.3	10.6
Transport Equipment	125–131	1133.4	132.14	149.9	95.9	119.9	8.9	5.7	7.2
Nonelectrical Machinery	132–140	2266.8	174.08	103.5	90.6	96.8	14.4	12.6	13.4
Electrical Machinery	141–144	773.6	100.04	82.0	78.2	80.1	9.9	9.4	9.7
Other Durables	145–146	289.7	40.41	42.5	39.0	40.7	18.4	16.9	17.6
Government	149–153	8522.8	766.26	37.0	26.4	31.2	42.2	30.1	35.6
Compensation	149–152	3677.2	412.20	30.1	22.0	25.7	40.5	29.7	34.7
Commodities	153	4845.6	354.06	45.0	31.0	37.4	44.1	30.4	36.6
Gross Domestic Product	1–153	62775.9	6192.20	48.5	32.5	39.7	31.2	20.9	25.5
Aggregates									
ICP Concepts[f]									
Consumption (CEP)[c,d]	1–110	28875.9	4210.62	47.7	27.8	36.4	24.6	14.4	18.8
Capital Formation (GCF)[e]	111–148	25377.2	1215.39	58.8	44.3	51.0	47.2	35.5	40.9
Government (PFC)	149–153	8522.8	766.26	37.0	26.4	31.2	42.2	30.1	35.6
Gross Domestic Product	1–153	62775.9	6192.20	48.5	32.5	39.7	31.2	20.9	25.5
SNA Concepts[f]									
Consumption (PFCE)	1–110	26930.7	3771.67	50.7	29.4	38.6	24.3	14.1	18.5
Capital Formation (GCF)	111–148	25377.2	1215.39	58.8	44.3	51.0	47.2	35.5	40.9
Government (GFCE)	149–153	10468.0	1202.06	31.5	23.6	27.3	36.9	27.7	31.9
Gross Domestic Product	1–153	62775.9	6189.04	48.6	32.5	39.7	31.2	20.9	25.5

Note: See end of Summary Binary Table 5.30 for notes.
Exchange rate: Rls68.72 = US$1.00.

Summary Binary Table 5.23. Italy and United States: Expenditures per Capita, Purchasing-Power Parities, and Quantity per Capita, 1973

Category	Line numbers[a]	Expenditure per capita Italy (lire)	Expenditure per capita United States (dollars)	Purchasing-power parities (lira/dollar) U.S. weight	Purchasing-power parities (lira/dollar) Italy weight	Purchasing-power parities (lira/dollar) Ideal[b]	Quantity per capita (United States=100) U.S. weight	Quantity per capita (United States=100) Italy weight	Quantity per capita (United States=100) Ideal[b]
Consumption, ICP[c,d]	1–110	1013091.	4210.62	585.	446.	511.	54.0	41.1	47.1
Food, Beverage, and Tobacco	1– 39	364139.	671.52	692.	540.	611.	100.3	78.4	88.7
Food,	1– 33	305315.	536.26	735.	540.	630.	105.5	77.4	90.4
Bread and Cereals	1– 6	38192.	61.64	528.	401.	460.	154.4	117.4	134.6
Meat	7– 12	110599.	149.85	655.	634.	645.	116.3	112.7	114.5
Fish	13– 14	10308.	20.22	719.	698.	708.	73.1	70.9	72.0
Milk, Cheese, and Eggs	15– 17	41741.	79.79	633.	642.	638.	81.4	82.6	82.0
Oils and Fats	18– 20	19924.	23.99	683.	661.	672.	125.5	121.5	123.5
Fruits and Vegetables	21– 26	65305.	120.11	689.	382.	513.	142.3	78.9	106.0
Coffee, Tea, and Cocoa	27– 29	5698.	17.67	1728.	1767.	1747.	18.3	18.7	18.5
Spices, Sweets, and Sugar	30– 33	13549.	62.99	1095.	1123.	1109.	19.1	19.6	19.4
Beverages	34– 37	34620.	72.84	512.	555.	533.	85.7	92.8	89.2
Tobacco	38– 39	24203.	62.42	526.	528.	527.	73.5	73.7	73.6
Clothing and Footwear	40– 51	87838.	299.03	618.	579.	598.	50.8	47.6	49.1
Clothing	40– 47	71264.	250.54	613.	572.	592.	49.8	46.4	48.1
Footwear	48– 51	16574.	48.48	642.	611.	626.	56.0	53.3	54.6
Gross Rent and Fuel	52– 57	131012.	730.16	452.	447.	449.	40.2	39.7	39.9
Gross Rents	52– 53	103642.	595.67	384.	407.	395.	42.8	45.3	44.0
Fuel and Power	54– 57	27370.	134.49	750.	712.	731.	28.6	27.1	27.9
House Furnishings and Operations	58– 71	58042.	308.72	594.	558.	575.	33.7	31.7	32.7
Furniture and Appliances	58– 66	34888.	190.86	651.	567.	607.	32.3	28.1	30.1
Supplies and Operation	67– 71	23154.	117.86	501.	544.	522.	36.1	39.2	37.6
Medical Care	72– 78	75340.	433.93	253.	188.	218.	92.3	68.7	79.7
Transport and Communications	79– 91	106394.	611.80	924.	535.	703.	32.5	18.8	24.7
Equipment	79– 80	30869.	236.83	912.	675.	785.	19.3	14.3	16.6
Operation Costs	81– 84	50191.	263.91	1113.	641.	845.	29.7	17.1	22.5
Purchased Transport	85– 89	15718.	35.18	454.	279.	356.	160.3	98.4	125.6
Communications	90– 91	9616.	75.88	522.	524.	523.	24.2	24.3	24.2
Recreation and Education	92–103	115478.	655.22	504.	359.	426.	49.0	34.9	41.4
Recreation	92– 98	52338.	310.36	662.	503.	577.	33.5	25.5	29.2
Education	99–103	63140.	344.86	362.	291.	324.	63.0	50.5	56.4
Other Expenditures	104–109	92351.	475.51	592.	576.	584.	33.7	32.8	33.2
Personal Care	104–106	14296.	108.46	706.	457.	568.	28.9	18.7	23.2
Miscellaneous Services	107–109	78055.	367.05	558.	605.	581.	35.1	38.1	36.6
Capital Formation[e]	111–148	308852.	1215.39	530.	442.	484.	57.5	48.0	52.5
Construction	111–124	174141.	697.45	349.	367.	358.	68.1	71.5	69.8
Residential	111–112	90985.	301.71	397.	406.	402.	74.2	75.9	75.1
Nonresidential Bldgs	113–120	54017.	212.43	382.	405.	394.	62.7	66.5	64.6
Other Construction	121–124	29139.	183.31	232.	247.	240.	64.3	68.4	66.3
Producers Durables	125–146	134910.	446.67	788.	617.	698.	48.9	38.3	43.3
Transport Equipment	125–131	30887.	132.14	1009.	990.	999.	23.6	23.2	23.4
Nonelectrical Machinery	132–140	53777.	174.08	710.	580.	642.	53.2	43.5	48.1
Electrical Machinery	141–144	38936.	100.04	594.	474.	531.	82.1	65.6	73.4
Other Durables	145–146	11309.	40.41	887.	904.	896.	31.0	31.5	31.2
Government	149–153	149882.	766.26	513.	446.	479.	43.8	38.1	40.9
Compensation	149–152	104717.	412.20	450.	428.	439.	59.3	56.4	57.9
Commodities	153	45165.	354.06	587.	494.	539.	25.8	21.7	23.7
Gross Domestic Product	1–153	1471802.	6192.20	565.	445.	502.	53.4	42.0	47.4

(Table continues on following page.)

Summary Binary Table 5.23 continued.

Category	Line numbers[a]	Expenditure per capita		Purchasing-power parities (lira/dollar)			Quantity per capita (United States=100)		
		Italy (lire)	United States (dollars)	U.S. weight	Italy weight	Ideal[b]	U.S. weight	Italy weight	Ideal[b]
Aggregates									
ICP Concepts[f]									
Consumption (CEP)[c,d]	1–110	1013091.	4210.62	585.	446.	511.	54.0	41.1	47.1
Capital Formation (GCF)[e]	111–148	308852.	1215.39	530.	442.	484.	57.5	48.0	52.5
Government (PFC)	149–153	149882.	766.26	513.	446.	479.	43.8	38.1	40.9
Gross Domestic Product	1–153	1471802.	6192.20	565.	445.	502.	53.4	42.0	47.4
SNA Concepts[f]									
Consumption (PFCE)	1–110	942381.	3771.67	613.	492.	549.	50.8	40.8	45.5
Capital Formation (GCF)	111–148	308852.	1215.39	530.	442.	484.	57.5	48.0	52.5
Government (GFCE)	149–153	220592.	1202.06	454.	318.	380.	57.7	40.5	48.3
Gross Domestic Product	1–153	1471802.	6189.04	565.	445.	502.	53.5	42.1	47.4

Note: See end of Summary Binary Table 5.30 for notes.
Exchange rate: Lit583.0 = US$1.00.

Summary Binary Table 5.24. Japan and United States: Expenditures per Capita, Purchasing-Power Parities, and Quantity per Capita, 1973

Category	Line numbers[a]	Expenditure per capita		Purchasing-power parities (yen/dollar)			Quantity per capita (United States=100)		
		Japan (yen)	United States (dollars)	U.S. weight	Japan weight	Ideal[b]	U.S. weight	Japan weight	Ideal[b]
Consumption, ICP[c,d]	1–110	556310.	4210.62	306.	233.	267.	56.8	43.2	49.5
Food, Beverage, and Tobacco	1– 39	167913.	671.52	406.	339.	371.	73.7	61.6	67.4
Food,	1– 33	135131.	536.26	443.	354.	396.	71.1	56.9	63.6
Bread and Cereals	1– 6	27838.	61.64	282.	379.	327.	119.3	160.2	138.2
Meat	7– 12	18647.	149.85	506.	484.	495.	25.7	24.6	25.1
Fish	13– 14	26621.	20.22	341.	341.	341.	385.7	386.1	385.9
Milk, Cheese, and Eggs	15– 17	10135.	79.79	398.	338.	367.	37.6	31.9	34.6
Oils and Fats	18– 20	2027.	23.99	413.	397.	405.	21.3	20.4	20.9
Fruits and Vegetables	21– 26	31487.	120.11	375.	297.	334.	88.2	70.0	78.6
Coffee, Tea, and Cocoa	27– 29	2433.	17.67	701.	321.	474.	42.9	19.7	29.0
Spices, Sweets, and Sugar	30– 33	15945.	62.99	612.	372.	477.	68.0	41.4	53.0
Beverages	34– 37	26492.	72.84	315.	328.	322.	110.8	115.4	113.1
Tobacco	38– 39	6290.	62.42	194.	194.	194.	52.0	52.0	52.0
Clothing and Footwear	40– 51	53113.	299.03	286.	322.	303.	55.2	62.1	58.6
Clothing	40– 47	49728.	250.54	297.	332.	314.	59.8	66.9	63.2
Footwear	48– 51	3385.	48.48	230.	222.	226.	31.5	30.4	30.9
Gross Rent and Fuel	52– 57	81071.	730.16	344.	303.	323.	36.6	32.3	34.4
Gross Rents	52– 53	66712.	595.67	301.	294.	298.	38.1	37.2	37.6
Fuel and Power	54– 57	14359.	134.49	535.	354.	435.	30.1	19.9	24.5

Summary Binary Table 5.24 continued.

Category	Line numbers[a]	Expenditure per capita Japan (yen)	United States (dollars)	Purchasing-power parities (yen/dollar) U.S. weight	Japan weight	Ideal[b]	Quantity per capita (United States = 100) U.S. weight	Japan weight	Ideal[b]
House Furnishings and Operations	58– 71	48417.	308.72	310.	297.	304.	52.8	50.5	51.7
Furniture and Appliances	58– 66	31755.	190.86	351.	365.	358.	45.6	47.4	46.5
Supplies and Operation	67– 71	16662.	117.86	244.	219.	231.	64.6	57.9	61.1
Medical Care	72– 78	44561.	433.93	99.	86.	92.	119.6	103.7	111.4
Transport and Communications	79– 91	24999.	611.80	431.	222.	309.	18.4	9.5	13.2
Equipment	79– 80	5854.	236.83	413.	354.	382.	7.0	6.0	6.5
Operation Costs	81– 84	6802.	263.91	527.	506.	516.	5.1	4.9	5.0
Purchased Transport	85– 89	6916.	35.18	184.	111.	143.	177.6	106.7	137.7
Communications	90– 91	5427.	75.88	270.	269.	270.	26.6	26.5	26.5
Recreation and Education	92–103	66020.	655.22	247.	218.	232.	46.3	40.8	43.5
Recreation	92– 98	22549.	310.36	300.	321.	310.	22.7	24.2	23.4
Education	99–103	43471.	344.86	199.	186.	192.	67.6	63.5	65.5
Other Expenditures	104–109	66941.	475.51	225.	189.	206.	74.4	62.6	68.3
Personal Care	104–106	8362.	108.46	247.	219.	233.	35.1	31.2	33.1
Miscellaneous Services	107–109	58579.	367.05	218.	186.	201.	86.0	73.1	79.3
Capital Formation[e]	111–148	406660.	1215.39	305.	287.	296.	116.6	109.8	113.2
Construction	111–124	232753.	697.45	292.	276.	284.	120.8	114.2	117.5
Residential	111–112	89705.	301.71	271.	272.	271.	109.3	109.8	109.6
Nonresidential Bldgs	113–120	90473.	212.43	379.	335.	356.	127.1	112.4	119.5
Other Construction	121–124	52576.	183.31	227.	217.	222.	132.5	126.3	129.3
Producers Durables	125–146	140721.	446.67	316.	301.	308.	104.7	99.7	102.2
Transport Equipment	125–131	21913.	132.14	348.	348.	348.	47.7	47.7	47.7
Nonelectrical Machinery	132–140	45811.	174.08	304.	289.	296.	91.2	86.6	88.9
Electrical Machinery	141–144	35941.	100.04	304.	299.	302.	120.0	118.2	119.1
Other Durables	145–146	37056.	40.41	294.	294.	294.	311.9	311.9	311.9
Government	149–153	54477.	766.26	272.	195.	230.	36.5	26.1	30.9
Compensation	149–152	34103.	412.20	196.	165.	180.	50.2	42.3	46.1
Commodities	153	20374.	354.06	362.	280.	318.	20.6	15.9	18.1
Gross Domestic Product	1–153	1017446.	6192.20	301.	249.	274.	66.0	54.5	60.0
Aggregates									
ICP Concepts[f]									
Consumption (CEP)[c,d]	1–110	556310.	4210.62	306.	233.	267.	56.8	43.2	49.5
Capital Formation (GCF)[e]	111–148	406660.	1215.39	305.	287.	296.	116.6	109.8	113.2
Government (PFC)	149–153	54477.	766.26	272.	195.	230.	36.5	26.1	30.9
Gross Domestic Product	1–153	1017446.	6192.20	301.	249.	274.	66.0	54.5	60.0
SNA Concepts[f]									
Consumption (PFCE)	1–110	518839.	3771.67	320.	246.	280.	55.9	43.0	49.1
Capital Formation (GCF)	111–148	406660.	1215.39	305.	287.	296.	116.6	109.8	113.2
Government (GFCE)	149–153	90237.	1202.06	241.	162.	198.	46.3	31.2	38.0
Gross Domestic Product	1–153	1015736.	6189.04	301.	249.	274.	65.9	54.5	59.9

Note: See end of Summary Binary Table 5.30 for notes.
Exchange rate: ¥272.19 = US$1.00.

Summary Binary Table 5.25. Kenya and United States: Expenditures per Capita, Purchasing-Power Parities, and Quantity per Capita, 1973

Category	Line numbers[a]	Expenditure per capita Kenya (shillings)	Expenditure per capita United States (dollars)	Purchasing-power parities (shilling/dollar) U.S. weight	Purchasing-power parities (shilling/dollar) Kenya weight	Purchasing-power parities (shilling/dollar) Ideal[b]	Quantity per capita (United States=100) U.S. weight	Quantity per capita (United States=100) Kenya weight	Quantity per capita (United States=100) Ideal[b]
Consumption, ICP[c,d]	1–110	853.96	4210.62	5.72	2.69	3.92	7.6	3.5	5.2
Food, Beverage, and Tobacco	1– 39	407.25	671.52	5.62	3.13	4.19	19.4	10.8	14.5
Food,	1– 33	370.28	536.26	5.34	2.97	3.98	23.2	12.9	17.3
Bread and Cereals	1– 6	156.78	61.64	3.75	4.17	3.96	60.9	67.8	64.3
Meat	7– 12	34.92	149.85	3.57	2.62	3.06	8.9	6.5	7.6
Fish	13– 14	9.05	20.22	5.95	3.97	4.86	11.3	7.5	9.2
Milk, Cheese, and Eggs	15– 17	43.06	79.79	4.21	3.58	3.88	15.1	12.8	13.9
Oils and Fats	18– 20	14.26	23.99	8.08	6.46	7.22	9.2	7.4	8.2
Fruits and Vegetables	21– 26	86.27	120.11	4.92	1.69	2.88	42.6	14.6	24.9
Coffee, Tea, and Cocoa	27– 29	5.29	17.67	6.51	3.22	4.58	9.3	4.6	6.5
Spices, Sweets, and Sugar	30– 33	20.66	62.99	11.76	4.75	7.47	6.9	2.8	4.4
Beverages	34– 37	26.22	72.84	8.91	8.88	8.90	4.1	4.0	4.0
Tobacco	38– 39	10.75	62.42	4.16	4.22	4.19	4.1	4.1	4.1
Clothing and Footwear	40– 51	37.74	299.03	5.26	4.80	5.03	2.6	2.4	2.5
Clothing	40– 47	28.27	250.54	5.64	5.45	5.54	2.1	2.0	2.0
Footwear	48– 51	9.47	48.48	3.29	3.55	3.41	5.5	5.9	5.7
Gross Rent and Fuel	52– 57	104.77	730.16	8.74	5.16	6.72	2.8	1.6	2.1
Gross Rents	52– 53	90.95	595.67	8.64	6.75	7.64	2.3	1.8	2.0
Fuel and Power	54– 57	13.83	134.49	9.20	2.02	4.31	5.1	1.1	2.4
House Furnishings and Operations	58– 71	54.05	308.72	7.79	2.31	4.24	7.6	2.2	4.1
Furniture and Appliances	58– 66	13.47	190.86	9.88	7.43	8.57	0.9	0.7	0.8
Supplies and Operation	67– 71	40.58	117.86	4.41	1.88	2.88	18.3	7.8	12.0
Medical Care	72– 78	38.94	433.93	1.55	1.22	1.37	7.4	5.8	6.5
Transport and Communications	79– 91	59.36	611.80	6.85	4.09	5.30	2.4	1.4	1.8
Equipment	79– 80	12.55	236.83	7.50	7.38	7.44	0.7	0.7	0.7
Operation Costs	81– 84	7.18	263.91	7.46	3.30	4.97	0.8	0.4	0.5
Purchased Transport	85– 89	37.84	35.18	6.09	3.76	4.79	28.6	17.7	22.5
Communications	90– 91	1.79	75.88	3.04	3.17	3.11	0.7	0.8	0.8
Recreation and Education	92–103	96.07	655.22	4.90	1.42	2.64	10.3	3.0	5.6
Recreation	92– 98	38.35	310.36	7.86	4.03	5.63	3.1	1.6	2.2
Education	99–103	57.72	344.86	2.24	0.99	1.49	16.9	7.5	11.2
Other Expenditures	104–109	55.77	475.51	3.54	2.53	2.99	4.6	3.3	3.9
Personal Care	104–106	7.08	108.46	6.65	6.22	6.43	1.1	1.0	1.0
Miscellaneous Services	107–109	48.69	367.05	2.62	2.33	2.47	5.7	5.1	5.4
Capital Formation[e]	111–148	311.83	1215.39	6.49	5.32	5.88	4.8	4.0	4.4
Construction	111–124	154.82	697.45	3.64	4.11	3.86	5.4	6.1	5.7
Residential	111–112	36.60	301.71	3.18	3.08	3.13	3.9	3.8	3.9
Nonresidential Bldgs	113–120	31.75	212.43	3.34	3.52	3.43	4.2	4.5	4.4
Other Construction	121–124	86.47	183.31	4.73	5.15	4.93	9.2	10.0	9.6
Producers Durables	125–146	136.04	446.67	10.82	10.15	10.48	3.0	2.8	2.9
Transport Equipment	125–131	36.07	132.14	10.38	10.52	10.45	2.6	2.6	2.6
Nonelectrical Machinery	132–140	78.24	174.08	11.12	10.34	10.72	4.3	4.0	4.2
Electrical Machinery	141–144	19.55	100.04	11.55	8.96	10.18	2.2	1.7	1.9
Other Durables	145–146	2.18	40.41	9.12	9.38	9.25	0.6	0.6	0.6
Government	149–153	125.36	766.26	3.68	0.94	1.86	17.3	4.4	8.8
Compensation	149–152	95.26	412.20	1.94	0.77	1.23	29.9	11.9	18.9
Commodities	153	30.10	354.06	5.70	3.13	4.22	2.7	1.5	2.0
Gross Domestic Product	1–153	1291.14	6192.20	5.62	2.53	3.77	8.2	3.7	5.5

Summary Binary Table 5.25 continued.

Category	Line numbers[a]	Expenditure per capita		Purchasing-power parities (shilling/dollar)			Quantity per capita (United States=100)		
		Kenya (shillings)	United States (dollars)	U.S. weight	Kenya weight	Ideal[b]	U.S. weight	Kenya weight	Ideal[b]
Aggregates									
ICP Concepts[f]									
Consumption (CEP)[c,d]	1–110	853.96	4210.62	5.72	2.69	3.92	7.6	3.5	5.2
Capital Formation (GCF)[e]	111–148	311.83	1215.39	6.49	5.32	5.88	4.8	4.0	4.4
Government (PFC)	149–153	125.36	766.26	3.68	0.94	1.86	17.3	4.4	8.8
Gross Domestic Product	1–153	1291.14	6192.20	5.62	2.53	3.77	8.2	3.7	5.5
SNA Concepts[f]									
Consumption (PFCE)	1–110	800.23	3771.67	6.14	3.03	4.31	7.0	3.5	4.9
Capital Formation (GCF)	111–148	311.83	1215.39	6.49	5.32	5.88	4.8	4.0	4.4
Government (GFCE)	149–153	179.09	1202.06	3.08	0.96	1.72	15.5	4.8	8.7
Gross Domestic Product	1–153	1291.14	6189.04	5.61	2.53	3.77	8.2	3.7	5.5

Note: See end of Summary Binary Table 5.30 for notes.
Exchange rate: KSh7.0012 = US$1.00.

Summary Binary Table 5.26. Republic of Korea and United States: Expenditures per Capita, Purchasing-Power Parities, and Quantity per Capita, 1973

Category	Line numbers[a]	Expenditure per capita		Purchasing-power parities (won/dollar)			Quantity per capita (United States=100)		
		Korea Republic of (won)	United States (dollars)	U.S. weight	Korea Republic of weight	Ideal[b]	U.S. weight	Korea Republic of weight	Ideal[b]
Consumption, ICP[c,d]	1–110	101570.	4210.62	304.	160.	220.	15.1	7.9	10.9
Food, Beverage, and Tobacco	1– 39	56766.	671.52	378.	230.	295.	36.8	22.4	28.7
Food,	1– 33	47827.	536.26	378.	217.	286.	41.1	23.6	31.1
Bread and Cereals	1– 6	24797.	61.64	260.	263.	261.	153.2	154.8	154.0
Meat	7– 12	4223.	149.85	269.	263.	266.	10.7	10.5	10.6
Fish	13– 14	3070.	20.22	119.	119.	119.	127.3	127.3	127.3
Milk, Cheese, and Eggs	15– 17	1847.	79.79	377.	321.	348.	7.2	6.1	6.7
Oils and Fats	18– 20	512.	23.99	400.	437.	418.	4.9	5.3	5.1
Fruits and Vegetables	21– 26	7258.	120.11	291.	128.	193.	47.1	20.8	31.3
Coffee, Tea, and Cocoa	27– 29	250.	17.67	964.	975.	970.	1.5	1.5	1.5
Spices, Sweets, and Sugar	30– 33	5870.	62.99	833.	286.	488.	32.6	11.2	19.1
Beverages	34– 37	4789.	72.84	484.	483.	484.	13.6	13.6	13.6
Tobacco	38– 39	4151.	62.42	254.	254.	254.	26.2	26.2	26.2
Clothing and Footwear	40– 51	11244.	299.03	208.	198.	203.	19.0	18.1	18.5
Clothing	40– 47	10418.	250.54	214.	214.	214.	19.4	19.4	19.4
Footwear	48– 51	825.	48.48	174.	102.	133.	16.7	9.8	12.8
Gross Rent and Fuel	52– 57	7464.	730.16	375.	430.	402.	2.4	2.7	2.5
Gross Rents	52– 53	3375.	595.67	333.	334.	334.	1.7	1.7	1.7
Fuel and Power	54– 57	4089.	134.49	560.	564.	562.	5.4	5.4	5.4

(Table continues on following page.)

Summary Binary Table 5.26 continued.

Category	Line numbers	Expenditure per capita		Purchasing-power parities (won/dollar)			Quantity per capita (United States = 100)		
		Korea Republic of (won)	United States (dollars)	U.S. weight	Korea Republic of weight	Ideal[e]	U.S. weight	Korea Republic of weight	Ideal[e]
House Furnishings and Operations	58– 71	3080.	308.72	228.	94.	146.	10.6	4.4	6.8
Furniture and Appliances	58– 66	1819.	190.86	278.	359.	316.	2.7	3.4	3.0
Supplies and Operation	67– 71	1260.	117.86	147.	45.	82.	23.5	7.3	13.1
Medical Care	72– 78	3376.	433.93	93.	58.	74.	13.3	8.4	10.6
Transport and Communications	79– 91	5801.	611.80	631.	100.	251.	9.5	1.5	3.8
Equipment	79– 80	249.	236.83	815.	842.	829.	0.1	0.1	0.1
Operation Costs	81– 84	10.	263.91	700.	318.	472.	0.0	0.0	0.0
Purchased Transport	85– 89	5183.	35.18	119.	101.	110.	145.4	124.3	134.5
Communications	90– 91	358.	75.88	53.	54.	54.	8.7	8.8	8.8
Recreation and Education	92–103	7976.	655.22	135.	78.	102.	15.7	9.0	11.9
Recreation	92– 98	3263.	310.36	181.	151.	165.	7.0	5.8	6.4
Education	99–103	4713.	344.86	93.	58.	73.	23.5	14.8	18.6
Other Expenditures	104–109	7237.	475.51	199.	109.	147.	13.9	7.7	10.3
Personal Care	104–106	3299.	108.46	141.	78.	105.	39.2	21.5	29.0
Miscellaneous Services	107–109	3937.	367.05	216.	166.	189.	6.5	5.0	5.7
Capital Formation[e]	111–148	33149.	1215.39	296.	185.	234.	14.7	9.2	11.7
Construction	111–124	19286.	697.45	139.	142.	140.	19.4	20.0	19.7
Residential	111–112	4467.	301.71	112.	118.	115.	12.5	13.2	12.9
Nonresidential Bldgs	113–120	7507.	212.43	168.	166.	167.	21.2	21.0	21.1
Other Construction	121–124	7312.	183.31	148.	139.	144.	28.7	27.0	27.8
Producers Durables	125–146	15013.	446.67	526.	380.	447.	8.9	6.4	7.5
Transport Equipment	125–131	6044.	132.14	643.	562.	601.	8.1	7.1	7.6
Nonelectrical Machinery	132–140	7185.	174.08	577.	355.	452.	11.6	7.2	9.1
Electrical Machinery	141–144	1301.	100.04	399.	256.	320.	5.1	3.3	4.1
Other Durables	145–146	483.	40.41	237.	140.	182.	8.5	5.0	6.6
Government	149–153	11028.	766.26	174.	81.	119.	17.7	8.3	12.1
Compensation	149–152	6206.	412.20	57.	59.	58.	25.4	26.5	25.9
Commodities	153	4822.	354.06	310.	157.	220.	8.7	4.4	6.2
Gross Domestic Product	1–153	145746.	6192.20	286.	154.	210.	15.3	8.2	11.2
Aggregates									
ICP Concepts[f]									
Consumption (CEP)[c,d]	1–110	101570.	4210.62	304.	160.	220.	15.1	7.9	10.9
Capital Formation (GCF)[e]	111–148	33149.	1215.39	296.	185.	234.	14.7	9.2	11.7
Government (PFC)	149–153	11028.	766.26	174.	81.	119.	17.7	8.3	12.1
Gross Domestic Product	1–153	145746.	6192.20	286.	154.	210.	15.3	8.2	11.2
SNA Concepts[f]									
Consumption (PFCE)	1–110	98374.	3771.67	328.	171.	237.	15.2	8.0	11.0
Capital Formation (GCF)	111–148	33149.	1215.39	296.	185.	234.	14.7	9.2	11.7
Government (GFCE)	149–153	14225.	1202.06	145.	73.	103.	16.3	8.2	11.5
Gross Domestic Product	1–153	145746.	6189.04	286.	154.	210.	15.3	8.2	11.2

Note: See end of Summary Binary Table 5.30 for notes.
Exchange rate: W398.54 = US$1.00.

Summary Binary Table 5.27. Malaysia and United States: Expenditures per Capita, Purchasing-Power Parities, and Quantity per Capita, 1973

Category	Line numbers[a]	Expenditure per capita Malaysia (M. dollars)	Expenditure per capita United States (dollars)	Purchasing-power parities (M. dollar/dollar) U.S. weight	Purchasing-power parities (M. dollar/dollar) Malaysia weight	Purchasing-power parities (M. dollar/dollar) Ideal[b]	Quantity per capita (United States=100) U.S. weight	Quantity per capita (United States=100) Malaysia weight	Quantity per capita (United States=100) Ideal[b]
Consumption, ICP[c,d]	1–110	951.64	4210.62	1.94	1.23	1.54	18.4	11.6	14.6
Food, Beverage, and Tobacco	1– 39	389.78	671.52	2.37	1.75	2.04	33.2	24.5	28.5
Food,	1– 33	324.32	536.26	2.36	1.65	1.98	36.5	25.6	30.6
Bread and Cereals	1– 6	89.47	61.64	2.47	1.76	2.09	82.5	58.7	69.6
Meat	7– 12	57.57	149.85	1.94	2.06	2.00	18.7	19.8	19.2
Fish	13– 14	48.65	20.22	1.26	1.28	1.27	187.5	190.5	189.0
Milk, Cheese, and Eggs	15– 17	30.80	79.79	3.05	2.08	2.51	18.6	12.7	15.4
Oils and Fats	18– 20	13.52	23.99	1.92	1.83	1.88	30.8	29.3	30.0
Fruits and Vegetables	21– 26	43.96	120.11	2.08	1.14	1.54	32.2	17.6	23.8
Coffee, Tea, and Cocoa	27– 29	6.22	17.67	4.00	2.81	3.35	12.6	8.8	10.5
Spices, Sweets, and Sugar	30– 33	34.13	62.99	2.98	2.11	2.51	25.7	18.2	21.6
Beverages	34– 37	22.47	72.84	2.36	2.28	2.32	13.5	13.1	13.3
Tobacco	38– 39	43.00	62.42	2.50	2.51	2.50	27.5	27.6	27.5
Clothing and Footwear	40– 51	47.20	299.03	1.04	1.39	1.20	11.3	15.2	13.1
Clothing	40– 47	41.41	250.54	1.10	1.67	1.36	9.9	15.0	12.2
Footwear	48– 51	5.79	48.48	0.71	0.63	0.67	18.9	16.9	17.9
Gross Rent and Fuel	52– 57	109.43	730.16	1.49	1.18	1.33	12.7	10.0	11.3
Gross Rents	52– 53	88.25	595.67	1.08	1.02	1.05	14.5	13.7	14.1
Fuel and Power	54– 57	21.18	134.49	3.31	3.36	3.33	4.7	4.8	4.7
House Furnishings and Operations	58– 71	53.09	308.72	1.93	1.59	1.75	10.8	8.9	9.8
Furniture and Appliances	58– 66	21.79	190.86	2.10	1.67	1.87	6.8	5.4	6.1
Supplies and Operation	67– 71	31.30	117.86	1.66	1.53	1.59	17.3	16.0	16.7
Medical Care	72– 78	36.94	433.93	0.88	0.43	0.61	19.9	9.7	13.9
Transport and Communications	79– 91	137.88	611.80	3.36	1.50	2.24	15.0	6.7	10.0
Equipment	79– 80	28.96	236.83	5.09	4.51	4.79	2.7	2.4	2.6
Operation Costs	81– 84	53.66	263.91	2.70	1.97	2.31	10.3	7.5	8.8
Purchased Transport	85– 89	48.24	35.18	1.52	0.92	1.18	148.8	90.2	115.9
Communications	90– 91	7.02	75.88	1.11	1.18	1.14	7.8	8.3	8.1
Recreation and Education	92–103	107.71	655.22	1.51	0.67	1.00	24.7	10.9	16.4
Recreation	92– 98	45.75	310.36	2.26	1.23	1.67	11.9	6.5	8.8
Education	99–103	61.96	344.86	0.83	0.50	0.64	36.1	21.6	27.9
Other Expenditures	104–109	69.63	475.51	2.31	1.34	1.76	10.9	6.3	8.3
Personal Care	104–106	28.21	108.46	2.02	1.31	1.63	19.9	12.9	16.0
Miscellaneous Services	107–109	41.42	367.05	2.40	1.37	1.81	8.3	4.7	6.2
Capital Formation[e]	111–148	410.43	1215.39	1.61	1.28	1.44	26.3	21.0	23.5
Construction	111–124	150.72	697.45	0.71	0.72	0.72	30.1	30.3	30.2
Residential	111–112	41.11	301.71	0.66	0.66	0.66	20.8	20.8	20.8
Nonresidential Bldgs	113–120	47.34	212.43	0.60	0.61	0.60	36.8	37.3	37.0
Other Construction	121–124	62.27	183.31	0.94	0.90	0.92	37.7	36.0	36.8
Producers Durables	125–146	128.65	446.67	2.91	2.79	2.85	10.3	9.9	10.1
Transport Equipment	125–131	31.69	132.14	3.48	3.47	3.47	6.9	6.9	6.9
Nonelectrical Machinery	132–140	76.53	174.08	3.03	2.99	3.01	14.7	14.5	14.6
Electrical Machinery	141–144	16.19	100.04	2.33	2.02	2.17	8.0	6.9	7.4
Other Durables	145–146	4.24	40.41	1.89	1.26	1.54	8.3	5.6	6.8
Government	149–153	184.14	766.26	1.33	1.03	1.17	23.3	18.1	20.6
Compensation	149–152	114.82	412.20	0.82	0.92	0.87	30.2	33.8	31.9
Commodities	153	69.32	354.06	1.91	1.28	1.56	15.3	10.3	12.5
Gross Domestic Product	1–153	1546.21	6192.20	1.80	1.21	1.48	20.6	13.9	16.9

(Table continues on following page.)

Summary Binary Table 5.27 continued.

Category	Line numbers[a]	Expenditure per capita		Purchasing-power parities (M. dollar/dollar)			Quantity per capita (United States=100)		
		Malaysia (M. dollars)	United States (dollars)	U.S. weight	Malaysia weight	Ideal[b]	U.S. weight	Malaysia weight	Ideal[b]
Aggregates									
ICP Concepts[f]									
Consumption (CEP)[c,d]	1–110	951.64	4210.62	1.94	1.23	1.54	18.4	11.6	14.6
Capital Formation (GCF)[e]	111–148	410.43	1215.39	1.61	1.28	1.44	26.3	21.0	23.5
Government (PFC)	149–153	184.14	766.26	1.33	1.03	1.17	23.3	18.1	20.6
Gross Domestic Product	1–153	1546.21	6192.20	1.80	1.21	1.48	20.6	13.9	16.9
SNA Concepts[f]									
Consumption (PFCE)	1–110	876.73	3771.67	2.06	1.45	1.73	16.1	11.3	13.5
Capital Formation (GCF)	111–148	410.43	1215.39	1.61	1.28	1.44	26.3	21.0	23.5
Government (GFCE)	149–153	259.04	1202.06	1.19	0.75	0.94	28.9	18.1	22.9
Gross Domestic Product	1–153	1546.21	6189.04	1.80	1.21	1.48	20.6	13.9	16.9

Note: See end of Summary Binary Table 5.30 for notes.
Exchange rate: M$2.4426 = US$1.00.

Summary Binary Table 5.28. Netherlands and United States: Expenditures per Capita, Purchasing-Power Parities, and Quantity per Capita, 1973

Category	Line numbers[a]	Expenditure per capita		Purchasing-power parities (guilder/dollar)			Quantity per capita (United States=100)		
		Netherlands (guilders)	United States (dollars)	U.S. weight	Netherlands weight	Ideal[b]	U.S. weight	Netherlands weight	Ideal[b]
Consumption, ICP[c,d]	1–110	7583.77	4210.62	3.82	2.75	3.24	65.4	47.1	55.5
Food, Beverage, and Tobacco	1– 39	1863.84	671.52	3.39	2.77	3.06	100.3	81.9	90.6
Food,	1– 33	1437.50	536.26	3.56	3.01	3.27	89.1	75.4	82.0
Bread and Cereals	1– 6	180.06	61.64	3.00	2.52	2.75	116.1	97.2	106.3
Meat	7– 12	384.60	149.85	3.55	3.42	3.48	75.0	72.4	73.7
Fish	13– 14	37.20	20.22	3.56	2.84	3.18	64.7	51.7	57.9
Milk, Cheese, and Eggs	15– 17	263.39	79.79	2.61	2.54	2.57	130.1	126.7	128.4
Oils and Fats	18– 20	69.20	23.99	3.41	3.32	3.36	86.8	84.7	85.7
Fruits and Vegetables	21– 26	281.32	120.11	3.19	2.47	2.80	94.9	73.5	83.5
Coffee, Tea, and Cocoa	27– 29	82.59	17.67	5.99	4.95	5.45	94.4	78.0	85.8
Spices, Sweets, and Sugar	30– 33	139.14	62.99	5.40	5.44	5.42	40.6	40.9	40.7
Beverages	34– 37	247.77	72.84	2.34	2.26	2.30	150.4	145.1	147.7
Tobacco	38– 39	178.57	62.42	3.19	2.08	2.58	137.6	89.6	111.1
Clothing and Footwear	40– 51	673.36	299.03	3.14	3.24	3.19	69.6	71.7	70.6
Clothing	40– 47	580.36	250.54	3.12	3.25	3.18	71.3	74.3	72.8
Footwear	48– 51	93.01	48.48	3.24	3.17	3.21	60.5	59.1	59.8
Gross Rent and Fuel	52– 57	909.30	730.16	2.37	2.38	2.37	52.4	52.5	52.4
Gross Rents	52– 53	645.83	595.67	2.21	2.18	2.19	49.8	49.0	49.4
Fuel and Power	54– 57	263.47	134.49	3.08	3.07	3.08	63.7	63.6	63.7

Summary Binary Table 5.28 continued.

Category	Line numbers[a]	Expenditure per capita		Purchasing-power parities (guilder/dollar)			Quantity per capita (United States = 100)		
		Netherlands (guilders)	United States (dollars)	U.S. weight	Netherlands weight	Ideal[b]	U.S. weight	Netherlands weight	Ideal[b]
House Furnishings and Operations	58– 71	756.62	308.72	3.49	3.45	3.47	71.1	70.3	70.7
Furniture and Appliances	58– 66	518.38	190.86	3.78	3.72	3.75	73.0	71.9	72.4
Supplies and Operation	67– 71	238.24	117.86	3.02	2.97	2.99	68.0	67.0	67.5
Medical Care	72– 78	690.48	433.93	2.21	1.63	1.90	97.8	72.1	83.9
Transport and Communications	79– 91	680.73	611.80	8.23	3.45	5.33	32.3	13.5	20.9
Equipment	79– 80	209.08	236.83	12.85	4.91	7.94	18.0	6.9	11.1
Operation Costs	81– 84	288.69	263.91	5.99	3.62	4.66	30.2	18.3	23.5
Purchased Transport	85– 89	92.19	35.18	6.37	2.43	3.93	107.9	41.1	66.6
Communications	90– 91	90.77	75.88	2.46	2.44	2.45	48.9	48.7	48.8
Recreation and Education	92–103	1282.66	655.22	3.87	3.43	3.64	57.1	50.5	53.7
Recreation	92– 98	547.62	310.36	3.59	2.94	3.25	59.9	49.2	54.3
Education	99–103	735.04	344.86	4.13	3.90	4.01	54.6	51.6	53.1
Other Expenditures	104–109	716.44	475.51	3.08	2.66	2.86	56.7	48.9	52.6
Personal Care	104–106	86.24	108.46	3.37	2.97	3.16	26.8	23.6	25.1
Miscellaneous Services	107–109	630.21	367.05	3.00	2.62	2.80	65.5	57.3	61.3
Capital Formation[e]	111–148	3402.75	1215.39	3.38	2.55	2.94	109.6	82.9	95.3
Construction	111–124	1676.64	697.45	2.20	1.94	2.07	123.7	109.5	116.4
Residential	111–112	789.43	301.71	2.43	1.90	2.15	137.7	107.5	121.6
Nonresidential Bldgs	113–120	562.28	212.43	2.51	2.51	2.51	105.5	105.5	105.5
Other Construction	121–124	324.93	183.31	1.44	1.45	1.45	121.9	123.0	122.4
Producers Durables	125–146	1203.79	446.67	5.11	4.19	4.63	64.3	52.8	58.2
Transport Equipment	125–131	363.76	132.14	6.24	6.10	6.17	45.1	44.1	44.6
Nonelectrical Machinery	132–140	530.51	174.08	4.17	3.75	3.95	81.2	73.1	77.1
Electrical Machinery	141–144	279.32	100.04	4.57	3.41	3.94	82.0	61.2	70.8
Other Durables	145–146	30.21	40.41	6.83	7.11	6.97	10.5	11.0	10.7
Government	149–153	1318.38	766.26	3.41	2.94	3.17	58.5	50.4	54.3
Compensation	149–152	959.00	412.20	3.13	2.94	3.03	79.2	74.3	76.7
Commodities	153	359.37	354.06	3.74	2.95	3.32	34.4	27.1	30.5
Gross Domestic Product	1–153	12304.83	6192.20	3.68	2.71	3.16	73.2	53.9	62.8
Aggregates									
ICP Concepts[f]									
Consumption (CEP)[c,d]	1–110	7583.77	4210.62	3.82	2.75	3.24	65.4	47.1	55.5
Capital Formation (GCF)[e]	111–148	3402.75	1215.39	3.38	2.55	2.94	109.6	82.9	95.3
Government (PFC)	149–153	1318.38	766.26	3.41	2.94	3.17	58.5	50.4	54.3
Gross Domestic Product	1–153	12304.83	6192.20	3.68	2.71	3.16	73.2	53.9	62.8
SNA Concepts[f]									
Consumption (PFCE)	1–110	6834.90	3771.67	3.85	2.71	3.23	66.9	47.0	56.1
Capital Formation (GCF)	111–148	3402.75	1215.39	3.38	2.55	2.94	109.6	82.9	95.3
Government (GFCE)	149–153	2067.26	1202.06	3.47	3.04	3.25	56.5	49.5	52.9
Gross Domestic Product	1–153	12304.83	6189.04	3.68	2.71	3.16	73.2	54.0	62.9

Note: See end of Summary Binary Table 5.30 for notes.

Exchange rate: f2.7956 = US$1.00.

Summary Binary Table 5.29. Philippines and United States: Expenditures per Capita, Purchasing-Power Parities, and Quantity per Capita, 1973

Category	Line numbers[a]	Expenditure per capita		Purchasing-power parities (peso/dollar)			Quantity per capita (United States=100)		
		Philippines (pesos)	United States (dollars)	U.S. weight	Philippines weight	Ideal[b]	U.S. weight	Philippines weight	Ideal[b]
Consumption, ICP[c,d]	1–110	1255.36	4210.62	3.87	1.83	2.66	16.3	7.7	11.2
Food, Beverage, and Tobacco	1– 39	741.64	671.52	4.28	3.65	3.95	30.3	25.8	28.0
Food,	1– 33	667.70	536.26	4.67	3.96	4.30	31.4	26.7	29.0
Bread and Cereals	1– 6	308.48	61.64	4.86	4.93	4.90	101.6	102.9	102.2
Meat	7– 12	108.84	149.85	3.03	2.68	2.85	27.1	24.0	25.5
Fish	13– 14	115.51	20.22	3.21	3.06	3.13	186.9	177.8	182.3
Milk, Cheese, and Eggs	15– 17	32.05	79.79	5.45	5.77	5.61	7.0	7.4	7.2
Oils and Fats	18– 20	13.35	23.99	6.85	6.70	6.77	8.3	8.1	8.2
Fruits and Vegetables	21– 26	14.69	120.11	4.52	2.38	3.28	5.1	2.7	3.7
Coffee, Tea, and Cocoa	27– 29	13.35	17.67	8.27	7.92	8.09	9.5	9.1	9.3
Spices, Sweets, and Sugar	30– 33	61.43	62.99	6.29	5.08	5.65	19.2	15.5	17.2
Beverages	34– 37	44.41	72.84	2.58	1.79	2.15	34.0	23.7	28.4
Tobacco	38– 39	29.53	62.42	2.94	2.95	2.95	16.0	16.1	16.0
Clothing and Footwear	40– 51	80.93	299.03	1.90	2.91	2.35	9.3	14.3	11.5
Clothing	40– 47	70.41	250.54	1.94	3.26	2.51	8.6	14.5	11.2
Footwear	48– 51	10.52	48.48	1.71	1.69	1.70	12.8	12.7	12.8
Gross Rent and Fuel	52– 57	115.45	730.16	2.35	1.17	1.66	13.5	6.7	9.5
Gross Rents	52– 53	80.28	595.67	1.51	0.86	1.14	15.6	8.9	11.8
Fuel and Power	54– 57	35.17	134.49	6.09	6.21	6.15	4.2	4.3	4.3
House Furnishings and Operations	58– 71	77.59	308.72	4.21	1.76	2.72	14.3	6.0	9.2
Furniture and Appliances	58– 66	40.78	190.86	4.74	3.63	4.15	5.9	4.5	5.2
Supplies and Operation	67– 71	36.81	117.86	3.36	1.12	1.94	27.9	9.3	16.1
Medical Care	72– 78	38.07	433.93	1.88	1.15	1.47	7.6	4.7	6.0
Transport and Communications	79– 91	24.47	611.80	9.56	1.08	3.21	3.7	0.4	1.2
Equipment	79– 80	2.89	236.83	18.78	13.41	15.87	0.1	0.1	0.1
Operation Costs	81– 84	3.35	263.91	4.49	4.68	4.59	0.3	0.3	0.3
Purchased Transport	85– 89	17.07	35.18	1.95	0.80	1.25	60.3	24.9	38.7
Communications	90– 91	1.16	75.88	1.99	2.10	2.04	0.7	0.8	0.8
Recreation and Education	92–103	90.63	655.22	2.41	0.50	1.09	27.9	5.7	12.7
Recreation	92– 98	15.92	310.36	3.95	1.67	2.57	3.1	1.3	2.0
Education	99–103	74.70	344.86	1.03	0.43	0.66	50.3	21.1	32.6
Other Expenditures	104–109	86.60	475.51	2.99	1.18	1.88	15.4	6.1	9.7
Personal Care	104–106	28.36	108.46	2.58	1.36	1.87	19.3	10.1	14.0
Miscellaneous Services	107–109	58.24	367.05	3.11	1.11	1.86	14.3	5.1	8.5
Capital Formation[e]	111–148	399.90	1215.39	4.99	3.50	4.18	9.4	6.6	7.9
Construction	111–124	110.87	697.45	2.56	1.60	2.02	10.0	6.2	7.9
Residential	111–112	34.86	301.71	1.96	1.93	1.95	6.0	5.9	5.9
Nonresidential Bldgs	113–120	34.47	212.43	2.84	2.65	2.74	6.1	5.7	5.9
Other Construction	121–124	41.54	183.31	3.21	1.08	1.86	20.9	7.1	12.2
Producers Durables	125–146	203.35	446.67	8.80	8.26	8.52	5.5	5.2	5.3
Transport Equipment	125–131	54.59	132.14	10.68	10.23	10.45	4.0	3.9	4.0
Nonelectrical Machinery	132–140	101.80	174.08	9.41	8.88	9.14	6.6	6.2	6.4
Electrical Machinery	141–144	31.36	100.04	7.00	6.60	6.79	4.8	4.5	4.6
Other Durables	145–146	15.60	40.41	4.48	5.07	4.77	7.6	8.6	8.1
Government	149–153	95.40	766.26	1.87	0.73	1.17	17.1	6.7	10.7
Compensation	149–152	42.39	412.20	0.51	0.51	0.51	20.2	20.3	20.3
Commodities	153	53.01	354.06	3.45	1.11	1.96	13.5	4.3	7.7
Gross Domestic Product	1–153	1750.66	6192.20	3.84	1.88	2.69	15.0	7.4	10.5

Summary Binary Table 5.29 continued.

Category	Line numbers[a]	Expenditure per capita		Purchasing-power parities (peso/dollar)			Quantity per capita (United States = 100)		
		Philippines (pesos)	United States (dollars)	U.S. weight	Philippines weight	Ideal[b]	U.S. weight	Philippines weight	Ideal[b]
Aggregates									
ICP Concepts[f]									
Consumption (CEP)[c,d]	1–110	1255.36	4210.62	3.87	1.83	2.66	16.3	7.7	11.2
Capital Formation (GCF)[e]	111–148	399.90	1215.39	4.99	3.50	4.18	9.4	6.6	7.9
Government (PFC)	149–153	95.40	766.26	1.87	0.73	1.17	17.1	6.7	10.7
Gross Domestic Product	1–153	1750.66	6192.20	3.84	1.88	2.69	15.0	7.4	10.5
SNA Concepts[f]									
Consumption (PFCE)	1–110	1204.36	3771.67	4.16	2.21	3.03	14.5	7.7	10.5
Capital Formation (GCF)	111–148	399.90	1215.39	4.99	3.50	4.18	9.4	6.6	7.9
Government (GFCE)	149–153	146.40	1202.06	1.69	0.54	0.95	22.6	7.2	12.8
Gross Domestic Product	1–153	1750.66	6189.04	3.84	1.88	2.69	15.0	7.4	10.5

Note: See end of Summary Binary Table 5.30 for notes.
Exchange rate: P6.7629 = US$1.00.

Summary Binary Table 5.30. United Kingdom and United States: Expenditures per Capita, Purchasing-Power Parities, and Quantity per Capita, 1973

Category	Line numbers[a]	Expenditure per capita		Purchasing-power parities (pound/dollar)			Quantity per capita (United States = 100)		
		United Kingdom (pounds)	United States (dollars)	U.S. weight	United Kingdom weight	Ideal[b]	U.S. weight	United Kingdom weight	Ideal[b]
Consumption, ICP[c,d]	1–110	905.541	4210.62	0.391	0.313	0.350	68.6	55.0	61.4
Food, Beverage, and Tobacco	1– 39	246.430	671.52	0.412	0.394	0.403	93.2	89.1	91.1
Food,	1– 33	146.626	536.26	0.357	0.321	0.338	85.1	76.7	80.8
Bread and Cereals	1– 6	19.404	61.64	0.278	0.262	0.270	120.3	113.1	116.6
Meat	7– 12	45.876	149.85	0.340	0.320	0.330	95.6	90.0	92.8
Fish	13– 14	5.516	20.22	0.503	0.492	0.498	55.4	54.3	54.8
Milk, Cheese, and Eggs	15– 17	22.885	79.79	0.337	0.349	0.343	82.2	85.1	83.6
Oils and Fats	18– 20	5.552	23.99	0.403	0.298	0.346	77.7	57.5	66.8
Fruits and Vegetables	21– 26	26.330	120.11	0.359	0.301	0.329	72.9	61.0	66.7
Coffee, Tea, and Cocoa	27– 29	4.248	17.67	0.350	0.216	0.275	111.4	68.7	87.5
Spices, Sweets, and Sugar	30– 33	16.815	62.99	0.430	0.460	0.445	58.0	62.1	60.0
Beverages	34– 37	65.084	72.84	0.582	0.549	0.565	162.7	153.5	158.1
Tobacco	38– 39	34.720	62.42	0.689	0.689	0.689	80.7	80.7	80.7
Clothing and Footwear	40– 51	69.297	299.03	0.367	0.349	0.358	66.3	63.2	64.7
Clothing	40– 47	57.354	250.54	0.390	0.385	0.387	59.4	58.8	59.1
Footwear	48– 51	11.942	48.48	0.249	0.242	0.245	101.8	99.0	100.4
Gross Rent and Fuel	52– 57	154.820	730.16	0.392	0.377	0.384	56.2	54.1	55.2
Gross Rents	52– 53	120.939	595.67	0.372	0.376	0.374	54.1	54.6	54.3
Fuel and Power	54– 57	33.881	134.49	0.479	0.383	0.428	65.7	52.6	58.8

(Table continues on following page.)

Summary Binary Table 5.30 continued.

Category	Line numbers[a]	Expenditure per capita		Purchasing-power parities (pound/dollar)			Quantity per capita (United States=100)		
		United Kingdom (pounds)	United States (dollars)	U.S. weight	United Kingdom weight	Ideal[b]	U.S. weight	United Kingdom weight	Ideal[b]
House Furnishings and Operations	58– 71	60.907	308.72	0.442	0.385	0.412	51.3	44.6	47.9
Furniture and Appliances	58– 66	37.879	190.86	0.491	0.431	0.460	46.0	40.5	43.1
Supplies and Operation	67– 71	23.027	117.86	0.363	0.326	0.344	59.9	53.8	56.7
Medical Care	72– 78	54.284	433.93	0.185	0.152	0.168	82.4	67.5	74.6
Transport and Communications	79– 91	111.192	611.80	0.585	0.361	0.460	50.4	31.1	39.6
Equipment	79– 80	36.558	236.83	0.800	0.478	0.618	32.3	19.3	25.0
Operation Costs	81– 84	38.486	263.91	0.514	0.386	0.445	37.8	28.4	32.7
Purchased Transport	85– 89	25.652	35.18	0.457	0.294	0.366	248.2	159.7	199.1
Communications	90– 91	10.496	75.88	0.222	0.235	0.229	58.7	62.3	60.5
Recreation and Education	92–103	132.720	655.22	0.342	0.240	0.286	84.3	59.3	70.7
Recreation	92– 98	65.512	310.36	0.397	0.248	0.314	85.1	53.1	67.2
Education	99–103	67.208	344.86	0.292	0.233	0.261	83.7	66.8	74.8
Other Expenditures	104–109	75.866	475.51	0.349	0.272	0.308	58.7	45.7	51.8
Personal Care	104–106	12.031	108.46	0.301	0.208	0.250	53.3	36.8	44.3
Miscellaneous Services	107–109	63.834	367.05	0.364	0.288	0.324	60.3	47.8	53.7
Capital Formation[e]	111–148	234.630	1215.39	0.374	0.340	0.357	56.7	51.6	54.1
Construction	111–124	118.922	697.45	0.281	0.287	0.284	59.4	60.6	60.0
Residential	111–112	48.376	301.71	0.240	0.234	0.237	68.5	66.9	67.7
Nonresidential Bldgs	113–120	51.196	212.43	0.358	0.362	0.360	66.6	67.4	67.0
Other Construction	121–124	19.350	183.31	0.262	0.292	0.277	36.1	40.3	38.2
Producers Durables	125–146	128.508	446.67	0.507	0.423	0.463	68.0	56.7	62.1
Transport Equipment	125–131	37.772	132.14	0.771	0.742	0.756	38.5	37.1	37.8
Nonelectrical Machinery	132–140	49.875	174.08	0.413	0.390	0.401	73.4	69.5	71.4
Electrical Machinery	141–144	21.367	100.04	0.411	0.371	0.390	57.6	51.9	54.7
Other Durables	145–146	19.493	40.41	0.290	0.290	0.290	166.1	166.1	166.1
Government	149–153	138.451	766.26	0.311	0.259	0.284	69.7	58.2	63.7
Compensation	149–152	79.240	412.20	0.236	0.206	0.220	93.4	81.3	87.1
Commodities	153	59.211	354.06	0.397	0.385	0.391	43.5	42.2	42.8
Gross Domestic Product	1–153	1278.617	6192.20	0.378	0.311	0.343	66.4	54.7	60.3
Aggregates									
ICP Concepts[f]									
Consumption (CEP)[c,d]	1–110	905.541	4210.62	0.391	0.313	0.350	68.6	55.0	61.4
Capital Formation (GCF)[e]	111–148	234.630	1215.39	0.374	0.340	0.357	56.7	51.6	54.1
Government (PFC)	149–153	138.451	766.26	0.31!	0.259	0.284	69.7	58.2	63.7
Gross Domestic Product	1–153	1278.617	6192.20	0.378	0.311	0.343	66.4	54.7	60.3
SNA Concepts[f]									
Consumption (PFCE)	1–110	789.817	3771.67	0.408	0.350	0.378	59.8	51.3	55.4
Capital Formation (GCF)	111–148	234.630	1215.39	0.374	0.340	0.357	56.7	51.6	54.1
Government (GFCE)	149–153	245.983	1202.06	0.286	0.215	0.248	95.2	71.5	82.5
Gross Domestic Product	1–153	1270.424	6189.04	0.378	0.311	0.343	66.1	54.3	59.9

Exchange rate: £0.4078 = US$1.00.

a. Line numbers refer to Appendix Tables 4.1–4.5 and show the detailed categories included in each aggregation.

b. The ideal, or Fisher, index is the geometric mean of the indexes with weights of the United States and of the country compared with the United States.

c. Expenditures for lines 1 through 110 (Consumption, *ICP*) include both household and government expenditures. The latter are shown separately in Table 2.1. Consumption, *SNA*, excludes these government expenditures.

d. The consumption aggregate (lines 1–110) includes net expenditure of residents abroad (line 110), not shown separately in these summary binary tables. See Appendix Table 5.1 for this item.

e. The capital formation aggregate (lines 111–148) includes increase in stocks (line 147) and net exports (line 148), not shown separately in these summary binary tables. See Appendix Table 5.1 for these items.

f. Letters in parentheses are: *CEP*, consumption expenditures of the population; *GCF*, gross capital formation; *PFC*, public final consumption expenditure; *PFCE*, private final consumption expenditure; *GFCE*, government final consumption expenditure. See Glossary for definitions.

**Table 5.31. Exchange-Rate Conversions, Binary and Multilateral Indexes of GDP
per Capita, 1970 and 1973**

(United States=100)

Country	Ex-change-rate-con-verted index (1)	Binary indexes — Own weights (2)	Binary indexes — U.S. weights (3)	Binary indexes — Ideal index (4)= $\sqrt{(2)\times(3)}$	Multi-lateral index (5)	Exchange-rate-deviation index with respect to — Ideal index (6)= (4)÷(1)	Exchange-rate-deviation index with respect to — Multi-lateral index (7)= (5)÷(1)	Binary index spread (8)= (3)÷(2)	Binary/multilateral spread — Own weights (9)= (2)÷(5)	Binary/multilateral spread — U.S. weights (10)= (3)÷(5)	Binary/multilateral spread — Ideal index (11)= (4)÷(5)
				1970							
Kenya	3.0	4.0	8.2	5.7	6.3	1.90	2.10	2.05	0.63	1.30	0.90
India	2.1	4.2	8.2	5.9	6.9	2.81	3.29	1.95	0.61	1.19	0.86
Philippines	3.9	6.9	14.2	9.9	12.0	2.54	3.08	2.06	0.58	1.18	0.82
Korea, Republic of	5.4	6.7	13.6	9.6	12.1	1.78	2.24	2.03	0.55	1.12	0.79
Colombia	7.2	11.8	22.7	16.3	18.1	2.26	2.51	1.92	0.65	1.25	0.90
Malaysia	8.1	13.9	20.6	16.9	19.1	2.09	2.36	1.48	0.73	1.08	0.88
Iran	8.4	14.0	21.9	17.5	20.3	2.08	2.42	1.56	0.69	1.08	0.86
Hungary	21.6	33.5	49.1	40.6	42.7	1.88	1.98	1.47	0.78	1.15	0.95
Italy	36.0	44.3	55.5	49.6	49.2	1.38	1.37	1.25	0.90	1.13	1.01
Japan	39.8	51.1	61.9	56.2	59.2	1.41	1.49	1.21	0.86	1.05	0.95
United Kingdom	45.7	57.3	68.8	62.8	63.5	1.37	1.39	1.20	0.90	1.08	0.99
Netherlands	50.8	57.1	74.8	65.4	68.7	1.29	1.35	1.31	0.83	1.09	0.95
Belgium	55.1	58.4	76.5	66.9	72.0	1.21	1.31	1.31	0.81	1.06	0.93
France	58.2	66.2	77.9	71.8	73.2	1.23	1.26	1.18	0.90	1.06	0.98
Germany, F.R.	64.1	68.0	80.8	74.1	78.2	1.16	1.22	1.19	0.87	1.03	0.95
				1973							
Kenya	3.0	3.7	8.2	5.5	6.1	1.83	2.03	2.22	0.61	1.34	0.90
India	2.1	3.8	7.9	5.5	6.4	2.62	3.05	2.08	0.59	1.23	0.86
Philippines	4.2	7.4	15.0	10.5	12.2	2.50	2.90	2.03	0.61	1.23	0.86
Korea, Republic of	5.9	8.2	15.3	11.2	14.6	1.90	2.47	1.87	0.56	1.05	0.77
Colombia	7.1	11.9	26.1	17.6	17.9	2.48	2.52	2.19	0.66	1.46	0.98
Malaysia	10.2	13.9	20.6	16.9	19.1	1.66	1.87	1.48	0.73	1.08	0.88
Iran	14.8	20.9	31.2	25.5	29.2	1.72	1.97	1.49	0.72	1.07	0.87
Hungary	26.2	36.0	51.7	43.1	45.1	1.65	1.72	1.44	0.80	1.15	0.96
Italy	40.8	42.0	53.4	47.4	47.0	1.16	1.15	1.27	0.89	1.14	1.01
Japan	60.4	54.5	66.0	60.0	64.0	0.99	1.06	1.21	0.85	1.03	0.94
United Kingdom	50.6	54.7	66.4	60.3	60.6	1.19	1.20	1.21	0.90	1.10	1.00
Netherlands	71.1	53.9	73.2	62.8	68.4	0.88	0.96	1.36	0.79	1.07	0.92
Belgium	74.6	57.6	80.0	67.9	75.3	0.91	1.01	1.39	0.77	1.06	0.90
France	77.2	68.0	80.5	74.0	76.1	0.96	0.99	1.18	0.89	1.06	0.97
Germany, F.R.	89.4	65.0	79.8	72.0	77.4	0.81	0.87	1.23	0.84	1.03	0.93

Consequently, when a country's quantities are valued at its own prices the aggregate produced by such a valuation will be smaller than when the quantities are valued at the prices prevailing in almost any other situation. Any extraneous price structure is apt to contain some relatively high prices for goods that are consumed in large quantities because own prices are low for them.

As was pointed out in Chapter 4, low-income countries tend to have low prices for service categories (for example, education or government employees) and to consume relatively large quantities of them. When U.S. prices, which are high for these kinds of goods, are used to value the quantities, the result is to push up the aggregate value of a low-income country's GDP substantially. The ideal index, simply a compromise between the own-weighted and the U.S.-weighted indexes, naturally produces results that are intermediate between its two component indexes.

The higher a country's per capita income, the closer will its price structure be to that of other high-income countries [5]—closer, in the present context, both to the U.S. price structure and to the average international price structure.[6] This affects the relationship between own-weighted and U.S.-weighted binary indexes and between each of these and the multilateral indexes.

The impact on the first of these relationships—on what may be called the "binary index spread" (column 8)—is to diminish the difference as per capita income rises. Thus, for the lowest-income countries (Kenya, India, the Philippines, the Republic of Korea, and Colombia) the U.S.-weighted indexes are twice the own-weighted indexes, whereas for countries with incomes closer to the United States (France and the Federal Republic of Germany) they are only about 20 percent higher.

When a country's price structure is very different from the international price structure, a much lower measure of its real income is produced when its own prices are the basis for the valuation of quantities than when international prices are used. Thus, the own-weighted indexes for the four lowest-income countries in both years are only about 60 percent of the multilateral indexes, whereas for the high-income countries they tend to be in the 80 to 90 percent range (column 9). The ratio of the U.S.-weighted binary indexes to the multilateral indexes (column 10) moves in the opposite direction (from high to low) across the countries arrayed in order of ascending per capita income. For the low-income countries, the U.S. price structure, which is more different from the local price structure than the international price structure, produces higher quantity indexes.

Even if the relationships among the alternative indexes (in columns 2 to 5) have been explained, the question of choice among them remains to be considered. The own-weighted and U.S.-weighted results provide extremes within which both the Fisher and the multilateral indexes fall in every instance in the table. The Fisher index is attractive as a compromise solution; it has little else to recommend it, even though it is often favored for this pragmatic reason.

Although the multilateral indexes also tend to yield results that are intermediate between the two primary binary indexes, they are usually above the average produced by the Fisher indexes. The relatively high indexes yielded by the multilateral method—especially for the low-income countries—may cause doubt. Is it not unrealistic to allow high international prices for services, for example, to drive up the aggregate product of the low-income countries? Does this not exaggerate their real product?

The answer is that the low-income countries do in fact absorb relatively (for their per capita income levels) large quantities of these goods that are high in price in the aggregate transactions of the world at large. The use of average international prices appears to be the most neutral way to place common values on these and other goods consumed in all the countries. Without some technique like this, comparisons that are transitive across countries and additive across categories could not be made.

It would, of course, be more comforting to find that the different index number methods yielded similar results. Although this cannot be claimed, it is usually true that the differences between the Fisher and the multilateral indexes are small relative to the differences between either one and the ex-

5. See the similarity indexes in Chapter 6.
6. The price structures of high-income countries are more similar to the international price structure because the latter is an average in which weights depend upon aggregate incomes. See Table 3.1.

change-rate–converted estimate of GDP per capita. Even in the case of the
largest Fisher–multilateral spread (column 11)—for the Republic of Korea
in 1973—the exchange-rate–derived index is 5.9, which is much farther off
from either the Fisher 11.2 or the multilateral 14.6 than the latter two are
from each other.

In Table 5.32, the comparisons of the various binary and multilateral
quantity indexes are extended to the major components of GDP—consumption, capital formation, and government. The relationships among the indexes
described above for GDP are found generally to exist for consumption also:
first, the lowest indexes are the own-weighted binaries and the highest ones
are the U.S.-weighted binaries; second, the multilateral indexes are usually
between the U.S.-weighted binaries and the Fisher indexes. For capital
formation the first of these generalizations is still clearly true but there are a

Comparisons for Subaggregates

**Table 5.32. Binary and Multilateral Indexes of per Capita Quantities of Consumption,
Capital Formation, and Government, 1970 and 1973**

(United States=100)

| | Consumption | | | | Capital formation | | | | Government | | | |
| | Binary indexes | | | Multi-lateral index | Binary indexes | | | Multi-lateral index | Binary indexes | | | Multi-lateral index |
Country	Own weights (1)	U.S. weights (2)	Ideal index (3)	(4)	Own weights (5)	U.S. weights (6)	Ideal index (7)	(8)	Own weights (9)	U.S. weights (10)	Ideal index (11)	(12)
					1970							
Kenya	4.0	7.8	5.6	6.4	4.3	4.8	4.6	4.7	3.6	14.4	7.2	8.6
India	4.5	7.9	6.0	7.2	3.5	6.4	4.8	5.3	3.7	11.9	6.7	8.2
Philippines	7.5	15.9	11.0	13.6	6.1	8.4	7.1	7.7	4.2	13.0	7.4	10.1
Korea, Republic of	6.9	13.6	9.7	12.7	6.2	11.4	8.4	9.1	6.7	16.0	10.4	13.4
Colombia	12.7	23.7	17.4	18.9	10.9	23.1	15.8	18.3	7.5	17.3	11.4	13.4
Malaysia	12.5	19.6	15.6	18.5	20.0	25.7	22.7	22.8	14.2	18.6	16.2	16.8
Iran	13.0	20.9	16.5	19.8	16.3	25.0	20.2	23.5	14.9	22.8	18.5	17.6
Hungary	29.6	49.5	38.3	41.3	47.7	60.2	53.6	54.6	27.9	33.2	30.4	30.5
Italy	42.0	54.8	48.0	47.9	65.1	73.1	69.0	66.2	30.8	36.1	33.4	28.6
Japan	40.1	54.1	46.6	49.3	108.4	114.5	111.4	113.7	21.9	32.5	26.7	24.8
United Kingdom	55.4	68.5	61.6	62.5	68.5	72.9	70.7	73.0	53.2	64.6	58.6	52.9
Netherlands	51.8	68.6	59.6	62.9	87.0	115.2	100.1	101.2	46.1	53.7	49.7	47.6
Belgium	54.3	74.6	63.6	69.8	85.8	104.8	94.8	98.8	40.7	49.9	45.0	40.3
France	59.0	71.9	65.1	65.9	110.3	119.5	114.8	111.8	49.5	54.2	51.8	50.5
Germany, F.R.	58.1	69.1	63.4	64.7	130.0	148.8	139.1	144.5	45.2	50.7	47.9	45.1
					1973							
Kenya	3.5	7.6	5.2	6.1	4.0	4.8	4.4	4.4	4.4	17.3	8.8	9.8
India	4.0	7.0	5.3	6.4	3.0	5.6	4.1	4.3	5.1	16.0	9.0	10.3
Philippines	7.7	16.3	11.2	13.5	6.6	9.4	7.9	8.2	6.7	17.1	10.7	11.7
Korea, Republic of	7.9	15.1	10.9	14.7	9.2	14.7	11.7	13.7	8.3	17.7	12.1	15.8
Colombia	12.5	26.3	18.1	18.5	9.8	21.9	14.7	17.5	14.1	31.6	21.2	14.3
Malaysia	11.6	18.4	14.6	17.5	21.0	26.3	23.5	23.3	18.1	23.3	20.6	20.5
Iran	14.4	24.6	18.8	23.1	35.5	47.2	40.9	46.7	30.1	42.2	35.6	32.7
Hungary	30.4	50.5	39.1	42.0	51.4	62.7	56.7	59.0	36.0	41.4	38.6	36.6
Italy	41.1	54.0	47.1	47.4	48.0	57.5	52.5	51.5	38.1	43.8	40.9	35.4
Japan	43.2	56.8	49.5	53.5	109.8	116.6	113.2	112.7	26.1	36.5	30.9	30.7
United Kingdom	55.0	68.6	61.4	62.2	51.6	56.7	54.1	56.3	58.2	69.7	63.7	59.0
Netherlands	47.1	65.4	55.5	60.3	82.9	109.6	95.3	101.2	50.4	58.5	54.3	52.2
Belgium	54.1	79.6	65.6	74.8	75.9	94.8	84.9	90.2	47.9	58.5	53.0	47.2
France	60.6	73.7	66.9	67.9	105.2	116.2	110.6	110.0	56.1	61.3	58.7	58.6
Germany, F.R.	56.5	68.1	62.0	63.9	110.6	134.5	122.0	130.0	50.8	57.0	53.8	55.1

few exceptions to the second, and for government the exceptions to both generalizations are more numerous.

Per capita quantity indexes for selected summary categories are presented in Table 5.33 for the same groups of countries, classified by real per capita GDP, as used in the analysis of the multilateral results in Chapter 4. Here only averages of the Fisher indexes are presented. (The own-weighted and U.S.-weighted indexes can be found in the summary binary tables.) The pattern of these results, whether assessed by scanning the rows or the columns, is very similar to that of the multilateral results in Table 4.12. Even the individual indexes tend to be more similar than was the case for the more aggregative indexes that were considered in Tables 5.31 and 5.32. This is to be expected; since the categories of Tables 4.12 and 5.33 generally involve lower levels of aggregation, there is less leeway for different aggregation methods to drive them apart. There are, however, some substantial differences. Among the most notable are the indexes for bread and cereals, which are much higher for the three lowest groups when international prices are used than the results embodied in the Fisher indexes.

Table 5.33. Average Quantities per Capita for Groups of Countries Classified by Real per Capita GDP, 1970 and 1973

(United States=100)

Category	1970 Group I	1970 Group II	1970 Group III	1970 Group IV	1970 Group V	1973 Group I	1973 Group II	1973 Group III	1973 Group IV	1973 Group V
Consumption										
Food	21.7	32.8	70.2	82.2	100.0	23.8	34.4	73.4	86.9	100.0
Bread and cereals	91.0	79.3	141.4	121.0	100.0	97.5	89.1	133.5	118.4	100.0
Meat	9.9	24.1	63.0	93.2	100.0	11.3	26.2	70.0	101.2	100.0
Fish	62.6	69.6	123.8	62.9	100.0	83.2	70.7	131.7	72.5	100.0
Milk	9.0	29.6	59.3	92.2	100.0	10.2	29.6	66.0	103.3	100.0
Oils	14.4	25.0	69.9	122.6	100.0	14.4	27.8	72.4	130.0	100.0
Fruits and vegetables	16.6	29.8	68.5	64.8	100.0	18.6	33.5	77.0	77.4	100.0
Clothing and footwear	7.6	17.5	53.1	67.4	100.0	9.0	17.7	53.4	67.5	100.0
Clothing	7.8	15.2	51.4	65.9	100.0	9.1	15.0	52.4	68.5	100.0
Footwear	6.7	34.4	63.8	76.0	100.0	8.4	35.1	59.5	62.8	100.0
Gross rents and fuels	4.4	13.6	38.1	56.4	100.0	4.2	15.3	37.9	56.5	100.0
Gross rents	4.8	17.0	39.5	58.1	100.0	4.5	18.1	38.3	56.9	100.0
House furnishings and operations	5.5	13.8	38.0	82.0	100.0	5.7	16.6	40.8	81.3	100.0
Medical care	7.4	15.8	91.0	94.4	100.0	7.2	14.4	84.0	90.7	100.0
Transport and communications	2.2	9.6	22.1	30.5	100.0	2.1	10.2	22.5	27.6	100.0
Personal equipment	0.4	2.1	13.1	22.1	100.0	0.3	2.1	13.5	17.8	100.0
Public transport	47.5	118.8	140.5	118.7	100.0	55.2	157.4	149.8	115.7	100.0
Recreation and education	9.1	13.7	51.0	59.5	100.0	8.7	15.8	50.7	58.7	100.0
Recreation	3.0	6.6	41.7	52.4	100.0	2.8	7.4	40.2	52.2	100.0
Education	19.2	26.1	63.0	67.1	100.0	18.4	32.0	64.4	64.5	100.0
Capital formation										
Construction	9.7	30.8	80.6	122.0	100.0	10.2	34.2	79.7	115.3	100.0
Producers' durables	4.4	7.5	60.6	84.7	100.0	4.4	8.3	59.8	75.9	100.0
Government										
Compensation	20.0	27.8	54.7	72.3	100.0	21.8	40.0	58.0	80.7	100.0
Commodities	2.9	8.1	23.5	27.4	100.0	4.9	18.0	30.6	29.0	100.0

Note: Group I includes India, Kenya, the Republic of Korea, and the Philippines; Group II, Colombia, Iran, and Malaysia; Group III, Hungary, Italy, Japan, and the United Kingdom; Group IV, Belgium, France, the Federal Republic of Germany, and the Netherlands; and Group V, the United States.

An important source of difference between binary and multilateral estimates arises in connection with detailed categories for which prices had to be imputed from other categories. The country–product–dummy method used in the multilateral comparisons sometimes produced very different PPPs from those obtained by the methods used in the binary comparisons (see Chapter 3). Table 5.34 giving binary PPPs for detailed categories indicates the categories for which prices were imputed. The corresponding multilateral PPPs may be found in Appendix Table 4.3.

This appendix presents the purchasing-power parities used for each detailed category in the binary comparisons. For some categories, direct price comparisons could not be made; such exceptions are indicated in the footnotes to the table. These detailed purchasing-power parities in conjunction with the detailed expenditures in Table 4.1 provide the basis for producing the 1970 data in the summary binary tables in this chapter.

Appendix to Chapter 5

Detailed Binary Table

Appendix Table 5.1. Purchasing-Power Parities per U.S. Dollar, 1970

Code	Category	Belgium (B. francs)	Colombia (pesos)	France (francs)	Germany (DM)	Hungary (forints)	India (rupees)	Iran (rials)
01.101	Rice	69.8	12.1	4.81	5.20	49.4	4.51	72.4
01.102	Meal, other cereals	59.1	17.2	6.98	5.51	19.3	2.88	49.9
01.103	Bread, rolls	22.1	11.8	2.47	2.45	5.4	3.13	20.1
01.104	Biscuits, cakes	94.0	22.8	11.36	6.17	20.0	8.56	57.8
01.105	Cereal preparations	67.2	20.8	8.28	4.56	5.4 a	—	51.7
01.106	Macaroni, spaghetti	68.4	7.4	4.08	3.38	16.5	10.59	47.2
01.111	Fresh beef, veal	49.1	10.1	4.47	3.20	40.3	3.79	57.8
01.112	Fresh lamb, mutton	—	3.1	4.45 a	—	13.0	4.70	69.2
01.113	Fresh pork	41.5	8.9	4.42	3.38	45.7	1.86	—
01.114	Fresh poultry	72.3	21.0	7.37	5.84	35.6	7.66	98.3
01.115	Other fresh meat	43.7	9.8	4.91	3.68	16.0	3.99 a	39.6
01.116	Frozen, salted meat	52.7	12.2	6.08	4.38	25.0	4.64	60.2
01.121	Fresh, frozen fish	46.6	11.6	5.42	3.27	14.9	1.34	29.2
01.122	Canned fish	88.3	18.1	9.44	5.58	73.1	8.25	115.9
01.131	Fresh milk	29.1	7.8	3.05	2.29	11.9	2.88	64.8
01.132	Milk products	36.0	14.6	3.69	3.04	15.5	4.76	13.5
01.133	Eggs, egg products	50.6	17.4	5.54	3.76	31.1	5.36	66.9
01.141	Butter	55.0	15.6	6.17	4.00	26.2	4.01	99.6
01.142	Margarine, edible oil	41.1	17.1	4.15	4.22	28.7	6.71	96.3
01.143	Lard, edible fat	—	44.6	—	—	39.1	1.86 a	62.3 a
01.151	Fresh fruits, tropical	75.7	3.1	7.71	5.03	51.5	2.95	86.7
01.152	Other fresh fruits	26.9	22.8	2.95	2.13	11.6	3.38	36.3
01.153	Fresh vegetables	28.2	7.3	3.00	2.16	8.0	1.43	19.1
01.161	Fruit other than fresh	60.5	22.1	8.18	4.87	63.9	6.03	38.9
01.162	Vegetables other than fresh	83.0	34.6	8.83	6.73	36.7	6.26	37.8
01.170	Tubers, including potatoes	17.5	8.7	2.59	3.70	14.8	3.82	35.2
01.191	Coffee	97.5	11.4	8.90	11.17	115.7	10.48	147.4
01.192	Tea	52.6	18.9	6.49	8.55	52.1	2.71	76.8
01.193	Cocoa	71.6 a	11.9	5.40	4.98	45.2	15.22	108.3
01.180	Sugar	55.3	10.2	4.77	4.54	33.7	7.39	82.9
01.201	Jam, syrup, honey	40.9	13.4	4.67	3.26	18.6	8.51	110.4
01.202	Chocolate, ice cream	60.6	11.7	9.00	5.60	31.9	6.73	65.3
01.203	Salt, spices, sauces	104.0	6.6	12.47	6.84	14.7	2.45	22.6
01.310	Nonalcoholic beverages	27.7	9.4	3.25	2.82	22.4	4.98	56.7
01.321	Spirits	33.2	9.4	3.30	2.16	24.0	10.37	38.1
01.322	Wine, cider	33.2	22.4	3.18	3.08	18.4	19.78	55.3
01.323	Beer	30.7	8.3	2.96	2.23	17.2	9.97	53.6
01.410	Cigarettes	31.3	3.1	3.77	4.21	8.3	8.13	43.2
01.420	Other tobacco	18.2	10.4	2.43	2.11	18.6	2.51	43.2 a
02.110	Clothing materials	51.9	17.1	6.54	3.97	56.5	6.72	81.0

Italy (lire)	Japan (yen)	Kenya (shillings)	Korea (won)	Malaysia (M. dollars)	Netherlands (guilders)	Philippines (pesos)	U.K. (pounds)	Category	Code
590	441	4.15	241.	1.55	4.38	3.18	0.390	Rice	01.101
875	347	4.72	119.	1.72	4.38	8.99	0.355	Meal, other cereals	01.102
292	187	3.04	213.	1.42	1.55	3.53	0.203	Bread, rolls	01.103
704	300	1.06	506.	6.91	4.86	6.26	0.247	Biscuits, cakes	01.104
1,137	563	10.22	—	3.99	3.77	5.72	0.291	Cereal preparations	01.105
466	340	11.41	92.	1.79	5.23	5.52	0.384	Macaroni, spaghetti	01.106
573	568	3.14	225.	1.59	3.20	2.03	0.214	Fresh beef, veal	01.111
592 [a]	504 [a]	2.76	—	1.71	—	—	0.207	Fresh lamb, mutton	01.112
612	447	6.83	221.	1.83	2.99	2.01	0.347	Fresh pork	01.113
935	444	5.12	355.	3.84	5.02	3.15	0.351	Fresh poultry	01.114
474	483 [a]	4.17 [a]	287.	—	2.73	2.60	0.324	Other fresh meat	01.115
641	455	5.35	301.	2.83	3.80	3.82	0.323	Frozen, salted meat	01.116
678	260	4.11	148.	1.70	2.57	2.63	0.270	Fresh, frozen fish	01.121
877	422	11.63	148. [a]	0.83	5.04	3.31	0.511	Canned fish	01.122
507	375	4.14	387.	5.00	2.16	5.17	0.362	Fresh milk	01.131
609	405	6.11	337.	2.05	2.65	3.93	0.220	Milk products	01.132
707	261	5.64	306.	2.04	3.26	4.03	0.376	Eggs, egg products	01.133
904	411	4.48	104.	2.49	3.82	5.22	0.217	Butter	01.141
596	389	8.51	336.	2.07	3.33	6.50	0.421	Margarine, edible oil	01.142
—	680	13.10	776.	—	—	6.14	0.466	Lard, edible fat	01.143
870	496	2.48	1,559.	0.78	4.36	1.70	0.447	Fresh fruits, tropical	01.151
272	386	15.77	170.	2.65	1.48	1.82	0.369	Other fresh fruits	01.152
324	210	2.06	132.	1.33	2.06	1.88	0.253	Fresh vegetables	01.153
960	417	4.93	439.	2.70	3.88	4.74	0.365	Fruit other than fresh	01.161
970	519	5.90	—	2.86	5.12	4.62	0.407	Vegetables other than fresh	01.162
508	365	2.00	96.	1.20	2.74	2.40	0.258	Tubers, including potatoes	01.170
1,902	709	7.63	1,035.	4.53	6.61	6.71	0.369	Coffee	01.191
1,087	236	2.88	615.	1.67	2.55	6.52	0.180	Tea	01.192
1,145	409 [a]	8.70	1,245.	3.54	3.75	5.63	0.293	Cocoa	01.193
887	508	5.49	523.	2.03	4.13	3.43	0.291	Sugar	01.180
527	375	3.49	512.	3.33	2.58	3.54	0.189	Jam, syrup, honey	01.201
1,083	604	32.71	1,148.	3.76	4.60	5.45	0.568	Chocolate, ice cream	01.202
925	163	5.39	150.	1.09	5.26	2.46	0.403	Salt, spices, sauces	01.203
608	353	14.69	691.	2.20 [a]	2.33	4.97	0.396	Nonalcoholic beverages	01.310
395	263	6.85	455.	1.86	1.59	0.99	0.440	Spirits	01.321
417	269	7.79	93.	2.20 [a]	3.27	1.53 [a]	0.690	Wine, cider	01.322
408	332	8.21	505.	2.61	2.05	2.37	0.572	Beer	01.323
572	208	4.35	271.	2.70	3.48	3.03	0.693	Cigarettes	01.410
551	208 [a]	3.82	—	2.07	1.40	3.08	0.714	Other tobacco	01.420
577	400	7.94	610.	2.09	2.70	5.11	0.382	Clothing materials	02.110

(*Table continues on the following page.*)

Appendix Table 5.1 continued.

Code	Category	Belgium (B. francs)	Colombia (pesos)	France (francs)	Germany (DM)	Hungary (forints)	India (rupees)	Iran (rials)
02.121	Men's clothing	41.8	10.1	5.47	3.13	23.5	3.25	19.7
02.122	Women's clothing	59.5	15.9	8.93	4.67	25.7	3.88	80.1
02.123	Boys', girls' clothing	34.2	11.5	4.86	4.25	21.1	2.39	44.3
02.131	Men's, boys' underwear	66.9	13.6	6.95	5.62	27.0	1.95	37.3
02.132	Women's, girls' underwear	65.8	12.2	8.77	4.97	24.7	5.90	40.1
02.150	Other clothing	56.3	10.1	6.64	4.44	18.3	4.77	24.6
02.160	Clothing rental, repair	18.0	5.6	2.81	3.26	9.3	1.26	9.1
02.211	Men's footwear	37.6	7.9	5.71	3.51	21.0	4.01	25.5
02.212	Women's footwear	39.2	6.4	5.41	2.68	20.3	4.02	10.6
02.213	Children's footwear	34.3	7.0	3.76	2.77	11.4	2.55	18.7
02.220	Footwear repairs	34.4	6.3	5.00	2.55	16.9	3.54	19.8
03.110	Gross rents	33.3	12.2	3.25	2.53	10.0	1.89	19.1
03.120	Indoor repair, upkeep	27.2	7.3	3.25	2.38	6.5	0.46	15.3
03.210	Electricity	81.6	7.2	7.65	4.17	30.0	6.98	105.2
03.220	Gas	86.8	4.4	9.25	7.56	20.7	6.17	50.0
03.230	Liquid fuels	51.3	10.7	5.61	3.33	41.9	12.96	60.0
03.240	Other fuels, ice	56.7	7.0	5.92	4.45	7.0	3.26	66.0
04.110	Furniture, fixtures	38.4	11.0	4.58	2.92	23.3	4.21	30.0
04.120	Floor coverings	51.0	12.0 [a]	5.80	3.65	28.7	2.98	15.7
04.200	Household textiles, etc.	72.5	13.2	7.22	6.29	26.7	2.11	54.9
04.310	Refrigerators, etc.	37.7	31.9	4.86	2.65	44.0	14.43	107.5
04.320	Washing appliances	77.5	56.4	9.13	5.22	29.5	—	103.1
04.330	Cooking appliances	39.4	23.0	5.12	3.56	14.3	6.12	41.3
04.340	Heating appliances	54.6	20.8	7.75	3.97	34.9	3.11	74.0
04.350	Cleaning appliances	72.4	59.4	7.81	4.94	29.1	—	76.3 [a]
04.360	Other household appliances	57.2	54.2	7.90	4.86	24.4	4.93	76.3 [a]
04.400	Household utensils	30.7	10.2	3.81	2.41	20.8	4.74	42.3
04.510	Nondurable household goods	43.2	12.1	5.60	3.33	36.1	7.00	41.9
04.520	Domestic services	—	1.0	—	—	9.3	0.24	15.3 [a]
04.530	Household services	50.9	5.9	6.95	4.58	14.9	1.10	31.0
04.600	Household furnishings, repairs	—	—	—	—	9.4	0.46 [a]	15.3 [a]
05.110	Drugs, medical preparations	25.4	14.8	2.77	3.34	10.7	3.23	35.8
05.120	Medical supplies	62.9	—	7.13	4.61	21.5	2.41	22.2
05.200	Therapeutic equipment	21.6	9.4	3.77	2.71	—	0.72	17.6
05.310	Physicians' services	31.2	4.9	4.82	2.34	1.3	0.13	14.7
05.320	Dentists' services	18.7	3.3	7.46	2.60	0.7	0.01	11.6
05.330	Nurses' services	258.3	4.5	5.81	6.91	13.5	4.70	86.6
05.410	Hospitals, etc.	5.0	2.3	0.36	0.22	3.5	0.20	25.6
06.110	Personal cars	89.7	31.6	6.11	4.99	53.6	9.17	156.0
06.120	Other personal transport	61.1	30.9	5.63	3.04	20.8	6.35	61.7

Italy (lire)	Japan (yen)	Kenya (shillings)	Korea (won)	Malaysia (M. dollars)	Netherlands (guilders)	Philippines (pesos)	U.K. (pounds)	Category	Code
524	244	4.66	150.	1.06	2.38	1.71	0.317	Men's clothing	02.121
792	234	7.71	263.	1.05	3.40	0.93	0.457	Women's clothing	02.122
464	280	2.80	275.	1.03	2.97	1.64	0.307	Boys', girls' clothing	02.123
689	230	8.06	167.	1.20	4.18	2.14	0.497	Men's, boys' underwear	02.131
740	249	4.17	163.	1.42	3.85	1.45	0.351	Women's, girls' underwear	02.132
586	218	4.73	189.	0.81	3.24	1.78	0.258	Other clothing	02.150
182	112 [a]	3.56	108.	—	1.66	0.30	0.331	Clothing rental, repair	02.160
622	179	2.72	125.	0.91	2.69	2.25	0.208	Men's footwear	02.211
449	211	1.80	254.	0.93	2.36	1.05	0.252	Women's footwear	02.212
410	158	1.59	49.	0.39	2.20	1.23	0.174	Children's footwear	02.213
311	112	4.01	121.	—	2.21	2.53	0.220	Footwear repairs	02.220
328	277	6.44	329.	0.97	1.70	1.00	0.291	Gross rents	03.110
207	191	3.15	61.	1.82	1.79	0.75	0.356	Indoor repair, upkeep	03.120
756	326	9.10	474.	4.57	2.95	3.16	0.327	Electricity	03.210
1,225	1,353	8.30	—	3.11	3.51	6.19 [a]	0.890	Gas	03.220
645	414	17.17	383.	3.62	2.87	12.13	0.436 [a]	Liquid fuels	03.230
667	186	1.67	452.[a]	3.72 [a]	4.04	7.99	0.285	Other fuels, ice	03.240
424	335	4.44	120.	0.88	2.54	2.04	0.500	Furniture, fixtures	04.110
659	313	8.63	—	1.47	3.75	7.89	0.303	Floor coverings	04.120
827	428	7.36	310.	1.26	4.36	1.62	0.321	Household textiles, etc.	04.200
422	639	8.93	891.	4.10	2.70	10.12	0.525	Refrigerators, etc.	04.310
591	225	11.53 [a]	—	3.75 [a]	4.97	6.99 [a]	0.344	Washing appliances	04.320
355	259	10.41	459.	2.48	2.44	6.65	0.382	Cooking appliances	04.330
790	426	11.53 [a]	370.	3.03	4.85	6.54	0.556	Heating appliances	04.340
926	426	11.53 [a]	533.[a]	3.75 [a]	4.90	6.99 [a]	0.729	Cleaning appliances	04.350
769	375	16.48	533.[a]	6.40	4.45	5.41	0.643	Other household appliances	04.360
332	204	3.25	93.	0.94	2.13	5.36	0.351	Household utensils	04.400
686	340	7.73	237.	1.87	3.42	3.52	0.418	Nondurable household goods	04.510
—	136	0.68	29.	1.82 [a]	—	0.35	0.185	Domestic services	04.520
754	205	4.09	139.	—	3.48	1.37	0.272	Household services	04.530
—	191 [a]	0.89	8.	1.82 [a]	—	0.75 [a]	0.111	Household furnishings, repairs	04.600
397	155	3.31	86.	1.86	1.97	3.50	0.164	Drugs, medical preparations	05.110
308	191	3.68	90.	1.13	3.72	1.64	0.207	Medical supplies	05.120
588	69	1.44	65.	0.47	1.60	1.86	0.171	Therapeutic equipment	05.200
246	34	0.98	20.	0.79	2.09	1.18	0.097	Physicians' services	05.310
224	21	1.13	14.	1.32	4.93	1.83	0.130	Dentists' services	05.320
812	260	3.14	147.	1.69	1.28	13.88	1.631	Nurses' services	05.330
37	31	1.04	84.	0.10	0.12	0.26	0.080	Hospitals, etc.	05.410
660	373	7.64	697.	4.66	7.11	16.56	0.570	Personal cars	06.110
539	436	8.61	462.	3.10	4.35	4.49	0.522	Other personal transport	06.120

(*Table continues on the following page.*)

Appendix Table 5.1 continued.

Code	Category	Belgium (B. francs)	Colombia (pesos)	France (francs)	Germany (DM)	Hungary (forints)	India (rupees)	Iran (rials)
06.210	Tires, tubes, accessories	56.2	16.8	6.38	4.99	29.5	8.12	75.2
06.220	Repair charges	67.6	5.1	8.92	6.42	13.6	1.15	20.8
06.230	Gasoline, oil, etc.	85.1	7.1	10.94	6.73	38.9	11.57	59.1
06.240	Parking, tolls, etc.	23.6	3.0 ª	2.21	1.76	3.9	1.57 ª	13.4
06.310	Local transport	29.6	2.4	3.40	2.56	7.9	1.23	6.6
06.321	Rail transport	35.9	3.7	3.22	2.62	11.9	2.19	18.9
06.322	Bus transport	33.3	3.7	5.18	2.68	15.0	2.00	10.2
06.323	Air transport	65.1	11.8	6.60	4.70	18.4 ª	7.21	99.5
06.330	Miscellaneous transport	—	—	—	—	35.1	1.57 ª	8.2 ª
06.410	Postal communication	29.0	7.0	3.62	1.94	11.1	1.88	97.3
06.420	Telephone, telegram	69.2	2.6	6.60	3.80	5.0	1.10	12.9
07.110	Radio, TV, phonograph, etc.	72.5	29.0	8.91	4.13	43.5	7.91	110.6
07.120	Major durable recreation equipment	56.1	23.1	6.81	3.70	19.2	7.91 ª	149.2
07.130	Other recreation equipment	56.4	24.5	6.03	4.09	26.9	5.95	37.3
07.210	Public entertainment	14.8	4.5	1.85	1.20	3.1	1.99	11.2
07.220	Other recreation, cultural	24.4	9.3	3.02	2.19	2.8	0.83	39.8
07.310	Books, paper, magazines	43.2	10.0	4.07	3.30	15.2	2.68	45.7
07.320	Stationery	31.8	10.8	3.71	2.99	52.5	2.59	30.1
07.411	Teachers, 1st and 2nd level	33.1	1.5	3.53	1.98	4.0	0.32	8.2
07.412	Teachers, college	5.2	4.6	7.80	5.80	4.3	0.77	31.8
07.420	Educational facilities	49.8 ª	9.3 ª	5.63 ª	3.66 ª	22.7 ª	5.02 ª	44.6 ª
07.431	Educational supplies	43.2 ª	10.0 ª	4.07 ª	3.30 ª	15.2 ª	2.68 ª	45.7 ª
07.432	Other educational expenditures	55.8 ª	12.4 ª	5.54 ª	4.50 ª	26.1 ª	4.67 ª	54.0 ª
08.100	Barber, beauty shops	18.7	4.3	2.62	1.81	3.4	1.31	12.8
08.210	Toilet articles	55.3	14.9	5.72	3.89	14.4	5.09	48.5
08.220	Other personal care goods	57.9	8.0	6.35	4.17	34.9	4.12	23.9
08.310	Restaurants, cafes	39.4	9.4	4.85	3.63	17.9	3.66	62.3
08.320	Hotels, etc.	26.4	8.1	3.03	3.06	16.8	3.80	36.9
08.400	Other services	28.9 ª	3.8 ª	3.60 ª	2.30 ª	6.5 ª	0.94 ª	23.8 ª
08.900	Net expenditure abroad	49.7 ª	—	5.53 ª	3.65 ª	—	—	—
10.100	One and two dwelling buildings	47.4	4.6	5.19	3.59	17.7	1.55	15.6
10.200	Multi-dwelling buildings	31.5	3.9	3.78	2.03	15.0	1.69	23.1
11.100	Hotels, etc.	25.3	3.8	1.97	1.39	17.2	1.65	38.5
11.200	Industrial buildings	36.7	6.6	4.04	2.44	22.4	2.62	24.2 ª
11.300	Commercial buildings	30.2	4.2	2.47	1.65	19.6	1.85 ª	32.1

Italy (lire)	Japan (yen)	Kenya (shillings)	Korea (won)	Malaysia (M. dollars)	Netherlands (guilders)	Philippines (pesos)	U.K. (pounds)	Category	Code
513	304	10.76	313.	2.13	3.48	5.05	0.240	Tires, tubes, accessories	06.210
654	362	1.77	177.	1.32	5.05	2.18	0.172	Repair charges	06.220
1,457	571	10.81	971.	4.24	6.01	3.40	0.698	Gasoline, oil, etc.	06.230
167	370	2.23 [a]	143.	0.22	1.10	10.95	0.295	Parking, tolls, etc.	06.240
296	101	1.90	66.	1.14	1.95	0.63	0.214	Local transport	06.310
255	117	3.16	75.	1.23	1.87	2.00	0.283	Rail transport	06.321
333	144	2.62	137.	0.82	2.05	1.08	0.236	Bus transport	06.322
660	251	12.01	178.	2.75	9.43	2.93	0.397	Air transport	06.323
—	121 [a]	2.23 [a]	95. [a]	0.97 [a]	—	0.82 [a]	0.997	Miscellaneous transport	06.330
453	258	4.33	162.	1.84	2.06	2.63	0.268	Postal communication	06.410
449	296	2.73	47.	1.19	2.10	1.80	0.187	Telephone, telegram	06.420
849	210	11.25	301.	2.41	4.72	7.81	0.576	Radio, TV, phonograph, etc.	07.110
747	218	8.46	278.	1.69	4.33	4.05	0.403	Major durable recreation equipment	07.120
643	269	7.33	121.	2.62	4.09	3.88	0.437	Other recreation equipment	07.130
287	408	1.35	45.	0.56	0.79	0.85	0.084	Public entertainment	07.210
422	165	2.30	77.	2.51	1.47	0.59	0.370	Other recreation, cultural	07.220
524	366	6.85	226.	1.88	2.91	2.73	0.166	Books, paper, magazines	07.310
354	262	16.17	100.	1.28	2.06	4.31	0.339	Stationery	07.320
224	118	0.92	29.	0.46	3.45	0.31	0.165	Teachers, 1st and 2nd level	07.411
400	231	4.48	63.	0.95	4.15	0.77	0.530	Teachers, college	07.412
679 [a]	367 [a]	5.61 [a]	298. [a]	2.41 [a]	3.01 [a]	3.47 [a]	0.414 [a]	Educational facilities	07.420
524 [a]	366 [a]	6.85 [a]	226. [a]	1.88 [a]	2.91 [a]	2.73 [a]	0.166 [a]	Educational supplies	07.431
632 [a]	311 [a]	5.05 [a]	334. [a]	2.41 [a]	3.82 [a]	5.18 [a]	0.357 [a]	Other educational expenditures	07.432
247	135	2.55	40.	0.41	1.45	0.38	0.118	Barber, beauty shops	08.100
732	279	8.65	193.	3.19	3.52	2.67	0.366	Toilet articles	08.210
730	178	5.48	135.	1.67	3.95	2.15	0.268	Other personal care goods	08.220
645	194	2.84	243.	3.35	2.92	3.81	0.408	Restaurants, cafes	08.310
446	267	4.01	107.	0.63	2.49	1.00 [a]	0.285	Hotels, etc.	08.320
290 [a]	153	1.98	74. [a]	0.92 [a]	2.14 [a]	1.02 [a]	0.210 [a]	Other services	08.400
627 [a]	358 [a]	—	310. [a]	—	3.62 [a]	—	0.417 [a]	Net expenditure abroad	08.900
449	266	3.33	121.	0.63 [a]	2.74	1.84	0.186	One and two dwelling buildings	10.100
291	227	3.64	92.	0.63	1.52	1.71	0.222	Multi-dwelling buildings	10.200
229	274	4.81	154.	0.58 [a]	1.63	2.23	0.402	Hotels, etc.	11.100
413	543	5.21	169.	0.58 [a]	2.42	3.49	0.379	Industrial buildings	11.200
257	453	3.79	169.	0.58 [a]	1.70	3.50	0.348	Commercial buildings	11.300

(*Table continues on the following page.*)

Appendix Table 5.1 continued.

Code	Category	Belgium (B. francs)	Colombia (pesos)	France (francs)	Germany (DM)	Hungary (forints)	India (rupees)	Iran (rials)
11.400	Office buildings	36.2	2.8	3.45	2.03	12.7	1.56	16.1
11.500	Educational buildings	57.4	2.7	6.45	3.60	14.8	1.74	18.6
11.600	Hospital buildings	39.7 ª	4.1 ª	3.98 ª	2.44 ª	12.2	1.36	16.8
11.700	Agricultural buildings	62.8	4.1 ª	6.00	4.35	21.6	1.85 ª	40.1
11.800	Other buildings	39.7 ª	4.1 ª	3.98 ª	2.44 ª	17.6	1.85 ª	23.5
12.100	Roads, highways	26.3	4.4	2.59	1.75	19.0	1.59	53.2
12.200	Transmission, utility lines	26.9	4.3	2.72	1.99	14.8	1.62	40.4
12.300	Other construction	16.9	4.4 ª	1.83	0.89	12.1	1.36 ª	22.4
13.000	Land improvement	42.9	4.4 ª	4.46	2.45	9.3	1.36 ª	—
14.110	Locomotives	113.1 ª	16.5	8.93	4.95	62.2	8.35	82.9 ª
14.120	Other	113.1	16.5 ª	9.22	3.83	42.5	7.61	82.9
14.200	Passenger cars	76.7	35.0	4.65	5.61	69.5	8.98	145.1
14.300	Trucks, buses, trailers	76.5 ª	31.6	5.79	4.84 ª	27.8	9.62	163.1
14.400	Aircraft	67.8	28.1	4.91	3.35	39.7 ª	9.53	77.8
14.500	Ships, boats	76.5 ª	32.1 ª	5.52 ª	4.84 ª	39.7 ª	8.93 ª	95.4 ª
14.600	Other transport	—	34.3 ª	5.49	4.11	39.7 ª	5.88	51.7
15.100	Engines and turbines	52.0 ª	28.7	5.28 ª	3.69 ª	50.6	10.81	89.6 ª
15.210	Tractors	50.1	19.5	4.89	3.41	30.7	5.25	44.2
15.220	Other agricultural machinery	62.7	32.7	5.39	3.90	24.9	6.00	143.4
15.300	Office machinery	51.5	45.8	5.54	3.67	45.1	6.43	98.5
15.400	Metalworking machinery	44.9	14.2	2.78	2.66	33.6	5.15	47.5
15.500	Construction, mining machines	72.8	31.6	7.88	5.63	31.7	11.01	91.6
15.600	Special industrial machinery	44.6	22.7	4.76	3.18	36.0	5.97	103.7
15.700	General industrial machinery	45.6	31.0	3.98	2.99	33.5	8.19	55.2
15.800	Service industrial machinery	56.3	36.4	8.99	6.80	37.4	7.77	185.6
16.100	Electrical transmission	41.9	30.8	3.61	2.83	22.4	7.71	75.3 ª
16.200	Communication equipment	111.9	23.7	5.46	3.67	21.2	9.74	75.3 ª
16.300	Other electrical	28.5	13.2	3.60	2.97	27.1	7.32	46.9
16.400	Instruments	36.8	24.9	3.71	2.67	23.8	3.13	101.1
17.100	Furniture, fixtures	46.8	20.2	4.96	4.39	25.6	5.19	43.9
17.200	Other durable goods	75.8	16.7	6.61	4.67	51.2	5.19 ª	34.0
18.000	Increase in stocks	47.3 ª	11.8 ª	4.98 ª	3.67 ª	20.1 ª	4.20 ª	41.8 ª
19.000	Exports less imports	49.7	18.4	5.53	3.65	30.0	7.50	76.4
20.100	Blue collar, unskilled	27.0	1.9	3.53	3.01	4.7	0.33	17.0
20.210	Blue collar, skilled	20.8	2.4	3.09	2.45	5.0	0.37	22.5
20.220	White collar	29.0	2.8	3.96	2.85	5.4	0.56	35.1
20.300	Professional	38.5	4.7	4.13	3.59	5.9	1.20	46.1
21.000	Government expenditure on commodities	44.8	10.4	4.69	3.31	19.1	2.83	40.8

—. The country reported no expenditure in the category.
a. The PPP for this category was imputed.
b. Blue collar workers include both first- and second-level blue collar workers.

Italy (lire)	Japan (yen)	Kenya (shillings)	Korea (won)	Malaysia (M. dollars)	Netherlands (guilders)	Philippines (pesos)	U.K. (pounds)	Category	Code
327	285	2.64	177.	0.67	2.17	1.82	0.260	Office buildings	11.400
460	210	2.55	137.	0.51	3.72	1.51	0.312	Educational buildings	11.500
375 [a]	181	3.03	176.	0.58 [a]	2.54 [a]	1.66	0.244	Hospital buildings	11.600
542	622	2.23	121.	0.58 [a]	4.21	3.95	0.250	Agricultural buildings	11.700
375 [a]	264	3.64 [a]	162. [a]	0.58 [a]	2.54 [a]	2.00	0.304	Other buildings	11.800
215	286	4.61 [a]	134.	1.05 [a]	1.13	0.69	0.241	Roads, highways	12.100
265	170	4.61	148.	0.78	1.46	3.57	0.186	Transmission, utility lines	12.200
83	195	9.03	132.	0.86 [a]	1.27	3.26	0.315	Other construction	12.300
416	173	3.83	93.	0.86 [a]	1.94	2.44	0.351	Land improvement	13.000
986	374 [a]	6.84	275. [a]	6.01	5.69 [a]	11.67	0.640	Locomotives	14.110
1,328	374 [a]	9.46	275.	—	5.69 [a]	11.67 [a]	0.640 [a]	Other	14.120
783	374	8.15	697.	4.40	6.39	15.89	0.670	Passenger cars	14.200
803 [a]	374 [a]	6.99	551. [a]	3.38	5.69 [a]	9.73	0.640 [a]	Trucks, buses, trailers	14.300
660	374 [a]	7.67 [a]	487.	—	4.41	9.54	0.640 [a]	Aircraft	14.400
803. [a]	374 [a]	7.67 [a]	551. [a]	3.66 [a]	5.69 [a]	11.65 [a]	0.640 [a]	Ships, boats	14.500
821	374 [a]	8.21	236.	2.88	4.71	4.32	0.530	Other transport	14.600
533 [a]	300 [a]	8.42	497.	2.79 [a]	3.79 [a]	8.01	0.310	Engines and turbines	15.100
557	300 [a]	6.82	—	2.65	3.64	7.98	0.320	Tractors	15.210
868	300 [a]	9.56	1,066.	2.65 [a]	4.23	9.20	0.390	Other agricultural machinery	15.220
669	300 [a]	9.85	407.	2.10	4.09	6.38	0.410	Office machinery	15.300
300	427	4.39	109.	5.28	3.40	4.38	0.300	Metalworking machinery	15.400
842	302	9.29	377.	3.57	5.52	8.45	0.370	Construction, mining machines	15.500
519	230	6.60	316.	3.02 [a]	3.02	6.25	0.370	Special industrial machinery	15.600
433	292	7.84	284.	2.59	3.22	4.95	0.320	General industrial machinery	15.700
522	300 [a]	11.09	527.	3.02 [a]	4.74	11.24	0.350 [a]	Service industrial machinery	15.800
401	354 [a]	5.48	251.	1.53 [a]	2.96	8.72	0.340 [a]	Electrical transmission	16.100
591	354 [a]	11.94	543.	3.55	6.39	6.28 [a]	0.540	Communication equipment	16.200
272	280	4.83	184.	0.66	3.85	4.87	0.150	Other electrical	16.300
522	388	7.28	97.	1.53 [a]	2.43	5.52	0.160	Instruments	16.400
693	323 [a]	5.82	38.	1.15	4.13	2.64	0.210	Furniture, fixtures	17.100
786	323 [a]	6.65	417.	2.59	6.40	3.58	0.210 [a]	Other durable goods	17.200
548 [a]	309 [a]	5.22 [a]	259. [a]	1.92 [a]	3.16 [a]	3.24 [a]	0.331 [a]	Increase in stocks	18.000
627	358	7.14	310.	3.08	3.62	6.06	0.417	Exports less imports	19.000
378	142	0.51	36.	0.36	2.64	0.54	0.149 [b]	Blue collar, unskilled	20.100
341	118	1.18	41.	0.33	1.88	0.47	—	Blue collar, skilled	20.210
387	124	1.91	49.	0.78	2.45	0.56	0.201	White collar	20.220
473	244	4.26	56.	1.48	3.71	0.65	0.274	Professional	20.300
478	261	4.76	184.	1.58	2.94	2.20	0.337	Government expenditure on commodities	21.000

Chapter 6

Some Relations Between Quantities and Prices

IN THE PRESENT CHAPTER the masses of data generated in Chapter 4 by the methods described in Chapter 3 are subjected to some simple analyses, partly to check on the coherence of the numbers and partly to take advantage of the rich opportunities provided by these data for new insights into international economic structure. On the first count, the main question is whether the data hang together in the ways that an economist would expect. (Intriguing questions not taken up here are the versions of the last sentence with "economist" replaced by "geographer," or "political scientist," or "sociologist," and so forth.) On the second count, the outputs set out in the tables of Chapter 4 provide an opportunity to investigate price and quantity relations for sixteen countries varying widely in income level, economic organization, and geographical location that has not previously been available. The network of PPPs for each country, for 36 summary categories and for 153 detailed categories, make it possible to compare price structures across countries. Similarly, the vector of quantities for each of the summary and detailed categories, expressed in international dollars, reflects the physical quantity structure of each country in a comparable way, so that detailed international comparisons can be made of the composition of real final expenditures on GDP.

The forays into the use of these materials in this chapter follow closely the lines pursued in the Phase I report: first, measures of similarity of the price structures and of the quantity structures are calculated and efforts are made to account for the patterns found; and, second, explanations are sought for the quantity of each category absorbed by each of the countries. The addition of six new observations significantly expands the number available in the Phase I report and provides an opportunity to check on its tentative findings with respect to quantity and price relationships.

In addition, further insight is sought into relative prices by attempting to decompose them into category and country components which are amenable to economic interpretations.

The Similarity of Quantity and Price Structures

If the world works the way economists' models suggest—quantities consumed depend upon opportunities as defined by prices and income—countries that have similar price structures and similar incomes should have similar quantity structures. That is, they ought to absorb the various categories of goods in the same proportions.

To verify this proposition, measures of the similarity of the price and of the quantity structures of the different countries were formulated. As in the Phase I report, the measure of similarity between the vectors of quantities (or prices) referring to any pair of countries is their weighted "raw correlation" coefficient. This is defined as the ratio of the weighted cross moment to the square root of the product of the two weighted second moments, each moment being computed relative to the origin rather than the mean. The formulas are:

$$(6.1) \qquad S_{jk}{}^{q} = \frac{\sum\limits_{\alpha=1}^{n} q_{\alpha j} q_{\alpha k}}{\sqrt{\sum\limits_{\alpha=1}^{n} q_{\alpha j}{}^{2} \sum\limits_{\alpha=1}^{n} q_{\alpha k}{}^{2}}},$$

$$(6.2) \qquad S_{jk}{}^{p} = \frac{\sum\limits_{\alpha=1}^{n} w_{\alpha} R_{\alpha j} R_{\alpha k}}{\sqrt{\sum\limits_{\alpha=1}^{n} w_{\alpha} R_{\alpha j}{}^{2} \sum\limits_{\alpha=1}^{n} w_{\alpha} R_{\alpha k}{}^{2}}},$$

where

$S_{jk}{}^{q}$ = quantity similarity index between countries j and k;
$S_{jk}{}^{p}$ = price similarity index between countries j and k;
$q_{\alpha j}$ = quantity valued in international dollars of the αth category in the jth country
$R_{\alpha j}$ = ratio of the percentage of expenditure on the αth category in country j, measured in domestic currency units to the corresponding percentage measured in international dollars;
n = number of categories; and
w = weight.

The measure is the same as the cosine of the angle between the 153 dimensional quantity (or price) vectors.[1] No ws appear in the $S_{jk}{}^{q}$ formula because the category quantities, expressed in international dollars, were self-weighting in the sense that the quantities in important categories would already be large compared with the quantities in unimportant categories.[2] Category Rs were weighted by the ratio of the total world output in the category to total world GDP both valued in international prices.[3] These weights were obtained through the use of the supercountry method.

The Rs serve as measures of relative price structures. As pointed out in Chapter 4 (page 121), the value of $R_{\alpha j}$ for GDP as a whole is 1. For example, a value above 1 for a given α for a given j indicates that relative to the relationship of js prices to international prices for GDP as a whole, its price for α is high.[4]

It should be noted that, unlike the Phase I similarity indexes, which were based on U.S.-weighted binary indexes, those presented here are based on the multilateral price and quantity indexes.

Similarity indexes were computed for each pair of countries for each of four different vectors in each of the two reference years, 1970 and 1973. The

1. Irving B. Kravis, Zoltan Kenessey, Alan Heston, and Robert Summers, *A System of International Comparisons of Gross Product and Purchasing Power* (Baltimore: Johns Hopkins University Press, 1975), p. 268; referred to as *A System*.

2. The summary category quantities are from Summary Multilateral Tables 4.5 and 4.10. Those for the detailed categories are from Appendix Table 4.5 for 1970 and from the corresponding unpublished table for 1973.

3. The summary category Rs are from Summary Multilateral Tables 4.1 and 4.5 for 1970 and 4.6 and 4.10 for 1973. Those for the detailed categories are from Appendix Tables 4.1 and 4.5 for 1970 and the corresponding unpublished tables for 1973.

4. Note that in *A System,* the price similarity indexes were based upon category PPPs with the United States as the base. The new formulation, using Rs, is superior in that relative price structures are expressed in terms of the average international price structure rather than that of the United States. This is preferable conceptually, though it must be said that it makes little substantive difference in the empirical results.

four vectors consisted of indexes referring to: 34 summary categories of GDP, 150 detailed categories of GDP, 25 summary categories of consumption, and 109 detailed categories of consumption. Three categories in which expenditures can be negative—net expenditures of residents abroad, exports minus imports, and increase in stocks—were omitted. For each of the four vectors, there are 120 quantity and 120 price similarity indexes $[n(n-1)/2]$, one for each possible pair among the sixteen countries.

Analysis of similarity indexes

The similarity indexes for quantities and prices are set out for the thirty-four summary categories of 1970 GDP in Table 6.1. The countries are arrayed in both the rows and the columns in order of increasing size of real GDP per capita. An inspection of the quantity part of the table is an easy way of seeing the role of real per capita income in determining the similarity of quantity compositions. There is a distinct tendency for the size of the similarity indexes to diminish as the distance from the principal diagonal (from upper left to lower right) increases along any row or column. That

Table 6.1. Indexes of Similarity for Quantity Structures and Price Structures for the Thirty-four Summary Categories of GDP, 1970

Country	Kenya	India	Philippines	Korea, Republic of	Colombia	Malaysia	Iran	Hungary
				Quantities				
Kenya	1.000	0.923	0.835	0.905	0.742	0.844	0.753	0.704
India	0.923	1.000	0.864	0.953	0.661	0.846	0.749	0.638
Philippines	0.835	0.864	1.000	0.856	0.701	0.882	0.795	0.690
Korea, Republic of	0.905	0.953	0.856	1.000	0.714	0.878	0.740	0.725
Colombia	0.742	0.661	0.701	0.714	1.000	0.815	0.696	0.791
Malaysia	0.844	0.846	0.882	0.878	0.815	1.000	0.893	0.855
Iran	0.753	0.749	0.795	0.740	0.696	0.893	1.000	0.797
Hungary	0.704	0.638	0.690	0.725	0.791	0.855	0.797	1.000
Italy	0.721	0.616	0.721	0.676	0.793	0.872	0.882	0.896
Japan	0.648	0.586	0.658	0.672	0.721	0.802	0.748	0.908
United Kingdom	0.708	0.602	0.743	0.676	0.750	0.867	0.851	0.913
Netherlands	0.659	0.566	0.646	0.657	0.766	0.842	0.819	0.935
Belgium	0.685	0.581	0.726	0.631	0.828	0.837	0.816	0.920
France	0.664	0.544	0.672	0.619	0.758	0.833	0.829	0.916
Germany, F.R.	0.615	0.528	0.619	0.617	0.717	0.815	0.788	0.906
United States	0.607	0.512	0.633	0.574	0.678	0.810	0.808	0.866
				Prices				
Kenya	1.000	0.897	0.829	0.942	0.939	0.916	0.904	0.918
India	0.897	1.000	0.861	0.860	0.885	0.923	0.900	0.882
Philippines	0.829	0.861	1.000	0.836	0.892	0.923	0.906	0.862
Korea, Republic of	0.942	0.860	0.836	1.000	0.907	0.895	0.858	0.872
Colombia	0.939	0.885	0.892	0.907	1.000	0.923	0.914	0.880
Malaysia	0.916	0.923	0.923	0.895	0.923	1.000	0.958	0.901
Iran	0.904	0.900	0.906	0.858	0.914	0.958	1.000	0.908
Hungary	0.918	0.882	0.862	0.872	0.880	0.901	0.908	1.000
Italy	0.893	0.817	0.801	0.839	0.850	0.915	0.907	0.927
Japan	0.928	0.822	0.804	0.886	0.868	0.899	0.892	0.927
United Kingdom	0.940	0.836	0.806	0.892	0.873	0.924	0.905	0.907
Netherlands	0.883	0.803	0.812	0.826	0.861	0.914	0.908	0.908
Belgium	0.920	0.835	0.838	0.849	0.888	0.921	0.930	0.941
France	0.881	0.780	0.779	0.808	0.838	0.882	0.879	0.910
Germany, F.R.	0.890	0.795	0.786	0.830	0.857	0.903	0.903	0.910
United States	0.871	0.717	0.729	0.780	0.814	0.837	0.862	0.850

is, the similarity of quantity composition diminishes as the per capita income gap between countries increases.

A comparison of the matrix of price similarity indexes with that of the quantity ratios indicates that price structures are generally more similar than quantity compositions. This is to be expected since there are more direct links between prices in different countries than between quantities. The similarity indexes for the Rs also show some tendency for figures near the principal diagonal to be larger than figures distant from it. The implication is that countries with such similar income levels are apt to have not only similar quantity structures but also similar price structures.

Tables in the format of Table 6.1, omitted here for reasons of space, for detailed GDP and for consumption in 1970 and the corresponding 1973 tables provide the following information:

First, the similarity indexes for 150 categories are uniformly smaller than those for 34 categories. In the case of quantities, most of them fall between 50 percent and 85 percent of the corresponding similarity indexes for the

Italy	Japan	United Kingdom	Nether- lands	Belgium	France	Germany, F.R.	United States	Country
				Quantities				
0.721	0.648	0.708	0.659	0.685	0.664	0.615	0.607	Kenya
0.616	0.586	0.602	0.566	0.581	0.544	0.528	0.512	India
0.721	0.658	0.743	0.646	0.726	0.672	0.619	0.633	Philippines
0.676	0.672	0.676	0.657	0.631	0.619	0.617	0.574	Korea, Republic of
0.793	0.721	0.750	0.766	0.828	0.758	0.717	0.678	Colombia
0.872	0.802	0.867	0.842	0.837	0.833	0.815	0.810	Malaysia
0.882	0.748	0.851	0.819	0.816	0.829	0.788	0.808	Iran
0.896	0.908	0.913	0.935	0.920	0.916	0.906	0.866	Hungary
1.000	0.867	0.947	0.939	0.925	0.961	0.917	0.886	Italy
0.867	1.000	0.855	0.921	0.897	0.907	0.915	0.780	Japan
0.947	0.855	1.000	0.939	0.918	0.956	0.923	0.950	United Kingdom
0.939	0.921	0.939	1.000	0.938	0.969	0.981	0.897	Netherlands
0.925	0.897	0.918	0.938	1.000	0.945	0.922	0.882	Belgium
0.961	0.907	0.956	0.969	0.945	1.000	0.968	0.904	France
0.917	0.915	0.923	0.981	0.922	0.968	1.000	0.892	Germany, F.R.
0.886	0.780	0.950	0.897	0.882	0.904	0.892	1.000	United States
				Prices				
0.893	0.928	0.940	0.883	0.920	0.881	0.890	0.871	Kenya
0.817	0.822	0.836	0.803	0.835	0.780	0.795	0.717	India
0.801	0.804	0.806	0.812	0.838	0.779	0.786	0.729	Philippines
0.839	0.886	0.892	0.826	0.849	0.808	0.830	0.780	Korea, Republic of
0.850	0.868	0.873	0.861	0.888	0.838	0.857	0.814	Colombia
0.915	0.899	0.924	0.914	0.921	0.882	0.903	0.837	Malaysia
0.907	0.892	0.905	0.908	0.930	0.879	0.903	0.862	Iran
0.927	0.927	0.907	0.908	0.941	0.910	0.910	0.850	Hungary
1.000	0.947	0.964	0.971	0.981	0.980	0.989	0.939	Italy
0.947	1.000	0.948	0.940	0.962	0.940	0.947	0.907	Japan
0.964	0.948	1.000	0.956	0.958	0.955	0.966	0.946	United Kingdom
0.971	0.940	0.956	1.000	0.969	0.983	0.985	0.948	Netherlands
0.981	0.962	0.958	0.969	1.000	0.978	0.983	0.946	Belgium
0.980	0.940	0.955	0.983	0.978	1.000	0.990	0.960	France
0.989	0.947	0.966	0.985	0.983	0.990	1.000	0.961	Germany, F.R.
0.939	0.907	0.946	0.948	0.946	0.960	0.961	1.000	United States

summary categories. The lower values are found for low-income countries, a point to which further reference will be made. All but a few of the indexes of price similarity for 150 categories are between 85 percent and 95 percent of the 34-category price similarity indexes. The fact that quantity patterns throughout the world are more similar when broad categories are considered points to the importance of substitutions in the form in which GDP is absorbed at detailed category levels.

Second, when the capital formation and government categories are excluded and similarity indexes are calculated for the twenty-five categories of consumption, the results are almost the same as those for the thirty-four categories of GDP. This is true both of quantities and of prices.

Third, the relationships for 1973 are very close to those for 1970.

*Regression
analysis*

The relationship between similarity of quantities and similarity of prices and incomes is examined by means of regression analysis. The investigation is carried out in the context of a simple extension of conventional demand theory, which asserts that the extent of similarity in quantity composition for various pairs of countries ($S_{jk}{}^q$) should be directly related to the extent of similarity in price structure ($S_{jk}{}^p$) and in similarity of real per capita income level ($S_{jk}{}^y$). Per capita income similarity is defined as:

$$(6.3) \qquad S_{jk}{}^y = \frac{2 \cdot \min(Y_j, Y_k)}{Y_j + Y_k},$$

so it takes on values between 0, approached when the two incomes are very different, and 1, approached when the two incomes are identical.[5] (The values of Y_j and Y_k that are used in calculating $S_{jk}{}^y$ are taken from Table 1.2.) The equation employed for regression analysis of this relationship is:

$$(6.4) \qquad S_{jk}{}^q = \alpha S_{jk}{}^p + \beta S_{jk}{}^y + \gamma + u_{jk},$$

where it is expected that α and β will both be greater than 0. Furthermore, if prices and incomes alone were the only systematic determinants of quantities, then $\alpha + \beta + \gamma$ should equal 1. (When $S_{jk}{}^p = 1$ and $S_{jk}{}^y = 1$, $S_{jk}{}^q = 1$. Therefore, $1 = \alpha \cdot 1 + \beta \cdot 1 + \gamma$).

Results of running the regression equation 6.4 appear in Table 6.2. It can be seen from the values of $\overline{R}^2$ that, generally speaking, between two-thirds and three-fourths of the variation in similarity of quantity composition is explained by similarity in price structure and income level. The coefficients of $S_{jk}{}^p$ and $S_{jk}{}^y$ are uniformly of the right sign and well in excess of twice their standard errors.[6] Furthermore, the sums of the coefficients (column 5) are close to unity. When formal F-tests are applied, the hypothesis that the sum is equal to 1 passes at the 5 percent level in all four sets of summary categories, and in two of the four sets of the detailed categories.[7]

The stability of equation 6.4 was investigated in two ways: by seeing if

5. Note that this definition of the income term differs from that used in the Phase I report. We are indebted to Lawrence Summers for suggesting this formulation.

6. The usual multiple regression assumption of independent disturbances may not be justified in this similarity index regression. If one country is an outlier, the residuals for the observations involving that country and each of the other fifteen countries all will be affected.

7. The possible clustering of residuals referred to in an earlier footnote may make the usual F-test misleading in this case because it assumes that the disturbances in each of the regressions are independent. Clustering probably would make the critical values of the test statistic larger than those found in the F table. Also, it should be emphasized that the eight regressions are not independent: the 1970 and 1973 observations are not completely independent and there is overlap between the summary and the detailed sets and between the GDP and the consumption sets.

Table 6.2. Regression Coefficients for $S_{jk}{}^q = \alpha S_{jk}{}^p + \beta S_{jk}{}^y + \gamma + u_{jk},$

(1970 and 1973)

Year	$S^p{}_{jk}$ (1)	$S^y{}_{jk}$ (2)	Constant (3)	$\bar{R}^2$ (4)	Sum of coefficients (5)
\multicolumn{6}{c}{**GDP: 34 summary categories**}
1970	0.7664 (0.1313)	0.2563 (0.0279)	−0.0386 (0.1069)	0.764 (0.059)	0.9841 [a]
1973	0.8345 (0.1544)	0.2662 (0.0321)	−0.1145 (0.1245)	0.779 (0.059)	0.9862 [a]
\multicolumn{6}{c}{**GDP: 150 detailed categories**}
1970	0.8510 (0.1780)	0.3208 (0.0440)	−0.2605 (0.1286)	0.689 (0.090)	0.9113
1973	0.7258 (0.1787)	0.3637 (0.0457)	−0.1862 (0.1274)	0.706 (0.090)	0.9003
\multicolumn{6}{c}{**Consumption: 25 summary categories**}
1970	0.9504 (0.1381)	0.2920 (0.0307)	−0.2404 (0.1134)	0.743 (0.070)	1.0020 [a]
1973	1.0719 (0.1857)	0.3048 (0.0349)	−0.3759 (0.1546)	0.727 (0.075)	1.0008 [a]
\multicolumn{6}{c}{**Consumption: 109 detailed categories**}
1970	0.8709 (0.1820)	0.4119 (0.0493)	−0.3339 (0.1302)	0.666 (0.120)	0.9489 [a]
1973	0.8209 (0.2027)	0.4312 (0.0538)	−0.3140 (0.1456)	0.633 (0.119)	0.9381 [a]

a. Insignificantly different from 1 at the .05 level of significance.
$S_{jk}{}^q$ = Quantity similarity index between countries j and k.
$S_{jk}{}^p$ = Price similarity index between countries j and k.
$S_{jk}{}^y$ = Per capita income level similarity index between countries j and k: in GDP equations y refers to GDP, in consumption equations to consumption.
$\bar{R}^2$ = Coefficient of determination adjusted for degrees of freedom.
Notes: Numbers in parentheses in columns 1–3 are coefficient standard errors. Number in parentheses in column 4 are standard errors of estimate (SEE).

the results reported in Phase I could be replicated with the six new Phase II countries; and by seeing if the results for 1970 and 1973 are consistent. The standard analysis of covariance test [8] was used for both 1970 and 1973. Are the regression coefficients of equation 6.4 based on the forty-five observations from the first ten countries and the regression coefficients based upon the fifteen observations of the additional six countries significantly different? Are the coefficients for 1973 significantly different from those for 1970? In the main, these questions were answered negatively. In one of the four groupings in one of the years—the twenty-five summary consumption categories for 1970—the hypothesis of the equality of ten-country and six-country coefficients could be accepted only at the 0.04 level; in all the other seven cases the hypothesis could be accepted at a significance level greater than 0.10.

The regression coefficients of equation 6.4 were estimated for each of the four groupings for both 1970 and 1973 using the similarity index data of all sixteen Phase II countries, the original ten Phase I countries, and the six new Phase II countries. In ten of the twelve cases—three out of four for both sixteen-country and ten-country cases and all of the six-country cases—the hypothesis of temporal stability can be accepted at a significance level greater

8. See J. Johnston, *Econometric Methods* (New York: McGraw-Hill, 1972), p. 199.

than 0.10. In only two cases—thirty-four summary GDP categories for sixteen and ten countries—must one unequivocally reject the hypothesis of stability.

Though it must be admitted that the analysis of covariance does not have great power in these applications because of lack of complete independence of the observations,[9] still it is encouraging to find that the original similarity index findings of Phase I hold up reasonably well under replication over space and time.

A search for other variables that would improve the explanation of the variation in $S_{jk}{}^q$ was conducted along two lines. One avenue of exploration was the grouping of the pairs of countries by common stage of economic development, and the other was concerned with other characteristics that pairs of countries had in common, namely, geographical location, trading association (that is, British Commonwealth and the European Economic Community), degree of income inequality, and climate. Some of the failures to find significant relationships—notably, for inequality and climate—may conceivably reflect the difficulty of devising within the limited attention that could be given to the task adequate measures of the relevant variables. The geographical factor was treated simply by assigning dummy variables for different continental locations. Only the coefficient of the dummy variable representing a European location for both members of a pair (D_E) yielded a positive coefficient that was rather consistently greater than its standard error (and for the GDP sets, more than twice as great). The inference is that for any degree of similarity of prices and income European countries are more similar in quantity composition than non-European countries.

The grouping of pairs according to stage of economic development was intended to see if income plays a more complicated role than the one specified in equation 6.4. Perhaps an income difference of the same size between two countries has a different impact on the similarity of quantity composition if both countries are relatively poor than if both are relatively rich. This possibility was investigated by means of a dummy variable for pairs both members of which were among the lowest seven in per capita income among the sixteen countries.[10] The coefficient of this dummy variable was consistently negative and uniformly strongly significant.[11]

It is possible that the significance of the European dummy is simply another manifestation of the stage-of-development effect, since all the European countries are relatively affluent. This was investigated by retaining the low-income dummy variable (D_L) while replacing the European variable (which places countries with middling or high incomes together) with dummy variables for pairs comprising the four middle-income countries (D_M) and for pairs composed of the four highest-income countries (D_H) other than the United States, leaving pairs involving the United States and mixed pairs as the reference group. The low-income dummy again exhibits substantial statistical significance: its t-ratio is below -2.5 in six of the eight cases and is below -1 in the other two cases.[12] The coefficient for the middle-income countries exceeds its standard error in seven out of the eight sets (the exception being the 25 consumption category set for 1970 and 1973), and the coefficient for the upper-income countries exceeds its standard error in four

9. See the previous footnotes.

10. The array of countries from low to high per capita income may be found in a number of preceding tables including Tables 1.2 and 6.1.

11. Similar treatment of the five lowest-income countries yielded much less significant coefficients.

12. The combination of D_L and D_E performed less satisfactorily than the combination of D_L and D_M, and D_H.

out of the eight sets. The size of the coefficients, however, progressively changes from one income group to the next higher one in five of the eight sets from a relatively large negative number to a smaller negative number or a positive one.[13] The equation for 109 consumption categories in 1970, to take one of the clearest examples, is:

$$(6.5) \qquad S_{jk}{}^q = 0.6187 \; S_{jk}{}^p + 0.5357 \; S_{jk}{}^y - 0.1098 \; D_L - 0.0885 \; D_M$$
$$\qquad\qquad (0.2012) \qquad (0.0574) \qquad (0.0303) \qquad (0.0477)$$

$$\qquad - 0.0521 \; D_H - 0.1771.$$
$$\qquad (0.0508) \qquad (0.1441)$$

$$\bar{R}^2 = 0.696$$
$$\mathrm{SEE} = 0.1048$$

Equation 6.5 says that the low-income countries are relatively much less alike in quantity composition than would be inferred from their $S_{jk}{}^p$ and $S_{jk}{}^y$ values, the middle-income countries somewhat less alike, and the upper-income countries only a little less alike. The clear implication that emerges from the various regressions is that pairs of countries at lower stages of the development process with like incomes and price structures have less similar quantity compositions than similarly situated pairs at a higher development stage.[14]

After weighing the evidence obtained from introducing D_E and the income dummies in various combinations, it was concluded that the effect not captured by $S_{jk}{}^p$ and $S_{jk}{}^y$ in fact was related to income and not to geographical propinquity or some factor associated with it.[15] Both economic and statistical explanations present themselves. In economic terms, low-income countries may be bound to traditional patterns of production and consumption that reflect their particular environment and history, and it is only after modernization and industrialization begin to take hold that quantities become more closely adapted to price and income similarities.

An alternative explanation is that errors in measurement of quantities, especially at the detailed category level, are associated with levels of development. If expenditure distributions are subject to measurement errors to a greater extent for low-income countries, the derived quantities will show less similarity to those of other countries, including other low-income countries. Support for this view comes from the fact that the pattern in equation 6.5 holds for the 150 detailed categories but is weaker for the summary category regressions. Since many of the measurement errors will cancel out within summary categories, one would expect the similarity in quantities to be closer across countries at the summary category level than at the detailed level.

This investigation of price and quantity structures thus clearly confirms the findings of *A System:* The more similar that countries are with respect to their per capita incomes and price structures, the more similar they are in the composition of the physical bundles of goods they take from the productive process to use for consumption, investment, and governmental services.

A second line of investigation relating to applications of the data set out in Chapter 4 involves simple demand analyses. The various quantities ab-

Demand Analyses

---

13. In the other three sets, D_L and D_M fall into this order but D_H does not.

14. This same effect was originally observed in Phase I on the basis of only forty-five observations entering into the regressions.

15. When a squared term for income similarity was added, it was significant ($t > 2$) in seven out of the eight sets and raised the $\bar{R}$s to the middle 0.70s. It did not, however, substantially change the behavior of the coefficients of the dummy variables, D_E, D_L, D_M, and D_H.

sorbed by different countries expressed in international dollars, the $q_{\alpha j}$s, are treated as functions of prices and incomes. No attempt was made here to estimate complete demand systems. The basic regression equation investigated was:

$$(6.6) \qquad \ln q_{\alpha j} = \beta_{\alpha 1} \ln \left(\frac{p_{\alpha j}}{p_{c j}} \right) + \beta_{\alpha 2} \ln C_j + \beta_{\alpha 0} + \mu_{\alpha j}$$

$$\alpha = 1, \ldots, m; j = 1, \ldots, 16,$$

where

$\ln$ = natural logarithm;

$q_{\alpha j}$ = real quantity per capita of the αth good consumed in the jth country (denominated in international dollars and given in either Summary Multilateral Table 4.5 or Appendix Table 4.5);

$p_{\alpha j}$ = purchasing-power parity for the αth good in the jth country (as given in either Summary Multilateral Table 4.3 or Appendix Table 4.3);

$p_{c j}$ = purchasing-power parity for consumption in the jth country (denominated in international dollars and given in line 1 of Summary Multilateral Table 4.3); and

C_j = real consumption per capita in the jth country (denominated in international dollars and given in line 1 of Summary Multilateral Table 4.5).[16]

Since C is expressed relative to the United States, the demand function is homogeneous of degree zero, as it should be. Placing $p_{c j}$ in the denominator in the price term takes account of substitution possibilities with no loss of scarce degrees of freedom. The regression coefficients $\beta_{\alpha 1}$ and $\beta_{\alpha 2}$ may be interpreted as price and income elasticities. They have been estimated by the ordinary least squares method, one equation at a time, for each of the subaggregate groupings defined in the summary multilateral tables of Chapter 4, and also for most of the commodities defined by the detailed categories.[17]

There are reasons for thinking that simultaneity rising from a possible endogenous character of prices may not be a major problem. Price differences between countries for a given category may be attributable not to the influence of quantities but to varying income levels and to differences in transfer costs and government policies. Also, it is possible that differing factor intensities from country to country may lead to price differences that are not completely eradicated by competitive forces. Finally, it may be mentioned that the experiments with various exogenous variables, reported in the Phase I report, produced price elasticity estimates that varied over a wide range depending on which combination of exogenous variables was used, but, for the most part, the consumption elasticities were fairly robust.[18]

16. The table references in the text are for 1970 data. For 1973, the $q_{\alpha j}$s come from Summary Multilateral Table 4.10 or an unpublished table corresponding to Appendix Table 4.5 and the $p_{\alpha j}$s from Summary Multilateral Table 4.8 or an unpublished table corresponding to Appendix Table 4.3.

17. On the face of it, it is implausible that tastes will be satisfied in the same way in countries as diverse in climate as the sixteen studied here. As in the case of the similarity analyses of the previous section, attempts to allow climate to help in the explanation of quantities consumed were not successful. When the mean temperature of the capital was introduced as an additional independent variable, its coefficient was insignificant for most categories. When the coefficient was significant, it was not always of the right sign.

18. Recent econometric research suggests that ordinary least squares (OLS) may not be inferior to, say, two-stage least squares as an estimating procedure for the demand regressions. When misspecification is a serious possibility—and it surely is here—the relative insensitivity of OLS to specification error outweighs its disadvantages in terms of

The regression equations of the form given in equation 6.6 are set out in Table 6.3 for twenty-five summary categories of consumption. The empirical results yielded by the 1970 and 1973 equations are very similar, but it should be borne in mind that in many cases the underlying 1973 data were extrapolated from the 1970 data.

The equations taken as a group are well behaved. Relative prices and incomes (that is, consumption levels) explain the variations in quantities consumed among the sixteen countries very well; for seventeen of the categories in 1970 and sixteen in 1973, the $\bar{R}^2$s exceed 0.80 and only two (bread and cereals and fish) fail to produce substantial explanatory power.

The coefficient of the price variable is negative with but a single exception (oils and fats in 1970) and is significant at the 5 percent level in eleven of the categories in 1970 and twelve in 1973. Milk, eggs, and cheese; personal transport equipment; personal care; and fruits and vegetables seem to have high price elasticities. Tobacco rather clearly has a low price elasticity.

The coefficient of the income variable is positive in almost every case. Elasticities are significantly above unity in one or both years for clothing, rents, fuel and power, furniture and appliances, medical care, communications, recreation, personal transport operating costs, and miscellaneous services. They are significantly below unity for milk, cheese, and eggs; fruits and vegetables; spices, sweets, and sugar; and public transport.

When these results based on sixteen countries are compared with those of the Phase I report based on ten countries, the coefficients of the income (consumption) term are found to be very similar. The price elasticities differ more, though their general pattern remains similar.[19] The differences between the two sets of price elasticities are not surprising in view of the relatively large standard errors associated with the price coefficients in both the Phase I and the present equations. (Compare the standard errors of the price coefficients with those of the income coefficients in Table 6.3.) When Phase II data are used for both the original ten and the six new countries, the standard analysis of covariance test indicates (at the 5 percent level of significance) that in all but two of the categories (gross rents and personal care) the hypothesis cannot be rejected that the coefficients of the equation for the ten countries are equal to those of the equation for the six countries.[20] A joint test of all twenty-five analyses of covariance can be carried out using the Kolmogoroff-Smirnov test.[21] Under the null hypothesis that the new six countries are like the old ten for all twenty-five categories, the set of twenty-five analysis of covariance F-statistics constitute twenty-five random drawings [22] from the distribution of $F(3,10)$. The Kolmogoroff-Smirnov test that indeed these twenty-five observations may be regarded as such drawings is passed at the 0.12 significance level.

bias and mean-square error. See C. Hale, R. S. Mariano, and J. G. Ramage, "Finite Sample Analysis of Misspecification in Simultaneous Equation Models," Discussion Paper no. 357 (Philadelphia: Department of Economics, University of Pennsylvania, February 1978, processed); also *Journal of American Statistical Association* (in press).

19. The rank correlation between the Phase I and the present 1970 price elasticities is 0.58, significant at the 1 percent level.

20. See Johnston, *Econometric Methods.*

21. See W. L. Hays and R. L. Winkler, *Statistics: Probability Inference and Decision* (New York: Holt, Rinehart, and Winston, 1971), pp. 817–21.

22. The interdependence of consumption for the twenty-five categories make these drawings not quite independent even under the null hypothesis.

Table 6.3. Regressions of Real per Capita Quantities on Relative Price and per Capita Consumption, 1970 and 1973: Twenty-five Summary Groupings

Category	Natural log of relative price (1)	Natural log of per capita consumption (2)	Constant (3)	$\bar{R}^2$ (4)
1970				
Bread and Cereals	−0.5709	0.0092	4.0744	−0.0632
	(0.5526)	(0.1099)	(0.7643)	(0.3696)
Meat	−0.9810	1.1654	−3.7312	0.7822
	(0.6389)	(0.1702)	(1.2485)	(0.5632)
Fish	−0.1341	0.4545	−0.7532	0.0113
	(0.8915)	(0.3118)	(2.1483)	(1.0212)
Milk, Cheese, and Eggs	−2.0345	0.5323	0.1350	0.9080
	(0.4097)	(0.1260)	(0.9303)	(0.2964)
Oils and Fats	0.1299	1.0533	−4.6701	0.6238
	(0.7432)	(0.3023)	(2.3859)	(0.6609)
Fruits and Vegetables	−1.3786	0.7047	−0.8135	0.5910
	(0.7979)	(0.1640)	(1.1637)	(0.5499)
Coffee, Tea, and Cocoa	−0.9782	1.0312	−4.3658	0.7591
	(0.2989)	(0.2006)	(1.4911)	(0.6547)
Spices, Sweets, and Sugar	−0.4857	0.5804	−0.4717	0.7752
	(0.4289)	(0.1121)	(0.8977)	(0.3059)
Beverages	−1.0885	1.1070	−4.0731	0.8160
	(0.5723)	(0.3294)	(2.4421)	(0.6738)
Tobacco	−0.2844	1.0089	−3.8288	0.8811
	(0.2258)	(0.1086)	(0.7695)	(0.3395)
Clothing	−0.4222	1.1745	−3.8584	0.9468
	(0.3349)	(0.0728)	(0.5161)	(0.2447)
Footwear	−0.6343	1.2259	−6.0742	0.8528
	(0.4205)	(0.1324)	(0.9380)	(0.4206)
Gross Rents	−0.9377	1.2608	−4.3940	0.9200
	(0.2347)	(0.1131)	(0.7826)	(0.3696)
Fuel and Power	−0.5547	1.2017	−4.7850	0.9119
	(0.2377)	(0.1034)	(0.7485)	(0.3427)
Furniture and Appliances	−0.6793	1.7021	−8.1667	0.9573
	(0.4516)	(0.1097)	(0.8330)	(0.3282)
Supplies and Operations	−0.7285	1.0931	−4.2227	0.8599
	(0.3978)	(0.1127)	(0.8004)	(0.3735)
Medical Care	−0.7557	1.3588	−5.7671	0.9587
	(0.1852)	(0.0729)	(0.5618)	(0.2340)
Personal Transport Equipment	−1.9288	1.2648	−4.8832	0.9019
	(0.4947)	(0.3299)	(2.6446)	(0.6890)
Operation Costs	−1.3965	1.8906	−9.7596	0.8463
	(0.5897)	(0.2124)	(1.4957)	(0.7179)
Public Transport	−0.4012	0.5039	−0.3029	0.4545
	(0.4464)	(0.1325)	(0.9168)	(0.4393)
Communications	−1.0716	1.6094	−9.7082	0.8690
	(0.4113)	(0.1603)	(1.1598)	(0.5101)
Recreation	−1.0702	1.5076	−6.6818	0.9149
	(0.4874)	(0.1330)	(0.9441)	(0.4285)
Education	−0.5445	0.9262	−2.5322	0.8696
	(0.2365)	(0.1313)	(1.0320)	(0.2294)
Personal Care	−1.8097	1.0711	−4.3854	0.8766
	(0.4980)	(0.1124)	(0.7873)	(0.3791)
Miscellaneous Services	−1.0156	1.3943	−5.6228	0.9331
	(0.4259)	(0.0995)	(0.7409)	(0.3054)

Table 6.3 continued.

Category	Natural log of relative price (1)	Natural log of per capita consumption (2)	Constant (3)	$\bar{R}^2$ (4)
1973				
Bread and Cereals	−0.4969	−0.0174	4.4937	−0.0790
	(0.5239)	(0.1150)	(0.8288)	(0.3888)
Meat	−0.7590	1.1581	−3.8596	0.7845
	(0.6238)	(0.1609)	(1.1993)	(0.5482)
Fish	−0.4226	0.4513	−0.5841	0.0079
	(0.6820)	(0.3130)	(2.2518)	(1.0280)
Milk, Cheese, and Eggs	−1.5502	0.6335	−0.6032	0.8942
	(0.3704)	(0.1183)	(0.8992)	(0.3106)
Oils and Fats	−0.2289	0.8837	−3.3583	0.5954
	(0.6046)	(0.2801)	(2.2262)	(0.6741)
Fruits and Vegetables	−1.6957	0.6264	−0.2036	0.6865
	(0.6294)	(0.1562)	(1.1599)	(0.5044)
Coffee, Tea, and Cocoa	−0.7822	0.9781	−4.2766	0.7774
	(0.2669)	(0.1685)	(1.2957)	(0.5604)
Spices, Sweets and Sugar	−0.0318	0.6721	−1.3027	0.7746
	(0.3641)	(0.1102)	(0.9298)	(0.3182)
Beverages	−0.9151	1.2077	−4.9125	0.7696
	(0.6629)	(0.3475)	(2.6653)	(0.7647)
Tobacco	−0.1746	1.0014	−3.8799	0.8623
	(0.2998)	(0.1186)	(0.8731)	(0.3631)
Clothing	−0.3950	1.1514	−3.7531	0.9397
	(0.4213)	(0.0773)	(0.5766)	(0.2613)
Footwear	−0.4949	1.1118	−5.2750	0.8410
	(0.3996)	(0.1245)	(0.9051)	(0.4115)
Gross Rents	−0.8854	1.2681	−4.4669	0.8972
	(0.2603)	(0.1274)	(0.9181)	(0.4265)
Fuel and Power	−0.7510	1.1836	−4.7106	0.9555
	(0.1800)	(0.0736)	(0.5494)	(0.2463)
Furniture and Appliances	−0.1860	1.7785	−9.0301	0.9653
	(0.5641)	(0.1383)	(1.1455)	(0.3045)
Supplies and Operation	−0.5394	1.0671	−3.9983	0.8431
	(0.4293)	(0.1175)	(0.8573)	(0.4022)
Medical Care	−0.8448	1.4154	−6.2589	0.9620
	(0.1920)	(0.0751)	(0.6156)	(0.2275)
Personal Transport Equipment	−1.8358	1.3274	−5.3752	0.9000
	(0.4926)	(0.3025)	(2.5234)	(0.6763)
Operation Costs	−1.3561	1.9184	−10.1618	0.8357
	(0.5992)	(0.2220)	(1.6150)	(0.7624)
Public Transport	−0.8072	0.4753	−0.0062	0.4604
	(0.3838)	(0.1369)	(0.9854)	(0.4662)
Communications	−1.1795	1.6593	−10.2082	0.8738
	(0.3477)	(0.1616)	(1.2173)	(0.5118)
Recreation	−0.4041	1.5422	−7.1186	0.9140
	(0.4969)	(0.1292)	(0.9542)	(0.4260)
Education	−0.7168	1.0340	−3.3537	0.9318
	(0.1526)	(0.0924)	(0.7415)	(0.1685)
Personal Care	−1.9789	1.0421	−4.1577	0.9024
	(0.4524)	(0.1055)	(0.7792)	(0.3546)
Miscellaneous Services	−1.0214	1.4142	−5.8902	0.9476
	(0.3667)	(0.0873)	(0.6714)	(0.2794)

Notes: The basic equation for these regressions in equation 6.6 in the text. The numbers in parentheses in columns 1–3 are coefficient standard errors. $\bar{R}^2$ is the coefficient of determination. The numbers in parentheses in column 4 are standard errors of estimate (SEE).

Detailed categories

The results of the demand equations for the detailed categories in Table 6.4 are similar in broad pattern to those for the summary categories. The description of the equations that follows is based on 109 detailed consumption categories for 1970, but it fits the 1973 results almost as well.

The proportion of variance in quantities explained tends to be smaller than for the summary categories. Although 79 percent of the $\bar{R}^2$s are 0.50 or higher, only 34 percent exceed 0.80. In all but 10 percent of the equations, the price coefficients are negative, virtually half of the coefficients being significantly different from zero at the 5 percent level. Indeed, about 10 percent are significantly elastic. About an equal proportion of the price coefficients are significantly inelastic.

All but five of the income coefficients are positive, more than 80 percent of them are significantly different from zero at the 5 percent level, and nearly 40 percent are significantly above 1.0 (that is, the categories are income elastic). The negative coefficients are generally found for categories in which it would be expected that the income inelasticity would be very low: rice; meal and other cereals; cereal preparations; salt, spices, and sauces; and bus transport.

A comparison of the new six countries with the original ten was made for about two-thirds of the 109 detailed categories. As in the case of the summary category comparisons, the demand relationships for the new six countries tend to be the same as for the original ten.

The conclusion of this demand investigation is a confirmation of the Phase I results: prices and income indeed explain consumption patterns, and this appears to hold over a diverse set of countries and at least for time periods not far apart.[23]

Category and Country Influences on Relative Prices

In this section the relationship of price structures to country and commodity characteristics is explored briefly. A crudely empirical approach would be to employ the technique of analysis of variance to decompose the price of a category in a country into a "country effect" and a "category effect." This could be accomplished by regressing price, denoted R_{ij}, on two sets of dummy variables, one representing the different countries and the other representing the categories.[24] (Observe that this is what was done in the application of the CPD method described in Chapter 3, but that application was for a different purpose.) Were such a procedure carried out, the obvious next step would be to seek an explanation of the observed pattern of the dummy coefficients. One would want to know why the coefficients for some countries indicated higher prices than the coefficients for others, and why some commodities tend to have higher relative prices than others. Such a research strategy would lead to a search for country characteristics that would explain the country dummies and for category characteristics that would explain the category dummies. At a deeper level of analysis, an interaction term might be included.

In fact, a more efficient procedure than this is to attempt to explain the R_{ij}s directly in terms of country and category characteristics. The analysis

23. In the next phase of the ICP work, enough categories will be included finally to make possible verification of this proposition using a full-scale interdependent system demand analysis.

24. As explained earlier in this chapter and more fully in Chapter 4, each R_{ij} is a measure of the relative price of a particular category (i) in a particular country (j) compared with the relative international price for the category. R_{ij} is obtained by dividing the j'th country's percentage share of GDP devoted to the i'th category as valued in its own currency by the percentage share when its GDP is valued at international prices.

Table 6.4. Regressions of Real per Capita Quantities on Relative Price and per Capita Consumption, 1970: Sixty-seven Detailed Categories

Code	Category	Natural log of relative price (1)	Natural log of per capita consumption (2)	Constant (3)	$\bar{R}^2$ (4)
1.101	Rice	0.7960 (1.3201)	−1.0242 (0.4968)	8.4675 (3.6046)	0.1717 (1.6597)
1.102	Meal and Other Cereals	−0.8587 (0.5308)	−0.8259 (0.2499)	8.0437 (1.7438)	0.4465 (0.8436)
1.104	Biscuits, Cakes and the like	−0.8656 (0.2082)	1.4004 (0.1642)	−7.5971 (1.1687)	0.8724 (0.5475)
1.111	Fresh Beef and Veal	−1.6337 (0.8938)	1.2855 (0.3505)	−5.9053 (2.4380)	0.4832 (1.1825)
1.114	Fresh poultry	0.4365 (0.7258)	1.3380 (0.2714)	−7.6664 (2.1589)	0.6445 (0.7899)
1.121	Fresh and Frozen Fish	0.6225 (0.8713)	0.4031 (0.2965)	−0.8410 (2.0604)	0.0414 (0.9941)
1.122	Canned Fish	−1.8606 (0.4937)	0.7295 (0.3314)	−3.3613 (2.3078)	0.5233 (1.1194)
1.131	Fresh Milk	−2.4353 (0.3945)	0.3047 (0.2411)	0.7539 (1.7319)	0.8202 (0.6756)
1.132	Milk Products	−2.0583 (0.7056)	0.7932 (0.3194)	−3.0982 (2.3160)	0.7270 (0.8187)
1.133	Eggs and Egg Products	1.7634 (0.8391)	1.9289 (0.2892)	−12.2925 (2.3085)	0.8060 (0.6423)
1.141	Butter	−0.6657 (0.7501)	1.3635 (0.3658)	−8.1853 (2.6493)	0.5114 (1.1918)
1.142	Margarine and Edible Oil	−1.8958 (0.9706)	0.2367 (0.5194)	1.0984 (4.0041)	0.5399 (0.9326)
1.153	Fresh Vegetables	−1.5968 (0.5820)	0.6414 (0.1656)	−2.3061 (1.1622)	0.5878 (0.5594)
1.170	Potato, Manioc, and Tubers	−1.5731 (0.5376)	0.4538 (0.2222)	−1.7784 (1.5512)	0.4157 (0.7510)
1.180	Sugar	−1.0532 (0.4451)	0.1196 (0.2034)	1.9959 (1.5638)	0.3831 (0.5616)
1.201	Jam, Syrup, and Honey	−1.4029 (0.6060)	0.5917 (0.3579)	−3.0523 (2.6634)	0.5905 (0.9036)
1.203	Salt, Spices, and Sauces	−1.3824 (1.1016)	−0.0239 (0.3091)	1.5770 (2.1231)	−0.0249 (1.0113)
1.310	Nonalcoholic Beverages	−0.4826 (0.6173)	1.3293 (0.4043)	−7.7268 (3.0444)	0.7913 (0.7083)
1.321	Spirits	−0.7620 (0.5872)	1.0289 (0.3838)	−5.1383 (2.7215)	0.5600 (1.0241)
1.323	Beer	−0.3932 (0.7612)	1.4740 (0.4903)	−8.2417 (3.5867)	0.6537 (1.0310)
1.410	Cigarettes	−0.6441 (0.2629)	1.0427 (0.1486)	−4.2221 (1.0600)	0.8383 (0.4647)
2.110	Clothing Materials	−0.3618 (0.6338)	0.1547 (0.2533)	1.4210 (1.9550)	−0.0676 (0.8067)
2.121	Men's Clothing	−1.0035 (1.0649)	1.5722 (0.2670)	−8.2827 (1.8624)	0.6967 (0.9005)
2.122	Women's Clothing	−0.1717 (0.3834)	1.7973 (0.1705)	−10.1147 (1.2010)	0.8799 (0.5757)
2.131	Men's and Boys' Underwear	−0.4491 (0.7475)	1.5595 (0.2354)	−9.3221 (1.6447)	0.7369 (0.7953)
2.132	Women's and Girls' Underwear	0.0603 (0.4656)	1.9207 (0.1540)	−11.7079 (1.0794)	0.9111 (0.5204)

(Table continues on the following page)

Table 6.4 continued.

Code	Category	Natural log of relative price (1)	Natural log of per capita consumption (2)	Constant (3)	$\bar{R}^2$ (4)
2.150	Haberdashery and Millinery	−1.0070 (0.7860)	1.3374 (0.1911)	−7.7239 (1.3309)	0.7673 (0.6453)
2.211	Men's Footwear	−0.4053 (0.4929)	1.0727 (0.1331)	−5.9737 (0.9254)	0.8076 (0.4478)
2.212	Women's Footwear	−1.0614 (0.3325)	1.4075 (0.1526)	−8.5055 (1.0707)	0.8484 (0.5001)
2.213	Children's Footwear	−0.7590 (0.4795)	1.2674 (0.2125)	−8.2094 (1.5509)	0.7004 (0.6419)
3.110	Rents	−0.9402 (0.2575)	1.2304 (0.1256)	−4.2788 (0.8690)	0.9083 (0.3997)
3.120	Indoor Repair and Upkeep	−0.9558 (0.5265)	1.8159 (0.3070)	−11.0081 (2.2118)	0.6886 (0.9628)
3.210	Electricity	−0.7396 (0.2856)	1.6927 (0.1483)	−9.3678 (1.1451)	0.9518 (0.3840)
3.230	Liquid Fuels	−0.8221 (0.6101)	1.1996 (0.4315)	−6.4730 (3.3602)	0.7975 (0.7462)
3.240	Other Fuels and Ice	−0.7340 (0.4717)	0.5825 (0.2783)	−2.1017 (1.9184)	0.1879 (0.9075)
4.110	Furniture and Fixtures	−0.6009 (0.6085)	1.9599 (0.2003)	−11.2645 (1.3959)	0.8635 (0.6769)
4.200	Household Textiles and the like	−1.0904 (0.5253)	1.6074 (0.1824)	−8.9674 (1.2931)	0.8435 (0.6163)
4.310	Refrigerators and Freezers	−0.0998 (0.3041)	1.9218 (0.2610)	−12.5509 (2.0148)	0.9065 (0.5537)
4.400	Household Utensils	−0.8151 (0.4143)	1.3804 (0.1873)	−7.4652 (1.3044)	0.8307 (0.5987)
4.510	Nondurable household goods	−1.9260 (0.7600)	0.7743 (0.2886)	−2.3970 (2.2147)	0.8306 (0.5586)
5.110	Drugs and Medical Preparation	−0.8401 (0.2646)	1.3339 (0.1289)	−6.5051 (0.8874)	0.9206 (0.3953)
5.310	Physicians' Services	−0.3524 (0.1008)	1.2644 (0.1067)	−6.3748 (0.7914)	0.9070 (0.3125)
5.320	Dentists' Services	−0.1506 (0.0986)	1.6485 (0.1832)	−10.1851 (1.3291)	0.8559 (0.5433)
5.330	Nurses' Services	−0.4887 (0.1643)	0.9881 (0.1543)	−5.2061 (1.0742)	0.7558 (0.5212)
5.410	Hospitals	−0.3936 (0.1444)	1.2228 (0.1569)	−6.3916 (1.0850)	0.8311 (0.5248)
6.110	Personal Automobiles	−1.7069 (0.5153)	1.4004 (0.3703)	−6.0993 (2.9622)	0.8848 (0.7750)
6.310	Local Transport	−1.3932 (0.4918)	1.0445 (0.2305)	−6.1152 (1.7691)	0.5554 (0.6551)
6.321	Rail Transport	−3.1831 (1.0315)	1.0548 (0.3163)	−7.0712 (2.2142)	0.5604 (1.0690)
6.322	Bus Transport	0.4656 (0.6643)	−0.1210 (0.2322)	2.4876 (1.6896)	−0.1042 (0.7403)
6.410	Postal Communication	−2.1066 (0.3942)	1.4228 (0.1812)	−9.5567 (1.2627)	0.8982 (0.5760)
6.420	Telephone and Telegraph	−1.1179 (0.3779)	1.6117 (0.2069)	−10.1802 (1.4962)	0.7984 (0.6157)
7.110	Radios, Televisions, and Phonographs	−1.0691 (0.3381)	1.3429 (0.1751)	−6.7859 (1.4103)	0.9293 (0.4249)
7.130	Other Recreational Equipment	−0.5638 (0.6151)	2.2856 (0.2437)	−14.1261 (1.8458)	0.8964 (0.7088)
7.210	Public Entertainment	−0.7820 (0.6661)	1.5927 (0.3475)	−9.8113 (2.4342)	0.5823 (1.1735)

Table 6.4 continued.

Code	Category	Natural log of relative price (1)	Natural log of per capita consump- tion (2)	Constant (3)	$\bar{R}^2$ (4)
7.230	Other Recreational and Cultural Actvities	−0.9947 (0.3024)	1.2780 (0.2113)	−7.5339 (1.4985)	0.7157 (0.6900)
7.310	Books, Papers, and Magazines	−0.9402 (0.6819)	1.5357 (0.2239)	−8.6360 (1.6253)	0.8532 (0.6198)
7.411	First- and Second- level Teachers	−0.2675 (0.1313)	0.6341 (0.1025)	−0.8160 (0.8156)	0.8475 (0.1696)
7.412	College Teachers	−0.9882 (0.1797)	1.3376 (0.1536)	−7.7844 (1.0829)	0.8498 (0.5009)
7.420	Physical Facilities for Education	−1.2658 (1.2156)	1.2654 (0.2764)	−6.7147 (2.2463)	0.7856 (0.6638)
7.431	Educational Books and Supplies	−1.2217 (0.8677)	0.5626 (0.2876)	−3.4039 (2.0698)	0.4185 (0.8090)
7.432	Other Educational Expenditures	−0.5847 (1.1800)	0.9010 (0.3033)	−4.9992 (2.4102)	0.4903 (0.8310)
8.100	Barber and Beauty Shops	−1.9510 (0.5300)	1.3502 (0.2455)	−9.3821 (1.8611)	0.6917 (0.8010)
8.210	Toilet Articles	−0.4627 (0.5790)	1.2692 (0.2204)	−7.0400 (1.6936)	0.8449 (0.5176)
8.220	Other Personal Care Goods	−0.0832 (0.4498)	1.0911 (0.1611)	−5.8923 (1.1046)	0.7533 (0.5304)
8.310	Restaurants and Cafes	−1.0801 (0.3555)	1.5903 (0.1617)	−7.5098 (1.1298)	0.8962 (0.5266)
8.320	Hotels and Lodgings	−2.4402 (0.8876)	1.2700 (0.3357)	−6.9167 (2.3308)	0.6820 (1.0550)
8.400	Other Services	−2.5665 (1.2890)	1.4763 (0.4835)	−8.6594 (3.9061)	0.3710 (0.8366)

Notes: The basic equation for these regressions is equation 6.6 in the text. The numbers in parentheses in columns 1–3 are coefficient standard errors. $\bar{R}^2$ is the coefficient of determination. The numbers in parentheses in column 4 are standard errors of estimate (SEE).

below follows this approach, but it is limited to only the most obvious characteristics. The characteristics included are country per capita income and category income elasticity of demand. In addition, variables from the supply side reflecting factor intensities are considered. It will be seen that the empirical analysis is enlightening, but it cannot be regarded as entirely successful.

The role of income and income elasticity in explaining R_{ij}s has been the subject of speculation in the economic literature. One way in which these variables have been linked together is in the presumption that luxuries tend to be cheap in rich countries and dear in poor ones, and that the opposite is the case for necessities. If true, this would have important implications for international comparisons of real income. The implications, which relate to the behavior of index numbers when different weights are used, have been explored by P. A. Samuelson and much of what follows rests heavily on his work.[25]

As already commented upon, the income of one country relative to another

The demand side

25. See P. A. Samuelson, "Analytical Notes on International Real Income Measures," *Economic Journal*, September 1974.

Figure 6.1

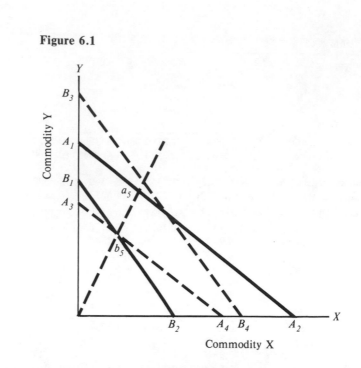

Commodity X

will usually appear higher when its quantities are valued in the other country's prices than when valued in its own prices. Thus, the own-weighted binary indexes of per capita GDP reported in Chapter 5 were consistently lower than the corresponding U.S.-weighted indexes.[26] This "own-weight" effect has generally been observed in other studies also.[27]

The "luxuries-are-cheaper-in-rich-countries" proposition is a sufficient condition for this phenomenon to hold. The sufficiency condition may be explained in terms of Figures 6.1 and 6.2. In the first figure, B_1B_2 and A_1A_2 are the budget constraints of a poor country, B, and a rich country, A. Observe that without loss of generality the price ratio p_x/p_y facing A is chosen lower than the ratio facing B. Simple recourse to Euclidean geometry will show that, if A's consumption point, a^*, on A_1A_2 is to the right of (below) a_5, the intersection of A_1A_2 and the ray emanating from the origin through b_5, then the own-weight effect will show up. That is, the comparison of B with A using B's prices will make B look worse than the comparison using A's prices.[28] If a^* is to the left (above), the converse will hold.

Is there reason to expect a^* to be on the segment a_5A_2? The answer depends upon substitution and income effects. (Note that throughout this discussion it is assumed that tastes are the same in A and B, and that they can be represented by the indifference map of representative persons from each country.) In the unlikely event of a zero substitution effect and an income elasticity of precisely 1, a^* will be right at a_5, and B will look just as good

26. Incidentally, the Geary–Khamis international price-weighted indexes were consistently between the two.

27. In the intertemporal context, this is equivalent to what might be called the "excess Laspeyres effect"; that is, a Laspeyres quantity index will usually indicate the current year's quantity to be larger than will the current year Paasche index. This has sometimes been referred to as the "Gerschenkron effect."

28. At A's prices, given by the slope of A_1A_2, the ratio of B's income to A's is OA_3/OA_1. At B's prices, given by the slope of B_1B_2, the ratio is OB_1/OB_3. The latter ratio will be larger than, equal to, or smaller than the former depending upon whether A's consumption point (shown by the intersection of A_1A_2 and B_3B_4) is to the left of a_5, at a_5, or to the right of a_5. The proof draws upon similar triangles to show that when A's consumption point is at a_5, $OB_1/OB_3 = Ob/Oa_5 = OA_3/OA_1$.

Figure 6.2

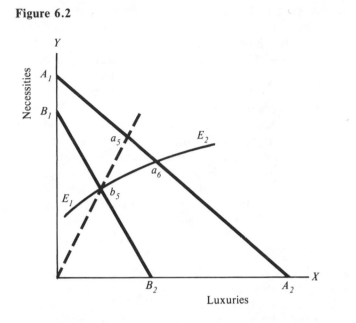

(or bad) relative to A whichever country's prices are used. Since substitution effects are never positive, an income elasticity of greater than 1.0 is enough to assure that a^* will lie to the right of a_5.

Now impose the "luxuries-are-cheaper-in-rich-countries" empirical proposition. Since p_x/p_y is smaller for A than B, x must be a luxury and y a necessity. Because luxuries are goods for which the income elasticity is greater than 1.0 (by definition), the income-consumption curve (that is, the Engel curve) based upon B's prices, E_1E_2 in Figure 6.2, must intersect A_1A_2 to the right of a_5. If the substitution effect is zero, a^* will be at a_6; if it is nonzero, a will lie even further down a_5A_2. Thus, if luxuries are cheaper in rich countries, the own-weight effect will definitely be observed.

It is important to note, however, that the premise is not a necessary condition. If necessities are cheaper in the rich country—now y is the luxury and x is the necessity—then the intersection of E_1E_2 and A_1A_2, a_6 will lie to the left of a_5. Whether the own-weight effect will show up in this case turns on the relative strength of the income and substitution effects and on the magnitude of the differences in income and relative prices between A and B. The substitution effect pushes a^* to the right (downward) along A_1A_2. The more powerful the substitution effect, the more likely a^* will lie to the right of a_5; the effect of a large price difference will be similar.

Thus, the commonly observed own-weight effect cannot be invoked as indirect evidence that luxuries are cheap in rich countries. Cheap necessities in rich countries with extensive price-induced substitution could also produce the effect. The actual reason for the observed effect is an empirical question upon which ICP data can be brought to bear.

As Samuelson has pointed out, it is possible to conjure up various situations in which luxuries may be dear or cheap in rich countries.[29] For example, with appropriate attendant assumptions, luxuries may be dear in rich countries because they are labor intensive and labor is expensive there; or because the demand for luxuries is higher relative to other goods, and the law of diminishing returns comes into play. On the other hand, luxuries may be cheap be-

29. Samuelson, "Analytical Notes on International Real Income Measures," p. 596.

cause the greater demand makes it possible to take advantage of scale economies; or because, though they are labor intensive, the rich country enjoys a
markedly higher productivity of labor relative to its margin of superiority in
the productivity of other factors. These alternatives are not explored here.
Rather, an attempt is made to ascertain whether there is any systematic tendency for luxuries to be relatively low in price in high-income countries.

The data required for this investigation are relative prices, per capita income
levels, and indicators of the degree to which each good may be considered a
necessity or a luxury. Relative prices were measured by the same R_{ij}'s that
were used in the section on the similarity of quantity and price structures.
Real consumption per capita (designated in this section as "y" to denote
the role it serves) was used as the income variable, since the analysis was
confined to consumption. The income elasticities (η) estimated in the demand
equations of the section on demand analyses above served as a continuous
variable to provide a gauge of the extent to which each expenditure category
was a necessity ($\eta < 1$) or a luxury ($\eta > 1$).

The relationship was specified in the simplest way consistent with the
possibility that the association between R_{ij} and y varied with the income
elasticity. The relationship between R_{ij} and y_j was assumed to be linear with
the slope and intercept depending systematically on the income elasticity. The
luxuries-are-cheaper-in-rich-countries proposition implies that the slope will
be negative for income-elastic categories and positive for income-inelastic
categories. By introducing into a regression of R_{ij} on income (y_j) a linear
term for η and an interaction term, the data were allowed to show whether the
slopes do indeed vary. The equation estimated was:

$$(6.7) \qquad R_{ij} = \alpha_1 y_j + \beta_1 \eta_i + \gamma_1 y_j \eta_i + \delta_1 + u_{ij}{}^1. \qquad \begin{array}{l} i = 1, \ldots, m \\ j = 1, \ldots, 16 \end{array}$$

The number of observations available for estimating the parameters is 16
times the number of categories.

Equation 6.7 can be rewritten to make explicit the dependence of the
slope in the (R_{ij}, y_j) space upon η_i:

$$(6.8) \qquad R_{ij} = \gamma_1 y_j \left(\eta_i + \frac{\alpha_1}{\gamma_1} \right) + (\beta_1 \eta_i + \delta_1) + u_{ij}{}^1$$

The luxuries-are-cheaper-in-rich-countries notion in a literal sense implies
that $\frac{\alpha_1}{\gamma_1} = -1$ and $\gamma_1 < 0$. This asserts that $\alpha_1 = -\gamma_1$, $\gamma_1 < 0$, $\alpha_1 > 0$. (Incidentally, also implied is $\beta_1 > 0$ and $\beta_1 + \delta_1 = 1$.) A more liberal interpretation
would only demand that $\frac{\alpha_1}{\gamma_1}$ be in the neighborhood of 1 (and β_1 be in the
neighborhood of $1 - \delta_1$).

Each country's observations were introduced into the regression with a
weight equal to the importance of the category in the country's consumption
as measured by international prices. Weighting is necessary to ensure that
each country's average R_{ij} is equal to 1. This avoids the possibility that the
average R_{ij}s will be correlated with the y_js, an economic anomaly. Equations
6.9 and 6.10 give the regressions for 25 summary categories and 109 detailed
categories, respectively.

$$(6.9) \qquad R_{ij} = -0.0392 \, y_j + 0.0031 \, \eta_i + 0.0293 \, y_j \eta_i + 0.9995$$
$$\qquad\qquad (0.1534) \quad\; (0.0566) \quad\;\; (0.1316) \qquad (0.0583)$$

$$\bar{R}^2 = -0.0071$$
$$SEE = 0.3054$$
$$N = 400$$

(6.10) $R_{ij} = -0.0038\,y_j + 0.0268\,\eta_i - 0.0177\,y_j\eta_i + 0.9824$
$\qquad\qquad (0.0814)\quad (0.0226)\quad (0.0583)\quad\;\; (0.0268)$

$$\bar{R}^2 = -0.0005$$
$$\text{SEE} = 0.4451$$
$$\text{N} = 1{,}744$$

It is apparent that the data lend no support to the proposition. None of the coefficients is significantly different from 0; what is more, the signs of three of the four slope coefficients are wrong. Other experiments with the data including the use of alternative functional forms, the omission of weights, and the use of other combinations of categories produced equivalent results. Clearly, the own-weight effect cannot be ascribed to any general tendency for luxuries to be cheap in rich countries. Although the converse is not true either—that luxuries are cheap in poor countries—the implication is that the own-weight effect must be attributable to sufficiently large price elasticities for the mix of goods (both luxuries and necessities) that are cheap in rich countries to bring about a compensating expansion in their consumption in the rich country.

An alternative line of investigation into the determinants of relative product prices is the varying intensities with which various factors are employed in the production of different goods. It is a familiar proposition that the price of a good will be relatively high if its production is intensive in a factor that is relatively high in price. Since labor is relatively expensive in rich countries and capital relatively cheap, and since the opposite is true in poor countries, the R_{ij}s for labor-intensive goods should be relatively low in poor countries and high in rich countries whereas the opposite should be true for capital-intensive goods. If these statements about the factor intensities were to hold empirically, then there would be a strong presumption that the luxuries-are-cheaper-in-rich-countries proposition foundered because necessities are generally not labor intensive and luxuries are generally not capital intensive.

An investigation of the relationship between relative product prices on the one hand and factor intensities on the other would ideally entail information on each of these variables in each country. The relative commodity prices, the R_{ij}'s, are, of course, available. Factor prices are notoriously difficult to obtain on an internationally comparable basis, but there is a very strong presumption that relative factor prices (price ratios of labor to capital) are highly correlated with per capita income. Real GDP per capita, therefore, is used as a proxy for relative factor prices.[30] Unfortunately, data on factor intensities for the various commodities are difficult to obtain on a country-by-country basis.[31] The compromise followed here is the usual one of using

The supply side

30. GDP seems to be the appropriate income concept here, rather than consumption per capita, which was used in equations 6.9 and 6.10.

31. For present purposes, labor per unit of output for consumption categories was taken from an updated version of Table B-16 in U.S. Department of Labor, *Structure of the U.S. Economy in 1980 and 1985*, Bureau of Labor Statistics Bulletin 1831 (1975). The table gives direct and indirect employment per billion U.S. dollars of delivery to final demand in 1970 (in terms of 1963 producers' values) for each of 129 industries. (Note that this measure does not take account of the difference in quality mix of labor across industries.) Capital per unit of output was taken from U.S. Department of Commerce, *A Study of Fixed Capital Requirements of the U.S. Business Economy, 1971–1980* PB–248–690 (Springfield, Va.: National Technical Information Service, December 1975), Appendix Table 5. The table gives the direct and indirect capital requirements per dollar of output for 1967 in 1958 dollars for 77 industries. A matching of the classifications used in the Bureau of Labor Statistics and Commerce Department tabulations and the ICP classification produced twenty categories for which both relative prices and factor intensities were available. Of these, one category was food, eight were at

data on factor intensities for a single country—the United States—and relying on the absence of reversals of factor intensities.[32] The common, but unsatisfactory, practice of excluding natural resources from consideration is followed.

When the factor intensities were correlated with income elasticity, the r's were -0.12 and 0.02 for the labor and capital intensities, respectively. Thus, whatever is found about the empirical relation between the R_{ij}s and the factor intensities, the fact that luxuries are not consistently either labor intensive or capital intensive removes the basis for expecting luxuries in rich countries to be generally either expensive or cheap.

Turning now to the relationship between R_{ij} and income and the factor intensities, equations 6.11 and 6.12 are written in a form parallel with 6.9.

$$(6.11) \qquad R_{ij} = \alpha_2 y_j + \beta_2 L_i + \gamma_2 y_j L_i + \delta_2 + u_{ij}^2,$$

$$i = 1, \ldots, 20$$
$$j = 1, \ldots, 16$$

$$(6.12) \qquad R_{ij} = \alpha_3 y_j + \beta_3 K_i + \gamma_3 y_j K_i + \delta_3 + u_{ij}^3,$$

where L_i is the labor output ratio and K_i the capital output ratio for the i'th category. Rearranging terms, as when dealing with the income-elasticity equation, produces equations 6.13 and 6.14:

$$(6.13) \qquad R_{ij} = \gamma_2 y_j \left(L_i + \frac{\alpha_2}{\gamma_2} \right) + (\beta_2 L_i + \delta_2) + u_{ij}^2,$$

$$(6.14) \qquad R_{ij} = \gamma_3 y_j \left(K_i + \frac{\alpha_3}{\gamma_3} \right) + (\beta_3 K_i + \delta_3) + u_{ij}^3.$$

Since it is to be expected that labor and therefore labor-intensive goods are more expensive in rich countries, then α_2 and γ_2 should be opposite in sign:

$\gamma_2 > 0$, $\beta_2 < 0$, and $\beta_2 \left(-\dfrac{\alpha_2}{\gamma_2} \right) + \delta_2 = 1$. The value of $-\dfrac{\alpha_2}{\gamma_2}$ cannot be specified

because it depends upon the critical value of L at which the R_{ij}s are independent of a country's income level. With respect to equation 6.14, since capital and therefore capital-intensive goods tend to be cheap in rich countries, α_3 and γ_3 should be opposite in sign: $\gamma_3 < 0$, $\beta_3 > 0$, and $\beta_3(-\alpha_3/\gamma_3) + \delta_3 = 1$. As in the case of labor, the value of (α_3/γ_3) cannot be specified.

The regressions of equations 6.11 and 6.12 were run using a hybrid set of 21 categories for which matches could be established between the classifications for which factor intensities were available and the ICP categories for which relative prices were in hand.

The fitted equations, in which the observations were weighted, were as follows:

---

the summary category level, and eleven were at the detailed category level. The large preponderance of consumption was covered by these categories; the chief omissions were services of medical personnel and personal care services.

32. This common empirical procedure is not universally accepted. See, for example, the assessment of the literature on factor reversal in R. Baldwin, "Determinants of the Commodity Structure of U.S. Trade," *American Economic Review* (March 1971), p. 129. If the assumption of no factor reversals could be relied upon, the disadvantage of not having factor intensities for each of the countries would be sharply reduced. There may be differences in overall or average labor and capital intensities for various countries, but these would not in themselves contribute anything to the explanation of the R_{ij}'s not already accounted for by the relative intensities for different goods and by relative factor prices. The relative factor intensities would be substantially similar for all countries in the absence of factor reversals, whereas the relative factor prices, proxied by y, vary from country to country.

(6.15) $R_{ij} = -0.2272\ y_j - 0.2029\ L_i + 0.3703\ y_j \cdot L_i + 1.1189;$
          $(0.0771)\quad (0.0527)\quad (0.0967)\qquad (0.0400)$

$$\bar{R}^2 = 0.0407$$
$$SEE = 0.3148$$
$$N = 320$$

(6.16) $R_{ij} = -0.6219\ y_j - 0.00034\ K_i + 0.00058\ y_j \cdot K_i + 1.3654.$
          $(0.1380)\quad (0.00007)\quad (0.00013)\qquad (0.0758)$

$$\bar{R}^2 = 0.0666$$
$$SEE = 0.3105$$
$$N = 320$$

The empirical results are a mixed bag. The coefficients of equation 6.15 appear to lend clear support to the hypothesis that labor-intensive goods tend to be expensive in rich countries. The coefficients of L_i and of the interaction term conform to expectations and $\beta_2(-\alpha_2/\gamma_2) + \delta_2 = 1$. Unfortunately, equation 6.16 comes out precisely contrary to expectations. Furthermore, the contrary coefficients are even statistically significant. Note that the highly significant t-ratios arise because of the relatively large samples. The coefficients of determination are very small, indicating that income per capita and these measures of factor intensity provide only a little explanation of relative prices. The implication is that capital-intensive goods also tend to be relatively expensive in rich countries.

It is tempting to try to explain away the latter result and retain the former on grounds that the measures of capital intensities are less reliable or less representative of countries other than the United States than the measures of labor intensities. Without further work, it would appear to be more appropriate to adopt a reserved position about the roles of both labor and capital intensities in explaining relative prices. Better results might be obtained with other measures of factor intensities such as those based on value added or those incorporating technological elements.[33] These and other possibilities are the subject of continuing work by the authors.

What can be concluded from this brief exploration of the determinants of relative prices across countries? The highly plausible conjecture that factor intensities and relative factor prices are key elements has not been confirmed, although there was some evidence in favor of a positive finding with respect to labor. It was possible to arrive at a definite assessment of the luxuries-are-cheaper-in-rich-countries proposition. The connection between factor intensities and income elasticities was very weak, and this alone is probably enough to foreclose the possibility that the proposition would hold. In addition, the proposition is undermined by the tenuous empirical connection between factor intensities and relative prices. Finally, it was found that the reason for the prevalence of the own-weight effect must lie in strong substitution effects.

Summary

This first effort to identify variables that might explain the differences in relative prices cannot be adjudged a success. The analysis in the previous sections of this chapter, however, had a happier outcome. It was shown that quantities, prices, and incomes—viewed across countries—are related in the way that the basic working models of economists posit: quantities (examined

---

33. The former would involve wage and nonwage value added per man and the latter would take account of such inputs as research and development or engineering and scientific personnel.

product category by product category) are negatively related to relative prices and are positively related to incomes. Or, to put it another way, the more similar are price structures and income levels, the more similar are the proportions in which the countries consume various products. With respect to these relationships of quantity, price, and income, the sixteen-country data of the present report confirm the findings of the Phase I report.

Glossary

Additivity: The property that makes it possible to have correct country-to-country quantity relationships for each detailed category, and, at the same time, to obtain the correct country-to-country quantity relationships for any desired aggregation of categories simply by summing the quantities for the included categories. This requires that the quantities be stated in value terms so that (1) the values for any category are directly comparable between countries and (2) the values for any country are directly comparable between categories.

Binary comparison: A price or quantity comparison between two countries without regard to the consistency of this comparison with comparisons of each of the countries with any third countries. (See **Circularity or transitivity.**)

Bridge-country binary comparison: A price or quantity comparison between a pair of countries derived from the comparison of each country with a third country. For example, given $I_{j/k}$ and $I_{l/k}$, the bridge-country method of obtaining $I_{j/l}$ is to divide $I_{j/k}$ by $I_{l/k}$, where I is a price or quantity index and j, k, and l are countries. (See also **Original-country binary comparison.**)

CEP (consumption expenditures of the population): The ICP concept of "consumption" that includes both household expenditures and expenditures of government on such categories as health and education. (See Table 2.1.)

Characteristicity: The property whereby the sample of prices or quantities and the weights used in an international comparison conform closely to a representative sample of items and to the weights of each of the countries included in the comparison.

Circularity or transitivity: There is circularity or transitivity if the indexes expressing the price or quantity relationships between any two among three or more countries are the same whether derived (1) from an original-country comparison between them or (2) from the comparison of each country with any third country. In the case of three countries, where I is a price or quantity index and j, k, and l are countries, the circular test is satisfied if: $I_{j/k} = I_{j/l} \div I_{k/l}$. When this test is satisfied, there is a unique cardinal scaling of countries with respect to relative quantities and prices.

Country-product–dummy (CPD) method: A generalized bridge-country method employing regression analysis to obtain transitive price comparisons for each detailed category. The basic data for a given category consist of all the prices available for the various specifications for the entire collection of countries. The prices are regressed against two sets of dummy variables: one set contains a dummy for each specification; the second set, a dummy for each country other than the numéraire country. The transitive price comparisons are derived from the cofficients of the country dummies. (See Chapter 3.)

Country-reversal test: This test is satisfied if, when country j is taken as the base country, the price or quantity index for countries j and k is the reciprocal of the index when country k is the base country. For example, $I_{j/k} \cdot I_{k/j} = 1$, where I is a price or quantity index.

Detailed categories: The subdivisions of final expenditure for which the first aggregation of price (or quantity) ratios for individual specifications or items takes place. (See Appendix Tables 4.1–4.5 and Appendix Table 5.1.)

255

Direct price or quantity comparison: One made by comparing for two or more countries the prices or quantities for a representative sample of equivalent commodities. (See also **Indirect price or quantity comparison.**)

Doubled-weighted CPD: A weighted CPD method in which the weights are the products of (1) the importance of each cell in the column in which it falls (the percentage of the country's expenditure) and (2) the importance of the cell in the row in which it falls (the percentage of the total quantity of the category in the sixteen countries). The double-weighted CPD is used to obtain PPPs for categories for which no price comparisons were made. The CPD is applied in this case to the matrix of PPPs in which the columns represent countries and the rows detailed categories. (See **Country-product–dummy method.**)

Exchange-rate–deviation index: The ratio of the real GDP per capita relative to the United States as estimated by the ICP to the GDP per capita relative to the United States when the exchange rate is used to convert nondollar currencies to dollars.

Factor-reversal test: The condition that, for any given item, category, or aggregate and for any given pair of countries, the product of the price ratio (or index) and the quantity ratio (or index) be equal to the expenditure ratio.

Final products: Products purchased for own use and not for resale or for embodiment in a product for resale; those purchased by households, by government, or by business on capital account.

Fisher, or "ideal," index: The geometric mean of two indexes: one, the harmonic mean of price (or quantity) relatives weighted by the numerator country's expenditures; the other, the arithmetic mean weighted by the denominator country's expenditures. (The more usual definition is the geometric mean of the own-weighted and base-country–weighted indexes.)

GCF (gross capital formation): Includes fixed capital formation, change in stocks, and net exports. Definitions of these three components correspond to SNA concepts, although the SNA does not include net exports in its definition of GCF.

GDP: Gross domestic product.

Geary-Khamis method: An aggregation method in which category international prices (reflecting relative category values) and country PPPs (depicting relative country price levels) are estimated simultaneously from a system of linear equations. (See Chapter 3.)

GFCE (government final consumption expenditure): The SNA concept of "government" that includes public expenditures on education, health, and similar categories. (See Table 2.1.)

ICP: International Comparison Project.

"Ideal" index: See **Fisher, or "ideal," index.**

Index spread: The ratio of a U.S.-weighted quantity index to an own-weighted quantity index.

Indirect price or quantity comparison: A comparison made by dividing the price or quantity ratio into the expenditure ratio. That is, the indirect quantity comparison between country j and country k for commodity i, $\frac{q_{ij}}{q_{ik}}$, is obtained from: $\frac{p_{ij}}{p_{ik}} \frac{q_{ij}}{q_{ik}} \div \frac{p_{ij}}{p_{ik}} = \frac{q_{ij}}{q_{ik}}$, where the ps are the commodity prices. (See also **Direct price or quantity comparison.**)

International dollars (I\$): Dollars with the same purchasing power over total U.S. GDP as the U.S. dollar, but with a purchasing power over subaggregates and over detailed categories determined by average international prices rather than by U.S. relative prices.

International prices: Average prices based on the prices of the sixteen included countries, each weighted by the GDP of the supercountry to which it is assigned, expressed relative to the numéraire country.

Multilateral comparison: A price or quantity comparison of more than two countries simultaneously that produces consistent relations among all pairs; that is, one that satisfies the circular test or the transitivity requirement.

Original-country binary comparison: A price or quantity comparison between two countries based on the data of the two countries and no others. (See also **Bridge-country binary comparison.**)

Own weights: The weights of the numerator country: that is, the weights of country j in the index $I_{j/k}$. The term is used to refer mainly to the weights of a country other than the United States in comparisons in which the United States is the base country, k.

Partner country: A country compared to the base country, the United States in the present study.

PFC (public final consumption expenditure): The ICP concept of "government" that excludes public expenditures for education, health, and like categories. (See Table 2.1.)

PFCE (private final consumption expenditure): The SNA concept of "consumption" that excludes public expenditures on education, health, and similar categories. (See Table 2.1.)

PPP: See **Purchasing-power parity.**

Price index: The price level for a category or aggregate of goods in one country expressed as a percentage of the price level for the same category or aggregate in another country, when prices in both countries are expressed in a common currency, usually the U.S. dollar, with the official exchange rate being used for currency conversions. A price index may be derived from a purchasing-power parity by dividing by the exchange rate. (See **Purchasing-power parity.**)

Purchasing-power parity (PPP): The number of currency units required to buy goods equivalent to what can be bought with one unit of the currency of the base country, usually the U.S. dollar in the present study.

Quantity index: The quantity per capita of a category or aggregate of goods in one country expressed as a percentage of the quantity per capita in another country.

Quantity ratio: The quantity of a particular commodity in one country as a proportion of the quantity of the same commodity in another country.

Real product or real quantity: The final product or quantity in two or more countries that is valued at common prices and, therefore, valued in comparable terms internationally.

Representative country: One of the sixteen included countries regarded as a representative of a larger group of countries that together with it form a supercountry. All the countries in the world are assigned to one of the sixteen supercountries. (See also **Supercountry.**)

Similarity index: The similarity index for quantities is the weighted "raw correlation" coefficient between the quantity vectors of two countries. The coefficient is the ratio of the cross moment to the square root of the product of the two second moments, where each moment is computed relative to the origin rather than to the mean. The similarity index for prices is the corresponding measure for the price vectors of two countries, with the category prices weighted by the relative importance of each category in total world GDP. The similarity index for incomes for a pair of countries is the ratio of (1) twice the index of the real GDP per capita (with the United States equal to 100) of the member of the pair with the smaller index to (2) the sum of the indexes of the two members of the pair.

SNA: The U.N. System of National Accounts.

Specification: A description of an item for which a price comparison is to be made. The description is designed to ensure that goods of equivalent quality are compared.

Supercountry: A group of countries assumed to have the price and quantity structure of the representative country. The aggregate GDP of the supercountry is used to weight the prices of the representative country in the process of deriving average international prices. (See also **Representative country.**)

Transitivity requirement: See **Circularity or transitivity.**

Index

Accounting: problems in, 28–30

Additivity: consistency, 71; defined, 255

Aggregation methods, 79–84, 114, 115, 116, 173–221

Automobiles: binary price comparisons of, 37–38; as a category, 35–39; data for regressions, 36–37; multilateral price comparisons of, 38–39

Balassa, B., 9

Baldwin, R., 252n

Barber and Beauty Shops: classifications of, 60

Base-country invariance, 75; as methodological criterion, 5, 71

Belgium: prices in, 25, 33

Benchmark years, 3, 7, 9–19, 22–23, 24–25, 128, 130–34

Beverages. *See* Food, Beverages, and Tobacco

Binary comparisons, 2; aggregation methods in, 173–221; of automobile prices, 37–38; defined, 4, 255; disadvantages of, 5; methods of, 4–5, 68–70; original country, 172, 257; and PPPs, 223–31; of rents, 44–45; results of, 172–231. *See also specific categories; specific countries*

Blue collar employees: defined, 67n

Bread and Cereals: classifications of, 54–55; prices in Iran, 34

Bridge-country binary comparison, 44–45, 173; and CPD method, 72–73; defined, 255

Brooms: prices in Iran, 34

Buildings, Nonresidential: classifications of, 61

Buildings, Residential: classifications of, 61

Capital formation. *See* Gross capital formation

Capital goods: classification of, 62–64; prices of, 16–17

Categories. *See* Detailed categories; *specific categories;* Summary categories

CEP. *See* Final consumption expenditure of the population

Characteristicity: defined, 5, 70, 255

Circularity or transitivity: defined, 6, 255

Classification system, 4, 25–28, 54–67

Climate: as variable, 240n

Clothing and Footwear: classifications of, 56–57

Cocoa. *See* Coffee, Tea, and Cocoa

Coffee, Tea, and Cocoa: classifications of, 56

Commodities: and GDP, 17–23; and price comparisons, 127–28

— expenditure on: comparisons for, 123–28; quantity index for, 127

Commodity Stocks: classifications of, 64

Communication Equipment: classifications of, 64

Communication and Transport: classifications of, 59

Comparisons. *See* Binary comparisons; Bridge-country binary comparison; Consumer-goods prices; International comparisons; Multilateral comparisons; Original-country binary comparison; Price, comparisons; Quantity, comparison; Similarity indexes; Simultaneous comparisons

Compensation of Employees, 51–52; classifications of, 65, 67n

Construction: classifications of, 61–62; cost estimates in, 48–50

Consumers' goods specifications, 32

Consumption: and GDP, 4, 14–17; and price comparisons, 32–46. *See also* Final consumption expenditure of the population